HISTORY

I0197779

OF

ANCIENT EGYPT.

BY

GEORGE RAWLINSON, M.A.,

CAMDEN PROFESSOR OF ANCIENT HISTORY IN THE UNIVERSITY OF OXFORD; CANON
OF CANTERBURY; AUTHOR OF "SEVEN GREAT MONARCHIES OF
THE ANCIENT EASTERN WORLD."

IN TWO VOLUMES

VOL. I.

ISBN: 978-1-63923-598-8

Printed: January 2023

Published and Distributed By:
Lushena Books
607 Country Club Drive, Unit E
Bensenville, IL 60106
www.lushenabks.com

ISBN: 978-1-63923-598-8

PREFACE.

The work here offered to the public, conceived and commenced in the year 1876, was designed to supply what seemed a crying need of English literature—viz., an account of Ancient Egypt, combining its antiquities with its history, addressed partly to the eye, and presenting to the reader, within a reasonable compass, the chief points of Egyptian life—manners, customs, art, science, literature, religion—together with a tolerably full statement of the general course of historical events, whereof Egypt was the scene, from the foundation of the monarchy to the loss of independence. Existing English histories of Ancient Egypt were either slight and scantly illustrated, like those of Canon Trevor and Dr. Birch, or wanting in illustrations altogether, like Mr. Kenrick's, or not confined to the period which seemed to deserve special attention, like the 'Egypt' of Mr. Samuel Sharpe. Accordingly, the present writer, having become aware that no 'History of Egypt' on a large scale was contemplated by Dr. Birch, designed in 1876 the work now published, regarding it in part as necessary to round off and complete his other principal labours in the historical field, in part as calculated to fill up a gap, which it was important to fill up, in the historical literature of his country. Since his intention was announced, and the sheets of his first volume to some extent printed off, English literature has been enriched by two most important publications on the subject of Egypt—Dr. Birch's excellent edition of Wilkinson's 'Manners and Customs of the Ancient Egyptians,' and the translation of Dr. Brugsch's 'Geschichte Aegyptens' made by the late Mr. Danby Seymour and Mr. Philip Smith. Had these works existed in the year 1876, or had he then known that they were forthcoming, the author feels that the present volumes would never have seen the light. But, as they were tolerably advanced when he first became aware to what rivalry his poor efforts would be subjected, it was scarcely possible for him to draw back and retract his announced intentions. Instead of so doing, he took refuge in the hope that neither of the two new works would altogether pre-occupy the ground which he had marked out for himself, and in the pleasing persuasion that the general public, when books are published on a subject in which it feels an interest, and are devoured with avidity, has its appetite rather whetted by the process than satisfied. He trusts therefore to find, in England and America, a sufficient body of readers to justify his present venture, and prevent his publishers from suffering any loss through him.

In preparing the volumes, the author has endeavoured to utilise the enormous stores of antiquarian and historical material accumulated during the last

eighty years, and laid up in works of vast size and
enormous cost, quite inaccessible to the general public.
Of these the most magnificent are the 'Description de
l'Egypte,' published by the French savants who accompanied the expedition of the great Napoleon; the
'Monumenti dell' Egitto e della Nubia' of Ippolito
Rosellini; and the 'Denkmäler aus Aegypten und
Aethiopien' of Professor Lepsius. M. Mariette's
'Monuments Divers recueillis en Egypte et en Nubie'
have also furnished him with a considerable number of
illustrations. Possessing only a rudimentary knowledge of the Egyptian language and writing, he has
made it his aim to consult, as far as possible, the various
translations of the Egyptian documents which have
been put forth by advanced students, and to select the
rendering which seemed on the internal evidence most
satisfactory. He has based his general narrative to a
large extent on these translations; and, where they
failed him, has endeavoured to supply their place by a
careful study, not only of finished 'Histories of Egypt,'
like those of Lenormant, Birch, and Brugsch, but of
those elaborate 'monographs' upon special points, in
which French and German scholars subject to the
keenest scrutiny the entire evidence upon this or that
subject or period. Such books as De Rougé's 'Recherches sur les Monuments qu'on peut attribuer aux
six premières dynasties de Manéthon,' Chabas' 'Pas-
teurs en Egypte,' 'Mélanges Egyptologiques,' and
'Recherches pour servir à l'histoire de la XIXme
Dynastie et spécialement à celle des temps de l'Exode,'

Lepsius's pamphlet 'Ueber die XXII. ägyptische Kö-
nigsdynastie, nebst einigen Bemerkungen zu der XXVI.
und andern Dynastien des neuen Reichs,' and his
'Königsbuch der alten Aegypter,' Dümichen's 'Flotte
einer ägyptischen Königin ' and ' Historische Inschriften
alt-ägyptischer Denkmäler,' are specimens of the class
of works to which allusion is here made, and have
been the sources of the present narrative much more
than any methodised 'Histories.' The author, however, is far from wishing to ignore the obligations under
which he lies to former historians of Egypt, such as
Bunsen, Kenrick, Lenormant, Birch, and Brugsch,
without whose works his could certainly not have been
written. He is only anxious to claim for it a distinct
basis in the monographs of the best Egyptologists and
the great collections of illustrations above noticed, and
to call attention to the fact that he has endeavoured
in all cases to go behind the statements of the his-
toriographers, and to draw his own conclusions from
the materials on which those statements were based.

In conclusion he would express his obligations to
his engraver and artist, Mr. G. Pearson and Mr. P.
Hundley, in respect of his illustrations; to the late
Colonel Howard Vyse in respect of all that he has
ventured to say concerning the Pyramids; to Mr.
James Fergusson in respect of his remarks on the rest
of Egyptian architecture; to his old friend and col-
league, the late Sir Gardner Wilkinson, in respect of
the entire subject of Egyptian customs and manners;
to M. Wiedemann in respect of the history of the

twenty-sixth dynasty ; and to Mr. R. Stuart Poole, Dr. Eisenlohr, M. Deveria, and other writers on Egyptian subjects in the ' Dictionary of the Bible,' the ' Revue Archéologique,' and the ' Transactions of the Society of Biblical Archæology.' He has lived to feel, continually more and more, how small a part of each ' History ' is due to the nominal author, and how large a share belongs to the earlier workers in the field. He trusts that in the past he has never failed conspicuously in the duty of acknowledging obligations ; but, however that may be, he would at any rate wish, in the present and in the future, not to be liable to the charge of such failure. To all those whose works he has used he would hereby express himself greatly beholden ; he would ask their pardon if he has involuntarily misrepresented them, and would crave at their hands a lenient judgment of the present volumes.

CANTERBURY : *December* 31, 1880.

CONTENTS.

CHAPTER VIII.

MIMETIC ART.

CHAPTER IX.

SCIENCE.

CHAPTER X.

RELIGION.

CHAPTER XI.

MANNERS AND CUSTOMS.

LIST OF ILLUSTRATIONS.

HISTORY

OF

ANCIENT EGYPT.

―――――•◊•―――――

CHAPTER I.

THE LAND.

Geography of Egypt. Boundaries, Dimensions, and Character of the Country. Proportion of cultivable Territory. Dependence on the Nile. Course of the Nile—its Tributaries—Time and Causes of the Inundation. Chief Divisions of the Territory: the Nile Valley; the Delta; the Fayoum; the Eastern Desert; the Valley of the Natron Lakes. Character of the adjoining Countries.

Αἴγυπτος . . . ἐπίκτητός τε γῆ καὶ δῶρον τοῦ ποταμοῦ.—HEROD. ii. 5.

THE broad stretch of desert which extends from the shores of the Atlantic Ocean across Africa and Western Asia, almost to the foot of the Zagros mountain-range, is pierced in one place only by a thin thread of verdure. A single stream, issuing from the Equatorial regions, has strength to penetrate the 'frightful desert of interminable scorching sand,'[1] and to bring its waters safely through 2,000 miles of arid, thirsty plain, in order to mingle them with the blue waves of the

―――――

[1] Baker's *Albert Nyanza*, vol. i. p. xxvii.

Mediterranean. It is this fact which has produced Egypt. The life-giving fluid, on its way through the desert, spreads verdure and fertility along its course on either bank; and a strip of most productive territory is thus created, suited to attract the attention of such a being as man, and to become the home of a powerful nation. Egypt proper is the land to which the river gave birth,[1] and from which it took name,[2] or, at any rate, that land to a certain distance from the Mediterranean; but, as the race settled in this home naturally and almost necessarily exercises dominion beyond the narrow bounds of the valley, it is usual[3] and it is right to include under the name of 'Egypt' a certain quantity of the arid territory on either side of the Nile, and thus to give to the country an expansion considerably beyond that which it would have, if we confined the name strictly to the fluvial and alluvial region.

The boundaries of Egypt are, by general consent, on the north the Mediterranean, on the east the Red Sea, and a line drawn from the head of the Gulf of Suez to the Wady-el-Arish, or 'River of Egypt' of the Hebrews;[4] on the south the first cataract (lat. 24° 5'), and a line drawn thence to the Red Sea at the ruins of Berenice; on the west the great Libyan Desert. The

[1] See Herod. ii. 18; Strab. xvii. 1, § 4. Compare the *Mémoire* of M. Jomard in the *Description de l'Egypte,* 'Antiquités,' vol. ii. p. 89.
[2] The term 'Egypt,' which was not known to the Egyptians themselves, appears to have been first used by the Greeks as a name for the Nile (Hom. *Od.* iv. 477, xiv. 257; Strab. i. 2, § 22), and thence to have extended itself to the country. Its derivation is uncertain.
[3] See Jomard in the *Description de l'Egypte,* l.s.c.; Kenrick, *Ancient Egypt,* vol. i. p. 61; Russell, *Ancient and Modern Egypt,* p. 419; Smith, *Dict. of Greek and Roman Geography,* vol. i. p. 36, &c.
[4] See 1 Kings viii. 65; 2 Kings xxiv. 7; Is. xxvii. 12. 'The torrent of Egypt' would be a better translation than 'the river;' since in the Hebrew it is הנחל, not הנהר.

tract included within these limits is, in the main, an irregular parallelogram, lying obliquely from N.N.W. to S.S.E., and extending about 520 miles in this direction, with a width of about 160 miles. From the parallelogram thus formed lie out two considerable projections, both triangular, one of them on the south-east, having its apex at Berenice, a little outside the tropic of Cancer;[1] the other on the north-east, having its base along the line of the Suez Canal, and its apex at the mouth of the El-Arish river. The area of the entire tract, including the two projections, is probably not much short of 100,000 square miles. Egypt is thus almost twice the size of England, and rather larger than the peninsula of Italy.[2]

Within these limits the character of the territory presents some most extreme and violent contrasts. A narrow strip of the richest soil in the world is enclosed on either side by regions of remarkable sterility: on the west by wastes of trackless and wholly unproductive sand, on the east by a rocky region of limestone and sandstone, penetrated by deep gorges, and presenting occasionally a scant but welcome vegetation. Towards the north the sandy region, interrupted by the Nile deposit, is continued again eastward of the Suez Canal in the desert, which stretches thence to the borders of Palestine; while towards the south the

---

[1] The ruins of Berenice are placed by the French savants in lat. 23° 48′, by Mr. Donne (*Dictionary of Greek and Roman Geography*, sub voc. Berenice) in lat. 23° 56′. This latter view is now generally taken.

[2] Very exaggerated estimates of the size of Egypt have been formed by some writers. Heeren says (*Handbuch*, p. 47) that it equals two-thirds of Germany, which would give it an area of above 160,000 square miles. A school geography which has come into my hands (Anderson's) goes beyond this, making the area 177,800 square miles. The real area is certainly not over—it is perhaps somewhat under—100,000 square miles.

rocky tract is prolonged a distance of 160 miles from Assouan (Syené) to Berenice.

It is difficult to calculate with exactness the proportion of the cultivable to the unproductive territory. The Nile Valley, if we take its curves into account, extends from Syené to the Mediterranean, a distance of nearly 700 miles.[1] From Cairo to the Mediterranean it is not so much a real valley as a vast plain, from seventy to a hundred miles wide,[2] with a superficies of at least 7,000 square miles.[3] Above Cairo the Nile is hemmed in for above 500 miles between two rocky barriers, and the width of the valley varies from two to twelve, or even in some places fifteen miles, the average being calculated at about seven miles.[4] This would appear to give an additional cultivable territory of above 4,000 square miles. Further, the district of the Fayoum is reckoned

---

[1] From the old apex of the Delta, nearly opposite Heliopolis, to the Sebennytic mouth is 110 miles (Wilkinson, in Rawlinson's *Herodotus*, vol. ii. p. 8); from Thebes to the apex is 456 miles; from Elephantiné to Thebes 124 miles (ib. p. 10); total, 690 miles. The distance from Elephantiné to the Mediterranean at Rosetta is given by Mr. Kenrick (*Ancient Egypt*, vol. i. p. 34, note) as 739 miles; but this is, I think, an over-estimate.

[2] By measurement of the large French map published in the *Description de l'Égypte*, on which there has been scarcely any improvement in more recent times, I find the distance from the present apex of the Delta to Canopus, to Pelusium, to the Damietta and Rosetta mouths, in every case a mile or two over, or the same distance under 100 miles. The plain is narrowest between the Lake Menzaleh and the Libyan hills, about lat. 30° 35′, and again between Lake Bourlos and the Arabian hills in the

vicinity of Tel Basta (Bubastis). The width in these places is about 65 miles.

[3] Here, again, I have had recourse to measurement, and though my estimate exceeds that of some writers, I believe it is not excessive. A writer in the *Edinburgh Review* (Jan. 1877) estimates the area of the Delta in the time of Herodotus at 8,000 sq. miles (p. 120). M. Jomard assigns to Lower Egypt an area of 1,500 French leagues (*Description*, 'Antiquités,' vol. ii. p. 92), or above 11,000 English sq. miles. He appears, however, to include in this estimate the area of the four great lakes, Mareotis, Edkou, Bourlos, and Menzaleh, which must cover a space of from 2,000 to 3,000 sq. miles.

[4] So Mr. Donne, in Dr. Smith's *Dict. of Greek and Roman Geography*, vol. i. p. 36. Dr. Russell, in his *Ancient and Modern Egypt*, gave the average width of the valley as nine miles (p. 31). But this is certainly too much. See M. Girard's 'Essaie' in the *Description*, 'Histoire Naturelle,' vol. ii. p. 344.

to have a superficies of 400 square miles. The entire result would thus seem to be that the cultivable area of Egypt is 11,400 square miles, or 7,296,000 acres.[1] It was found, however, by the scientific men who accompanied the great French expedition at the close of the last century that the land actually under cultivation amounted to no more than 1,907,757 hectares,[2] or 4,714,543 acres. But they saw and noted that, besides this cultivated territory, there were considerable tracts quite fit for crops, which remained untilled. These they estimated to amount to 465,873 hectares,[3] which is equivalent to 1,151,290 acres ; so that the total *cultivable* land at the time of their observations was 5,865,833 acres. Another estimate,[4] somewhat less exact, reduced the amount to 5,189,625 acres.

The difference between the cultivable area, and the actual superficies of the Nile valley, which appears to exceed 1,430,000 acres, is due chiefly to the fact that a considerable portion of the low country is occupied by sands. The verdure spread by the Nile reaches in few places the foot of the hills which enclose its vale. Sands intervene on both sides, or at any rate on one ; and while the entire width of the valley is estimated to average seven miles, the width of the productive tract is thought scarcely to average more than five.[5] Sands also occur within the actual limits of the cultivated region.[6] Again, the space occupied by the Nile itself

---

[1] Dr. Russell (l.s.c.) estimated the cultivable area at *ten* millions of acres.
[2] *Description*, 'Antiquités,' vol. ii. p. 90.
[3] Ibid.
[4] That of M. Girard (*Description*, 'Hist. Nat.' vol. ii. p. 351 : 'Ainsi l'Egypte entière, depuis la dernière cataracte jusqu'à la pointe de Bourlos, comprend en latitude une intervalle de sept degrés et demi, et une superficie d'environ 2,100,000 hectares de terrains cultivables.')
[5] Donne, in Smith's *Dictionary of Greek and Roman Geography*, l.s.c.
[6] Jomard, *Description*, 'Antiquités,' vol. ii. p. 92.

and its canals, as well as by the Lake Mœris and various ponds and reservoirs, has to be deducted from the gross superficies. As the Nile itself averages probably a mile in width from the point where it enters Egypt to the commencement of the Delta, and after dividing occupies certainly no less a space, and as the Lake Mœris is calculated to have an area of 150 square miles,[1] the entire water surface is manifestly considerable, being probably not far short of 850 square miles,[2] or 542,000 acres. The sands cannot be reckoned at much less than 1,500 square miles, or 960,000 acres.[3]

It is argued by M. Jomard that the occupation of the Nile valley by sands is wholly and entirely an encroachment, due to the neglect of man, and maintained that anciently, under the Pharaohs, the sands were successfully shut out, and the whole of the plain country between the Libyan and the Arabian ranges brought under cultivation. He believes that the additional quantity of cultivable soil thus enjoyed by the ancient Egyptians was not much less than one-half of the present cultivable area. This calculation is probably in excess; but we shall scarcely transcend the limits of moderation if we add one-fourth in respect of this difference, and view the productive area of the Nile valley in ancient times as somewhat exceeding seven millions of acres.

A certain addition might be made to this amount in respect of the fertile territory included within the limits

---

[1] See the essay on Lake Mœris in Bunsen's *Egypt*, vol. ii. p. 329, E.T.

[2] Allowing the Nile a course of 690 miles through Egyptian territory, and an average width of a mile, its waters would cover 690 square miles. Add to this 150 square miles

for the superficies of Lake Mœris, and the amount is 840 square miles.

[3] The estimate of M. Jomard exceeds this. He speaks (l.s.c.) of the sands covering 558 square leagues, or between two and three millions of acres.

of the Eastern desert; but the quantity of such territory is so small, and its productiveness so slight, that
it will perhaps be better to make no estimate at all in
respect of it.

If, then, we regard the entire area of ancient Egypt
as amounting to from ˙95,000 to 100,000 square miles,
and the cultivable surface as only about seven millions of
acres, we must come to the conclusion that considerably
more than seven-eighths of the soil, perhaps not much
short of eight-ninths, was infertile and almost worthless.

In fact, Egypt depends for her fertility almost
wholly upon the Nile. The Arabian desert, which
fences her in upon the right, is little less unproductive than
the ' frightful' Sahara upon the left ; and, had the Nile
not existed, or had it taken a different course, the
depressed tract through which it runs from Syené to
the Mediterranean would have been no less barren and
arid than the Wadys of Arabia Petræa or even than the
Sahara itself.   The land, if not ' the gift of the river'
in the sense which Herodotus intended,[1] is at any rate,
as a country, created by the river[2] and sustained by
it ; and hence the necessity, felt by all who have ever
made Egypt the subject of their pens, of placing the
Nile in the forefront of their works,[3] and describing
as fully as they could its course and its phenomena.

---

[1] See the passage quoted at the
head of this chapter.   Herodotus
imagined that the Nile Valley as far
as Syené had been originally a narrow
inlet of the Mediterranean Sea, which
the alluvial deposit had gradually
filled up.   An examination of the
tract in question has disproved this by
showing that there are no marine remains between the sandstone or limestone which forms the original bed of
the valley and the deposit from the

river (see Wilkinson, in the author's
Herodotus, vol. ii. p. 5, and compare
the Description de l'Egypte, ' Hist.
Nat.' vol. ii. p. 361).
[2] Compare Sir S. Baker's remarks
in his Albert Nyanza, vol. i. Introduction, p. xxvii.: ' Egypt has been
an extraordinary instance of the
actual formation of a country by
alluvial deposit ; it has been created
by a single river.'
[3] See Hecatæus, Frag. 278, 279.

The duty thus incumbent on every historian of Ancient
or Modern Egypt is, at the present day, happily beset
with fewer difficulties than at any former time. The
long untrodden interior of Africa has been penetrated
by British enterprise, and the hitherto inscrutable
Sphinx has been forced to reveal her secrets. Speke
and Grant, Baker, Livingstone, Gordon, and Cameron
have explored, till there is little left to learn, the water
system of the African interior ; and the modern historian, thanks to their noble labours, can track the mighty
stream of the Nile from its source to its embouchure,
can tell the mystery of its origin, describe its course,
explain its changes and account for them, declare the
causes of that fertility which it spreads around and of
that unfailing abundance whereof it boasts, paint the
regions through which it flows, give, at least approxi-
mately, the limits of its basin, and enumerate—in some
cases describe—its tributaries. The profound ignorance
of seventeen centuries was succeeded, about ten years
since, by a time of half-knowledge, of bold hypothesis,
of ingenious, unproved, and conflicting theories. This
twilight time of speculation has gone by.[1]   The areas
occupied by the basins of the Nile, the Congo, and the
Zambesi are tolerably nearly ascertained. The great
reservoirs from which the Nile flows are known ; and
if any problems still remain unsolved,[2] they are of an

295, 296 ; Herod. ii. 5–34 ; Diod.
Sic. i. 10, 19, 32-38 ; Kenrick, Ancient Egypt, vol. i. pp. 5–60 ; Russell,
Ancient and Modern Egypt, pp. 32–
53 ; Sharpe, History of Egypt, vol. i.
pp. 4–7, &c.
   [1] The main doubt has recently
been with respect to the basins of
the Nile and Congo. It was thought,
till 1875, that Lake Tanganyika
might drain into the Albert Nyanza.

Lieut. Cameron's travels have shown
that this is not the case, and that
the Lualaba and L. Tanganyika belong to the upper waters of the
Congo.
   [2] The extent of the Upper Nile
basin towards the west is unknown.
Schweinfurth traced it as far as long.
26°, but it is conjecture alone that
extends it to long. 23°, as Sir S.
Baker does (see his map, vol. i. opp.

insignificant character, and may properly be considered as mere details, interesting no doubt, but of comparatively slight importance.

The Nile, then, rises in Equatorial Africa from the two great basins of the Albert and Victoria Nyanzas. which both lie under the Equator, the former in long. 29° to 31° 30′, the latter in long. 32° to 36°, E. from Greenwich.[1] The Victoria Nyanza is a c -shaped lake, with the 'stalk' at Muanza in long. 33° and south latitude 3° nearly. It swells out to its greatest width between south latitude 1° and the Equator, where it attains a breadth of above four degrees, or nearly three hundred miles. After this it contracts rapidly, and is rounded off towards the north at the distance of about ten or fifteen miles above the Equator. From the ' stalk' at Muanza to the opposite coast, where the great issue of the water takes place (long. 33° nearly), is a distance of not quite four degrees, or about 270 miles. The entire area of the lake cannot be less than 40,000 square miles. Its surface is estimated to be about 3,500 feet above the level of the ocean.[2] The other great reservoir, the Albert Nyanza, is a long and, comparatively speaking, narrow lake, set obliquely from S.S.E. to N.N.W., and with coasts that undulate somewhat, alternately projecting and receding. Its shores are still incompletely explored ; but it is believed to have a length of nearly

---

p. xxi). There is also a doubt whether the Victoria Nyanza does not communicate with a series of lakes towards the east.

[1] According to Sir S. Baker the Albert Nyanza extends westward nearly to long. 28° (see his large map). He places the western shore of the Victoria in long. 31° 35′ nearly, and the eastern in long. 36°.

[2] Speke in 1858 made the elevation 3,740 feet, while his observations in 1862 gave the result of 3,308 feet (so Livingstone in 1873). The *mean* of these would be 3,524 feet. Lieut. Cameron, however, in 1875 argues for an elevation of not more than 2,000 feet ! (See *Geographical Journal*, vol. xlvi. p. 222.)

six degrees, or above four hundred miles, and a width in places of about ninety miles. Its average width is probably not more than sixty miles, and its area may be reckoned at about 25,000 square miles. Its elevation above the ocean is about 3,000 feet.[1]

The Albert and Victoria Nyanzas are separated by a tract of mountain ground, the general altitude of which is estimated at from 4,200 to 5,000 feet. The Victoria Nyanza receives the waters which drain from the eastern side of this range, together with all those that flow from the highlands south and east of the lake, as far in the one direction as lat. 4° south, and in the other as long. 38° east. Its basin has thus a width of eight degrees. The Albert Nyanza receives the streams that flow westward from the tract between the reservoirs, together with all those from the southwest and west, to a distance which is not ascertained, but which can scarcely fall short of the 27th or 26th meridian.[2] Its basin is thus at the least from four to five degrees in width, and is considerably longer than that of its eastern sister. Moreover, the Albert Nyanza receives, towards its northern extremity, the whole surplus water of the Victoria by the stream known as the River Somerset or Victoria Nile, which flows northwards from that lake as far as the Karuma Falls (lat. 2° 15′ north) and then westward by Murchison's Falls and Magungo into the Albert. The stream which thus joins the two lakes may be regarded as in some sense the Nile, or not so regarded, according as we please;

---

[1] Baker (*Albert Nyanza*, vol. ii. p. 153) made the elevation 2,720 feet. So Livingstone (*Last Journals*, map). But Sir H. Rawlinson on the whole is inclined to regard the Albert as not more than 500 feet below the Victoria Nyanza (MS. note communicated to me in 1876).

[2] It has been already noticed that Sir S. Baker extends conjecturally the basin of the Albert N. to long. 23° (see above, note [2], p. 8).

but the river which issues from the north-eastern extremity of the Albert Nyanza, and which runs thence,
with a course only a very little east of north, by Gondokoro to Khartoum, is undoubtedly the Nile [1]—all other
streams that join it from right or left are mere affluents
—and a description of the course of the Nile commences, therefore, most properly at this point, where the
head-streams are for the first time joined together, and
the whole waters of the Upper Nile basin flow in one
channel.

The Nile quits the Albert Nyanza [2] in about N. lat.
2° 45′, and runs with a course that is very nearly north-
east to the first cataract [3] (lat. 3° 36′, long. 32° 2′),
receiving on its way a small tributary, the Un-y-Amé,
from the S.E., which enters it a few miles above the
cataract, in lat. 3° 32′. Below the junction the river
has a width between the reeds that thickly fringe its
banks of about 400 yards,[4] which expands to 1,200 a
little lower,[5] where its course is obstructed by numerous islands. A rocky defile is then entered, through
which the stream chafes and roars, reduced to a width
of 120 yards, and forming a series of falls and rapids.[6]
At the same time the direction is altered, the river
turning to the west of north, and running N.W. by N.
till it touches long. 31° 30′, when it once more resumes
its north-eastern course, and so flows to Gondokoro.
On the way are at least three further rapids; but the

[1] See Baker's *Albert Nyanza,* vol. ii. pp. 94–103.
[2] The issue of the Nile from the Albert Nyanza, which until 1876 had only been *seen* from a distance of about 100 miles, not actually visited by a European (Baker, vol. ii. pp. 134-5), was experimentally proved by Col. Gordon in that year.
[3] See Baker's large map. Lieut.

Julian Baker places Afuddo, which is very near the first cataract, in lat. 3° 34′ (*Geograph. Journal* for 1874, p. 76).
[4] *Albert Nyanza,* vol. ii. p. 283.
[5] Ibid. p. 286.
[6] Ibid. p. 287. In fifteen miles, between Afuddo and the Asua, the fall is 222 feet, or nearly fifteen feet a mile (*Athenæum,* No. 2551, p. 372).

stream is said in this part not to be unnavigable,[1] as the
volume of water is increased by numerous tributaries
flowing in from the eastern mountains, one of which, the
Asua, or Ashua,[2] is of some importance.   From Gondokoro the Nile is without obstruction until it reaches
Nubia.   The river in this part of its course flows
through an almost interminable region of long grass,
swamps, and marshes, with endless windings and a
current varying from one to three miles an hour.[3]   Its
banks are fringed with reeds and with tangled masses
of water-plants, which make it impossible to calculate
the real width of the stream ; the clear space between the
water-plants is sometimes as little as 100, and scarcely
anywhere more than 500 yards.   The general course
is from south to north, but with a strong bend to the
west between lat. 6° and 9° 30′ ; after which the direction is east, and even partly south of east, to the junction with the Sobat (lat. 9° 21′).   This river, which
has a long and circuitous course from the Kaffa country
augments the main stream with a considerable body
of water.   It is 120 yards wide at its mouth in the dry
season, and is sometimes from twenty-seven to twenty-
eight feet deep, with a current of between two and three
miles an hour.[4]   Between Gondokoro and the Sobat
the Nile receives on its left bank the Bahr Ghazal from
the Darfur country, and sends off on its right bank a

---

[1] Col. Gordon's steamers have
ascended all the rapids but one, and
have shown the Nile to be navigable
from the Mediterranean to the Albert Nyanza, except for the space of
about three miles.
[2] Asua is the form used by Sir S.
Baker (*Albert Nyanza*, vol. ii. pp.
287, 308, &c.), Ashua that preferred by his nephew, Lieut. Baker

(*Geographical Journal* for 1874, p.
46).   This river, below its junction
with the Atabbi, was 130 yards
broad, and knee-deep in March 1871
(ibid.).   It is said to be 'important
from April 15 to November 15 ; dry
after that date' (*Albert Nyanza*, vol.
ii. p. 308).
[3] *Albert Nyanza*, vol. i. pp. 33–84.
[4] Ibid. p. 46.

branch—the Bahr Zaraffe or Giraffe river,[1]—-which
leaves the main stream in lat. 5° 20' and rejoins it in
lat. 9°, about thirty-six miles above the entrance of the
Sobat river.[2] After receiving the Sobat, the Nile,
which has now about 700 yards of clear water,[3] runs
through a flat and marshy country, with a slow stream
and a course that is a very little east of north to Khartoum,[4] in lat. 15° 36' 6'[1], where it receives its chief
affluent, the Bahr el Azrek or Blue Nile, which, until
the recent discoveries, was considered by most geographers to be the main river.

The Blue Nile rises in the highlands of Abyssinia,
in lat. 11°, long. 37° nearly,[5] at an elevation of above
6,000 feet.[6] Its course is N.N.W. to Lake Tzana or
Dembea, which it enters at its south-western and
leaves at its south-eastern corner. From this point it
flows S.E. and then S. to the tenth parallel of north
latitude, .when it turns suddenly to the west, and, passing within seventy miles of its source, runs W. by N.
and then almost due north-west to Khartoum.[7] It
receives on its way the waters of numerous tributaries,

---

[1] *Albert Nyanza*, vol. i. p. 48.
[2] *Geograph. Journal* for 1876, p.
38. In this part of its course, where
the water is most dispersed, the Nile
is often obstructed by great masses
of floating vegetation, which even
form dams across the river. Channels have to be cut through these
obstructions in order that boats may
pass up or down stream. (Lieut.
Baker in *Geograph. Journal* for
1874, pp. 38–40; *Albert Nyanza*,
vol. ii. pp. 329–332.)
[3] *Albert Nyanza*, vol. i. p. 44.
[4] Sir S. Baker makes the latitude
of Khartoum 15° 29', but the mean
result of a number of observations
taken recently is 15° 36' 6" (see the

Geographical Journal for 1874, p.
71).
[5] So Bruce (*Travels*, vol. v. p.
308). I am not aware that there
have been any more recent observations.
[6] Humboldt (*Central Asien*, p.
93) gives the elevation as 955 toises,
or 6,106 English feet.
[7] The courses of the Blue Nile and
its affluents were in part explored by
Sir S. Baker in 1861-2. He descended the Dinder from about lat.
14° nearly to its junction with the
Blue Nile, and then the Blue Nile
itself to Khartoum (see his *Nile Tributaries*, pp. 357-375).

whereof the chief are the Rahad, the Dinder, and the Tumet. In the dry season the stream is small;[1] but during the great rains it brings with it a vast volume of water, charged heavily with earthy matter of a red colour, and contributes largely to the swell of the Nile and the fertilising deposit which gives its productiveness to Egypt.[2]

The White (or true) Nile at its junction with the Blue is about two miles in width, when the water is at a medium height.[3] From this point it flows at first nearly due north, but after a while inclines towards the east, and where it receives its last tributary, the Atbara, has reached its extreme easterly limit, which is E. long. 34° nearly.   The latitude of the junction is 17° 37′, according to Sir Samuel Baker.[4]   Here—1,100 miles from its mouth—the river has its greatest volume. Between the Atbara junction and the Mediterranean not a single stream is received from either side ; and the Nile runs on for 1,100 miles through dry regions of rock and sand, suffering a constant loss through absorption and evaporation,[5] yet still pouring into the Mediterranean a volume of water, which has been estimated at 150,566 millions of cubic mètres a day in the low, and at 705,514 millions of cubic mètres a day in the high season.[6] In lat. 17° 37′ the volume must be very much more considerable.

After receiving the Atbara, the direction of the Nile is N.N.W. for about 150 miles to Abu Hamed, after which it proceeds to make the greatest and most remarkable bend in its entire course, flowing first south-

[1] Baker, *Albert Nyanza*, vol. i. p. 7.
[2] Ibid. p. 8 ; *Nile Tributaries*, pp. 373 et seqq. (4th edition).
[3] *Albert Nyanza*, vol. i. p. 33.
[4] *Nile Tributaries*, Preface, p. viii.
[5] Baker, *Albert Nyanza*, vol. i. p. 6.
[6] See Wilkinson in the author's *Herodotus*, vol. ii. p. 8 (3rd edit.).

west, then north, then north-east, and finally, for a short
distance, south-east, to Korosko, in lat. 22° 44'.
Cataracts are frequent in this portion of the river,[1] and,
at once to avoid them and shorten the circuitous route,
travellers are accustomed to journey by camels for
230 miles across the Nubian desert,[2] leaving the Nile at
Abu Hamed and reaching it again at Korosko in about
seven or eight days.[3]   From Korosko the general
course is north-east for about sixty or seventy miles,
after which it is north and a little west of north, to
Assouan (lat. 24° 5'). Here Egypt begins—the
longest cataract is passed—the Nubian granite and
syenite give place to sandstone[4]—and the river, having
taken its last plunge, flows placidly between precipitous
cliffs, less than three miles apart, with narrow strips of
cultivable soil between them and the water.[5]   The
course is north, with slight deflections to east and west,
past Ombos (Koum-Ombos) to Silsilis,[6] where the sandstone rocks close in and skirt the river for a distance of
three-quarters of a mile.[7]   The valley then expands a
little ; there is a broadish plain on the left, in which stand
the ruins of important cities ;[8] the stream bends some-

---

[1] Three main cataracts are commonly reckoned between Abu
Hamed and Korosko ; but Belzoni
notes five between Korosko and
Koké (see his map, opp. p. 485), and
there are at least two others between Koké and Abu Hamed.
[2] This was the route taken by
Bruce in 1772, by Burckhardt in
1814, and by Baker in 1861. It is
now almost invariably followed.
[3] Baker, *Albert Nyanza*, vol. i. p.
4 ; *Nile Tributaries*, p. 4.
[4] See Girard in the *Description
de l'Egypte*, 'Hist. Nat.' vol. ii. p.
343 : ' L'Egypte semble commencer
en quelque sorte à où finit le sol gra-

nitique.' Compare Wilkinson, *Topography of Thebes*, p. 452 ; Kenrick,
Ancient Egypt, vol. i. pp. 33–5, &c.
[5] *Description*, 'Hist. Nat.' vol. ii.
p. 344.
[6] See the map attached to Belzoni's *Travels*, and compare the still
more exact one of the *Description*
('Antiquités,' vol. ii. *ad fin.*), which
leaves nothing to be desired.
[7] *Description*, 'H. N.,' l.s.c. Compare Wilkinson, *Topography*, pp.
438–447. Champollion observes
that the river here ' makes a second
entrance into Egypt.'
[8] Especially Edfou (Apollinopolis
Magna) and Esné (Latopolis), both

what to the west, until a little below Esné (Latopolis), the hills again approach, the defile called the Gibeleïn, or 'the two mountains,' is passed, the sandstone ends, and is succeeded by limestone ranges;[1] and the Nile, turning to the north-east, flows through the plains of Hermonthis and of Thebes, the first really wide space on which it has entered since it issued from the Nubian desert. Below Thebes the northern course is again resumed and continued to Dendyra (Tentyris), when the stream turns and flows almost due west to Abydos (Arabat-el-Matfour), thence procee dingnorth-west across the 27th parallel to Cusæ (Qousyeh) in lat. 27° 27'. The valley between Abydos and Cusæ is from six to ten miles wide,[2] and the left bank is watered by canals derived from the main stream. Beyond Cusæ the course of the Nile is once more nearly due north to Cynopolis (Samallout), in lat. 28° 18', after which it is N.N.E. to the convent of St. Antony (lat. 29° 14'). A little below Cusæ[3] the Great Canal of Egypt, known as the *Bahr-Yousuf*, or 'River of Joseph,' goes off from the Nile on its left bank, and is carried along the base of the Libyan range of hills a distance of 120 miles to Zâouy[4] or Zouyieh (lat. 29° 22'), where it rejoins the main river.

---

of which are on the *left* bank (*Description*, 1 s.c. ; *Topography of Thebes*, pp. 425 and 435). Kenrick (vol. i. p. 37) wrongly places Edfou on the right bank.

[1] Strictly speaking, the sandstone ends and the limestone begins *before* Gibeleïn. The exact point of the change is opposite El Qenán, about fourteen miles above Esné (*Topography*, p. 429).

[2] *Description*, p. 345, and map.

[3] At Darout-el-Sherif, in lat. 27° 34' (*Description*, p. 345). Mr.

Kenrick regards this canal as branching off more than a hundred miles higher up the stream, at Chenoboscion, near Diospolis Parva (*Ancient Egypt*, vol. i. p. 45). But the French savants distinguish between the Bahr Yousuf and the branch stream, which extends from Chenoboscion to Syout (Lycopolis), a little north of which it terminates.

[4] Zouyieh is the form used by Belzoni, Zâouy that of the French savants. This place is probably the Iseum of the Greeks and Romans.

The Nile itself skirts the base of the Arabian range; and the flat tract left between it and the Bahr-Yousuf, which is from seven to twelve miles wide, forms the richest and most productive portion of Middle Egypt.[1] From the Convent of St. Antony to the ruins of Memphis (lat. 29° 50′), the course of the Nile is again nearly due north, but about lat. 29° 55′ it becomes west of north, and so continues till the stream divides in lat. 30° 13′, long. 31° 10′ nearly. In ancient times the point of separation was somewhat higher up the stream,[2] and the water passed by three main channels:[3] the Canopic branch, which corresponded closely with the present Rosetta one; the Sebennytic, which followed at first the line of the Damietta stream, but left it about Semennoud, and turning west of north ran into the Mediterranean through Lake Bourlos, in long. 30° 55′; and the Pelusiac, which, skirting the Arabian hills, ran by Bubastis and Daphne through Lake Menzaleh to Tineh or Pelusium. The courses of these streams were respectively about 130, 110, and 120 miles.

Thus the entire course of the Nile, from the point where it quits the Albert Nyanza (lat. 2° 45′) to that of its most northern issue into the Mediterranean (lat. 31° 35′) was a distance of nearly twenty-nine degrees, which is about 2,000 English miles. Allowing the moderate addition of one-fourth for main windings, we must assign to the river a further length of 500 miles, and make its entire course 2,500 miles.[4] This is a

---

[1] *Description*, 'Hist. Nat.' vol. ii. p. 345: 'Ces terres, pouvant être facilement arrosées, sont les plus productives de l'Egypte moyenne.'
[2] Wilkinson, in the author's *Herodotus*, vol. ii. p. 8, note [2], 3rd edition.
[3] Herod. ii. 17. To these three main branches Herodotus adds two

minor ones, the Saitic and Mendesian, branching from the Sebennytic, and two artificial branches or canals.
[4] If we add to this the flow through the Albert Nyanza, and the course of the Somerset from the Ripon falls, we shall have a total

length more than double that of the Tigris, more than one-fourth longer than that of the Euphrates, and considerably beyond that of the Indus, Oxus, or Ganges. The Nile, it will have been seen, has not many tributaries. The chief are the Atbara and Bahr-el-Azrek (or Blue Nile) from Abyssinia, the Sobat from the Kaffa country, and the Asua from the Madi and adjacent mountains. These all flow in from the east or right bank. From the other side the only tributaries received are the Bahr-el-Ghazal, which is said to give 'little or no water,'[1] the Yé, which is described as a third-class stream,[2] and another unnamed river of the same character.[3] The important affluents are thus only the Sobat, the Bahr-el-Azrek, and the Atbara.

Of these, the Bahr-el-Azrek has been described already.[4] The Sobat is known only in its lower course. It is 'the most powerful affluent of the White Nile,'[5] and is said to be fed by numerous tributaries from the Galla country about Kaffa, as well as by several from the Berri and Latooka countries. The course of the main stream[6] is believed to be at first south, between the 10th and the 15th parallels, after which it runs south-west, and then north-west to its junction with the White Nile in lat. 9° 21' 14". It has a strong current, and in the rainy season (June

length of about 300 miles more, or 2,800 miles.

[1] Baker, *Albert Nyanza*, vol. i. p. 49; vol. ii. p. 308. The upper portion of the streams forming the Bahr-el-Ghazal has been explored by Herr Schweinfurth, and is carefully laid down in his large map (see *Heart of Africa*, vol. i. opp. p. 1).

[2] Baker, *Albert Nyanza*, vol. ii.

p. 308.
[3] Ibid.
[4] See above, pp. 13–4.
[5] Baker, *Albert Nyanza*, vol. ii. p. 309.
[6] See Baker's small map, *Albert Nyanza*, vol. i. opp. p. xxi. (repeated in his *Nile Tributaries* and his *Ismailia*).

to January) brings down a large body of water, being
at its mouth sometimes 250 yards wide [1] and nearly
thirty feet deep.[2] The Atbara is not a permanent river. In the
spring and early summer, from the beginning of March
to June, it is for upwards of 150 miles from its junction with the Nile perfectly dry, except in places.[3] In
the deeper hollows of its sandy channel, at intervals of
a few miles, water remains during these months; and
the denizens of the stream, hippopotamuses, crocodiles,
fish, and large turtle, are crowded together in discon-
tinuous pools, where they have to remain until the
rains set them at liberty.[4] This change occurs about
the middle of June, from which time until the middle
of September the storms are incessant, and the Atbara
becomes a raging torrent, bringing down with it in wild
confusion forest trees, masses of bamboo and drift-
wood, bodies of elephants and buffaloes, and quantities
of a red soil washed from the fertile lands along its
course and the courses of its tributaries. These are the
Settite, the Royân, the Salaam, and the Angrab—all of
them large rivers in the wet season, and never without
water even at the driest time.[5] Increased by these
streams, the Atbara is, from June to September, a great
river, being 450 yards in average width and from twenty-
five to thirty feet deep[6] for many miles above its junction with the Nile, in lat. 17° 37′ nearly.

---

[1] *Geograph. Journal* for 1874, p.
38.
[2] Baker's *Albert Nyanza*, vol. i.
p. 47.
[3] Ibid. p. 8.   Compare *Nile Tributaries*, pp. 22–3.
[4] *Albert Nyanza*, vol. i. p. 9 ; *Nile
Tributaries*, p. 25.

[5] *Albert Nyanza*, vol. i. p. 10.
[6] Ibid. p. 5.   The courses of the
Blue Nile and Atbara, together
with their tributaries, are well given
by Sir S. Baker in the map accompanying his *Nile Tributaries of Abyssinia*, opp. p. i.

The great inundation of the Nile, which causes the peculiar fertility of Egypt, commences ordinarily towards the end of June or beginning of July, and continues till November or December. The rise at Cairo is in average years between twenty-three and twenty-four feet ;[1] but it is sometimes as much as twenty-six, and sometimes as little as twenty-two feet.[2] In Upper Egypt, where the valley is narrower, the rise of course is greater. At Thebes the average increase is reckoned at thirty-six feet, while at Syênê (Assouan) it is about forty feet.[3] On the other hand, in the open plain of the Delta the height to which the water rises is very much less, being about twenty feet near Heliopolis, eleven at Xoïs and Mendes, and no more than four at the Rosetta and Damietta embouchures.[4] The extent to which the inundation reaches depends upon the height attained by the river. If the rise is under the average, much of the higher ground is left uncovered, and has to be irrigated with great trouble by means of canals and shadoofs or hand-swipes. If, on the contrary, the average is much exceeded, calamitous results ensue ;[5] the mounds which keep the water from the villages are overflowed or broken down ; the cottages, built of mud, collapse and are washed away ; the cattle are drowned ; the corn in store is spoiled, and the inhabitants with difficulty save their lives by climbing trees or making their way to some neighbouring eminence.

---

[1] The French savants made the average rise 7·419 mètres (Description, 'Hist. Nat.' vol. ii. p. 352), which is 23·721 English feet. Sir G. Wilkinson says the rise at Old Cairo is sixteen cubits, or twenty-four feet. (See the author's Herodotus, vol. ii. p. 297, 3rd ed.)

[2] Description, l.s.c.

[3] Wilkinson, in the author's Herodotus, l.s.c.

[4] Ibid.

[5] See the description of an unusual rise in Belzoni's Operations and Discoveries, pp. 299–303. Extraordinary inundations in ancient times were equally disastrous (Plin. H. N. v. 9).

Providentially, these excessive inundations occur but
seldom; the uniformity which characterises the operations of nature is nowhere more observable than in
Egypt; and a rise of even two feet above the average is
a rare and unusual occurrence.

It has sometimes been supposed that, although
within the time since Egypt has been subjected to
modern scientific observation the results presented are
thus uniform, yet in the course of ages very great
changes have happened, and that still greater may be
expected if the world continues to exist for a few
more thousand years. Herodotus declares[1] that less
than nine hundred years before his visit to Egypt, or
in the fourteenth century B.C.,[2] the Nile overflowed all
the country below Memphis as soon as it rose so little as
eight cubits; and as in his own day, for the inundation to be a full one, the rise required was sixteen cubits,
he concludes that the land had risen eight cubits in
nine centuries. At such a rate of growth, he observes,[3]
it would not be long before the fields would cease to be
inundated, and the boasted fertility of Egypt would
disappear altogether. Had the facts been as he supposed, his conclusion would not have been erroneous;
but all the evidence which we possess seems to show,
that the rise of the Nile during the flood time has never
been either greater or less than it is at present;[4] and that,

[1] Herod. ii. 13.
[2] The visit of Herodotus to Egypt
was *probably* during the Athenian
occupation, which was from B.C. 460
to B.C. 455. Nine hundred years
before this would be B.C. 1360–1355.
[3] Herod. l.s.c. The views of
Herodotus were adopted by Dr.
Shaw in the last century, who argued that 'in process of time the

whole country might be raised to
such a height that the river would
not be able to overflow its banks,
and Egypt, consequently, from being
the most fertile, would, for want of
the annual inundation, become one
of the most barren parts of the universe' (*Travels*, vol. ii. p. 235).
[4] Herodotus tells us that sixteen
cubits, or twenty-four feet, was the

though the land is upraised, there is no need of any greater rise of the river to overflow it. The explanation is,[1] that the bed of the river is elevated in an equal ratio with the land on either side of it; and the real effect of the elevation is rather to extend the Nile irrigation than to contract it; for as the centre of the valley rises, the waters at the time of their overflow spread further and further over the base of the hills which bound it—the alluvium gradually extends itself and the cultivable surface becomes greater.[2] If the soil actually under cultivation be less now than formerly, it is not nature that is in fault. Mohammedan misrule checks all energy and enterprise ; the oppressed *fellahin*, having no security that they will enjoy the fruits of their labours, are less industrious than the ancient Egyptians, and avail themselves more scantily of the advantages which are offered them by the peculiar circumstances of their country.

In one part of Egypt only does it seem that there has been any considerable change since the time of the Pharaohs. A barrier of rock once crossed the river at Silsilis, and the water of the Nile south of that point stood at a much higher level.[3] Broad tracts were overflowed at that period which the inunda-

normal rise in his day (B.C. 460–450). A statue of the Nile at Rome, surrounded by sixteen diminutive figures, indicates that the rise was sixteen cubits in the time of the Roman Empire. Sixteen cubits is assigned by Abd-allatif, the Arabian historian, as the medium between excess and defect (ab. A.D. 1200) ; and twenty-four feet is said to be the usual rise of the river at Cairo in our own day (Wilkinson, in the author's *Herodotus*, vol. ii. p. 297, 3rd edit.).

[1] *Description de l'Egypte*, 'Hist. Nat.' vol. ii. p. 366: 'En effet, si les dépôts de limon exhaussent le sol de l'Egypte, la même cause exhausse aussi le fond du Nil, de sorte que la profondeur de ce fleuve au-dessous de la plaine doit rester à peu près la même.'
[2] Kenrick, *Ancient Egypt*, vol. i. p. 80; Wilkinson in the author's *Herodotus*, vol. ii. p. 15, note [4].
[3] See Wilkinson in the author's *Herodotus*, vol. ii. p. 298.

tion now never reaches.[1] But these tracts belonged to
Ethiopia rather than to Egypt; and within the latter
country it was only the small portion of the Nile Valley
between 'the first cataract' and Silsilis that suffered
any disadvantage. In that tract the river does not
rise now within twenty-six feet of the height to which
it attained anciently;[2] and though the narrowness of
the valley there prevented the change from causing a
very sensible loss, yet no doubt some diminution of the
cultivable territory was produced by the giving way of
the barrier.

It has long been known[3] that the annual inundation
of the Nile is caused, at any rate mainly,[4] by the rains
which fall in Abyssinia between May and September;[5]
but it is only recently that the entire Nile system, and
the part played in its economy by the Abyssinian and
Equatorial basins, have come to be clearly understood
and appreciated. The White Nile is now found to be,
not only the main, but the only true river. Fed by
the great Equatorial lakes, and supported by a rainfall
which continues for more than nine months of the year,
from February to November,[6] this mighty and unfailing
stream carries down to the Mediterranean a vast and
only slightly varying[7] body of water, the amount of

---

[1] Especially in the plains of Don-
gola, about lat. 19°.
[2] Wilkinson, l.s.c.
[3] See Agatharcides ap. Biod. Sic.
i. 41; Plutarch, De Isid. et Osir. p.
366,C; Abd-allatif, quoted by Shaw,
Travels, vol. ii. p. 215; Russell,
Ancient and Modern Egypt, p. 46,
&c.
[4] The first inundation is beyond
all question caused by the Abyssinian rivers; but the flooding would
scarcely continue so long as it does,

if it were not for the White Nile,
which is highest in November.
[5] Baker found the first rains commence in Abyssinia 'in the middle
of May' (Victoria Nyanza, vol. i.
p. 9). The last shower fell on September 15 (Nile Tributaries, p. 142).
[6] Albert Nyanza, vol. ii. p. 307.
[7] This expression is not to be
taken quite strictly. The White
Nile rises at Ismailia, near Gondokoro, a little more than four feet
(Geograph. Journal for 1874, p. 44);

which may be estimated by considering the volume
poured into the sea, even when the Nile is lowest, which
is said to be above 150,000 millions of cubic mètres
daily.[1] The contribution of the Blue Nile at this season
is so small,[2] that it must be considered a barely sufficient
set-off against the loss by absorption and evaporation
which the stream must suffer in the 1,400 miles
between Khartoum and the sea, and thus the whole
of the 150,000 millions of mètres may be put to the
account of the White Nile. Were the White Nile
diverted from its course above Khartoum, the Blue
Nile alone would fail in the dry season to reach the
Mediterranean ; it would shrink and disappear long
before it had passed the Nubian desert,[3] and Egypt
would then be absolutely without water and uninhabit-
able. But the abundant reservoirs under the Equator
forbid this result, and enable the river to hold its own
and make head against the absorbing power of the
desert and the evaporating power of the atmosphere
while it traverses a space of above sixteen degrees with
a course which, including only main bends, cannot be
far short of 1,400 miles.

On the other hand, without the Abyssinian streams,
it is doubtful whether the Nile would ever rise above
its banks or flood Egypt at all. If it did, it is certain
that it would leave little deposit, and have but a slight
fertilising power.[4] The Atbara and Blue Nile bring
down the whole of that red argillaceous mud,[5] which

at Towfikia, in lat. 9° 25′, as much
as 14 feet 3 inches (ibid. p. 42) ; at
Khartoum, certainly more than 5
feet (Baker, *Albert Nyanza*, vol. i.
p. 34). But its rise is slight compared with that of the Blue Nile and
the Atbara.
[1] See above, p. 14.

[2] Baker, *Albert Nyanza*, vol. i. p.
7 ; *Nile Tributaries*, p. 373.
[3] Baker, *Albert Nyanza*, vol. i.
p. 10.
[4] Wilkinson in the author's *Herodotus*, vol. ii. p. 29, note [8].
[5] The analysis made by the French
savants showed the Nile deposits to

being spread annually over the land forms a dressing of such richness that no further manure is needed to main- tain Egypt in perpetual fertility and enable it to pro- duce an endless series of the most abundant harvests that can be conceived. The fat soil is washed year by year from the highlands of Abyssinia by the heavy summer rains, and spread from Syênê to Alexandria over the Egyptian lowlands, *tending* to fill up the hollow which nature has placed between the Libyan and Arabian hills. There will be no diminution of Egyptian fertility until the day comes when the Abys- sinian mountains have been washed bare, and the rivers which flow from them cease to bring down an earthy deposit in their flood-time, remaining equally pellucid during all seasons, whatever their rise or fall. That day must, however, be almost indefinitely distant ; and the inhabitants of Egypt will not need for long ages to be under any apprehension of its productiveness suffer- ing serious diminution.

It has been customary among writers on Egypt to divide the country either into two or into three portions;[1] but to the present author it seems more convenient to make a fivefold division of the Egyptian territory. The

contain nearly one-half argillaceous earth (alumen), about one-fifth car- bonate of lime, one-tenth water, and the remainder carbon, carbonate of magnesia, oxide of iron, and silica. The oxide of iron gives it its reddish hue.

[1] The ancient Egyptians them- selves made a twofold division, viz. into the Upper and the Lower coun- try, the latter corresponding to the Delta. Hence the Hebrews desig- nated Egypt by a dual form, Mizraim, or the two Mizrs. Herodotus makes a similar distinction (ii. 7, 8). The Ptolemies seem to have introduced a threefold division : that into Lower Egypt, or the Delta ; Middle Egypt, or the Heptanomis ; and Upper Egypt, or the Thebaid (Strab. xvii. 1, § 3 ; Plin. *H. N.* v. 9, § 9 ; Ptol. *Geogr.* iv. 5). The Romans maintained this division, but sub- divided the Delta and the Thebaid, and called the Heptanomis Arcadia. After the Arab conquest Upper Egypt became known as the Said, Middle Egypt as the Vostani, and Lower Egypt as the Bahari, or 'maritime country.'

Nile Valley, the great plain of the Delta, the curious
basin of the Fayoum, the Eastern Desert, and the
Valley of the Natron Lakes are regions which have a
natural distinctness, and which seem to deserve separate
treatment. It is proposed, therefore, to describe these
five tracts severally before proceeding to an account of
the countries by which Egypt was bordered.

The Nile Valley from Syêné to the apex of the Delta
is a long and narrow strip of the most fertile land in the
world, extending from lat. 24° 5' to 30° 10', a distance
of above six degrees, or 360 geographical miles. The
general direction of the valley is from south to north ;
but during the greater portion of the distance there is
a tendency to incline towards the west ; this prevails as
far as lat. 28° 18', where E. long. 30° 40' is touched ;
after which the inclination is for above a degree to the
east of north as far as Atfieh, whence the valley runs
almost due north to the old apex of the Delta near
Heliopolis. Through these deflections the length of the
valley is increased from 360 to about 500 geographical
miles, or 580 miles of the British statute measure. The
valley is extremely narrow from Syêné to near Thebes,[1]
where it expands ;[2] but it contracts again below the
Theban plain, and continues narrowish until How or
Diospolis Parva, whence it is, comparatively speaking,
broad[3] to about Atfieh. It is then again narrow[4] till it
expands into the Delta below Cairo. The greatest
width of the valley is about fifteen, the least about two

[1] Description de l'Egypte, 'Hist.
Nat.' vol. ii. p. 344; Wilkinson,
Topography of Thebes, pp. 451-2;
Kenrick, Ancient Egypt, vol. i. p. 35.
[2] Description, l.s.c.; Kenrick, p.
41.

[3] That is, from twelve to fifteen
miles (Wilkinson in the author's
Herodotus, vol. ii. p. 11, note [1]).
[4] Description, 'H. N.' vol. ii. p.
346. Compare Herod. ii. 8, and
Scylax, Peripl. p. 103.

miles.[1]   In many parts, on the western side especially, a sandy tract intervenes between the foot of the hills and the cultivated territory,[2] which is thus narrowed to a width that rarely exceeds ten miles.

The great plain of the Delta is, speaking roughly, triangular; but its base towards the sea is the segment of a circle and not a straight line. The deposit which the Nile has brought down during the long course of ages causes a projection of the coast line, which in E. long. 31° 10′ is more than half a degree in advance of the shore at Pelusium and at Marea. Like the Nile valley, the Delta is bounded on either side by hills; on the west by a range which runs N.W. from Memphis to Lake Marea, and then W. to the coast near Plinthiné (long. 29° nearly); on the east by one which has a general north-easterly direction from Cairo to Lake Serbônis and Mount Casius.[3] The distance along the coast-line from Plinthiné to Mount Casius is about 300 miles;[4] that from the apex of the Delta to the sea about a hundred miles.[5] It is believed that the old apex was about six miles higher up the stream than the present point of separation,[6] which is in lat. 30° 13′, whereas the old point of separation was about lat. 30° 8′. The entire Delta is a vast alluvial plain without a natural elevation of any kind; it is intersected by numerous streams derived from the two great branches of the Nile, and has experienced in the course of time very great

---

[1] Occasionally, as the first cataract at Silsilis, and at Gibeleïn, the hills close in and leave little or no ground between the cliffs and the river. (See above, pp. 15–6, and compare the *Description*, 'H. N.' vol. ii. p. 436.)

[2] *Description*, pp. 345, 395, &c.

[3] The western chain is continuous; the eastern one is penetrated by a valley in lat. 30° 32′, along which was carried anciently the line of the canal which united the Nile with the Red Sea.

[4] See Wilkinson in the author's *Herodotus*, vol. ii. p. 7, note [7].

[5] Ibid. p. 9, note [6].

[6] *Description*, 'Hist. Nat.' vol. ii. p. 553; Wilkinson, *Modern Egyptians*, vol. i. p. 401.

changes in respect of its watercourses.[1] The general tendency has been for the water to run off more and more towards the west. The Pelusiac branch, which was originally a principal one,[2] is now almost entirely dried up; the Tanitic and Mendesian branches have similarly disappeared ; the present most easterly mouth of the Nile is the Damietta one, which was originally the fourth, as one proceeded along the coast from east to west. Even this conveys but a small proportion of the Nile water, and tends to silt up. At Rosetta there is a bar across the mouth of the river ; and the Mahmou- diyeh canal, which connects Alexandria with the Nile at Foueh, forms the only permanently navigable channel between the coast and the capital. The cause of this gradual change seems to be the current in the Mediter- ranean, which runs constantly from west to east along the Egyptian coast, and carries the Nile mud eastward, depositing it little by little as it goes. Port Said is con- tinually threatened with destruction from this cause, and it is only by constant dredging that the mouth of the canal can be kept clear.

About one-fourth of the natural area of the Delta is occupied by lakes, which are separated from the sea by thin lines of rock or sand-bank. Commencing on the west we find, first, Lake Marea or Mareotis, which extends from Plinthiné for thirty-five miles in a north- east direction, and runs inland a distance of five-and- twenty miles towards the south-east. Adjoining it on the east, and separated from it by only a narrow strip of alluvium,[3] is Lake Menelaites (now Ma'dyeh), a basin

---

[1] On these changes see the *Des- cription*, ' H. N.' vol. ii. pp. 367–70, and compare Wilkinson in the au- thor's *Herodotus*, vol. ii. p. 26, note [1].

[2] Herod. ii. 17.

[3] *Description*, ' Hist. Nat.' vol. ii. p. 348. Along this strip runs the line of the Alexandrian canal.

of no great size, its dimensions being about ten miles
by seven or eight. Both these lakes are protected from
the sea by a low limestone range,[1] which terminates in
the rock forming the western extremity of Aboukir Bay.
From this point as far as Mount Casius, the rest of the
coast consists entirely of sand and alluvium.[2] South of
Aboukir Bay is Lake Metelites (*Edkou*), with a length
of twenty miles and a width of about ten, reaching on
the one side nearly to Lake Ma'dyeh, and on the other
to the Bolbitine or Rosetta branch of the Nile. At a
little distance beyond the Rosetta branch commences
Lake *Bourlos* (Lacus Buticus), which has a breadth of
twenty miles with a length of nearly forty,[3] and is
divided from the Mediterranean by a thin tongue of
sand extending from the Rosetta mouth to the most
northerly point of Egypt, opposite Beltym. A broad
tract of land now intervenes between Lake Bourlos and
the Damietta branch of the Nile; but east of the Damietta branch occurs almost immediately another lake,
the greatest of all, the Lake *Menzaleh*, which has a length
of forty-five miles and a width in places of nearly thirty.
The country south and south-west of this lake is a vast
marsh,[4] containing only occasional dry spots, but the
resort in all times of a numerous and hardy population.[5] Still further to the east, beyond the Pelusiac
mouth, and beyond the limits of the Delta proper, is
Lake Serbônis, which has a length of fifty miles, but a
width varying from one mile only to six or seven. A

---

[1] Ibid. Compare Wilkinson in
the author's *Herodotus*, vol. ii. p. 6,
note [4].
[2] *Description*, pp. 348-51.
[3] Ibid. p. 349.
[4] See the French map, and compare that given by Dr. Brugsch in
his pamphlet on the Exodus of the
Israelites.
[5] Herod. ii. 92, 140; Thucyd. i.
109, &c. Compare Brugsch, *L'Exode
et les Monuments Égyptiens*, p. 11.

low and narrow sand-bank,[1] midway in which the Mons
Casius rises, separates this lake from the sea.

It has been much disputed whether the Delta projects increasingly into the Mediterranean, and whether
consequently it is now larger than in ancient times.
The French savants who examined the country at the
time of Napoleon's great expedition were decidedly of
opinion that the coast-line advanced constantly,[2] and
regarded the general area of the Delta as thus considerably augmented. They thought, however, that as
much land had been lost internally by the neglect of
the old dykes, and the enlargement of Lakes Bourlos
and Menzaleh,[3] as had been gained from the sea, and
believed that thus the cultivable area of the Delta was
about the same in their own day as anciently.

On the other hand, Sir Gardner Wilkinson declares
that the 'Mediterranean has encroached, and that the
Delta has lost instead of gaining along the whole of its
extent from Canopus to Pelusium.' He maintains that
'the land is always sinking along the north coast of
Egypt,' and appears to think that the Nile deposit is
barely sufficient to compensate for this continued
subsidence. According to him [4] 'the Nile now enters
the sea at the same distance north of the Lake Mœris
as it did in the age of early Kings of Egypt,' and 'the
sites of the oldest cities are as near the seashore as
they ever were.' He thus believes the coast-line to
have made no advance at all in historical times, and
appears even to regard the remarkable projection of the

---

[1] Brugsch supposes the Israelites
to have marched along this sand-
bank.

[2] *Description de l'Egypte*, 'Hist.
Nat.' vol. ii. pp. 372–3, 398–404, &c.

[3] Ibid. 'Antiquités,' vol. ii. p.

91; 'Hist. Nat.' vol. ii. p. 436.

[4] See the author's *Herodotus*, vol.
ii. p. 6, note [4]; and compare Wilkinson, *Ancient Egyptians*, vol. i.
p. 7.

land between the Canopic and Pelusiac mouths as an
original formation and not the result of deposit.
It is difficult to decide between two such weighty
authorities; but it may be observed that the English
Egyptologist is scarcely consistent with himself, since,
while stating that the sea 'has encroached,' he allows
that the Nile enters it at the *same* distance below Lake
Mœris as formerly, which implies that the sea has not
encroached. It may further be remarked that he
gives no proof of the subsidence of the coast along the
north of Egypt, and that his statement on the subject
is open to question. On the whole, we may perhaps
with most reason conclude that there is an advance,
especially towards the east, whither the mud is swept
by the current, but that the progress made is slow and
the gain of territory inconsiderable.

The curious basin of the Fayoum has from a remote
antiquity attracted the attention of geographers,[1] and
in modern times has been carefully examined and
described by M. Jomard[2] and M. Linant de Bellefonds.[3]
It is a natural depression in the Libyan chain of hills,
having an area of about 400 square miles,[4] of which
150 are occupied by a long and narrow lake,[5] the Birket-
el-Keroun (or 'Lake of the Horn'), whose waters cover
the north-western portion of the basin. The whole

---

[1] Herod. ii. 149; Strab. xvii. 1–3;
Plin. *H. N.* v. 9, § 9; Diod. Sic. i.
52; Pomp. Mel. i. 9.

[2] See the 'Mémoire sur le lac
Mœris' in the *Descript. de l'Egypte,*
'Antiquités,' vol. i. pp. 79–114.

[3] Linant's account is given in a
Mémoire which was published at
Alexandria in 1843 by the 'Société
Egyptienne.' It is entitled '*Mé-
moire sur le lac Mœris, présenté et
lu à la Société Egyptienne le 5 juillet*

1842, par Linant de Bellefonds, etc.'
[4] Bunsen, *Egypt's Place in Universal History,* vol. ii. p. 335 (translated by Cottrell).
[5] Bunsen says the lake is 'about
33 miles long, and has an average
width of about four miles' (ibid. p.
337). Dean Blakesley (*Herodotus,*
vol. i. p. 304) extends the length to
35 or 36 miles. Other estimates
will be found in Jomard's *Mémoire,*
pp. 83–4.

tract lies at a much lower level than that of the Nile valley, with which it is connected by a rocky ravine about eight miles in length,[1] having a direction from N.W. to S.E., and lying in about lat. 29° 20′. Originally the basin was most probably cup-shaped; but at present the ground within it slopes from the opening of the gorge in all directions—to the north, the west, and the south—the upper ground consisting of deposits of Nile mud, which have accumulated in the course of ages. A branch from the Bahr-Yousuf—still in use—was conducted in ancient times through the gorge; and an elaborate system of irrigation,[2] involving the construction of numerous dykes, canals, and sluices, brought almost the whole tract under cultivation, and rendered it one of the most productive portions of Egypt. The lake itself—which is a construction of nature and not of art—was of great value as a fishery,[3] and the Arsenoïte nome, as the whole tract was called, took rank among the chief wonders of a most wonderful country.[4]

The Eastern Desert is by far the largest of all the divisions of Egypt. Its length may be estimated at above 500 miles, and its average width at 130 or 140 miles.[5] Its entire area is probably not less than 65,000 square miles, or considerably more than two-thirds of the area of Egypt. It is in the main a region of rock, gravel, and sand, arid, waterless, treeless.[6] On the side

[1] Bunsen, p. 325.
[2] An account of the system employed will be given in the chapter on the Agriculture of the Egyptians.
[3] Herod. ii. 149. The Birket-el-Keroun is said still to produce excellent fish. (*Description*, 'Etat Moderne,' vol. ii. p. 213.)
[4] Strab. xvii. 1: ἀξιολογώτατος τῶν ἀπάντων ὁ ᾿Αρσινοΐτης νόμος κατά τε τὴν ὄψιν καὶ τὴν κατασκευήν.

[5] Mr. Kenrick says: 'The Red Sea is nowhere more than 150 miles from the valley of the Nile' (*Ancient Egypt*, vol. i. p. 61); but this is untrue. Sir G. Wilkinson estimates the distance in lat. 24° at 175 miles. (See the author's *Herodotus*, vol. ii. p. 11, note [9].) The French map in the *Description* shows the same.
[6] See Belzoni's *Travels*, pp. 305–7.

of the Nile, the ridge rises in terraces,[1] which are steep and precipitous, presenting towards the west ranges of cliffs like walls; after this, mountains alternate with broad gravelly or sandy plains; the land gradually rises; the elevation of the hills is sometimes as much as 6,000 feet,[2] and is greatest about half way between the Nile and the Red Sea. The geological formation is limestone towards the north, sandstone about lat. 25°, and granite in lat. 24°; but occasionally masses of primitive rock are intruded into the secondary regions,[3] extending as far northward as lat. 27° 10′. In a few places the desert is intersected by rocky gorges of a less arid character, which furnish lines of communication between the Nile Valley and the Red Sea;[4] of these the most remarkable are, one about lat. 30°, connecting Cairo with the Gulf of Suez;[5] a second, in lat. 26°, uniting Coptos and Thebes with Cosseir;[6] and a third, branching off from the Nile in lat. 25°, and joining Edfou (Apollinopolis Magna) with Berenicé,[7] in lat. 23° 50′. Other similar gorges or ravines penetrate into the desert region for a longer or a shorter distance,

---

Compare the *Description*, 'Hist. Nat.' vol. ii. pp. 449–57 and pp. 611–21; and see also Russell, *Ancient and Modern Egypt*, pp. 419–20; and Kenrick, *Ancient Egypt*, vol. i. pp. 61–66.

[1] *Description*, 'Hist. Nat.' vol. ii. p. 437: 'La chaîne orientale présente, dans sa partie septentrionale, des escarpements semblables à de longues murailles formées d'assises horizontales. Le nom de *Gebel el-Mokattam* (montagne taillée) qu'elle porte dans le pays, lui a été donné sans doute à cause de ces formes escarpées.'

[2] Kenrick, p. 62.

[3] Russegger, *Geognostiche Karte*,

quoted by Kenrick, vol. i. p. 62, note [2].

[4] *Description*, 'Hist. Nat.' vol. ii. p. 345.

[5] This is well marked in Belzoni's map. The *Description* also gives it very clearly in the general 'Carte de l'Egypte,' at the end of the 'Antiquités,' vol. ii.

[6] *Description*, 'Hist. Nat.' l.s.c.; Wilkinson, *Topography of Thebes*, p. 412; Kenrick, *Ancient Egypt*, vol. i. p. 62.

[7] This was traversed by Belzoni (*Travels*, pp. 304–330). It is noticed by Mr. Kenrick (l.s.c.), and represented in the 'Carte de l'Egypte' of the *Description*.

and then suddenly terminate. For the most part these valleys are, to a certain extent, fertile. Trees grow in them ;[1] and they produce in abundance a thorny plant, called *basillah*,[2] which affords a sufficient nourishment for camels, goats, and even sheep. In places the vegetation is richer. 'Delightful ravines, ornamented with beautiful shrubs,' and producing date-trees and wild wheat, are said to exist in the northern portion of the desert,[3] while near the Red Sea, in lat. 28° 45', the monasteries of St. Antony and St. Paul are situated in 'verdant spots,' and 'surrounded with thriving orchards of dates, olives, and apricots.'[4] The great want of the region is water, which exists only in wells, scattered at wide intervals over its surface, and is always of an unpleasant and sometimes of an unwholesome character.[5] The only really valuable portion of the Eastern desert is that of Mount Zabara,[6] the region of the emerald mines, in lat. 24° 25', long. 35° nearly.

The valley of the Natron Lakes[7] is a long and narrow depression in the Libyan desert, lying chiefly between lat. 30° and 31°. It may be viewed as branching off from the valley of the Nile about Abousyr, between the great pyramids of Gizeh and those of Sakkara. Its general direction is from S.E.E. to N.W.W. ; and it thus runs parallel with the western skirt of the Delta, from which it is separated by an

---

[1] Belzoni, *Travels*, pp. 305, 307, 308, &c. The trees mentioned are the sont and sycomore.
[2] Ibid. p. 395 and Pl. 36.
[3] Russell, *Ancient and Modern Egypt*, p. 413.
[4] Ibid.
[5] Belzoni, *Travels*, pp. 309, 314, 320, &c.
[6] Ibid. pp. 313–315. Compare

Wilkinson, *Topography of Thebes*, p. 420; and Russell, *Ancient and Modern Egypt*, pp. 418–9.
[7] The chief authorities for this description are the French savants General Andréossy and M. Gratian le Père, whose Memoirs on the valley will be found in the *Description*, 'État Moderne,' vol. i. pp. 279–298, and vol. ii. pp. 476–480.

arid tract of limestone rock and gravelly desert, from thirty to fifty miles in width. The length of the valley from the point where it quits the Nile to the place where it is lost in the sands south of Marea a little exceeds ninety miles. The lakes occupy the central portion of the depression, lying between lat. 30° 16′ and lat. 30° 24′. They are six in number, and form a continuous line, which is reckoned at six French leagues,[1] or about sixteen and a half English miles. Their ordinary width is from 100 to 150 yards. The water is supplied from springs, which rise in the limestone range bounding the valley on the north-east, and flow copiously from midsummer till December, after which they shrink and gradually fail till the ensuing June.[2] During the time of their failure some of the lakes become dry. Though the water of the springs which supply the lakes is quite drinkable, yet it contains in solution several salts, as especially the muriate of soda or common sea salt, the subcarbonate of soda,[3] or natron, and the sulphate of soda ; and these salts, continually accumulating in the lakes, which have no outlet, crystallise on their surface in large quantities, and become valuable objects of commerce.[4] Excepting immediately round the lakes, there is little vegetation ;[5]

---

[1] *Description*, 'Etat Moderne,' vol. i. p. 281.

[2] Gen. Andréossy argues from this, with considerable force, that the water must be really derived from the Nile, and filter through the thirty miles of intervening soil, since the copious flow of the springs is exactly coincident with the time of the inundation.

[3] Gen. Andréossy says 'the carbonate' (p. 282); but Wilkinson (in my *Herodotus*, vol. ii. p. 142,

note [4]) 'the subcarbonate.' I am not chemist enough to know which is right.

[4] The salt from one of the lakes is said to be of a red colour, and to have an odour like that of a rose (Andréossy, l.s.c.).

[5] A few palms grow in places, and there are numerous tamarisk bushes. Otherwise, the vegetation consists merely of the 'flags, sedge, and rushes, which thickly fringe the margins of the lakes' (ibid. p. 285).

yet the valley is permanently inhabited at the present day by the monks of three convents, besides being visited from time to time by caravans of merchants, bent on conveying its treasures to Cairo or Alexandria. South of the Natron Valley, and separated from it by a low ridge, is a waterless ravine, containing a quantity of petrified wood, which has been regarded by some as an old branch of the Nile,[1] and supposed to have a connection with the Birket-el-Keroun ;[2] but this latter supposition is entirely erroneous,[3] and it may be doubted whether the presumed connection with the Nile is not equally without foundation.[4]

The countries whereby ancient Egypt was bordered were three only, Ethiopia, Libya, and Syria including Palestine. Ethiopia, which lay towards the south, was a tract considerably larger than Egypt, comprising, as it did, not only Nubia, but the whole of the modern Abyssinia, or the tract from which flow the Atbara and Blue Nile rivers. It was also, in part, a region of great fertility, capable of supporting a numerous population, which, inhabiting a mountain territory, would naturally be brave and hardy.[5] Egypt could not but have something to fear from this quarter ; but a certain degree of security was afforded by the fact, that between her frontier and the fertile portion of Ethiopia lay a desert tract, extending for above six degrees, or more

---

[1] Andréossy, p. 208 ; Russell, p. 61, and map.
[2] Russell, l.s.c.
[3] The supposed connection has depended very much on the name Bahr-bela-ma, or 'river without water,' which, however, is really applied by the Arab to any waterless ravine. There is a Bahr-bela-ma in the Fayoum, which has no issue from it (Bunsen's Egypt, vol. ii.

pp. 340-2) ; another between the Fayoum and the oasis of Ammon (Belzoni, Travels, p. 401) ; and a third near the Natron Valley (Description, ' Etat Moderne,' vol. i. p. 286).
[4] See the remarks of Mr. Kenrick, Ancient Egypt, vol. i. p. 70.
[5] Compare Herod. ix. 122. The warlike qualities of the modern Abyssinians are undeniable.

than 400 miles, between the mouth of the Atbara and
Syêné. The dangers of the desert might indeed be
avoided by following the course of the Nile; but the
distance was under such circumstances very considerably increased, the march from Meroë to Syêné being
augmented from one of 450 to one of 850 miles.
Hence the ordinary route followed was that across the
Nubian desert,[1] a distance of not less than ten days'
march for an army; and thus, practically, it may be
said that a barrier difficult to surmount protected
Egypt on the south, and rendered her, unless upon rare
occasions, secure from attack on that side.

The vast tract, known to the ancients vaguely as
Libya, and inhabited by Libyans, extended from the
Delta and the Nile valley westward across the entire continent,[2] comprehending all North Africa west of Egypt,
excepting the small Greek settlements of Cyrene and
Barca, and the Phœnician ones of Carthage, Utica, and
Hippo. The geographical area was enormous; but the
inhospitable nature of the region, which is for the most
part an arid and unproductive desert, though dotted
with palm-bearing oases,[3] rendered it in the main unfit
for the habitation of man, and kept the scattered tribes
that wandered over its surface from multiplying. The
portion of North Africa which borders on Egypt is
particularly sterile and unattractive; a scant and
'sparse population can alone contrive to find subsistence
amid its parched and barren wastes; and this population, engaged in a perpetual struggle for existence, is

[1] Herod. iii. 25. Compare Burckhardt, Travels in Nubia, p. 171;
Baker, Albert Nyanza, vol. i. p. 4;
Nile Tributaries, p. 4, &c.
[2] Herod. iv. 197.
[3] Ibid. iv. 181. The oases are
more numerous than Herodotus
imagined; but still they bear only a
small proportion to the arid territory. (See Barth's Maps in the
fifth volume of his Travels, opp. p.
1 and opp. p. 457.)

naturally broken up into tribes which regard each other with animosity, and live in a state of constant war, rapine, and mutual injury. Combination is almost impossible under such circumstances ; and thus the great and powerful monarchy of Egypt could have little to fear from the tribes upon its western frontier, which were individually weak,[1] and were unapt to form leagues or alliances. Once alone in the history of Egypt does any great attack come from this quarter, some peculiar circumstances having favoured a temporary union between races ordinarily very much disinclined to act together.

On the east Egypt was protected along the greater portion of her frontier by a water barrier, a broad and impassable[2] moat, the Red Sea and its western prolongation, the Gulf of Suez. It was only at the extreme north, where Africa is joined on to Asia, that on this side she had neighbours. And here, again, she enjoyed to some extent the protection of a desert. Egypt is separated from Syria by the sandy tract, known to the Arabs as El-Tij, the 'Wilderness of the Wanderings.' The width of the desert is, however, not great ; armies have at all times traversed it without much difficulty ;[3] and with the support of a fleet, it is easy to conduct a force

---

[1] The Maxyes seem to have been the most powerful of the tribes (Lenormant, *Manuel*, vol. i. p. 427). They are mentioned by Herodotus (iv. 191),and others (Hecat. Fr. 304; Justin, xviii. 6; Steph. Byz. *ad voc.*), and take a leading part in the great Libyan attack on Egypt,which will be described in a later chapter.

[2] In the infancy of nations seabarriers were of great importance, and could with difficulty be surmounted, owing to the dangers of navigation. The Red Sea, with its rock-bound coast, its want of harbours, and its liability to sudden storms, was peculiarly dreaded.

[3] The Pharaohs frequently, perhaps generally, conveyed their armies into Syria by sea; but their enemies, the Hyksos, the Assyrians, Babylonians, and Persians, traversed the desert when they made their invasions. The early Arab conquerors and the Crusaders marched through the desert frequently, as in more recent times did Napoleon and Ibrahim Pasha.

along the coast route from Gaza to Pelusium. Accordingly, we shall find that it was especially in this quarter,
on her north-eastern border, that Egypt came into
contact with other countries, made her own chief military
expeditions, and lay open to attack from formidable
enemies. The strip of fertile land—alternate mountain
and rich plain—which intervenes between the eastern
Mediterranean and the Palmyrene or Syrian desert, has
at all times been a nursery of powerful and warlike
nations—Emim, Rephaim, Philistines, Canaanites,
Israelites, Hittites, Jews, Saracens, Druses. Here in
this desirable region, which she could not help coveting,
Egypt was brought into collision with foemen ' worthy
of her steel '—here was the scene of her early military
exploits—and hence came the assault of her first really
dangerous enemy.[1] Moreover, it was through this
country alone, along this fertile but somewhat narrow
strip, that she could pass to broader and richer regions
—to Mesopotamia, Assyria, Asia Minor—seats of a
civilisation almost as ancient as her own—wealthy,
populous, well-cultivated tracts,—next to the Nile
valley, the fairest portions of the earth's surface. Thus
her chief efforts were always made on this side, and her
history connects her not so much with Africa as with
Asia. For twenty centuries the struggle for the first
place among the nations of the earth was carried on
in these regions—Egypt's rivals and enemies were
Syria, Assyria, Babylonia, Persia—her armies and those
of her adversaries were perpetually traversing the
• Syrian and Palestinian plains and valleys—the country
between the ' river of Egypt ' and the Euphrates at
Carchemish was the battle-ground of the 'Great

---

[1] The nation, called Hyksos by Manetho, probably a Semitic race.

Powers'—and the tract is consequently one with which
Egyptian history is vitally connected. Its main features
are simple and easily intelligible. A spur from Taurus [1]
detaches itself in E. long. 37°, and, skirting the Gulf of
Issus, runs south and a little west of south from the
37th parallel to beyond the 33rd, where we may regard it as terminating in Mount Carmel. Another
parallel range [2] rises in Northern Syria about Aleppo,
and, running at a short distance from the first, culminates
towards the south in Hermon. Between them lies the
deep and fertile valley of Cœlesyria, watered in its more
northern parts by the Orontes, and in its more southern
by the Litany. Extending for above 200 miles from
north to south, almost in a direct line, and without
further break than an occasional screen of low hills,
Cœlesyria furnishes the most convenient line of passage
between Africa and Asia, alike for the journeys of
merchants and the march of armies.[3] Below Hermon.
the mountains cease, and are replaced by uplands of a
moderate elevation. The country is everywhere travers-
able ; but the readiest route is that which, passing from
the Bukaa [4] over the hills of Galilee, descends into the
plain of Esdraëlon, and then, after crossing the low
range which joins Carmel to the Samaritan highland,
proceeds along the coast through the plain of Sharon
and the Shephelah to the Egyptian frontier at the
Wady-el-Arish. Such are the chief features of Syria

[1] This spur is known as Amanus
in the north, then as Casius and
Bargylus; towards the south as
Libanus or Lebanon ('the White
Mountain').
[2] This range bears various names.
Towards the south it is known as
Anti-libanus, or the range over
against Lebanon.

[3] See *Ancient Monarchies*, vol. iv.
p. 291 (1st ed.).
[4] This is the native name of the
more southern part of the Cœlesyrian valley (see Tristram, *Land
of Israel*, p. 620; and compare
Smith's *Dict. of the Bible*, vol. iii.
p. 1405).

considered strategically. It presents one, and one only, *regular* line of march for the passage of armies. This line of march is from south to north, by Philistia, Sharon, the Esdraëlon plain, Galilee, and the Cœlesyrian valley, to the latitude of Aleppo, whence are several routes to the Euphrates. There is also one *secondary* line, which passing out of Galilee to the north-cast, and leaving Hermon and Anti-libanus to the left, proceeds by way of Damascus along the eastern skirt of the mountains to Chalcis, Gabbula, and Hierapolis. But directly, from west to east, through the Syrian desert, there is no route that an army can traverse. Caravans may pass from Damascus by Palmyra to Circesium, and possibly may cross the desert by other lines and in other directions ; but such routes must be left out of sight when the tract is viewed strategically. The line of communication between Africa and Asia, between Egypt and the Mesopotamian plain, so far as armies are concerned, lies north and south, by Palestine and Cœlesyria to the latitude of Antioch and Aleppo.

Politically, Syria, though scarcely suitable for the seat of a great power, is a country that may well hold a high secondary rank. Well watered and well wooded, possessing numerous broad valleys and rich plains, she can nurture a population of many millions, and in her mountain fastnesses can breed races of a high physical development and excellent moral qualities. The classical idea of Syrian weakness and sensuality[1] belongs to comparatively late times, and applies especially to the inhabitants of luxurious and over-civilised cities. In the mountain regions of Libanus and Anti-libanus,

---

[1] See Hor. *Od.* ii. 7, 8 ; *Sat.* i. 2, 1 ; Propert. *Eleg.* ii. 23, 21 ; iii. 4, 30 ; Juven. *Sat.* iii. 62–66, &c,

on the table-land of Moab and Ammon, and even in
the hill-tracts of Galilee, Samaria, and Judæa, the
natives are naturally hardy, warlike, even fierce. The
land itself is favourable for defence, possessing many
strong positions, capable of being held by a handful of
brave men against almost any numbers. Syria was
thus by far the most powerful of the countries bordering
upon Egypt; and it was natural that she should play an
important part in Egyptian history. Libya was too
weak for offence, too poor to tempt aggression; Ethiopia
was too remote and isolated; Syria alone was near, rich,
attractive; too strong to be readily overpowered, too
freedom-loving to be long held in subjection, of sufficient force to be occasionally aggressive; sure therefore to come frequently into collision with her neighbour,
and likely to maintain an equal struggle with her for
centuries. Above all, she lay on the road which
Egyptian effort was sure to take; she was the link
between Africa and Asia; she at once separated and
united the countries which were the earliest seats of
empire. If Egypt were ambitious, if she strove to
measure her strength against that of other first-rate
powers, she could only reach them through Syria; if
they retaliated, it was on the side of Syria that she
must expect their expeditions. We shall find in the
sequel that, from the time of the twelfth to that of the
twenty-sixth dynasty, connection between Egypt and
Syria, generally hostile, was almost perpetual, and that
consequently to all who would understand Egyptian
history, a knowledge of Syria, both geographically and
politically, is indispensable.

CHAPTER II.

CLIMATE AND PRODUCTIONS.

Climate of Egypt—of the Nile Valley—of the Eastern Highland. Vegetable Productions—Indigenous Trees and Plants—Plants anciently cultivated. Indigenous Wild Animals—Domesticated Animals. Birds, Fish, Reptiles, and Insects. Mineral Products.

'Provincia . . omni granorum ac leguminum genere fertilis.'
LEO AFRIC. viii. 1.

In considering the climate of Egypt, we must begin by making a distinction between Egypt proper or the valley of the Nile, including the Delta, and that desert and (comparatively speaking) mountainous tract which intervenes between the Nile valley and the Red Sea, and which we have reckoned to Egypt in the preceding chapter.[1] The difference between the climates of the two regions is considerable; and no description which should extend to both could be at once minute and accurate.

The leading characteristics of the climate of the Nile valley are, combined warmth and dryness. In Southern Egypt, which lies but a very little outside of the tropic of Cancer, the heat during the summer time is excessive, being scarcely surpassed even by that of Central Bengal, which lies under the same parallel. The range of the thermometer throughout this portion of the year is from 100° to 112° in the shade during

---

[1] See above, pp. 32-4.

the daytime.[1] At night, of course, the heat is less,
but still it is very great. In Northern Egypt several
causes combine to keep the summer temperature at a
lower level. The difference in latitude, which is seven
degrees, by substituting oblique for vertical rays, causes
a certain diminution in the solar power. The spread
of the inundation over the low lands, happening at this
time,[2] produces a general absorption, instead of a reflection, of the sun's rays; while the prevalence of
northerly and north-westerly winds, noted by Herodotus[3]
as well as by modern observers,[4] brings into the valley
a continual current of air, coming from a cool quarter,
and still further cooled by its passage over the Mediterranean. The summer may be considered to commence
in April, and to terminate at the end of October. The
heats at this time subside, and a mild pleasant temperature succeeds, which continues with little change
throughout the remainder of the year, until summer
comes round again. Hence, Egypt has been said to
have but two seasons, spring and summer.[5] Snow and
frost are wholly unknown, and the temperature rarely
falls below 40° of Fahrenheit.[6]

The dryness of the Nile valley is very remarkable.
In ancient times it was even believed that rain scarcely

[1] Russell, *Ancient and Modern Egypt*, pp. 53–4.
[2] Supra, p. 20.
[3] Herod. ii. 20. Compare Diod. Sic. i. 39, and Aristot. *Meteor.* ii. 6.
[4] Wilkinson in the author's *Herodotus*, vol. ii. p. 26, note [1] (2nd Edition); Andréossy in the *Description de l'Egypte*, 'Etat Moderne,' vol. i. p. 267.
[5] See Anderson's *Geography*, p. 152. The Egyptians themselves spoke of three seasons—Spring,

Summer, and Winter (Diod. Sic. i. 11).
[6] The lowest temperature registered at Cairo during the French occupation was 2° of Réaumur, or 36½° of Fahrenheit, which was reached on one night during January, 1799; 37½° was registered on one other night. The average temperature at night was about 46°. (See the *Description de l'Egypte*, 'Hist. Nat.' vol. ii. p. 332.)

ever fell in any part of it. Mela[1] calls Egypt 'a land devoid of showers;' and Herodotus regards even a slight drizzle[2] in the Thebaid as a prodigy. These views are exaggerated, but rest upon a basis of truth. There is less rain in Egypt than in almost any other known country. In the upper portion of the valley, showers ordinarily occur only on about five or six days in the year,[3] while heavy rain is a rare phenomenon, not witnessed more than once in every fifteen or twenty years. A continuance of heavy rain for two or three days is almost unheard of,[4] and would cause the fall of many buildings, no provision being made against it. In Lower Egypt the case is somewhat different. At Alexandria and other places upon the coast, rain is as common in winter as it is in the south of Europe. But during the rest of the year, as little falls as in the upper country; and at fifty or sixty miles from the coast the winter rains cease, the climate of Cairo being no less dry than that of the Thebaid. At the same time it must be noted that, notwithstanding the rarity of rain, the air is moderately moist, evaporation from the broad surface of the Nile keeping it supplied with a fair degree of humidity.

In the desert tract between the Nile valley and the Red Sea the air is considerably drier than in the valley itself, and the alternations of heat and cold are greater. In the summer the air is suffocating, while in winter the days are cool, and the nights positively cold. Heavy rain and violent thunderstorms are frequent at this season; the torrent beds become full of water, and

---

[1] *De situ Orbis*, i. 9.
[2] Herod. iii. 10 (τότε ὕσθησαν αἱ Θῆβαι ψακάδι). Mons. Courtelle in the *Description* ('Hist. Nat.' vol.

ii. p. 321) echoes Herodotus.
[3] Wilkinson in the author's *Herodotus*, vol. ii. p. 14.
[4] Ibid. p. 15.

pour their contents into the Nile on the one hand and the Red Sea on the other. A month or two later these beds are perfectly dry, and are covered with a drapery of green herbage, interspersed with numerous small flowers, until about May, when the heat of the sun and the oppressive wind from the Desert, known as the Khamseen, withers them up, and nothing remains except a few acacia trees and some sapless shrubs from which only a camel can derive any sustenance.[1]

The Khamseen wind is one of the chief drawbacks upon the delights of the Egyptian climate. It arises for the most part suddenly, and without warning, from the south or south-west. 'The sky instantly becomes black and heavy; the sun loses its splendour and appears of a dim violet hue; a light warm breeze is felt, which gradually increases in heat till it almost equals that of an oven. Though no vapour darkens the air, it becomes so grey and thick with the floating clouds of impalpable sand that it is sometimes necessary to use candles at noonday. Every green leaf is instantly shrivelled, and everything formed of wood is warped and cracked.'[2] The animal creation suffers. The pores of the skin are closed, and fever commences; the hot sand, entering the lungs, irritates them, and the breathing grows difficult and quick. Intense thirst is felt, which no drinking will assuage, and an intolerable sense of discomfort and oppression spreads over the whole frame. In towns and villages the inhabitants remain secluded in their houses, striving, but in vain, to prevent the sand from entering through their doors and windows. In the open

---

[1] Russell, *Ancient and Modern Egypt*, pp. 419–20; Belzoni, *Re-searches*, pp. 305, 307, 311, &c.
[2] Russell, p. 55.

fields and deserts, where shelter is unattainable, they
wrap their cloaks or shawls around their heads while
the storm lasts, and pray that it may cease.   If it continues for more than a day, their danger is great.
Whole caravans and even armies are said in such cases
to have been destroyed by its effects ; [1] and the solitary
traveller who is caught in one can scarcely hope to
escape.   Fortunately, however, prolonged storms of the
kind are rare ; their duration very seldom exceeds a
day ; [2] and thus upon the whole the Khamseen winds
must be regarded rather as an annoyance and discomfort than as an actual peril to life.[3]

The vegetable productions of Egypt may be
enumerated under the six heads of trees, shrubs,
esculent plants, wild and cultivated, grain, artificial
grasses, and plants valuable for medicinal or manufacturing purposes.   The trees are few in number,
comprising only the *dom* and date palms, the sycamore,
the tamarisk, the *mokhayt* or myxa, the *sunt* or
acanthus, and three or four other kinds of acacias.

The *dom* palm (*cucifera Thebaica*) is among the
most important of the vegetable products.   It first
appears a little north of Manfaloot [4] (lat. 27° 10'), and
is abundant throughout the whole of Upper Egypt.
The wood is more solid and compact than that of the
ordinary date tree.   It is suitable for beams and rafters,
as well as for boats, rafts, and other purposes which ne-
cessitate contact with water.   The fruit is a large rounded
nut, with a fibrous exterior envelope ; it has a sweet
flavour, very similar to our gingerbread.   The natives

---

[1] See Herod. iii. 26.
[2] Wilkinson in the author's *Herodotus*, vol. ii. p. 427, 3rd edition.

[3] Burckhardt's *Travels in Nubia*,
p. 190; Baker, *Nile Tributaries*, p. 17.
[4] Wilkinson's *Topography of
Thebes*, p. 387.

eat it both unripe and ripe : in the former case its
texture is like that of cartilage or horn ; in the latter,
it is very much harder, and has been compared with

Dom and Date Palms (from the *Description*).

the edible part of the cocoa-nut.[1] The wood of the
dom palm was used by the ancient Egyptians for the

[1] Wilkinson, *Ancient Egyptians*, vol. ii. p. 179.

handles of their tools,[1] and for all other purposes for
which a hard material was requisite; from the shell of
the nut they made beads, which took a high polish;[2]
the leaves served them for baskets, sacks, mats,
cushions, and other textile fabrics, for fans, fly-flaps,
brushes, and even for certain parts of their sandals.[3]
The *dom* palm is a picturesque tree, very different
in its growth from the ordinary palm. Instead of the
single long slender stem of its date-bearing sister, with
a single tuft of leaves at the top, the *dom* palm, by a
system of bifurcation, spreads itself out on every side
into numerous limbs or branches, each of which is
crowned by a mass of leaves and fruit.[4] The bifurcation begins generally about five feet from the ground,[5]
and is repeated at intervals of nearly the same length,
till an elevation is reached of about thirty feet. The
blossoms are of two kinds, male and female,[6] from the
latter of which the fruit is developed. This grows in
large clusters, and attains the size of a goose's egg
externally, but the nut within is not much bigger than
a large almond.[7]
The date palm is too well known to require description here. In Egypt the trees are of two kinds,
cultivated and wild. The wild tree, which springs
from seed, bears often an extraordinary number of
dates;[8] but being of small size and bad quality, they are

[1] Wilkinson, *Ancient Egyptians*, vol. ii. p. 180.
[2] Ibid.
[3] Ibid. p. 181.
[4] See the *Description de l'Égypte*, 'Hist. Nat.' vol. i. p. 53; Wilkinson, *Ancient Egyptians*, vol. ii. p. 179. See also the plate in the *Description*, 'Hist. Nat.' Planches, vol. iii. pl. 1. Compare Theophrast. *H.P.* ii. 7; p. 68.
[5] Wilkinson, l. s. c.
[6] *Description*, 'Hist. Nat.' vol. ii. p. 145.
[7] Ibid. Planches, vol. iii. pl. 2.
[8] Sir G. Wilkinson found a single bunch, which he gathered from a wild palm, to have on it between 6,000 and 7,000 dates. The tree was one of a cluster, each of which bore from 5 to 22 bunches. It may be concluded that each tree pro-

rarely gathered. The cultivated kind is grown from
offsets, which are selected with care, planted out at
regular intervals,[1] and abundantly irrigated. They
begin to bear in about five or six years, and continue
to be productive for sixty or seventy. In Roman times
it was said that the dates grown in Lower Egypt were
bad, while those of the Thebaïd were of first-rate
quality;[2] but under the Pharaohs we may be tolerably
sure that a good system of cultivation produced fruit
of fair quality everywhere. The wild tree furnishes,
and has probably always furnished, the principal
timber used in Egypt for building purposes. It is employed for beams and rafters either entire or split in
half,[3] and though not a hard wood, is a sufficiently good
material, being tough and elastic. The leaves, branches,
and indeed every part of the tree, serve some useful
purpose or other;[4] the dates have always constituted
a main element in the food of the people; from the
sap is derived an exhilarating drink; from the fruit
may be made, without much difficulty, wine, brandy,
and vinegar.

duced from 30,000 to 100,000 dates
(see Wilkinson, *Ancient Egyptians*,
vol. ii. p. 177, note).

[1] A single *feddan* (about 1¾ acre)
is sometimes planted with as many
as 400 trees. (Ibid. p. 178, note.)

[2] Strab. xvii. 1, § 51.

[3] *Description de l'Egypte*, 'Hist.
Nat.' vol. ii. p. 318; Wilkinson,
l.s.c.

[4] Wilkinson says:—'No portion
of this tree is without its peculiar
use. The trunk serves for beams,
either entire or split in half; of the
gereet, or branches, are made wicker
baskets, bedsteads, coops, and ceilings of rooms, answering every
purpose for which laths or any thin
wood-work are required; the leaves
are converted into mats, brooms,
and baskets; of the fibrous tegu-
ment at the base of the branches
strong ropes are made; and even
the bases of the *gereet* are beaten
flat and formed into brooms. Nor
are the stalks of the branches without their use: their fibres, separated by the mallet, serve for making
ropes, and for the *leef*, which is so
serviceable in the bath. Besides
the brandy, the *lowbgeh*, and the
date-wine, a vinegar is also extracted from the fruit; and the
large proportion of saccharine matter contained in the dates might, if
required, be applied to useful purposes.' (*Ancient Egyptians*, vol. ii.
p. 178.)

CH. II.]   THE FIG SYCAMORE AND MOKHAYT.   51

The Egyptian sycamore (*Ficus sycamorus*) is another tree of considerable value. The fruit, indeed, which ripens in the beginning of June, is not greatly esteemed, being insipid, though juicy;[1] but the shade is welcome, and the wood is of excellent quality. It is hard and close-grained, well fitted for all kinds of furniture. The ancient Egyptians used it for head-rests,[2] for figures or images,[3] for coffins,[4] and probably for many other purposes. Its superiority to most woods is shown in the fact, that the existing mummy-cases, which are in most instances made of it, have resisted the powers of decomposition for twenty, thirty, or even forty centuries. The tree grows to an extraordinary size in Egypt, some specimens, which have been measured, exceeding fifty feet in circumference.

The *mokhayt* (*Cardia myxa*) grows to the height of about thirty feet, and has a diameter of three feet at the base.[5] The stem is straight, and rises without branches to a height of ten or twelve feet, when it separates into a number of boughs, which form a large rounded head, rather taller than it is broad. The wood, which is hard and white, is employed in the manufacture of saddles.[6] The tree blossoms in May, and exhales at that time a delicious odour. Its fruit ripens about June, and is of a pale yellow colour, with two external skins, and a nut or stone in the centre. The texture of the fruit is viscous, and the flavour not very agreeable; but it is eaten by the natives, and the Arabs employ it as a medicine. In ancient times the Egyptians, we are told,

---

[1] Russell, *Ancient and Modern Egypt*, p. 475.
[2] Wilkinson, *Ancient Egyptians*, vol. ii. p. 205.
[3] Wilkinson, *Topography of*

[1 col 2] *Thebes*, p. 208, note.
[4] Ibid.   Compare *Russell*, l.s.c.
[5] *Description de l'Egypte*, ' Hist. Nat.' vol. ii. p. 191.
[6] Ibid. p. 193.

E 2

obtained from it a fermented liquor, which was regarded as a species of wine.[1]

The *sont* or acantha (*Mimosa Nilotica*) is a tree of no great size, groves of which are found in many parts of Egypt. At present it is valued chiefly on account of its producing the gum arabic;[2] but anciently it would appear to have been largely used in the construction of the boats engaged in the navigation of the Nile.[3] This is a purpose to which it is still applied to some extent;[4] but the wood of the *dom* palm, being found to answer better, is now employed more commonly. Herodotus says that the Nile boats were not only built of the acantha, but had also a mast of the same material. This, however, seems to be unlikely, as the wood is quite unsuited for that purpose.

The other acacias which grow in Egypt are the *lebbekh* (*Mimosa Lebbeck* of Linnæus), the *tuhl* (*Acacia gummifera*), the *fitneh* (*Acacia Farnesiana*), the *harras* (*Acacia albida*), and the *seyal* (*Acacia Soyal*). Of these the last is the most important, since it furnishes the great bulk of the gum arabic of commerce,[5] while at the same time its wood is valuable, being both by colour and texture well adapted for cabinet work. The general hue is orange with a darker heart: the grain is close, and the material hard. It is generally believed to be the 'shittim wood' of Scripture, which was employed for the Ark of the Covenant, and all the other furniture of the Tabernacle.[6] The *seyal* is 'a

---

[1] Plin. *H. N.* xiii. 5: 'Ex myxis in Ægypto et vina fiunt.'

[2] The pods of the *sont* are also valued, as they answer well for tanning (Wilkinson, *Topography of Thebes*, p. 210). This is a use to which they were applied anciently (Plin. *H. N.* l.s.c., and xxiv. 12).

[3] Herod. ii. 96; Plin. *H.N.* xiii. 9.

[4] Wilkinson in the author's *Herodotus*, vol. ii. p. 154, note [1] (3rd edition).

[5] *Description*, 'Hist. Nat.' vol. ii. p. 286.

[6] See the *Speaker's Commentary*, vol. i. p. 359.

gnarled and thorny tree, somewhat like a solitary haw-
thorn in its habit and manner of growth, but much
larger.'[1] Its height, when full grown, is from fifteen
to twenty feet.[2] It flourishes in the driest situations,
and is common in the Suez desert, in the tract between
the Nile and Red Sea, in the plain of Medinet-Habou,
and in the environs of Syêné.

Among the shrubs and fruit-trees of Egypt the most
important are the fig, the pomegranate, the mulberry,
the vine, the olive, the apricot, the peach, the pear, the
plum, the apple, the orange, the lemon, the banana, the
carob or locust tree (*Ceratonia siliqua*), the persea, the
palma Christi or castor-oil plant (*Ricinus communis*),
the *nebk* (*Rhamnus nabeca*), and the prickly pear or *shôk*
(*Cactus opuntia*). Of these, the orange, lemon, apricot,
and banana are probably importations of comparatively
recent times; but the remainder may be assigned, either
positively or with a high degree of probability, to the
Egypt of the Pharaohs.

It is unnecessary to describe the greater number
of these products; but there are some with which the
ordinary reader is not likely to be familiar, and of these
some account must be given. The persea (*Balanites
Ægyptiaca*), which is now rare in the Nile valley,[3]
but is met with in the Ababdeh desert, and grows in
great profusion on the road from Coptos to Berenice,[4]
is a bushy tree or shrub, which attains the height
of eighteen or twenty feet under favourable circum-

---

[1] Tristram (quoted in the *Speaker's Commentary*, l.s.c.).

[2] *Description*, l.s.c.

[3] Wilkinson says it is not now found in the valley below Ethiopia (*Topography of Thebes*, p. 209); but it was seen growing near Cairo at the time of the French Expedi-

tion (*Description*, 'H. N.' vol. ii. p. 223). The ancients regarded it as undoubtedly Egyptian (Theophrast. *H. P.* iii. 3; iv. 2; Plin. *H. N.* xiii. 9).

[4] Belzoni, *Researches*, pp. 320-1; Wilkinson, *Topography of Thebes*, p. 209.

stances.[1] The bark is whitish, the branches gracefully
curved, the foliage of an ashy grey, more especially on
its under surface. The lower branches are thickly
garnished with long thorns, but the upper ones are
thornless. The fruit, which grows chiefly on the upper
boughs, and which the Arabs call *lalôb*,[2] is about the
size of a small date, and resembles the date in general
character.[3] Its exterior is 'a pulpy substance of a
subacid flavour;'[4] the stone inside is large in proportion to the size of the fruit, and contains a kernel of
a yellowish-white colour, oily and bitter.[5] Both the
external envelope and the kernel are eaten by the
natives.

The sillicyprium, or castor-oil tree (*Ricinus communis*), grows abundantly in Egypt.[6] It is a plant of
a considerable size, with leaves like those of the vine,[7]
and bears a berry from which the oil is extracted.
This has medicinal qualities, and was used anciently
for medical purposes;[8] but its main employment has
always been as a lamp oil of a coarse kind. According
to Strabo, the common people in Egypt applied it also
to the anointment of their persons.[9]

The *nebk* or *sidr* (*Rhamnus nabeca*) is a fruit tree
common in Egypt, and in the interior of Africa,[10] but
not found in many other places. The fruit, which
ripens very early in the year, usually in March or
April,[11] is a fleshy substance of a texture not unlike that

[1] *Description de l'Egypte*, 'H. N.'
vol. ii. p. 222.
[2] Wilkinson, l.s.c.
[3] Abd-allatif says (*Relation de
l'Egypte*, traduite par M. de Sacy,
p. 17): 'Son fruit ressemble à la
datte.'
[4] Wilkinson, ut supra.
[5] *Description*, p. 223.
[6] Wilkinson in the author's *He-*

rodotus, vol. ii. p. 153.
[7] Wilkinson,   *Topography   of
Thebes*, p. 210.
[8] Plin. *H. N.* xv. 7.
[9] Strab. xvii. 2, § 5.
[10] *Description de l'Egypte*, 'Hist.
Nat.' vol. ii. p. 2.
[11] Wilkinson,   *Topography   of
Thebes*, p. 265.

of the date, with a hard stone in the centre. It is
eaten both raw and dried in the sun, the fleshy part
being in the latter case detached from the stone. Its
flavour is agreeable, and it is recommended as well
suited for sustenance during a journey.[1]
One species of fig, called *hamát* in Arabic, is indigenous in Egypt, and may often be found in desert
situations, growing wild from clefts in the rocks.[2] The
fruit, called by the Romans 'cottana,'[3] and by the
modern Arabs ' qottáyn,' is small in size, but remarkably
sweet.
The esculent plants of Egypt may be divided into
the wild and the uncultivated : among those which grew
wild, the most important were the byblus, or papyrus.
the *Nymphæa lotus*, the *Lotus cærulea*, and the *Nymphæa
nelumbo.*
The byblus, or papyrus (*Cyperus papyrus*), anciently
so common in Egypt, is not now found within the
limits of the country. It is a tall smooth flag or reed,
with a large triangular stalk,[4] inside of which is contained the pith from which the Egyptians made their
paper. The paper was manufactured by cutting the
pith into strips, arranging them horizontally, and then
placing across them another layer of strips, uniting the
two layers by a paste, and subjecting the whole to a
heavy pressure.[5] The upper and middle portions of
the reed were employed for this purpose ; the lower
portion, together with the root, was esteemed a delicacy.
and was eaten after it had been baked in a close vessel.[6]

---

[1] Burckhardt, *Travels in Nubia*,
p. 281.
[2] Wilkinson, *Topography*, p. 208.
[3] See Plin. *H. N.* xiii. 5; and
Martial, *Epig.* xiii. 28.
[4] Wilkinson in the author's *He-*
rodotus, vol. ii. p. 150 ; Cowan in
the *Encyclopædia Britannica*, vol.
xvii. pp. 246-8.
[5] Plin. *H. N.* xiii. 12.
[6] Herod. ii. 92.

The papyrus needed a moist soil, and was carefully cultivated in the shallow lakes and marshes, more especially those of the Sebennytic nome in the central part of the Delta. There was a second coarser kind— probably the *Cyperus dives* of botanists,[1]—which was employed in the construction of boats,[2] of sails,[3] of mats, baskets, sandals, and the like.[4]

The *Nymphœa lotus*, which nearly resembles our white water-lily,[5] grows freely in the lowlands of the Delta during the time of the inundations, being found at that period in ponds and channels which are ordinarily dry.[6] In ancient times the peasants collected and dried the seed-vessels of this plant, which they crushed and made into cakes that served them for bread.[7] They also ate the rest of the plant, which was considered to have ' a pleasant sweet taste,'[8] and was eaten either raw, baked, or boiled. A recent writer compares the flavour to that of ' a bad truffle,' and complains that the taste is ' exceedingly insipid;'[9] but it seems to have commended itself to the Egyptian palate, which was probably less fastidious than that of modern Europeans.

The *Lotus cœrulea* is scarcely more than a variety of the Nymphæa.[10] Its blossoms, which are of a pale blue colour, have fewer petals than those of the ordinary plant ; its leaves have a somewhat more oval shape, and are darker on their under surface. The seed-vessels

---

[1] Wilkinson in the author's *Herodotus*, l.s.c.

[2] Plin. *H. N.* vi. 22; vii. 16; xiii. 11; Theophrast. *H. P.* iv. 9; Plut. *de Isid. et Osir.* § 18; Lucan, *Pharsalia*, iv. 136; Isaiah, xviii. 2.

[3] Herod. ii. 96.

[4] Theophrastus, l.s.c. ; Plin. l.s.c.

[5] Wilkinson in the author's *He-*

rodotus, vol. ii. p. 148.

[6] Ibid.

[7] Herod. ii. 92. Theophrastus represents the cakes as formed of the seeds only (*Hist. Plant.* iv. 10).

[8] Herod. l.s.c.

[9] Wilkinson, *Topography of Thebes*, p. 205, note.

[10] *Description de l'Egypte*, ' H. N.' vol. ii. p. 307.

and roots are almost exactly similar, though the Arabs
pretend to make a distinction and to prefer the blue
variety, which they call *beshnin a'raby*, 'the lotus of
Arabs,' while they term the white *beshnin el-khanzyr*,
'the lotus of pigs.'[1]   Both the ordinary lotus and the
cærulea were valued on account of their flowers, which
were employed at banquets and woven into garlands
for the guests.[2]

The Nelumbium, or *Nymphæa nelumbo*, though not
now found in Egypt, nor indeed in Africa,[3] was beyond
all doubt a denizen of the country in ancient times,
though it may not have been indigenous.[4]   The Greeks
and Romans knew it as 'the Egyptian bean;'[5] and the
latter people regarded it as so characteristic of Egypt
that they used it constantly where they wanted an
Egyptian emblem.[6]   It has the general features of the
lotus tribe, growing in water, with round leaves which
float on the top, and having a large conical bud, from
which bursts a corolla of petals, that curve inwards, and
form a sort of cup.[7]   The peculiarities of the *nelumbo*
are the large size of its leaves, and the size and lovely
colour of its blossoms.   The diameter of the leaf varies

---

[1] *Description de l'Egypte*, vol. ii.
p. 306.
[2] Wilkinson, *Ancient Egyptians*,
vol. ii. p. 183.
[3] *Description*, 'H. N.' vol. ii. p.
309.
[4] Wilkinson in the author's *Herodotus*, vol. ii. p. 149.
[5] The *Nelumbo* is the κύαμος
Αἰγύπτιος of Theophrastus (*H. P.*
iv. 10); Diodorus Siculus (i. 9, 30);
Strabo (xvii. 2, § 4) ; and Dios-
corides (ii. 128); and the *faba
Ægyptia* of Pliny (*H. N.* xvii. 12),
which he also calls by its Greek
name of *cyamos*.   Its fruit is
thought by some to be the 'bean'

which Pythagoras forbade his fol-
lowers to eat.
[6] The *Nelumbo* is represented as
an Egyptian type on the large
statue of the Nile-God in the Vatican.   It appears in the mosaic of
Palestrina with a similar import
(*Histoire de l'Académie des Inscriptions* for 1790), and is employed to
express the same idea on various
Roman coins. (See Spanheim, *De
præstantia et usu numismatum*, vol.
i. p. 302, Lond. 1706 ; Zoega,
Numism. Ægypt. p. 193, Pl. 12,
No. 253; Morell, *Thesaur. Num.*
vol. ii. p. 391, Pl. 14, No. 5.)
[7] *Description*, l.s.c.

from a foot to a foot and a half; the petals are six inches in length, and of a beautiful crimson or rose-purple hue. They are arranged in two rows, one inner and one outer, while within them, at their base, is a dense fringe of stamens, surrounding and protecting the ovary. Here the fruit forms itself. It consists of a fleshy substance, shaped like the rose of a watering-pot;[1] and studded thickly with seeds, which project from the upper surface of the fruit, a circle about three inches in diameter.

Fruit of the *Nymphæa nelumbo.*

The number of the seeds is from twenty to thirty.[2] They are about the size of a small acorn, and contain inside their shell a white sweet-flavoured nut or almond, divided into two lobes, between which is a green leaf or ' corculum,' which is bitter, and should be removed before the nut is eaten. This nut, and also the root of the plant, were employed as food by the poorer classes among the ancient Egyptians.[3]

The cultivated vegetables of Egypt resemble in

[1] Wilkinson, *Topography of Thebes*, p. 206, note.
[2] *Description*, l.s.c.   Wilkinson

says 'about twenty-five.'
[3] Herod. ii. 92; Theophrast. *Hist. Plant.* iv. 10.

most respects those of the same class in other countries. They comprise peas, beans, lentils of two kinds, the *loobieh* (a sort of French bean), the endive, leeks, garlic, onions, melons, cucumbers, radishes, lettuce, capers, cumin, mustard, coriander, aniseed, and various others.[1] There is a perpetual succession of these different esculents, some of which are constantly in season, while others have a longer or a shorter term. The melon and cucumber class flourishes especially, the varieties being numerous,[2] and the fruit growing to a great size. The lentils, which form the chief food of the lower classes,[3] are of good quality. The mustard, aniseed, and coriander seed were anciently in especial repute.[4] The caper plant (*Capparis spinosa*) bears a fruit called *lussuf* by the Arabs, which is shaped like a small cucumber, and is two and a half inches long.[5]

Only three kinds of grain seem to have been cultivated by the ancient Egyptians. These were wheat, barley, and the *Holcus sorghum*, or modern *doora*.[6] Of wheat, there are now produced in Egypt six varieties;[7] and it is supposed that the same sorts existed in ancient as in modern times.[8] All of them but one are bearded.

---

[1] The subject of Egyptian vegetables has been carefully elaborated by Sir Gardner Wilkinson (*Topography of Thebes*, pp. 211–266; *Ancient Egyptians*, vol. iv. pp. 54–77); to whose works the reader is referred for further information.

[2] Eleven varieties of the melon and eight of the cucumber are mentioned. (Wilkinson, *Topography*, p. 262.)

[3] Wilkinson in the author's *Herodotus*, vol. ii. p. 203, note [6].

[4] See Plin. *H. N.* xix. 8; xx. 17, 20.

[5] Wilkinson, *Ancient Egyptians*, vol. iv. p. 69.

[6] On the cultivation of these three kinds of grain see Exod. ix. 31, 32; and compare Wilkinson, *Ancient Egyptians*, vol. iv. pp. 61, 97, &c.

[7] These are: 1. the *Towálee*, or long-eared wheat; 2. the *Dthukr Yousefee*, which is large-eared, and has a black beard; 3. the *Nayyeh*, small-eared, with black beard and husk; 4. the *Zerra el-Nebbi*, which is red, and without any beard; 5. the *Moghúyuz*, which has a short, broad ear; and 6. the *Tubbánee*, or white wheat, the kind most commonly cultivated. (See Wilkinson's *Topography of Thebes*, p. 261, note.)

[8] Wilkinson, *Ancient Egyptians*, vol. iv. p. 85.

the others differing chiefly in colour, and in the size of the ear. The common Egyptian wheat is white; it is sown in November, and reaped early in April, after an interval of about five months.[1] The barley cultivated is of two kinds, one red, and the other white. The two kinds are grown in about equal quantities, and are in equal repute.[2] The time of sowing, as with the wheat, is the month of November; but the grain is reaped much earlier, some coming to maturity in the latter half of February, while the remainder is harvested during the month of March.[3] There are five varieties of the *doora*;[4] but their differences are not important. Some is sown in November, and this ripens early in May; some in April, which ripens in July; and some in August, which comes to maturity in December. The doora is probably the '*olyra*' or '*zea*' of Herodotus, which (according to him) was the grain whereon the Egyptians mainly subsisted.[5]

Of artificial grasses, or plants cultivated as fodder for cattle, there were produced in ancient Egypt these four[6]—clover, vetches, lupins, and a plant called *gilbán* by the Arabs, and known to Pliny as the *Lathyrus sativus*.[7] The clover is thought to have been either the *Trifolium Alexandrinum* or the *Trigonella fœnumgræcum*, both of which are now common in Egypt.[8] The vetch was the *Cicer arietinum* of Linnæus and Pliny;[9] the lupin was the *Lupinus termis*, which

[1] Wilkinson, *Ancient Egyptians*, vol. iv. p. 53.
[2] Wilkinson, *Topography*, l.s.c.
[3] Ibid. Compare the *Speaker's Commentary*, vol. i. p. 286; note on Ex. ix. 31.
[4] Wilkinson, *Topography*, pp. 263-4.
[5] Herod. ii. 36.
[6] Wilkinson, *Ancient Egyptians*, vol. iv. pp. 61, 62, 97; *Topography*, p. 217.
[7] Plin. *H. N.* xviii. 12.
[8] Wilkinson, *Topography*, p. 218.
[9] Plin. l.s.c.

is still known as *termes* to the Arabs.[1] These plants
were, all of them, of rapid growth, and some were
capable of yielding three and even four crops in a year.[2]
They were eaten green, and also made into hay, and
stored up for the use of the cattle during the time of
the inundation.[3]

Among plants valuable for manufacturing and
medicinal purposes may be mentioned, in the first
place, those from which the Egyptians obtained oil for
lamps and for anointing themselves. For the former
purpose oil was obtained chiefly from three plants—the
'kiki,' or castor-oil plant (*Ricinus communis*), the
seemga (*Raphanus oleifer*), and the *simsim* or sesame.
The castor-oil plant has been already described:[4] it
gives out an oil with an unpleasant smell, but one which
is well suited for burning.[5] The Egyptians obtained it
either by pressing the berries, or by boiling them down
and then skimming the oil from the surface.[6] The
seemga, which now grows only in Nubia and the adjoining parts of Upper Egypt,[7] was largely cultivated in
ancient Egypt; and, in Roman times at any rate, its
seeds furnished the great bulk of the oil consumed.[8]
The sesame plant was also largely cultivated,[9] as it is at
the present day, the oil extracted from its seeds being
now reckoned the best lamp oil in the country.[10]

For anointing the body a greater number of oils
were used. The poorer classes applied to the purpose

[1] The Coptic name is ΘΑΡΜΟϹ OC,
'tharmos' (Wilkinson, *Ancient Egyptians*, vol. iv. p. 53).
[2] As the *Trifolium Alexandri-num*, which gives ordinarily three crops, and sometimes four. (Wil-kinson, l.s.c.)
[3] Wilkinson, *Topography*, p.218.
[4] Supra, p. 54.
[5] Pliny calls it 'cibis fœdum, lucernis utile' (*H. N.* xv. 7).
[6] Herod. ii. 94; Plin. *H. N.* l.s.c.
[7] Wilkinson, *Ancient Egyptians*, vol. iv. p. 55; *Topography of Thebes*, p. 220.
[8] Plin. *H. N.* xv. 7; xix. 5.
[9] Ibid. xv. 7, &c.
[10] Wilkinson, *Topography*, p. 219.

even the unpleasant-smelling 'kiki ; '[1] and the sesame oil
was used largely for adulterating the oils and unguents
regarded as appropriate to the person.[2]   But the richer
classes employed either olive oil or unguents of a more
expensive kind, such as were the 'metopion' or bitter-
almond oil (amygdalinum),[3] the 'cyprinum,'[4] which
was derived from the cypros, 'a tree resembling the
ziziphus in its foliage, with seeds like the coriander,'[5]
the 'œnanthinum,'[6] the 'amaracum' or 'sampsuchum,'[7]
the 'cnidinum,' yielded by a kind of urtica, or nettle,[8]
and an oil derived from a species of grass called
'chorticon.'[9]   Altogether Egypt was considered to be
better adapted for the manufacture of unguents than any
other country,[10] and by a mixture of various ingredients
recondite ointments were produced, which were regarded as of very superior quality.[11]

For manufacturing purposes the plants chiefly cultivated by the Egyptians were flax, which was very
largely grown, cotton, indigo, and the safflower or
Carthamus tinctorius. Linen was the ordinary material
of the under garment with all classes in Egypt ;[12] the
priests could wear nothing else when officiating ;[13] all

---

[1] Herod. ii. 94; Strab. xvii. 2, § 5.
[2] Plin. *H. N.* xiii. 1.
[3] The 'metopion' contained various other ingredients, but the Egyptian oil of bitter almonds pre-dominated. (See Plin. *H. N.* xiii. 1 — 'metopion — oleum hoc est amygdalis amaris expressum in Ægypto, cui addidere omphacium,' &c.; and compare xv. 7: 'Amygdalinum, quod aliqui metopium vocant.' Compare Dioscorid. i. 39.)
[4] Plin. *H. N.* xiii. 1; xv. 7.
[5] Ibid. xii. 24.
[6] Ibid. xiii. 1.   Compare xv. 7 and xxiii. 4.
[7] Plin. *H.N.* xxi. 11, 22. The 'sampsuchus' was a plant which grew in Cyprus and Mitylene (ibid. xiii.1).
[8] Ibid. xv. 7 ; xxii. 13.
[9] Ibid. xv. 7.
[10] Ibid. xiii. 3: 'Terrarum omnium Ægyptus adcommodatissima unguentis.'
[11] Especially the 'telinon' (Athen. *Deipn.* v. p. 195; Plin. xiii. 1), and the 'Mendesium' (Plin. l.s.c.).
[12] Herod. ii. 81, with Wilkinson's note. (Rawlinson's *Herodotus,* vol. ii. p. 132, note [8].)
[13] Herod. ii. 63.

dead bodies were wrapped in it previous to interment;[1] and it was employed also for ropes,[2] corslets,[3] and various other purposes. The representation of the flax harvest is frequent upon the monuments.[4] The kind chiefly cultivated is believed to have been the *Linum usitatissimum*,[5] which is now the only sort that is thought worth growing;[6] but anciently cultivation extended, we are told, to four varieties, which were known respectively as the Butic flax, the Tanitic, the Tentyric, and the Pelusiac.[7] Cotton (*Gossypium herbaceum*) was a product of the more southern parts of Egypt;[8] it was in almost equal repute with linen as a material for dress,[9] being preferred on account of its softness, though not regarded as possessing the highest degree of purity. Indigo and safflower were grown for the sake of the dyes which they furnished. Mummy-cloths were frequently stained with the safflower;[10] while indigo was used to colour textile fabrics of all kinds,[11] and also for the ornamental painting of walls.[12]

The number of medicinal plants and herbs produced in Egypt was matter of comment as early as the time of Homer.[13] Some of these grew naturally, while others were carefully cultivated. Among the former may be

---

[1] Herod. ii. 86. Wilkinson confirms the statement of Herodotus.
[2] Wilkinson in the author's *Herodotus*, vol. iv. p. 27, note [8].
[3] Ibid. vol. ii. pp. 271-2.
[4] Wilkinson, *Ancient Egyptians*, vol. iii. pp. 138-9; vol. iv. p. 98, &c.
[5] Ibid. vol. iv. p. 70.
[6] Wilkinson, *Topography of Thebes*, p. 262.
[7] Plin. *H. N.* xix. 1.
[8] Ibid.
[9] Wilkinson in the author's *Herodotus*, vol. ii. pp. 63 and 142. Pliny says: 'Vestes inde' (*i.e.* e

gossipio) 'sacerdotibus Ægypti *gratissimæ*' (l.s.c.).
[10] Wilkinson in the author's *Herodotus*, vol. ii. p. 143.
[11] Ibid. p.132; *Ancient Egyptians*, vol. iv. p. 62.
[12] Belzoni, *Researches*, p. 175.
[13] See *Odyss.* iv. 228-30:

'Εσθλὰ,τά οἱ Πολύδαμνα πόρεν,Θῶνος
παράκοιτις,
Αἰγυπτίη,τῇ πλεῖστα φέρει ζείδωρος
ἄρουρα
Φάρμακα, πολλὰ μὲν ἐσθλὰ μεμιγ-
μένα, πολλὰ δὲ λυγρά.

mentioned the colocinth,[1] the cassia senna,[2] the *Origanum Ægyptiacum*,[3] the myrobalanus[4] or *Moringa aptera*,[5] the *Clematis Ægyptia* (*Daphnoeides* or *Polygonoeides*),[6] and two arums,[7] probably the *Arum arisarum* and the *Arum colocasia*.[8] Among the latter, the most important were the anise[9] (*Pimpinella anisum*), an endive called 'seris'[10] (*Cichorium endivia?*), the coriander plant[11] (*Coriandrum sativum*), the Corchorum[12] (*Corchorus olitorius*), and the 'cnecum' or 'atractilis,'[13] which is thought to be the *Carthamus Creticus*.[14] Besides these, we find mentioned as medicinal plants produced in Egypt, the '*Apsinthius marinus*,'[15] the balsam,[16] the 'acacalis,'[17] the 'cyprus,'[18] the 'helenium,'[19] the 'myosotis,'[20] and the 'stratiotes.'[21] There was also a medicinal use of the tamarisk,[22] the papyrus,[23] the *Mimosa Nilotica*,[24] the *dom* and date palm,[25] the pomegranate,[26] the myrtle,[27] the locust-tree,[28] the 'persea,'[29] and many other plants.

Among the wild animals indigenous in Egypt the principal were the hippopotamus, the crocodile, the lion, the hyæna, the wolf, the jackal, the fox, the ichneumon, the hare, the jerboa, the rat, the mouse,

[1] 'An indigenous plant' (Wilkinson, *Ancient Egyptians*, vol. iv. p. 62).
[2] Ibid.
[3] Plin. *H. N.* xix. 8; xx. 16.
[4] Ibid. xxiii. 5.
[5] Wilkinson, *Ancient Egyptians*, vol. iv. p. 64.
[6] Plin. *H. N.* xxiv. 15.
[7] Ibid. 16.
[8] Wilkinson, *Ancient Egyptians*, vol. iv. p. 70.
[9] Plin. *H. N.* xx. 17.
[10] Ibid. xx. 8.
[11] Ibid. xx. 20.
[12] Ibid. xxi. 32.
[13] Ibid.
[14] Wilkinson, *Ancient Egyptians*, vol. iv. p. 74.
[15] Plin. *H. N.* xxvii. 7, ad fin.
[16] Dioscorid. *Mat. Med.* i. 18.
[17] Ibid. i. 118.
[18] Ibid. i. 124.
[19] Ibid. i. 28.
[20] Plin. *H. N.* xxvii. 12.
[21] Ibid. xxiv. 18.
[22] Dioscorid. *Mat. Med.* i. 116.
[23] Ibid. i. 115.
[24] Ibid. i. 133.
[25] Ibid. i. 143, 144.
[26] Ibid. i. 154.
[27] Ibid. i. 155.
[28] Ibid. i. 158.
[29] Ibid. i. 187.

the shrew-mouse; the porcupine, the hedgehog, and
perhaps the bear, the wild boar, the ibex, the gazelle,
three kinds of antelopes, the stag, the wild sheep, the
Monitor Niloticus, and the wild cat or *Felis chaüs*. The
hippopotamus seems in ancient times to have been
common, even in the more northern parts of Egypt,[1]
and to chase it was a favourite amusement. By degrees
it was driven southwards, and it is now uncommon
even in Nubia,[2] although occasionally it has been
known to descend the river beyond the First Cataract,
and to pass Syêné or Assouan.[3]

The crocodile is still very common in Upper Egypt,
but at present seldom descends below Manfaloot (lat.
27° 10').[4] Anciently, however, it was found along the
whole lower course of the Nile, even to the close vicinity of the sea,[5] as well as in the Fayoum or Arsinoïte
canton.[6] Notwithstanding its great size and strength,
it is a timid animal, 'flying on the approach of man,
and, generally speaking, only venturing to attack its
prey on a sudden.'[7] It will, however, seize and destroy
men, if it take them at a disadvantage; and instances
of its sweeping incautious persons from the bank of the
river into the water by the force of its tail, catching
them as they fall in its huge jaws, and carrying them
instantaneously to the bottom, are of no rare occurrence.[8] Still, for the most part, it lives on fish, which
abound in the Nile, and only occasionally indulges

[1] See Herod. ii. 71; and compare
Biod. Sic. i. 35; and Wilkinson,
Ancient Egyptians, vol. iii. p. 75.
[2] Wilkinson, *Ancient Egyptians*,
vol. v. p. 178.
[3] Burckhardt, *Travels in Nubia*,
p. 62; Wilkinson, *Ancient Egyptians*, vol. iii. p. 74.
[4] Wilkinson, l.s.c.

[5] Seneca, *Nat. Quæst.* iv. 2.
[6] Herod. ii. 69, 148; Ælian. x. 24.
[7] Wilkinson, *Ancient Egyptians*,
vol. iii. p. 78; *Topography*, p. 400.
Compare the remarks of M. Geoffr'y
St. Hilaire in the *Description*,' H.N.'
vol. ii. p. 144.
[8] Wilkinson, l.s.c.

itself in the luxury of devouring warm-blooded animals. It is very unwieldy upon land, and never goes far from the water's edge, but still it passes a good deal of its time in the air, more especially during the summer months, when it delights in frequenting the sand banks, where it sleeps with its mouth wide open and turned to the prevailing wind.[1]

Lions are not now found in any part of Egypt, nor anywhere in the Nile valley lower down than the junction with the Atbara.[2] It is believed, however, that anciently they inhabited the Egyptian deserts on either side of the river;[3] and the monuments show us that they were tamed and used by the upper classes in the chase of gazelles and ibexes.[4]

Hyænas, wolves, jackals, and foxes are among the most common of Egyptian wild animals.[5] The hyæna of the country is the ordinary, or striped hyæna (*Hyæna vulgaris*). It is both carnivorous and graminivorous, feeding in part upon wheat and *doora*, and doing great mischief to the standing crops,[6] while it will also attack cattle, and, on occasions, even man. In these cases, 'it is a rude and dangerous antagonist.'[7] It attacks by rushing furiously forward and throwing its adversary down by a blow of its large bony head, after which it uses its fangs and claws. In a sandy place it will even (we are told)[8] begin by throwing up a cloud of dust with

---

[1] Herod. ii, 68; Diod. Sic. i. 35; Wilkinson, *Ancient Egyptians*, vol. iii. p. 80.
[2] Wilkinson, *Ancient Egyptians*, vol. iii. p. 29.
[3] Ibid. Athenæus says that a lion was hunted and killed by the Emperor Hadrian near Alexandria (*Deipn.* xv. 6); and Amenemhat I. of the 12th dynasty speaks of hunt-ing the lion and the crocodile (*Records of the Past*, vol. ii. p. 14).
[4] Wilkinson, *Ancient Egyptians*, vol. iii. p. 16.
[5] Ibid. iii. 24; v. 145, 149, &c.
[6] Wilkinson, *Topography of Thebes*, p. 243, note.
[7] Wilkinson, *Ancient Egyptians*, vol. v. p. 159.
[8] Ibid.

its hind legs, and, after thus disconcerting its opponent, make its charge and bring him to the ground. The hyæna was much dreaded by the Egyptian peasants, who lost no opportunity of checking its ravages, by hunting it or catching it in traps.[1] There is nothing that is remarkable in the jackals or foxes of Egypt; but the wolves are peculiar. They are small in size,[2]

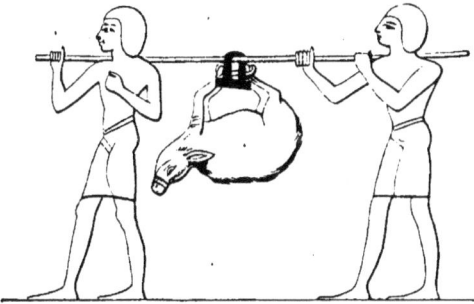

Hyæna caught in a trap (from the Monuments).

inactive in their habits,[3] and never gregarious. Usually they are met with prowling about singly; and it scarcely ever happens that more than two of them are seen together.[4]

The ichneumon (*Viverra ichneumon*) is a species of mangoust.[5] It lives principally in Lower Egypt and the Fayoum,[6] and haunts the borders of the Nile and the cultivated fields, where it conceals itself in the shallow ditches constructed for the irrigation of the crops.[7] It is excessively timid, and in the wild state is rarely seen. In length a full-grown specimen measures

[1] Wilkinson, *Ancient Egyptians*, vol. iii. p. 2.
[2] Herod. ii. 67; Aristot. *Hist. An.* viii. 28; Plin. *H. N.* viii. 22. Compare Wilkinson, *Ancient Egyptians*, vol. iii. p. 27.
[3] Plin. *H. N.* l.s.c.
[4] Wilkinson, vol. iii. p. 27; vol. v. pp. 145-6.
[5] *Description de l'Egypte*, tt. II. N.' vol. ii. p. 138.
[6] Wilkinson, vol. iii. p. 30; vol. v. p. 151.
[7] *Description*, p. 141.

about two feet and a half, the body being fifteen inches long, and the tail of the same (or a little greater) length with the body.[1] In a state of nature, it subsists chiefly upon eggs, and is said[2] to discover and devour great numbers of the eggs which the crocodile lays and leaves to hatch in the sand. It will also eat young birds and field-mice, if it finds the opportunity. The ichneumon has a singular antipathy to snakes. No sooner does it see one, than it advances to the attack. On the snake

Ichneumon (from the *Description*).

raising its head from the ground, the ichneumon springs upon it, seizes it at the back of the neck, and with a single bite lays it dead at its feet.[3] Ichneumons are frequently tamed, and, when made inmates of houses, answer the purpose of cats, clearing the residence of rats and mice with great rapidity.[4] It is difficult, how-ever, to prevent them from appropriating such things as eggs, poultry, pigeons, and the like, on which

---

[1] Wilkinson, vol. v. p. 152. M. St. Hilaire makes the length twenty French inches (*Description*, p. 139), which is less than two feet.

[2] *Description*, p. 143; Wilkinson, vol. v. p. 150.

[3] Wilkinson, vol. iii. p. 30; vol. v. p. 155. Compare Strab. xvii. 1,

§ 39; Plin. *H. N.* viii. 24; Ælian, *Nat. An.* vi. 38.

[4] *Description*, p. 141; Wilkinson, vol. iii. p. 31; vol. v. p. 153. Hence the name of 'Pharaoh's Cat,' by which the ichneumon is known to the modern Arabs.

account their services are for the most part dispensed with.[1] Many extraordinary tales were told of the ichneumon by the ancient naturalists,[2] who, like the early historians,[3] aimed at amusing rather than instructing their readers.

Egyptian Hare (from the *Description*).

The Egyptian hare is in no respects peculiar, excepting that it is smaller than that of Europe, and has

[1] Wilkinson, *Ancient Egyptians,* vol. v. p. 152.

[2] According to Diodorus (i. 35) the ichneumon broke the eggs of the crocodile, not to eat them, but to benefit mankind. It also destroyed the full-grown crocodile by a wonderful contrivance. Covering itself with a coat of mud, it watched till the crocodile was asleep, with its mouth gaping; when suddenly it sprang into the creature's jaws, glided down its throat, and gnawed through its stomach, so making its escape (i.

87). Strabo told a similar tale (xvii. 1, § 39), while Pliny and Ælian stated that, before attacking the asp, it covered itself with a coat of mud. The modern Arabs have a story that, if bitten by the asp, the ichneumon runs to a certain plant, eats some, and puts some on the wound, thereby rendering the poison harmless ! (See Wilkinson, vol. iii. p. 30.)

[3] Thucyd. i. 21 : 'Ως λογογράφοι ξυνέθεσαν ἐπὶ τὸ προσαγωγότερον τῇ ἀκροάσει, ἢ ἀληθέστερον.

longer ears.[1] The jerboa (*Dipus jaculus*), which is
common both in the upper and the lower country,
presents (it is said[2]) two varieties, and can scarcely
have been absent from ancient Egypt, though it is not
represented on the monuments. The rat, mouse, and
hedgehog, all of which are represented, require no
description. The porcupine, which appears on the
monuments frequently,[3] is also too well known to need
any comment.

It is a disputed point whether bears were ever
indigenous in Egypt. On the one hand, we have the
positive statement of Herodotus,[4] that in his time they
were not unknown there, although uncommon ; on the
other, we have the facts, that they appear on the monuments only among the curiosities brought by foreigners,[5]
that they are not now found there, and that no other
author besides Herodotus assigns them to the locality.
On the whole, it is perhaps best to suppose that Herodotus was, for once, mistaken.

It seems very improbable that Egypt could have
been in ancient times without the wild boar. Egypt is
of all countries the one which pre-eminently suits the
habits of the animal ; and it now abounds in the marshy
regions of the Delta, and also in the Fayoum.[6] Yet
representations of it are entirely absent from the monuments.[7] We may perhaps conjecture that the impurity,
which attached to the domestic animal,[8] extended also
to his wild congener ; and that though the wild boar
existed in the country, he was not hunted, and so

---

[1] Wilkinson, *Ancient Egyptians*,
vol. iii. p. 28.
[2] Ibid. vol. v. p. 175.
[3] Wilkinson, *Ancient Egyptians*,
vol. iii. pp. 9, 14, 19, &c.
[4] Herod. ii. 67.
[5] Wilkinson in the author's *He-*
rodotus, vol. ii. p. 114, note [6].
[6] Wilkinson, *Ancient Egyptians*,
vol. iii. p. 21 ; vol. v. p. 183.
[7] Ibid.
[8] Herod. ii. 47; Horapollo, ii. 37;
Ælian. *N. A.* x. 16.

escaped representation in the only sculptures in which he was likely to have appeared, namely, those representing hunting scenes.

The ibex, gazelle, oryx, antelope, stag, and wild sheep were certainly hunted by the Egyptians,[1] and were therefore, it is probable, denizens of some part or other of their country. The habits of these animals

Ibex, Oryx, and Gazelle (from the Monuments).

unfit them for such a region as Egypt Proper—the valley of the Nile and the Delta—but if we use the term 'Egypt' in a looser sense, including under it the tract between the Nile Valley and the Red Sea, together with a strip of the Western or Libyan Desert, we shall

Gazelles (from the Monuments).

find within such limits a very suitable *habitat* for these wild ruminants. The gazelle, the ibex, and the wild sheep are still to be met with in the Eastern Desert,

[1] Wilkinson, *Ancient Egyptians*, vol. iii. pp. 17-22.

especially in the more southern part of it,[1] and the stag, according to some accounts, is occasionally to be seen in the vicinity of the Natron Lakes.[2]   The oryx, the antelope *beïsa,* and the antelope *addax* inhabit Abyssinia;[3] while the antelope *defassa,* which seems to be one of those most frequently hunted by the Egyptians, is found in the Western Desert.[4]   This last is a large animal, standing about four feet high at the shoulder, of a reddish sandy colour, with a black tuft at the end of its tail.   It is not improbable, that anciently these several varieties of the antelope tribe had, one and all, a wider *habitat* than at present, and one which brought them within the limits of Egypt, in the more extended sense of the term.

The wild cat, or *Felis chaüs* of Linnæus, is now common in the vicinity of the Pyramids and of Heliopolis,[5] but is neither depicted on the monuments[6] nor mentioned by any of the ancient writers on Egypt.   It is, therefore, doubtful whether it inhabited the Egypt of the Pharaohs or not, though, as its introduction at any later period is highly improbable, it seems best, on the whole, to regard it as belonging to the class of indigenous animals.

The monitor of the Nile (*Lacerta Nilotica*) is another animal, which, though not represented upon the sculptures, and not even distinctly alluded to by any ancient writer,[7] must almost necessarily be regarded as

---

[1] Wilkinson, *Ancient Egyptians,* vol. iii. pp. 24–6.

[2] Ibid. p. 25.   [3] Ibid. p. 24.

[4] Ibid. p. 25.   The *defassa* is thought to be the real animal intended, where the artist seems to be representing wild cattle.   (See Wilkinson, vol. iii. pp. 18, 19.)

[5] Wilkinson, *Ancient Egyptians,* vol. iii. p. 31.

[6] Ibid. vol. iii. p. 21; vol. v. p. 174.

[7] It is probable that Herodotus may intend the monitor of the Nile by his ἔνυδρις, since the otter, which is what ἔνυδρις ordinarily means, was certainly not a native of Egypt. (See Wilkinson, vol. v. p. 137.)

an indigenous animal, an inhabitant of the Nile from remote antiquity.   It is a species of lizard, about three feet long,[1] which passes its time mainly in the water, and is therefore called *wurran-el-bahr*, 'the wurran of

The Smaller Monitor (from the *Description*).

the river,' by the Arabs.   There is also another and even larger[2] lizard (the *Lacerta scincus*), which is a native of Egypt, a land animal, frequenting dry places,

The Great Monitor (from the same).

and called by the Arabs *wurran-e'-gebel*, 'wurran of the mountains,' or *wurran-el-ard*, 'wurran of the earth.'[3] This also, like the former, was probably included among

---

[1] Three feet, three inches, according to M. Geoffroy St. Hilaire (*Description,* 'H. N.' vol. i. p. 122).

[2] Herodotus (iv. 192) speaks of the land monitor as three cubits (4 feet 6 inches) long. But this is an excessive estimate. The largest seen by Sir G. Wilkinson measured about four feet. (See his note in the author's *Herodotus*, vol. iii. p. 167, note ⁸.)

[3] Wilkinson, l.s.c. Compare *Description,* 'H. N.' vol. i. p. 125.

the ancient denizens of the country, since its artificial·
introduction would be very unlikely; though, no doubt,
it is possible that it may have come in from the more
western parts of Africa, where it was certainly found
in ancient times.[1]

The domestic animals of ancient Egypt were the
horse, the ass, the camel, the Indian or humped ox, the
cow, the sheep, the goat, the pig, the cat, and the dog.
Horses seem not to have been known in the early times,[2]
and were probably introduced from Arabia, bringing

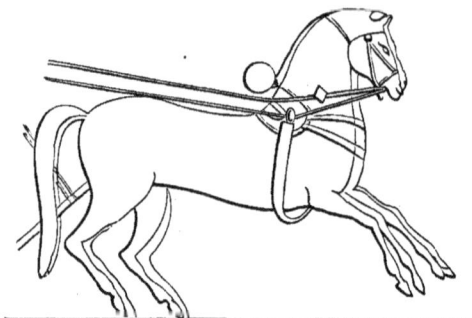

Egyptian Horses (from the Monuments).

with them their Semitic name.[3]   From the time, how-'
ever, of their introduction great pains were bestowed
upon the breed,[4] which seems to have resembled the
best Arab stock, being light, agile, and high-spirited.
Egyptian horses were, in consequence, highly esteemed,
and were largely exported to neighbouring countries.[5]

The ass was known in Egypt much earlier than the
horse,[6] and was probably employed as the chief beast

---

[1] See Herod. iv. 192.
[2] Wilkinson in the author's *Hero-dotus*, vol. ii. p. 178, note.
[3] The identity of the Egyptian *sus*, 'mare,' with the Hebrew סוס is generally admitted.

[4] Wilkinson, *Ancient Egyptians*, vol. iii. p. 35; iv. p. 20.
[5] See 1 Kings, x. 28, 29.
[6] Gen. xii. 16; Wilkinson, *Ancient Egyptians*, vol. iii. p. 34.

of burden from a remote antiquity. We may assume that it resembled the modern animal, so familiar to travellers, which is of small size, but active, and capable of bearing great fatigue.

The camel is placed among the domestic animals of Egypt,[1] partly on account of its being mentioned in Genesis among the elements of Abraham's wealth while he was in that country, but partly also on grounds of probability,[2] since without the camel it would have

Egyptian Ass (from the Monuments).

been scarcely possible to keep up communication with Syria, or with the Sinaitic Desert, where from a very remote time the Egyptians had valuable possessions.

The Indian or humped ox is represented upon the monuments in such a way as to imply that it was bred by the Egyptian farmers, and used largely both for sacrifice and for the table.[3] It is not now found in Egypt, though it is common in Abyssinia. Cows and oxen of the ordinary kind were also kept in considerable numbers, the flesh of the males being freely eaten,[4] and the oxen employed for various purposes connected with husbandry.[5] Sheep and goats were numerous in

. [1] Wilkinson, vol. v. p. 118.
[2] See the *Speaker's Commentary,* vol. i. p. 445.
[3] Wilkinson, vol. v. p. 199.

[4] Herod. ii. 41.
[5] Wilkinson in the author's *Herodotus,* vol. ii. pp. 18, 19, 22, &c.

all parts of the country.[1] Sheep were kept chiefly for the sake of their wool,[2] since it was unlawful to eat them in most parts of Egypt. They were usually sheared twice in the year, and bred twice.[3] Pigs, although reckoned unclean,[4] formed a portion of the stock on most farms; according to Herodotus, they were universally employed to tread in the corn ;[5] at any rate, they were so numerous, that their keepers—the

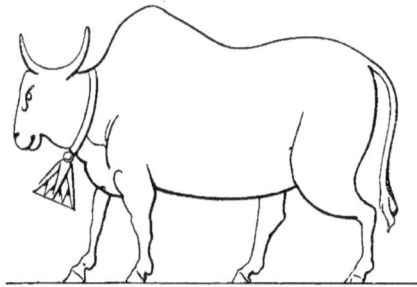

Egyptian Humped Ox (from the Monuments).

caste, or class, of swineherds—obtained mention as a special section of the population.[6]

Cats were great favourites with the ancient Egyptians.[7] Herodotus assures us [8] that, when a fire occurred in an Egyptian town, the chief attention of the inhabitants was directed to the preservation of the cats. Allowing the houses to burn, they formed themselves into bodies all round the conflagration, and endeavoured

[1] Wilkinson, *Ancient Egyptians*, vol. iii. p. 33; vol. v. pp. 190–193.
[2] Diod. Sic. i. 87. The milk of the sheep was also used for food, and cheese was made of it (ibid.).
[3] Diod. Sic. l.s.c. Compare Hom. *Od.* iv. 86.
[4] Herod. ii. 47.
[5] Ibid. ii. 14.
[6] Ibid. ii. 164.
[7] Diodorus tells us that the cats were valued on account of their destroying asps and other reptiles (i. 87). It is said that at the present day they do attack and kill asps and also scorpions (Wilkinson, *Ancient Egyptians*, vol. v. p. 155). Cicero says that no one ever heard tell of an Egyptian killing a cat (*De Nat. Deor.* i. 29).
[8] Herod. ii. 66. Compare Ælian, *Nat. An.* vii. 27.

to prevent the cats from rushing into the flames. We
see on the monuments pet cats seated by the master of
the house when he entertains a party of friends, or
accompanying him in his fowling excursions abroad.[1]
Cats were favoured when living and mourned when
dead.[2] Numerous mummies of cats have been found ;
and the care bestowed on them must have been almost
equal to that which was given to the bodies of men.[3]

Dogs were also great favourites, and were of several
kinds. The most common was a sort of fox dog (No. 2),

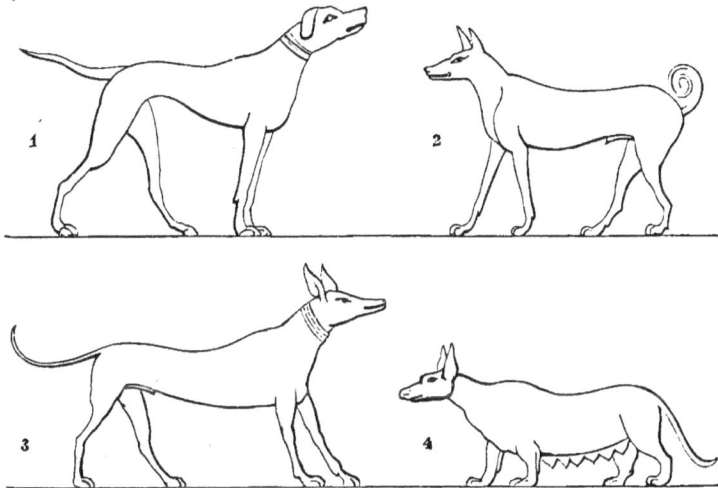

Egyptian Dogs (from the Monuments).

with erect ears, and a short curly tail, which is thought [4]
to have been the parent stock of the modern red dog of
Egypt, so common at Cairo and other towns of the lower
country. Another kind, which occurs often (No. 1), is

---

[1] Wilkinson, vol. iii. p. 42; vol.
v. p. 166.
[2] Herod. II. l.s.c.; Diod. Sic. i. 83.
[3] Numerous embalmed cats have
been found at Thebes and other
places, both in Upper and Lower
Egypt (Wilkinson, vol. v. p. 167).
They are carefully wrapped in linen
bandages, with the face and ears
painted outside, and are deposited
in wooden coffins or mummy cases.
[4] Wilkinson, vol. iii. p. 33.

a hound, tall and with a long straight tail, which was used to hunt the antelope[1] and other wild animals.[2] There was also a short-legged dog (No. 4), not unlike our turnspit,[3] with a pointed nose, erect ears, and a moderately long tail; which is said to have been fashionable about the time of Osirtasen I.[4]   Finally, we see represented on the sculptures a tall thin animal (No. 3), about the size of a hound, but with ears like a wolf, and a long thin tail.[5]

The most remarkable among the existing birds of Egypt are the eagle, which is of four kinds,[6] the falcon (three varieties),[7] the Ætolian kite, the black vulture, the bearded vulture, the *Vultur percnopterus*, the osprey, the horned owl, the screech-owl, the raven, the ostrich, the ibis, the pelican, the vulpanser or fox-goose, the Nile duck (*Anas Nilotica*), the hoopoe (*Upupa epops*), the sea-swallow (*Sterna Nilotica*), the Egyptian kingfisher (*Alcedo Ægyptiacus*), the quail, the oriental dotterell, the henno (*Ardea bubulcus*), and the sicsac (*Charadrius melanocephalus*). Besides these, there are found the common swallow, the sparrow, the wagtail, the crested plover, the heron and various other wading birds, the common kite, several kinds of hawks, the common vulture, the common owl, the white owl, the turtle-dove, the missel thrush, the common kingfisher,

---

[1] Wilkinson, vol. iii. p. 13.
[2] See the plate at the end of Wilkinson's *Ancient Egyptians*, vol. i.
[3] Ibid. vol. iii. p. 32.
[4] Ibid. p. 33.
[5] Ibid. p. 32; No. 7.
[6] These are given by M. Geoffroy St. Hilaire as the *Aquila heliaca*, or 'eagle of Thebes,' which is large and of a blackish colour; the *fulva*,

or common brown eagle; the *melanœtos*, a small black variety; and the *haliœetos*, or 'sea eagle.' (*Description*, 'H.N.' vol. i. pp. 82–87.)
[7] These are: 1. *Falco tinnunculus*, the 'cenchris' of Pliny (*H.N.* x. 52; xxix. 6), and *cresserelle* of Buffon; 2. *F. smirillus* (the *émérillon* of Buffon); and 3. *F. communis*, probably the 'sacred hawk' of Herodotus (ii. 65).

two kinds of larks, and various finches.[1] As most of
these birds are well known, it will not be necessary to
describe them; but a few words will be said with
respect to such of them as are either peculiar to Egypt,
or may be presumed to be unfamiliar to most readers.

The Ætolian kite (*Milvus Ætolius*) is of a greyish-
brown hue, smaller and with the tail less forked than
the ordinary kite.[2]   It is common in Egypt during the
autumn, and is at that time so tame as to come and
sit on the window-sills of the houses.[3]   The bearded
vulture (*Phene gigantea* of St. Hilaire) is a huge bird,
blackish brown with patches of grey.   One shot in the
desert between Cairo and the Red Sea during the
French occupation of Egypt measured about fifteen feet
from tip to tip of the wings.[4]   A bearded vulture of
a smaller kind is described and figured by Bruce as a
'golden eagle;'[5] but there can be no doubt that it
is rightly assigned to the vulture tribe.   The *Vultur
percnopterus* is a small white variety,[6] known to the
Arabs by the name of *rokhama*, and to the modern
Egyptians as 'Pharaoh's hen.'[7]   It is most valuable as
a scavenger, and, though unpleasing in its appearance,
enjoyed a considerable degree of favour among the
ancient Egyptians, as it still does among their successors.[8]

Two varieties of the ibis existed in ancient Egypt.[9]

---

[1] See Wilkinson, *Ancient Egyptians*, vol. iii. pp. 51-2; vol. v. pp.
120-122.
[2] *Description*, 'H. N.' vol. i. p. 89.
[3] Belon, *Nature des Oyseaux*, vol.
ii. p. 27.
[4] *Description*, 'H. N.' vol. i. p. 80.
[5] *Travels*, vol. v. p. 155, and
plate opposite.
[6] *Description*, pp. 76-7; Wilkinson, vol. iii. p. 51.
[7] Wilkinson, vol. v. p. 204.   The
Arabic *rokhama* is no doubt identical with the Hebrew רחם, wrongly
translated in the Authorised Version by 'gier-eagle' (Lev. xi. 18).
[8] Hasselquist, *Voyage dans le
Levant*, p. 195.
[9] Herod. ii. 76.

One was probably the *Ibis falcinella*, or ' glossy ibis,'
which measures about a foot from the breast to the
tail, and is of a reddish-brown colour, shot with dark
green and purple.[1]   The other was the *Ibis religiosa*
or *Ibis Numenia*, the *abou hannes* of Bruce.   This is
a bird of the stork class, standing about two feet high,

1. The Glossy Ibis; 2. The *Ibis Religiosa* (from the *Description*).

and measuring about two feet six inches from the tip
of the beak to the extremity of the tail.   The bill is
long and curved, measuring about six or seven inches.
The head and neck, for more than six inches below the
eyes, are entirely bare of feathers, and present nothing
but a black cutaneous surface.   The greater part of the
body is of a yellowish-white colour ; but the wings are
tipped with a greenish black, while on either side of
the tail, which is white, ' long funereal-looking plumes,
of a purplish-black colour, proceeding from beneath

---

[1] Wilkinson in the author's *Herodotus*, vol. ii. p. 125, note [6].

the tertiary wing feathers, hang not ungracefully.'[1]
The legs and feet are of a deep leaden hue, and the
claws are black. The *Ibis religiosa* rendered important
services to the Egyptians by destroying snakes and
various insects, and was therefore greatly esteemed,
and placed under the protection of Thoth, the Egyptian
Mercury.

The vulpanser or fox-goose (*Anser Ægyptius*) was
a wild goose of no very peculiar character.[2]   It is said
by Herodotus to have been sacred;[3] but this is questioned,[4] since it was certainly used freely for food by
the natives.[5]   The Egyptian duck (*Anas Nilotica*) has a
more distinctive character. 'The neck and inferior part
of the head are white, with black spots, and a grey line
runs lengthways behind the eyes; the under part of
the body, and the thighs, are of the same colour.'[6]   It
occurs wild in Upper Egypt, and in the lower country
is seen not unfrequently domesticated among the occupants of the farmyard.

The sea-swallow (*Sterna Nilotica*) is a small but
beautiful bird.   It frequents both the Nile itself and
the various canals which are led off from the main
stream.   The beak is black; the head and neck greyish,
with small white spots; the back, wings, and tail grey;
the belly and under part of the neck white; the feet
red, and the claws black.[7]   The oriental dotterel, a
species of *Charadrius*,[8] is said to be about the size of a

[1] Russell, *Ancient and Modern
Egypt*, p. 466. Compare Wilkinson
in the author's *Herodotus*, vol. ii.
p. 125, note [6]; and *Ancient Egyptians*, vol. v. p. 220.
[2] Wilkinson in the author's *Herodotus*, vol. ii. p. 121; *Ancient Egyptians*, vol. v. pp. 226-7.
[3] Herod. ii. 72.
[4] See Wilkinson's note on Hero-

dotus, ii. 72.
[5] Wilkinson, *Ancient Egyptians*,
vol. ii. p. 368; vol. iii. p. 47.
[6] Russell, *Ancient and Modern
Egypt*, p. 469.
[7] Ibid. pp. 469, 470.
[8] *Charadrius œdicnemus*, known
to the Arabs as the *Kerran*, or
Karawan.   (Wilkinson, *Ancient
Egyptians*, vol. v. p 255.)

crow, and to have a shrill but pleasing note, like that of the black woodpecker.[1] It feeds chiefly on rats and mice, with which Egypt abounds, and is thus of considerable service to the inhabitants. The places which it chiefly frequents are the acacia groves in the neighbourhood of villages; but it ·is found also in various parts of the desert. The *benno* (*Ardea bubulcus*) is a bird of the crane or heron kind. It is of a pure white colour, and is specially distinguished from all other herons, cranes, or storks, by having a tuft formed of two long feathers which stream from the back of the head. In ancient Egypt it was sacred to Osiris, the god of agriculture; and moderns remark that to the present day it lives in the cultivated fields and follows the plough, in order to feed on the worms and insects which are exposed when the soil is turned up.[2] It is often represented in the Egyptian sculptures.[3]

The sic-sac (*Charadrius melanocephalus*) is a small species of plover, not more than 9½ inches long. The head is black (whence Linnæus's name), with two white stripes running from the bill and meeting at the nape of the neck. The back and tail are slate-colour; the neck and abdomen white; the wings white tipped with black, and with a broad transverse black band; moreover, a sort of black mantle extends from the shoulders to the

The sic-sac or Trochilus.

[1] Russell, *Ancient and Modern Egypt*, p. 468.
[2] Wilkinson, *Ancient Egyptians*, vol. v. p. 225.
[3] Ibid. vol. iii. p. 41; vol. v. p. 262, &c.

tail. The beak is black, and the feet blue.[1] The sic-sac haunts the sand-banks, which are frequented also by the crocodile, and chirps loudly with a shrill note on the approach of man ;[2] whence the bird has been supposed to be the crocodile's friend, and to give him warning, *intentionally*, of the advent of danger.[3]

The 'river of Egypt' was celebrated for its fish, and not only produced a most abundant supply[4] of a food excellently suited for such a climate, but had several varieties which either were, or at any rate were thought to be, peculiar to itself.[5] Among these,

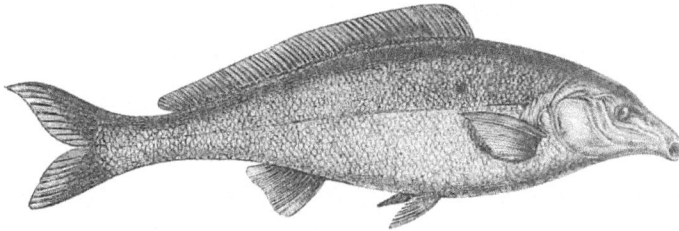

The Oxyrhynchus or Mizdeh.

those most highly regarded were the oxyrhynchus, the lepidotus, and the latus. The oxyrhynchus is now generally considered to be the *Mormyrus oxyrhynchus*,[6] the *mizdeh* of the modern Arabs, which has a long

[1] Wilkinson, *Ancient Egyptians*, vol. v. p. 226.
[2] Ibid. vol. iii. p. 80. Compare Wilkinson's note in the author's *Herodotus*, vol. ii. p. 97.
[3] Herod. ii. 68; Ælian, *Nat. An.* viii. 25. The idea, once started, that the bird was the crocodile's friend, led on to statements for which there was no foundation at all in fact, as that the bird hopped into the crocodile's mouth when he was asleep, and ate the leeches that were annoying him ! (See Herod. l.s.c.)
[4] Herodotus reckons the annual

supply taken in one of the Nile canals—that joining the river to the Lake Mœris—as equal in value to about 60,000*l.* of our money (ii. 149). Diodorus (i. 52) and Strabo (xvii. 2, § 4) also notice the excellence of the Nile fisheries.
[5] Strabo (l.s.c.) enumerates no fewer than *fourteen* sorts which had peculiar characteristics. See *Ancient Monarchies*, vol. iv. pp. 86 -7, note [1], 1st edition.
[6] Wilkinson, *Ancient Egyptians*, vol. iii. p. 58; vol. v. p. 249; *Description de l'Égypte*, 'H. N.' vol. i. p. 270.

pointed nose curving downwards. It is a smooth-skinned fish, apparently of the barbel class, and is at the present day not much esteemed for food.[1] Anciently it was sacred to Athor, and in some places might not be eaten.[2] The *lepidotus* has been identified with the *Salmo dentex*, the *Perca Nilotica*, and the binny,[3] all of them fish with large scales, which is what the word 'lepidotus' signifies. On the whole, the binny (*Cyprinus lepidotus*) is thought to have a claim superior to that of the other two, though the question cannot be considered to be as yet decided.[4] The binny is a fish of a good flavour, one of the best and wholesomest that the Nile produces. The *latus*, which was a sacred fish at Latopolis (*Esneh*), may perhaps be the *Perca Nilotica*,[5] another excellent fish, white-fleshed and delicate in flavour, much sought after by the present inhabitants.

Among other delicate fish produced by the Nile may be mentioned the *bulti*, or *Labrus Niloticus*, now the most highly esteemed of all ;[6] the *nefareh*, or Nile salmon (*Salmo Niloticus*), which ascends the stream to the latitude of Cairo, and has been known to weigh, when caught, above a hundred pounds, a fish pronounced to be 'very delicate eating ;'[7] the *sagboza* (*Clupea alosa*), a kind of herring ;[8] the spar (*Sparus Niloticus*) ;[9] the mullet (*Mugil cephalus*) ;[10] and the *garmoot* (*Silurus carmuth*).[11] The eels of the Nile are reckoned unwholesome, more especially in the summer

[1] Wilkinson, vol. v. p. 251.
[2] Herod. ii. 72; Plut. *De Is. et Osir.* § 18.
[3] Wilkinson, vol. v. p. 252.
[4] Wilkinson in the author's *Herodotus*, vol. ii. p. 101, 2nd edition.
[5] So De Pauw, *Travels*, vol. i. p. 136.

[6] Wilkinson, *Ancient Egyptians*, vol. iii. p. 60.
[7] Russell, p. 471.
[8] Hasselquist, *Voyage dans le Levant*, p. 223.
[9] Russell, p. 470.
[10] Ibid. p. 471.
[11] Wilkinson, vol. iii. p. 58.

months;[1] and the *tetraodon* is said to be actually
poisonous.[2] But, besides the fish named above as
delicacies, there were many others, which, though not
greatly esteemed, were good for food: e.g. the shall
(*Silurus shall*), the shilbeh (*Silurus schilbe Niloticus*),
the byad (*Silurus bajad*), the arabrab, the kelb-el-bahr
or Nile dog-fish (*Salmo dentex*), and a species of carp
(*Cyprinus rubescens Niloticus*).[3] In a country where,
owing to the high temperature, the flesh of land
animals was unsuited for general use, it was of the
greatest advantage that there should be, as there was,
an almost unlimited supply of a healthy pleasant food,
sufficiently nourishing, without being stimulating, and
readily available at all seasons.

Egypt was less happily circumstanced in respect of
reptiles and insects, which were as abundant as fish
without (for the most part) serving any useful purpose.
Of reptiles, we have already described the crocodile
and the two monitors,[4] creatures which, from their size
and their habits, are naturally classed with the larger
animals. We have now to notice the chief remaining
reptiles, which were the turtle (*Trionyx Niloticus*), two
species of iguana (*Stellio vulgaris* and *Stellio spinipes*),
two geckos, the chameleon, several snakes, more especially the horned snake (*Coluber cerastes*) and the asp
(*Coluber haje*), and several lizards. The turtle of the
Nile is of the soft kind, the upper and lower shells
being united by a mere coriaceous membrane. It is
a trionyx of a large size, sometimes even exceeding three
feet in length. The upper shell is very handsomely

[1] Wilkinson, vol. iii. pp. 58-9;
vol. v. p. 251.
[2] Russell, p. 471.
[3] Wilkinson, vol. iii. pp. 58-9.
[4] See above, pp. 65-6, and 72-3.

marked.[1] The common iguana (*Stellio vulgaris*) is a creature shaped like a lizard, of a dark olive-green colour shaded with black. It seldom exceeds a foot in length.[2] The Mohammedans dislike it and persecute it, since they regard its favourite attitude as a derisive imitation of their own posture in prayer.[3] The other species (*Stellio spinipes*) is a much larger animal, varying in length from two to three feet. It is found chiefly in Upper Egypt, and is of a bright grass-green colour.[4]

The two geckos, which are small lizards, are known respectively as *Lacerta gecko* and *Lacerta caudiverbera*. The former, called also *Gecko ptyodactylus*, or 'the fan-footed gecko,' is remarkable for the shape and physical qualities of its feet. These divide into five toes, which are spread out and do not touch one another. Each is armed on its under surface with a peculiar structure of folds, by means of which the animal is able to run up perpendicular walls of the smoothest possible material, and even to walk on ceilings, like house flies, or adhere to the underside of leaves.[5] This gecko is a frequent inmate of houses in Egypt; it conceals itself during the day and is very active at night, when it preys upon the flies and other insects which are at that time taking their repose. The natives might be expected to value it on this account, but they have a prejudice that it is poisonous, and communicates a species of leprosy to persons over whom it walks,[6] whence they term it *abu*

[1] *Description de l'Égypte*, 'H. N.' vol. i. pp. 115–120. (Compare 'Planches,' vol. i. pl. i.)

[2] Ibid. p. 126.

[3] *Encyclopædia Britannica*, vol. xix. p. 31.

[4] *Description*, 'Hist. Nat.' vol. i. pp. 125-6.

[5] See Mr. Houghton's account of this animal in Dr. Smith's *Dictionary of the Bible*, vol. ii. pp. 126-7; and compare the *Description*, 'H. N.' vol. i. pp. 132-3, and 'Planches,' vol. i. pl. v. fig. 5.

[6] Hasselquist, *Voyage dans le Levant*, p. 220.

burs, ' the father of leprosy.' [1] Some go so far as to maintain that it renders food unwholesome by walking upon it ; but this belief seems to be quite without foundation, and the irritating effects of its feet on the human skin have probably been exaggerated.[2] The house gecko is of a reddish-brown colour, spotted with white. It is about five inches in length.

The other Egyptian gecko (*Lacerta caudiverbera*) is larger. Its usual length is about eight inches,[3] and its habits are quite unlike those of the house gecko. Both kinds are oviparous, and produce a round egg with a hard calcareous shell. The *geckos* have the power of uttering a note like the double ' click ' used to urge a horse on in riding ; and it is said to be from this circumstance that they derive their name.[4]

The horned snake (*Coluber cerastes*) is so called on account of two curious excrescences above the eyes, to which the name of ' horns ' has been given ; they are small protuberances, erect, pointed, and leaning a little towards the back of the head; it is remarkable that no naturalist has been able to assign them any use. The colour of the cerastes is pale brown, with large irregular black spots.[5] Herodotus remarks that it is of small size ; [6] and modern specimens vary between one foot five inches and about two feet and a half in length.[7] The cerastes is exceedingly poisonous,[8] and, having the habit of partially burying itself in the sand,[9] which is

---

[1] *Description*, 'H. N.' vol. i. p. 134; Forskål, *Descript. Animal.* 13; Wilkinson, *Ancient Egyptians*, vol. v. p. 124.
[2] So Mr. Houghton (*Dict. of the Bible*, vol. ii. pp. 126–7).
[3] *Description*, p. 130.
[4] Mr. Houghton in the *Dict. of the Bible*, vol. ii. p. 127.

[5] *Description*, pp. 155-6.
[6] Herod. ii. 74.
[7] *Description*, l.s.c.
[8] Wilkinson in the author's *Herodotus*, vol. ii. p. 104, note [2], 2nd edition.
[9] Wilkinson, *Ancient Egyptians*, vol. v. p. 246.

nearly of the same colour, it is the more dangerous as
being difficult of avoidance.   The African snake-
charmers succeed, however, in handling it and escaping
all hurt, since it is one of the few vipers over which
their ' charming ' has influence.[1]

The asp, or *Coluber haje*, ' the Egyptian cobra,' as
it has been termed, is even more deadly than the
cerastes.   It is a large snake, varying from three to six
feet in length,[2] and has an extraordinary power of

The Egyptian asp (*Coluber haje*).

dilating its breast when angry.   Torpid during the
winter,[3] it appears on the approach of spring in the
Egyptian gardens, and is of great use, feeding on mice,
frogs, and various small reptiles.   It is easily tamed,
and is the favourite snake of the serpent-charmers, who
wind it about their necks, put it in their bosoms, and
make it perform various antics to the sound of the flute,

[1] Houghton in *Dict. of the Bible*, vol. ii. p. 127.
[2] Wilkinson, *Ancient Egyptians,* vol. v. p. 241.   The French savants made the length a little short of five feet (*Description*, 'H. N.' vol. i. p. 157); but Sir G. Wilkinson had one in his possession which measured exactly six feet.
[3] Wilkinson, p. 242.

without exhibiting any fear, and with absolute and
entire impunity.[1]

The chameleon is the quaintest of reptiles. The
strange shape of its head, the position and character of
the eyes, which are almost completely covered with the
skin and move independently of each other, the curious
structure of the tongue, which is cylindrical and
capable of great and sudden extension, the prehen-
sile power of the tail, the dry dull skin, and the division
of the claws into two sets, one opposed to the other,
are all of them remarkable features,[2] and their combination produces a most grotesque creature. The
change of colour under certain circumstances, which
the ancients thought so extraordinary,[3] is a subordinate
and secondary feature, and has been greatly exaggerated. One of the small Egyptian lizards, the *agame
variable* of St. Hilaire, which has never attracted much
attention, varies its hue to a much greater extent.[4]
The chameleon is naturally of a pale olive green, and
its changes are limited to a warming up of this tint
into a yellowish brown, on which are seen some faint
patches of red, and a fading of it into a dull ashen grey.[5]
The animal does not really alter its hue at will, but
turns colour, as men do, in consequence of its emotions,
becoming pale through fear, and warming to a sort of
redness through anger or desire. What is most notice-

---

[1] Bruce, *Travels*, vol. vii. pp. 302–3; Lane, *Modern Egyptians*, vol. ii. p. 106.
[2] See the observations of M. Geoffroy St. Hilaire in the *Descrip-tion*, 'Hist. Nat.' vol. i. p. 134.
[3] Democrit. ap. Flin. *H.N.* xxviii. 8; Aristot. *Eth. Nic.* i. 10, § 8; *Hist. Anim.* ii. 11, § 1; Ælian, *Nat. Anim.* iv. 33; Ovid, *Met.* xv. 411; Solin. *Polyhist.* § 43; Leo African. *Descr. Afric.* ix. p. 298, &c.
[4] See the *Description*, 'H. N.' vol. i. pp. 127, 167.
[5] *Encyclopædia Britannica*, vol. xix. p. 37. The author had a chameleon in his own house for some months, about the years 1846-7, and was convinced that the changes of colour were emotional.

able in its habits is the slow, stealthy, almost imperceptible movement by which it gradually approaches its prey, combined with the sudden rapid dart of the tongue by which the victim is surprised and devoured.

The most remarkable of the Egyptian insects are the scorpion, the locust, and the *solpuga* spider. The scorpion (*Scorpio crassicauda*), though classed with the *Aráchnidœ*,[1] has rather the character of an enormous beetle. It has two large horns, eight legs, and a long stiff tail of several joints, which it carries erect in a threatening manner.[2] It is not aggressive, however, but always seeks to hide itself, frequenting ruins and dark places, where it lies concealed among stones and in crannies. Sometimes, unfortunately, it enters houses, and hides under cushions and coverlets, where, if it suffers molestation, it will sting, and inflict a painful, though not dangerous, injury. In Egypt cats often attack it. Turning it over on its back by a pat of their paw upon its side, and then placing one fore foot on its body, they tear off the tail with the other. The creature is then easily killed, and the cat not unfrequently eats it.[3]

The locust is one of the permanent 'plagues of Egypt.' Swarms arrive with considerable frequency from Arabia, and, descending upon the gardens and cornfields, cover the whole ground, and in a short time destroy all but the very coarsest kinds of vegetation.[4] The hopes of the farmer disappear, and famine threatens, where, till the visitation came, there was

---

[1] Houghton in the *Dict. of the Bible*, vol. iii. p. 1161 ; Wilkinson, *Ancient Egyptians*, vol. v. p. 126.
[2] See the representation in the author's *Ancient Monarchies*, vol. iii.
p. 65, 1st edition.
[3] Wilkinson, vol. v. p.155. (Compare p. 166.)
[4] Russell, *Ancient and Modern Egypt*, p. 464.

every prospect of teeming abundance. The varieties of
the insect are numerous, and Egypt appears to suffer
from the attacks of some five or six species.[1] But the
deadliest inroads are made by the *Acridium peregrinum*
and the *Œdipoda migratoria*, the two most destructive
specimens of the locust tribe,[2] the latter of which has
been known to visit our own country.[3] Fortunately
these inroads are only occasional, and seldom extend to
a very large portion of the country. When they occur,
the principal check upon them is that arising from the
habits of the jackals, which issue from the mountains
at night, and, spreading themselves over the plains,
devour the locusts, apparently with great satisfaction,
and seriously diminish their numbers.[4]

The solpuga is a strong and active spider, possessing venomous qualities, and esteemed by the modern
Egyptians on account of its enmity to the scorpion.
The scorpion's sting is fatal to it; but in general it
succeeds in avoiding its adversary's tail, and, running
round it, fastens upon the head and kills it without
difficulty.[5]

Egypt was not very well provided by nature with
minerals. Stone indeed of many excellent kinds
abounded. The magnesian limestone of the Gebel
Mokuttam range,[6] opposite the site of Memphis, is a
good material, since it is hard and close-grained with-

[1] Four species are said to be
peculiar to Egypt, viz. *Truxalis
nasuta*, *Tr. variabilis*, *Tr. procera*,
and *Tr. miniata*. (Houghton in the
Dict. of the Bible, vol. ii. p. 129.)
[2] Ibid. p.132.
[3] See *Gentleman's Magazine* for
July, 1748, pp. 331 and 414.
[4] Wilkinson, *Ancient Egyptians*,

vol. v. p. 149. The ibis also (ib. p.
221), and no doubt other Egyptian
birds, help to destroy the locusts.
[5] Ibid. p. 155.
[6] Ibid. vol. iii. p. 322. Compare
Topography of Thebes, p. 319, and
the author's *Herodotus*, vol. ii. pp. 9
and 170.

out being difficult to work. The sandstone of the Gebel Silsilis and its neighbourhood is perhaps even superior, its texture being remarkably compact and even,[1] and its durability in the dry climate of Egypt almost unlimited. Further, porphyry and alabaster were readily obtainable, the former from various parts of the Eastern Desert,[2] the latter from quarries between Malawi and Manfaloot. Finally, there was an inexhaustible supply of the best possible granite in the vicinity of the First Cataract and of Syêné,[3] and therefore within the limits of Egypt, though close to her southern border. The same material was also abundant in the Eastern Desert, more especially in the mountains between Thebes and Kosseir. Syenite was likewise obtainable in the neighbourhood of Syêné,[4] as might be safely concluded from the name itself.

It added practically to the wealth of Egypt with respect to building material, that all the best kinds of stone were found in inexhaustible abundance within a short distance of the river, since it was thus possible to convey the several kinds by water-carriage from one end of Egypt to the other,[5] and to use each over the whole country for the purposes for which it was best fitted. More especially it was easy to float *down* the stream, from the First Cataract, the granite and syenite

---

[1] *Ancient Egyptians*, vol. iii. pp. 322-3; *Topography*, p. 442.
[2] There are porphyry quarries at Gebel e' Dokhan, nearly opposite Manfaloot (*Topography*, p. 363); and blocks of porphyry strew the surface of the Western Desert in some places (ibid. p. 451). There is also porphyry near Syêné.
[3] Stanley, *Sinai and Palestine*, 'Introduction,' p. xlvi.; Wilkinson,

Topography of Thebes, pp. 457-8.
[4] *Topography*, p. 459.
[5] Herodotus gives an indication of the actual practice when he tells us that *boatmen* conveyed a monolithic chamber from Elephantiné to Sais in the Delta (ii. 175). That it took three years to convey the block, he was no doubt told, but the fact may well be doubted.

of the far south, and to employ it at Thebes, or Memphis, or Saïs,[1] or other cities of the Delta. Thus the
best material of all was most readily distributed, and
might be employed with almost equal ease in the extreme north and the extreme south of the empire.

In metals Egypt was deficient. Gold mines, indeed,
seem to have existed, and to have been worked,[2] in the
more southern portion of the Eastern Desert, and these
in ancient times may have been fairly productive,
though they would not now repay the cost of ex-
tracting the gold from them. According to Diodorus,[3]
silver was also a product of Egypt under the Pharaohs,
and was obtained in tolerable abundance ; but no traces of
silver mines have been remarked by any modern observer,
and the unsupported authority of Diodorus is scarcely
sufficient to establish a fact which did not fall under
his own observation. Copper, iron, and lead do however exist in portions of the Eastern Desert,[4] and one
iron mine shows signs of having been anciently worked.[5]
The metal is found in the form of specular and red iron
ore. Still none of these metals seem to have been
obtained by the Egyptians from their own land in any
considerable quantity. The copper so necessary to
them for their arms, tools, and implements, was procured chiefly from the mines of Wady Maghara in the

---

[1] The granite of Syêné is found
in abundance at Thebes and Memphis. Its conveyance to Saïs rests
on the testimony of Herodotus.

[2] Their existence is testified by
Agatharcides (De Rub. Mar. p. 23),
Diodorus (iii. 12), and others ; and
the fact that they were worked
under the Pharaohs is thought to
be sufficiently indicated by the remains which still exist in the East-

ern Desert about Wady Foakbir
and Wady Allaga. (Wilkinson,
Ancient Egyptians, vol. iii. pp.
228-9.)

[3] Diod. Sic. i. 49.

[4] Wilkinson, vol. i. p. 234.

[5] Ibid. vol. iii. p. 246. This mine
'lies in the Eastern Desert, between
the Nile and the Red Sea, at a place
called Hammámi.'

Sinaitic peninsula,[1] which was beyond the limits of
Egypt; and it is most likely that lead, iron, and tin were
supplied to them by the Phœnicians.[2]

Among other mineral productions of Egypt the
most important were natron, salt, sulphur, petroleum,
chalcedonies, carnelians, jaspers, green breccia, and
emeralds. Natrum, or the subcarbonate of soda, is
yielded largely by the Natron Lakes beyond the
western limits of the Delta,[3] and is also found in Upper
Egypt near Eilethyias, and again near the village of
El Helleh.[4] It was greatly prized by the ancient
Egyptians, since it was the chief antiseptic material
made use of in the process of embalming.[5] Salt is
also furnished by the Natron Lakes in considerable
quantity.[6] The Gebel-el-Zayt, at the south-western extremity of the Suez inlet (lat. 27° 50′ to 28° 3′), abounds
in petroleum;[7] and at El Gimsheh, near the south-
western extremity of the Zayt inlet, are sulphur mines.[8]
Chalcedonies have been found in the range of Gebel
Mokuttam near Cairo,[9] jaspers and carnelians in
the granite rocks near Syêné,[10] and jaspers again in
the dry valley called by the Arabs *Bahr-bela-ma*, or
'the river without water.'[11] Breccia verde was obtained
by the ancient Egyptians from quarries in the Eastern
Desert,[12] and the emerald mines of *Gebel Zabara* were

[1] Brugsch, *Hist. d'Égypte*, p. 47; Wilkinson in the author's *Herodotus*, vol. ii. pp. 292 and 350, note [10].
[2] Iron may also have been imported from the countries on the Upper Nile, where it is abundant.
[3] *Description de l'Égypte*, 'État Moderne,' vol. i. p. 282; Russell, *Ancient and Modern Egypt*, p. 60; Wilkinson in the author's *Herodotus*. vol. ii. p. 121, note [4].
[4] Wilkinson, *Topography* of
[...]*Thebes*, pp. 428 and 433.
[5] Herod. ii. 86–88; Diod. Sic. i. 91.
[6] *Description*, 'État Moderne,' vol. i. p. 282.
[7] Wilkinson, *Topography*, p. 364.
[8] Ibid.
[9] Ibid. p. 319.
[10] Russell, p. 450.
[11] Ibid. p. 61.
[12] Wilkinson, *Ancient Egyptians*, vol. i. p. 45; *Topography*, p. 421; Russell, p. 451.

diligently worked by them.[1]   Agate and rock-crystal
are likewise occasionally met with, and also serpentine,
compact felspar, steatite, hornblende, basanite, actino-
lite, and the sulphate of barytes.[2]

---

[1] Wilkinson, *Ancient Egyptians,*   [2] Russell, pp. 450-5; Wilkinson,
vol. i. p. 231; *Topography,* p. 420.   *Topography,* p. 419.

CHAPTER III.

THE PEOPLE AND THEIR NEIGHBOURS.

The Egyptians of Asiatic Origin—Immigrants from the East—Not a Colony from Ethiopia—Proof of this—So far peculiar as to constitute a distinct Race—Their complexion dark, but not black—their Hair not woolly. Description of their Features; of their Form. Their Subdivisions, original and later. Their Intellectual Characteristics. Their Artistic Powers. Their Morality, theoretic and practical. Their Number. Nations bordering upon Egypt: The Libu (*Libyans*), *or* Tahennu, *on the West; the* Nahsi (*Negroes*) *and* Cush (*Ethiopians*) *on the South; the* Amu (*Shemites*) *and* Shasu (*Arabs*) *on the East. Nascent Empires in this quarter.*

'Die Aegypter ein von allen angrenzenden Menschenracen wesentlich ver-
schiedener Stamm waren.'—Niebuhr, *Vorträge über alte Geschichte,* vol.
i. p. 57.

It is generally allowed by modern ethnologists that the ancient Egyptians, although located in Africa, were not an African people.[1] Neither the formation of their skulls, nor their physiognomy, nor their complexion, nor the quality of their hair, nor the general proportions of their frames connect them in any way with the indigenous African races—the Berbers and the negroes. Nor, again, is their language in the least like those of the African tribes.[2] The skull and facial outline, both of the ancient Egyptian and of the modern

---

[1] See Lenormant, *Hist. Ancienne de l'Orient,* vol. i. p. 329; Brugsch, *Histoire d'Égypte,* première partie, pp. 5-6; Donne in Smith's *Dictionary of Greek and Roman Geography,* vol. i. p. 38; Stuart Poole in Smith's *Dictionary of the Bible,* vol. i. p. 501.

[2] See Brugsch, p. 6: 'La langue des Égyptiens . . . n'offre aucune analogie avec les langues des peuples d'Afrique.'

Copt, his existing representative, are Caucasian ;[1] and the Egyptian language, while of a peculiar type, has analogies which connect it both with the Semitic and with the Indo-European forms of speech, more espe- cially with the former.[2] We must regard the Egyp- tians, therefore, as an Asiatic people, immigrants into their own territory, which they entered from the east, and nearly allied to several important races of South- Western Asia, as the Canaanites, the Accadians or primitive Babylonians, and the Southern or Himyaritic Arabs.

It has been maintained by some[3] that the immi- gration was from the south, the Egyptians having been a colony from Ethiopia which gradually descended the Nile, and established itself in the middle and lower portions of the valley; and this theory can plead in its favour, both a positive statement of Diodorus,[4] and the fact, which is quite certain, of an ethnic connection between the Egyptians and some of the tribes who now occupy Abyssinia (the ancient Ethiopia). But modern research has shown quite unmistakably that the movement of the Egyptians was in the opposite direction. 'The study of the monuments,' says the latest historian of Egypt,[5] 'furnishes incontrovertible

---

[1] Dr. Birch observes, with more refinement than most previous writers, that 'on the earliest monu- ments the Egyptians appear as a red or dusky race, with features neither entirely Caucasian nor Ni- gritic; more resembling at the ear- liest age the European' (i.e. the Caucasian), 'at the middle period of the empire the Nigritic races, or the offspring of a mixed population, and at the most flourishing period of the empire the sallow tint and refined type of the Semitic families

of mankind.' (Egypt from the Ear- liest Times, Introduction, p. ix.)
[2] See Bunsen, Egypt's Place in Universal History, vol. v. pp. 745– 787 ; Philosophy of History, vol. iii. pp. 185–9.
[3] Especially Heeren, African Na- tions, vol. ii. pp. 101–109. E.T.; Manual of Ancient History, p. 57, E.T.
[4] Diod. Sic. iii. 11.
[5] Brugsch, Histoire d'Egypte, pre- mière partie, p. 7.

evidence that the historical series of Egyptian temples, tombs, and cities, constructed on either bank of the Nile, follow one upon the other in chronological order in such sort that the monuments of the greatest antiquity, the Pyramids for instance, are situated furthest to the North ; while the nearer one approaches the Ethiopian cataracts, the more do the monuments lose the stamp of antiquity, and the more plainly do they show the decline of art, of beauty, and of good taste. Moreover, in Ethiopia itself the existing remains present us with a style of art that is absolutely devoid of originality. At the first glance one can easily see that it represents Egyptian art in its degeneracy, and that art ill understood and ill executed. The utmost height to which Ethiopian civilisation ever reached was a mere rude imitation, alike in science and in art, of Egyptian models.'

We must look then rather to Syria or Arabia than to Ethiopia as the cradle of the Egyptian nation. At the same time we must admit that they were not mere Syrians or Arabs,[1] but had, from the remotest time whereto we can go back, distinct characteristics,' whereby they have a good claim to be considered as a separate race. What was the origin of these special characteristics cannot indeed be determined until the nature of differences of race is better understood than it is at present. Perhaps in ancient times the physical traits of an ancestor were, as a general rule, more completely reproduced in his descendants than they now are ; perhaps climate and mode of life had originally

---

[1] Niebuhr remarks on the difficulty of distinguishing the bulk of the modern Egyptians from Arabs (*Vorträge über alte Geschichte*, vol. i. p. 57), but notes that the pure Copts are clearly distinct and different.

greater effect. Some of the Egyptian characteristics
may be ascribed to these influences; some may, on
the other hand, be confidently attributed to intermixture with African races, from which they were far from
holding altogether aloof. Their complexion was probably rendered darker in this way; their lips were
coarsened; and the character of their eye was perhaps modified.[1]

The Egyptians appear to have been among the
darkest races with which the Greeks of the early times
came into direct contact. Herodotus calls them
'blacks;'[2] but this is an extreme exaggeration, akin
to that by which all the native inhabitants of Hindustan
have been termed 'niggers.' The monuments show
that the real complexion of the ordinary Egyptian man
was brown, with a tinge of red—a hue not very
different from that of the Copt at the present day.
The women were lighter, no doubt because they were
less exposed to the sun: the monuments depict them
as yellow; but there can scarcely have been as much
difference between the men's colour and the women's
as existing paintings represent.

The hair was usually black and straight. In no
case was it 'woolly,'[3] though sometimes it grew in
short crisp curls. Men commonly shaved both the
hair and the beard, and went about with their heads
perfectly bare, or else wore wigs or a close-fitting cap.[4]
Women always wore their own hair, and plaited it in

[1] See Donne in Smith's *Dictionary of Greek and Roman Geography*, vol. i. p. 38.
[2] Herod. ii. 146. It has been
argued that the term used (μελάγ-
χροες) means no more than
'swarthy;' but its literal rendering
is 'black-skinned,' and there is nothing to show that Herodotus did
not intend it literally.
[3] As Herodotus represents (ii.
104).
[4] Wilkinson in the author's *Herodotus*, vol. ii. p. 146, note [4], and p.
49, note [6].

long tresses sometimes reaching to the waist.[1] The
hair of the wigs, as also that which is found sometimes
growing on the heads of the mummies, is coarse to the
eye of a European, but has no resemblance to that of
the negro.

The Egyptians had features not altogether unlike
those of their neighbours, the Syrians, but with distinguishing peculiarities. The forehead was straight,
but somewhat low; the nose generally long and straight,
but sometimes slightly aquiline. The lips were over-
full; but the upper lip was short,
and the mouth was seldom too wide.
The chin was good, being well-
rounded, and neither retreating nor
projecting too far. The most marked
and peculiar feature was the eye,
which was a long narrow slit, like
that of the Chinese, but placed horizontally and not obliquely. An eyebrow, also long
and thin, but very distinctly pencilled, shaded it. The
colouring was always dark, the hair, eyebrows, eye-
lashes, and beard (if any) being black,
or nearly so, and the eyes black or
dark brown.

Head of Egyptian man.

In form the Egyptian resembled
the modern Arab. He was tall; his
limbs were long and supple; his head
was well placed upon his shoulders;
his movements were graceful; his
carriage dignified. In general, however, his frame was
too spare; and his hands and feet were unduly large.
The women were as thin as the men, and had forms

Egyptian child.

---

[1] See Wilkinson's *Ancient Egyptians*, vol. iii. pp. 368-70.

nearly similar. Children, however, appear to have been sufficiently plump; but they are not often represented.

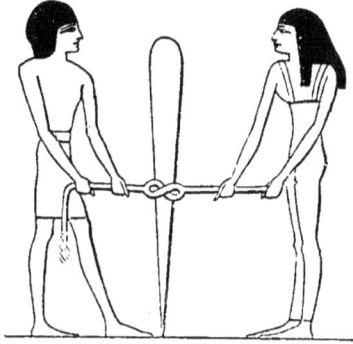

Egyptian man and woman (from the monuments).

The most ancient document which has come down to us bearing on the history of Egypt represents the Egyptian people as divided into a number of distinct races. We read of Ludim, Anamim, Lebahim, Naphtuhim, Pathrusim, Casluhim, and Caphtorim [1] as distinct 'sons of Mizraim,' *i.e.* as separate tribes of the powerful people which inhabited the 'two Egypts.' [2] It is suggested [3] that the Ludim were the ' dominant race, or Egyptians proper, who were called in Egyptian *lut* or *rut, i.e.* men *par excellence* ;' that the Anamim were the *Anu* of the monuments, who were dispersed widely over the Nile valley, and gave name to On (Heliopolis) and other cities ; that the Naphtuhim (*Na-Phtah*) were ' the domain of Phtah,' or people of Memphis ; the Pathrusim (*P-to-res*) ' the people of the South,' or in-

---

[1] Gen. x. 13, 14.
[2] ' Misraim ' is a dual form, and means 'the two Misrs,' or ' Egypts.' The names of the ' sons of Mizraim ' are all plural in form, and, it is gene-

rally allowed, represent tribes or races.
[3] See Lenormant, *Histoire Ancienne de l'Orient*, vol. i. p. 330.

habitants of the Thebaïd, &c. But these identifications are, all of them, more or less uncertain; and it would seem that, whatever tribal differences may have existed at the first, they had disappeared, or all but disappeared, by the time that the history of Egypt becomes known to us. The only real distinction that remained was one between the people of the south country and those of the north, who had their respective peculiarities, and even spoke dialects that were somewhat different.[1] Otherwise the various Egyptian tribes had been fused together and moulded into one compact and homogeneous people before the time when history first takes cognisance of them.

Intellectually, the Egyptians must take rank among the foremost nations of remote antiquity, but cannot compare with the great European races, whose rise was later, the Greeks and Romans. Their minds possessed much subtlety and acuteness; they were fond of composition, and made considerable advances in many of the sciences; they were intelligent, ingenious, speculative. It is astonishing what an extensive literature they possessed at a very early date[2]— books on religion, on morals, law, rhetoric, arithmetic, mensuration, geometry, medicine, books of travels, and, above all, novels! But the merit of the works is

[1] Brugsch, *Histoire d'Egypte*, p. 12. The distinction between the north and south country is constant in the Egyptian inscriptions. The kings term themselves 'lords of the thrones of the two countries,' or 'kings of the upper and lower countries' (*Records of the Past*, vol. iv. pp. 11, 14, 16, &c.; vol. vi. pp. 19, 23, 87, &c.). They wear two crowns, one the crown of Upper, the other that of Lower Egypt.

[2] Some idea of the extent and variety of Egyptian literature may be obtained by the ordinary student from the specimens contained in the unpretending but most valuable series published by Messrs. Bagster under the title of *Records of the Past*, vols. ii., iv., and vi. He may also with advantage cast his eye over the 'List of Further Texts,' arranged by M. Renouf, and given in vol. vi. pp. 162-5 of the same work.

slight. The novels are vapid, the medical treatises interlarded with charms and exorcisms, the travels devoid of interest, the general style of all the books forced and stilted. Egypt may in some particulars have stimulated Greek thought,[1] directing it into new lines, and giving it a basis to work upon ; but otherwise it cannot be said that the world owes much of its intellectual progress to this people, about whose literary productions there is always something that is weak and childish.

In art the power which the Egyptians exhibited was doubtless greater. Their architecture ' was on the grandest scale, and dwarfs the Greek in comparison.'[2] But even here it is to be noted that the higher qualities of art were wanting. The architecture produces its effect by mere mass. There is no beauty of proportion. On the contrary, the gigantic columns are clumsy from their undue massiveness, and are far too thickly crowded together. They are rather rounded piers than pillars, and their capitals are coarse and heavy. The coloured ornamentation used was over-glaring. The forms of the ornamentation were almost always stiff, and sometimes absolutely hideous.[3] In mimetic art the Egyptians might perhaps have done better, had they been at liberty to allow their natural powers free scope. But they worked in shackles ; a dull dead conventionalism

---

[1] The Greeks themselves always spoke with respect of the Egyptian progress in the sciences, and Greeks of high culture constantly visited Egypt with a view of improving themselves. It has been questioned whether the Egyptians had much to teach them (Cornewall Lewis, *Astronomy of the Ancients*, pp. 277-287) ; but the Greeks themselves were probably the best judges on such a point. Among those who sought improvement in Egypt are said to have been Hecatæus, Thales, Solon, Pythagoras, Herodotus, Œnopides, Democritus, Plato, and Eudoxus.

[2] Birch, *Egypt from the Earliest Times*, Introduction, p. xvi.

[3] See especially Wilkinson, *Ancient Egyptians*, vol. vi. pls. 24 A, 33, 40, 43 A, 55, &c.

bore sway over the land ; and though some exceptions occur,[1] Egyptian mimetic art is in the main a reproduction of the same unvarying forms, without freedom of design or vigour of treatment.

In morals, the Egyptians combined an extraordinary degree of theoretic perfection with an' exceedingly lax and imperfect practice. It has been said[2] that 'the forty-two laws of the Egyptian religion contained in the 125th chapter of the Book of the Dead fall short in nothing of the teachings of Christianity,' and conjectured that Moses, in compiling his code of laws, did but ' translate into Hebrew the religious precepts which he found in the sacred books' of the people among whom he had been brought up. Such expressions are no doubt exaggerated ; but they convey what must be allowed to be a fact, viz. that there is a very close agreement between the moral law of the Egyptians and the precepts of the Decalogue. But with this profound knowledge of what was right, so much beyond that of most heathen nations, the practice of the people was rather below than above the common level. The Egyptian women were notoriously of loose character, and, whether as we meet with them in history, or as they are depicted in Egyptian romance, appear as immodest and licentious.[3] The men practised impurity openly, and boasted of it in their writings ;[4] they were industrious, cheerful, nay, even gay, under hardships,[5]

---

[1] As the wooden statue in the museum of Boulaq, described by Dr. Birch (*Egypt from the Earliest Times*, p. 43), and the animal forms on several bas-reliefs (see Wilkinson, *Ancient Egyptians*, vol. iii. pp. 9, 13, 22 ; vol. iv. p. 139, &c.).

[2] Brugsch, *Histoire d'Egypte*, p. 17.

[3] See Gen. xxxix. 12 ; Herod. ii.

60, 111, 121, § 5, 126 ; Diod. Sic. i. 59 ; *Records of the Past*, vol. ii. p. 140 ; vol. vi. pp. 153–6, &c.

[4] *Records of the Past*, vol. ii. p. 113.

[5] See Brugsch, *Histoire d'Egypte*, p. 15 : ' Rien de plus gai, de plus amusant, de plus naïf que le bon peuple égyptien, qui aimait la vie, et qui se réjouissait profondément

and not wanting in family affection ; but they were
cruel, vindictive, treacherous, avaricious, prone to
superstition, and profoundly servile. The use of the
stick was universal. Not only was the bastinado the
ordinary legal punishment for minor offences,[1] but
superiors of all kinds freely beat their inferiors ; the
poor peasantry were compelled by blows to satisfy the
rapacity of the tax-gatherers ;[2] and slaves everywhere
performed their work under fear of the rod, which was
applied to the backs of laggards by the taskmaster.[3]
The passions of the Egyptians were excessive, and often
led on to insurrection, riot, and even murder ; they
were fanatical in the extreme, ever ready to suspect
strangers of insulting their religion, and bent on wash-
ing out such insults by bloodshed. When conquered,
no people were more difficult to govern ; and even
under their native kings they needed a strong hand to
keep them in subjection. But though thus impetuous
and difficult to restrain when their passions were
roused, they were at other times timid, cringing,
submissive, prone to fawn and flatter. The lower
classes prostrated themselves before their superiors ;
blows were quietly accepted and tamely submitted to.
The great nobles exhibited equal servility towards the
monarch, whom they addressed as if he were a god,[4]
and to whose kind favour they attributed it that they

de son existence. . . . On s'adon-
nait aux plaisirs de toute espèce, on
chantait, on buvait, on dansait, on
aimait les excursions à la campagne,
&c. Conforme à ce penchant pour
le plaisir, les gais propos, la plai-
santerie un peu libre, les bons-mots,
la raillerie et le goût moqueur
étaient en vogue, et les badinages
entraient jusque dans les tombeaux.'
[1] Birch, *Egypt from the Earliest*

Times, Introduction, p. xvi. ; Wilkinson, *Ancient Egyptians*, vol. ii.
p. 41.
[2] Brugsch, p. 18.
[3] See Wilkinson, *Ancient Egyptians*, vol. ii. p. 42 ; Rosellini, *Monumenti dell'Egitto*, vol. ii. p. 249,
&c. Compare Exod. v. 14.
[4] *Records of the Past*, vol. vi. pp.
16, 102, &c.

were allowed to continue to live.[1] Altogether the Egyptians were wanting in manliness and spirit. They at no time made good soldiers; and though they had some considerable successes in their early wars, when they attacked undisciplined hordes with large bodies of well-disciplined troops, yet, whenever they encountered an enemy acquainted with the art of war, they suffered defeat. As allies, they were not to be depended on. Always ready to contract engagements, they had no hesitation in breaking them where their fulfilment would have been dangerous or inconvenient; and hence their neighbours spoke of Egypt as a 'bruised reed, whereon if a man lean, it will go into his hand and pierce it.'[2]

Another defect in the Egyptian character was softness and inclination to luxurious living. Drunkenness was a common vice among the young;[3] and among the upper class generally sensual pleasure and amusement were made, ordinarily, the ends of existence. False hair was worn; dyes and cosmetics used to produce an artificial beauty;[4] great banquets were frequent; games and sports of a thousand different kinds were in vogue;[5] dress was magnificent; equipages were splendid; life was passed in feasting, sport, and a constant succession of enjoyments. It is true that some seem not to have been spoiled by their self-

---

[1] Birch, p. 50: 'I have passed 110 years of my life *by the gift of the king.*'

[2] Isaiah xxxvi. 6; 2 Kings xviii. 21. Compare Ezekiel xxix. 6, 7: 'And all the inhabitants of Egypt shall know that I am the Lord, because *they have been a staff of reed* to the house of Israel. When they took hold of thee by thy hand, thou didst break and rend all their shoulder; and when they leaned upon thee, thou brakest, and madest all their loins to be at a stand.'

[3] Birch, *Egypt from the Earliest Times*, Introduction, p. xvi.

[4] Ibid. p. xv.

[5] See Wilkinson in the author's *Herodotus*, vol. ii. pp. 271-277, where many of the games are represented.

indulgence, or at any rate to have retained in old age a theoretic knowledge of what was right ;[1] but the general effect of such a life cannot but have been hurtful to the character ; and the result is seen in the gradual decline of the Egyptian power, and the successive subjections of the country by hardier and stronger races, Ethiopians, Assyrians, Persians, and Macedonian Greeks.

There is considerable difficulty in determining the amount of the population of ancient Egypt. Josephus gave the number at 7,800,000 in his day,[2] when the population was probably less numerous than under the native kings. Diodorus prefers the round number of 7,000,000, and says that in his time the population was not less than it had been under the Pharaohs.[3] An English scholar of repute[4] regards 6,000,000 as the maximum of the census of ancient Egypt, while another[5] is convinced that the real amount was not above 5,000,000. If the class of professional soldiers really numbered above 400,000 men, as Herodotus declares,[6] that class being only one out of seven, distinct altogether from the priests, the herdsmen, the shopkeepers, the boatmen, the swineherds, and the interpreters,[7] it is difficult to resist the conviction that the *native* Egyptians alone must have amounted *at the*

---

[1] The 'Book of Egyptian Wisdom,' written by Prince Phthaophis in his 110th year (Birch, pp. 49, 50), shows an excellent perception of moral truth, and has not unaptly been compared with the Proverbs of Solomon.

[2] Joseph. *Bell. Jud.* ii. 16. The number given in this place is 7,500,000; but it is exclusive of the Alexandrians, who are elsewhere reckoned at 300,000. (Diod. Sic. xvii. 52.)

[3] Diod. Sic. i. 31.

[4] Mr. Donne. (See Dr. Smith's *Dictionary of Greek and Roman Geography,* vol. i. p. 38.)

[5] Mr. Kenrick. (See his *Ancient Egypt,* vol. i. p. 181.)

[6] Herod. ii. 165–6. Diodorus made the number 624,000 in the reign of Sesostris (i. 54); and the Egyptian priests told Germanicus that it had amounted to 700,000 (Tacit. *Ann.* ii. 60).

[7] Herod. ii. 164.

least to five millions. To this a considerable addition,
an addition of probably not less than one-third, must
be made for slaves[1] and casual visitors, which would
raise the sum total of the population nearly to the
estimate of Diodorus. As such an estimate, even if
confined to the Nile valley, the Delta, and the Fayoum
alone, would not imply a density of more than about
600 to the square mile—a rate less than that of East
Flanders and of many English counties which are not
particularly thickly peopled[2]—it may well be accepted
as probably not in excess of the truth.

We have now to pass from the consideration of the
Egyptians themselves to that of the peoples, or nations,
who inhabited the neighbouring countries.

The nations which bounded Egypt on the east, the
west, and the south, belonged to three distinct races,
and bore in the Egyptian language three distinct appel-
lations. To the west were the *Ribu* or *Libu*, who may
safely be identified with the Libyans of the Greek
historians and geographers, the inhabitants of the entire
north coast from Egypt to the Atlantic Ocean,[3] after
whom the Greeks called the whole continent 'Libya.'
The monuments represent this people as a white race,
with blue eyes and fair hair ; it has been conjectured that
they came originally from Northern Europe,[4] and crossed
into Africa by way of Spain and Italy. Probably they
found in the countries which they overran a darker
people, with whom they intermingled, and into which

---

[1] The slave class was large and
very important. See Brugsch (*Histoire d'Egypte*, p. 16), who says:
'Les esclaves, pour la plupart sortis
du nombre des prisonniers de guerre,
formaient un élément très-impor-
tant de la population.'
[2] As Lancashire, Surrey, Staf-
fordshire, Warwickshire, and the
West Riding of Yorkshire.
[3] Herod. iv. 168-97.
[4] Brugsch, *Histoire d'Egypte*, p. 8.

they were ultimately absorbed; but in the earlier Egyptian period this change had not taken place, and the Egyptians represented them as described above, emphasising (it may be) and exaggerating the tints which were to them strange and unaccustomed. The Ribu, or Libyans, called sometimes Tahennu,[1] were numerous and warlike; but under ordinary circumstances they were greatly divided, and the occasions were ' few and far between' on which union was so far established that they became formidable to any of their neighbours. Once only in Egyptian history was the kingdom of the Pharaohs seriously threatened from this quarter, when in the reign of Menephtah, the son of Rameses II. (about B.C. 1250), a great invasion of Western Egypt took place under the conduct of the ' chief of the Ribu,'[2] and a doubtful contest was waged for some time between this prince and the Egyptian monarch.

Towards the south, Egypt had for her immediate neighbours the *Nahsi* or *Nahasu*,[3] who were blacks and (it is thought) true negroes, with out-turned lips and woolly hair, and who were found in the Nile valley beyond the First Cataract, and in the country on either side of it, or in all the more northern portion of the tract which is now known as Nubia. The tribes of the Nahsi were numerous; their temper was ' turbulent and impatient of subjection;'[4] they rejected civilisation, wore scarcely any clothes,[5] and made frequent inroads on the more southern of the Egyptian provinces with a view to plunder and rapine. The Egyptian kings were

---

[1] *Records of the Past*, vol. ii. p. 33; vol. iv. p. 42, &c.

[2] Ibid. vol. iv. p. 44.

[3] See Birch, *Egypt from the Earliest Times*, Introduction, p. ix.; Brugsch, *Histoire d'Egypte*, p. 8.

[4] Birch, l.s.c.

[5] ' Leur costume était d'une simplicité toute primitive.' (Brugsch, l.s.c.) Compare the representation in the author's *Herodotus*, vol. ii. p. 170.

forced to lead expeditions against them continually, in order to keep them in check and punish their depredations; but no serious danger could ever menace the monarchy from enemies who, though numerous, were ill-armed, scattered, and quite incapable of coalescing.

Beyond the Nahsi, however, further to the south, and inclining to the east of south, was a formidable power—a nation known to the Egyptians as the Kish or Kush, and to the Greeks and Romans as the Ethiopians, who occupied the broad tract lying between the Nile and Bahr-cl-Azrek on the one hand, and the Atbara on the other,[1] extending perhaps also across the Atbara, and at times holding the Nile valley along its entire course from Khartoum to the borders of Egypt.[2] This people was not of negro blood, but is to be regarded as Caucasian.[3]   It was ethnically connected with the Canaanites, the southern Arabians, the primitive Babylonians or Accadians, and with the Egyptians themselves.   Its best modern representatives are probably the Gallas, Agau, Wolaitsa, &c., of modern Abyssinia.   This people formed, at any rate in the later Egyptian times, a single settled monarchy, with a capital at Napata (*Gebel Berkel*) or at Meroë (*Dankalah*).[4] They were to a considerable extent civilised, though their civilisation does not appear to have been self-originated, but was due to Egyptian influence.   They were numerous, warlike, of great strength,[5] and more than common height;[6] they possessed a fair amount of discipline, and were by far the most important of the

[1] Wilkinson in the author's *Herodotus*, vol. ii. p. 41, note [8].
[2] See Ezek. xxix. 10; Herod. ii. 29.
[3] Donne in Smith's *Dictionary of Greek and Roman Geography*, vol.

i. p. 57.
[4] Wilkinson in the author's *Herodotus*, l.s.c.
[5] Herod. iii. 21, 30.
[6] Ibid. iii. 20, 114.   Compare Isaiah xlv. 14.

enemies against whom the Egyptians had to contend in Africa.

On their eastern border, where it was not washed by the Red Sea, the Egyptians came into contact with tribes which they called by the generic name of *Amu*, 'people,' or perhaps 'herdsmen,'[1] whom they seem to have regarded with a special contempt and dislike.[2] They had from a remote period been subject to aggression in this quarter; and a portion of the Amu had actually effected a lodgment within the territory naturally belonging to Egypt,[3] and held all the north-eastern portion of the Delta about the Lake Menzaleh and the cities known as Zoan (Zan, Tanis) and Rameses.[4] These Amu were, of course, Egyptian subjects; but there were likewise Amu beyond the Egyptian borders, in Syria and Palestine, who were almost perpetually at war with Egypt in the earlier times. Of these Amu the most important tribes were those of the Khita or Kheta ('Children of Heth,' 'Hittites'), the Kharu (Cherethites?), and the Rutennu, who seem to represent the Syrians. Another enemy of the Egyptians in this quarter was the people called *Shasu*, perhaps identical with the Hyk-sos,[5] and seemingly Arabs. Ordinarily the Shasu were not regarded as a formidable foe;[6] but

---

[1] Both Pierret and Brugsch suggest the root ☐𝕐, 'people,' as that from which Amu is derived (Pierret in the *Records of the Past*, vol. vi. p. 83; Brugsch, *Histoire*, p. 8). Brugsch, however, adds that possibly the root may be the Coptic *ame*, which is in the plural *ame'ou*, and means 'a herdsman.'

[2] Brugsch, l.s.c.

[3] Birch, *Egypt*, p. 129.

[4] Brugsch, p. 9.

[5] According to Manetho, *hyk* meant 'king,' and *sôs*, 'shepherd'

(Joseph. *c. Apion.* i. § 14). It is generally believed that Shasu is the same word as *sôs*. (See Birch, *Egypt*, p. 75; Wilkinson in the author's *Herodotus*, vol. ii. p. 351; Lenormant, *Histoire Ancienne de l'Orient*, vol. i. p. 360, &c.)

[6] They are sometimes spoken of with great contempt, as in the Tablet of Aahmes (*Records of the Past*, vol. iv. p. 8), where the writer says, 'I brought as tribute from the land of the Shasu very many prisoners—*I do not reckon them.*'

once in the course of Egyptian history, owing to circumstances that are unexplained, they made a great invasion, conquered all the lower country, and for many years held it in subjection. Otherwise one would have said that Egypt had little to fear from her immediate neighbours upon the east, who were at once numerically weak, and powerless through their multitudinous divisions.[1]

There was, however, a danger in this quarter, at which it is necessary to glance. Beyond the line of Egypt's immediate neighbours, beyond the Amu and the Shasu, Syria and Arabia, further to the east and the north-east, in the great Mesopotamian plain, and the highland by which it is overlooked, were to be seen, hazily and dimly through the intervening space, the forms of giant empires, already springing into being when monarchy in Egypt was still young, from whose rivalry the foresight of the wise may have discerned that peril would ultimately ensue, though the day of contact, and so of trial, might be far distant. A civilised State arose in the alluvial plain upon the Lower Tigris and Euphrates not very long after the birth of civilisation in Egypt.[2] As time went on, a second great monarchy and a third were formed in the countries above the alluvium. These empires were,

---

[1] The Arabians have always been divided into a multitude of tribes, and have never been united, except under Mohammed and his immediate successors. The Hittites seem to have had a number of kings (*Ancient Monarchies*, vol. ii. p. 363, note 2. 1 Kings x. 29; 2 Kings vii. 6). The Syrians formed several states, Aram-Beth-Rehob, Aram-Dammesek, Aram-Maachah, Aram-Zobah, &c.

[2] The early Egyptian and early Babylonian chronology are both of them uncertain ; but individually I incline to place the commencement of monarchy in Egypt about B.C. 2450, and its commencement in Babylonia about B.C. 2300. At any rate, it can scarcely be supposed that the monarchy mentioned in Gen. x. 10 was much later than that of which we hear in Gen. xii. 15-20.

like Egypt, aggressive, aiming at a wide, if not a universal, dominion.   Collision between them and Egypt was inevitable ; and the only question was when it would occur.   Its occurrence was the great danger with which Egypt was threatened from the first.   When the collision came, it would be seen whether Asia or Africa was the stronger, whether Egyptian discipline and skill and long experience were a match for the spirit, the dash, the impetuous valour of the Asiatics.   Until such time, the great African kingdom was, comparatively speaking, secure, and might calmly address itself to the maintenance and development of its arts, its industries, and its material prosperity generally.

CHAPTER V.

LANGUAGE AND WRITING.

Proposed Mode of Treatment. General Character of the Language. Connection of the Ancient Egyptian with the Coptic. Three Forms of Egyptian Writing. The Hieroglyphic Signs Pictorial. The Signs of four sorts, Representative, Figurative, Determinative, and Phonetic. Table of the most common Phonetics: other Phonetics. Number of the Signs. Arrangement of the Writing. Signs for Numerals—for Gods—for Months. Egyptian Grammar.

Αἰγύπτιοι . . . διφασίοισι γράμμασι χρέωνται.—HEROD. ii. 36.

IT is not proposed in the present chapter to attempt anything more than a popular, and so a superficial, account of the subjects put forward in the heading. To discuss thoroughly the Egyptian language and writing would require a work of the full dimensions of that which is here offered to the public, and would besides demand an amount of linguistic knowledge to which the present writer makes no pretension. It may be added that such a discussion would scarcely be suited to the general reader, who cannot be expected to interest himself deeply in a matter which is confessedly of a recondite character, not to be mastered without prolonged study, and, when mastered, only of value to persons who intend to devote themselves to the sciences of Egyptology or comparative philology. Such persons may be referred, though the reference is scarcely necessary, to the excellent works of Champollion, Lepsius, Brugsch, Birch, and De Rougé, on the writing,

the grammar, and the vocabulary of the ancient Egyptians [1]—works which treat the difficult subject in a most
masterly way, and which leave no branch of it un-
touched or even incompletely examined.

Speaking generally, the Egyptian language may be
described as 'an agglutinate monosyllabic form of
speech,' [2] presenting analogies, on the one hand, with
Turanian, on the other with Semitic tongues. The
grammar is predominantly Semitic: the pronouns,
prepositions, and other particles, are traceable for the
most part to Semitic roots; the Semitic system of
pronominal suffixes is used, at any rate partially. On
the other hand, the vocabulary is Semitic in comparatively few instances, its main analogies being with the
Accadian, Mongolian, and other Turanian tongues. As,
however, is generally the case with Turanian languages,[3]
the bulk of the roots are peculiar, standing separate
and unconnected with any other form of speech.

.The modern representative of the ancient Egyptian
is the Coptic, which, though corrupted by an Arabic
infusion, is its legitimate descendant, and which continued to be spoken in the lower part of the Nile valley
until the seventeenth century. At present a dead
language, it is known to us chiefly from the translations
into it of the Old and New Testament,[4] which are still

[1] See Champollion, *Grammaire Egyptienne*, Paris, 1836; *Diction-naire Egyptienne*, Paris, 1841; Lepsius, *Lettre à M. Rosellini sur le système Hiéroglyphique*, Rome, 1837; Birch, *Egyptian Grammar and Dictionary* in Bunsen's *Egypt*, vol. v.; Brugsch, *Scriptura Ægyp-tiorum demotica*, Berlin, 1848 : *Grammaire démotique*, Berlin, 1856; *Hieroglyphisch-demotisches Wörter-buch*, Leipsic, 1868; DeRougé, *Gram-maire Egyptienne*, Paris, 1867, &c.

[2] Stuart Poole in Smith's *Dict. of the Bible*, vol. i. p. 501.
[3] See Max Müller, *Languages of the Seat of War*, p. 88.
[4] There appears to have been three varieties of Coptic, the Mem-phitic, the Thebaic (or Sahidic), and the Bashmuric, but they do not greatly differ. (See *Dictionary of Languages*, p. 53; and compare the article on 'Versions' in Smith's *Dictionary of the Bible*.)

I 2

in use in Egypt, being read in the Coptic churches, though not 'understanded of the people.' It is mainly through the Coptic that the ancient Egyptian language has received its interpretation.

Egyptian writing is of three distinct kinds, which are known respectively by the names of Hieroglyphic, Hieratic, and Demotic or Enchorial.[1] The hieroglyphic is that of almost all monuments, and is also found occasionally in manuscripts. The hieratic and demotic occur with extreme rarity upon monuments, but are employed far more commonly than the hieroglyphic in the papyrus rolls or 'books' of the Egyptians. Both of them are cursive forms of the hieroglyphic writing, invented to save time, and suited for rapid writing with the pen, but in no way suited for carving upon stone and manifestly not intended for it. They have been called 'abbreviated forms;'[2] but this is scarcely correct, for they occupy more space than the corresponding hieroglyphics; but they could be written in (probably) one-tenth of the time. There is not much difference

between the hieratic and the demotic. The former was the earlier of the two, having been employed as far back as the time of the eighteenth and nineteenth dynasties, or perhaps even earlier;[3] it preserved the

---

[1] Lepsius, *Lettre à M. Rosellini,* p. 17; Lenormant, *Histoire Ancienne de l'Orient,* vol. i. pp. 498–506; Birch in Bunsen's *Egypt,* vol. v. p. 590.

[2] Lenormant, p. 505.

[3] The 'Great Harris Papyrus,' which has been translated by Dr. Birch and Professor Eisenlohr in the *Records of the Past,* vol. vi.

hieróglyphic forms to a certain extent. These are nearly lost in the demotic, which appears to have been introduced about the seventh century B.C.,[1] and which rapidly superseded the hieratic, being simpler and consequently easier to write. Both the hieratic and the demotic were written from right to left.

It is the essential characteristic of the hieroglyphic writing, that all the forms used, if we except those expressive of number, are pictures of objects. At the first glance, we see in a hieroglyphic inscription a multitude of forms, those of men, women, children, beasts, birds, reptiles, insects, human hands, legs, eyes, and the like, with which we are familiar ; but these shapes are mixed up with others, not so readily recognised, which seem to us at first sight not imitative but conventional, as circles, squares, half-circles, ovals, triangles, curved lines, wavy lines, small segments of circles, circles crossed diagonally, and the like. Investigation, however, shows that this apparent difference is not a real one. ALL the forms used are pictures, more or less successful, of objects which they were intended to represent. The circle o represents the sun, the curved line, placed either way, (or ⌢ , the moon ; the oval ◌, an egg ; the square, with an opening, ◻ a house ; the pointed oval, ⬄ a mouth, &c. Originally, it would seem, Egyptian writing was entirely picture writing, nothing being capable of being represented by it but objects and actions that the eye could see.

Ultimately, however, the system became much

---

pp. 21-70, vol. viii. pp. 5-52, is in hieratic, and belongs to the time of Rameses III., a king of the 19th dynasty.   Some of the hieratic papyri at Berlin are ascribed to the 12th or 13th (ibid. vol. vi. pp.

131-4). Dr. Birch speaks of works on medicine in the hieratic character as 'attributed to the kings of the Old Empire' (*Egypt from the Earliest Times*, p. 25).

[1] Lenormant. l.s.c.

more complicated; and the hieroglyphics, as employed
in the historical times, must be divided into at least
four classes. First, there were some which continued
to be used in the old way, to designate the object
represented, which have been called 'ikonographic,
representational, or imitative hieroglyphics.'[1] These
were such as the circle for the sun, the curved line or
crescent for the moon; a figure of a man, a woman, or
a child for an actual man, woman, or child; a picture
of a soldier armed with bow and quiver for a soldier;
&c. These direct representations were used in two
ways: either they stood alone to represent the object
intended, or they followed the name of the object
written phonetically. 'Thus the word *Ra*, " sun," might
be written in letters only, or be also followed by the
ikonograph of the solar disk (which, if alone, would
still have the same meaning); and as we might write
the word " horse," and place after it a figure of that
animal, so did they after their word *htr* or *htor*, " horse "
. So too the word *Aah* or *Joh*, " moon,"
was followed by the crescent , and *rôt*,
" mankind," by a figure of a man and woman .'[2]
In these cases it is evident that the ikonograph was mere
surplusage; but perhaps it facilitated the rapid reading
of the word preceding it.

Secondly, the characters were used figuratively, or
symbolically. Thus a circle o represented not only
'the sun,' but also 'a day,' and the curved line or
crescent not only 'the moon,' but also 'a month.'
Similarly, the representation of a pen and inkstand
stood for 'writing,' 'to write,' 'a scribe;' a man

---

[1] Wilkinson in the author's *Herodotus*, vol. ii. p. 258.   [2] Ibid. p. 259.

pouring out a libation from a vase ⚱, or a vase with liquid pouring from it ⌐, or even a simple vase inverted |, signified ' a priest;' an egg ○ meant 'a child,' 'a son;' a seated figure with a curved beard 'a god' 𓀭 ; and, with a remote connection, but still with a connection that can be easily traced, a bee 𓆤 stood for 'king,'[1] a vulture 𓃀 for 'mother,'[2] a serpent for 'god' 𓆓, a palm-branch ⌐ for 'year,' a 'goose' 𓅨 for 'son,' two water-plants of different kinds for 'the Upper and the Lower Egypt.' Again, the fore-part of a lion ⌐ meant 'the beginning' of anything, and the hind-quarters 𓄀 'the end;' a leg within a trap 𓌙 meant 'deceit;' the head and neck of a lion erect 𓄃 meant 'vigilance;' and, with a symbolism that was obscurer and more recondite, a beetle (scarabæus) 𓆣 meant the 'world,' an ostrich feather 𓆄 'justice,' and a man killing himself 𓀸 'wickedness' or 'atrocity.'[3]

A third use of the hieroglyphics was as 'determinatives.' These were most commonly added after proper names, and showed the class to which they belonged. Thus a word followed by the sitting figure with a curved beard 𓀭 is known to be the proper name of a god;[4] one followed by the figure of a man 𓀀 is the designation of a man; one accompanied by a circle

---

[1] The monarchical government of the beehive was early noticed, and led, no doubt, to this symbolism, which is believed to have been adopted in Babylonia no less than in Egypt. (See Oppert, *Voyage en Mésopotamie*, vol. ii. p. 68.)

[2] The Egyptians, it is said, thought there were no male vultures, so that each vulture was a mother. (Lenormant, *Histoire An-*

cienne de l'Orient, vol. i. p. 504.)

[3] The Egyptians regarded suicide as the worst of all crimes.

[4] See the so-called 'Egyptian altar' at Turin, where this determinative follows the names of fourteen deities, of all, in fact, but Horus and Nephthis. (*Transactions of Bibl. Archæology Society*, vol. i. opp. p. 112.)

with a cross inside it ⊕ is the name of a place in
Egypt; one followed by a sign intended to represent
mountains ⊔⊔ is the name of a foreign country; and
so on. Names moreover which are not, strictly speaking, proper names, but designate classes, have determinatives attached to them marking their genus. The
name of any particular kind of animal, as *ana*, 'ibex,'
mau, 'cat,' etc., has a determinative after it resembling
a short mallet ▶, which is supposed to represent the
skin and tail of an animal,[1] and shows that the word
whereto it is attached designates some species of beast.
So the names of classes of birds are followed by the
figure of a bird ⟁, of reptiles by a snake ⟋⟍, of
plants by a water-plant ⎜, of flowers by three blossoms
⚘, of buildings by the sign for house ⊓.[2]

Finally, the great bulk of the hieroglyphics in all
inscriptions are phonetic, standing either for letters
or for syllables,[3] most commonly the former.[4] The
Egyptians, like the Phœnicians, resolved speech into
its elements, and expressed these elements by signs,
which had the exact force of our letters. In choosing
their sign, they looked out for some common object,
with a name of which the initial element was identical
with the sound they wanted to express. Thus, *akhôm*
being the name of an eagle in Egyptian, the eagle was

---

[1] Wilkinson in the author's *Herodotus*, vol. ii. p. 262; Birch in Bunsen's *Egypt*, vol. v. p. 597.
[2] Some   determinatives   were
merely grammatical. The papyrus
roll ⎯⎯ was added as a tacit sign
to substantives, adjectives, and verbs.
Two human legs walking ⋀ marked
activity of any kind.
[3] Some signs stand for words of
two syllables, as the flag on a flag-
staff ⎮ for *neter*, 'a god,' the guitar

⎮ for *nefer*, 'good,' &c.
[4] Dr. Birch argues (Bunsen's *Egypt*,
vol. v. p. 599) that every hieroglyphic
character represents a syllable, each
consonant having a vowel sound
inherent in it: practically, however,
he represents the alphabetic hieroglyphs by single letters. Thus he
reads ⌁ ⎮⌒ not as *hu-bu-su*, but as
hebs.

made the sign of its initial sound, A ; the name of an owl in Egyptian being *moulag*, the figure of an owl was made to express M.[1] But, unfortunately, the Egyptians did not stop here. Not content with fixing on one such sign in each case to express each elementary sound, they for the most part adopted several. An eagle, the leaf of a water-plant, and a hand and arm to the elbow were alike employed to represent the sound A. The sound B was expressed by a human leg and foot, and also by a bird like a crane, and by an object resembling a flower-pot.[2] For M there were four principal signs, an owl, two parallel straight lines joined at one end by a diagonal, a form something like a sickle, and a sort of double-headed baton. There were four forms for T, three for N, for K, for S, for J,[3] for KH, and for H, while there were two for L or R (which the Egyptians regarded as the same), two for SH, two for I, for U, and for P. The letters F and D were about the only ones that were represented uniformly by a single hieroglyphic, the former by the cerastes or horned snake, the latter by a hand with the palm upwards.[4]

The subjoined table will give the general phonetic

---

[1] Lepsius, *Lettre à M. Rosellini*, p. 44 ; Wilkinson in the author's *Herodotus*, vol. ii. p. 262.

[2] Dr. Birch regards this as ' a vase of fire ' (Bunsen's *Egypt*, vol. v. p. 599).

[3] I follow here Dr. Eisenlohr's rendering of the hieroglyphs ⌐, ⌐, and ⌐ (*Transactions of Bibl. Arch. Society*, vol. i. pp. 358 and 367). Dr. Birch renders ⌐ by TH (ibid. vol. iv. p. 172). And ⌐ is generally rendered by the same in the name

of Kambath or Kenbuth, for 'Cambyses.' But the Persian letter to which the ⌐ corresponds in this word is a J undoubtedly. M. Lenormant considers all three forms, ⌐, ⌐, and ⌐, to represent the sound TS (*Histoire Ancienne de l'Orient*, vol. i. p. 501). So Birch with regard to ⌐ and ⌐ in Bunsen's *Egypt*, vol. v. p. 603.

[4] Birch regards this form as merely another representation of T.

alphabet of the Egyptians according to the best recent
authorities :—

Signs in common use.	Signs employed more rarely.	Equivalent in English.
		A (as in father).
		I (sounded as ee in see).
		U (sounded as oo in food)
		B
		P
		F
		G (deep guttural).
		K
		KH (sounded like the Hebrew ח).
		D
		T
		M
		N
		L
		S
		SH
		H
		J

Besides these ordinary phonetics, the Egyptians had a multitude of signs which could be used phonetically in certain groups, more especially at the beginning of words, but which were of comparatively rare occurrence. Lepsius gave, in 1837, a list of fifty-four such signs;[1] but the subsequent course of research has added largely to them. There are probably not less than a hundred signs of this kind, some of which represent letters, some syllables, their special characteristic being that they can only be used in certain groups. Many of them occur only in single words, as the *crux ansata* ♀, in *ankh*, 'life,' 'living,' 'flower,'[2]—the outstretched arms with palms downwards, ⏦, in *nen*, the negative particle[3]—the crocodile's tail, ▰, in *Kem*, *Kemi*, 'Egypt' or 'black;'[4] and the like.

Altogether the number of signs used is not less than from nine hundred to a thousand;[5] and hence the difficulty of reading the inscriptions, even now that—thanks to the Rosetta stone—the veil has been lifted. The student has to bear in mind the force of (say) a thousand characters, and not only so, but the various forces that many of them havê, as representative, as symbolic, as determinative, and as phonetic. He has to settle to his own satisfaction, first, the class to which they belong in each instance, and secondly, the value which they have.

---

[1] *Lettre à M. Rosellini*, pp. 48–56, and Planche A, parti ii. at the end of the work.

[2] Wilkinson in the author's *Herodotus*, vol. ii. p. 260; Lepsius, *Lettre à M. Rosellini*, p. 49.

[3] Dr. Birch gives this sign the sound of *nen* (*Dictionary of Hieroglyphics* in Bunsen's *Egypt*, vol. v. p. 453). But Dr. Eisenlohr prefers to render it by *an* (*Transactions of Bibl. Arch. Society*, vol. i. p. 360, line [1]).

[4] Dr. Birch (*Dictionary*, p. 420) notes *one* other word (*kamut*, 'to place' or 'carve') where the crocodile's tail is used.

[5] The fount of hieroglyphic type employed in the present work contains about eight hundred forms; but there are many other forms besides, which occur so rarely that they have hitherto not been expressed in type.

He has also to determine whether any are purely
superfluous, the Egyptians having had a fancy both for
repeating characters unnecessarily, and also for expressing the same sound twice over by variant signs.

The hieroglyphics are sometimes written in column,
one over another ; but this is, comparatively speaking, a
rare arrangement. In general, as in most other forms
of writing, the characters are in line, with only an
occasional superinscription of one sign over that which
in pronunciation follows it. They are read, when
written in line, from left to right, or from right to left,
according to the direction in which the characters face.[1]
This direction is most clearly seen in the human and
animal forms ; but it is not confined to these, most
characters fronting one way or the other. The direction
is from left to right, if the characters face to the left,
and *vice versa*.

In hieroglyphical writing, the numerals from one to
nine are expressed by vertical strokes, which, between
three and ten, are collected in two groups, thus :—

1	2	3	4	5	6	7	8	9
I	II	III	‖	⦀	⦀	⦀	⦀	⦀

Ten is expressed by a sort of arch or doorway, ∩;
twenty by two such arches ∩∩; thirty by three ∩∩∩; and
so on. For the hundreds the sign is the same as one of
those employed to express *u*, ⊕; for the thousands, it
is the same as one of those employed to express *kh*, ⌇;
and for tens of thousands, it is a form used also to express *h*, ⌇. The number 21,553 would be expressed
in a hieroglyphical inscription thus :— ⌇⌇⌇ ⊕⊕⊕ ∩∩∩ / ⊕⊕ ∩∩⦀

---

[1] There are occasional exceptions
to this rule (Birch in Bunsen's
Egypt, vol. v. p. 595); but they are
so rare as scarcely to deserve mention.

It may be added that most of the Egyptian gods have special signs significative of them, which are either human or animal figures, or the two intermixed. Their names, however, are also expressed phonetically, as Amun (Ammon) by ❘ 〰 , Phthah or Ptah by ❚ 𝑄, and the like. Signs which cannot be regarded as phonetic designate the several months, as ⌒ ⨇, which designates Thoth, the first month, corresponding to our September; ⌒ ⨇, which designates Paopi, the second month; ⌒ ⬭ which designates Phamenoph, the seventh month; ⌒ ▭▭, which is the sign for Mesoré, the twelfth month.[1]

In conclusion, a few remarks will be added on the subject of Egyptian grammar. The Egyptian language admitted all the nine parts of speech, but was very deficient in conjunctions and interjections. It had a single article only, which was the definite one, corresponding to the English 'the.' The article was declined, being *pâ* 🦅🦅 in the masculine singular,[2] *tâ* ⬭🦅 in the feminine singular,[3] and *nâ* 🦅 in the plural of both genders.[4]

Substantives form the plural by adding *u*, as *neter*, 'a god,' *neteru*, 'gods,' *ta*, 'a land,' *tau*, 'lands,' *uar*, 'a prince,' *uaru*, 'princes,' &c. Adjectives, participles, and possessive pronouns do the same. The feminine is made by adding *t* (•), as *sa* or *se*, 'a son,' *set*, 'a

---

[1] Wilkinson in the author's *Herodotus*, vol. ii. p. 238.
[2] A later form of the masculine article is ❚〰, *pi*, and a still later one, ▭▭, *pe*.
[3] The *t* is sometimes expressed in the later times by ❘.
[4] The *n* was expressed in later times by ⅄; and a full form *naiu* was sometimes used.

daughter;' *pâ neter aa*, 'the great god;' *tâ asbutu aat*, 'the great throne;' *sa neb*, 'every man;' *kat nebt*, 'every building;' and the like. There is said to be no dual;[1] but we find the form *ta* ($\overline{}$), 'land;' doubled for two lands $\overline{}$, and tripled for more than two thus, $\overline{}$. Tripling a sign is a common mode of expressing the plural, which is otherwise signified by the addition of three vertical lines (either ııı or ¦).

Pronouns were either used independently or suffixed. The independent form for 'I' was *anak* or *anuk*, which is plainly identical with the Hebrew אָנֹכִי, the Assyrian *anaku*, and the Moabite *anak*. The form for 'thou' was *ntek* (fem. *net*); for 'he,' *ntef*, or *su*; for 'she,' *ntes*; for 'we,' *nenanen*; for 'ye,' *ntuten*; for 'they,' *ntesen* (*natsen*), or *sen* The forms *su* and *sen* may compare with the Hebrew הוּא and הֵן; but otherwise the resemblance to the Semitic is not close.

The suffixed pronoun of the first person singular was *-a*, which might be expressed either phonetically by ▌, or by the figure of the speaker; that of the second person singular was, in the masculine *-k* (expressed by ▬, ℩, or 𝒞), in the feminine *-t* (expressed by either ▭ or ▬); the ordinary suffix of the third person masculine was *-f* (expressed by ⌣), of the third person feminine *-s* (expressed by either ─ or ∏); but there was also a masculine form *-su* (∐ ⌐ or ⌐ ⊚) to express 'him,' and a feminine form *-st* (⸗ or ∏ ⌐ or ∏ ▭) to express 'she,' 'her,' &c. In the plural the suffix of the first person was *-n* (﹏) or *-nu* (﹏ or ⌇ ¦); of the second *-ten* (≣) or *-tenu*

---

[1] Wilkinson in the author's *Hero-* however, allows a dual. (See Bun-*dotus*, vol. ii. p. 263. Dr. Birch, sen's *Egypt*, vol. v. p. 619.)

(⟨≡⟩ or ⟨≈⟩ or ⟨♦⟩ ¦); of the third -u (⟨⟩ ¦)-su (⟨≡⟩),
or (most commonly) -senu (expressed variously).[1] The
form -stu (⟨⟩ ⟨⟩ or ⟨⟩) is likewise found.

There were also in Egyptian a set of independent
possessive pronouns, produced by combining the article
in its three forms (pa, ta, and na) with the above
suffixes, the form of the article being determined by
the object possessed, that of the suffix by the possessor.
Thus 'my father' is expressed by pa-i-a atef, 'thy
father' by pa-i-k atef, 'his father' by pa-i-f atef, 'our
father' by pa-i-nu atef, 'your father' by pa-i-tenu atef,
and 'their father' by pa-i-u or pa-i-senu atef. If
'mother' be substituted for 'father,' the pronouns
become ta-i-a, ta-i-k, ta-i-f, ta-i-nu, ta-i-tenu, and ta-i-u
or ta-i-senu. If the noun which follows the pronoun
be in the plural number, the initial syllable becomes
na. Thus for 'my enemies' we must say na-i-a kheftu,
for 'thy enemies' na-i-k kheftu, 'his enemies' naif
kheftu, 'her enemies' nais kheftu, 'our enemies' nainu
kheftu, 'your enemies' naitenu kheftu, and 'their
enemies' naisenu kheftu.

The conjugation of the tenses of verbs was by
means of the suffixed pronouns. To mark the first
person, the verb was followed by a figure of the
speaker, which is supposed to have been pronounced a;
to mark the second person, k was suffixed, or t if the
agent was a female; to mark the third, f, or s in case
of a female; in the plural, the ordinary terminations[2]

---

[1] Compare the Hebrew suffixes :—
1st pers. sing. ‫י‬-   2nd (masc.) ‫ך‬- (fem.) ‫ך‬-   3rd (masc.) ‫ו‬- (fem.) ‫ה‬ּ-
„ plur. ‫נו‬-   „   ‫כם‬-   „   ‫כן‬-   „   ‫הם‬-   „   ‫הן‬ּ-.
The 2nd pers. sing. masc. and 1st pers. pl. are identical: the rest show a
connection.
[2] Instead of -nenu we sometimes find -:nu, as in the declension of au,

were *nenu, tenu,* and *senu,* for 'we,' 'you,' 'they;' as will be best seen by an example.

<table>
<tr><td align="center">Singular.</td><td align="center">Plural.</td></tr>
<tr><td>*jet-a,* 'I say.'</td><td>*jet-nenu,* 'we say.'</td></tr>
<tr><td>*jet-k, jet-t,* 'thou sayest.'</td><td>*jet-tenu,* 'ye say.'</td></tr>
<tr><td>*jet-f, jet-s,* 'he says,' 'she says.'</td><td>*jet-senu,* 'they say.'</td></tr>
</table>

The perfect tense was marked by interposing *n* between the verb and the pronoun, thus : ≃, *arf,* 'he makes,' ≋, *arnf,* 'he made' or 'has made.' The future was formed by prefixing the auxiliary verb | ⍨, *au,* 'to be,' together with the pronoun, and then placing *r* before the verb,[1] as ⍨, *ara,* 'I make,' | ⍨ ⍨≃, *auarar,* 'I am for making' or 'I will make.'

To form the passive, *tu* was added to the root of the verb, the pronominal suffix following. Thus from ⟨⟩, *mes,* 'born,' we have ⟨⟩ ⍨, *mestu-f,* 'he was born,' &c.

A remarkable peculiarity of Egyptian grammar is the *declension of prepositions.* It has been generally recognised by modern comparative grammarians that

---

to be, which is :—
aua, I am
auk, thou art (*m.*)
aut, thou art (*f.*)
auf, he is
aus she is
aunu, we are
autenu, ye are
ausenu, they are

[1] The *r* is no doubt the preposition *er,* 'for' or 'to,' and *au-a-r-ar* = 'I am for making,' or 'I am to make,' *i.e.* 'I will make.' (See Birch, p. 661.)

prepositions are in reality abraded forms of nouns or pronouns. Declension may therefore be said to belong to them naturally; though in very few languages does any vestige of their inflection remain. In Egyptian, however, 'all prepositions admit of a plural;'[1] and feminine forms are also not uncommon. For instance, the preposition ⌇⌇⌇, *en*, ' of,' becomes frequently ⌇⌇⌇, *ent*, after feminine nouns; and ⬤ or ⬤, *na* or *nu*, after plural ones. *Am*, 'in,' 'into,' has the plural form + 🦅 🦆 ⸰, *amu*; *er* or *ari*, ' to,' ' on,' has a plural *aru* (⬤⬤⬤); and so on. Egyptian prepositions are very numerous; but their sense is somewhat indeterminate: *her* (⬤), for example, has the nine meanings of ' above,' ' up,' ' upon,' ' for,' ' by,' ' from,' ' out of,' ' in,' and ' about ' or ' in the act of.' *Er* commonly means ' to,' or ' for '; but it is found also in the senses ' with,' ' by,'[a] ' than,'. ' as,' ' as far as,' ' in,' and ' at.' *Em* also is said[2] to have the senses of ' as,' ' in,' ' for,' ' throughout,' ' towards,' ' by means of,' ' to,' ' from,' and ' with.'

The rarity of conjunctions in Egyptian has been already mentioned.[3] The original language possessed no word corresponding to the ordinary copulative ' and '; nor was it until the Ptolemaic age that a real ' and ' (⳼, *ha*) was invented.[4] Previously the usual

----

[1] See an article on Egyptian prepositions by Mr. Le Page Renouf in the *Transactions of the Society of Biblical Archæology*, vol. ii. p. 301 et seqq.

[2] Birch in Bunsen's *Egypt*, vol. v.

p. 675.
[3] See above, page 125.
[4] In Roman times *ha* was re-placed by *her* ⳼ , which is also used in the sense of ' with.'

practice was to let the connective be supplied by inference, as—

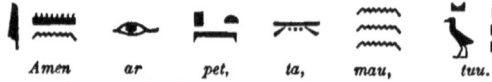

Amen   ar   pet,   ta,   mau,   tuu.

'Ammon has made heaven, earth, waters, (and) hills.'

But sometimes the preposition *h'na* ( ), 'with,' was employed as a conjunction. Thus we find *Har h'na Set* = 'Horus with Set' for 'Horus and Set'; *pet h'na amus*, 'heaven with its inhabitants,' for 'heaven and its inhabitants.' There were conjunctions, however, expressive of 'or,' 'nor,' 'for' or 'because,' 'when,' 'after' or 'while,' 'how,' and a few others.[1] The place of conjunctions in the construction of sentences was taken generally by prepositions, which were used, though not very freely, to bind the different clauses of a sentence together.

The only interjections which have been recognised in the inscriptions are: *A!* ( ), equivalent to our 'Ah!' or 'Oh!' *hai!* ( ), a stronger form of the same, and *ask!* or *ast!* (or), which has the force of 'Lo!' or 'Behold!'

The following are the chief points remarkable in Egyptian syntax or construction :—1. The sentences are short, rarely exceeding in length ten words. The construction is simple, and the order uniform.[2] 2. The adjective always follows the noun, and the nominative case almost always follows the verb. 3. The adverb generally follows the adjective or verb which it qualifies. 4. Neither nouns nor adjectives, nor even pronouns, have cases. The want is supplied by a free

---

[1] Birch in Bunsen's *Egypt,* vol. v. pp. 710-713.   [2] Ibid. p. 714.

use of prepositions. 5. Prepositions are always pre-
fixed to the words which they govern. 6. A conjunction used to join two words together is sometimes
placed after the second word.[1] 7. When two nouns
come together, and are not in apposition, the latter is
in regimen, as *neb ta*, 'lord of earth'; *sa Ra*, 'son of
Ra'; and the like. 8. There are several forms of the
substantive verb, two of which (*au*, | ⟩, and *an* ⟩)
are used as auxiliaries. 9. The negative is commonly
placed at the beginning of a sentence.

---

[1] This is the case with ⟩ ⟩ ⟩ conjunction. (Compare the Latin
rupu, 'or,' but not with any other   use of *ve* and *que*.)

CHAPTER V.

LITERATURE.

General Character of the Egyptian Literature, mediocre—perhaps at present not fairly appreciated. Variety and Extent of the Literature. Works on Religious Subjects—' Ritual of the Dead.' Shorter Works on Religion —Specimen. Historical Poems—Specimens. Lyrical Poems—Specimen from the ' Song of the Harper.' Travels. 'Romances. Autobiographies —Sketch of the ' Story of Saneha'—Specimen. Correspondence. Scientific Treatises. Works on Magic.

'La littérature égyptienne était nombreuse et célèbre.'—LENORMANT, *Manuel d'Histoire Ancienne de l'Orient*, vol. i. p. 306.

THE literature of the Egyptians, although it is remarkable for the extent and variety of the subjects comprised within its range, is, beyond a doubt, far inferior to the literatures of Greece, of Rome, and of the more eminent among modern countries. Its general character must be pronounced mediocre. History, whether as recorded on monuments, or as enshrined in books, was either written in a forced and stilted, or in a dry and wholly uninteresting style.[1] Poetry was in a more advanced condition. Like the Hebrew poetry, it delighted in parallelisms and antitheses; while it transcended Hebrew poetry in its rhythmic arrangement, in the balance of the lines, the close correspondence of

---

[1] Dr. Birch appears to me to speak somewhat too favourably when he says of the historical texts: 'The narrative is clear; and the metaphors, sparingly introduced, are at once simple and intelligible : the text marches to the cadence of an harmonious syntax.' (*Records of the Past*, vol. ii. preface, p. iii.) But I differ with great diffidence from so high an authority.

clause to clause, and the strict observance of rhythmic law in most cases.[1] Other branches of literature, as romance, travels, letters, are chiefly remarkable for an extreme and almost childish simplicity ; while the characteristic of some classes of composition is obscurity and confusion.[2] A general feature of Egyptian writing, in its more ambitious flights, is a frequent and abrupt change from the first or second to the third person, with as sudden a return from the third to the first or second, and an equally abrupt change of tense.[3] It is supposed that these startling transitions, for which there is no discernible reason and no discoverable, or at any rate nó discovered, law, were viewed as elegances of style, under the Egyptian standard of taste, and were thus especially affected by those who aspired to be considered 'fine writers.'[4] No doubt it may be urged, with a good deal of reason, that different ages and different nations have each their own peculiar styles, and that we modern Europeans are scarcely fair critics of a literature so remote in date as the Egyptian, and one so different in character from our own ; but as, on the other hand, their remoteness and peculiarity do not prevent us from appreciating the masterpieces of Greece and Rome, the Vedic hymns, the Norse sagas, or even the Davidical psalms, so it is probable that wherever there is real merit in a literature, however peculiar it may be, the merit will reveal itself to the candid critic, and will extort his admiration. A better

[1] Compare the remarks of M. Ludwig Stern in the *Records of the Past*, vol. vi. p. 127.

[2] What, for instance, can be made of the following, which is given as a translation of one of the 'Magical Texts' (*Records*, vol. vi. p. 121)?—

The burning brasier,
The great fire-basin,
Prepared by him who affrights
The overthrown : he that is headless,
The place of death, the place
Of life ; the great rock
Throwing fire against Set and his companions.

[3] Birch in the *Records*, vol. ii. preface, p. ii.   [4] Ibid.

argument for our, at present, suspending our judgment, and passing no sentence of unqualified condemnation on any branch of Egyptian writing, is furnished by the consideration that the Egyptian language is still imperfectly understood, and that the true force of numerous expressions, which it is easy enough to translate literally, is probably missed even by the advanced scholar. Much patient study, not only of linguistic forms, but of Egyptian ideas and modes of thought, is still requisite before a final judgment can be confidently given as to the position which Egyptian literature is entitled to hold in the literature of the world.

Whatever the opinion entertained of its degree of excellence, concerning the extent and variety of Egyptian literature there can be no dispute. A recent writer, of great authority in his day, did indeed venture to lay it down in so many words, that 'the Egyptians had no literature or history;'[1] but he would be a bold man who at the present date should venture to maintain this paradox. Besides the testimony of the classical writers,[2] which, even if it stood alone, legitimate criticism could not safely set aside,[3] we have now, in the discovered and deciphered inscriptions and papyri,

[1] Cornewall Lewis, *Astronomy of the Ancients*, p. 340.

[2] See Herod. ii. 3, 77; Plat. *Tim.* § 5; Diod. Sic. i. 44; Manetho ap. Joseph. *Contr. Ap.* i. 12, 26; Apollodor. ap. Syncell. *Chronograph.* vol. i. p. 171, &c.

[3] Sir G. C. Lewis (*Astronomy*, pp. 262-275) rejects all these testimonies unhesitatingly, on the ground that 'the later Greeks (is Herodotus a late Greek?) were wanting in that national spirit which leads moderns to contend for the claims of their own countrymen to inventions and discoveries,' and to priority in the various walks of literature; but he does not attempt to explain how the Greeks came to be destitute of a feeling which is so natural and (unless they are an exception) so absolutely universal. He seems really to assume that his favourite Greeks *must* have been the originators of all science, learning, and literature, and to be determined, on account of this foregone conclusion, to reject all statements—even those made by themselves—to the contrary.

a mass of literary matter, which those best entitled to pronounce an opinion declare to rival in extent the existing remains of any other known ancient literature.[1] Four volumes of Egyptian texts have been already published in English ;[2] while in France and Germany the number of the translations made is far greater.[3] All that has hitherto been done is, we are told, but as a drop in the bucket, compared with that which remains to be done. We are promised a long succession of volumes similar to those that have already appeared in English ; and even this extensive series will only contain 'the most important portions of this ancient literature.'[4]

If the extent of the literature is thus great and surprising, still more remarkable is the variety of subjects which it embraces. Besides history, which is largely represented on the monuments, and is occasionally illustrated by the papyri, Egyptologers enumerate works on religion and theology ; poems, historical and lyrical; travels; epistolary correspondence ; reports, military and statistical ; romances, or rather short tales; orations; treatises on morals and rhetoric ; mathematical and medical works ; books on geography, astronomy, astrology, and magic ; collections of proverbs ; calendars; books of receipts ; accounts; catalogues of libraries, and various others.[5] The first place in the

---

[1] Birch in *Records of the Past,* vol. ii. preface, p. ix.

[2] *Records of the Past,* vols. ii., iv., vi., and viii.

[3] See the *Recherches sur les Monuments des six premières Dynasties* of the late Vicomte Em. de Rougé ; the *Histoire d'Egypte* and *Recueil de Monuments Egyptiens* of Dr. Brugsch ; the *Denkmäler* of Lepsius ; the *Mélanges*

Egyptologiques and other works of M. Chabas ; the *Monuments divers* of M. Mariette ; and numerous articles in the *Zeitschrift für ägyptische Sprache,* the *Revue Archéologique,* and the *Mémoires de l'Académie des Inscriptions et Belles Lettres* during recent years.

[4] Birch in *Records of the Past,* vol. ii. preface, p. ix.

[5] See Lenormant, *Manuel d'His-*

literature is occupied undoubtedly by the religious books,[1] which are longer, more elaborate, and more carefully composed than the rest, and which held a position in the thoughts of the people analogous to that of the Vedas in India, and of the Bible and ecclesiastical literature in Europe during the middle ages.

Of all the religious works the most important was the one which is commonly called 'The Funereal Ritual,'[2] or 'The Ritual of the Dead,'[3] but of which the Egyptian title was 'The Manifestation to Light,' or, in other words, the Book revealing light to the soul. This book claimed to be a revelation from Thoth, or Hermes, who through it declared the will of the gods and the mysterious nature of divine things, to man.[4] Portions of it are expressly stated to have been written by the very finger of Thoth himself, and others to have been the composition of a 'great god.'[5] It was in such high esteem, that from the time of the eleventh dynasty some extracts from it were regularly placed in the coffins of the dead, either on the inner sides of the rectangular chests which held the mummies, or on the linen bandages in which the corpse was wrapped, or on the inner walls of the tomb, or sometimes on all three. Besides this, copies on papyrus, more or less complete, were frequently buried with the deceased,[6] more especially in the later Pharaonic times, when the book had taken its definitive form through an

toire Ancienne de l'Orient, vol. i. pp. 506–20; Birch, Egypt from the Earliest Times, Introduction, p. xiii.; and Records of the Past, vol. vi. pp. 162–5.

[1] Lenormant, p. 506: 'Le premier rang appartient aux livres religieux.'

[2] Bunsen's Egypt, vol. v. pp.

125–326; Lenormant, l.s.c.

[3] Birch's Egypt from the Earliest Times, l.s.c.; Records of the Past, vol. vi. p. 164, &c.

[4] Bunsen, p. 133.

[5] Ritual, ch. lxv. ad finem (Bunsen, p. 209).

[6] Lenormant, l.s.c.

authoritative revision made under the twenty-sixth dynasty.

The 'Ritual'' has been divided into three,[1] and again into twenty-three[2] portions. According to the former division, the first part consists of the first sixteen chapters, and contains forms of invocation and of prayer to be used over the dead from the moment of his decease to the commencement of the process of embalming.[3] The second part opens with a long chapter which has been considered to contain 'the Egyptian faith.'[4] It is mystical in the highest degree, and quite unintelligible to a modern, after all the explanations which it has received.[5] This creed is followed by a series of prayers, contained in three chapters, which refer to the justification of the deceased, and seem intended for use during the enrolment of the mummy in its bandages.[6] Then come prayers or spells, in six chapters, for the reconstruction of the deceased

[1] Champollion was the first to make this division (Bunsen, p. 137). It is the one preferred by M. Lenormant (*Manuel*, vol. i. pp. 507–515).

[2] Birch in Bunsen's *Egypt*, vol. v. pp. 138–56.

[3] Lenormant, pp. 507–9.

[4] Birch in Bunsen's *Egypt*, vol. v. pp. 139, 172, &c.

[5] What, for instance, can be more obscure than such passages as these, which are fair specimens of the document?—
'I am Yesterday. I know the morning. Let him explain it. Yesterday is Osiris, the Morning the Sun; the day on which are strangled the deriders of the universal Lord, when his son Horus has been invested; or the day is the victory of his arms, when the chest of Osiris has been confronted by his father the Sun.' (ch. xvii.

p. 172.)
'Tum has built thy house; the two Lion-gods have founded thy abode. Ptah going round thee, divine Horus purifies thee, the god Set does so in turn. The Osiris has come from the earth. He has taken his legs; he is Tum. He is from his city. Behind thee is a white lion to claw the head. The Osiris has turned back (or, Osiris has turned thee back) to guard thee. It is invisible to the guardians, said by the Osiris. It is Isis whom thou hast seen. He has stroked his locks for him. He has directed his face to the mouth of his road, or its horn. He is conceived by Isis, engendered by Nephthys.' (Ibid. p. 179.)

[6] See the rubrics at the end of chapters xviii., xix., and xx.; and compare Lenormant, *Manuel*, vol. i. p. 509.

in Hades; others, in thirty-seven chapters, for his preservation from all the dangers of Hades, from Typhonian animals, from the Eater of the Ass, and from the
awful block of the executioner; finally, others, in sixty
chapters, which are best described as 'forms for various
occasions.'[1] The third part of the 'Ritual' opens with
the famous chapter (ch. cxxv.) known as the 'Hall of
the Two Truths.'[2] Here the deceased is represented as
brought before the judgment-seat of Osiris, in order
that after a searching investigation it may be decided
whether he shall be admitted into heaven or excluded
from it. Osiris sits on a lofty throne, surrounded by
forty-two assessors. An interrogatory commences.
The dead person must give proof that he is worthy of
the life to come, that his spiritual knowledge is sufficient, and that his life on earth has been pure. Each
of the forty-two assessors in turn questions him, bids
him tell his mystic name and its meaning. In reply,
he addresses each in turn by name, and to each declares his innocence of some class of sin or other. 'I
have not blasphemed,' he says;[3] 'I have not deceived;
I have not stolen; I have not slain any one treache-
rously; I have not been cruel to any one; I have not
caused disturbance; I have not been idle; I have not
been drunken; I have not issued unjust orders; I have
not been indiscreetly curious; I have not multiplied
words in speaking; I have struck no one; I have
caused fear to no one; I have slandered no one; I
have not eaten my heart through envy; I have not
reviled the face of the king, nor the face of my father;

[1] *Ritual*, ch. cxvi. *ad fin.* (Bunsen, p. 248).
[2] Ibid. ch. cxxv.(Bunsen,p.252).
[3] I have followed chiefly the
translation of Lenormant, but have
adopted some idiomatic phrases
from Dr. Birch (Bunsen's *Egypt*,
vol. v. pp. 253–6).

I have not made false accusations; I have not kept
milk from the mouth of sucklings; I have not caused
abortion; I have not ill-used my slaves; I have not
killed sacred beasts; I have not defiled the river; I
have not polluted myself; I have not taken the clothes
of the dead.' Nor is he content with this negative vin-
dication; he goes on, and, addressing the great conclave
of the gods, exclaims: 'Let me go ; ye know that I am
without fault, without evil, without sin, without crime.
Do not torture me ; do not aught against me.   I have
lived on truth ; I have been fed on truth ; I have made
it my delight to do what men command and the gods
approve.   I have offered to the deities all the sacrifices that were their due; I have given bread to the
hungry and drink to him that was athirst; I have
clothed the naked with garments. . . . My mouth
and my hands are pure.' [1]   The justification of the deceased is allowed, and he passes from the Hall of Truth
into Elysium.   The remainder of the 'Ritual' consists
of about forty chapters,[2] and is still more mystical
and obscure than the earlier portions.   The deceased
appears to be identified with the sun, and to go forth
with the sun through the various regions of the heavens,
seated in the solar boat.   Finally he rises to such a
pitch of perfection as to become identical with the utmost that the Egyptians could imagine of divine, and
to be represented by a symbolical figure which unites
the attributes of all the divinities contained within the
Egyptian Pantheon.[3]

---

[1] Lenormant, *Manuel*, vol. i. p.
514; Birch in Bunsen's *Egypt*, vol.
v. p. 256.
[2] Birch in Bunsen's *Egypt*, vol. v.
pp. 260–309.

[3] Lenormant, *Manuel*, vol. i. p.
516.   It is remarkable that the
'Ritual of the Dead,' like the *Er-
tang* of Manes (*Seventh Monarchy*,
p. 97), is accompanied by pictures,

Among other religious books are 'The Tears of Isis,' of which a translation will be found in the 'Records of the Past;'[1] the 'Book of the Respirations' (*Sai-an-Sinsin*) or 'of the Breaths of Life,' which appears in an English dress in the same work;[2] the legend of the 'Destruction of Mankind by Ra;'[3] numerous Solar Litanies, collections of hymns, and the like. A general harmony pervades the various treatises upon religion; and if differences are to be traced, they will be found chiefly within the 'Ritual' itself, which contains signs of having been composed at several distinct epochs. The compositions are always rhythmical, though not (so far as appears) tied down by very strict laws. We subjoin an extract from the 'Book of the Respirations,' which will show the general character of the shorter religious works.[4]

> Hail to the Osiris, . . . ![5]
> AMMON is with thee each day,
> To render thee life :
> APHERU openeth to thee the right way.
> Thou seest with thine eyes ;
> Thou hearest with thine ears ;
> Thou speakest with thy mouth ;
> Thou walkest with thy legs ;
> Thy soul is made divine in heaven,
> And can effect the transformations it desireth.
> Thou formest the joy of the sacred persea-tree [6] in On.[7]
> Thou awakest each day ;

which form an essential portion of it, and are reproduced in the various copies.

[1] *Records*, vol. ii. pp. 119–26.
[2] Ibid. vol. iv. pp. 121–28.
[3] Ibid. vol. vi. pp. 105–12.
[4] Ibid. vol. iv. pp. 123–4.
[5] Here occurs the name of the deceased person, with whom the copy of the book is buried. It is

believed that the book was deposited exclusively with the mummies of priests or priestesses of Ammon-Ra. A dead person is always termed by the Egyptians an 'Osiris.'
[6] See above, p. 53.
[7] 'On,' or 'An,' is the city called by the Greeks 'Heliopolis,' or 'the City of the Sun.' (See the *Speaker's Commentary*, vol. i. p. 206.)

Thou seest the rays of the sun ;
AMMON cometh to thee with the breath of life ;
He granteth thee to breathe in thy coffin.
Thou comest on earth each day ;
Thine eyes behold the rays of the *disk ;
Truth is spoken to thee before OSIRIS;
The formulæ of justification are on thy body.
HORUS, the defender of his father, protecteth thee ;
He maketh thy soul like the souls of the gods.
The soul of RA giveth life to thy soul ;
The soul of SHU filleth thy lungs with soft breath.

The Egyptian poems hitherto discovered are of no
great length. The historical pieces, which have been
dignified with the name of 'Epic Poems,'[1] do not fill,
at the utmost, more than ten or a dozen pages, or extend to much above a hundred and twenty lines. Their
style will be sufficiently indicated by a couple of extracts. The first shall be from the composition of
Penta-our on an exploit of Rameses II. in one of his
campaigns against the Hittites.[2]

'Glorious is thy deed of valour! Firm in heart, thou hast saved
  thine army ;
Saved thy bowmen and thy horsemen ; son of TUM, sure none is
  like thee,
Spoiler of the land of Khita, with thy [keen] victorious falchion.
King that fightest for thy soldiers [stoutly] in the day of battle,
Great of heart, in fray the foremost, all the world cannot resist thee,
Mighty conqueror, victorious in the sight of all thy soldiers.
No gainsayer [doubts thy glories].   Thou art Egypt's [strength
  and] guardian ;
All thy foes thou crushest, bowest down the Hittites' backs for ever.'

---

[1] Goodwin, *Cambridge Essays*, 1858, p. 230; Lenormant, *Manuel d'Histoire Ancienne*, vol. i. p. 517 ; Birch, *Egypt from the Earliest Times*, p. 120.
[2] A complete translation of this composition will be found in the *Records of the Past*, vol. ii. pp. 67–78. A version of certain parts of the poem was published by Mr. Goodwin in 1858 (*Cambridge Essays*, pp. 240–2). The trans-lation in the text follows these authorities.

Then the King addressed his footmen, and his horsemen, and his chieftains—

All who in the fight were backward—'Well it was not done of any,

That ye left me [unsupported] singly with the foe to combat.

Not a chieftain, not a captain, not a sergeant came to aid me—

All alone I had to battle with a host that none could number.

Nechtu-em-djom, Nehr-ahruta, they, my horses, [and they only]

Gave me succour in my danger, when I singly fought the foemen.

Therefore do I grant them henceforth, when I rest within my palace,

Peacefully to champ their barley in the sight of RA for ever.

As for Menna, who was with me, [doughty] squire and armour-bearer,

Him I give the suit of armour clad in which I fought and conquered,

When with sword of might I battled, and ten thousand fell before me.

Our remaining example is from a tablet of Thothmes II., one of the greatest monarchs of the eighteenth dynasty. It has been described as a 'kind of hymn or song, recounting the victories of Thothmes,' with allusions to his principal conquests and exploits in an antithetical strain.[1] In length it only extends to twenty-five hieroglyphical lines ; but each line forms a sort of stanza, and the whole could scarcely be expressed in less than a hundred lines of our heroic measure. The entire poem is put into the mouth of Ammon-Ra,[2] the special god of Thebes, where the inscription was found, and whom Thothmes regarded as his father.

> Come, Ra-men-Kheper, come to me, my son,
> My best supporter, come and glad thyself
> In my perfections. Everlastingly

[1] Birch in *Records of the Past,* vol. ii. p. 30.
[2] The poem is entitled 'The Speech of Ammon-Ra, Lord of the Seats of the Upper and Lower World.'

I shine but as thou wishest. My full heart
Dilates whene'er thou comest to my temple.
Thy limbs I fondle and inspire with life
Delicious, till thou hast more power than I.
Set up in my great hall, I give thee wealth,
I give thee strength and victory o'er all lands.
The terror and the dread of thee I have spread
Through every country to the furthest poles
Of heaven—I make all hearts to quake at thee—
Yea, e'en the mighty nation of Nine Bows
I have made to fear the echoes of thy voice.
The chiefs of lands are clutched within thy fist.
Extending mine own hands, I tie for thee
In bundles the fierce Amu—thousands, ay,
And tens of thousands—with the Northern hordes,
In myriads upon myriads—that they yield
To be thy captives; underneath thy shoes
I have thrown down thy foemen ; prostrate crowds
Of the perverse lie in the dust before thee.
For thee the Earth, throughout its length and breadth,
I have ordered ; for thy seat, both East and West ;
There is no land whereto thou hast not reached ;
There is no nation that resists thy will.

The poems called 'lyrical' are such as the 'Song
of the Harper,' a composition of the period of the
eighteenth dynasty, which has been translated by M.
Dümichen and others.[1] This song belongs to the class
of poems which ' delight in parallelisms and antitheses,
and in the ornament of a burden.'[2] It is divided into
short verses of about equal length, and may be sufficiently represented by the following version of its
opening :—

    The Great One has gone to his rest,
    Ended his task and his race :
    Thus men are aye passing away,
    And youths are aye taking their place.

[1] See Dümichen, *Historische In-schriften*, ii. 40; Stern in the *Zeitschrift für ägyptische Sprache* for 1873, p. 58; and *Records of the Past*, vol. vi. pp. 120–30.

[2] *Records*, vol. vi. p. 127.

As RA rises up every morn,
    And TUM [1] every evening doth set,
So women conceive and bring forth,
    And men without ceasing beget.
Each soul in its turn draweth breath—
Each man born of woman sees Death.

Take thy pleasure to-day,
    Father! Holy One! See,
Spices and fragrant oils,
    Father, we bring to thee.
On thy sister's bosom and arms
    Wreaths of lotus we place ;
On thy sister, dear to thy heart,
    Aye sitting before thy face.
Sound the song ; let music be played ;
And let cares behind thee be laid.

Take thy pleasure to-day :
    Mind thee of joy and delight !
Soon life's pilgrimage ends,
    And we pass to Silence and Night.
Patriarch perfect and pure,
    Neferhotep, blessed one ! Thou
Didst finish thy course upon earth,
    And art with the blessed ones now.
Men pass to the Silent Shore,
And their place doth know them no more.

They are as they never had been,
    Since the Sun went forth upon high ;
They sit on the banks of the stream
    That floweth in stillness by.
Thy soul is among them ; thou
    Dost drink of the sacred tide,
Having the wish of thy heart—
    At peace ever since thou hast died.
Give bread to the man who is poor,
And thy name shall be blest evermore.

---

[1] The Egyptians distinguished the Rising from the Setting Sun, calling the former Ra and the latter Tum.

One work only has been discovered, which can be regarded as a book of 'Travels.' It seems intended to give an account of a 'Tour in Palestine,' accomplished by a Mohar, or engineer officer,[1] in about the fourteenth century B.C. ; but its exact purpose is somewhat uncertain, from the rhetorical style in which it is written. The subjoined extract will give a sufficient idea of it.

'Thou yokest thy horses, swift as jackals, to the chariot; their eyes flash ; they are like a gust of wind, when it bursts forth. Thou takest the reins ; thou seizest thy bow; we behold the deeds of thy hand. (Here I send thee back the Mohar's portrait, and make thee to know his actions.) Didst thou not go then to the land of the Khita (Hittites)? Didst thou not behold the land of Aup? Khatuma,[2] dost thou not know it? Ikatai, likewise, how great it is? The Tsor[3] of Rameses, the city of Khaleb (Aleppo) in its neighbourhood—how goes it with its ford? Hast thou not journeyed to Qodesh[4] and Tubakhi? Hast thou not gone with bowmen to the Shasu?[5] Hast thou not trodden the road to the Mountain of Heaven,[6] where flourish the cypresses, the oaks, and the cedars which pierce the sky? There are the numerous lions, the wolves, and the hyænas, which the Shasu track on every side. Didst

---

[1] The 'Tour' was partially translated by Mr. Goodwin in 1858 (*Cambridge Essays*, pp. 266–9). In 1866 a full translation in French was published by M. Chabas under the title of *Voyage d'un Egyptien en Syrie et Phénicie*. M. Drach, of the British Museum, contributed an English translation to the *Records of the Past* in 1873 (vol. i. pp. 109–116).

[2] Khatuma is perhaps Edom (אדוֹם) ; *Hudum* in Assyrian.

[3] Tsor seems to be the same word as the Hebrew *tsur* (צוֹר), which the Greek rendered by Τύρος (*Tyre*). The word means 'rock,' and was probably applied to any fort situated on a rocky eminence.

[4] Qodesh may be one of the many Syrian towns called Kadesh = 'holy,' whence the modern Arabic name for Jerusalem, Al-Kods.

[5] On the Shasu, see above, p. 111.

[6] Perhaps Mount Lebanon, or else Hermon.

thou not ascend the mountain of Shaoua ? Oh ! come to
. . . . barta. Thou hastenest to get there ; thou crossest
its ford ; thou hast experience of a Mohar's trials ; thy
car is a weight on thy hand ; thy strength fails. It is
night when thou arrivest ; all thy limbs are wearied ;
thy bones ache ; thou fallest asleep from excess of
somnolence—thou wakest up suddenly. It is the hour
when sad night begins, and thou art all alone. Comes
there not a thief to steal what lies about? See ! he
enters the stable—the horses are disquieted—he goes
back in the dark, carrying off thy clothes. Thy groom
wakes, and sees the thief retreating. What does he
do? he carries off the rest. Joining himself to the
evil-doers, he seeks refuge among the Shasu ; he trans-
forms himself into an Asiatic.'

The Egyptian novels, or romances, have attracted
more attention than any other portion of their literature. The ' Tale of the Two Brothers,' the ' Possessed
Princess,' and ' The Doomed Prince ' are well-known in
many quarters,[1] and need not be reproduced here.

---

[1] The 'Tale of the Two Brothers'
was first noticed by M. de Rougé
in the *Revue Archéologique* (vol. ix.
p. 385 *et seqq.*). A considerable
portion of it was translated by
Mr. Goodwin in 1858 (*Cambridge
Essays*, pp. 223–238). In 1860
Dr. Birch published the text. M.
Le Page Renouf translated a part
in 1863 (*Atlantis*, vol. iv.). Complete translations have since been
made by Dr. Brugsch in 1864
(German) ; by M. Maspero in 1867
(French), and by M. Renouf in
1873 (English). This last translation will be found in the *Records
of the Past*, vol. ii. pp. 139–152.
The ' Possessed Princess ' was first
translated by Dr. Birch in 1853
(*Transactions of Royal Society of
Literature*, vol. iv. p. 217 *et seqq.*).

This translation was reviewed and
another given by De Rougé in the
Revue Asiatique, 1856–8, who accompanied his translation with a
representation of the text. Dr.
Brugsch published a German translation in his *Geschichte Aegyptens*,
in 1859. Finally, Dr. Birch has re-
published his translation, with a
few corrections, in the *Records of
the Past* (vol. iv. pp. 55–60). The
story of the ' Doomed Prince ' has,
so far as I know, been translated only
by Mr. Goodwin, whose version first
appeared in the *Transactions of the
Society of Biblical Archæology* (vol.
iii. pp. 349–356), whence it has
been transferred, almost without
alteration, to the *Records of the
Past*, vol. ii. pp. 155–160.

Their character is that of short tales, like the ' Novelle ' of Boccacio, or the stories in the collection of the ' Thou-sand and One Nights.' They are full of most impro-bable adventure, and deal largely in the supernatural. The doctrine of metempsychosis is a common feature in them; and the death of the hero, or heroine, or both, causes no interruption of the narrative. Animals address men in speech, and are readily understood by them. Even trees have the same power. The dead constantly come to life again; and not only so, but mummies converse together in their catacombs, and occasionally leave their coffins, return to the society of the living, and then, after a brief sojourn, once more re-enter the tomb. The state of morals which the novels describe is one of great laxity—not to say, disso-luteness. The profligacy of the men is equalled or exceeded by that of the women, who not unfrequently make the advances, and wield all the arts of the se-ducer. The moral intention of the writers seems, however, to be in general good, since dissolute courses lead in almost every case to some misfortune or disaster.

With the romantic character of the Egyptian tales contrasts very remarkably the prosaic tone of one or two autobiographies. Sancha, an officer belonging to the court of Osirtasen I. and his co-regent, Amenemha, having fallen into disgrace with his employers, quits Egypt and takes refuge with Ammu-anshi, king of the Tennu, by whom he is kindly treated, given his daughter in marriage, and employed in the military service. The favour shown him provokes the jealousy of a native officer, formerly the chief confidant of the king; and this jealousy leads to a challenge, a duel, the defeat of the envious rival, and the establishment of Sancha in his office. After this Sancha accumulates wealth, has many children, and lives to a good old age in his adopted country. But at length, as he approaches his end, the 'home-sickness' comes upon him ; he is possessed with an intense desire of revisiting Egypt, and of being· 'buried in the land where he was born ; '[1] he therefore addresses a humble petition to Osirtasen, beseeching his permission to return.[2] The King of Egypt grants his request, accords him an amnesty, and promises him a restoration to favour when he reaches his court. The arrival of the good news makes Sancha, according to his own account, almost beside himself with joy ;[3] but he arranges his affairs in the land of Tennu with a great deal of good sense, divides his possessions among his children, establishes his eldest son as a sort of general supervisor, and makes provision for having from time to time a statement of accounts sent to him in Egypt. He then bids his family adieu, sets off on his journey, and, having accomplished it, is well received by the monarch, notwithstanding the opposition of the royal children. The promises made to him are performed, and he remains in favour with Osirtasen 'until the day of his death.'[4] Such are the meagre materials, out of which a work is composed which extends to above five hundred lines—an unusual length for an Egyptian

---

[1] *Records of the Past,* vol. vi. p. 142 (line 230 of the story).

[2] It is not quite clear whether Saneha's prayer is addressed to the King of Egypt or to Heaven ; but on the whole I incline to think that the king is intended, and that Saneha, though he does not expressly say so, adopted the very prosaic expedient of sending to his Majesty Osirtasen I. a petition for pardon and restoration. The prayer of the petition seems to be contained in lines 226–232 :—

Grant me to return home—
Permit me to show myself.
Have I not suffered anxiety ?
What more is there to boast ?
Let me be buried in the land of my birth ;
Let me have a fortunate lot hereafter ;
Grant me pardon.

[3] *Records of the Past,* vol. vi. p. 144 (line 311 of the tale).

[4] Ibid. p. 150 (line 511 of the tale).

composition. The opening of this story will show the mode in which so poor a theme was expanded and made to serve as the subject of a volume.

' When I was on the point of setting out [from Egypt],[1] my heart was troubled; my hands shook; numbness fell on all my limbs. I staggered; yea, I was greatly perplexed to find myself a place of repose. In order to account for my travels, I pretended to be a herbalist; twice I started forth on my journey, and twice I returned back. I desired to approach the palace no more. I longed to become free; I said there is no life like that. Then [at last] I quitted the House of the Sycamore; I lay down at the station of Snefru; I passed the night in a corner of the garden; I rose up when it was day and found one preparing for a journey. When he perceived me he was afraid. But when the hour of supper was come, I arrived at the town of * * *; I embarked in a barge without a rudder; I came to Abu * * *; I made the journey on foot, until I reached the fortress which the king [of Egypt] had made in order to keep off the Sakti.[2] An aged man, a herbalist, received me. I was in alarm when I saw the watchers upon the wall, watching day after day in rotation. But when the hours of darkness had passed, and the dawn had broken, I proceeded on from place to place, and reached the station of Kamur.[3] Thirst overtook me on my journey; my throat was parched: I said, " This is a foretaste

---

[1] The MS. is imperfect at the beginning, and opens in the middle of a sentence. We gather from a later passage that Saneha was quitting Egypt because he had fallen into disgrace at court.

[2] The Sakti were enemies of Egypt towards the east, probably a tribe of Arabs.

[3] According to Brugsch (*Geographische Inschriften*, vol. i. pp. 150, 260), Kamur was a town of Lower Egypt, situated in the Heliopolite canton.

of death." Then I lifted up my heart; I braced my
limbs. I heard the pleasant sound of cattle—I beheld
a Sakti. He demanded to know whither I journeyed,
and addressed me thus: "O thou that art from
Egypt!" Then he gave me water, he poured out milk
for me; I went with him to his people, and was conducted by them from place to place. I reached * * * ;
I arrived at Atima.'

It is impossible, within the limits of the present work, to trace in detail the Egyptian literature
any further. The epistolary correspondence and despatches present much that is interesting,[1] since they
have every appearance of being what they profess to
be—real letters and real despatches—though they have
reached our time in 'Collections,' where they were
placed to serve as patterns, the collections in question
corresponding to modern 'Complete Letter-Writers.'
Some of the letters were perhaps written with a view to
publication, and are therefore to a certain extent forced
and artificial; but the majority seem to be the spon-
taneous production of writers only intent upon amusing
or instructing their correspondents. The scientific treatises, on the other hand, are disappointing. The medical works which have been examined give a poor idea
of the point reached by the physicians of Pharaonic
times. They imply indeed a certain knowledge of
anatomy, and contain some fairly good·observations
upon the symptoms of different maladies; but the
physiology which they embody is fantastic, and they
consist in the main of a number of prescriptions for
different complaints, which are commonly of the most

---

[1] See the account of them given by Mr. Goodwin in the *Cambridge
Essays* for 1858, pp. 246–265.

absurd character.[1] The geometry is said to be respect-
able,[2] but has perhaps not been as yet sufficiently
studied. The astronomy is tainted by the predomi-
nance of astrological ideas. But the lowest intellectual
depth seems to be reached in the 'Magical Texts,'
where the happiness and misery of mankind appear to
be regarded as dependent upon spells and amulets, and
receipts are given to protect men against all the accidents of life, against loss of fortune, against fire, against
death by violence, and even (it would seem) against
suffering in the world to come.[3] It is to be feared that
the belief in magic was widely spread among the ancient
Egyptians, and that the elevating tendency of their
religious ideas was practically neutralised by this de-
basing and most immoral superstition.

[1] See Lenormant, *Manuel d'His-
toire Ancienne*, vol. i. p. 519; and
Brugsch, *Etudes sur un Papyrus
Médical de Berlin*, Leipsic, 1853.

[2] Lenormant, l.s.c.

[3] See *Records of the Past*, vol. vi.
pp. 115-126; and note especially
the receipt (p. 126) with the statement appended of its effects on
those who use it: 'Thou art protected against the accidents of life;
thou art protected against a violent
death; thou art protected against
fire; thou *escapest in heaven*, and
thou art not ruined upon earth.'

CHAPTER VI.

AGRICULTURE.

Extraordinary Productiveness of Egypt in Ancient Times. Tenure of Land under the Pharaohs—Absence of Governmental Interference with the Cultivation. Farming Operations—Preparation of the Soil. Character of the Plough used. Mode of Ploughing. Use of the Hoe. Sowing. Kinds of Corn grown. Cultivation of Wheat—of Barley—of the Doora or Holcus Sorghum. Great Variety of other Crops. System of Irrigation employed. Use of the Shadoof. Hydraulic Works of the Fayoum. Cultivation of the Olive. Cultivation of the Vine. Care of Cattle.

'Απονητότατα καρπὸν κομίζονται ἐκ γῆς.—HEROD. ii. 14.

THE extraordinary fertility of Egypt, consequent upon the abundance of water, the good qualities of the alluvial soil, and the rich dressing of mud which it receives every year by means of the annual inundation, has been noted in a former chapter ; [1] where some notion has been also given of the great abundance and variety of its vegetable productions—natural and artificial— during the period with which we are here especially concerned [2]—that of the independent monarchy. Egypt was reckoned in ancient times the principal granary of the civilised world.   In any famine or scarcity else-where it was to this quarter that the nations looked for the supplies which were necessary to enable them to tide over the existing distress, and save them from actual starvation. [3]   Under the Persians, the country,

---

[1] See above, ch. ii. pp. 59–61.
[2] Ibid. pp. 47–64.
[3] Gen. xii. 10 ; xli. 57 ; xlii. 1–3.

Compare *Records of the Past*, vol. iv. p. 43 ; and Birch, *Egypt from the Earliest Times*, p. 63.

besides feeding itself, supplied corn regularly for its
garrison of 120,000 Persian troops, and also paid to
the treasury at Susa an annual tribute of money,
amounting to nearly 170,000l. sterling.[1] In Roman
times its cereal exports were of such importance to
Italy that the trade enjoyed the peculiar protection
of the State,[2] and the general imperial system of pro-
vincial government received special modifications in its
adaptation to Egypt in consequence of the almost absolute dependence of the Roman people on the produce
of the Egyptian cornfields.[3]   This vast superabundance
of the food produced in the country beyond the needs
of the inhabitants arose, no doubt, in great part from
the natural advantages of the position ; but it was due
also, to a considerable extent, to the industrious habits
of the people and to their employment of good methods
of husbandry.   Their natural intelligence, which was
remarkable, having been applied for many centuries to
making the most of the capabilities of their excep-
tionally favoured region, led them by degrees to the
general adoption of a system and of methods which
were in the highest degree successful,[4] and which are
rightly regarded as among the main causes of that

---

[1] Herod. iii. 91.
[2] The Alexandrian corn-fleet enjoyed the protection of a convoy of
war-galleys; it was met at Puteoli
by a deputation of senators, and the
appearance of its topsails above the
horizon was the signal for the pro-
clamation of a general holiday (see
Merivale, *Roman Empire*, vol. iv.
p. 392).
[3] Tacitus says: ' Augustus, inter
alia dominationis arcana, vetitis
nisi permissu ingredi senatoribus
aut equitibus Romanis inlustribus,
seposuit Ægyptum ; ne fame ur-
geret Italiam, quisquis eam provin-
ciam claustraque terræ ac maris,
quamvis levi præsidio adversum
ingentes exercitus insedisset' (*Ann.*
ii. 59).   Again, it is noted that the
danger which would result to Rome
from the revolt of Egypt caused the
rule to be made that its governor
should be, not a senator, but a
knight.   Pliny says : 'Pererebuerat
antiquitus Urbem nostram, nisi opi-
bus Ægypti, ali sustentarique non
posse' (*Paneg.* § 31).
[4] See Diod. Sic. i. 74.

extraordinary wealth, prosperity, and eminence whereto
Egypt attained under the Pharaohs.

It cannot be said with truth that there was anything in the tenure of land in ancient Egypt which
much favoured production, or which accounts for its
agricultural pre-eminence. Peasant proprietors seem
not to have existed. The owners of the soil were [1] the
kings, the priestly communities attached to the different
temples, and the ' territorial aristocracy ' [2] or wealthy
upper class, which was numerous and had considerable
political influence. These last cultivated their estates
chiefly by means of slave-labour,[3] which is naturally a
wasteful and extravagant mode, though doubtless strict
and severe superintendence may, where the work required is of a simple kind, obtain from those employed a
large amount of toil, and so of produce. The kings and
the communities of priests were in the habit of letting
their lands in small allotments to *fellahin*, or peasants ; [4]
and the nobles may likewise have done this in some
cases, or may have employed free instead of slave
labour on the farms which they kept in their own
hands.[5] It is unfortunate that we do not know what
proportion the ordinary rent bore to the annual produce or profit.[6] Diodorus seems to have thought that
the rate established in his time was low ; but, if it be

[1] Diod. Sic. i. 73. Though the kings had once been owners of *all* the land except that of the priests (Gen. xlvii. 20–26), they must subse-quently have made grants to in-dividuals by which they parted with their property. Diodorus and Herodotus agree as to the triple ownership of the land—by the king, by the priests, and by mem-bers of the military class (Diod. S. l.s.c. ; Herod. ii. 168) ; and the monuments show a large class of rich private proprietors who are not priests.
[2] Birch, *Egypt from the Earliest Times*, ' Introduction,' p. xviii.
[3] Ibid. p. 44. ' In private the Egyptian lord led a charmed life—his estate was cultivated by slaves.'
[4] Diod. Sic. i. 74.
[5] Wilkinson, *Ancient Egyptians*, vol. iv. p. 35.
[6] The royal lands were, in the time of Joseph, let for one-fifth of the produce—a moderate rate, and

true that price is determined by the proportion of
demand to supply, and if the demand for land must
always have been great in Egypt owing to the numerous population, and the supply limited owing to the
small amount of cultivable territory, it is reasonable
to conclude that rents were at least as high there as in
other countries.   The only advantage—and it was
certainly no inconsiderable advantage—which the ancient Egyptian peasantry enjoyed over their modern
representatives in the same country, or in the East
generally, would seem to have been, that they were
not vexatiously interfered with by the government,
which (unless in extraordinary cases) neither required
of them forced labour, nor limited their freedom of
choice with respect to crops, nor in any way cramped
them in any of their farming operations.[1]   It is governmental interference which is the curse of the labouring
class in the East—the liability to be impressed for military service or for employment upon the public works—
roads, canals, bridges, palaces, temples—the liability to
be forbidden to grow one kind of produce and commanded to grow another—and the crowning vexation[2]
of having to adjust one's harvest operations to the convenience or caprice of the tax-gatherer, who prevents
the crops from being gathered in until he has taken his
share.   If the Egyptian peasant under the Pharaohs
was really free from this entire class of restrictions and
interferences, it must be allowed that, so far, his condition contrasted favourably with that of Oriental field-

one not uncommon in the East.
(See the author's *Seventh Monarchy*,
pp. 441-2.)   But it is uncertain
whether this continued.   Diodorus
seems to speak of a money rent.

[1] There is no *positive* evidence of
this ; but it is the impression of

those most familiar with the monuments.   (See Wilkinson, *Ancient
Egyptians*, vol. iv. p. 34.)

[2] On the oppressiveness of this
system, which still prevails in parts
of Turkey, see the author's *Seventh
Monarchy*, p. 441, note [2].

labourers generally. But this difference does not appear
sufficient to account for the enormous produce which
the land was made to yield. We return, therefore, to
our previous statement—that the patient and untiring
industry of the labourer, and the excellence of the
methods which he employed, were main causes in
bringing about the wonderful result.

Though there was no season of the year in which
agricultural labours were suspended in Egypt, yet the
special time for the activity of the husbandman, which
may consequently be regarded as the commencement
of the agricultural year, was upon the subsidence of the
waters. As the most elevated lands, which were those
nearest the river,[1] began to reappear, which was generally early in October, preparations were at once made
for the sowing of the grain upon the alluvium just
deposited. According to Herodotus,[2] there were parts
of Egypt where it was unnecessary to use either plough
or hoe; the seed was scattered upon the rich Nile
deposit, and was trodden in by beasts—sheep, goats,
or pigs,[3]—after which the husbandman had nothing to
do but simply to await the harvest. This state of
things must, however, in every age have been exceptional. For the most part, upon ordinary lands it was
necessary, or at any rate desirable, to make some
preparation of the ground; and the plough, or the hoe,

---

[1] Wilkinson, vol. iv. p. 106, and
pl. 18, fig. 1. Some land at the
edge of the desert must have reappeared about the same time as the
river banks.
[2] Herod. ii. 14.
[3] Herodotus says, 'by pigs'
(l.s.c.); and though this has been
objected to, it has been regarded as
not improbable by some good mo-

dern authorities (see Larcher's note
on Herod. ii. 14 in his *Histoire
d'Hérodote*; and Wilkinson, *Ancient
Egyptians*, vol. iv. p. 46). Goats are
represented upon the monuments as
treading in the grain. According
to Wilkinson, sheep, oxen, and even
asses were occasionally employed
for the purpose (ib. p. 39).

or both, were put into active employment over the greater part of the territory.

The plough used was of a simple character. It consisted of the indispensable plough-share, a double handle, and a pole or beam, whereto the animals that drew the implement were attached. The beam and stilt were fastened together by thongs or by a twisted rope, which kept the share and the beam at a proper

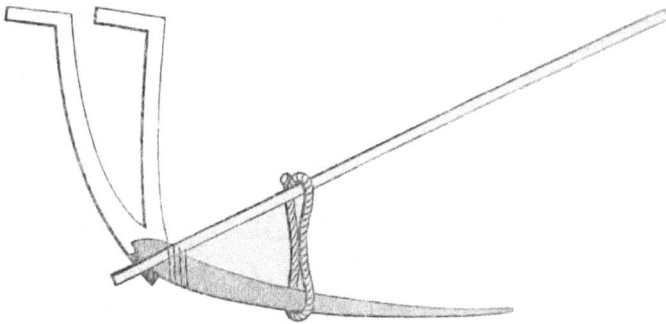

Egyptian Plough.

distance, and helped to prevent the former from penetrating too deeply into the earth. It is uncertain whether the share was ever shod with metal.[1] Apparently it was simply of wood, which may have been sufficient with a soil so light and friable as the Egyptian.[2] There were, of course, no wheels and no coulter. In general character the implement did not much differ from that of the modern Turks and Arabs.[3] Its chief peculiarity was the rounded sweep of the stilt and

[1] Rosellini believed that metal ploughshares were represented on the monuments (*Mon. Civ.* vol. i. p. 299). Wilkinson questions this.

[2] St. Hilaire says that even at the present day the plough used in Egypt is 'seldom furnished with an iron share' (*Egypt and the Suez Canal*, p. 100).

[3] For representations of these see Fellows's *Asia Minor*, p. 71 ; *Lycia*, p. 174 ; C. Niebuhr, *Description de l'Arabie*, opp. p. 137 ; Smith, *Dictionary of the Bible*, vol. i. p. 20 ; and compare the author's *Ancient Monarchies*, vol. i. p. 567.

handles, which (to judge by the monuments) was nearly, though not quite, universal.[1]

The plough was commonly drawn by two oxen or two cows,[2] which were either yoked to it by the shoulders, or else attached by the horns. In the former case a somewhat elaborate arrangement of shoulder-pieces and pads was employed;[3] in the latter, the cross-bar in which the pole terminated was simply lashed with four thongs to the base of the horns. Sometimes a single ploughman guided the

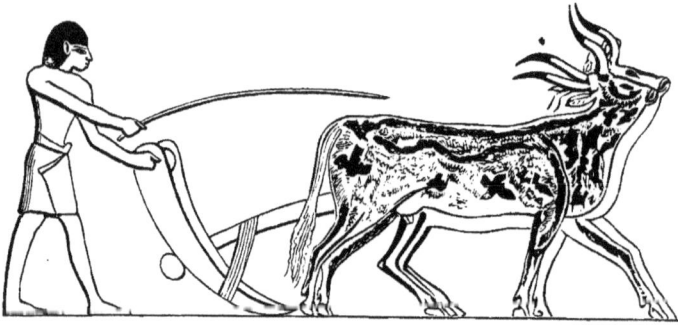

Mode of Ploughing.

plough by one of the handles with his left hand, while in his right he carried a whip or a goad. More often the implement gave employment to two labourers, one of whom held the two handles in his two hands, while the other drove the animals with whip or goad, and no doubt turned them when the end of the furrow was reached.

---

[1] An exception occurs in a tomb near the Pyramids, where the stilt is flat, and the handles which rise from it curve in a direction opposite to the usual one. (See the author's *Herodotus*, vol. ii. p. 18; and compare Lepsius, *Denkmäler*, vol. iii. part ii. pls. 51 and 56.)

[2] Occasionally a cow, when ploughing, was accompanied by her calf, which disported itself in the vicinity of the mother, but was muzzled to prevent its sucking. (See Rosellini, *Monumenti Civili*, pl. xxxii. 2.)

[3] A full description of the arrangement employed will be found in Wilkinson (*A. E.* vol. iv. pp. 42-3).

In soils whose quality was very light and loose, the
hoe took the place of the plough.   Three   or   four

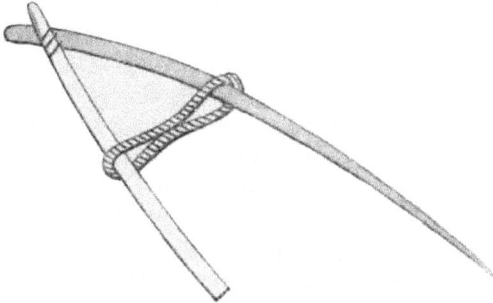

Egyptian Hoe.

peasants provided with hoes went over the ground
about to be sown,[1] and sufficiently prepared the surface
by a slight ' scarification.' [2]   The hoe, like the plough,
was of wood.[3]   It consisted of three parts—a handle,
a pick or blade, and a twisted thong connecting them

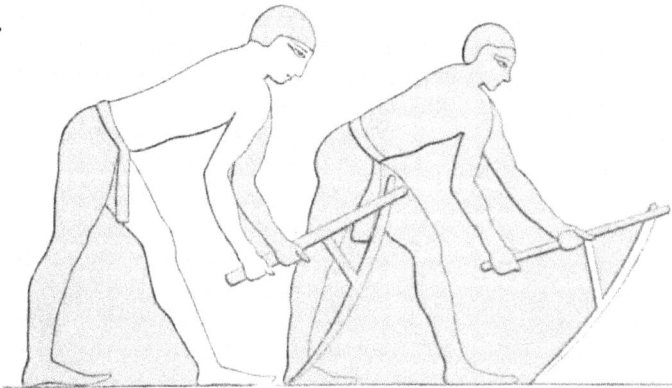

Egyptians Hoeing.

It was sometimes rounded, sometimes sharpened to a

[1] Three are represented as thus
employed in a tomb at Thebes
(Wilkinson, *A. E.* vol. iv. p. 46).
[2] The Roman *scarificatio* (Plin.
II. N. xviii. 17) was a light *ploughing*; but the term seems equally
applicable to the still lighter

' scratching ' of the soil by the hoe.
[3] Several hoes have been found
in tombs.   Sir G. Wilkinson says
that in no instance had he seen a hoe
with a metal blade (*A. E.* vol. iv.
p. 45).

point, but never (so far as appears) sheathed with metal
at the end. The shape was curious, and has been
compared to our letter A.[1] It required the labourer
to stoop considerably to his work, and cannot be
regarded as a very convenient implement.

As soon as the ground was prepared sufficiently,
the sowing took place. Drill-sowing, though practised
by the Assyrians from a very early date,[2] seems to have
been unknown in Egypt; and the sower, carrying with
him the seed in a large basket, which he held in his
left hand, or else suspended on his left arm (sometimes
supporting it also with a strap passed round his neck),
spread the seed broad-cast over the furrows.[3] No
harrow or rake was employed to cover it in. It lay as
it fell, and, rapidly germinating, soon covered the bare
soil with verdure.

The grain most largely cultivated by the Egyptians
was probably the modern *doora*, which Herodotus
called *zea* or *olyra*,[4] and which is a kind of spelt.
This grain takes from three to four months to ripen,
and, if sown in October, might be reaped in February.
It is now, however, not often sown till April, and we
may perhaps conclude that the primary attention of the
husbandman was directed, in ancient as in modern
times, to the more valuable cereals, wheat and barley,
which were required by the rich ; and that the *doora*,
which was needed only by the poor, was raised chiefly

---

[1] Wilkinson, *A. E.* vol. iv. p. 45; .Kenrick, vol. i. p. 185.

[2] See the author's *Ancient Monarchies*, vol. i. p. 567.

[3] Wilkinson, *A.E.* vol. ii. p. 136; vol. iv. p. 48.

[4] Herod. ii. 36. Though Herodotus was in error in supposing that all the Egyptians 'made their bread of the olyra,' yet no doubt his error had a foundation in fact. The *doora* bread was eaten by the great mass of the Egyptians. (See Wilkinson in the author's *Herodotus*, vol. ii. p. 58.)

as an after-crop. Wheat and barley would be put
into the ground in November, and would then be left
to the genial influences of sun and air,[1] which, under
ordinary circumstances, would ripen the barley in four,
and the wheat in five months. No hoeing of weeds,
no frightening of birds,[2] no calling upon heaven for

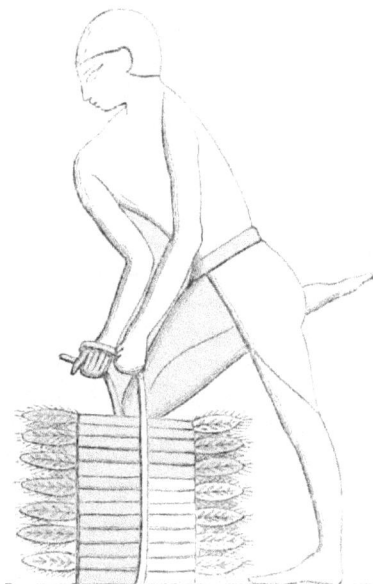

Binding Wheat in Sheaves.

rain,[3] seems to have been required. The husbandman
might safely trust to nature for an ample return.
Bounteous Mother Earth gave from her teeming breast
' the staff of life ' in prodigal abundance, and corn was
gathered ' as the sand of the sea—very much '—till
men ' left numbering.'[4]

[1] Kenrick, vol. i. p. 186.
[2] The Egyptians thought that the
'Nile-God' protected the newly-
sown fields from the birds. See
Records of the Past, vol. iv. p. 108,
note [1].

[3] As in Italy. See Virg. Georg.
i. 155-158.
[4] Gen. xli. 49. According to
Pliny (H. N. xviii. 7), the return on
the corn sown was a hundredfold.
The grain, however, was light (ib.).

The wheat grown was always bearded,[1] and comprised numerous varieties, one of which bore several ears
upon a single stalk.[2] It was cut with a toothed sickle,
a little below the ear, and was either put into baskets,
like hops in England, or sometimes bound up in sheaves,
arranged so that the ears appeared at both ends of the
sheaf. When the baskets were full they were conveyed,
either by men or donkeys, to the threshing-floor, and
their contents emptied into a heap. An ass carried two
baskets, which were placed across his back like panniers; but a single basket was regarded as a load for
two men, and was slung upon a pole which they bore
upon their right shoulders. Sometimes, instead of
being carried straight to the threshing-floor, the corn
was borne from the harvest-field to a storehouse or
granary, and retained there as much as a month.[3]
Threshing was effected by the tread of cattle,[4] which

Oxen treading out Corn.

were driven round and round the threshing-floor, while
a labourer with a pitchfork threw the unthreshed ears
into their path. The threshed corn was immediately

---

[1] It is, at any rate, always represented as bearded on the monuments.
[2] Wilkinson, *A. E.* vol. iv. p. 85.
[3] Birch, *Egypt from the Earliest
Times*, p. 64.
[4] The statement of Herodotus,
that pigs not only trod in the grain

on moist soils, but also trod it out
upon the threshing-floors (ii. 14), is
discredited by the fact that the
treading-out of the corn is always
represented on the monuments as accomplished either by oxen or by asses
(Wilkinson, *A. E.* vol. iv. p. 92).

winnowed by being tossed into the air with shovels in a draughty place,[1] so that, while the corn fell, the chaff was blown off. When this operation was over, the cleansed grain was collected into sacks, and carried to the granary, where it was stored until required for use.

Winnowing.

The cultivation of barley was similar to that of wheat, and commenced at the same time; but the harvest took place a month earlier. A large quantity must have been grown; for barley bread was in much request, and the grain was also malted, and beer brewed from it.[2] Horses were no doubt fed largely on it, as they are universally throughout the East; and it may have been employed also to fatten cattle.[3]

The *doora* harvest is represented on the monuments as taking place at the same time as the wheat

[1] Wilkinson, *A.E.* vol. iv. pp. 86, 89, and 90.

[2] Birch, *Egypt from the Earliest Times*, p. 64. Compare Herod. ii. 77; Diod. Sic. i. 52; Strab. xvii. 1, § 37; Athen. *Deipn.* i. 25. Sir Gardner Wilkinson found malt at Thebes. (See the author's *Herodotus*, vol. ii. p. 127, note [1].)

[3] In a harvest song, discovered by Champollion at Eilethyias, the oxen are represented as in the main threshing *for themselves*. The song runs as follows :—

Thresh for yourselves, thresh for yourselves,
O oxen, thresh for yourselves, for yourselves :
Measures for yourselves, measures for your masters!

(See Champollion's *Lettres sur l'Égypte*, pp. 146 and 196.)

harvest;[1] but this is perhaps not intended as the assertion of a fact. In modern Egypt the chief crop is
sown in April and reaped in July;[2] and the ancient
practice may have been similar. The *doora* was not
cut with the sickle, but pulled up by the roots, which
were then freed from earth by means of the hand.[3] It
was bound in sheaves and carried to a storehouse, where
it probably remained till it was dry. It was then un-
bound, and drawn by the hand through an instrument

Doora Harvest.

armed at one end with a set of metal spikes, which
detached the heads from the straw.[4] These were
then, it is probable, threshed and winnowed in the
usual way.

When the wheat and barley had been put into the
ground, the labourer proceeded to make preparations
for other crops. Several kinds of pulse were largely
cultivated, as beans,[5] peas, and lentils of two distinct

---

[1] Wilkinson, *A. E.* vol. iv. p. 98.
[2] Ibid. p. 59.
[3] Wilkinson, *A. E.* vol. iv. pp. 98 and 99.
[4] Ibid. p. 99.
[5] Herodotus thought that the Egyptians never ate beans and never sowed them (ii. 37); but in this he was mistaken, and is to be corrected from Theophrastus (*H. P.* vol. ii. p. 323), Diodorus (i. 89), and Pliny (*H. N.* xviii. 12). Probably only the priests were forbidden to eat them. (Wilkinson in the author's *Herodotus*, vol. ii. p. 66.)

varieties.[1]   Artificial grasses, as clover, lupins, and
vetches, were grown to furnish provender for the cattle
during the time of the inundation.[2] Flax was raised in
large quantities for the linen garments which were so indispensable ; cotton was cultivated to some extent, as
were safflower, indigo, the castor-oil plant, sesame, and
various medicinal herbs.   Again, there was a most
extensive cultivation of esculent vegetables, as garlic,
leeks, onions, endive, radishes, melons, cucumbers, lettuces, &c., which formed a most important
element in the food of the people.   The raising of these
various crops, of which each farmer cultivated such as
took his fancy or suited his soil, gave constant employment to the agricultural class throughout the entire
year, and rendered every season an almost equally
busy time.

This constant cultivation resulted, in part, from the
mild climate, which favoured vegetation and rapid
growth at all seasons, in part from the system
of irrigation, which had been established at a very
ancient date, and which was maintained with the
greatest care by the government.   The Egyptians were
not content with the mere natural advantages of the
Nile inundation.   By an elaborate system of canals,
with embankments, sluices, and flood-gates, they retained the overflow in what were in fact vast reservoirs,
from which, after the Nile had retired, the greater part
of the cultivable territory could obtain a sufficient supply
of the life-giving fluid during the remainder of the
year.   By embankments they also kept out the Nile

---

[1] Plin. *H. N.* xviii. 12. The
lentils grown near Pelusium were
especially celebrated (Virgil, *Geor-
gica*, i. 228 ; Martial, *Epigrammata*,
xiii. 9, 1).

[2] The wheat straw which was
cleared from the fields after the
reaping of the ears was also used
for the same purpose (Wilkinson,
A. E. vol. iv. p. 95).

water from gardens and other lands where its admission would have been injurious, watering these in some other way, as from wells or tanks.[1] The government had a general control over the main cuttings, opening and closing them according to certain fixed rules, which had for their object the fair and equitable distribution of the water supply over the whole territory. Each farm received in turn sufficient to fill its own main reservoir, and from this by a network of water-courses continually diminishing in size the fluid was conveyed wherever needed, and at last brought to the very roots of the plants. The removal or replacing of a little mud, with the hand or with the foot,[2] turned the water hither or thither, at the pleasure of the husbandman, who distributed it as his crops required.

On the banks of the Nile, which (as already observed [3]) were more elevated than the rest of the land, and in gardens, and other places occasionally, the *shadoof*, or hand-swipe, was used,[4] and water raised from the river or from wells to the height of the soil, over which it was then spread in the usual way. Ground thus cultivated was commonly portioned out into square beds, ' like salt-pans,' [5] each enclosed by its own raised border of earth, so that the water could be kept in or kept out of each bed without difficulty.

In one part of Egypt a large district, naturally barren, was rendered richly productive by hydraulic works of an extraordinarily grand and elaborate cha-

---

[1] Wilkinson, *A. E.* vol. ii. p.187.
[2] Deut. xi. 10.
[3] Supra, p. 156.
[4] As in Assyria (Layard, *Nineveh and Babylon*, p. 109, and pl. opp. p. 110); and in modern Egypt (Wilkinson, *A. E.* vol. ii. vignette on p. 1). Representations of the ancient

Egyptian hand-swipe will be found in the author's *Herodotus*, vol. ii. p. 21; in Wilkinson's *Ancient Egyptians*, vol. ii. p. 4; in Rosellini's *Monumenti Civili*, pl. xl. No. 2; and elsewhere.
[5] Wilkinson, vol. ii. p. 141.

racter.[1]   This was the tract called now the Fayoum,
which is a natural depression in the Libyan desert,
lying at the distance of eight or ten miles from the Nile
valley, and occupied in part by the natural lake known
as Birket-el-Keroun, the 'Lake of the Horn.'   A canal
derived from the Nile, 30 feet deep and 160 feet wide,
was carried westward through a gorge in the Libyan
hills a distance of at least eight miles to the entrance of
this basin, the south-eastern portion of which was separated from the rest by a vast dam or dyke,[2] within
which the water introduced by the canal accumulated,
and which formed the artificial 'Lake Mœris' of Herodotus.[3]   From this vast reservoir canals were carried
in all directions over the rest of the basin, which sloped
gently towards the Keroun ; and the Nile water, with
its fertilising deposit and prolific qualities, was thus
spread over the entire region,[4] which was as large as
many an English county.

   The land of this tract, which was irrigated but not
overflowed by the Nile water, admitted the growth of
at least one valuable product 'for which the rest of
Egypt was unsuitable.   The olive was cultivated,
according to Strabo,[5] only in the Arsinoïte nome (the
Fayoum), and in some of the gardens of Alexandria.
It produced a fruit which was remarkably fleshy,[6] but

---

[1] See the *Mémoires ur le Lac
Mœris* of M. Jomard in the *Description de l'Egypte*, and of M.
Linant de Bellefonds. published at
Alexandria in 1843. Compare Bunsen's *Egypt*, vol. ii. pp. 209-232.
   [2] Some remains of this am or
dyke, in the most southern art of
the basin, are still above 3 feet
broad and nearly 40 feet high
   [3] Herod. ii. 101 and 149;
iii. 91.
   [4] It is thought by some thatthe

reservoir, besides rendering possible
the cultivation of the Fayoum, was
also of service in relieving the Nile
valley of superfluous water when
the inundation was excessive, and
furnishing a supply when it was in
defect (Birch, *Egypt from the Earliest Times*, p. 68) : but the size of
the reservoir was scarcely sufficient
to make it of much service in these
respects.
   [5] Strab. xvii. 1, § 35.
   [6] Plin. *H. N.* xv. 3.

which did not yield much oil,[1] nor that of a very good quality.[2] Still the cultivation was pursued, and the oil extracted was doubtless superior to the kinds, which were more largely produced, from the sesame and from the castor-oil plant.[3]

A more important and far more widely spread cultivation was that of the vine.[4] The edge of the Nile valley towards the desert, the *Háger*, as it is now called, being a light soil, consisting of clay mixed with sand or gravel,[5] was suitable for the growth of the vine, which is found to have been largely cultivated along the whole tract from Thebes to Memphis, particularly in the vicinity of the great towns. It was also grown in the Fayoum,[6] and towards the western skirt of the Delta, at Anthylla,[7] in the Mareotis,[8] and at Plinthiné,[9] still further to the westward. The alluvial soil, which constituted nine-tenths of cultivable Egypt, was ill suited for it; but still there were places within the alluvium where vines were grown, as about Sebonnytus, the produce of which tract is celebrated by Pliny.[10]

Vines were sometimes kept low (as now in France and Germany), and grew in short bushes, which, apparently, did not need even the support of a vine-stake;[11] but more commonly they were allowed to spread them-

---

[1] Plin. *H. N.* xv. 3.
[2] Strab. l.s.c.
[3] See above, p. 61.
[4] Herodotus says the vine was not cultivated in Egypt (ii. 77); and some moderns have caught at this assertion and made much of it as discrediting the Pentateuch (Gen. xl. 9); but there is abundant evidence that the 'Father of History' was in this instance mistaken, the vine being really cultivated very widely. (See Hengstenberg, *Egypt and Moses*, p. 16; Wilkinson, *A.E.* vol. ii. pp. 143–171.)

[5] Wilkinson, *Ancient Egyptians,* vol. iv. p. 21.
[6] See Strabo, l.s.c. The roots are still found there (Wilkinson, vol. ii. p. 161).
[7] Athenæus, *Deipnosoph.* i. p. 25, E.
[8] Ibi. Compare Plin. *H. N.* xiv. 3; Virg. *Georg.* ii. 91; Horat. *Od.* i. 31, 14; Strab. l.s.c.; &c.
[9] Hellanicus, *Fr.* 155.
[10] Plin. *H. N.* xiv. 7.
[11] See a representation in Wilkinson, vol. ii. p. 151.

selves, and were trained either in bowers or on a framework of posts and poles—as now in Italy—which
formed shady alleys raised about seven feet from the

Vines grown in Bowers.

ground.   Sometimes, especially where the vineyard
was attached to a garden, the posts were replaced by
rows of ornamental columns, painted in bright colours,
and supporting rafters, and perhaps a trellis-work, from
which the grapes hung down.   This mode of growth

Vines trained on Posts.

shaded the roots of the plants, and facilitated the reten-
tion of moisture, which would have evaporated if the
culture had been more open, owing to the intense heat

of the sun.   There was generally a tank of water near
the vines, from which they could be supplied if needful;[1] but great caution was required when recourse
was had to this method, since too much moisture was
very hurtful to the vine.

As the fruit approached maturity, it was apt to
invite the attack of birds; and boys were constantly
employed in the vineyards at this period to alarm the
depredators with shouts, and sometimes to thin their
numbers with slings.[2]   Finally, the bunches were
carefully gathered by the hand, and, if intended to be
eaten, were arranged in flat open baskets, or, if destined

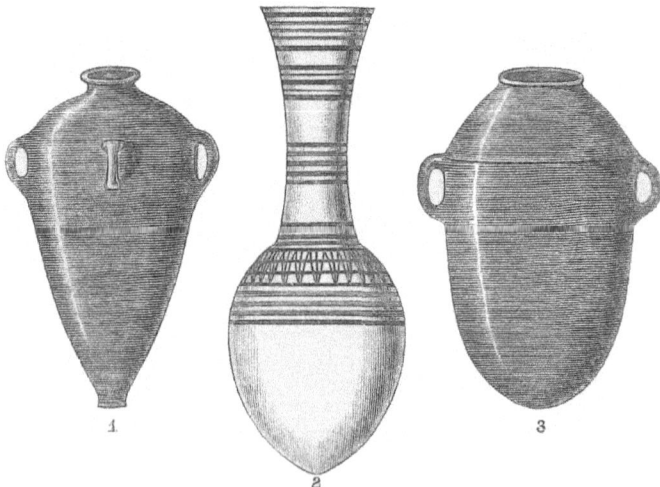

Egyptian Vase and Amphoræ.

for the winepress, were closely packed in deep baskets
or hampers, which men carried on their heads, or by
means of a yoke upon their shoulders, to the storehouse
or shed, where the pressing was accomplished either
by treading or by squeezing in a bag.   The juice seems

[1] Wilkinson, vol. ii. p. 148.   [2] Ibid. p. 149.

sometimes to have been drunk unfermented ;[1] but more
commonly fermentation was awaited, after which the
wine was stored away in vases or amphoræ of an elegant
shape, which were closed with a stopper, and then
hermetically sealed with moist clay, pitch, gypsum,
or other suitable substance.[2] The wines in best repute
were those made at Anthylla,[3] and in the Mareotis,[4] or
tract about Lake Marea, now *Mariout* ; the Sebennytic
wine was also highly esteemed,[5] while that made in the
Thebaïd, and especially about Coptos, was regarded as
peculiarly light and wholesome.[6]

Though Egypt was in the main an agricultural
rather than a pastoral country, yet the breeding and
rearing of cattle and other animals was everywhere
a part of the farmer's business, and in some districts
occupied him almost exclusively.   Large tracts in the
Delta were too wet for the growth of corn, and on
these cattle were grazed in vast quantities by ' the
marshmen,' as they were called,[7] a hardy but rude and
lawless race [8] who inhabited the more northern parts of
Egypt, in the vicinity of the great lakes.   Elsewhere,
too, cattle were reared, partly for agricultural work, as
ploughing, treading in, and again treading out the
grain ; [9] partly for draught ; and partly also for the
table, beef and veal being common articles of food.[10]
Three distinct varieties of cattle were affected, the long-
horned, the short-horned, and the hornless.[11]   During
the greater part of the year they were pastured in open

---

[1] See Genesis xl. 11: 'I took the
grapes, and pressed them into Pharaoh's cup, and I gave the cup into
Pharaoh's hand.'
[2] Wilkinson, *A. E.* vol. ii. p. 158.
[3] Athenæus, i. p. 25, *E.*
[4] Plin. *H. N.* xiv. 3 ; Athenæus,
l.s.c. ; Strab. xviii. 1, § 14.

[5] Plin. *H. N.* xiv. 7.
[6] Athen. l.s.c.
[7] Herod. ii. 94 ; Thucyd. i. 109-10.
[8] Diod. Sic. i. 43.
[9] See above, pp. 156 and 162.
[10] Birch, *Egypt from the Earliest
Times,* p. 45.
[11] Ibid.

fields on the natural growth of the rich soil, or on artificial grasses, which were cultivated for the purpose ;
but at the time of the inundation it was necessary to
bring them in from the fields to the farmyards, or
the villages, where they were kept in sheds or pens
on ground artificially raised, so as to be beyond the
reach of the river.[1] At times, when there was a
sudden rise of the water, much difficulty was experienced in the removal of the cattle from their summer
to their autumn quarters; and the monuments give
frequent representations of the scenes which occurred
on such occasions—scenes of a most exciting character.[2]

Rescuing Cattle from the Inundation.

As the waters overflow the fields and pastures, the
peasants appear, hurrying to the spot on foot or in
boats, intent on rescuing the animals. 'Some, tying
their clothes upon their heads, drag the sheep and
goats from the water, and put them into boats; others
swim the oxen to the nearest high ground;'[3] here
men drive the cattle towards the vessels which have
come to save them; there nooses are thrown over their
horns or heads, by which they are drawn towards
their rescuers. For some months from this time, the

[1] Wilkinson, A. E. vol. iv. p. 95.
[2] See Wilkinson in the author's
Herodotus, vol. ii. p. 161; and compare Lepsius, Denkmäler, vol. iii.
part ii. pls. 60, 132, &c.
[3] Wilkinson, A.E. vol. iv. p.101.

whole of the cattle in Egypt were fed in stalls,[1] partly on wheaten straw, partly upon artificial grasses, cut previously and dried for the purpose. They passed the night in sheds, and were tethered during the day in straw-yards, where their wants were carefully attended to.[2] Sick cattle received medical treatment, drugs being administered to them in balls, which were

Medicine administered to Cattle.

forced down their throats in the exact style of modern veterinary art.[3]

In some parts of Egypt herds were fed upon common pastures, or, at any rate, were liable to become intermixed, and owners had to secure themselves against losses by putting a mark upon their beasts. This was effected by tying their legs together, throwing them down, and then branding them with a red-hot iron upon their shoulders. The paintings in the tombs at Thebes exhibit to us this process in detail, showing the heating of the iron at a fire, its application to the

---

[1] Wilkinson, *A.E.* vol. iv. pp. 95, 122, &c.

[2] See the representation in Wilkinson, vol. ii. p. 134.

[3] Wilkinson, vol. iv. p. 139. Compare Rosellini, *Monumenti Civili,* vol. i. p. 270 and pl. xxxi.

174   HISTORY OF ANCIENT EGYPT.   [Ch. VI.

prostrate cows, and the distress of the calves at the
struggles and moans of their mothers.

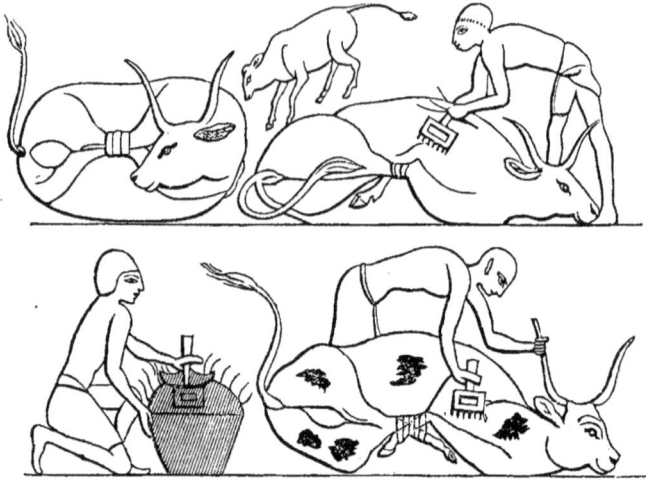

Marking of Cattle.

Besides cattle, the Egyptian farmers bred considerable numbers of sheep, goats, and pigs. A single in-

Egyptian Sheep.

dividual in one instance records upon his tomb that he
was the owner of 834 oxen, 220 cows, 2,234 goats,

760 donkeys, and 974 sheep.[1] Mutton was not held in much esteem,[2] and sheep were consequently but seldom killed for food. The Egyptians kept them mainly for the sake of their wool, which was required for the manufacture of the cloak or ordinary outer garment of the people,[3] for carpets and rugs,[4] and perhaps for the coverings of couches and chairs. Egyptian sheep are said to have yielded two fleeces each year, and also to have produced lambs twice,[5] which would cause the increase of the flock to be rapid. It is

Egyptian Goats.

uncertain for what purpose goats were kept. They were occasionally sacrificed,[6] and therefore, no doubt, employed as food ; but this practice does not seem to have been frequent, and will not account for the large numbers which were bred and reared. Possibly their

---

[1] Rosellini, *Monumenti Civili*, pl. xxx.; Wilkinson, vol. iv. p. 130; Lepsius, *Denkmäler*, vol. iii. pt. ii. pl. 9.

[2] 'Veal and beef, not pork and mutton, were the principal meats that appeared at an Egyptian's table.' (Birch, *Egypt from the Earliest Times*, p. 45.)

[3] Wilkinson, vol. i. p. 280; Vol. iii. p. 146, &c. Compare Herod. ii. 81.

[4] Wilkinson, vol. iii. pp. 141-2.

[5] Diod. Sic. i. 36. Sir G. Wilkinson observes that this is still the case in Egypt, but only when the sheep are very carefully fed and attended to. (*A.E.* vol. ii. p. 17, note.)

[6] Herod. ii. 42.

milk was an article of Egyptian diet,[1] or their hair may
have been used, as it was by the Israelites when they
quitted Egypt,[2] in the manufacture of certain fabrics,
as tent-coverings and the like. The Egyptian goats
are not, however, represented as long-haired.

It is certain that swine were largely kept in Egypt,
since the swineherds were sufficiently numerous to form
one of the recognised classes into which the population
was divided.[3]　According to Herodotus,[4] there were
occasions upon which the Egyptians were bound to
sacrifice them, and once a year each Egyptian partook
of the flesh ; but otherwise this was regarded as utterly
unclean ; the swineherds were despised and disliked ;
and pork was a forbidden food. Still swine 'frequently
formed part of the stock of the farmyard,'[5] either on
account of their usefulness in treading in the grain
after it was sown,[6] or perhaps because they cleared
land rapidly of roots and weeds, whose growth was
greatly favoured by the inundation.[7]　Pork may also,
though forbidden by the ordinances of the religion,
have been eaten by many of the lower orders, who had
not much to lose in social rank, were free from religious prejudice, and found the meat palatable and
savoury.

The pig of Egypt, if we may trust the monuments,[8]
was a hideous-looking animal, long-legged and long-

---

[1] That the Egyptians drank milk
is stated by Birch (l.s.c.), but whether the produce of cows or goats,
or both, he does not mention. Goats'
milk was drunk by the Israelites
(Prov. xxvii. 27).

[2] Exod. xxv. 4 ; xxvi. 7 ; xxxvi.
14.

[3] Herod. ii. 47, 164.

[4] Ibid. ii. 47, 48.

[5] Wilkinson, vol. iii. p. 33.

[6] See above, p. 156.

[7] This is the view to which Wilkinson, on the whole, inclines.
(Compare *A. E.* vol. iv. pp. 39 and
49, with the author's *Herodotus,*
vol. ii. p. 20, note [2].)

[8] See Wilkinson's representation
taken from a tomb at Thebes (*A. E.*
vol. iii. p. 34) ; and compare Rosellini, *Mon. Civ.* vol. i. p. 269, and
pl. xxx. 3.

necked, covered with rough hair, and with a crest of bristles along the whole neck and back. The hog was especially ugly; in the sow the worst features were somewhat modified, while in the sucking-pig there was nothing particular or fitted to attract remark.

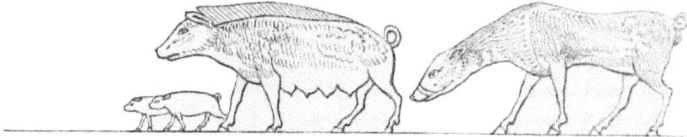

Egyptian Pigs, Hog, and Sow.

Egyptian cultivators, while depending for their profits mainly upon the growth of grain and vegetables and the increase of their flocks and herds, did not neglect those smaller matters of the dovecote and the poultry-yard, which often eke out a modern farmer's income and are sometimes not unimportant to him. The domestic fowl was perhaps not known under the Pharaohs;[1] but the absence of this main support of the poultry-yard was compensated for by the great abundance of the ducks and geese, more especially the latter, which constituted one of the main articles of food in the country,[2] were offered to the gods,[3] and were reckoned among the most valuable of farming products. The very eggs of the geese were

[1] So Birch: 'The domestic fowl *was unknown to him*' (*i.e.* the Egyptian lord); 'it had not been brought by the hands of tributaries to the valley of the Nile, where it never appears in Pharaonic times' (*Egypt from the Earliest Times*, p. 45). Wilkinson agrees as to the fact of the non-appearance, but does not draw the conclusion that fowls were therefore unknown. On the contrary, he supposes them to have always 'abounded in Egypt' (*A.E.* vol. v. p. 214; compare vol. ii. p. 18, and vol. iv. p. 133). Fowls were certainly common in Egypt in Roman times. It seems to be, on the whole, most probable that they were introduced by the Persians.

[2] Birch, l.s.c.; Wilkinson, *A. E.* vol. ii. pp. 18, 21, and 380. Compare Herod. ii. 37.

[3] Herod. ii. 45; Wilkinson, vol. v. p. 227; *Records of the Past*, vol. ii. pp. 57-8, &c.

counted in the inventories wherewith land-stewards
furnished their masters.[1]   The geese themselves, in
flocks of fifty or more, were brought under the
steward's eye to be inspected and reckoned. Goslings
for the service of the table were delivered to him in
baskets.[2]   Ducks, though less common than geese,
were likewise among the produce of the farmyard ; [3]
and pigeons, which were a favourite article of food,[4]
must also have engaged the attention of the producing
class.

It is among the most remarkable features of Egyptian farming, that not domestic animals only, but wild
ones also, were bred and reared on the great estates.
Wild goats, gazelles, and oryxes appear among the possessions of the larger land-owners,[5] no less than oxen,
sheep, and goats ; and similarly, in the poultry-yard,
the stork, the vulpanser, and other wild fowl share the
farmer's attention with ordinary ducks and geese.[6]
Probably no sharp line of distinction had been as yet
drawn between domestic and wild animals ; it was not
known how far domestication might be successfully
carried ; experiments, in fact, were in progress which
ultimately proved failures, the birds and beasts either
not being capable of being thoroughly tamed, or not
flourishing under human control sufficiently to make
it worth the breeder's while to keep on with them.

Another curious feature of Egyptian husbandry
was the entire absence of wagons[7] and the very rare

[1] Wilkinson, *Ancient Egyptians*, vol. iv. p. 132.
[2] Ibid.
[3] Herod. ii. 77.
[4] Wilkinson, *A.E.* vol. v. p. 216; Birch, *Egypt from the Earliest Times*, p. 45; Horapollo, *Hierogl.* i. 57.
[5] Wilkinson, vol. iii. p. 7; vol. iv. p. 140.
[6] Ibid. Compare Rosellini, *Mon. Civ.* pl. xxx. 2 ; and Lepsius, *Denkmäler*, vol. iii. pt. ii. pl. xvii. b.
[7] In our Authorised Version Joseph is said to have sent 'wagons'

use of carts.[1] Agricultural produce was transported
from the field to the barn or farm-yard mainly by
human labour,[2] the peasants carrying it in bags or
baskets on their shoulders, or slung between two men
on a pole, or sometimes by means of a yoke. Where
this simple method was insufficient, asses were com-
mouly employed to remove the produce, which they
carried in panniers or else piled upon their backs.[3] In
conveying grain, or provender, or cattle even, to a distant market, it is probable that boats were largely used,[4]
water communication between all parts of Egypt being
easy by means of the Nile and the extensive canal-
system, while roads did not exist, and the country, being
everywhere intersected by water-channels, was ill
adapted for wheeled vehicles.[5]

The beasts of burden used in Egypt were asses, cows,
and oxen. Horses, which were carefully bred from
the time of their introduction, probably under the
eighteenth dynasty,[6] were regarded as too noble, and
perhaps too valuable, for such a purpose. They were
commonly either ridden[7] or employed to draw cur-

---

into Palestine to fetch Jacob and
his brothers' families (Gen. xlv.
19, 27; xlvi. 5). And some modern
commentators justify the rendering. (See the *Speaker's Commentary*,
vol. i. p. 216.) But, as 'wagon'
in modern English means a four-
wheeled vehicle, the word is inap-
propriate in Genesis xlv. and xlvi.,
where two-wheeled vehicles, or
carts, are certainly intended. (See
Wilkinson, *A. E.* vol. iii. pp. 178–
80.)

[1] The carts represented on the
monuments belong for the most
part to foreigners (Wilkinson, vol. i.
p. 369). But I believe there are
instances of their employment in the

carriage of native agricultural produce.
[2] See above, p. 162.
[3] Wilkinson, *A. E.* vol. iv. p. 87.
[4] Ibid. vol. iii. p. 195. Compare
Lepsius, *Denkmäler*, vol. iii. pt. ii.
pl. civ. *b.*
[5] See Herod. ii. 108.
[6] Birch, *Egypt from the Earliest
Times*, p. 82; Wilkinson in the
author's *Herodotus*, vol. ii. p. 177,
note [2]; Pickering, *Races of Man*,
p. 373.
[7] Birch, l.s.c.; Herod. ii. 162;
Wilkinson, *A. E.* vol. i. pp. 289
and 406. It is curious how unfrequently the Egyptians are represented on horseback.

ricles and chariots,[1] chiefly by men of the upper classes.
Farmers are said to have made use of them occasionally
to draw the plough ;[2] but this cannot have been a
common practice. Great numbers were required for
the war-chariots, which formed so important an element
in the Egyptian military force ; the cavalry employed
almost as many ;[3] a brisk trade in them was also carried on with Syria and Palestine, where they were in
great request, and fetched high prices.[4] They seem
not to have been allowed to graze in the fields, but to
have been kept constantly in stables and fed on straw
and barley.[5] On the whole it is clear that their connection with agriculture was but slight ; and this brief
notice of them will therefore suffice for the purposes of
the present chapter.

---

[1] Rosellini, *Monumenti Civili*, pls. cxvi., cxx., cxxii., &c. ; Wilkinson, *Ancient Egyptians*, vol. i. pp. 336, 338, 354, &c.
[2] Birch, *Egypt from the Earliest Times*, p. 82.
[3] Diodorus makes the cavalry of Sesostris amount to 24,000, when the chariots are 27,000 (i. 54). That of Shishak (Sesonchis) was 60,000, when the chariots were no more than 1,200 (2 Chron. xii. 3). There can be no doubt that the Egyptians maintained a large cavalry force from the time of the eighteenth dynasty, though repre-
sentations of horsemen on the monu-
ments are scanty in the extreme. (See Ex. xiv. 9; 2 Kings xviii. 24; Jerem. xlvi. 9; Herod. ii. 162; Wilkinson, *Ancient Egyptians*, vol. i. pp. 288-292, &c.)
[4] See 1 Kings x. 29; 2 Chron. i. 17.
[5] *Records of the Past*, vol. ii. p. 75; Diod. Sic. i. 45, *ad fin.*

CHAPTER VII.

ARCHITECTURE.

Earliest Egyptian Architecture, sepulchral. Most ancient Tombs. Primitive stepped Pyramids—Pyramid of Meydoun—of Saccarah. Great Pyramids of Ghizeh. Intention of the Pyramids. Their technic excellence. Their æsthetic merit. Pyramids of two elevations. Rock Tombs. Primitive Temples. Later ones—Temple at Medinet Abou—Rameseum—Great Temple of Karnak. Obelisks. Southern Karnak Temple. Mammeisi. Beauties of the Architecture—Massiveness—Elegance of Columns and Capitals—Caryatide Piers—Employment of Colour. Egyptian domestic Architecture. Pavilion of Rameses III. Houses of Private Persons. Chief Peculiarities of Egyptian Construction. Non-employment of the Arch—Symmetrophobia—Contrivances for increasing apparent Size of Buildings.

Φασὶν [Αἰγύπτιοι] δεῖν θαυμάζειν μᾶλλον τοὺς ἀρχιτέκτονας τῶν ἔργων ἢ τοὺς βασιλεῖς.—Diod. Sic. i. 64.

THE origin of Architecture, in the proper sense of the term,[1] is different in different countries. In most it springs from the need which man has of shelter, and the desire which he entertains of making his dwelling-place not merely comfortable, but handsome. In some this desire seems not to have been early developed ; but in lieu of it, the religious sentiment brought architecture into life,[2] the desire which worked being that of giving to the buildings wherein God was worshipped

---

[1] By 'architecture' I understand not the mere 'technic art' of constructing buildings for various uses, but the 'æsthetic' one of constructing buildings which shall not be merely useful, but shall likewise affect the mind with the sense of beauty, of grandeur, or of both together. (See Fergusson, *Hist. of Architecture*, vol. i. pp. 10–16, 2nd edition.)

[2] This was the case in the ancient Chaldæa or Babylonia. (See the author's *Ancient Monarchies*, vol. i. p. 71, 2nd edition.)

a grandeur, a dignity, and a permanency worthy of Him. According to Herodotus,[1] the first Egyptian edifice of any pretension was a temple; and, could we depend on this statement, it would follow that Egypt was one of the countries in which architecture sprang from religion. The investigations, however, conducted on Egyptian soil by modern inquirers, have led most of them to a different conclusion, and have seemed to them to justify Diodorus in the important place which he assigns, in speaking of Egyptian architecture, to the Tomb. 'The inhabitants of this region,' says the learned Siceliot, 'consider the term of man's present life to be utterly insignificant, and devote by far the largest part of their attention to the life after death. They call the habitations of the living "places of sojourn," since we occupy them but for a short time; but to the sepulchres of the dead they give the name of "eternal abodes," since men will live in the other world for an infinite period. For these reasons they pay little heed to the construction of their houses, while in what concerns burial they place no limit to the extravagance of their efforts.'[2]

The early Egyptian remains are in entire harmony with this statement. They consist almost exclusively of sepulchral edifices. While scarcely a vestige is to be found of the ancient capital, Memphis, its necropolis on the adjacent range of hills contains many hundreds of remarkable tombs, and among them the 'Three Pyramids' which, ever since the time of Herodotus, have attracted the attention of the traveller beyond all the other marvels of the country. The art of pyramid building, which culminated in these mighty efforts, must have been practised for a considerable period before it

---

[1] Herod. ii. 99, ad fin.   [2] Diod. Sic. i. 51.

reached the degree of perfection which they exhibit ; and it is an interesting question, whether we cannot to a certain extent trace the progress of the art in the numerous edifices which cluster around the three giants, and stretch from them in two directions, northward to Abu-Roash, and southward as far as the Fayoum.[1] The latest historian of architecture has indeed conjectured that one, at any rate, of the most interesting of these subordinate buildings is of later date than the Three ;[2] but the best Egyptologists are of a different opinion, and regard it as among the most ancient of existing edifices.[3] It is not improbable that some of the smaller unpretentious tombs are earlier, as they are simpler, than any of the pyramidal ones, and it is therefore with these that we shall commence the present account of Egyptian sepulchral architecture.

Around the pyramids of Ghizeh, and in other localities also, wherever pyramids exist, are found numerous comparatively insignificant tombs which have as yet been only very partially explored and still more imperfectly described. ' Their general form is that of a truncated pyramid, low, and looking externally like a house with sloping walls, with only one door leading to the interior, though they may contain several apartments; and no attempt is made to conceal the entrance. The body seems to have been preserved from profanation by being hid in a well of considerable depth, the opening into which was concealed in the thickness of

[1] See Howard Vyse's *Pyramids of Ghizeh*, vol. iii. p. 2, and map.
[2] Fergusson, *Hist. of Architecture*, vol. i. p. 100.
[3] Birch ascribes the great pyramid of Saccarah to Ouennephes, a Manethonian king of the first dynasty (*Egypt from the Earliest Times*, p. 25). Lenormant regards its builder as *Kekeou* (Cechous) of the second Manethonian dynasty (*Manuel d'Histoire Ancienne*, vol. i. p. 332). The pyramids of Ghizeh are universally ascribed to kings of the fourth dynasty.

the walls.'¹ The ground-plan of these tombs is usually an oblong square, the walls are of great thickness, and the roofs of the chambers are in some instances supported by massive square stone piers. There is little external ornamentation ;² but the interior is in almost every instance elaborately decorated with coloured bas-reliefs, representing either scenes of daily life or religious and mystic ceremonies.

It was no great advance on these truncated pyramids to conceive the idea of adding to their height and solidity by the superimposition of some further storeys, constructed on a similar principle, but without internal chambers. An example of this stage of construction seems to remain in the curious monument at Meydoun, called by some a 'pyramid,' by others a 'tower,'³ of which the opposite page contains a representation.

¹ Fergusson, vol. i. p. 102.
² External ornamentation is confined to the doorways or entrances, which are sometimes carved curiously. The lintels are rounded. Door-posts are represented in the stone on either side of the doorway ; an imitation of lattice-work appears above ; at the side are alternate pilasters and depressions adorned with a sort of panelling. The whole appears to be an imitation of the façade of a house, in which the main material used was wood.
This would seem to indicate that there was a wooden architecture in Egypt anterior to the stone one. Of this wooden architecture there are, however, no remains.
³ Vyse (*Pyramids of Ghizeh*, vol. iii. p. 78), Birch (*Egypt from the Earliest Times*, p. 28), and others call it a 'pyramid.' Fergusson says (*Hist. of Architecture*, vol. i. p. 100) that it is not so much a pyramid as a 'tower.'

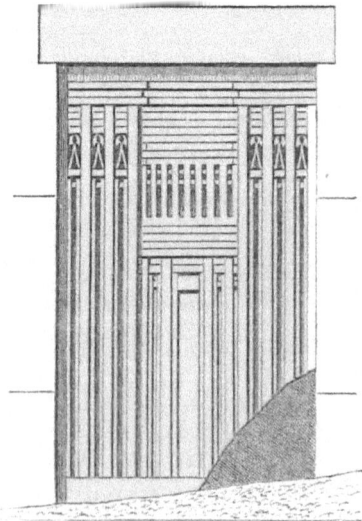

Doorway of Tomb, near the Pyramids.

This monument, which is emplaced upon a rocky knoll, has a square base, about 200 feet each way, and rises at an angle of 74° 10′, in three distinct stages, to an elevation of nearly 125 feet. The first stage is by far the loftiest of the three, being little short of seventy feet; the second somewhat exceeds thirty-two feet, while the third (which, however, may originally have been higher) is at present no more than twenty-two feet six inches.[1] The material is a compact limestone, and must have

Pyramid of Meydoun.

been brought from a considerable distance. The blocks, which vary in length, have a thickness of about two feet, and 'have been worked and put together with great skill.'[2] No interior passages or chambers have as yet been discovered in this edifice, which has, however, up to the present date, been examined very insufficiently.

After the idea of obtaining elevation, and so grandeur, by means of stages had been once conceived, it

[1] These are Perring's measurements, recorded by Vyse in the Appendix to his work, vol. iii. p. 79.
[2] Ibid.

was easy to carry out the notion to a much greater extent than that which had approved itself to the architect of the Pyramid of Meydoun. Accordingly we find at Saccarah an edifice similar in general character to the Meydoun pile, but built in six instead of three stages.[1] The proportions are also enlarged considerably, the circumference measuring 1,490 feet instead of 800, and the height extending to 200 feet instead of 125. The stages still diminish in height as they rise; but the diminution is only slight, the topmost stage of all falling short of the basement one by no more than eight feet and a half.[2] The sides of the several stages have a uniform slope, which is nearly at the same angle with that of the Meydoun building—viz. 73° 30′ instead of 74° 10′. The core of the Saccarah pyramid is of rubble;[3] but this poor nucleus is covered and protected on all sides with a thick casing of limestone, somewhat roughly hewn and apparently quarried on the spot. In the rock beneath the pyramid, and almost under its apex,[4] is a sepulchral chamber paved with granite blocks, which, when discovered, contained a sarcophagus,[5] and was connected with the external world by passages carefully concealed. A doorway

---

[1] This edifice has been briefly described by Dr. Birch (*Egypt*, p. 23), more elaborately by Baron Bunsen (*Egypt's Place*, vol. ii. pp. 379–84), and Mr. Fergusson (*Hist. of Architecture*, vol. i. pp. 100, 101). But the accounts of these writers are all taken from the work of Col. Howard Vyse, which is the authority followed in the text. (See *Pyramids of Ghizeh*, vol. iii. pp. 41–50.)

[2] The gradual diminution of the several stages is as follows:—

	Ft.	in.
Basement stage	37	8
Second stage	35	11
Third stage	34	3
Fourth stage	32	7
Fifth stage	30	10
Sixth stage	29	2

Dr. Birch regards the pyramid as having had originally seven stages; but there is no trace of a seventh stage, and neither Vyse nor Fergusson favours his theory.

[3] Vyse, vol. iii. p. 42.

[4] Ibid. p. 43. There is a deviation from the exact central point, whether intentional or not is uncertain, to the extent of 36 feet eastward.

[5] This had disappeared at the time of Col. Vyse's excavations; but it was seen at an earlier date by Minutoli.

leading into another smaller chamber, a low and narrow opening, was ornamented at the sides by green cubes of baked clay, enamelled on the surface, alternating with small limestone blocks; and the limestone lintel, which covered in the doorway at the top, was adorned with hieroglyphics.[1]

Great Pyramid of Saccarah—Present Appearance.

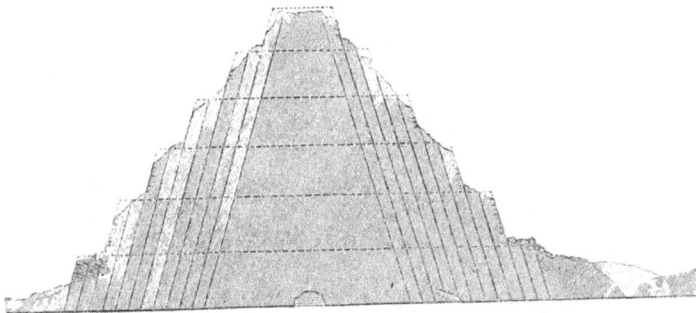

Section of same, showing Original Construction.

Among other peculiarities of this pyramid are its departure from correct orientation, and its *oblong*-square shape. It is said to be 'the only pyramid in Egypt the sides of which do not exactly face the cardinal points.'[2]

[1] The entire doorway has been removed to Europe, and is now in the Berlin Museum.   [2] Vyse, vol. iii. p. 41 ; Fergusson, vol. i. p. 100.

The departure is as much as 4° 35', and can therefore scarcely have been unintentional. To intention must also be ascribed the other peculiarity (which is not unexampled [1]), since the length by which the eastern and western sides exceeded the northern and southern was certainly as much as forty-three feet. According to a conjecture of the principal explorer, the *original* difference was even greater, amounting to sixty-three feet, or more than one-fifth of the length of the shorter sides.[2]

When multiplication of the stages had once been conceived of as possible, it became a mere question of taste for the designer or the orderer of a monument how numerous the stages should be. It was as easy to make them sixty as six, or two hundred as two. Evidence is wanting as to intermediate experiments; but it seems soon to have suggested itself to the Egyptian builders that the natural limit was that furnished by the thickness of the stones with which they built, each layer of stones conveniently forming a distinct and separate stage. Finally, when a *quasi*-pyramid was in this way produced, it would naturally occur to an artistic mind to give a perfect finish to the whole by smoothing the exterior, which could be done in two ways—either by planing down the projecting angles of the several stages to a uniform level,[3] or by filling up the trian-

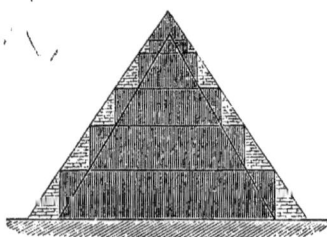

---

[1] A second instance of an oblong pyramid exists in the *Mustabet-el-Faraoun* or 'Throne of Pharaoh,' described by Vyse, vol. iii. p. 53.
[2] Vyse thinks that the N. and S. sides were originally no more than 331 feet, the E. and W. being 394

feet. Subsequently to the original construction a wall ten feet in thickness was (he says) built on at the northern and southern ends (*Pyramids of Ghizeh*, vol. iii. p. 42, note).
[3] Wilkinson (*Topography of Thebes*, p. 329) says that this was

gular spaces between the top of each step and the side
of the succeeding one.——

There are from sixty to seventy pyramids remaining in Egypt,[1] which appear to have been constructed
on these principles. Agreeing in form and in general
method of construction, they differ greatly in size, and
so in dignity and grandeur. As it would be wearisome
to the reader if we were to describe more than a few
of these works, and as it has been usual from the most
ancient times to distinguish three above all the rest,[2]
we shall be content to follow the example of most previous historians of Egypt, and to conclude our account
of this branch of Egyptian architecture with a brief
description of the Three Great Pyramids of Ghizeh.

The smallest of these constructions, which is usually
regarded as being the latest, was nearly of the same
general dimensions as the stepped pyramid of Saccarah
recently described. It a little exceeded the Saccarah
building in height, while it a little fell short of it in
circumference. The base was a square, exact or nearly
so, each side measuring 354 feet and a few inches.[3]
The perpendicular height was 218 feet, and the angle
of the slope fifty-one degrees. The pyramid covered
an area of two acres three roods and twenty-one poles,
and contained above nine millions of cubic feet of solid
masonry, calculated to have weighed 702,460 tons.[4]

---

the method employed in smoothing
the second pyramid. He mentions
both methods in the author's *Herodotus*, vol. ii. p. 201, note ³.
  ¹ Brugsch,*Histoire d'Egypte*,p. 52.
  ² See Herod. ii. 124–34; Diod.
Sic. i. 63, 64; Strabo, xvii. 1, § 33.
The last-named writer notices that
the three are only the chief among
many—πολλαὶ μέν εἰσι πυραμίδες,
τρεῖς δὲ ἀξιόλογοι.

  ³ Vyse makes the base 354 feet
6 inches (*Pyramids of Ghizeh*, vol.
ii. p. 120). Fergusson calls it 354
feet. Herodotus (ii. 134), curiously
enough, under-estimates the size of
this pyramid, making the length
of each side no more than 280
feet.
  ⁴ Vyse, *Pyramids of Ghizeh*, vol.
ii. p. 120.

Originally it was built in steps or stages,[1] like the Saccarah monument; the stages, however, were perpendicular, and not sloping; they seem to have been five in
number, and were not intended to be seen, the angles
formed by the steps being at once filled in with masonry.
Externally the lower half of the pyramid was covered
with several layers of a beautiful red granite,[2] bevelled
at the joints,[3] while the casing of the upper half as well

General View of the Tomb-chamber of the Third Pyramid.

as the main bulk of the interior was of limestone.
Nearly below the apex, sunk deep in the native rock

---

[1] Bunsen, *Egypt's Place in Univ.*
History, vol. ii. p. 166.
[2] Vyse, vol. ii. p. 120.

[3] Wilkinson in the author's *Herodotus*, vol. ii. p. 208, note [1].

on which the pyramid stands, is a sepulchral chamber, or rather series of chambers, in one of which was found the sarcophagus of the monarch whom tradition had long pointed out as the builder of the monument.[1] The chamber in question, which measures twenty-one feet eight inches in length, eight feet seven inches in breadth, and eleven feet three inches in its greatest height,[2] runs in a direction which is exactly north and south, and is composed entirely of granite. The floor was originally formed of large

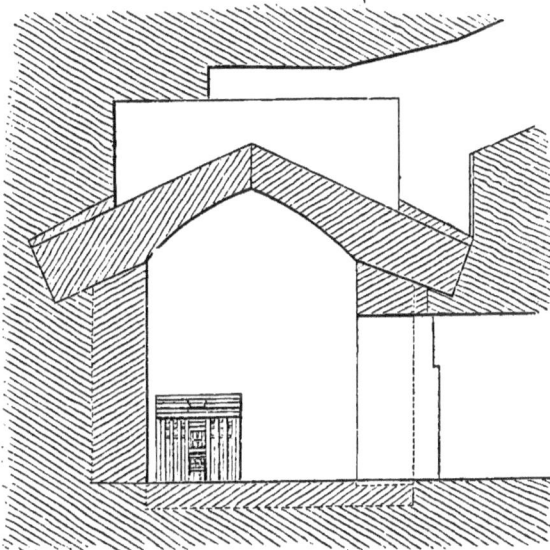

Arrangement of the Blocks forming the Roof.

masses well put together, but had been disturbed before any modern explorer entered the room ; the

---

[1] On the lid of the sarcophagus which occupied the sepulchral chamber of this pyramid was the cartouche—
which is read as Men-ka-re or Menker-re, undoubtedly the original or the Mencheres (Manetho), Mecherinus (Diod. Sic.), or Mycerinus (Herod.) of the Greek writers.
[2] Vyse, vol. ii. p. 122.

sides and ends were lined with slabs two and a half
feet thick; while the roof was composed of huge blocks
set obliquely, and extending from the side walls, on
which they rested, to the centre, where they met at an
obtuse angle. Internally these blocks had been caved
out after being put in place, and the roof of the chamber was thus a pointed arch of a depressed character.
The slabs covering the sides had been fastened to the

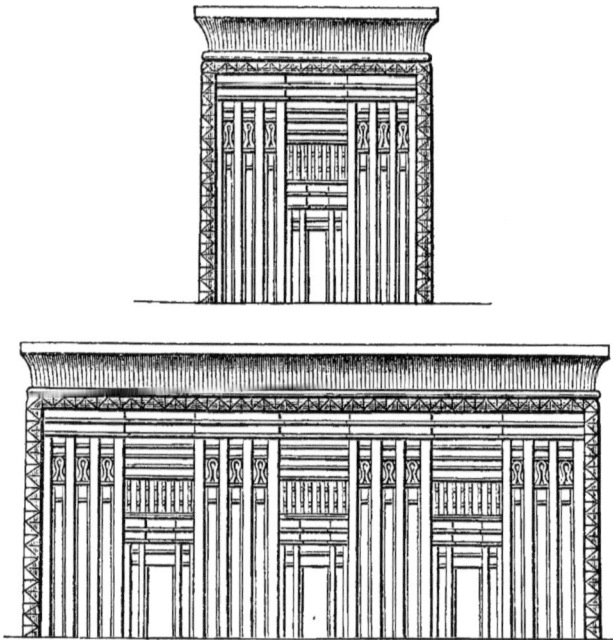

Sarcophagus of Mycerinus.

rock and to each other by means of iron cramps, two
of which were found *in situ*.[1]

The sarcophagus which the chamber contained was
extremely remarkable. Formed, with the exception
of the lid, of a single mass of blue-black basalt, and

---

[1] Vyse, vol. ii. p. 82, and compare pl. 3, figs. 7 and 9 (opp. p. 81).

the apex ; this was carved out of the solid rock, but covered in by the basement stones of the edifice, which were here sloped at an angle.[1]   The length of the chamber from east to west was forty-six feet, its breadth from north to south a little more than sixteen feet, its

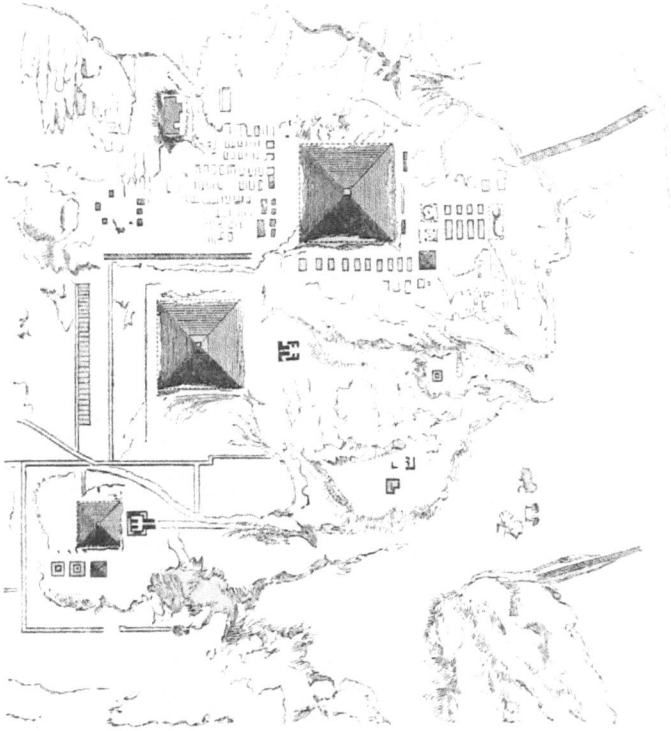

General Plan of the Pyramids of Ghizeh.

greatest height twenty-two feet.[2]   It contained a plain granite sarcophagus, without inscription of any kind, which was sunk into the floor,[3] and measured in length eight feet seven inches, in breadth three feet six inches, and in depth three feet.[4]   The chamber was connected

---

[1] Bunsen, vol. ii. p. 152.   [3] Belzoni, *Researches*, p. 271.
[2] Vyse, vol. ii. p. 118.   [4] Vyse, l.s.c.

o 2

with the world without by two passages, one of which, commencing in the north side of the pyramid, at the height of fifty feet above the base, descended to the level of the base at an angle of 25° 55', after which it became horizontal; while the other, beginning outside the pyramid in the pavement at its foot, descended at an angle of 21° 40' for a hundred feet, was horizontal for sixty feet, and then, ascending for ninety-six feet, joined the upper passage halfway between the outer air and

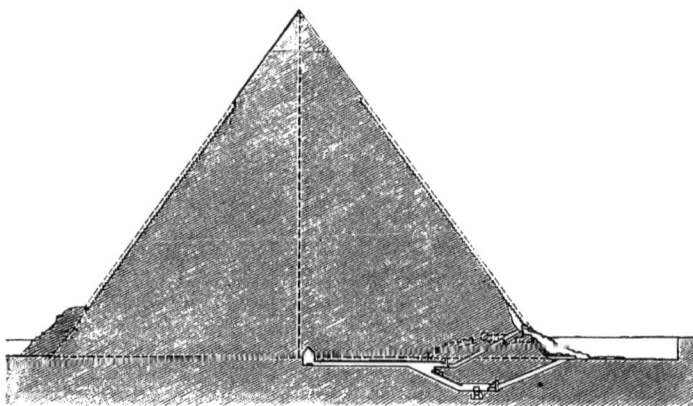

Section of the Second Pyramid.

the central chamber.[1]   Connected with the horizontal part of the lower passage were two other smaller chambers, which did not appear to have been sepulchral.   These measured respectively eleven feet by six and thirty-four feet by ten.[2]   They were entirely hewn out of the solid rock, and had no lining of any kind.   The passages were in part lined with granite;[3] and granite seems to have been used for the outer casing of the two lower tiers of the pyramid,[4] thus

[1] Vyse, vol. ii. pp. 118-9.
[2] Bunsen, *Egypt's Place*, vol. ii. p. 153.
[3] Ibid. vol. ii. p. 152.
[4] Herod. ii. 127; Vyse, vol. ii. p. 115; Wilkinson in the author's *Herodotus*, vol. ii. p. 204, note [2].

extending to a height of between seven and eight feet ; but otherwise the material employed was either the lime- stone of the vicinity, or the better quality of the same substance which is furnished by the Mokattam range. The construction is inferior to that of either the First or the Third Pyramid ; it is loose and irregular, in places ' a sort of gigantic rubble-work,' composed of large blocks of stone intermixed with mortar,[1] and seems scarcely worthy of builders who were acquainted with such far superior methods.

The First Pyramid of Ghizeh—the ' Great Pyramid,' as it is commonly called—the largest and loftiest build- ing which the world contains, is situated almost due north-east of the Second Pyramid,[2] at the distance of about 200 yards. It was placed on a lower level than that occupied by the Second Pyramid, and did not reach to as great an elevation above the plain.[3] In height from the base, however, it exceeded that pyramid by twenty-six feet six inches, in the length of the base line by fifty-six feet, and in the extent of the area by one acre three roods and twenty-four poles. Its original perpendicular height is variously estimated, at 480, 484, and 485 feet.[4] The length of its side was

---

[1] Vyse, l.s.c. ; Bunsen, vol. ii. p. 154.   Dr. Birch is less accurate than usual when he says that this pyramid was ' of admirable execu- tion' (*Egypt from the Earliest Times*, p. 38).

[2] Bunsen (vol. ii. plan opp. p. 147) and Wilkinson (plan in vol. ii. of the author's *Herodotus*, p. 199) represent the Great Pyramid as lying *exactly* north-east of the second. But the *expert*, Perring, lays down very positively the contrary (Vyse, vol. ii. plan of the pyramids opp. p. 148).

[3] The base of the Great Pyramid

was thirty-three feet below that of the Second Pyramid (Vyse, vol. ii. p. 106).   In vertical height it ex- ceeded the Second Pyramid by twenty-six feet six inches. Its ele- vation above the plain was conse- quently *less* than that of the Second Pyramid by six feet six inches. This fact has not been commonly noted.

[4] At 480 (or rather 480¾) by Vyse and Perring (vol. ii. p. 109) ; at 484 by Mr. Fergusson (*Hist. of Architecture*, vol. i. p. 95) ; and at 485 by Mr. Piazzi Smyth (*As- tronom. Observ.* p. 5).   The height depends on the exact angle of the

764 feet,[1] and its area thirteen acres one rood and twenty-two poles. It has been familiarly described as a building 'more elevated than the Cathedral of St. Paul's, on an area about that of Lincoln's Inn Fields.'[2] The solid masonry which it contained is estimated at more than 89,000,000 cubic feet, and the weight of the mass at 6,848,000 tons.[3] The basement stones are many of them thirty feet in length[4] and nearly five feet high. Altogether, the edifice is the largest and most massive building in the world,[5] and not only so,

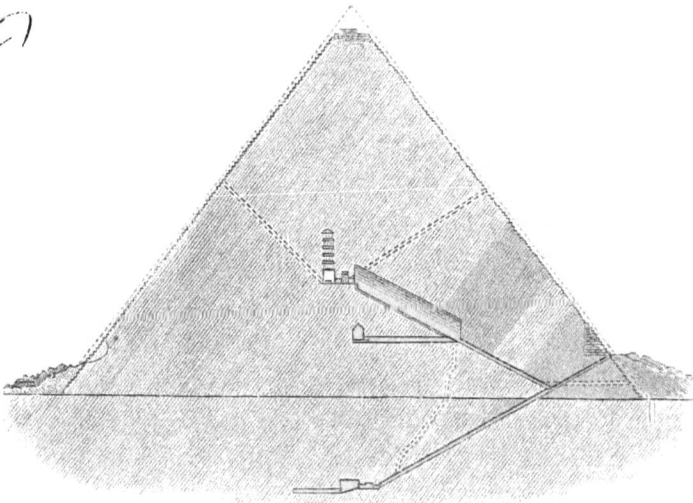

Section of the Great Pyramid.

casing stones, which is given as 51°50' by Vyse and Perring (vol. i. p. 261), but by Mr. Fergusson as 51°51' (*Hist. of Architecture*, vol. i. p. 95).
[1] So Vyse and Perring (l.s.c.). Mr. Fergusson says 760.
[2] Birch, *Egypt from the Earliest Times*, p. 32. Compare Wilkinson, *Topography of Thebes*, p. 323, note, where the comparison with Lincoln's Inn Fields was first made.
[3] These are Perring's estimates (Vyse, vol. ii. p. 113). They have

been generally accepted. (See Bunsen, vol. ii. p. 155; Wilkinson in the author's *Herodotus*, vol. ii. p. 200; Fergusson, *Hist. of Architecture*, vol. i. p. 95.)
[4] Herod. ii. 124, *ad fin.*, with Wilkinson's comment.
[5] Lenormant says (*Manuel d'Histoire Ancienne*, vol. i. p. 335): 'La pyramide de Khoufou est demeurée la plus prodigieuse des œuvres humaines, au moins par sa masse.'

but *by far* the largest and most massive—the building which approaches it the nearest being the Second Pyramid, which contains 17,000,000 cubic feet less, and is very much inferior in the method of its construction.

The internal arrangement of chambers and passages in the Great Pyramid is peculiar and complicated. A single entrance in the middle of the northern front, opening from the thirteenth step or stage from the base, conducts by a gradual incline, at an angle of

Relieving Stones at the entrance to the Great Pyramid.

26° 41′, to a subterranean chamber, deep in the rock, and nearly under the apex of the building, which measures forty-six feet by twenty-seven, and is eleven

feet high.[1] The passage itself is low and narrow,
varying from four to three feet only in height, and in
width from three feet six inches to two feet nine. It is
necessary to creep along the whole of it in a stooping
posture. The sides, which are perpendicular, are formed
of blocks of Mokattam limestone, and the passage is
roofed in by flat masses of the same. Above two such
masses are seen, at the entrance, two stones, and then
two more placed at an angle, and meeting so that they
support each other, and act as an arch, taking off the
pressure of the superincumbent masonry. It is supposed that the same construction has been employed
along the whole passage until.it enters the rock.[2] This
it does at the distance of about forty yards from the
outer air, after which it is carried through the rock in
the same line for about seventy yards, nearly to the
subterranean chamber, with which it is joined by a
horizontal passage nine yards in length. No sarcophagus
was found in this chamber, which must, however, it is
thought, have originally contained one.[3]

At the distance of twenty-one yards from the entrance to the pyramid an ascending passage goes off
from the descending one, at an angle which is nearly
similar,[4] and this passage is carried through the heart
of the pyramid, with the same height and width as the
other, for the distance of 124 feet. At this point it
divides.[5] A low horizontal gallery, 110 feet long,
conducts to a chamber, which has been called 'the

---

[1] Vyse, vol. ii. p. 110.
[2] Fergusson, *Hist. of Architec-ture*, vol. i. p. 99.
[3] Bunsen, *Egypt's Place*, vol. ii. p. 160. Compare Herod. ii. 124.
[4] The angle of the descending passage is 26° 41', that of the as-cending one 26° 18' (Vyse, vol. ii. p. 110).
[5] At first three feet ten inches high only; after 'the step' five feet eight inches (ibid. p. 112).

Queen's,'[1] a room about nineteen feet long by seventeen feet broad, roofed in with sloping blocks, and having a height of twenty feet in the centre.[2]   Another longer and much loftier gallery or corridor continues on in the line of the ascending passage for 150 feet, and is then joined by a short passage to the central or main chamber—that in which was found the sarcophagus of Cheops, or *Khufu*.[3]   The great gallery is of very curious construction.   It is five feet two inches wide at the base, and is formed of seven layers of stones, each layer projecting a little beyond the one below it, so that the gallery contracts as it ascends; and the ceiling, which measures only about four feet, is formed of flat stones laid across this space, and resting on the two uppermost layers or tiers.   The central chamber, into which this gallery leads, has a length (from east to west) of thirty-four feet, a width of seventeen feet, and a height of nineteen.[4] It is composed wholly of granite, beautifully polished,[5] and is roofed in a manner which shows great ingenuity and extreme care.   In the first place, nine enormous granite blocks, each of them measuring nearly nineteen feet long,[6] are laid across the room to form the ceiling ; then above these there

---

[1] Vyse, *passim* ; Bunsen, vol. ii. pp. 156, 158 ; Wilkinson, *Topo-graphy*, p. 324.   There is no ground for this appellation.

[2] Vyse, vol. ii. p. 113.

[3] The sarcophagus had no inscription ; but the walls of the chambers had roughly scrawled upon them in red ochre the names

of Khufu and

Khnum-Khufu

See Lepsius, *Denkmäler*, vol. iii. pt. ii. pl. 1.   Dr. Birch seems to regard these two cartouches as representing the same king (*Egypt from the Earliest Times*, pp. 32–8).

[4] Vyse, vol. ii. p. 111.

[5] Bunsen, vol. ii. p. 164.

[6] Ibid.   Compare Vyse, vol. ii. plan opp. p. 158.

Section of gallery in Great Pyramid.

is a low chamber, roofed in similarly; this is followed by a second chamber, a third, and a fourth; finally, above the fourth, is a triangular opening, roofed in by blocks that slope at an angle and support each other, like those over the entrance. Further, from the great chamber are carried, northwards and southwards, two ventilators or air-passages, which open on the outer surface of the pyramid, and are respectively 233 and 174 feet long.[1] These passages are square, or nearly so, and have a diameter varying between six and nine inches. Finally, it must be noted that from the subterranean chamber a passage is continued towards the south, which is horizontal, and extends a distance of fifty-three feet, where it abruptly terminates without leading to anything.[2]

[1] Vyse, vol. ii. p. 111.
[2] Ibid. p. 110. This fact would seem to show either a change of design on the part of the original

Many speculations have been indulged in, and various most ingenious theories have been framed, as to the object or objects for which the pyramids were constructed, and as to their perfect adaptation to their ends. It has been supposed that the Great Pyramid embodies revelations as to the earth's diameter and circumference, the true length of an arc of the meridian, and the proper universal unit of measure.[1] It has been conjectured that it was an observatory, and that its sides and its various passages had their inclinations determined by the position of certain stars at certain seasons.[2] But the fact seems to be, as remarked by the

King's Chamber and Chambers of Construction, Great Pyramid.

builder, or the passing of the building into new hands, and the substitution for the original design of an entirely new plan.

[1] See the work of Mr. Piazzi Smyth, entitled *Antiquity of Intel-* *lectual Man*, Edinburgh, 1865, p. 240, &c.

[2] These ideas, which originated with Signor Caviglia, were encouraged by Col. Howard Vyse (*Pyra-* *mids of Ghizeh*, vol. ii. pp. 105, 106)

first of living English Egyptologers,[1] that 'these ideas do not appear to have entered into the minds of the constructors of the pyramids,' who employed the measures known to them for their symmetrical construction,[2] but had no theories as to measure itself, and sloped their passages at such angles as were most convenient, without any thought of the part of the heavens whereto they would happen to point. The most sound and sober view seems to be, that the pyramids were intended simply to be tombs.[3] The Egyptians had a profound belief in the reality of the life beyond the grave, and a conviction that that life was, somehow or other, connected with the continuance of the body. They embalmed the bodies of the dead in a most scientific way; and having thus, so far as was possible, secured them against the results of natural decay, they desired to secure them also against accidents and against the malice of enemies. With this view they placed them in chambers, rock-cut, or constructed of huge blocks of stone, and then piled over these chambers a mass that would, they thought, make it almost impossible that they should be violated. The leading idea which governed the forms of their constructions

and, to some extent, by Wilkinson (*Topography of Thebes*, p. 328). Their entire falsity is sufficiently indicated by the facts, that no two pyramids have their sides inclined, or their entrance passages sloped, at the same angle.

[1] Birch, *Egypt from the Earliest Times*, p. 35.

[2] The symmetrical idea before the minds of the constructors of the pyramids seems to have been that each face of a pyramid should form an equilateral triangle. Their architectural skill was not sufficient to enable them to effect this quite

exactly, but they did not miss their aim by very much. The proportions of the bases to the sloping edges in the three pyramids are as follows:—

	Base.	Sloping edge.	Deficiency.
Great Pyramid	764 ..	723 ..	one-ninteenth
Second Pyramid	707 ..	672 ..	one-twentieth
Third Pyramid	354 ..	330 ..	one-fifteenth.

(See Fergusson's *History of Architecture*, vol. i. p. 96.)

[3] See Birch, *Egypt from the Earliest Times*, pp. 32–41; Lenormant, *Manuel d'Histoire Ancienne*, vol. i. pp. 537–8; Fergusson, *History of Architecture*, vol. i. p. 98; Brugsch, *Histoire d'Egypte*, pp. 51–59, &c.

was that of durability;[1] and the pyramid appearing to them to be, as it is, the most durable of architectural forms, they accordingly adopted it. The passages with which the pyramids are penetrated were required by the circumstance that kings built their sepulchres for themselves, instead of trusting to the piety of a successor, and thus it was necessary to leave a way of access to the sepulchral chamber. No sooner was the body deposited than the passage or passages were blocked. Huge portcullises, great masses of granite or other hard stone, were placed across them,[2] and these so effectually obstructed the ways that moderns have in several instances had to leave them where they were put by the builders, and to quarry a path round them.[3] The entrances to the passages were undoubtedly 'intended to be concealed,'[4] and were, we may be sure, concealed in every case, excepting the rare one of the accession, before the tomb was finished, of a new and hostile dynasty.[5] As for the angles of the passages, whereof so much has been said, they were determined by the engineering consideration, at what slope a heavy body like a sarcophagus could be lowered or raised to most advantage, resting without slipping when required to rest, and moving readily when required to move.[6]

---

[1] Lenormant, p. 537; Fergusson, p. 98.

[2] Vyse, vol. i. p. 288; vol. ii. pp. 73, 82, &c.; Belzoni, *Researches*, pp. 269, 274, &c.

[3] Fergusson, vol. i. p. 100.

[4] Ibid. p. 98.

[5] According to Diodorus (i. 64, § 8) the entrance to the Third Pyramid was not concealed, but, on the contrary, was pointed out for observation, by having the name of Mencheres inscribed over it. If this were so, we must attribute it to the carelessness or hostility of the kings of the fifth dynasty, who may have come into power before the works connected with the closing of the tomb of Mencheres were completed.

[6] This was first proved by Sir Henry James, of the Royal Engineers, whose models and lucid explanations convinced me of the fact, when I was at Exeter on the occasion of the meeting of the British Association in 1869. Mr. Fergusson adopts Sir H. James's

The ventilating passages of the Great Pyramid were simply intended to run in the line of shortest distance between the central chamber and the external air. This line they did not exactly attain, the northern passage reaching the surface of the pyramid about fifteen feet lower, and the southern one about the same distance higher than it ought, results arising probably from slight errors in the calculations of the builders.

In considering the architectural merit of the pyramids, two points require to be kept distinct—first their technic, and secondly their artistic or æsthetic value.

Technically speaking, a *simple* pyramid is not a work of much difficulty. To place masses of stone in layers one upon another, each layer receding from the last, and the whole rising in steps until a single stone crowns the summit; then to proceed downwards and smooth the faces, either by cutting away the projections or by filling up the angles of the steps, is a process requiring little constructive art and no very remarkable engineering skill. If the stones are massive, then, of course, a certain amount of engineering proficiency will be implied in their quarrying, their transport, and their elevation into place; but this last will be much facilitated by the steps, since they afford a resting-place for the block which is being raised, at each interval of two or three feet.[1] Had the Egyptian pyramids been nothing more than this—had they been merely solid

---

views (*Hist. of Architecture*, vol. i. p. 98).

[1] Herodotus (ii. 125) expressly notices that the stones were raised in this way, a step at a time, by machines placed on the step below. Mr. Perring found marks of the use of such machines wherever the upper surface of the original steps was exposed to view. He conjectured that the machine used was the *polyspaston* of Vitruvius (Vyse, *Pyramids of Ghizeh*, vol. i. p. 197, note).

masses of stone—the technic art displayed in them would not have been great. We should have had to notice for approval only the proper arrangement of the steps in a gradually *diminishing* series,[1] the prudent employment of the largest blocks for the basement and of smaller and still smaller ones above, and the neat

Outer Casing Stones of the Great Pyramid.

cutting and exact fitting of the stones that form the outer casing.[2] As it is, however, the pyramid-builders are deserving of very much higher praise. Their construc-tions were not solid, but had to contain passages and chambers—chambers which it was essential should

---

[1] *I.e.* diminishing as they ascend. | compare the frontispiece to the first
[2] See the above woodcut, and | volume of Col. Vyse's work.

remain intact, and passages which must not be allowed
to cause any settlement or subsidence of the building.
It is in the formation of these passages and chambers
that the architects of the pyramids exhibited their technic
powers. 'No one can possibly examine the interior of
the Great Pyramid,' says Mr. Fergusson, 'without
being struck with astonishment at the wonderful
mechanical skill displayed in its construction. The
immense blocks of granite brought from Syéné—a distance of 500 miles—polished like glass, and so fitted
that the joints can scarcely be detected. Nothing can
be more wonderful than the extraordinary amount of
knowledge displayed in the construction of the discharging chambers over the roof of the principal apartment, in the alignment of the sloping galleries, in the
provision of ventilating shafts, and in all the wonderful
contrivances of the structure. All these, too, are carried out with such precision that, notwithstanding the
immense superincumbent weight, no settlement in any
part can be detected to the extent of an appreciable
fraction of an inch. *Nothing more perfect mechanically
has ever been erected* since that time.'[1]

Æsthetically, the pyramids have undoubtedly far
less merit. 'In itself,' as the writer above quoted well
observes, 'there can be nothing less artistic than a

[1] Fergusson, vol. i. pp. 91, 92.
Compare Vyse, vol. i. p. 289: 'The
masonry of the [central] chamber
is probably the finest specimen in
the world. It consists entirely of
enormous masses of polished granite,
worked down and laid with the
greatest exactness, and has retained
its original perfection for unnum-
bered centuries, whilst other mighty
fabrics, composed of coarse workmanship and materials, have gradually crumbled away into shapeless
masses of stone and rubbish. In
this instance every block is as fresh
and as perfect as when taken from
the quarry; and such is the pon-
derous solidity and perfection of
their texture, and the labour and
science employed in their arrangement, that they seem to set at de-
fiance the effects of time and the
efforts of human violence.'

VIEW OF THE GREAT AND SECOND PYRAMIDS.

pyramid.'[1]   It has no element of architectural excellence but greatness, and this it conceals as much as
possible. 'A pyramid never looks as large as it is ;
and it is not till you almost touch it that you can realise
its vast dimensions. This is owing principally to all its
parts sloping away from the eye instead of boldly chal-
lenging observation.'[2]   Still, the great pyramids of
Egypt, having this disadvantage to struggle against,
must be said to have overcome it. By the vastness of
their mass, by the impression of solidity and durability.
which they produce, partly also perhaps by the symmetry and harmony of their lines and their perfect
simplicity and freedom from ornament, they do convey
to the beholder a sense of grandeur and majesty, they
do produce within him a feeling of astonishment and
awe, such as is scarcely caused by any other of the
erections of man. In all ages travellers have felt and
expressed the warmest and strongest admiration for
them.[3]   They impressed Herodotus as no works that
he had seen elsewhere, except perhaps the Babylonian.[4]
They astonished Germanicus, familiar as he was with
the great constructions of Rome.[5] They stirred the
spirit of Napoleon, and furnished him with one of his
most telling phrases.[6]   Greece and Rome reckoned

---

[1] Fergusson, vol. i. p. 105.
[2] Ibid. Compare Vyse, vol. i. p.
176.
[3] After noticing the fact that *at
first sight* the pyramids generally
disappoint travellers, Col. Vyse observes : 'A more deliberate examination, however, never fails to alter
and correct these opinions; and
it was *universally acknowledged* by
those who remained for any length
of time at Ghizeh, that the more
carefully and completely they were
inspected the more extraordinary

their grandeur appeared. . . . Pre-
eminent in dimensions and antiquity
over all other buildings in the world,
they are alike admirable for the
excellence of their masonry, the skill
and science displayed in their construction, and the imposing majesty
of their simple forms.' (*Pyramids of
Ghizeh*, l.s.c.)
[4] Herod. ii. 124-34 and 148.
Compare i. 93.
[5] Tacit. *Ann.* ii. 61.
[6] 'Soldiers, forty centuries look
down upon you from the top of

them among the Seven Wonders of the world.[1] Moderns have doubted whether they could really be the work of human hands.[2] If they possess one only of the elements of architectural excellence, they possess that element to so great an extent that in respect of it they are unsurpassed, and probably unsurpassable.

Before quitting altogether the subject of the pyramids it should perhaps be noted—first, that the Egyptians not unfrequently built brick pyramids,[3] and prided

the pyramids.' (See Alison, *History of Europe*, vol. iii. p. 433.)
[1] Diod. Sic. i. 63; ii. 11; Strab. xvii. 1, § 33.
[2] Richardson, *Travels along the*

70-1) gives a full account of two brick pyramids at Dashoor. They were composed of crude, not baked, bricks, and were cased with Mokattam limestone. The original bases

Section of Brick Pyramid at Illahoun.

Mediterranean and Parts adjacent, vol. i. p. 119, quoted by Dr. Russell in his *Egypt, Ancient and Modern*, p.124. Compare Diod. Sic i. 63,*sub fin.*
[3] Vyse (vol. iii. pp. 57-63 and

were estimated at 342 feet 6 inches and 350 feet, their perpendicular heights at 267 feet 4 inches and 215 feet 6 inches. There is also a pyramid chiefly built of crude brick

themselves upon constructing durable monuments with
so poor a material;[1] and secondly, that they occasionally built pyramids with two distinct inclinations.
The southern stone pyramid of Dashoor, which has a
base of nearly 617 feet, is commenced at an angle of
54° 15', and, if this slope had been continued, must
have risen to an elevation of nearly 400 feet. When,

Southern Stone Pyramid of Dashoor.

however, the work had been carried up to the height of
about 150 feet, the angle was suddenly changed to one
of 42° only, and the monument being finished at this low
slope, lost sixty feet of its proper elevation, falling short
of 340 feet by a few inches.[2] The effect of a pyramid
of this kind is pronounced to be unpleasant;[3] and there
can be little doubt[4] that the change of construction,

at Illahoun, on the way to the Fayoum. This had not only a casing of
stone, but was strengthened internally by a number of stone walls, the
arrangement of which will be best
understood by the representation on
the opposite page. There is another brick pyramid inside the

Fayoum, known as the Pyramid of
Howara (Vyse, vol. iii. p. 83).
[1] Herod. ii. 136.
[2] Vyse, vol. iii. pp. 65–7.
[3] Ibid. p. 66.
[4] So Wilkinson (*Topography of
Thebes*, p. 338). The Dashoor pyramid shows an inferiority of cou-

when made, was an after-thought resulting from a desire to complete the work more rapidly than had been at first intended.

Besides the brick and stone tombs thus elaborately constructed, the Egyptians were also in the habit of forming rock-sepulchres by excavations in the mountains whereby the Nile Valley was bordered. These excavated tombs belong to a period somewhat later than that of the pyramids, and have but few architectural features, being for the most part a mere succession of chambers and passages,[1] with walls and ceilings ornamented by painting and sculpture, but devoid of any architectural decoration. Still, there are certain exceptions to the general rule. Occasionally the entrances, and again the larger chambers, are supported by columns ; and these, though for the most part plain, have in some instances an ornamentation which is interesting, showing as it does the germ of features which ultimately came to be employed widely and recognised as possessing great merit. In the earliest of the rock-tombs the pillar is a mere pier,[2] at first

struction in the upper part; and it is doubtful if it was ever quite completed (Vyse, vol. iii. p. 66).

nearly 100 feet below the level of the entrance. It comprised five pillared chambers, numerous pas-

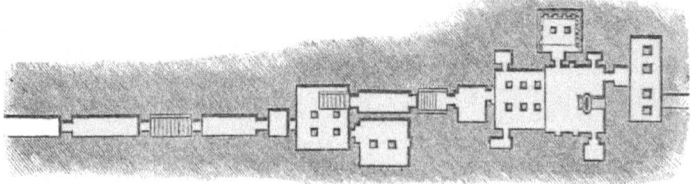

Rock Tomb near Thebes.

[1] See Mr. Fergusson's description of the 'Tomb of Menephthah' at Thebes (*Hist. of Architecture*, vol. i. p. 128). This excavation was 350 feet long, and descended gradually till it reached a depth of

sages or corridors, and a large room with a coved roof, in which Belzoni found the sarcophagus of Menephthah (*Researches*, p. 236).

[2] Fergusson, *Hist. of Architecture*, vol. i. p. 103.

square or, at any rate, rectangular; then the projecting
angles are cut away,
and the shape be-
comes octagonal;
finally, the octagon
is rounded off into
a circle. This form
being too simple, an
ornamentation of it
is projected, and that sort of shallow
fluting appears which characterises the
Doric order of the Greeks. Several
tombs at Beni Hassan, in Middle Egypt,
exhibit pillars so like the Grecian that
they have obtained the name of 'Proto-
Doric.'[1] Sixteen shallow curved inden-
tations, carried in straight lines from top
to bottom of the columns, streak them
with delicate varieties of shade and light,
adding greatly to their richness and
effect. The sides slope a little, so that
the column tapers gently; but there is
no perceptible *entasis* or hyperbolic
curve of the sides. The base is large,
and there is a square plinth between the
column and the architrave, which latter
is wholly unornamented. The entire effect is simple
and, pleasing.[2]

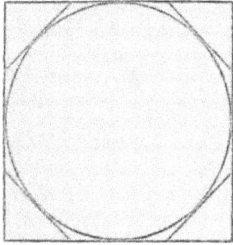

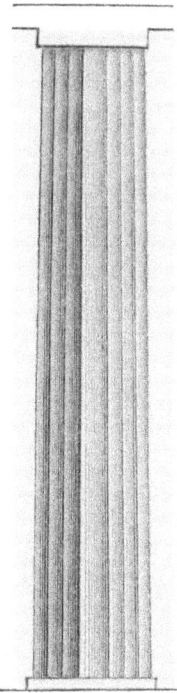

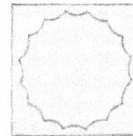

'Doric' Pillar and
Section of Base.

---

[1] Fergusson, *Hist. of Architecture*, vol. i. p. 103. Compare Falkener in *Museum of Class. Antiquities*, vol. i. p. 87. The resemblance to the Doric order was remarked by the architect Gaetano Rosellini, who accompanied the Tuscan expedition of the Grand Duke Leopold. (See Rosellini, *Monumenti Civili*, vol. i.

p. 65, note [4].) It is also noticed by Sir Gardner Wilkinson (*Ancient Egyptians*, vol. i. p. 44), and by Bunsen (*Egypt's Place*, vol. ii. p. 284).

[2] 'Tali colonne sono tra le più eleganti di quante se ne veggono negli antichi monumenti d'Egitto.' (Rosellini, *Mon. Civ.* l.s.c.)

Another still more elegant and thoroughly Egyptian column, which is found occasionally in the early tombs, seems to deserve description. This appears to imitate four reeds or lotus stalks, clustered together and bound round with a ligature near the top, above which they swell out and form a capital. This pillar stands— like the other—on its own base, and is rather more tapering. It was sometimes delicately coloured with streaks and bars of blue, pink, yellow, green, and white, which gave it a very agreeable appearance.[1]

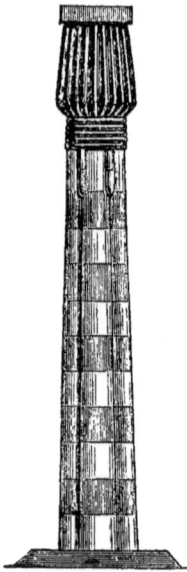

The spaces between the pillars are sometimes occupied by curvilinear roofs,[2] which, though not exhibiting any engineering skill, since they are merely cut in the rock, imply, at any rate, an appreciation of the beauty of coved ceilings, and suggest, if they do not prove, an acquaintance with the arch. Such a knowledge was certainly possessed by the later Egyptians, and may not improbably have been acquired even at the very remote date to which the tombs in question belong.

Egyptian Pillar and Section of Base.

Although their early architecture is almost entirely of a sepulchral character, yet we have a certain amount of evidence that, even from the first, the TEMPLE had a place in the regards of the Egyptians,

---

[1] 'A queste colonne, oltre l'eleganza della forma, aggiungono vaghezza i colori, che, disposti con bell' armonia, danno risalto agli steli, ai legami, ed ai bocciuoli' (Rosellini, p. 70).
[2] Ibid. p. 69; Fergusson, vol. i. p. 110.

though a place very much inferior to that occupied by the Tomb. Not only is the building of temples ascribed by the ancient writers to more than one of the early kings,[1] but remains have been actually found which the best authorities view as edifices of this class,[2] belonging certainly to a very ancient period. One such edifice has been discovered, and at least partially explored, in the immediate vicinity of the Second Pyramid—that of Chephren—and may be confidently regarded as of his erection. It consists mainly of a single apartment, built in the form of the letter T, and measuring about 100 feet each way. The entrance was in the middle of the cross-bar of the T, which was a sort of gallery 100 feet long by twenty-two wide, divided down the middle by a single range of oblong-square piers, built of the best Syenite granite. From this gallery opened out at right angles the other limb of the apartment, which had a length of nearly eighty feet with a breadth of thirty-three, and was divided by a double range of similar piers into three portions, just as our churches commonly are into a nave and two aisles. The temple has no roof, but is believed to have been covered with granite blocks, laid across from the walls to the piers, or from one pier to another. The walls were lined with slabs of alabaster, arragonite, or other rare stones, skilfully cut and deftly fitted together ; and the temple was further adorned with statues of the founder, having considerable artistic merit, and executed

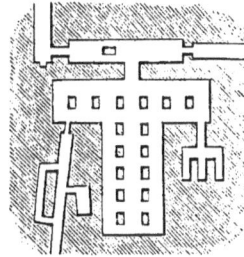

Plan of Temple.

[1] Herod. ii. 99; Diod. Sic. i. 45, 46, &c.

[2] Donaldson in the *Transactions* of the *Society of British Architects* for Feb. 1861 ; Fergusson, *Hist. of Architecture*, vol. i. p. 104.

in green basalt,[1] a close-grained and hard material.   A
certain number of narrow passages, leading to small
chambers, were connected with it, but these must be
regarded as mere adjuncts, not interfering with the
main building.

There is no beauty of ornamentation and but little
constructive skill in the temple which we have been
considering.   It has been described as 'the simplest
and least adorned in the world.'[2]   Still, we are told
that the effect is pleasing.   'All the parts of the building are plain—straight and square, without a single
moulding of any sort, but they are perfectly proportioned to the work they have to do.   They are *pleas-
ingly* and effectively arranged, and they have all that
lithic grandeur which is inherent in large masses of
precious materials.'[3]

The means do not exist for tracing with any completeness the gradual advance which the Egyptians
made in their temple building, from edifices of this
extreme and archaic simplicity to the complicated and
elaborate constructions in which their architecture ultimately culminated.   The dates of many temples are
uncertain ; others, of which portions are ancient, have
been so altered and improved by later builders that
their original features are overlaid, and cannot now be
recovered.   We can only say, that as early as the
time of the twelfth dynasty the obelisk was invented
and became an adjunct and ornament of the temple,[4]
its ordinary position being at either side of a doorway
of moderate height, which it overtopped ; and that

---

[1] Birch, *Egypt from the Earliest Times*, p. 38.
[2] Fergusson, vol. i. p. 105.
[3] Ibid. pp. 105–6.
[4] Wilkinson, *Ancient Egyptians*, vol. i. p. 45; Bunsen, *Egypt's Place*, vol. ii. p. 283, &c.

soon after the accession of the eighteenth dynasty—if not even earlier—round pillars were introduced[1] as a substitute for square piers, which they gradually superseded, retaining however to the last, in their massive form, a pier-like character. About the same time the idea arose (which afterwards prevailed universally) of forming a temple by means of a succession of courts, colonnaded or otherwise, opening one into another, and generally increasing in richness as they receded from the entrance, but terminating in a mass of small chambers, which were probably apartments for the priests.

The progress of the Egyptian builders in temples of this kind will perhaps be sufficiently shown if we take three specimens, one from Medinet-Abou, belonging to the early part of the eighteenth dynasty; another, that of the Rameseum, belonging to the very best Egyptian period—the reign of Rameses II., of the nineteenth dynasty; and the third, that magnificent temple at Karnak, the work of at least seven distinct monarchs, whose reigns cover a space of above five hundred years, which has been well compared to the greatest mediæval cathedrals,[2] gradually built up by the piety of successive ages, each giving to God the best that its art could produce, and all uniting to create an edifice richer and more various than the work of any single age could ever be, yet still not inharmonious, but from first to last repeating with modifications the same forms and dominated by the same ideas.

The temple at Medinet-Abou faces to the south-east.[3] It is entered by a doorway of no great height,

---

[1] See below, p. 219.
[2] Fergusson, *Hist. of Architecture*, vol. i. p. 118.
[3] See the plan in the *Description de l'Egypte*, 'Antiquités,' 'Planches,' vol. ii. pl. 4, fig. 1.

on either side of which are towers or 'pylons' of moderate elevation,[1] built (as usual) with slightly sloping sides, and crowned by a projecting cornice. The gateway is ornamented with hieroglyphics and figures of gods ;[2] but the pylons, except on their internal faces, are plain. Having passed through this portal, the traveller finds himself in a rectangular court, rather more than sixty feet long by thirty broad, bounded on either side by a high wall, and leading to a colonnaded building. This, which is the temple proper, consists of an oblong cell, intended, probably, to be lighted from the roof, and of a gallery or colonnade running entirely round the cell, and supported in front and at the sides by square piers. The side colonnades have a length of about fifty feet, while the front colonnade or porch has a length of thirty-five or forty. The space between the cell and the piers is a distance of about nine feet, and this has been roofed in with blocks of stone extending horizontally across it ; but the roof, thus formed, having, apparently, shown signs of weakness in places, and further support having been needed, four octagonal pillars have been introduced at the weak points.[3] The position of three of these is fairly regular : but one stands quite abnormally, as will be seen by reference to the plan. At either end of the front gallery or porch are apartments—one nearly square, about fifteen feet by twelve ; the other oblong, about twenty-seven feet by fifteen. In this latter are two round pillars with bell or lotus capitals,[4] intended to support the roof. In the rear

---

[1] According to the French savants the original height was about twenty-four feet (*Description de l'Egypte*, l.s.c. fig. 4).

[2] Ibid. 'Texte,' vol. i. ch. ix. p. 25.

[3] Ibid. p. 26 : 'On s'était aperçu sans doute que les pierres du plafond, trop pesantes, menaçoient de se rompre sous leur propre poids.'

[4] Ibid. p. 28.

of the temple, and in the same line with the side piers,
are a group of six apartments, opening one into another,
and accessible only from the gallery immediately be-

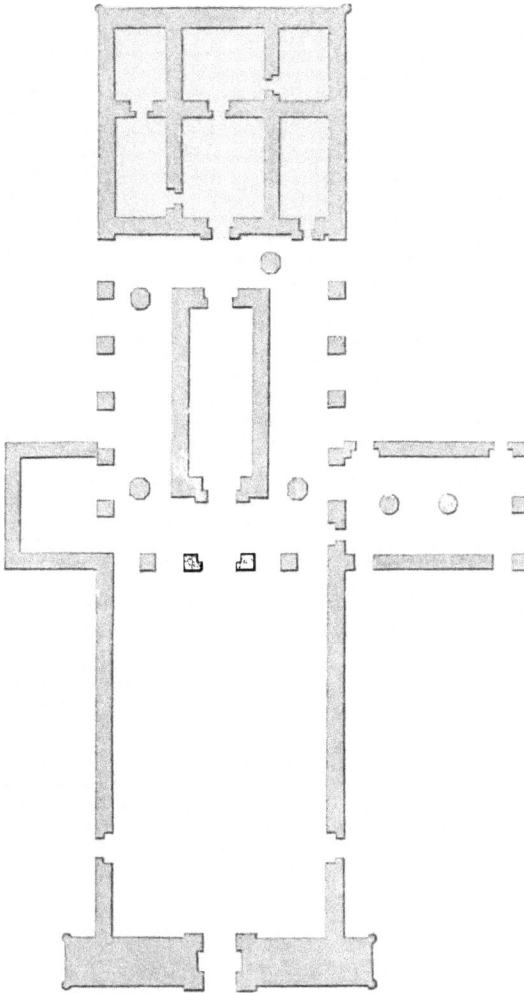

Ground-plan of Temple at Medinet-Abou.

hind the cell.   The whole interior of the temple is
profusely ornamented with hieroglyphics and sculp-

tures, chiefly of a religious character.   Externally this
building can have had but little grandeur or beauty ;
internally it can scarcely have been very satisfactory ;
but the sculptures, whose effect was heightened by
painting, may have given it a certain character of richness and splendour.

Section of Temple at Medinet-Abou.

A great advance upon this edifice had been made
by the time when Rameses II. constructed the building,
known formerly as the Memnonium,[1] and now commonly called the Rameseum,[2] at Thebes.   Still, the
general plan of the two buildings is not very dissimilar.
The entrance-gateway stood, similarly, between two
tall pylons, or ' pyramidal masses of masonry, which,
like the two western towers of a Gothic cathedral, are
the appropriate and most imposing part of the structure
externally.'[3]   It led, like the other, into a rectangular
courtyard, bounded on either side by high walls, which,

[1] D'Anville,   Mémoires   sur
l'Egypte, p. 205; Description, ' Antiquités,' vol. i. ch. ix. p. 121 ;
Wilkinson, Ancient Egyptians, vol.
i. pp. 114–6.
[2] Brugsch, Geschichte Aegyptens
unter den Pharaonen, p. 542 ; Fergusson, Hist. of Architecture, vol. i.
pp. 116–7 ; Birch, Egypt from the

Earliest Times, p. 127.
[3] Fergusson, p. 117.   Diodorus
gives the pylons a height of forty-five
cubits, or sixty-seven and a half feet
(i. 47).   The French savants (Description, ' Planches,' vol. ii. pl. 27)
represent it as somewhat greater
(about seventy-three feet).

however, were in this instance screened by a double

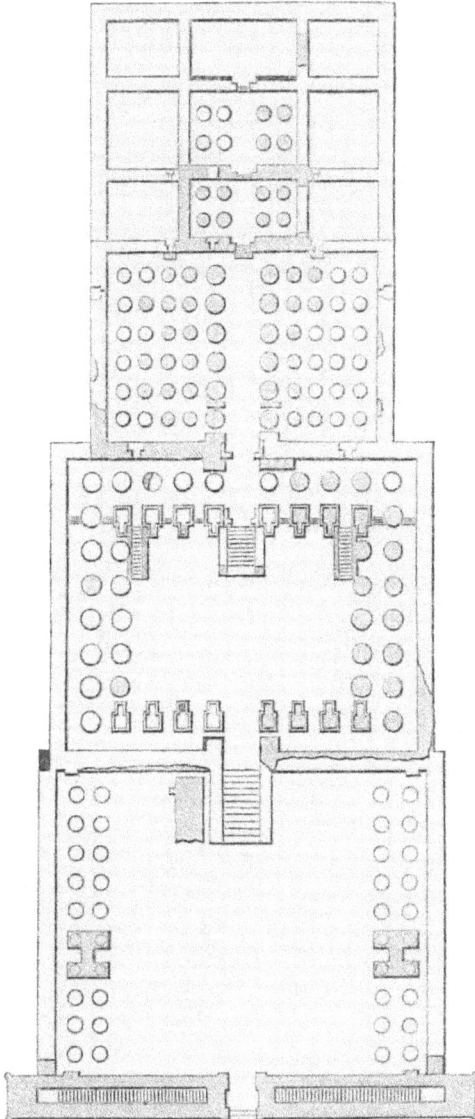

Ground-plan of the Rameseum.

colonnade, supported on two rows of round pillars, ten

in each row.[1]   From this courtyard a short flight of
steps, and then a broad passage, conducted into an
inner *peristyle* court,[2] a little smaller,[3] but very much
more splendid than the outer. On the side of entrance,
and on that opposite, were eight square piers, with
colossi in front, each thirty feet high ; while on the
right and left were double ranges of circular columns,
eight in each range, the inner one being continued on
behind the square piers which faced the spectator on
his entrance. Passing on from this court in a straight
line, and mounting another short staircase, the traveller
found himself in a pillared hall of great beauty, formed
by forty-eight columns in eight rows of six each,[4] most
of which are still standing. The pillars of the two
central rows exceed the others both in height and diameter.[5] They are of a different order from the side
pillars, having the bell-shaped or lotus capital which
curves so gracefully at the top ; while the side capitals
are contracted as they ascend, and are decidedly less
pleasing. The whole of the hall was roofed over with
large blocks of stone, light being admitted into it
mainly by means of a clerestory in the way shown
by the section opposite. All the columns, together
with the walls enclosing them, were beautifully orna-

[1] Wilkinson, *Ancient Egyptians,*
vol. i. p. 116 ; *Description,* 'Texte,'
vol. i. ch. ix. pp. 123–4 ; Fergusson,
p. 116.

[2] That is to say, a court with
colonnades all round it.

[3] The French savants made the
two courts, the hall, and the building beyond, all of them, of exactly
the same width ; but Sir G. Wilkinson and other authorities tell us
that the width of the edifice is contracted at each stage. (See the
plan, p. 221.)

[4] So Wilkinson (l.s.c.) and Fergusson (vol. i. p. 116). The French
explorers supposed that there had
been *ten* rows of six columns, and
thus made their number *sixty* (*Description,* 'Antiquités,' 'Texte,' vol. i.
ch. ix. p. 132 ; 'Planches,' vol. ii. pl.
27).

[5] The central pillars have a height
of thirty-five feet, the side ones of
twenty-four. The former are above
six feet in diameter, the latter about
five feet. (*Description,* 'Texte,'
l.s.c.)

mented with patterns, hieroglyphics, and bas-reliefs cut
in the stone and then brilliantly coloured.[1] Behind
the hall were chambers, probably nine in number,[2]
perhaps more, the two main ones supported by eight
pillars each, and lighted, most likely, by a clerestory ;
the others either dark or perhaps receiving light through
windows pierced in the outer walls.

A magnificent ornament of this temple, and probably its greatest glory, was a sitting colossus of enormous size, formed of a single mass of red Syenite

Section of Hall, Rameseum, Thebes.

granite, and polished with the greatest care, which
now lies in fragments upon the soil of the great courtyard and provokes the astonishment of all beholders.[3]
Its original height is estimated at eighteen yards, and its
cubic contents at nearly 12,000 feet,[4] which would
give it a weight of almost 900 tons! It was the
largest of all the colossal statues of Egypt, exceeding
in height the two seated colossi in its vicinity, one of

[1] *Description de l'Egypte,* pp.
132-3.
[2] So Wilkinson and Fergusson.
The French explorers thought that
there might originally have been
as many apartments in the rear of

the great hall as Diodorus states.
(See their plan, 'Antiquités,' pl. 33.)
[3] *Description,* 'Texte,' vol. i. ch.
ix. pp. 124-5; Wilkinson, *Topography of Thebes,* pp. 10-12.
[4] *Description,* p. 125, note [1].

which is known as 'the vocal Memnon,' by nearly seven feet.[1]

The Great Temple of Karnak is termed by the latest historian of architecture 'the noblest effort of architectural magnificence ever produced by the hand of man.'[2] It commences with a long avenue of crio-sphinxes[3] facing towards each other, and leading to a portal, placed (as usual) between two pylons, one of which is still nearly complete and rises to the height of 135 feet.[4] The portal gives access to a vast open court, with a covered corridor on either side resting upon round pillars, and a double line of columns down the centre. The court and corridors are 275 feet long, while the distance from the outer wall of the right to that of the left corridor is 329 feet.[5] The area of the court should thus be nearly 100,000 square feet. A portion of it, however, on the right is occupied by a building which seems to have been a shrine or sanctuary distinct from the main temple. This edifice, placed at right angles to the walls of the court, interrupts the colonnade upon the right after it has reached about half its natural length, and, projecting in front of it, contracts the court in this quarter, while at the same time it penetrates beyond the line of the walls to a distance of about 120 feet. It is constructed in the usual manner, with two pylons in front, an entrance court colonnaded on three sides, an inner pillared chamber lighted from the roof, and some apartments behind, one of which is thought to have been the sanctuary.[6] Small in proportion to the remainder of the vast pile

[1] *Description*, pp. 80–1.
[2] Fergusson, *Hist. of Architecture*, vol. i. p. 118.
[3] Wilkinson, *Topography of Thebes*, p. 173.
[4] *Description*, 'Antiquités,' vol. i. ch. ix. p. 208.
[5] Wilkinson, l.s.c.
[6] *Description*, 'Antiquités,' vol. i. ch. ix. p. 216.

INTERIOR OF THE SMALL TEMPLE AT KARNAK.

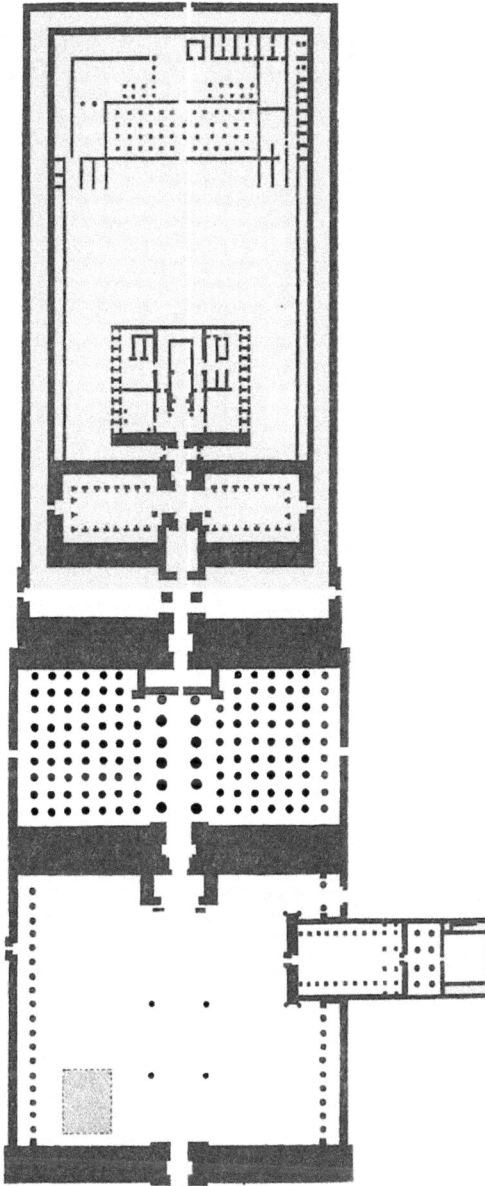

Ground-plan of Great Temple at Karnak.

whereof it forms a part, this temple has yet a length of
160 feet and a breadth of nearly eighty,[1] thus covering
an area of 12,500 square feet. It is ·ornamented
throughout with sculptures and inscriptions, which
have been finished with great care.

On the side of the court facing the great entrance
two vast pylons once more raised themselves aloft, to a
greater height, probably, than the entrance ones,[2] though
now they are mere heaps of ruins. In front of them projected two masses like the *antæ* of a portico, between
which a flight of seven steps[3] led up to a vestibule
or antechamber, fifty feet by twenty, from which a
broad and lofty passage conducted into the wonderful pillared hall which is the great glory of the Karnak
edifice. In length nearly 330 feet,[4] in width 170,[5] this
magnificent apartment was supported by 164 massive stone columns, divided into three groups—twelve
central ones, each sixty-six feet high and thirty-three in
circumference, forming the main avenue down its midst;
while on either side sixty-one, of slightly inferior dimensions,[6] supported the huge wings of the chamber, arranged in seven rows of seven each, and two rows of six.
The internal area of the chamber was above 56,000
square feet, and that of the entire building, with its walls

---

[1] *Description,* 'Antiquités,' vol. i.
ch. ix. p. 216.
[2] The bases of the second pylons
exceed in width those of the first by
about six feet (ibid., ' Planches,'
vol. iii. A. pl. 21). It is therefore
probable that they had a greater
weight to support.
[3] Ibid. 'Texte,' vol. i. ch. ix. p.
218.
[4] Mr. Fergusson says 340 (*Hist.
of Architecture,* vol. i. p. 118); but
I do not know on what authority.

Sir G. Wilkinson gives the length
as 329 feet (*Topography,* p. 174);
the French explorers at 100 mètres,
which is 328 feet (*Description,* vol.
i. ch. ix p. 220).
[5] So Wilkinson and Fergusson.
The *Description* (l.s.c.) makes the
width *exactly* half the length, or
164 feet.
[6] The side columns are said by
Wilkinson to be forty-one feet nine
inches high and twenty-seven feet
in circumference (*Topography,*l.s.c.).

INTERIOR OF THE GREAT HALL OF COLUMNS, KARNAK.

and pylons, more than 88,000 square feet, a larger area than that covered by the Dom of Cologne, the greatest of all the cathedrals of the North.[1]   The slight irregularity in the arrangement of the pillars above noticed was caused by the projection into the apartment at its further end of a sort of vestibule (enclosed by thick walls and flanked at the angles by square piers) which stood out from the pylons, wherewith the hall terminated towards the south-east.   These seem to have been of somewhat smaller dimensions than those which gave entrance to the hall from the courtyard;[2] but their height can scarcely have been less than a hundred or a hundred and twenty feet.

Passing through these inner propylæa, the visitor found himself in a long corridor open to the sky, and saw before him on either hand a tall tapering obelisk of rose-coloured granite covered with hieroglyphics,[3] and beyond them fresh propylæa—of inferior size to any of the others, and absolutely without ornament—which guarded the entrance into a cloistered court,[4] 240 feet long by sixty-two broad, running at right angles to the general axis of the edifice.   The roof of the cloister was supported by square piers with colossi in front, the number of such piers being thirty-six.   In the open court, on either hand of the doorway which gave entrance into it, stood an obelisk of the largest dimensions known to the Egyptians,[5] a huge monolith,

---

[1] See Fergusson, l.s.c.
[2] Their width was forty-eight feet, that of the western pylons fifty-two feet.
[3] See the *Description*, 'Antiquités,' vol. i. ch. ix. p. 228.   The total height of these obelisks is reckoned by the French savants at twenty-two mètres and three-quarters, or

seventy-four feet seven inches.
[4] Mr. Fergusson (*Hist. of Architecture*, vol. i. p. 118) calls this a 'hall,' but I do not suppose that he imagines the space between the piers, which was above thirty feet, to have been roofed in.
[5] *Description*, p. 229: 'Cet obélisque est le plus élevé des onze que

q 2

100 feet high and above eight feet square at the base, which is calculated to have contained 138 cubic mètres of granite, and to have weighed nearly 360 tons.[1]

Leaving these behind him, and ascending a second short flight of steps, the visitor passed through a portal opposite to that by which he had entered the cloistered court, and found himself in a small vestibule, about forty feet by twenty, pierced by a doorway in the middle of each of its four sides, and conducting to a building which seems properly regarded as the adytum or inmost sanctuary of the entire temple.[2] This was an edifice about 120 feet square, composed of a central cell of polished granite, fifty-two feet long by fourteen broad, surrounded by a covered corridor, and flanked on either side by a set of small apartments, accessible by twenty small doorways from the court in which the building stood. The style here was one of primitive simplicity. No obelisks, no colossi, no pillars even, if we except three introduced to sustain a failing roof,[3] broke the flat uniformity of the straight walls. Nothing was to be seen in the way of ornament excepting the painted sculptures and hieroglyphical legends wherewith the walls were everywhere adorned, and two short stelæ or prisms of pink granite, which stood on either side of the entrance to the granite cell. This cell itself was broken into three parts. Passing between the stelæ, one entered a porch or ante-room, sixteen feet broad and about six feet deep, from which a doorway about eight feet wide led into a first chamber, or ' Holy Place,' twenty feet long by fourteen. Hence, another doorway,

renferme encore l'Egypte, et il égale presque en hauteur les plus grands qui se trouvent à Rome.'

[1] *Description*, p. 230.

[2] Ibid. p. 234 : ' Tout semble in-diquer ici un lieu mystérieux et révéré, dans lequel les prêtres ou les ministres du roi avoient seuls la faculté d'entrer.'

[3] Ibid. p. 232.

of the same width as the first, conducted into the 'Holy of Holies,' an oblong square, twenty-seven feet by fourteen, richly decorated both on walls and ceiling with paintings. The general resemblance in plan of this sacred cell, with its inner and outer apartments, its porch, and its two

Stelæ in front of Granite Cell, Great Temple, Karnak.

stelæ before the porch, to the Temple of the Jews—similarly divided into three parts, and with 'Jachin and Boaz' in front[1]—must strike every student of architecture.

The entire square building here described, whereof the granite cell was the nucleus or central part, stood at one end of a vast open court[2] which surrounded it on three sides. The court itself was enclosed by high walls, behind which were long corridors, thought to have been divided formerly into numerous rooms for priests or guards,[3] and running the whole length of the court, from the south-eastern pylons of the cloister to an edifice at the further extremity of the court, which must now engage our attention. This was a pillared

[1] On the probability that 'Jachin and Boaz' stood in front of the Temple, and not under the porch, see the author's note on 1 Kings vii. 15–19, in the *Speaker's Commentary*.
[2] One hundred yards long by nearly eighty broad. (See the plan in the *Description,* 'Planches,' A. vol. iii. pl. 21; and compare above, p. 225.)
[3] *Description,* Texte, 'Antiquités,' vol. i. ch. ix. p. 237.

hall, 140 feet long by fifty-five feet wide,[1] containing two rows of massive square columns or piers, and two rows of round pillars with bell-shaped capitals reversed. The round pillars supported a lofty roof, with a clerestory admitting the light of day, while the square piers, rising to a less height, formed, comparatively speaking, low aisles on either side of the grand avenue. The axis of the hall was at right angles to the general axis of the temple. It was entered by three doors, two placed symmetrically in the centre of the north-western and south-eastern walls, the other, strangely and abnormally, at its southern corner. Around this hall were grouped a number of smaller chambers, some sup-

Section of smaller Pillared Hall, Great Temple, Karnak.

ported by pillars, some by square piers, while others were so narrow that they could be roofed over by blocks of stone resting only on the side walls. The number of these small apartments seems to have been not less than forty.[2]

It is time now to turn from the details of this vast edifice, or rather mass of edifices, to its broad features and general dimensions. It is in shape a rectangular oblong, nearly four times as long as it is wide, extending from N.W. to S.E. a distance of 1,200 feet, and in the opposite direction a distance of about 340 feet.[3] One

[1] Fergusson, Hist. of Architecture, vol. i. p. 119. The Description makes the length 143 feet.

[2] See the plan, supra, p. 225.
[3] Mr. Fergusson says ‘360 feet’ (l.s.c.), but this is more than the

projection only breaks the uniformity of the oblong, that of the dependent sanctuary, which interrupts the right-hand corridor of the entrance court. The entire area, including that of this dependent sanctuary, is about 396,000 square feet, or more than half as much again as that covered by St. Peter's at Rome.[1] The structure comprised two extensive courts—one colonnaded, the other plain ; an oblong cloister, supported on piers ornamented with colossi ; four splendid obelisks ; two sanctuaries, one central, one subordinate ; and two vast pillared halls, one of them exceeding in dimensions any other in Egypt, and covering with its walls and pylons more space than that occupied by the cathedral of Cologne. The French engineers observe that the cathedral of Notre Dame would have stood entirely within it ;[2] and this is perfectly true so far as area is concerned, though not, of course, in respect of elevation. The greatest height of the Karnak pylons was not more than about 140 feet, and the height from the floor to the roof of the Great Hall did not exceed seventy-six feet. Still, the dimensions of the hall, the mass of material which it contained, and the massive character of its construction, are truly wonderful and admirable ; and it is well said, that ' when we consider that this is only a part of a great whole, we may fairly assert that the entire structure is among the largest, as it undoubtedly is one of the most beautiful, buildings in the world.'[3] Moreover, it is to be remembered, that besides the buildings here described ' there are

extreme width of the propylæa in front, which does not exceed 345 feet.   In rear, the length of the wall which skirted the enclosure was not more than 330 feet.

[1] By exaggerating the width Mr. Fergusson is enabled to say, that the entire edifice ' occupies *nearly twice* the area of St. Peter's at Rome.' But this is an over-estimate.

[2] *Description,* ' Antiquités,' vol. i. ch. ix. p. 220.

[3] Fergusson, *Hist. of Architecture,* vol. i. p. 119.

other temples to the north, to the east, and, more
especially, to the south ; and pylons connecting these,
and avenues of sphinxes extending for miles, and
enclosing walls and tanks and embankments,' so that
the conclusion seems to be just, that the whole constitutes ' such a group as no other city ever possessed
either before or since,' and that ' St. Peter's with its
colonnades and the Vatican, make up a mass insignificant in extent . . . compared with this glory of Thebes
with its surrounding temples.' [1]

With respect to the æsthetic merit of the building
different estimates may be formed.   There are some
to whom Egyptian architecture is altogether distasteful,
and it must be granted to have faults which place it
considerably below the best and greatest styles ; but
few can visit the remains themselves and gaze upon
the ' long vista of courts and gateways and halls and
colonnades,' with ' here and there an obelisk shooting
up out of the ruins and interrupting the opening view
of the forest of columns,' [2] without being moved to
wonder and admiration at the sight.   The multiplicity
and variety of the parts, the grandeur of all, the beauty
of some, the air of strangeness and of remote antiquity
which hangs over the scene, the thousand associations—historical and other—which it calls up, evoke
an interest and a delight which overpower criticism,
and dispose the spectator to exclaim that never has he
beheld anything so glorious.   More especially is admiration excited by the ruins of the Great Hall.   ' No
language,' says a writer not given to strong displays
of feeling, ' no language can convey an idea of its
beauty, and no artist has yet been able to reproduce

---

[1] Fergusson, *Hist. of Architecture*,
vol. i. p. 119.

[2] Stanley, *Sinai and Palestine*,
' Introduction,' p. xxxviii.

its form so as to convey to those who have not seen it
an idea of its grandeur. The mass of its central piers,
illumined by a flood of light from the clerestory, and
the smaller pillars of the wings gradually fading into
obscurity, are so arranged and lighted as to convey an
idea of infinite space : at the same time the beauty and
massiveness of the forms, and the brilliancy of their ·
coloured decorations, all combine to stamp this as the
greatest of man's architectural works, but such a one
as it would be impossible to reproduce, except in such
a climate, and in that individual style, in which and for
which it was erected.' [1]

Among the ornaments of the Great Temple of
Karnak the obelisk has been mentioned. It is a creation purely Egyptian, which has scarcely ever elsewhere
been even imitated with success.[2] Such specimens as
exist—in Rome, Paris, Constantinople, London—are
the spoil which Egypt has yielded to her conquerors or
the tribute which she has paid to her protectors, not
the production of the countries which they adorn. It
is very remarkable that the Romans, fond as they
were of the gigantic in architecture, and special
admirers as they showed themselves to be of the
obelisk, never themselves produced one. Though in
possession for above six centuries of the granite quarries
of Syêné, whence the Egyptians obtained the greater
number of their huge monoliths, they preferred lower-
ing and carrying off the creations of Egyptian art to
exerting their own skill and genius in the production
of rival monuments. Rome boasted in the time of her

[1] Fergusson, vol. i. pp. 119-20.
[2] The monuments in the shape of
obelisks, which, like the one in
Kensington Gardens, are built up of
a number of moderately sized stones,
transgress against the fundamental
law of the obelisk's being, which is
to be monolithic. They offend
against good taste like sham carv-
ings on a ceiling, or wood painted to
imitate marble.

full splendour twelve obelisks, but every one of them had been transported from Egypt to Italy.[1] Architects commonly divide the obelisk into three parts,[2] the base, the shaft or obelisk proper, and the pyramidion which crowns the summit ; but, materially, the parts are two only, since the pyramidion is ordinarily in one piece with the shaft which it terminates. The base is always separate, and may consist of a single block or of two placed stepwise, which is the arrangement in the case of the obelisk before the church of St. John Lateran at Rome. This is the grandest monument of the kind that exists anywhere, or is known to have existed. Exclusively of the base, it has a height of 105 feet,[3] with a width diminishing from nine feet six inches to eight feet seven inches.[4] It is estimated to have contained 4,945 cubic feet (French), and to have weighed above 450 tons.[5] An ordinary height for an obelisk was from fifty to seventy feet,[6] and an ordinary weight from 200 to 300 tons.[7]

---

[1] The nearest approach to a Roman obelisk is that of the Piazza Navona, which appears to have been erected in Egypt to the honour of Domitian by his flatterers in that country. It belongs thus to Roman times, but was the production of Egyptian workmen.

[2] Fergusson, *Hist. of Architecture*, vol. i. p. 129 ; Smith, *Dict. of Greek and Roman Antiquities*, p. 816.

[3] *Description*, ' Antiquités,' vol. i. p. 229, note ; Fergusson, l.s.c.

[4] *Description*, l.s.c.

[5] Ibid.

[6] According to the French savants, the obelisks nearest in height to that of St. John Lateran are the *great* obelisks of Karnak, which they imagined to have measured 29·83 mètres, or ninety-seven feet eight inches, but which are now said to

have a height of only ninety-three feet (Stuart Poole in the *Encyclopædia Britannica, ad voc.* EGYPT, p. 508 ; Fergusson, *Hist. of Architecture*, vol. i. p. 129). Next to these comes the one before St. Peter's, which measures 25·135 mètres, or eighty-two feet four inches. Almost of the same size are the *great* obelisk of Luxor and its fellow, now the main ornament of the Place de la Concorde at Paris, which measure twenty-five mètres, or almost exactly eighty-two feet. The obelisk near the Porta del Popolo at Rome has a height of seventy-eight feet, that at Heliopolis of sixty-six, and that recently brought to England of sixty-seven feet.

[7] The obelisk in front of St. Peter's is estimated to weigh 694,000 lbs. (French), or 335 tons ;

Obelisks as erected by the Egyptians commonly stood in pairs. Their position was in front of a temple, on either side of its gateway. Some have conjectured that they represented solar rays,[1] and were specially dedicated to the sun ;[2] but both these views have been combated, and must be regarded as uncertain. Architecturally they served the purpose of the Roman column, the Gothic spire, and the Oriental minaret ; they broke the too frequent horizontal lines with their quasi-vertical ones, and carried the eye upwards from the flat earth to the dome of heaven. They were especially valuable in Egyptian architecture from the comparative lightness and slimness of their forms, where all otherwise was over-massive and heavy.[3] The proportions of the obelisk differed within certain limits ; but the most satisfactory had an elevation about eleven times their diameter at the base.[4]

Before quitting the subject of temples, it seems desirable to note that the Egyptian buildings to which this term is commonly applied are of two classes. Some, and especially the more magnificent, such as that at Karnak (above described), and again that at Luxor, seem to deserve the name which has been given them,[5]

---

that in the Place de la Concorde and its fellow at Luxor, 525,236 lbs. (French), or 254 tons ; the smaller one of those still standing at Luxor, 352,767 lbs. (French), or 170 tons. (See the *Description*, 'Antiquités,' vol. i. pp. 188, 229, and 230.)

[1] See Zoega, *De Obeliscis*; and compare Plin. *H. N.* xxxvi. 8, § 14.

[2] Plin. l.s.c.

[3] I cannot agree with those who see in obelisks nothing but 'grotesque and unsightly monuments of Eastern superstition' (Merivale, *Roman Empire*, vol. iv. p. 73).

[4] Mr. Fergusson says the *average* proportion is ten diameters (*Hist. of Architecture*, vol. i. p. 129). But in the best specimens, as in that of the Lateran obelisk, the height is so exactly eleven diameters that we must conclude that proportion to have been intended. (The French engineers give the diameter as 2·923 mètres, the height as 32·159. Now, 2·923 × 11 = 32·153.)

[5] The name was, I believe, first given by Sir Gardner Wilkinson (*Topography of Thebes*, pp. 28, 31, and 'Table of Contents,' p. xxiii. ;

of ' Palace Temples,' being places which were at once
the residences of the kings and structures in which the
people assembled for worship. Others are entirely
free from this double character. The southern temple
at Karnak is ' strictly a temple, without anything about
it that could justify the supposition of its being a
palace.'[1] It is a perfectly regular building, consisting of
two pylons, approached through an avenue of sphinxes,
of a hypæthral court, surrounded on three sides by a
double colonnade, of a pillared hall lighted from the roof
in the usual way, a cell surrounded by a corridor or
passage, and a small hall beyond supported by four
columns.[2] This temple is pronounced to have considerable 'intrinsic beauty,'[3] and is interesting as having
furnished a model which continued to be followed in
Greek and Roman times.

Ground-plan of Southern Temple, Karnak.

Another description of Egyptian temple, intended
for religious purposes only, is that which is known
under the title of *mammeisi*, an edifice dedicated to
the Mother of the Gods. Temples of this kind are
cells, containing either one or two chambers, and surrounded by a colonnade in front, flank, and rear. They

---

Ancient Egyptians, vol. i. p. 58). It
has been adopted by Fergusson
(*Hist. of Architecture*, vol. i. p. 118)
and others.
[1] Fergusson, vol. i. p. 123.

[2] See the plan in the *Description*,
'Planches,' vol. iii. A. pl. 54, which
is reproduced above.
[3] Fergusson, l.s.c.

are of oblong form, and are sometimes approached by a flight of steps in front, which conducts to the door-way.[1] The size is always small; and they would be unimportant were it not for the fact that they appear to have been selected by the Greeks as the models after which they should construct their own religious

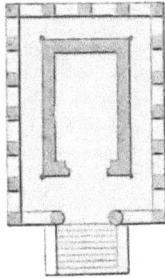

Mammeisi, or Temple of the 'Mother of the Gods.'

edifices, which were in most instances peristylar, and which changed but little from the Egyptian type be-yond rounding the square piers and surmounting the flat architrave with a pediment.

It will have been seen that Egyptian architecture depended for its effect, first, upon its size and massive-

---

[1] Fergusson, p. 126.

ness ; secondly, on the beauty of certain forms, which were constantly repeated, as the pillar, the caryatide pier, and the obelisk ; thirdly and lastly, on the richness and brilliancy of its sculptured and coloured ornamentation.   The massiveness appears most remarkably in the pyramids, and in the pylons or great flanking towers at the entrances of palaces and temples ; [1] but it is not shown only in these structures—it pervades the entire style, and meets us everywhere, in pillars, in lintels, in colossi, in monolithic chambers, in roofs, in walls, in obelisks.   However great the diameter of a column, it has usually in each of its layers no more than four stones, [2] while all the layers are of enormous thickness.   Lintels of doorways sometimes exceed forty feet in length ; [3] colossi weigh above 800 tons ; [4] monolithic chambers not much less ; [5] roofing stones have a length of thirty feet, and a weight of above sixty tons ; [6] obelisks, as we have seen, [7] range from 170 to 450 tons.   In mere ordinary walls the stones are usually of vast size, and the thickness of such walls is

[1] These were in every case solid structures, pierced (at the utmost) by a single narrow staircase, which led to the top (*Description*, ' Antiquités,' vol. i. ch. ix. p. 209).
[2] Ibid. p. 221.   Wilkinson says that the usual construction is by layers of *two* blocks each (*Architecture*, p. 44).
[3] Wilkinson, *Topography of Thebes*, p. 174, note ; *Ancient Egyptians*, vol. iii. p. 332.
[4] That of Rameses II. at the Rameseum weighed, according to Wilkinson (*Topography*, p. 12), 887 tons 5 cwt. and a half.   Those of Amenophis III., in the plain of Qurnah, which are said to contain 11,500 cubic feet (Wilkinson, *Ancient Egyptians*, vol. iii. p. 329), must be nearly as heavy.

[5] See Burton's *Excerpta*, pl. 41 ; and compare Wilkinson in the author's *Herodotus*, vol. ii. p. 263, note [3].   One such apartment is said to have weighed as much as 5,000 tons (!) ; but this estimate depends on the accuracy of Herodotus in the measurements which he gives of the monolithic chamber at Buto (ii.155), and on a calculation founded thereon by Wilkinson (*A. E.* vol. iii. p. 331).   It is scarcely possible that the chamber, if of the size stated, was really formed of a single block.
[6] *Description*, ' Antiquités,' vol. i. ch. ix. p. 221.   Wilkinson says, a length of ' above twenty-four feet ' (*Architecture of Ancient Egypt*, p. 18, note).
[7] Supra, p. 234 and note [7].

surprising. It is not as in Assyria and Babylonia, where the material used was crude brick, and the wall which had to sustain a serious weight was necessarily of great breadth ; the Egyptians used the best possible materials—sandstone, close-grained limestone, or gra- nite—yet still made their walls almost as broad as the Mesopotamians themselves. This could only be from a pure love of massiveness.

The column is undoubtedly among the most effec- tive of architectural forms. In Egypt its special cha- racteristic is its solidity, or the very large proportion borne by the diameter to the height. Whereas in the perfected architecture of the Greeks, the column where it is thickest must have a height at least equalling six diameters,[1] in Egypt the height rarely much exceeds four diameters, and is[2] sometimes not above three. In many cases it about equals the extreme circum- ference of the pillar. This extreme circumference is not always at the base. Columns are found which swell gradually as they ascend, and do not attain their full width till they have reached a fourth or fifth of their height. They then contract gently, and are narrowest just below the capital, where they commonly present the appearance of being bound round by cords. Other columns are, like the Greek, largest at the base, and taper gradually from bottom to top ; but in no case have they the Greek swell or *entasis*.

The shafts of Egyptian columns are sometimes plain, but more commonly have an ornamentation.

---

[1] This was the proportion ulti- mately fixed for the Doric order, in which the column was the thickest. Antique specimens are found which approach the proportions usual in Egypt. (See Smith's *Dict. of Greek and Roman Antiquities*, p. 325.)

[2] See Wilkinson's *Architecture of Ancient Egypt*, pp. 36, 43, &c.

This is effected by sculpture or painting, or both. Some, as already noticed,[1] are merely fluted like the Greek; others have a perfectly smooth surface, but are adorned with painting.[2] In general, however, the surface is more or less sculptured, and at the same time is painted—often with much taste and delicacy. For the most part vegetable forms have been imitated.

1.   2.   3.   4.
Egyptian Columns.

The column bulges out from its base like a water-plant, and is then sculptured so as to resemble a number of stalks tied together at the top or at intervals, and finally swelling above the last compression into a calix.[3] Or it has the leaves and flowers of water-plants delicately traced upon it and coloured naturally.[4] Or, finally, it retains the mere general form derived from pillars thus moulded, and substitutes

---

[1] See above, p. 213.
[2] Wilkinson, *Architecture*, p. 7.
[3] See the woodcut above, figs. 2

and 4.
[4] *Description*, 'Planches,' vol. i.
A. pls. 18, 88, &c.

hieroglyphics and human or divine figures for the simple decoration of earlier times.[1] Capitals are of four principal forms. One, which has been called the ' lotus blossom ' or ' bell ' capital,[2] begins with a slight swell above the top of the shaft—is then nearly cylindrical for a while ; after which it curves outwards very considerably, and terminates in a lip, which is rounded

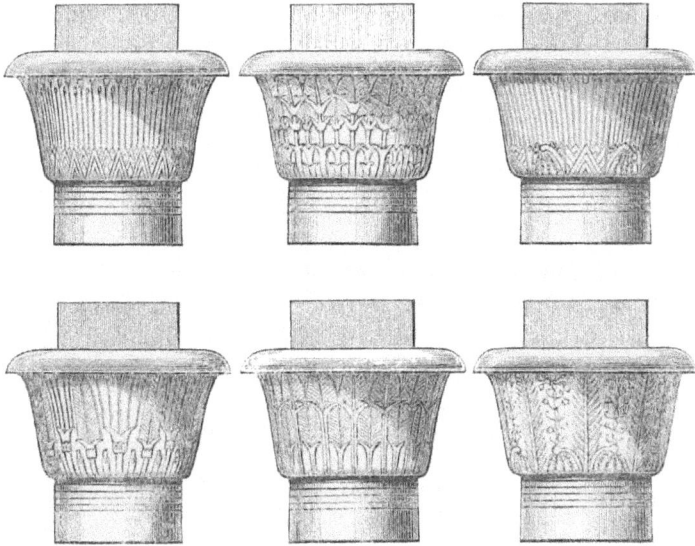

Egyptian Bell-Capitals.

off into a flat surface. Water-plants of various kinds are represented on these ' bell-capitals,' which are among the most beautiful of the architectural forms invented by the Egyptians. Another kind of capital is that which is thought to imitate a lotus bud, or a group of such buds, with the upper portion removed.[3]

<hr>

[1] See the woodcut on the preceding page, fig. 1.

[2] *Description*, 'Antiquités,' vol. i. ch. ix. p.35: 'Des chapiteaux à campanes '—p. 132 : 'Ce chapiteau a la

forme d'une fleur de lotus épanouie.'

[3] 'Chapiteaux à boutons de lotus tronqués ' (ibid. p. 127); the 'bud-capital' of Wilkinson (*Architecture of Ancient Egypt*, p. 33).

It swells out considerably from the top of the shaft, after which it contracts, and is terminated abruptly by a plain square stone, placed on it to receive the architrave. Capitals of this type are frequent at Thebes, but rare elsewhere.[1] The principal varieties are the following :—

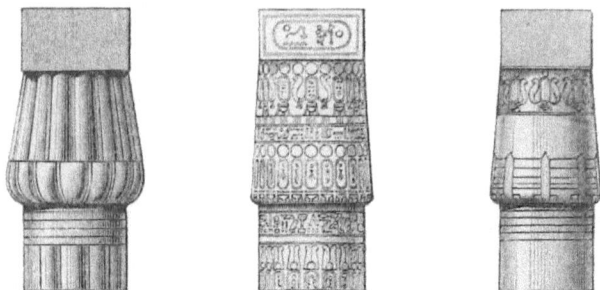

Egyptian Lotus-Capitals.

A third form, which is very unusual, consists of the

bell-capital *reversed*, a freak of the architect which is said not to add either to the beauty or the strength of the building.[2] There is also a compound capital which is decidedly unpleasing,[3] consisting of four human heads placed at the summit of the ordinary bell-capital, between it and the architrave.

The proportion of the capital to the shaft was considerably beyond that approved by the Greeks,[4] though less than the proportion which prevailed in

[1] ' Il est à remarquer que cet *ordre* est proprement celui de Thèbes ; partout il y est employé, et on ne le retrouve que rarement ailleurs ' (*Description*, p. 193).

[2] Fergusson, *Hist. of Architecture*, vol. i. p. 119 ; *Description*, ' Antiquités,' vol. i. ch. ix. p. 165 ; Wil-

kinson, *Topography of Thebes*, pp. 175–6.

[3] Fergusson, p. 123. This was commoner in the later than in the earlier times. Numerous specimens exist in Upper Egypt, as at Koum Ombou, at Esné, and elsewhere.

[4] The Doric capital was from

Judæa[1] and in Persia.[2] Instances are found in which the height of the capital is as much as one-third of the shaft,[3] though it is more commonly one-fourth, and some-times even as little as one-fifth.[4] The appearance of 'heaviness' produced by the thickness of the pillars is increased by the defect here noticed, which makes each column seem to be overloaded at the top and to be sinking under its own weight.

Another peculiarity in the Egyptian use of columns is the narrowness of the intercolumniation. Main avenues of pillars are, indeed, sometimes of a fair width, extending to nearly two diameters in some cases.[5] But the spaces left between the pillars at the sides, instead of being, as in Grecian art, the same or nearly the same, frequently do not equal a single diameter,[6] and are scarcely ever as much as a diameter and a half. Thus the columns are unduly crowded together, and in the great pillared halls the forest of stems stands so thick that, except in front and on either flank, the view is everywhere interrupted, and the immensity of the space enclosed cannot be seen from any point. The intention, seemingly, is to make sure that the roof

one-eighth to one-twelfth the height of the pillar, the Ionic from one-ninth to one-eleventh, the Corinthian between one-seventh and one-eighth (*Encyclop. Brit. ad voc.* Architecture, pp. 463–6).

[1] See 1 Kings vii. 15–19, which shows that in the pillars Jachin and Boaz, the proportion of the capital to the shaft of the column was as one to two !

[2] *Ancient Monarchies*, vol. iii. p. 306.

[3] For an example see *Encyclop. Brit.* vol. iii. pl. li. fig. 7.

[4] See the woodcut on p. 240, figs. 2 and 3.

[5] In the great pillared hall at Karnak the width of the central avenue is eighteen feet, the diameter of the columns at their base being eleven feet eight inches, which gives an intercolumniation of not much more than a diameter and a half; but in the temple of Rameses II., which projects into the great court at Karnak, and again in the larger of the two temples towards the south, the distance of two diameters is reached. See the *Description*, 'Planches,' A. pls. 21 and 55, fig. 3.

[6] *Description*, 'Antiquités,' vol. i. ch. ix. p. 212.

shall have an ample support, and to this desire is sacrificed every other consideration.

The caryatide piers of the Egyptians were even
more massive than their columns.   Square in plan,
slightly pyramidical in outline, narrowing (that is to
say) as they rose, and spaced at short distances one from
another, with a heavy cornice above them, they had
no ornament to take off from their solid strength beyond a few hieroglyphics and the figure from which
they take their name.   This was a colossus, generally
from twenty-five to thirty-five feet high,[1] which was
placed directly before the pier on a pedestal of one or
two steps.   Solemn and
stately stand the figures,
clothed, apparently, in
tight-fitting vests,[2] with
mitres upon their heads,
and arms crossed upon
their breasts, each exactly
like all the others, with expressionless countenances,
emblems of complete re-
pose. Unlike the similarly
named statues of the
Greeks, they do not afflict
the beholder with the spectacle of human forms op-
pressed by the burden of a crushing weight whereof
they can never be rid.   The caryatides of Egypt bear
no burden at all.   They stand *in front* of the piers,
entirely distinct from them, though touching them, and
for the most part do not even quite reach to the archi-

Caryatide Figures.

---

[1] *Description,* 'Antiquités,' vol. i.
ch. ix. pp. 35, 127, &c.

[2] 'Elles sont vêtues d'une tunique
longue et étroite.' (Ibid. p. 127.)

trave which the piers support.[1] They are not slaves
condemned to an ignominious punishment,[2] but emblems of a divine presence, impressing the spectator
with a sense that the place wherein they stand is holy
ground.

Obelisks, as already observed,[3] were among the
lightest of the forms used by the Egyptians. Architecturally they must have been intended to relieve the
eye, wearied by the too great massiveness of pillars,
piers, and pylons, with the contrast of a slim delicate
spire, rising gracefully among them and cutting the
horizontal lines at right angles. They were generally
placed at the entrances to temples, one on either
side of the main doorway; but sometimes they are
found in the interior of buildings. The great Palace-
Temple at Karnak was adorned, as we have seen, with
four; but in general a temple had no more than two,
and most temples were altogether without them. The
conventional necessity of setting them up in pairs[4]
gave rise to occasional awkwardness. When obelisks
of the largest size were ordered, it was difficult to find,
in the quarries two masses of granite ninety or a hundred feet long without break or flaw in them. Flaws
might even be discovered when the work had proceeded
to a certain point, and an obelisk intended to have
reached a certain length might in consequence have to
be shortened. The result was that in some instances the
pair of obelisks supplied were not of equal height; and

---

[1] An exception appears in a set
of caryatides belonging to the temple of Rameses II. at Karnak, where
the top of the mitre rises a little
above the line of the architrave.
(See *Description*, 'Planches,' vol.
iii. pls. 25 and 30, fig. 1.)

[2] As the Greek caryatides were
said to be (Vitruv. i. 1, § 5; Plin.
H. N. xxxvi. 45).

[3] See above, p. 235.

[4] Herod. ii. 111. Compare Plin.
H. N. xxxvi. 8, § 14, where *four*
are ascribed to Sesothes, *two* to
Rhamsesis (Rameses), *two* to Mes-
phres, &c.

this want of symmetry had to be met by artifice. The
shorter obelisk was given a higher pedestal than the
taller one, and was sometimes even advanced a little
towards the spectator that it might appear as large as
the other.[1] Obelisks seem most usually to have been
votive offerings set up by monarchs before temples,
partly to propitiate the gods, but mainly for their own
glory. The inscriptions upon them set forth in every
case the greatness and the victories of their erector.

It is difficult for one who has not visited Egypt to
pronounce positively on the merit or demerit of the
Egyptian coloured decoration. If we could feel sure
that the effect produced was really such as is represented by the French artists who made the drawings
for the ' Description,' we should have to assign it high
praise, as at once tasteful, rich, and harmonious. Nothing in decorative colour can well be more admirable
than the representation given in that magnificent work
of the interior of a temple at Philœ, restored to what
is supposed to have been its ancient condition.[2] The
design is excellent; the tints are pleasing; and the
arrangement by which thin hnes of white separate between colours that would otherwise offer too strong a
contrast, leaves nothing to be desired. The pale grey of
the stucco also, predominating throughout, subdues the
whole, and prevents any appearance of glare or gaudi-
ness. But it is difficult to decide how much this admirable drawing owes to the accurate observation of facts,

[1] See the remarks of the French engineers on the two obelisks of Luxor (*Description,* 'Antiquités,' vol. i. ch. ix. pp. 188–9).
[2] See the plates, vol. i. A. pl. 18. The temple at Philæ is a late construction, and the character of its ornamentation would scarcely be a sure indication of the character of decorative árt under the Pharaohs. Still, it is a thoroughly Egyptian building, and, considering how disinclined the Egyptians were to change of any kind, might not improbably repeat more ancient work.

how much it is indebted for its beauties to the imagination and the good taste of the designers. Egyptian colouring in its primitive aspect is to be seen only in the rock-tombs, where, we are told, the paintings have all the freshness of works executed but yesterday.[1] Much admiration is expressed for these paintings by many who have visited the tombs and described them;[2] but nothing can well be more disappointing than to turn from the glowing descriptions that have been given by these writers to the representations made by artists in the magnificently illustrated works of Rosellini and Lepsius, on which no expense has been spared. Of crude, coarse, and inharmonious colouring we behold in these works abundant specimens; of what is really harmonious and artistic in colour we observe scarcely anything. A few vases and some of the patterns upon ceilings are fairly good;[3] but these are exceptions, and in general the colouring is about as bad as colouring can be. A coarse and violent red, a dull blue, and a staring yellow predominate; white, the great chastener and subduer of colour, is introduced but scantily. Strong tints prevail: half tones are scarcely to be seen. Shading is of course unknown: and the whole style cannot but be pronounced crude, harsh, and unpleasing. Still, it is to be borne in mind that these illustrated works are not the originals, and that what they present to us are fragments detached from their surroundings; and it would evidently be unsafe to conclude upon such data that the general effect

---

[1] Belzoni, Researches, pp. 231, 234, &c.; Rosellini, Monumenti Civili, vol. i. pp. 54, 106, &c.; Sharpe, History of Egypt, vol. i. p. 73.
[2] Belzoni, p. 234; Stanley, Sinai and Palestine, 'Introduction,' pp.
xxxix–xl.; Fergusson, Hist. of Architecture, vol. i. p. 129.
[3] See Rosellini, Monumenti Civili, Plates, vol. ii. pl. 53, figs. 16 and 17; pl. 59, figs. 1 and 2; pl. 71, fig. 11, &c.

actually produced upon the beholder by an Egyptian temple, seen as a whole, was not heightened and improved by the painted decoration,[1] which was certainly rich and brilliant, though we may suspect that it wanted delicacy and would have seemed to moderns over-glaring.

Before this chapter is brought to a close a few words must be said, first, with regard to the domestic architecture of the Egyptians, and, secondly, concerning some peculiarities of their construction.

The specimens which exist of the domestic architecture are few and fragmentary. Excluding the great buildings above described, which seem to have been at once temples and royal residences, there is but one example remaining of a mere dwelling-house, and that example is believed to be at the present time incomplete.[2]   It stands in the near vicinity of the temple at Medinet-Abou, which has already engaged our attention,[3] and is commonly called a 'pavilion,'[4] having been built for himself as a sort of private residence by one of the kings.[5]   It consists at present of a court in the form of a cross, surrounded on three sides by buildings three storeys high, which attain an elevation of thirty-seven feet above the actual ·level of the soil, and must have had originally an elevation of above

---

[1] Wilkinson says: 'No one who understands the harmony of colours will fail to admit that they (i.e. the Egyptians) perfectly understood their distribution and proper combinations, and that an Egyptian temple was greatly improved by the addition of painted sculptures.' (*Ancient Egyptians*, vol. iii. p. 298.)

[2] So Fergusson, *Hist. of Architecture*, vol. i. p. 131. The point admits of a doubt.

[3] See above, pp. 217–20.

[4] The term was first used by the French savants in the *Description* ('Antiquités,' vol. i. ch. ix. pp. 30–33). It has been adopted from them by Sir G. Wilkinson (*Ancient Egyptians*, vol. ii. p. 116; vol. v. p. 345) and Mr. Fergusson (*Hist. of Architecture*, vol. i. p. 130).

[5] Rameses III., of the twentieth dynasty.

fifty feet.[1] The buildings consist of three rectangular blocks, with three rooms in each, one above the other, and two narrow erections enclosing passages that con-

Ground-plan and View of the Pavilion of Rameses III.

nect the three sets of rooms together. All the rooms are small, the largest not exceeding seventeen feet by

[1] These measures are taken from the *Description*, 'Planches,' vol. ii. A. pl. 16.

thirteen, and the smallest being about nineteen feet by nine. All were lighted by windows except the ground-floor room of the main block at the end of the court, which obtained light only from its doorways. The walls are of great strength and solidity; the roof and the ceilings of the chambers, except perhaps in one instance, were of stone. A wooden ceiling is thought to have separated the ground-floor room of the main block from the apartment above it;[1] but this has been destroyed, and the two rooms form now only one. The buildings are ornamented, both externally and internally, with hieroglyphics and sculptures of the usual type;[2] but the ornamentation is on the whole somewhat scanty. The entire edifice was of the same height, and was crowned with a sort of battlement, of which the annexed is a representation. Its plan was remarkably varied in outline, and the nume-

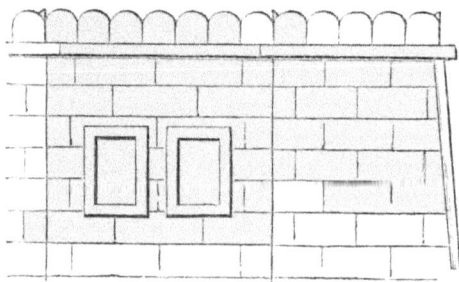

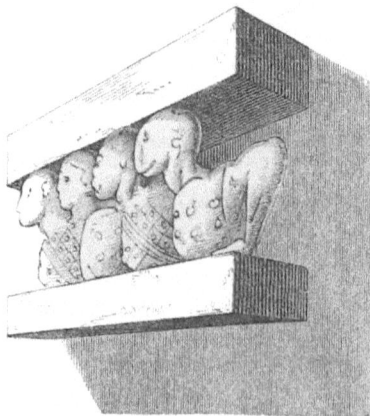

[1] *Description,* 'Antiquités,' vol. i. ch. ix. p. 32.

[2] One very peculiar ornamentation requires special notice. The sills of several blank windows are supported by a row of heads, apparently those of captives, which seem crushed beneath the weight that presses on them. (See the *Description,* 'Planches,' vol. ii. A. pl. 17, fig. 7; and compare Wilkinson, *Ancient Egyptians,* vol. v. pp. 345–6, and *Architecture,* p. 64.) This ornament is nowhere else repeated.

rous projections and recesses must have rendered the play of light and shade upon the building curious and striking.

In the pictorial representations which ornament the rock-tombs we sometimes meet with buildings which appear to be private residences. In one case [1] we have what seems to represent the exterior façade of a house, on the side on which it was ordinarily approached. The building divides itself into three portions, a centre

An Egyptian Dwelling-house, viewed in Front.

and two wings. The central part, which is higher than the rest, is crowned by a steep roof,[2] shaped like a truncated pyramid; below this is a projecting cornice, and below the cornice a plain wall, broken only by a door at the right-hand corner. Adjoining the door is

---

[1] See the woodcut, and compare Rosellini, *Monumenti Civili*, vol. ii. pp. 381-2, with the representation given in vol. ii. of the Plates (pl. 68, fig. 8).

[2] Rosellini argues that this represents a lantern, which acted at once as a skylight and a ventilator. But there is nothing to show this.

the right wing, which consists of two storeys—a basement one, ornamented with four pillars unequally
spaced, and a first floor, likewise with four pillars,
which are equally spaced, and thus not directly superimposed over those below them. Between the pillars
are represented stands with vases and eatables, from
which we gather that the pillars are detached from the
mansions, and form in the one case a colonnade, in the
other a gallery. The character of the left wing is

An Egyptian Dwelling-house, viewed from Internal Court.

similar, but it does not extend so far as the other, and
is ornamented with only four pillars, two to each
storey. The wings have an architrave above the
pillars, and are then crowned with a sort of double
cornice. The character of the pillars is thoroughly
Egyptian.

Another tomb exhibits to us the internal court-yard
of a three-storeyed mansion of much elegance, appa-

rently decorated for a festival.[1] A central doorway, supported on either side by thin pillars representing a lotus plant, gives entrance to a staircase, which rises directly from it, and conducts probably to the upper apartments.[2] The staircase seems to be carpeted and to have a mat at the foot of the first step. To the left we see on the ground-floor a doorway and three small windows protected by perpendicular bars. Above this rises a storey, built, seemingly, of wood or crude brick, and broken by two windows with the blinds[3] drawn down nearly to the bottom. At the top is an open gallery, supported on four pillars, which sustain a painted cornice. On the right of the main entrance the ground-floor is perfectly plain, except that it is pierced about its centre by a low doorway.[4] Above it the first floor presents to the eye nothing but a drapery or awning, which hangs in front of it and leaves its character a mystery. The second floor exhibits pillars at either end, and between them what is perhaps another awning, though this is not quite clear. Above this there is a long range of very short pillars, which seem to support an upper gallery, constituting on this side a sort of fourth storey,[5] though one too low to have been inhabited. Finally, the entire house is crowned by a cornice painted in stripes of red, blue, and white, and resting at either end on a lotus pillar of the same character with those at the main entrance.

[1] See Rosellini, *Mon. Civ.* vol. ii. ·pp. 382–6, and compare the illustration in his Plates, vol. ii. pl. 68, fig. 2, from which the woodcut in the text is taken.

[2] Fergusson, *Hist. of Architecture*, vol. i. p. 132.

[3] These 'blinds,' as I have called them, may possibly be shutters; but

they seem not quite to reach the bottom of the window.

[4] The artist has accidentally omitted this.

[5] Diodorus says that the Theban houses had occasionally four and even five storeys (i. 45). The tomb containing this representation is close to Thebes.

A third representation of an Egyptian house is given by Rosellini in his great work,[1] which has clearly four storeys, but it is drawn in so conventional a manner that but little can be concluded from it as to the actual Egyptian arrangements. The doors by which the house was entered being, as it would seem, at the side, are introduced *sideways* into the front wall above and below one of the windows. The three upper storeys are represented *in section*, and exhibit the contents of the apartments. No staircase by which they could be reached is visible, and their inhabitants must apparently have flown up into them. The cornice of the house, which is painted in the usual way, supports three large masses of the papyrus plant.

An Egyptian House, partly in section.

On the whole, we may perhaps conclude, with Mr. Fergusson,[2] that though the Egyptian houses 'exhibited nothing of the solidity and monumental character which distinguished their temples and palaces, they seem in their own way to have been scarcely less beautiful. They were, of course, on a smaller scale, and built of more perishable materials;[3] but they appear to have

[1] See the Plates, vol. ii. pl. 69; and compare the description given in the text (vol. ii. pp. 386–8).

[2] *History of Architecture*, vol. i. p. 131.

[3] Rosellini conceives the ordinary material to have been crude brick. (*Mon. Civ.* vol. ii. p. 380. Compare Wilkinson, *Topography*, p. 199.)

been as carefully finished and decorated with equal taste to that displayed in the greater works.' The peculiarities of Egyptian construction, whereto, in conclusion, it is desired to draw attention, are three in number, viz. : 1. Their non-employment of the arch as a constructive expedient and preference of perpendicular supports and horizontal imposts; 2. Their 'symmetrophobia,' or dislike of exactness and regularity either in the general arrangements or in the details of their buildings; and 3. Their skilful use of certain contrivances for increasing the apparent size, especially the apparent length, of their more important and more imposing edifices.   This last has been entirely left out of sight by recent writers on Egyptian architecture,[1] though it is a peculiarity well worthy of study and imitation.

That the Egyptians were acquainted with the principle of the arch, and made occasional use of it in their minor edifices, is now generally admitted.[2]   Not only do coved roofs appear in some of the rock-tombs,[3] which might lead one to suspect such an acquaintance, but actual arches have been found, both in brick and stone, in connection with hieroglyphical legends and in purely Egyptian buildings.   The latest historian of architecture goes so far as to maintain [4] that the Egyptians had all the knowledge needed for the employment of the arch to any extent in their constructions, and that they purposely abstained from its use from a dis-

---

[1] As Sir G. Wilkinson, Mr. Fergusson, and Mr. R. S. Poole, whose contribution to the *Encyclopædia Britannica* on the subject of Egypt is of great value.
[2] See Wilkinson, *Architecture of Ancient Egypt*, p. 17 ; *Topography of Thebes*, pp. 81, 201; *Ancient*

Egyptians, vol. ii. p. 116 ; vol. iii. p. 319 ; Sharpe, *Hist. of Egypt*, vol. i. pp. 49, 143 ; Vyse, *Pyramids of Ghizeh*, vol. ii. p. 131, &c.
[3] See above, p. 214.
[4] Fergusson, *Hist. of Architecture*, vol. i. 'Introduction,' p. 22.

like of the complexity which it would have introduced, and a conviction of its architectural weakness, as a form wanting in durability. ' The Arabs,' he observes, ' have a proverb that the arch never sleeps ; ' and it really exerts unceasingly a thrusting force laterally upon the walls at its side and centrically upon the keystone, which tends to destroy the building whereof it is a part. Its employment would not have accorded with the governing ideas of Egyptian architecture, which

Egyptian Arches.

were durability, repose, and strength ; and therefore they did not employ it. The position here laid down may be true; but it can never be more than a hypo- thesis, since it is quite impossible to prove that a people knew how to do that which they never attempted to do. The Egyptians never made any application of the arch on a grand scale or to large edifices. They were acquainted with the form as one that would bear a weight ; but it would seem to have had no charms for them. This is not surprising, since arches would not have given the same impression of stability, firmness, and strength which is produced by the solid masses of flat stone that compose their roofs. Instead of maintaining that they deliberately preferred these roofs to vaulted ones, it would probably be nearer the truth to say, that, being entirely content with flat roofs, the idea of constructing vaulted ones never occurred to them.

The 'symmetrophobia' of the Egyptians [1] is a peculiarity which developed itself gradually, and is strongest in the latest times. It appears most strikingly in such buildings as the great temples of Luxor and Philæ, where, on proceeding from one court to another, we find the axis of the building violently changed,[2] and the lines running in entirely new directions. But, apart from these extreme cases, it appears that the Egyptians had a general dislike to exact correspondency and uniformity, preferring variation within limits. The difference in the elevation of the four corners of the Great Pyramid, noticed by Fergusson,[3] is very remarkable, as also is the striking irregularity in the first or entrance court at Karnak, where the temple of Rameses II. breaks the line of the right-hand colonnade, while the left-hand one is continuous and complete.[4] Other lesser irregularities are such as the following.[5] Detached pylons have frequently their axis at an angle with that of the building whereon they depend ; the columns in a colonnade are often unequally spaced ; doorways that correspond in position are of different sizes ; caryatide piers and rounded columns are united in the same colonnaded court, occupying different sides ; columns contained within the same pillared hall have completely different

[1] Wilkinson, *Architecture of Ancient Egypt*, pp. 30 and 103 ; *Topography of Thebes*, pp. 3 and 54 ; Fergusson, *Hist. of Architecture*, vol. i. p. 115.
[2] See the *Description*, 'Planches,' vol. i. A. pl. 5; vol. iii. A. pl. 5.
[3] *Hist. of Architecture*, vol. i. p. 95, note.
[4] See page 224.
[5] See Wilkinson, *Architecture of Ancient Egypt*, pp. 29 and 43 ; *Topography of Thebes*, l.s.c. ; *Description,*'Antiquités,' vol.i.ch. ix. p. 214.

capitals, and arc of different heights; the wings of
houses do not match; courts are seldom square;
their angles and the angles of rooms are frequently
not right angles. It is manifest that the Egyptians
'purposely avoided regularity,' and the conjecture
is probable that they did this ' with a view of not fati-
guing the eye.'[1] The principle would seem to be sound
within certain limits. Absolute uniformity is wearisome, and to be eschewed; but violent irregularities
are displeasing. The Egyptians, even in the best times,
somewhat overstepped the true mean; their mingling
of different sorts of columns, and of columns with
caryatide or other piers, cannot be defended; but it was
not until their art had greatly declined under the de-
pressing influence of foreign conquest that they reached
their extreme practices, the complete change in the
axis of a building and the employment of twenty different capitals for the columns of a single apartment.[2]

The contrivance for augmenting the apparent size
of buildings, of which we have to speak in conclusion,
is the following. Egyptian buildings of large extent
for the most part rise as we penetrate into them. When
we pass from one limb to another, we generally ascend
a few steps. Sometimes, however, the ascent is more
gradual. At the Rameseum,[3] and again at Edfou,[4] the
level of the ground rises from column to column, each
column being placed on a low step a little above the
preceding one. The effect is similar to that produced
in a modern theatre by the slope of the floor from the
foot-lights to the back of the stage. It is aided by the

---

[1] Wilkinson, *Architecture*, p. 30.
[2] *Description*, 'Planches,' vol. i.
A. pls. 6, 8, &c.; Wilkinson, *Architecture*, p. 61.

[3] *Description*, 'Planches,' vol. ii.
A. pl. 28; and compare the text,
'Antiquités,' vol. i. ch. ix. p. 128.
[4] Ibid. 'Planches,' vol. i. A. pl. 50.

general arrangements of doors and pylons, which diminish in size as we advance. An illusory perspective is in this way produced ; the vistas of pillars seem twice the length that they really are, and the entire building appears to be of an extent almost interminable. If it be one of the worst faults that an architect can commit, to make his edifice appear smaller than it is, and if the constructors of the pyramids are to be considered blameable in this respect, the later Egyptian builders must be regarded as deserving of no small commendation for an arrangement which, without introducing any unworthy artifice, makes the size of their constructions even greater in appearance than it is in reality.

CHAPTER VIII.

MIMETIC ART.

Sculpture of Ancient Egypt—Single Statues of full size—peculiarities. Groups. Principal Defects and Merits. Statuettes. General Uniformity and its Causes. Works in high Relief, rare. Works in Bas-relief and Intaglio. Defects. Superiority of the Animal over the Human Forms. Examples— Gazelle Hunt—Lion Hunt. Foreshortening. Want of Proportion. Absence of Perspective. Ugliness. Four Classes of Subjects : 1. Religious; 2. Processional; 3. Military; and 4. Domestic. Playful Humour in the Domestic Scenes. Egyptian Painting—its general Character. Mechanism employed—Colours. Paintings good as Wall Decorations. Stages of Egyptian Mimetic Art.

' Les Egyptiens ont été, avant les Grecs, celui de tous les peuples de l'antiquité qui a porté les arts plastiques au plus haut degré de perfection et de grandeur.'—Lᴇɴᴏʀᴍᴀɴᴛ, *Manuel d'Histoire Ancienne de l'Orient*, vol. 1. p. 537.

Tʜᴇ sculpture of ancient Egypt falls under the three heads of statuary, or sculpture *in the round* ; relief, or representation of forms on a flat surface by means of a certain projection ; and intaglio, or representation by the opposite process of cutting the forms into the stone or marble, and thus sinking them below the surface. This last includes a process, almost peculiar to Egypt, which has been called *cavo-relievo*, or *intaglio-relievato*,[1] whereby the figures are first incised, and then given a slight relief, which raises them almost, but not quite, to the level of the stone outside them.

Completely detached statues of full size were, com-

---

[1] Birch, *Guide to the Egyptian Galleries of the British Museum*, p. 16 ; Wilkinson, *Ancient Egyptians*, vol. iii. p. 304.

paratively speaking, rare in Egypt; and when they occur, their merit is but slight. Only about six or seven attitudes seem to have been allowed ; and these are repeated with a monotony that is absolutely wearisome through the twenty centuries, or more, during which Egyptian civilisation lasts. Single figures usually stand upright with their arms dependent at their sides, or crossed upon their breast, and their feet equally advanced ; or they are in a walking attitude, with the *left* foot (invariably) set before the right,[1] and the arms pendent ; or they sit on thrones, with their arms laid along their thighs, and the hands extended with palms downward ; or they kneel upon the ground with both knees similarly placed, and hold in their two hands a shrine containing an image of some god ; or finally they are seated on the ground, with both knees drawn up nearly to the chin, and the arms resting upon them, the lower part of the person being enveloped in a robe or petticoat. No movement is exhibited, no energy, scarcely any action even. The faces are for the most part expressionless, though sometimes they are evidently intended for portraits, and great pains have been taken to render them close imitations of nature.[2] The mechanical finish is high, a perfectly smooth surface being produced, however stubborn the material.[3] But the artistic finish is the lowest conceivable. There is no rendering of veins or muscles, no indication of any anatomical study, no appearance even of acquaintance with the human skeleton.[4] The limbs are smooth and

[1] Birch, l.s.c.

[2] Lenormant, *Manuel d'Histoire ancienne*, vol. i. p. 540; Birch, *Egypt from the Earliest Times*, p. 43.

[3] The Egyptians carved their statues in calcareous stone, in dark and red granite, in porphyry, and in basalt. They also employed wood in the more ancient times, and bronze, ivory, and porcelain for statuettes.

[4] 'Les muscles, les veines, les plis et les contractions de la peau

rounded — the general proportions not bad—though altogether the forms are too slim to accord with Western notions of beauty : but all the higher qualities of art, as understood in the West, are wanting—there is composure and calm dignity, but there is no expression, no vigour, no life, no attempt to grapple with difficulties, no idealism.   The sculpture seems altogether incipient, undeveloped.   It is not, as has been justly observed, 'modelled grossly, but summarily'[1]—that is to say, it does not fail of its aims through inability to give effect

1. Egyptian walking Statue.   2. Egyptian sitting Statue.

to them, but its aims are low.   It seeks to indicate the human form, rather than to express it, to give the general contour rather than a representation of details, to embody repose and not action; there is nothing

n'y sont pas rendus, ni même la charpente osseuse.' (Lenormant, *Manuel*, vol. i. p. 539.)

[1] Ibid. 'La figure égyptienne est modelée, non pas grossièrement, mais sommairement.'

rude, gross, or coarse about it; on the contrary, the forms have delicacy and elegance, but they are incompletely rendered ; they are good, as far as they go, but they do not go far ; the artist has stopped short of the nature which he had before his eyes, and has preferred not to imitate too closely.

In the walking statues, the want of completeness is strikingly shown by the fact, that the legs, though represented as separate, are not disengaged from the stone, the space between them not having been hollowed out. This peculiarity does not extend, however, except occasionally, to figures in bronze or wood, which, so far, are superior to the stone figures.

Another curious peculiarity of Egyptian stone statues is the support which is given to them at the back. Except in the case of sitting figures, which have the support of their chairs or thrones, Egyptian stone statues have almost invariably at their back an upright slab or plinth, sometimes resembling an obelisk, against which the figures lean, and with which they are in a manner blended. This is probably explained rightly, as the reminiscence of a time when all statues were attached to walls, and constituted mere architectural adornments.[1]

The Egyptian statuaries did not stop at single figures, but sometimes proceeded to the composition of groups. Two figures, a husband and a wife, not unfrequently occupy a single seat. Generally they sit separate ; but sometimes they hold hands, or the husband has his arm placed around his wife's waist.[2] Occasionally, the man is seated on a chair, accompanied by standing figures of his wife and children,

---

[1] Kenrick, *Ancient Egypt,* vol. i. p. 265.
[2] See the woodcut overleaf.

sculptured on a smaller scale, and evidently intended
as accessories.[1] The composition is in every case rude
and inartificial, no attempt being made at 'grouping,'
in the technical sense, or at producing an effective
whole.

Besides the negative defects, which have been here

Group of two Statues, Husband and Wife.

noticed, there are some positive ones, which must not
be glossed over, whereby a great part of the statuary
is rendered repulsive, rather than attractive—at any

---

[1] Birch, *Guide to Museum*, p. 16.

rate, to the modern European. The figures are, for
the most part, too elongated ; and the limbs especially
are too long for the body. The ears are misplaced,
the hole of the ear being made parallel with the pupil
of the eye,[1] instead of with the nostrils. The inlaying
of the eye in a different material from the rest of the
statue, which is common, offends a correct taste ;[2] and
the prolongation of the eyebrows and eyelids nearly to

Bust of an Egyptian King.

the ears is unnatural and unpleasing. The great masses
of hair hanging down on either side of the face in
heavy blocks, concealing the neck and resting upon the
shoulders, the broad and depressed nose verging upon
a negro type, the prominent cheek-bones, the large
mouth, and full, half out-turned lips, are even more
disagreeable, and produce an *ensemble* from which the

[1] Birch, l.s.c. p. 17. Compare
Kenrick, vol. i. p. 266.

[2] This is done even in the remarkable wooden statue which forms
the glory of the museum of Boulaq,
and is said to exhibit 'a truth,
grace, and fidelity, which shows
the hand of a great master' (Birch,

Egypt from the Earliest Times, p.
43). There is no doubt some evidence that the practice was occasionally adopted by the Greeks ;
but, in spite of this, a true taste
will pronounce it ' more honoured in
the breach than the observance.'

eye instinctively turns away, and on which it can only
bring itself to gaze with difficulty.[1]   The dark material
commonly in use, and the smears of red paint often
observable, render the physiognomies even more repulsive than they would have been otherwise, and produce
disgust and aversion.   Again, the grotesque figures of
the gods, sometimes coarse-featured and dwarfish, often

Egyptian Figures of Phthah and Bes.

mixing together animal and human forms,[2] always
utterly devoid of the faintest trace of beauty, lower

---

[1] The author delivers here his
own impressions of the Egyptian
statues which have come under his
notice. He has not thought it
necessary to encumber his pages
with representations of the hideous
figures themselves. They may be
seen in all their native ugliness
in the Egyptian collection at the
British Museum, in the Louvre, at
Berlin, and elsewhere.

[2] See Wilkinson, *Ancient Egyptians*, vol. vi. Supplement, pls. 21,
22, 24, 25, 27, 35a, 40, &c.

the general character of the statuary where it might
have been expected to be highest, and tempt the
lover of high art to question whether the Egyptian
attempts ought to be allowed the name of Art at all. If
we pass from the contemplation of the Apollo Belve-
dere to that of an Egyptian representation of Phthah
or Bes,[1] we seem to step from one world to another,
from one pole of production to its opposite ; and it is
difficult to persuade ourselves that one and the same
term ought to embrace the two.

If, however, we contemplate Egyptian statuary in
Egypt itself—ou its native soil—as it was intended to
be seen by those who wrought it, we shall find reason
to modify some of these views, and to allow that, while
devoid of the excellencies which we commonly associate with Greek art, it had merits of its own, and was
not wholly contemptible. Sculpture in Egypt was
almost entirely 'architectonic,'[2] and was intended simply,
or at any rate mainly, for architectural embellishment.
The Great Colossi, the most remarkable of the Egyptian efforts, were set up in temples, or in their immediate neighbourhood, and to be rightly judged must be
viewed in connection with those buildings. The statues
of the gods had their proper place in shrines prepared
for them, and were not out of keeping with their surroundings. The grand effect of the Osiride images in
the temple courtyards has been already noticed.[3] Even
the private statues of individuals were intended for
ornaments of tombs, and seen, by torchlight only, in
those dark abodes, must have been impressive. Alto-

---

[1] The grotesque character of the figures of Phthah was noted by Herodotus (iii. 37), and, if we may believe him, attracted the attention of Cambyses. The figures of Bes are, according to Wilkinson (A.E. pl. 24A), even more hideous.
[2] Birch, *Guide to Museum*, p. 15.
[3] See above, pp. 244–5.

gether, the judgment appears to be sound, that 'the sculptures were well adapted for architectural effect, from their grand, simple, and vertical lines, their great regularity, squareness, and repose.'[1] They had strength and massiveness, majesty and grandeur, simplicity and

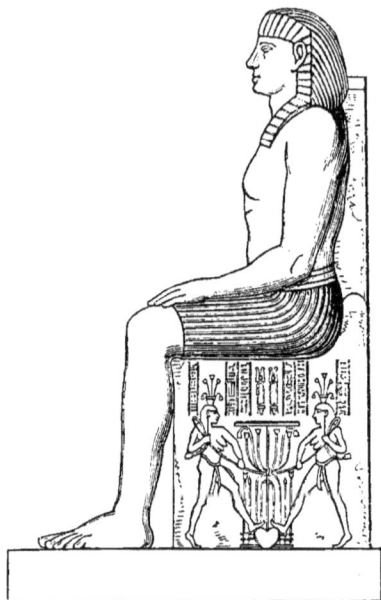

Colossal Figure of Rameses II.

dignity; above all, they had about them an air of profound, eternal, unchanging rest.

The smaller statuettes, in bronze, basalt, or clay, are less dignified than the statues, but have greater elegance and grace.[2] Some female figures, apart from their uncouth Egyptian head-dress, are decidedly pleasing, though it must be admitted that they are too slender to satisfy an eye accustomed to the rounded forms of the Greeks. Animals are also rendered suffi-

[1] Birch, *Guide to Museum*, p. 17.
[2] See the representations in the

Description de l'Egypte, 'Antiquités,' vol. v. pl. 64–72.

ciently well *in the round*. The pair of lions in the Southern Gallery at the British Museum have considerable artistic excellence. The Great Sphinx of the Pyramids, though scarcely deserving of all the praises which have been lavished upon it,[1] must be admitted to

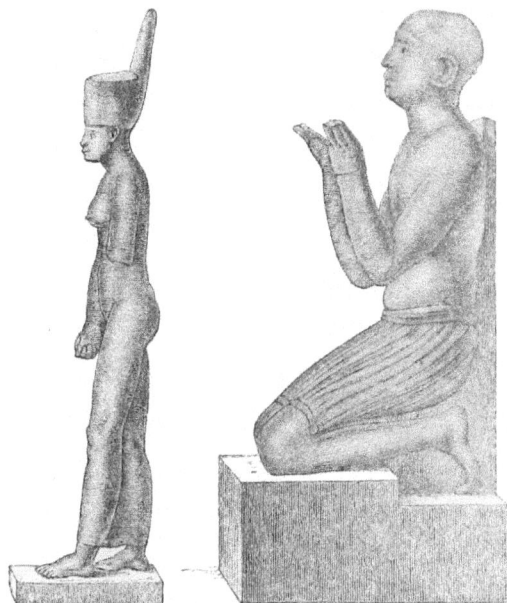

Egyptian Statuettes.

be a striking monument, and to impress the spectator, not only by its bulk, but by its air of impassive dignity. Other sphinx figures are considered to have a certain

[1] Professor Owen calls it 'a sculpture of exquisite art and finish' (*Leisure Hour* for May 1876, p. 324). Ampère says: 'Cette grande figure mutilée est d'un effet prodigieux; c'est comme une apparition éternelle. Le fantôme de pierre paraît attentif; on dirait qu'il entend et qu'il regarde. Sa grande oreille semble recueillir les bruits du passé; ses yeux tournés vers l'orient semblent épier l'avenir; le regard a une profondeur et une vérité qui fascinent le spectateur. Sur cette figure, moitié statue, moitié montagne, on découvre une majesté singulière, une grande sérénité, et même une certaine douceur.' (Quoted by Lenormant in his *Manuel d'Histoire ancienne*, vol. i. p. 541.)

calmness and grandeur.   There are also statuettes of
bulls, monkeys, and dogs,[1] which are characteristic and
fairly good.

It has been urged by many,[2] that the principal de-
ficiencies of Egyptian statuary—the general uniformity

Sphinx of the Pyramids.

of design, the stiffness and want of grace, the absence
of motion from the forms, and of character and expres-

---

[1] See Wilkinson, *Ancient Egyp-* | Kenrick, *Ancient Egypt*, vol. i. p.
tians, vol. vi. Supplement, pl. 43. | 264; Lenormant, *Manuel*, vol. i.
[2] Ibid. vol. iii. pp. 263–275; | pp. 353–4, &c.

sion from the faces, nay, even the incompleteness of
the representation—were the results, not so much of

Ordinary Sphinx.   Crio-Sphinx.

inability to do better on the part of the artists, as of a
constraint imposed upon them from without by the

Modelled Figures of Animals.

religious prejudices of a dominant hierarchy.[1]   It is
undoubtedly true that nothing more tends to cramp

---

[1] Lenormant, *Manuel d'Histoire*   iii. p. 87; Kenrick, *Ancient Egypt*
ancienne, vol. i. pp.   538-541 ; | *tians*, vol. i. pp. 264-5.
Wilkinson, *Ancient Egyptians*, vol. 1

Art and prevent its satisfactory development, than laws against change, especially when they are imposed from without, and rest upon a religious, rather than an artistic, basis. It is also tolerably certain that there existed in ancient Egypt a religious censorship of Art —that 'hieratic canons' were laid down and commanded to be observed [1]—and that a restraint was thus placed upon genius and invention. But it may be remarked, on the other hand, that the laws against change cannot have been absolute, since there are decided differences of style at different periods,[2] and that freedom of treatment must have been, to a certain extent, allowed, since the animal forms at any rate improve as time goes on, and are best about the period of the eighteenth and nineteenth dynasties. In representations that are strictly religious, the amount of change, it is true, was slight, and there it is probable that 'hieratic canons' really prevailed; but in the portrait statues and the statuettes this is scarcely likely to have been the case, and the uniformity which is observable must, it would seem, be attributed to some want of artistic conception or power. A similar conclusion is naturally drawn from a general consideration of the bas-reliefs and intaglios, which, though boasting more freedom of treatment than the statues, still participate in their characteristics of uniformity, stiffness, and want of finish.

High relief—the exhibition of human and animal forms in connection with a flat surface, but very much

[1] Birch, *Guide to British Museum*, p. 18; Wilkinson in the author's *Herodotus*, vol. ii. pp. 269–271, 3rd edition. The main authorities upon the points are Plato, Diodorus, and Synesius.

[2] Birch, *Egypt from the Earliest Times*, pp. 43, 129, 175, &c.; and see below, pp. 290–292.

raised above it—which was common in Persia,[1] Lycia,[2] and Greece, is very rarely found in Egypt. The few reliefs of the kind which occur possess scarcely any merit. It is scarcely necessary to present specimens of these uncouth works, which can possess no attraction for any but professional students of art, who may desire to see sculpture of every kind in its rudest and most primitive condition. For such persons a few references are given in the subjoined note.[3]

The bas-reliefs and intaglios of the Egyptians will be treated together, their general effect being very similar, and the composition in both kinds being marked by nearly the same characteristics, praiseworthy or the contrary. In general the defects are glaring, and preponderate greatly over the merits. With rare exceptions, the figures are represented in profile, stiffly erect, and standing still, or walking in a formal, stately manner. The eye is drawn in full, not as it really appears sideways, but as if seen from the front. It is long and narrow, often set a little obliquely ; and both eye and eyebrow are prolonged nearly to the ear. The ear is placed too high in the head, and is generally somewhat too large. The limbs are for the most part too slim, and the hands and feet are stiff, straight, and of undue size. Where variety of attitude occurs, the drawing is generally incorrect, and the new attitude impossible. For instance, sometimes the head is turned completely round, and the man who walks one way

[1] See the author's *Ancient Monarchies*, vol. iii. pp. 296, 301, and 334 (2nd edition).
[2] See the frontispiece to Sir C. Fellows's *Lycia*, and compare the Lycian sculptures in the British Museum.
[3] A somewhat high relief is ob- servable in the hideous monster figured by Wilkinson, *Ancient Egyptians*, vol. vi. Supplement, pl. 43 A. Also in Lepsius, *Denkmäler*, vol. iii. part ii. pls. 11 and 44 ; and in the *Description*, ' Antiquités,' vol. iii. pl. 31.

looks directly the other. Female tumblers lean backwards till their hands reach the ground with the palms
downward. Others defy all the laws of gravity, and

Figure of an Egyptian Priest.

lean back in a position which could not be retained for
a moment.[1]

Female tumbler, in an impossible attitude.

Composition is in general formal, artificial, and
constrained. In the processional scenes the same figure

---

[1] See Wilkinson, *Ancient Egyptians*, vol. ii. p. 416, Fig. 2, ᴀ.

AN EGYPTIAN KING DESTROYING HIS ENEMIES.

is reiterated twenty, thirty, fifty, or a hundred times. There is scarcely any idea of grouping, of balance, or even of a main point of interest to which the rest shall be subordinate. In the battle scenes, it must be admitted, this defect is not so apparent. There the monarch is the central object, and the whole remainder of the composition, being intended simply for his honour and glory, is intentionally subordinated to him. But in this case another defect obtrudes itself. The artist, distrusting his ability to give the necessary pre-eminence to the royal figure by the means ordinarily considered legitimate—position, finish, expression, convergence of the attention of the others to him —has had recourse to the rude and inartistic expedient of making his superiority apparent by mere difference of size. Rameses towers above his soldiers and his enemies, not as Saul above the children of Israel,[1] or Ajax above the Argives,[2] but as Gulliver above the people of Lilliput. The colossal figure of the great king dwarfs all the others, not into subordination merely, but into insignificance ;[3] and it is necessary that we should shut him out from our vision before we can take an interest in the details of the battle. These are sufficiently lively and varied ; they exhibit confusion, turmoil, strange attitudes of dying and dead, life, motion, energy ; but it can scarcely be said that they are artistic. The reliefs in question may represent truthfully enough the varied and separate incidents of an ancient battle-field ; but the want of mass, of

---

[1] 1 Sam. ix. 2.
[2] Hom. *Il.* iii. 226–7:
    ἀνὴρ ἠΰς τε μέγας τε,
"Εξοχος 'Αργείων κεφαλήν τε καὶ
εὐρέας ὤμους.

[3] See the *Description de l'Egypte*, 'Antiquités,' vol. iii. pls. 3, 6, 38, &c. ; and compare Lepsius, *Denk-mäler*, vol. vi. pt. iii. pls. 126, 127, 165, &c.

grouping, and of perspective renders them singularly
ineffective as pictures.[1]

Æsthetically, by far the best of the Egyptian reliefs
are those in which animals form the entire subject, or
at any rate constitute the preponderating element.[2]
The Pharaonic artists had a happy knack of catching
the leading characteristics of beast[3] and bird,[4] and
rendering them effectively though simply. A purely
animal scene, represented by Rosellini in his great
work,[5] is graceful and pleasing, full of life, and characterised by an artistic touch which is very unusual.
The subjoined woodcut repeats a portion of this
drawing, and will give a tolerable idea of its general
style : —

Hunting the gazelle and hare.

---

[1] One of the best of the battle-
scenes is reproduced in the woodcut opposite. It exists at Karnak,
on the northern wall of the central
building, and probably represents
Amenophis I. destroying his enemies (see the *Description*, ' Antiquités,' vol. iii. pl. 40, fig. 6).

[2] The remark of Madame de
Staël is quite just. ' Les sculpteurs
égyptiens saisissaient avec bien
plus de génie la figure des animaux
que celle des hommes ' (*Corinne*,
vol. i. p. 127).

[3] At first the animal forms are
weak, and sometimes absurd, as the

tall hare in the *Denkmäler* (vol. iii.
pt. ii. pl. 3), and the very feeble dogs
catching antelopes of different kinds
in the same (vol. iii. pt. ii. pl. 6).
But they became fairly satisfactory
not much later; and by the date of
the eighteenth dynasty they leave
but little to be desired.

[4] Compare Rosellini, *Monumenti
Civili*, vol. ii. pls. 6 to 13, with
Wilkinson, *Ancient Egyptians*, vol.
iii. pp. 36–51.

[5] Rosellini, *Monumenti Civili*,
vol. ii. pl. 15. The scene is taken
from a tomb at Beni Hassan, near
Thebes.

RAMESES III. HUNTING THE LION.

A nobler, grander, and altogether superior design may be seen at Medinet-Abou, on the external wall of the great palace, facing the north.[1] This is a compositiou in which the monarch, standing by himself in his chariot, advances at full speed in the chase of a wounded lion, while at the same time, attacked from behind, probably by another similar beast,[2] he turns himself round and directs his spear against the assailant. Under his horses, which, as usual, prance high in the air, lies the body of a lion pierced by two arrows, and struggling in the agonies of death. The hunted animal is in front. Though pierced by three arrows and a javelin, he continues his mad career, rushing through the water-plants, from which we may conclude that he has been aroused by the beaters. The whole piece is remarkable for the boldness and freedom of the outline, for the spirit of the composition, the good drawing of the lions, the expression of suffering in their countenances, and the contrast which they offer to each other and to the remaining figures of the design.[3] Their massive forms compare well with the slim and graceful horses ; their violent action sets off the comparative impassiveness of the main figure. Moreover, the balance of the composition, if we imagine another lion behind, is good ; part corresponds to part, yet not too closely or exactly ; and, by the

---

[1] See the *Description*, 'Antiquités,' Texte, vol. i. ch. ix. § i. p. 54, and Planches, vol. ii. pl. 9, fig. i.

[2] The wall is here interrupted by a doorway, which renders the composition imperfect, and can scarcely have been part of the original structure.

[3] Compare the *Description* (l.s.c.)

—'Ce bas-relief, précieux sous le rapport de l'histoire (?), ne l'est pas moins sous le rapport de l'art. On peut remarquer *la franchise et la hardiesse du dessin,* la variété et la fermeté des attitudes de toutes les figures ; *l'expression de la douleur* est surtout rendue avec beaucoup de vérité.'

greater elevation of the horses' crests and the hunter's spear, the 'principle of the pyramid' is asserted, and a unity given to the design which it might otherwise have lacked.

Like the human, the animal figures are drawn for the most part strictly in profile; but there are a certain number of exceptions, where the animal is turning round, and the form is to a certain extent fore-shortened.[1] Occasionally even more ambition is shown, and more difficult attitudes are attempted, as in the Beni Hassan scene above mentioned, where some of

Animals foreshortened.

the dogs turn their full faces to the spectator, and the antelopes are drawn in the act of falling prone to earth, or represented as struggling to shake off the hounds which have got hold of them.

Among the main defects of the Egyptian designs are the non-observance of proportion and the almost entire inability to represent anything in perspective, as

---

[1] See Wilkinson, *Ancient Egyptians,* vol. iii. pp. 16, 18, 22; Lep- | sius, *Denkmäler,* vol. ii. pt. ii. pls. 22, 46, &c.

it is really seen. Not only are royal personages drawn commonly on a larger scale than the officers and others in attendance upon them, but in the tomb scenes even the ordinary *paterfamilias* is given a similar advantage over his servants and labourers. This advantage he sometimes shares with his wife, who sits with him on the same seat[1] and is drawn on the same scale.[2] The animal forms are, on the other hand, frequently too small, cows being represented as about half the height of a man,[3] and donkeys as less than half.[4] When an elephant is depicted, the top of his back only just reaches his attendant's waist;[5] and the head of the giraffe a very little overtops that of the man who leads him.[6] The accessories of a battle scene, towns, forts, rivers, are on a scale absurdly disproportioned to the men, the horses, and the chariots;[7] while in domestic scenes the persons represented often exceed in height the doors of the mansions.[8]

The inability to present a scene in perspective is, no doubt, one common to the Egyptian artists with other primitive designers; but it is a defect which attains in Egypt an intensity almost without a parallel elsewhere. A phalanx of soldiers is represented by a mass of figures ranged one above the other, either in completely distinct lines, or in such a position that

---

[1] Lepsius, *Denkmäler*, vol. iii. pls. 10, 24, 25, 42, 57 *a*, &c. Sometimes both figures stand, the wife a little in the rear (ibid. pls. 13, 17 *a*, 21, &c.).

[2] Or on a scale slightly smaller (ibid. pls. 27, 38 *a*, &c.).

[3] Ibid. pls. 19, 47, &c.

[4] Ibid. vol. iii. pt. ii. pls. 47, 51 ; vol. vi. pt. iii. pl. 154.

[5] Rosellini, *Mon. Civ.* vol. ii. pl.

22, fig. 3.

[6] Ibid. fig. 2. Compare Wilkinson, *A. E.*, plate at the end of vol. i. line 3. A better representation of the real proportions will be found in Lepsius, *Denkmäler*, vol. vi. pt. iii. pl. 118.

[7] Lepsius, *Denkmäler*, vol. vi. pt. iii. pls. 158, 159, 164, 166, &c.

[8] Rosellini, pls. 68 and 69.

each more distant row shows above the nearer ones to the extent of half the height.[1] As a general rule, what is distant and would be partially or entirely

Egyptian drawing water from a reservoir.

hidden by intervening objects is raised up, if the artist wishes to show it, and exhibited at a higher level. The animals and the targets, whereat shooters aim, are represented as close to them ; and the full face of the target is shown, when it ought to be nearly, if not quite, invisible.[2] Where a river, pond, or pool has to be indicated, the entire surface is presented to view, being lifted up and placed at right angles to the eye

---

[1] Wilkinson, *A. E.* vol. i. p. 293.   [2] Ibid. vol. ii. pp. 188–9.

of the spectator.[1] Gardens are commonly given in
ground-plan, though the buildings which they contain
stand erect,[2] exhibiting their sides and not their roofs.
Altogether, the rules of perspective are completely
ignored or defied, and no representation is accurate,
unless limited to objects which are all at the same
distance and in the same plane.

Further, there is the same defect in the bas-reliefs
of the Egyptians which has been already noticed in
their statuary,[3] the frequent intrusion of simply hideous
forms into the designs, more especially where these
have a religious character. The three huge and
misshapen figures,[4] so frequent upon the ceilings of
temples, which are supposed to represent ' the heavens,'
oppress the imagination of one who stands under them
with the sense of a superincumbent nightmare. Bes in
all his forms is fearful to behold ; Taouris, Savak, and
Cerberus are not much better ; even Osiris has presenta-
tions which are repulsive ; and the constant recurrence
of the Priapic Khem is a perpetual eyesore. All the
forms of the gods are more or less disagreeable ; the
stiff constrained outlines, the tight-fitting robes, the
large clumsily-drawn hands and feet, the frequent
animal heads and enormous head-dresses, the ugly or
inexpressive faces, compose an *ensemble* as unpleasant
as can easily be conceived, and recall the monstrosities
of Brahminical and Buddhistic religious representations.

---

[1] A striking instance of this bad
drawing may be seen in Wilkinson,
vol. ii. p. 145, where a tank of
water interposed between two rows
of palm trees is made to show itself by being raised up to half their
height, and then placed at right
angles to the spectator, suspended
in air, like the coffin of Mohammed!

[2] See Wilkinson, vol. ii. pl. 9,
and woodcut, p. 142, No. 130; and
Rosellini, vol. ii. pl. 69.
[3] See above, p. 266.
[4] See the *Description de l'Egypte*,
' Antiquités,' vol. i. pl. 18; vol. ii.
pl. 37 ; and compare Wilkinson,
A. E. vol. vi. Supplement, pl. 55,
pt. iii.

It seems strange that artists, who occasionally at any rate show taste and æsthetic culture, should consent to reproduce from age to age stereotyped forms of a character which sound artistic judgment must always pronounce repulsive and disgusting.

Egyptian representations of Taouris, Savak, and Osiris.

The bulk of the drawings are of a sober and serious character. They may be divided into :—1. The strictly religious, where worship of some kind or other— generally sacrifice—is offered to the gods, or where they strengthen and sustain the monarch, or where the soul passes through some of the scenes which it will have to undergo after death. 2. The processional, where the king goes in state, or where tribute is brought to him, or where the pomp of a funeral, or the inauguration of an officer, or some other civil ceremony, forms the subject. 3. The war scenes, including battles by sea and land, the siege of forts, the

Head of female, in a good style.

march of armies, the return home with booty and captives, &c. ; and 4. The scenes of common life, represented exclusively in the tombs, where the deceased is presented with offerings, or with inventories of his worldly goods, or exhibits his skill in the chase, or depicts his house and its environs, or the processes of the trade which he followed when alive, or the entertainments which he gave and the large number of his guests and friends, or the amusements which he delighted in. These tomb scenes are the most numerous and the most interesting ; and, while perhaps the highest inventive qualities are displayed by

the artists who decorate the walls of temples and
palaces with gigantic battle-pieces, it is in the sepulchres that we observe the lightest touch, the freest
drawing, the greatest variety of artistic excellence.
Solemn as are the associations which attach to the
grave, it is here, and here only, in the sepulchral
chambers, in the close vicinity of the tombs, that the
Egyptian artists shake off the weight of seriousness
which elsewhere oppresses them, and condescend to
be sportive and amusing, to exhibit playfulness and
humour, to approach or even pass the line which
separates serious drawing from caricature. There is
a tomb near Thebes, where, in the middle of an
entertainment, a guest is represented as bringing down
the apartment upon the feasters by leaning against a
central pillar, and upsetting it.[1] In another tomb, ladies,
not of too refined an appearance, converse with animation about their ear-rings, and appraise them, or inquire
where they were bought. The humour is sometimes
even more broad.[2] 'In one of the royal sepulchres at
Thebes we see an ass and a lion singing and accompanying themselves on the phorminx and the harp.
Another design is the burlesque of a battle-piece.
A fortress is attacked by rats, and defended by cats,
who are mounted on the battlements. The rats bring
a ladder to the walls and prepare to scale them, while
a body armed with spear, shield, and bow protect the
assailants, and a rat of gigantic size, in a chariot drawn
by dogs, has pierced the cats with his arrows, and
swings round his axe in exact imitation of Rameses
dealing destruction on his enemies. In a papyrus of

[1] See Wilkinson, *Ancient Egyp-tians*, vol. ii. p. 366. Compare the passage of Horace to which he re-
fers (*Sat.* ii. 8, 54).
[2] Wilkinson, vol. ii. p. 367.

the Museum of Turin, a cat is seen with a shepherd's
crook watching a flock of geese, and a cynocephalus
ape playing on the flute.'[1]   Souls returning from
Hades after judgment in the form of pigs, under the
protection of monkeys, have a crest-fallen expression of
countenance which is quaint and ludicrous.[2]

Of painting, in the modern sense of the word, the
Egyptians knew absolutely nothing. No surface was
ever completely covered. The Egyptians drew figures
of men and animals, together with other objects, in
outline on a white or whitish background, and then
filled in the outline, or portions of it, with masses of
uniform hue. No shading or softening off of the tints
was practised.[3] All the exposed parts of a man's body
were coloured of a uniform red-brown; all the exposed
parts of a woman's of a lighter red or a yellow. Except
in the case of a few foreigners, the hair and beard were
pitch-black. Dresses were predominantly white, but
had their folds marked by lines of red or brown, and
were sometimes striped or otherwise patterned, generally with red or blue.[4] Most large surfaces[5] were
more or less patterned, in general with small patterns
of various colours, including a good deal of white.

[1] Kenrick, *Ancient Egypt*, vol. i.
pp. 269-70.
[2] *Description de l'Egypte*, ' Antiquités,' vol. ii. pl. 83, fig. 1 ; Wilkinson, *A. E.*, Supplement, vol. vi.
pl. 87.
[3] In the animal paintings there
seems to be some exception to this
rule. Rosellini has representations
of beasts, birds, and fish, where the
colour is softened off from dark to
light (*Monumenti Civili*, vol. ii. pls.
13, 16, 17, 20, and 25).
[4] Patterned dresses are common
in the case of foreigners, rare in
that of Egyptians. For examples,

see Lepsius, *Denkmäler*, vol. iv.
pt. ii. pl. 133 ; vol. vi. pt. iii. pls.
115-6, and 136.
[5] As particularly sails and cabins
of vessels (Rosellini, *M. C.* vol. ii.
pls. 107, 108 ; Wilkinson, *A. E.*
vol. iii. pl. xvi.), caparisons of
horses (*Description*, ' Antiquités,'
vol. iii. pl. 12; Wilkinson, vol. i.
pl. 1), seats (Wilkinson, vol. ii. pl.
11 ; vol. vi. pl. 20, &c.), frames of
harps (ibid. vol. ii. pl. 13, and
woodcut on p. 270), bow-cases
(ibid. vol. i. p. 346), and dresses of
deities (ibid. vol. vi. pls. 20, 23, 33,
50, &c.).

Altogether the effect was one of combined flatness
and spottiness, the white background showing far too
strongly and isolating the different parts of the picture
one from another.

The mechanism of painting was effected as follows.
First of all the stone, whether it were sandstone, or
fossiliferous limestone, or even granite, was covered over
with a coating of stucco,[1] which was white or whitish,
and which prevented the colours from being lost by
sinking into the ground. *Fresco* painting was unknown: the Egyptians allowed the composition
whereon they painted to become completely dry,
before they commenced even to sketch in their figures,
much less to paint them. An outline was first drawn
with red paint, or red chalk, on the prepared surface;
when this was satisfactorily executed, the filling in
began. The scale of colours known to the artists was
not extensive. Besides black and white, and the three
primitive colours, red, blue, and yellow, the Egyptians
employed only green and brown, together with a light
wash of the black, which produced a sort of grey.[2] The
black is a bone-black,[3] very decided and very durable;
the white is a preparation of pure chalk with a slight
trace of iron. The red and the yellow are ochres, the
colouring matter being iron, not however artificially
introduced, but mixed by nature with the earthy substance.[4]. The blue colour is derived from the oxide of
copper; but before becoming a pigment it has been
combined with glass, which has then by trituration
been reduced into a fine powder. The green is this

---

[1] Wilkinson, vol. iii. p. 300.
[2] This is found, I believe, only in representations of animals. See Rosellini, *Mon. Civ.* vol. ii. pl. xvii. figs. 6, 7, 10; pl. xx. figs. 4,
7, 8).
[3] Wilkinson, *A. E.* vol. iii. p. 303.
[4] Ibid. pp. 302–3.

same preparation, combined with a certain amount of yellow ochre.[1] The brown is probably a mixture of the blue-black with the red.

A somewhat narrow gamut of colour was thus formed. The Egyptian artists appear to have enlarged it by employing several shades of the primitive colours —three, at least, of blue, one very dark, another of medium hue, and a third very light, resembling our 'sky-blue;' two of red, a scarlet, and a red-brown; and at least two of yellow, a darker and a lighter.[2] They used also at least two shades of green, and several of brown, ranging from a light drab to a hue nearly approaching black. But they were ignorant of lilac, of purple, of orange, of crimson, of olive, and were thus compelled to abstain from all attempts to produce that sort of beauty which is caused by the employment of half-tints, and the 'soft and gradual transition from one tint to another,' which is to the eye what 'an harmonious concert of music is to the ear,'[3] and which especially characterises the Italian schools of Bologna and Venice. They had to depend on the broad contrasts of the primitive tints mainly, and were thus thrown upon the style of colouring which produces its effects by striking contrasts.[4] It is quite possible to obtain a good result in this way. Only let care be taken that the colours are strong and forcible, that a balance is maintained, and that the masses are broad, and not too much entangled or interspersed, and an effect is produced which is simple and grand, effective and pleasing. The Egyptians, unhappily,

---

[1] Wilkinson, *A. E.* vol. iii. p. 302.

[2] See particularly the *Description de l'Egypte*, ' Antiquités,' Planches, vol. ii. pl. 91.

[3] Sir J. Reynolds, *Discourses before the Royal Academy*, Discourse iv. p. 102.

[4] Ibid. Discourse iv. p. 89.

broke up their masses of colour, and intermixed them in such a way that a sense of unquiet is produced; there is a general flutter and disturbance; the eye finds nothing upon which it can dwell long, or repose with a feeling of satisfaction.

The painting was executed in a sort of distemper. The colours were mixed with water, and with a certain rather moderate amount of gum, which rendered the mixture more tenacious and adhesive.[1] They were applied, as already observed,[2] to a stuccoed surface, which might either be flat and unbroken, or already prepared by the chisel with figures in relief or intaglio. These figures, by the variations of their surfaces, enjoyed the advantage of a slight variety of light and shade, which helped to mark them out, and gave their contour greater definiteness. Some compensation was thus introduced for the absence of painted *chiaroscuro*; but the compensation was slight, and did not extend to all classes of paintings.

Altogether, it must be said that while, as artistic productions, the Egyptian paintings possess only a low degree of merit, as wall decorations they were undoubtedly effective and striking. Where the sun always shines and the air is always clear, where nature lights up the landscape upon every side with mellow hues and bright effects, pale plain surfaces of stone, such as match well with the dull grey of northern lands, are unsuitable, offend the eye, seem tame and out of harmony. The brilliant hues which covered the walls of the Egyptian temples, inside and outside, illuminated them with a warmth that well accorded with their surroundings, and rendered them the richest-looking and

---

[1] Wilkinson, *A. E.* vol. iii. p. 301.   [2] See above, p. 286.

brightest objects in a scene that was all brightness and richness. As the ancient Greeks employed colour externally in the pediments and other parts of their temples,[1] and the Italians of the Middle Ages warm marbles and stone of many different hues in their palaces and churches,[2] so these primitive builders made the exterior, as well as the interior, of their edifices to glow with colour, from an instinctive feeling of what was truly fitting and harmonious. Separately, the colours are often crude, if not coarse, and the contrasts sometimes over-violent;[3] but, in their entirety, the paintings had no doubt a pleasing effect, and 'greatly improved' the appearance of the buildings which they decorated.[4]

Egyptian mimetic art can scarcely be said to have a history. Its most notable characteristic is its general unchangingness and want of progress. Crystallised in its infancy, it presents to us from first to last a strange unparalleled sameness, an extraordinary monotony. Still, while this is its most striking feature, and the first and main impression which it produces on those who study it,[5] prolonged attention enables the inquirer to perceive certain minor differences which underlie this general uniformity, and prove that, whatever might be intended, change to a

---

[1] See K. O. Müller, *History of Greek Art*, pp. 48, 76, &c.; Falkener, *Ephesus*, pp. 260–1; Fergusson, *Hist. of Architecture*, vol. i. pp. 252-4.

[2] Ruskin, *Stones of Venice*, vol. i. pls. 1, 5, 8; vol. ii. pl. 5; *Seven Lamps of Architecture*, pp. 130–133.

[3] Compare above, p. 246.

[4] Wilkinson, *A. E.*, vol. iii. p. 298; Fergusson, *Hist. of Architecture*, vol. i. p. 120.

[5] 'L'art égyptien,' says Lenormant, 'semble être retenu par certains côtés dans une éternelle enfance' (*Manuel d'Histoire Ancienne*, vol. i. p. 539). 'It was the peculiarity of Egyptian art,' observes Mr. Kenrick, 'that the characteristics of its infancy were perpetuated through all the stages of its existence' (*Ancient Egypt*, vol. i. p. 264).

certain extent did in fact intrude itself, and that progress, development, decay, renaissance are consequently
terms not wholly inapplicable to the art of Egypt at
different periods. The earliest remains found at Saccarah and at Meydoun, consisting in part of statues,
in part of painted bas-reliefs, exhibit a certain amount
of rudeness and indecision, a certain weakness and want
of regular method, indicative of an incipient art which
is as yet imperfectly formed and does not know exactly
how to proceed.[1] When we reach the time of the
fourth dynasty, improvement is observable, more especially in the statuary, which rapidly attains the
highest degree of perfection that it ever reached in
Egypt. The portrait-statues of Chephren, and of
various private persons contemporary with him or with
the other Pyramid kings, are the best specimens which
occur of Egyptian sculpture ' in the round,' and are
regarded by some as ' rivalling the busts and statues
of Rome.'[2] Up to this time Egyptian art is thought
to have been wholly, or at any rate to a great extent,[3]
untrammelled by law ; and so far as statuary is concerned, it has a naturalness in the human forms that
disappears afterwards. But the bas-reliefs of the period
are decidedly inferior to those of a later time. Not
only is the aim low, scenes of common life being alone
exhibited, but the rendering is unsatisfactory, the
different representations being wanting in variety, and

---

[1] Lenormant, having mentioned
works of art which he attributes to
the second dynasty, says: 'En les
étudiant, on y remarque une ru-
desse et une indécision de style qui
montre qu'à la fin de la deuxième
dynastie l'art égyptien cherchait
encore sa voie, et n'était qu'impar-
faitement formé' (Manuel, vol. i.
p. 333).
[2] Birch, Ancient Egypt, p. 43.

A comparison of the busts in the
Roman room of the Brit. Museum,
ranging from Julius Cæsar to Ela-
gabalus, with the best specimens of
Egyptian art, will (I think) show
this judgment to be very much too
favourable.
[3] Wholly, according to Lenormant (Manuel, vol. i. p. 538) ; but
not so, according to Birch (Guide to
Museum, p. 18).

the best of them deficient in expression and life. A
new epoch introduces itself with the twelfth dynasty,
when hieratic canons were absolutely enforced,[1] and
art, cramped so far, found compensation in an increased
delicacy of rendering, an elegance and a harmony
never previously realised.[2] New ideas sprang into
being under the fostering influence of enlightened
princes. Obelisks were erected ; piers were superseded
by columns ; and an architectural order was elaborated, which at a later date approved itself to the
Greeks.[3] Sculpture at the same time took a fresh
start. The tombs of Beni-Hassan reproduce in a
general way those of a more primitive age at Saccarah
and Ghizeh ; but the touch is more delicate, the proportions are better, and the subjects are more varied.
After the time of the twelfth dynasty, Egyptian art
does not so much decline as disappear, until the great
reaction sets in under the eighteenth dynasty, when
the Egyptian nation attains its acmé, and the perfection
of art, as of most other things, is reached. The 'grand
style' is now brought into existence,[4] and supersedes
the humbler and more prosaic one that had hitherto prevailed. Colossi are erected ; huge battle-scenes are
composed, containing hundreds of figures ; variety of
attitude is studied ; life and energy are thrown into the
drawing ; even the countenances lose their immobility
and have a certain amount of feeling and expression.
But after the space of about three centuries a rapid
decline sets in [5]—the higher qualities of art disappear—

[1] Lenormant, *Manuel*, vol. i. p.
354.
[2] 'La qualité prédominante dans
la sculpture de cet âge est la finesse,
l'élégance, et l'harmonie des proportions' (ibid. p. 353).

[3] See above, p. 212.
[4] On the 'Grand Style,' see Sir
J. Reynolds's *Discourses before the
Royal Academy*, Discourse iii.
[5] Birch, *Ancient Egypt*, p. 129;
Wilkinson, *A. E.*, vol. iii. p. 305;

there is no more invention, no more expressiveness—
convention resumes the grasp upon art which it had
relaxed, and a dead period begins which continues till
the time of the first Psamatik.   Then there was a renaissance.[1]   By a not unnatural reaction, the style of the
eighteenth dynasty was discarded, and the artists took
the older productions of the fourth and fifth dynasties
for their models, imitating them in all their principal
details, but 'with greater smoothness, fineness, and
floridity.'[2]   Much grace is visible in the contour of
the figures—but the old vigour is not attained—all
is too rounded and smooth—the muscles cease to be
marked—and the attempted reproduction falls (as
commonly happens) very much below the antique
standard.[3]   Ultimately Egyptian art is debased by
intermixture with Greek,[4] most unpleasing effects being
produced by a barbarous attempt to combine two styles
absolutely and essentially incongruous.   But this last
stage of decline need not occupy us here, since it
falls beyond the time whereto the present history is
confined.

Lenormant, *Manuel*, vol. i. p. 426.
'Les monuments de Rameses II.,'
says the last-named writer, 'nous
font assister à une décadence radi-
cale de la sculp'ure égyptienne, qui
se précipite avec une incroyable
rapidité à mesure qu'on s'avance
dans ce long règne.   Il débute par
des œuvres dignes de toute admiration, qui sont le *ne plus ultra* de
l'art égyptien, comme les colosses
de Memphis et d'Ibsamboul; mais
bientôt l'oppression universelle, qui
pèse sur toute la contrée comme un
joug de fer, tarit la source de la
grande inspiration des arts. La sève
créatrice semble s'épuiser dans les
entreprises gigantesques conçues par
un orgueil sans bornes.   Une nou-
velle génération d'artistes ne vient

pas remplacer celle qui s'était for-
mée sous les souverains précédents.
A la fin du règne la décadence est
complète.'
[1] Lenormant, *Manuel*, vol. i. p.
469; Birch, *Ancient Egypt*, pp.
176-7; Wilkinson, *A. E.*, vol. iii.
p. 306.
[2] Birch, p. 177.
[3] 'L'art égyptien eut une dernière renaissance, qui se prolongea
pendant toute la durée de la dynastie Saïte, et qui, *sans atteindre à
la vérité et à la grandeur des anci-
ennes écoles*, produisit cependant un
grand nombre des œuvres char-
mantes par leur finesse' (Lenormant, *Manuel*, vol. i. p. 469).
[4] Birch, *Guide to Museum*, p. 17.

CHAPTER IX.

SCIENCE.

Egyptian Science. Arithmetic. Geometry. Astronomy—Observations of Eclipses—Planetary Occultations—Motions and Periods of the Planets— Tables of the Stars—Acquaintance with true Solar Year—General Character of the Astronomy. Egyptian Astrology. Medicine. Engineering Science.

Περὶ Αἴγυπτον αἱ μαθηματικαὶ πρῶτον τέχναι συνέστησαν.—ARISTOT. *Metaph.* i. 1.

THE sciences in which the ancient Egyptians appear to have made a certain amount of progress, and which will be alone considered in the present sketch, are astronomy, geometry, arithmetic, medicine, and engineering. The bulk of the physical sciences are of recent growth, and were utterly unknown, even to the ancient Greeks. Morals, metaphysics, logic, and political science, in which the Greeks made considerable advances, were either unknown to the Egyptians, or at any rate not cultivated by them in a scientific manner.[1] There remain the abstract sciences of arithmetic and geometry, together with the practical ones of astronomy, medicine, and engineering, with respect to which there is evidence that they engaged the attention of this primitive people, and were elaborated to a certain extent, though very different opinions may

---

[1] The Egyptian ideas on morals were sound, as has been observed in a previous chapter (ch. iii. p. 104). But they did not reduce morals to a science. Their only ethical works were collections of proverbs (see Chabas, *Le plus ancien livre du Monde*, Paris, 1867).

be entertained as to the degree of perfection which was reached in them.

Arithmetic is a science some knowledge of which must of necessity be possessed by every nation that is not wholly barbarous. Savages frequently cannot count, or, at any rate, not beyond some low number, as five, six, or ten;[1] but the needs of civilised life, of buying and selling, hiring and letting, even of knowing the extent of one's possessions, require a familiarity with tolerably high figures, and the power of performing certain numerical processes. The Egyptians had an arithmetical notation similar to that of the Phœnicians, the Etruscans, and the Romans, whereby distinct signs being attached to the unit, to ten, to a hundred, a thousand, ten thousand, &c., other numbers were expressed by repetition of these characters. Just as a Roman expressed 7,423 by MMMMMMMCCCCXXIII, so an Egyptian rendered it by ↑↑↑↑↑↑↑⌐⌐⌐||; and similarly with other numbers, excepting that the Egyptians did not have special signs for five, fifty, or five hundred, like the Roman v., L., and D. It has been observed,[2] and it is undoubtedly true, that 'the Egyptian method must have been very inconvenient for calculation;' but this difficulty was in practice overcome, and there can be no doubt that all the ordinary operations of arithmetic were performed as successfully in Egypt, or in Rome, as among ourselves. Numbers were dealt with readily as far as millions,[3] and, no doubt, would have

---

[1] The Weddas of Ceylon are said not to be able to count beyond three (see *Report of the British Association for* 1875, part iii. p. 175).

[2] Kenrick, *Ancient Egypt*, vol.

i. p. 345.

[3] The numbers of various objects mentioned in the 'Great Harris Papyrus' often exceed a million (*Records of the Past*, vol. vi. pp. 43, 45, 49, &c.; vol. viii. pp. 42–5).

been carried further, if it had been necessary for practical purposes. Speculative calculations seem not to have been indulged in, or at any rate we have no evidence that they were, and the generally practical character of the Egyptian mind is against the supposition. In this they differed from the Babylonians, who formed tables of squares, not for any immediate practical purpose, but as arithmetical exercitations.[1]

The geometry of the Egyptians originated, we are told,[2] from the peculiar conditions of their country, which, owing to the changes produced by the annual inundation, required the constant employment of land-surveying. Accurate land-surveying involves a knowledge of trigonometry, and it would seem to have been mainly in this direction that the Egyptians pushed their mathematical inquiries. Pythagoras, who studied mathematics on the banks of the Nile,[3] and is said to have 'introduced geometrical problems from Egypt into Greece,'[4] was especially proud of his demonstration of that fundamental problem of trigonometry, that in every right-angled triangle, the squares of the two sides containing the right angle equal the square of the hypothenuse, or side subtending the right angle.[5] It is not absolutely certain that the Samian philosopher learnt the demonstration of this truth, or even the truth itself, in Egypt; but we may at least suspect that his Egyptian studies either embraced, or at any rate led him on to the apprehension of the truth, which was clearly not known to the Greeks before his day. So,

---

[1] See the author's *Ancient Monarchies*, vol. i. p. 103, 2nd edition.
[2] Herod. ii. 109; Diod. Sic. i. 81.
[3] Isocrat. *Busir.* § 30, p. 227; Strab. xiv. 1, § 16; Diod. Sic. i. 96, 98; Cic. *De Fin.* v. 29; Justin, xx. 4; Val. Max. viii. 7, 2; Amm. Marc. xxii. 16, § 21, &c.
[4] Callimach. ap. Diod. Sic. x. 11.
[5] Cic. *De Nat. Deor.* iii. 36; Plutarch, *De Repugn. Stoic.* vol. ii. p. 1089.

too, with regard to the scanty remains which have
come down to us of Egyptian geometry, we are told
that the problems treated of belong to ' plane trigonometry,' including its simple necessary elements, and
going somewhat beyond them.[1] How far beyond, we are
not informed; but modern criticism is probably right
in questioning whether any very considerable advance
was ever made by the native Egyptians beyond mere
plane trigonometry, and in regarding spherical trigonometry and conic sections as outside the range of their
mathematical science.[2] It is quite possible, however,
that their geometry had a development of a different
kind—that it ' led on to geography,' and the formation
of maps,[3] the first employment of which is ascribed
by some Greek writers to the Egyptians.[4]

The early direction of Egyptian thought to the
subject of astronomy is so largely attested[5] that the
most sceptical of modern historical critics does not
attempt to deny it.[6] What is questioned, and what
must be allowed to be, to a considerable extent, ques-
tionable, is the degree of their proficiency in the science
—the amount of astronomical knowledge to which they
actually attained by their own unassisted efforts, prior to

---

[1] Lenormant, *Manuel d'Histoire
Ancienne*, vol. i. p. 519.
[2] Kenrick, *Ancient Egypt*, vol. i.
p. 328; Cornewall Lewis, *Astronomy of the Ancients*, p. 278.
[3] Wilkinson in the author's *Herodotus*, vol. ii. p. 328, 3rd edition.
[4] Eustath. *Comment. ad Dionys.
Per.* p. 214, ed. C. Müller.
[5] See Plat. *Epin.* § 9, p. 987;
Arist. *De Cœlo*, ii. 12, § 3; Cic. *De
Div.* i. 42; Diod. Sic. i. 50 and
69; Strab. xvii. 1, § 5; Manil. i.
40–5; Macrob. *Comment. in Somn.
Scip.* i. 21, § 9; Plin. *H. N.* vii. 56;

Diog. Laert. *Proœm.* § 2; Val. Max.
l.s.c.; Achill. Tat. *Isag.* i. p. 73;
Clem. Alex. *Strom.* i. 16, § 74;
Lactant. *Div. Inst.* ii. 13, &c.
[6] See Lewis's *Astronomy of the
Ancients*, p. 277. 'The true character both of the Babylonian and
the Egyptian priests, as astronomers,
seems to have been, that *from an
early period* they had, induced by
the clearness of their sky, and by
their seclusion and leisure—perhaps
likewise stimulated by some religious motive—been *astronomical
observers.*' Compare p. 157.

the time when the science passed from their hands into those of the Greeks. It seems not to be doubted by any that their attention was given :—1. To eclipses of the sun and moon ; 2. to occultations of the planets ; 3. to the motions of the planets and the determination of their periodic and synodic times ; 4. to the construction of tables of the fixed stars, and the mapping them out into constellations; and 5. to the settling of the exact length of the true solar year.[1]

Eclipses are phenomena which naturally attract the notice even of barbarous and ignorant peoples, by whom they are generally regarded as fearful portents, indicative of the divine anger and of coming calamity.[2] There can be no reasonable doubt that the Egyptians from an early date observed eclipses, both of the sun and moon,[3] and entered their occurrence in the books wherein all important events were registered by them.[4] Whether they knew their causes, whether they registered them *scientifically*, whether they could to any extent predict them, are matters on which it is impossible to come to definite conclusions in the present state of our knowledge, or rather of our ignorance. It has been conjectured[5] that Pythagoras derived from

[1] See Lewis, pp. 156-7 and 287-291 ; Kenrick, *Ancient Egypt*, vol. i. pp. 328-340.
[2] Herod. i. 74 ; vii. 37 ; Liv. xliv. 37 ; Plutarch, *Æmil.* § 17. Even nations so civilised as the Greeks and Romans participated in these apprehensions (Thucyd. vii. 50 ; Plut. *Pelop.* § 31 ; *Dion,* § 24 ; Q. Curt. *Vit. Alex.* iv. 39 ; Diod. Sic. xx. 5; Tacit. *Ann.* i. 24).
[3] 'It may be reasonably suspected,' says Sir G. C. Lewis, 'that the observations of the Egyptians were particularly directed to phenomena such as *eclipses*' (*As-*

tronomy of the Ancients, p. 278). Conon, who lived about B.C. 250, made a collection of the solar eclipses which the Egyptians had observed (Senec. *Nat. Quæst.* vii. 3). Their observation of eclipses, both solar and lunar, is attested by Diodorus (i. 50) and Diogenes Laertius (*Proœm.* § 1).
[4] These registers are mentioned by Strabo (xvii. i. § 5), Theophrastus (*De Lapid.* § 24), Valerius Maximus (viii. 7, 2), and others.
[5] Kenrick, *Ancient Egypt*, vol. i. p. 340.

Egypt his acquaintance[1] with the fact that the sun is
the true centre of the planetary system, and the earth
a spherical body revolving round it—a fact which,
when known, leads on naturally to true conceptions as
to the nature of eclipses.   But we cannot be certain
that the knowledge, if he possessed it, reached him in
this way.   Doubt is thrown on the scientific character
of the Egyptian registration by the circumstance that
neither Hipparchus nor Ptolemy, who both lived in
Egypt, availed themselves, so far as appears, of the
Egyptian records;[2] nor is it easy to see how, with their
loose ideas on the subject of chronology,[3] Egyptian
savants could assign to their observations such definite
dates as might render them of service in later ages.   With
regard to prediction we have no evidence beyond the
fact that Thales, who   studied in Egypt,[4] is said to
have on one occasion predicted an eclipse of the sun;[5]
but here again, even if we accept the fact, there is
nothing to prove that the advanced knowledge of the
Milesian sage was the result of his Egyptian studies.
It is quite conceivable that he derived it from Babylon,
where the cycle of 223 lunations (or eighteen years and
ten days), which is sufficient for the prediction of lunar,
and to some extent of solar eclipses, was certainly known.[6]

---

[1] Diog. Laert. *Pythag.* 81, 25.
It must be admitted to be doubtful whether Pythagoras really knew
this fact or not. (See Lewis, pp.
123–132.)

[2] Lewis, p. 287; Kenrick, vol. i.
p. 339.

[3] The Egyptians seem at no time
to have made use of any era. They
dated events by the regnal years of
their kings.   In default of any authoritative table of the kings—and
none such seems to have existed—
a Greek or Chaldean astronomer

would derive little advantage from
the statement that an eclipse, total
or partial, of the sun or moon, had
taken place (say) in the fourth year
of Rameses II.

[4] Hieronym. ap. Diog. Laert. i.
27; Plutarch, *De Placit. Phil.* i. 3;
Joseph. *c. Ap.* i. p. 2; Clem. Alex.
Strom. i. 15, § 66; Pamphila ap.
Diog. Laert. i. 24; Euseb. *Præp. Ev.*
x. 4, &c.

[5] Herod. i. 74.

[6] See the author's *Ancient Monarchies*, vol. ii. p. 575, 2nd edition.

That occultations of the planets by the moon were carefully noted by the Egyptians, we have the testimony of Aristotle, who, after describing an occultation of Mars by the moon, proceeds to state that similar occultations of other stars (*i.e.* planets) had been noted by the Egyptians and Babylonians, who had observed the heavens for many years and communicated to the Greeks many oral reports concerning each of the stars.[1] Such occultations are of primary importance for the determination of astronomical distances; but, in order to be of service, they must be carefully timed and repeated at several distant places. It is not quite clear that the Egyptians could measure time very accurately:[2] and though the priests at the various seats of learning—Heliopolis, Thebes, Memphis—would in all probability observe the phenomena of occultations from those different localities, yet we do not hear of their comparing notes or drawing any conclusions from recorded differences in their observations. Thus the knowledge obtained was scarcely so productive as we might have expected it to be; the results which modern science derives from an occultation or a transit were not attained, nor even apprehended as attainable; probably, the bare fact of the occultation, together with some rough note of its time, was all that was put on record; and thus not even was material of much value for future progress accumulated.

The motions of the planets, which were somewhat strangely neglected by the earlier Greek astronomers,[3]

---

[1] Aristot. *De Cœlo,* ii. 12, § 3.

[2] It is probable that the Egyptians had sun-dials at least as early as the Jews, i.e. by the beginning of the seventh century B.C. But sun-dials would be of no use for measuring the time of a *lunar* occultation, which could only be observed at night. For this purpose some kind of clock was necessary; but we have no evidence that the ancient Egyptians possessed clocks.

[3] Lewis, *Astronomy of the Ancients,* p. 156. The reason of the

attracted attention in Egypt from very primitive times, and must have been studied with great care, since conclusions not very remote from the truth were arrived at concerning them. Eudoxus, who is expressly stated to have derived his knowledge of the planetary movements from Egypt,[1] laid it down that the periodic time of Saturn, or the period in which that planet completes his orbit, was thirty years; the periodic time of Jupiter, twelve years; that of Mars, two years; that of Venus and of Mercury, like that of the Earth, one year.[2] The real times are, respectively :—

	years	days	hours
Saturn	29	174	1
Jupiter	11	315	14
Mars	1	321	23
Venus		234	16
Mercury		87	23

So that, with regard to three out of the five planets known to the ancients, the error is inconsiderable; while with regard to one (Mercury) the error, though great, may readily be condoned if we consider the nearness of Mercury to the sun, and the consequent difficulty of making exact observations respecting it. The somewhat large error observable in the case of Venus is curious, and not readily explicable. Perhaps Eudoxus only meant that the two planets nearest the sun completed their orbits *within* the space of one year, not that they took the full year to complete them. It is noticeable that, in laying down his periodic times, Eudoxus in no case introduces any fractions of years.

It is otherwise in his statement of the 'synodic

neglect seems to have been, that the planets, on account of their motion, 'were classed with wandering meteors and comets,' and consequently looked down upon, the admiration of the Greeks being reserved for the stars, as fixed and immutable.

[1] 'Eudoxus primus *ab Ægypto* hos motus in Græciam transtulit.' (Senec. *Nat. Quæst.* vii. 3.)

[2] Simplicius, in the *Schol. Aristot.* ed. Brandis, p. 4996.

periods' of the planets, or the times of their periodic conjunctions. Here, once more, he derives his knowledge from Egypt;[1] and the knowledge is, comparatively speaking, exact and accurate. The periods are given in months and days. The synodic period of Mercury is 110 days; of Venus, nineteen months; of Mars, eight (twenty-five?) months and twenty days; of Jupiter and Saturn, almost exactly thirteen months.[2] If the emendation proposed[3] in the case of Mars be accepted, these numbers give a very close approximation to the true times, as will be seen by the subjoined table :—

	Eudoxus' time	True time	Excess	Defect
Saturn .	. 390 days	378 days	$\frac{2}{65}$	
Jupiter .	. 390 ,,	399 ,,	—	$\frac{3}{140}$
Mars .	. 770 ,,	780 ,,	—	$\frac{1}{77}$
Venus .	. 570 ,,	584 ,,	—	$\frac{3}{285}$
Mercury.	. 110 ,,	116 ,,	—	$\frac{3}{55}$

The error is in no case so much as one-eighteenth, and in one case (if the proposed reading be right) is as little as one-seventy-seventh.

The Scholiast upon Aratus tells us that the Greeks derived their tables of the fixed stars from the Egyptians and Chaldeans.[4] The distribution or grouping of the stars was the subject of one of the astronomical books assigned to Thoth or Hermes, and required to be learnt by the horoscopus,[5] a priest of high rank in Egypt. This grouping, of course, included an arrangement of the constellations through which the sun travels; but the Egyptian arrangement did not correspond with that of the ordinary 'signs of the Zodiac,'

---

[1] Lewis, *Astronomy of the Ancients*, l.s.c.

[2] Simplicius, l.s.c.

[3] By Ideler (*Berlin Transactions* for 1830, p. 78). It is not easy, however, to see how KE could pass into H.

[4] Schol. ad Arat. l. 752.

[5] Clem. Alex. *Strom.* p. 757.

which the Greeks (apparently) derived from the Babylonians,[1] and which the later Egyptians borrowed
from the Greeks.[2] It is said indeed to have been, like
that, duodecimal ;[3] but the names of the groups, and
probably the groups themselves, were, at any rate for
the most part,[4] different. Hence there is much difficulty in interpreting the older astronomical monuments
of Egypt, it being seldom possible to identify the stars
mentioned under their obscure and strange nomen-
clature.[5]

The ordinary Egyptian year consisted, like our own
ordinary year, of 365 days, but was divided differently.
It contained twelve months, each of thirty days; after
the expiration of which, at the close of the year, five days
were intercalated.[6] All ordinary reckoning was by
this year ; and even the festivals followed it, with the
result that in the course of time they circled round the
entire range of the seasons, the festival which was
properly a summer one becoming in turn a spring
festival, a winter, and an autumn one.[7] This effect
followed from the omission from the calendar of the
quarter-day by which the true solar year is in excess
of 365 days, or of any compensation for it, such as is
furnished by the extra day of our 'leap-years.' Still,

[1] See the author's *Ancient Mo-narchies*, vol. ii. p. 573.
[2] The zodiacs at Denderah and Esneh, which at one time were re-garded as native Egyptian, are now proved to belong to Roman times, and rightly considered to be less Egyptian than Greek. The earlier astronomical monuments are alto-gether dissimilar.
[3] Kenrick, *Ancient Egypt*, vol. i. p. 341.
[4] Achilles Tatius says (*Fragm.* p. 96) that the Greeks and Romans

took the name of the Balance from the Egyptians.
[5] Lenormant, *Manuel d'Histoire Ancienne*, vol. i. p. 520.
[6] Herod. ii. 4 ; Syncell. *Chrono-graph.* p. 123. Lepsius believes that the five intercalary days are noticed in a monument belonging to the twelfth dynasty (see Kenrick, *Ancient Egypt*, vol. i. p. 330).
[7] This is distinctly stated by Geminus (*Isagog. in Arati Phæ-nom.* § 6).

this excess appears to have been known to the Egyptians, whose ' Sothiac Cycle' was founded upon it. This was a period of 1,461 vague, or 1,460 true years, which was certainly recognised by the later Egyptians,[1] and is believed to be indicated by monuments of the Pharaonic time.[2]   It was called by the Egyptians *Sothiac*, because they fixed its commencement at a date when the Dog Star, which they called *Sothis*, rose heliacally, on the first day of the month *Thoth*, which was the beginning of their year.   Now Sirius rose heliacally in Egypt, on the first of *Thoth*, in the years B.C. 2782 and 1322, and again in A.D. 138.   This last-named year was certainly known to the Egyptians as the first of a Sothiac cycle;[3] the year B.C. 1322 was probably so known;[4] concerning the year B.C. 2782 we have no evidence.   On the whole, however, there would seem to be grounds for believing that the Sothiac period was known and used even anterior to the time of the nineteenth dynasty, and therefore that the Egyptians had from a remote antiquity advanced so far on the road to accuracy and exactness as to fix the solar year, not at 365, but at $365\frac{1}{4}$ days.   They do not appear, on the other hand, to have been aware that that estimate is in excess, or to have made any arrangements for neutralising the error such as are carefully provided by the Gregorian calendar now in general use.

The Egyptians also knew the obliquity of the ecliptic to the equator,[5] and found a way of deter-

---

[1] Censorin. *De Die Natali*, § 18; Tac. *Ann.* vi. 28; Geminus, § 6, &c.

[2] Kenrick, *Ancient Egypt*, vol. i. p. 335; Wilkinson in the author's *Herodotus*, vol. ii. p. 4: Birch, *Egypt from the Earliest Times*, p.

127.

[3] Censorin. § 21.

[4] See the arguments in Kenrick, pp. 334-5; which, however, did not convince Sir G. C. Lewis.

[5] Kenrick, p. 340.

mining an *exact* meridian line.[1]   It has been supposed
that they were acquainted with the precession of the
equinoxes;[2] but the grounds for this opinion are insufficient.   Their astronomy must thus be pronounced
on the whole not very advanced, and rather empirical
than scientific, rather practical than speculative.   Brugsch
well says of it: 'Astronomy with the Egyptians was
not that mathematical science which calculates the
movements of the stars through the construction of
grand systems of the heavens.   It was rather a collection of the observations which they had made on the
periodically recurring phenomena of earth and sky
in Egypt, the bearings of which upon each other could
not long escape the notice of the priests, who in the
clear Egyptian nights observed the brilliant luminaries
of their firmament.   Their astronomical knowledge
was founded on the base of empiricism, not on that of
mathematical inquiry.'[3]

The astronomy of the Egyptians seems to have
been less tainted with astrology than that of most
ancient nations.   In their calendar, certain days were
reckoned as lucky and others as unlucky in connection
with stellar influences;[4] and horoscopes were occasionally cast for individuals from the general aspect of the
stars at their birth,[5] or from the supposed influence of
certain ruling constellations.[6]   But astrology did not hold

---

[1] Kenrick, p. 322.
[2] Lepsius, *Chronologie der Aegypter*, pp. 190 et sqq.
[3] Brugsch, *Histoire d'Egypte*, pt.
i. p. 39, 1st edition (quoted by
Lewis, *Astronomy of the Ancients*,
p. 278, note 135).
[4] Lenormant, *Manuel d'Histoire
Ancienne*, vol. i. p. 520.
[5] Birch, *Egypt from the Earliest*

Times, p. 127; Herod. ii. 82; Diod.
Sic. i. 81; Cic. *De Div.* i. 1; Jamblich. viii. 4; Lucan, i. 640.
[6] Wilkinson says that the horo-
scope was determined 'by observing
the constellations that appeared on
the eastern horizon at the moment
of birth' (see the author's *Herodotus*, vol. ii. p. 135, note [2], 3rd
edition).

in Egypt the place that it held in Babylonia. If not
altogether 'an exotic in the country,'[1] it was at any rate
of no great account; a very small proportion of the extant
literature bears upon it ;[2] and the references made to its
employment by the Egyptians in the works of the
classical writers are few and scanty.[3]

In medicine, the Egyptians were regarded by their
contemporaries as remarkably advanced ;[4] and it seems
to be certain that they had studied the subject from a
remote period. The composition of medical works
was assigned by tradition to more than one of the most
ancient kings,[5] while by some these antique productions
were regarded as composed by one of the native
deities.[6] All physicians were expected to study them ;
and were required to employ the prescribed remedies,
and in no case to resort to others, unless the regularly
authorised prescriptions proved unavailing. Any trans-
gression of this rule of practice, if followed by the
death of the patient, was a capital offence.[7] It is evident that, under such a system, while rash experiments
would almost certainly be prevented, the progress and
improvement of the healing art would suffer no inconsiderable hindrance. Still, medical knowledge seems
to have, notwithstanding, progressed. Homer praised
the skill of the Egyptian physicians ;[8] and no sooner
did the Persian kings become masters of Western Asia

---

[1] See Lewis, *Astronomy of the
Ancients*, p. 301.

[2] A 'Sallier papyrus' contains a
calendar of lucky and unlucky days,
which has probably an astrological
basis. Otherwise, though there is
much magic in the Egyptian remains, there is little that comes
under the head of astrology.

[3] See Lewis, *Astronomy of the
Ancients*, pp. 301-4, and compare

the references in note [5] on the preceding page. (Herod. ii. 82 does
not necessarily bear on the subject.)

[4] Jerem. lxvi. 11 ; Herod. ii. 84.

[5] Manetho ap. Euseb. *Chron.*
Can. i. 20.

[6] Clem. Alex. *Strom.* vi. p. 758.

[7] Diod. Sic. i. 82. Compare
Aristot. *Pol.* iii. 10.

[8] Hom. *Od.* iv. 229.

than they had recourse to Egypt for their medical advisers.[1] If it be true that *post-mortem* examinations were allowed, and indeed commanded by royal authority,[2] we can understand that advances would be made in Egypt, since elsewhere there was generally a prejudice against the dissection of the human subject. It is clear also that the subdivision of the medical profession, which prevailed among the Egyptians,[3] must have had a tendency, in some respects, to advance medical knowledge by specialising it. On the other hand, such information as has reached us of the treatment actually employed is not of a nature to raise our estimate of the proficiency attained. The monthly use of emetics and clysters for the purpose of purging the body of its ill humours,[4] though analogous to a practice widely current in Western Europe a hundred years ago, is scarcely one in accordance with modern notions of *hygiene*. The prescriptions of the medical treatises, so far as they have been deciphered and translated, are absurd, and their physiological views seem to be purely imaginary and fantastic.[5] On the whole, while there is reason to believe that the science of medicine was better understood in Egypt than in any other country during the period with which we are concerned in this history, the positive knowledge possessed must be pronounced to have been not very considerable.

In one respect, and in one only, do the scientific attainments of the Egyptians seem to have been really

[1] Herod. iii. 1 and 132.
[2] Pliny says (*H. N.* xix. 5): 'In Ægypto, *regibus* corpora mortuorum ad scrutandos morbos insecantibus,' &c.
[3] Herod. ii. 84. According to this writer, besides dentists and oculists, the Egyptians possessed doctors who treated diseases of the stomach only, diseases of the head only, and so of other parts of the body. He even goes so far as to say that 'each physician treated only one disorder.'
[4] Herod. ii. 77; Biod. Sic. i. 82.
[5] See above, pp. 150-1.

great and surprising. Their engineering science is certainly most remarkable; and, though it has perhaps been,
like their sculpture, over-praised,[1] yet beyond dispute
there is much in it that is truly deserving of our warm
admiration. In their cutting of hard materials, in their
finished polish of surfaces, in their exact production of
whatever angle they required, in their perfect fitting of
stone to stone, and again in their power of quarrying,
transporting, and raising into place enormous masses,
this ancient people was, and still is, unsurpassed. In
stone-cutting the results attained are with reason declared to equal those which are effected at the present
day by the aid of gunpowder and of steam machinery in
the quarries of Aberdeen.[2] In mechanical skill their
great works are as perfect as anything that has ever
been produced since.[3] In massiveness of construction
they far exceed all that any other nation has ever
attempted. The engineering student is naturally lost
in admiration when he contemplates the huge masses
so prodigally employed by the Egyptians in their
temples, their palaces, and their tombs—blocks of stone
thirty or forty feet long, used in walls or for the lintels
of doors—obelisks weighing from 200 to 450 tons,
each a wonder to the Western world, but in Egypt a
common ornamentation, sometimes set up in avenues—
monolithic chambers and colossi weighing 800 tons[4]
—and all apparently moved with ease to the point required, as though there were no mechanical difficulties
whatsoever in the transportation. At the first blush,
one is apt to suppose that practical mechanics must

---

[1] Vyse, *Pyramids of Ghizeh*, vol.
i. p. 289; Owen, in *Leisure Hour*
for 1876, p. 326.
[2] Owen, l.s.c.

[3] See Fergusson, *Hist. of Architecture*, vol. i. p. 92 (quoted above,
p. 207).
[4] See above, pp. 237-8.

have been profoundly studied and pushed to great perfection by a people which could with such apparent
ease produce such an enormous number of colossal
works. But such accounts as we obtain from the
classical writers of the manner in which their grandest
achievements were effected, and such representations
as they have themselves left us of their methods of
proceeding, are calculated to dispel these ideas, and to
lower very considerably our estimate of their mechanical
science. The transportation of the hugest colossi was
effected by the simple plan of attaching ropes to them
in front and dragging the enormous mass by main force
from the quarry where it was hewn to the place where
it was intended to set it up.[1] Human muscular power
was the motive force used ; and scarcely any mechanical
art or expedients were employed to facilitate the operation. No levers were made use of, so far as appears,
no rollers.[2] Beyond the rounding off in front of the
sledge whereon the colossus was placed, and the lubri-
cating of the ground over which it had to be dragged
by some oily substance, no ingenious contrivance was
had recourse to. Sheer strength accomplished the
object aimed at, which must have been achieved slowly,[3]
painfully, and with much waste of power. It is difficult to persuade oneself that horrible accidents did not
occur with some frequency, when blocks of such an

[1] Wilkinson, *Ancient Egyptians*, vol. iii. pp. 325–8 ; and compare the author's *Herodotus*, vol. ii. pl. opp. p. 177.
[2] Levers and rollers were known to the Assyrians at the time of Sennacherib (B.C. 690), and were employed by them in the transport of colossi. (See Layard's *Nineveh and Babylon*, pl. opp. p. 112; and

compare the author's *Ancient Mo-narchies*, vol. i. p. 402, 2nd ed.).
[3] On the time consumed in the transportation of the larger masses, see Herod. ii. 175, who says that it took *three years* to convey a certain monolith from the quarries near Elephantiné to Saïs in the Delta. Two thousand men were employed in effecting the transport.

enormous size and weight were moved long distances by large gangs of human labourers.[1] The raising into place of obelisks, lintels of doors, and roofing blocks, such as those which cover in the sepulchral chamber of the Great Pyramid,[2] must have called into play some larger amount of mechanical art, and can scarcely have been managed without machines. It is certainly curious that machines are nowhere represented in the Egyptian sculptures ;[3] but Herodotus tells us that they were really employed in the construction of the pyramids,[4] and modern observation confirms his statement.[5] The machines may have been simple, or they may have been complex. As we have no representations or descriptions of them, it is impossible to determine their character. But at any rate they were such that works, difficult of execution even at the present day, were accomplished by them. Obelisks of the largest size were emplaced upon their pedestals successfully ; pyramids were built up to the height of nearly 500 feet ; temples were roofed in with huge masses of limestone or granite. Whatever were the means employed, the ends were most certainly effected ; and the lower the opinion which we form of the mechanical appliances in use, the higher must be our admiration of the skill which, with such poor means, produced such vast results.

---

[1] The occurrence of accidents is indicated by one of the stories which Herodotus heard with respect to the site occupied by the monolith above referred to. It was evidently out of place ; and 'some said that one of the workmen engaged in moving the mass was crushed and killed by it, and that this was the reason of its being left where it stood' in his day. (See Herod. ii. 175, ad fin.)

[2] See above, p. 201.

[3] Wilkinson notes this (*Ancient Egyptians*, vol. iii. pp. 325, 334, &c.).

[4] Herod. ii. 125. The contrary statement of Diodorus, who lived more than four hundred years later, is of no weight.

[5] See above, p. 205, note [2].

CHAPTER X.

RELIGION.

Large share occupied by Religion in the Life of the Nation—Esoteric and Exoteric Systems. Nature of the Esoteric Religion. Opinions concerning God, concerning Evil, and concerning the Soul. Exoteric Religion. Local origin of the Polytheism. Egyptian Pantheon—Ammon—Kneph—Khem—Phthah—Maut—Sati—Neïth—the Sun-Gods, Ra, Osiris, &c. Osirid Myths. Minor Deities—Athor, Isis, Khons, Thoth, &c. Powers of Evil, Set, Nubi, Taouris, Bes, Apap. Genii, Anubis, Amset, Hapi, &c. Orders of Gods. Triads. Character of the Worship—Prayers, Hymns, Sacrifices. Animal Worship. Apis, Mnevis, and Bacis Bulls—Momemphite Cow. Origin of the Animal Worship. Outward Aspect of the Religion—Festivals, Processions, and Worship of Ancestors. The Mysteries.

'Tout en Egypte portait l'empreinte de la Religion.'—LENORMANT, *Manuel d'Histoire Ancienne de l'Orient*, vol. i. p. 521.

THE most important element in the thought of a nation, that which beyond aught else forms and influences its character, which underlies all its customs, and comes to the surface in ten thousand various and surprising ways, is its Religion. The Egyptians were profoundly religious. What most struck Herodotus, when, in the middle of the fifth century before our era, he visited the country, was the extreme devotion of its inhabitants. 'The Egyptians,' he says,[1] 'are religious to excess, far beyond any other race of men ; ' and, accordingly, the greater portion of his description of Egypt is occupied with an account of the priests, the temples, and the

---

[1] Herod. ii. 37, ad init.

religious ceremonies.[1] We have seen that, in the architectural remains, the Temple dominates over the Palace, and is itself dominated by the Tomb,[2] both the Temple and the Tomb being the expression of religious ideas. Everywhere in Egypt gigantic structures up-reared themselves into the air, enriched with all that Egyptian art could supply of painted and sculptured decoration, dedicated to the honour, and bearing the sacred name, of some divinity. The great temple of each city was the centre of its life. A perpetual cere-monial of the richest kind went on within its walls, along its shady corridors, or through its sunlit courts— long processions made their way up or down its avenues of sphinxes—incense floated in the air—strains of music resounded without pause—all that was brightest and most costly met the eye on every side—and the love of spectacle, if not deep religious feeling, naturally drew to the sanctuary a continual crowd of worshippers or spectators, consisting partly of strangers, but mainly of the native inhabitants, to whom the ceremonies of their own dear temple, their pride and their joy, fur-nished a perpetual delightful entertainment.[3] At times, the temple limits were overpassed, and the sacred pro-cessions were carried through the streets of the town, attracting the gaze of all; or, embarking on the waters of the Nile or of some canal derived from it, glided with stately motion between the houses on either side, a fairer and brighter sight than ever.[4] The calendar was crowded with festivals, and a week rarely passed with-out the performance of some special ceremony, possess-

[1] Forty-one consecutive chap-ters of the Second Book (chs. 36-76) are entirely devoted to this sub-ject, which is further treated in chs. 91, 122, 138, and 144-6.

[2] See above, ch. vii. pp. 182, 214, &c.
[3] See Wilkinson, *Ancient Egyp-tians*, vol. iv. p. 141.
[4] Herod. ii. 60.

ing its own peculiar attractions. Foreigners saw with amaze the constant round of religious or semi-religious ceremonies, which seemed to know no end, and to occupy almost incessantly the main attention of the people.

Nor was the large share which religion had in the outer life of the nation the sole or the most important indication of the place which it held in their thoughts and regards. Religion permeated the whole being of the people. 'Writing was so full of sacred symbols and of allusions to the mythology that it was scarcely possible to employ it on any subject which lay outside the religion. Literature and science were little more than branches of theology. The arts were scarcely employed for any other purpose than with a view to worship, and for the glorification of some god or of some deified monarch. Religious laws and precepts were so numerous, so multiplied, that it was impossible to exercise a profession, or even to obtain subsistence and provide for one's daily wants, without having constantly present to the memory the regulations established by the priests. Every province had its special divinities, its own peculiar rites, its special sacred animals. It even seems as if the sacerdotal element had presided at the original distribution of the country into nomes or cantons, and that these were, at the outset, not civil, but religious divisions.'[1]

To understand the Egyptians, it is thus absolutely necessary to have something like a clear idea of their religion. The subject is, no doubt, one of great complexity and considerable obscurity; the views of the best authorities with respect to it still differ to no small

---

[1] Lenormant, *Manuel d'Histoire Ancienne*, vol. i. p. 521.

extent;[1] but a certain number of characteristic features, belonging to the inner life, seem to have obtained general recognition, while there is a still more complete agreement as to the outward presentation of the religion in the habits and actions of the people. In the present sketch, mere speculation will be, as far as possible, avoided; and only those conclusions set forth, with regard to which there is something like a general accord among the persons best acquainted with the Egyptian remains, whether sculptured or literary.

First, then, it appears to be certain that the Egyptian religion, like most other religions in the ancient world, had two phases or aspects:[2] one, that in which it was presented to the general public or vast mass of the population; the other, that which it bore in the minds of the intelligent, the learned, the initiated. To the former it was a polytheism of a multitudinous, and in many respects of a gross, character: to the latter it was a system combining strict monotheism with a metaphysical speculative philosophy on the two great subjects of the nature of God and the destiny of man, which sought to exhaust those deep and unfathomable mysteries. Those who take the lowest views of the Egyptian religion[3] admit that 'the idea of a single

---

[1] Compare Lepsius, *Das Todten-buch der Aegypter*, passim; Bunsen, *Egypt's Place*, vol. i. pp. 357–444; vol. iv. pp. 305–60; Lenormant, *Manuel*, vol. i. pp. 520–36; Birch, *Egypt*, 'Introduction,' pp. ix–xii.; *Guide to British Museum*, pp. 11–21; and De Rougé, *Etudes sur le Rituel funéraire*, passim.

[2] Lenormant says, strongly and well: 'En Egypte, comme partout dans le paganisme, *il y avait, en ré-alité, deux religions*, l'une à l'usage des classes populaires, qui n'était

que la forme extérieure de la doc-trine ésotérique, et présentait un monstrueux assemblage des plus grossières superstitions; l'autre, con-nue seulement de ceux qui avaient approfondi la science religieuse, ren-fermait quelques dogmes plus re-levés et formait une sorte de théo-logie savante, au fond de laquelle se retrouvait la grande idée de l'unité de Dieu.' (*Manuel d'Histoire Ancienne*, vol. i. pp. 521–2.)

[3] As Dr. Birch, who lays it down that 'the religion of the Egyptians

self-existent deity' was involved in the conceptions
which it set forth,[1] and is to be found not unfrequently
in the hymns and prayers of the Ritual.[2] It is impossible that this should have been so, unless there were a
class of persons who saw behind the popular mythology,
understood its symbolical or metaphysical character, and
were able in this way to reconcile their conformity to
the established worship with the great truths of natural
religion which, it is clear, they knew and which they
must have cherished in their heart of hearts.

The primary doctrine of the esoteric religion undoubtedly was the real essential Unity of the Divine
Nature. The sacred texts taught that there was a single Being, 'the sole producer of all things both in
heaven and earth, Himself not produced of any '—'the
only true living God, self-originated'—'who exists
from the beginning '—'who has made all things, but
has not Himself been made.'[3] This Being seems never
to have been represented by any material, even symbolical, form.[4] It is thought that He had no name, or,
if He had, that it must have been unlawful either to
pronounce or write it.[5] He was a pure spirit, perfect
in every respect—all-wise, almighty, supremely good.

---

consisted of an extended polytheism
represented by a series of local
groups' (*Guide to Museum*, p. 4),
and holds moreover that 'their religious notions were chiefly connected with the worship of the Sun'
(*Ancient Egypt*, ' Introduction,'
p. ix.).

[1] Birch, *Guide to Museum*, l.s.c.

[2] Birch, *Egypt from the Earliest
Times*, ' Introduction,' p. x.

[3] Lenormant, *Manuel*, vol. i. p.
522. Compare *Records of the Past*,
where such phrases as the following are frequent :—'Hail to the

One in his works, single among
the gods;' 'Chief of all the gods;'
'Father of the gods;' 'Maker of
the gods;' 'Lord of the gods;'
'the One maker of existences;' 'the
One alone without peer;' 'the true
King of gods,' &c. (See vol. ii. pp.
129–32; vol. iv. pp. 99, 100; vol.
vi. p. 100; &c.)

[4] Wilkinson, *Ancient Egyptians*,
vol. iv. p. 178.

[5] Ibid. Curiously enough, these
high monotheistic ideas are applied
in the later times, where they are
manifestly inapplicable, as to the

The gods of the popular mythology were understood, in the esoteric religion, to be either personified attributes of the Deity, or parts of the nature which He had created, considered as informed and inspired by Him. Num or Kneph represented the creative mind, Phthah the creative hand, or act of creating; Maut represented matter, Ra the sun, Khons the moon, Seb the earth, Khem the generative power in nature, Nut the upper hemisphere of heaven, Athor the lower world or under hemisphere; Thoth personified the Divine wisdom; Ammon, perhaps, the Divine mysteriousness or incomprehensibility; Osiris (according to some) the Divine goodness. It is difficult in many cases to fix on the exact quality, act, or part of nature intended; but the principle admits of no doubt. No educated Egyptian priest certainly, probably no educated layman, conceived of the popular gods as really separate and distinct beings. All knew that there was but one God, and understood that when worship was offered to Khem, or Kneph, or Phthah, or Maut, or Thoth, or Ammon, the One God was worshipped under some one of His forms or in some one of His aspects. It does not appear that in more than a very few cases did the Egyptian religion, as conceived of by the initiated, deify created beings, or constitute a class of secondary gods who owed their existence to the supreme God. Ra was not a Sun-Deity with a distinct and separate existence, but the supreme God acting in the sun,

---

Nile-God, of whom we read in one of the hymns:

He is not graven in marble;
He is not beheld;
His abode is not known;
No shrine (of his) is found with painted figures.

And again:

Unknown is his name in Heaven;
He doth not manifest his forms;
Vain are all representations!

(See *Records of the Past*, vol. iv. pp. 109, 113; with Canon Cook's comment, p. 109.)

making His light to shine on the earth, warming,
cheering, and blessing it ; and so Ra might be worshipped with all the highest titles of honour,[1] as indeed
might any god,[2] except the very few which are more
properly called *genii*, and which corresponded to the
angels of the Christian system. Such is Anubis, the
conductor of souls in the lower world,[3] and such probably are the four ' genii of the dead,' Amset, Tuamutef,
Hapi (Apis), and Kebhsnauf, who perform so conspicuous a part in the ceremonial of Amenti.[4]

(It is difficult to decide what were the esoteric views
of the Egyptians with regard to Evil. Several deities,
as Set or Sutech, Nubi, or (as Wilkinson reads the
name) Ombo,[5] and Apepi or Apophis, the great serpent, seem to be personifications of evil;)(and the
strongest antagonism is represented as existing between
these and the favourite divinities of the Egyptians, as
Ammon, Khem, Phthah, Ra, Osiris ; but whether, as
among the Persians,[6] two original Principles, one of
Good, and the other of Evil, were intended, or whether
Evil was viewed as ' a necessary part of the universal
system, inherent in all things equally with good,'[7] and
so as one aspect of the Divine nature, is to some
extent doubtful. It is hard to believe that, if the
pantheistic notion, by which Sin and Evil generally are

---

[1] In the ' Litany of Ra,' translated by M. Edouard Naville (*Records
of the Past,* vol. viii. pp. 105–28),
Ra is called ' the Supreme Power ; '
' the master of the hidden spheres ; '
' the only One ; ' ' the supremely
great one ; ' ' the great lion that creates the gods ; ' ' the great eldest
one ; ' and the like.
[2] Even the Nile-God, as we have
seen (see above, p. 314, note [5]) could
be addressed as if the Supreme God.

[3] The *Hermes psychopompus* ('Eρ-
μῆς ψυχοπομπός) of Plutarch (*De
Is. et Osir.* § 11).
[4] Wilkinson, *Ancient Egyptians,*
vol. v. pp. 70–5 ; Bunsen, *Egypt's
Place,* vol. i. pp. 430–1.
[5] *Ancient Egyptians,* vol. iv. pp.
414–15, &c.
[6] See the author's *Ancient Monarchies,* vol. ii. pp. 331–7, and vol.
iii. pp. 348–9.
[7] Wilkinson, vol. iv. p. 423.

considered to be equally of the essence of God with goodness, had been the real belief of the Egyptian priesthood, their protests in favour of virtue and against vice of all kinds could have been so strong and earnest as they are.[1]   It is also difficult to imagine that the priests would have allowed the general obliteration of the monumental emblems of Set, which is noticed by Egyptologists,[2] if they had viewed him as really an aspect of the Supreme Being. Perhaps the Egyptian priests at no time thought out the problem of the origin and nature of evil, but were content with indistinct and hazy notions upon the subject. Perhaps their views varied at different times, inclining during the earlier ages to the pantheistic doctrine, in the later to the Persian tenet of Two Principles.[3]

The continuance of the soul after death, its judgment in another world, and its sentence according to its deserts, either to happiness or suffering, were undoubted parts both of the popular and of the more recondite religion. It was the universal belief that, immediately after death, the soul descended into the lower world and was conducted to the Hall of Truth (or ' of the Two Truths '),[4] where it was judged in the presence of Osiris and the forty-two dæmones, the ' Lords of Truth ' and judges of the dead. Anubis, ' the director of the weight,'[5] brought forth a pair of scales, and, placing in one scale a figure or emblem of Truth, set in the other a vase containing the good

---

[1] See above, pp. 104, 138-9, &c.
[2] Wilkinson, *Ancient Egyptians*, vol. iv. pp. 418–19 ; Bunsen, *Egypt's Place*, vol. i. p. 443, &c.
[3] The inscription of Set and his emblems on the monuments in the earlier times, and their subsequent obliteration, imply at any rate a serious change of opinion.
[4] *Ritual of the Dead*, ch. cxxv. (Bunsen, vol. v. p. 252.)
[5] Wilkinson, *A. E.* vol. iv. p. 315.

actions of the deceased, Thoth standing by the while,
with a tablet in his hand, whereon to record the result.[1]
According to the side on which the balance inclined,
Osiris delivered sentence. If the good deeds prepon-
derated, the blessed soul was allowed to enter the
'boat of the sun,'[2] and was conducted by good spirits
to Aahlu (Elysium), to the 'pools of peace,'[3] and the
dwelling-place of Osiris. If, on the contrary, the good
deeds were insufficient, if the ordeal was not passed,
then the unhappy soul was sentenced, according to its
deserts, to begin a round of transmigrations in the
bodies of more or less unclean animals;[4] the number,
nature, and duration of the transmigrations depending
on the degree of the deceased's demerits, and the con
sequent length and severity of the punishment which
he deserved, or the purification which he required.
Ultimately, after many trials, if purity was not attained,
the wicked soul underwent a final sentence at the
hands of Osiris, Judge of the Dead, and, being pronounced incurable, suffered complete and absolute
annihilation.[5] The good soul, having first been freed
from its infirmities by passing through the basin of
purgatorial fire guarded by the four ape-faced genii,[6]

---

[1] These details are represented
with a certain amount of variety.
Sometimes Anubis is assisted by
Horus, more frequently he is alone.
Sometimes the individual himself is
weighed in the balance instead of
his actions. Occasionally Harmachis
(Harpocrates) sits on the crook of
Osiris.

[2] *Ritual of the Dead*, ch. cxxix.
(Bunsen, vol. v. p. 263.)

[3] Birch, *Egypt from the Earliest
Times*, 'Introduction,' p. x.

[4] Usually he quits the presence of
Osiris in the form of a pig, and is

reconveyed to earth by Anubis in
a boat, guarded by monkeys. (See
Wilkinson, *A. E.* 'Supplement,' pl.
87; *Description de l'Égypte*, 'Antiquités,' Planches, vol. ii. pl. 83, fig. 1 ;
Rosellini, *Monumenti del Culto*, pl.
lxvi. &c.)

[5] So Lenormant, *Manuel*, vol. i.
p. 528: 'L'anéantissement de l'être
était tenu par les Egyptiens pour le
châtiment réservé aux méchants.'
This is not perhaps universally allowed.

[6] *Ritual of the Dead*, ch. cxlviii.
(Bunsen, vol. v. pp. 298–9.)

and then made the companion of Osiris for 3,000 years, returned from Amenti, re-entered its former body, rose from the dead, and lived once more a human life upon earth. This process was reiterated until a certain mystic cycle of years became complete, when finally the good and blessed attained the crowning joy of union with God, being absorbed into the Divine Essence, and thus attaining the true end and full perfection of their being.[1]

Such, in outline, was the general belief of educated Egyptians upon the highest subjects of human thought —the nature of God, and the ultimate destiny of man. On minor points varieties of opinion no doubt existed at different times and in different parts of the country. More especially was there diversity in the arrangements which were made of the Divine attributes and aspects into groups, and the subordination of some of those groups to others, arrangements which became the basis of the well-known disposition of the popular gods into ' orders,' forming a sort of divine hierarchy.[2] It would seem that the selection of attributes and aspects made by the Egyptians was not the result of exact thought or of philosophic analysis, but was casual and partial. The priests of one district made one selection, of another another. Even where the same selection was made, different names were given. The attributes noticed, and separated off, increased in number as time went on; and it was not until a comparatively late period that graduation and arrangement were attempted. Then, in different parts of the country, different views were taken. There must always be much that is

---

[1] See above, p. 139.
[2] Herod. ii. 145; Bunsen, vol. i. pp. 361-8; Wilkinson in the au-
thor's *Herodotus*, vol. ii. pp. 284, 291; Birch, *Egypt from the Earliest Times*, 'Introduction,' p. xi.

arbitrary in distinctions between the primary and secondary qualities of any existence. When the existence is the mysterious and inscrutable Author of Nature, the arbitrariness is apt to be excessive. Hence the remarkable diversity of the Egyptian groupings, the details of which will be given in a later portion of this chapter.

It has been supposed by some that the Egyptian esoteric religion comprised a recognition of the fact, first made known to mankind distinctly by Christianity, that the Divine nature is a Trinity in Unity. In the seventeenth century Cudworth strongly supported this view ;[1] and in modern times it has been favoured by some of those who are opposed to the doctrine and desirous of tracing it to a merely human origin. But the grounds upon which Cudworth rested his belief were long ago examined and refuted by Mosheim,[2] who showed, in the first place, that the authority on whom the English divine relied was untrustworthy, and, in the second, that he did not make the assertion which was ascribed to him. Modern investigation of the religious books and inscriptions of Egypt confirms the view of Mosheim ; for, though in the local worships of the country ' triads ' were very numerous, there is not the slightest indication of the Egyptians having possessed any such conception as that of a Trinity in Unity. The Supreme Being was viewed as in his essence absolutely One, and, when divided up, was divided not into three, but into a multitude of aspects. The 'triads' are not groups of persons, but of attributes ; the Three are not co-equal, but distinctly the reverse, the third

---

[1] See his *Intellectual System of the Universe*, ch. iv. p. 413.
[2] See Mosheim's Latin transla-tion of Cudworth's great work, vol. i. notes to p. 413.

in the triad being always subordinate ; nor is the division regarded as in any case exhaustive of the Divine
nature, or exclusive of other divisions. The doctrine
of the Trinity is thus in no sense an Egyptian doctrine ;
and it is quite fanciful to suppose that it even, in any
sense, grew out of the Egyptian affection for ' triads ; '
the doctrine, as has been frequently shown, underlies
the most ancient portions of the Pentateuch, and is
most reasonably regarded as involved in that primeval
revelation which God vouchsafed to our first parents in
Paradise.

It is essential to a true conception of the popular
Egyptian religion that we recognise the fact that the
polytheistic system ultimately adopted grew up gradually, its various parts having originated separately
in different portions of the country.[1] The geographical
conformation of Egypt has a natural tendency to produce separation ; and, historically, it seems certain, not
only that, owing to its conformation, Egypt was at
various times divided into several distinct kingdoms,
but that originally *all* the nomes were distinct communities, having their peculiar customs and ideas, among
which the most markedly peculiar were those connected
with religion. No doubt ' a certain unity of religious
conception ' prevailed throughout the whole country ;
but this unity, as has been well said,[2] ' was rather a
national agreement in the mode of expressing the
religious sentiment common to mankind ' than any
more definite acceptance of a single religious system.
Egyptian worships and gods were, primarily, local ;
and the Pantheon was gradually formed by joining

---

[1] See Bunsen's *Egypt*, vol. i. pp.
364-6 ; Wilkinson in the author's
Herodotus, vol. ii. p. 284 ; Kenrick,

Ancient Egypt, vol. i. p. 363.
[2] Kenrick, vol. i. p. 364.

together the various local groups and arranging them
into a sort of hierarchy. Even these arrangements,
though proceeding upon the same principle, were not
always uniform ; and the chief centres at any rate of
religious knowledge in the country had their separate
and, to some extent, conflicting systems.[1] In most
places there was very slight recognition of any deities,
except those of the district ; and thus the polytheism,
which theoretically was excessive, practically was confined within narrow limits.

In treating of the several Egyptian gods, it will be
convenient, first of all, to take them separately, and
describe, so far as is possible, their general character
and attributes, and then to arrange them in the recognised groups, whether these were strictly local, or
such as obtained more widely. The order followed in
the general description will be based upon that which,
in his later years, was advocated by Wilkinson.[2]

AMON or AMMON. (Egypt. *Am-n.*)

Ammon was the great god of Thebes, the southern
Egyptian capital. According to Manetho,[3] his name
signified ' concealment ' or ' that which is concealed ; '
and this meaning is confirmed both by the fact, which
is now certain, that the root *amn*, in the hieroglyphics has the signification ' to veil,' ' to hide,' [4] and
also by statements in the religious poems of the

[1] Birch, *Ancient Egypt*, 'Introduction,' p. x.
[2] See the author's *Herodotus*, vol.
ii. pp. 284–7.
[3] Ap. Plutarch, *De Is. et Osir.*
§ 9: τῶν πολλῶν νομιζόντων ἴδιον
παρ' Αἰγυπτίοις ὄνομα τοῦ Διὸς εἶναι

τὸν 'Αμοῦν, Μανεθὼς μὲν ὁ Σεβεν-
νύτης τὸ κεκρυμμένον οἴεται, καὶ τὴν
κρύψιν ὑπὸ ταύτης δηλοῦσθαι τῆς
φωνῆς.
[4] Birch, *Dictionary of Hieroglyphics*, in Bunsen's *Egypt*, vol. v.
pp. 344–5.

Egyptians.[1] We may therefore safely adopt the view
of Plutarch,[2] that the original notion of Ammon was
that of a concealed or secret god, one who hid himself
and whom it was difficult to find; or, in other words,
that the mysterious and inscrutable nature of the Deity
was the predominant idea in the minds of those who
first worshipped God under this name. Ammon's
most common title is *suten-neteru*, ⸗ 🝓 ⸗, 'king of the
gods,' and hence he was naturally identified by the
Greeks and Romans with their Zeus or Jupiter,[3] who
alone of their deities had that epithet.[4] He is also
called *hek* or *hyk*, 'the ruler.' Other titles borne by
him are—'the Lord of Heaven,' 'the Eldest of the
Gods,' 'the Lord of the Throne,' 'the Strong Bull,'
and 'the Horus (sun) of the two Egypts.'[5] To him
was dedicated the first mystic region in the other world.
Originally, he seems to have been worshipped only in
Thebes; but the conquests made by the Diospolite
kings carried his cult southwards into Nubia and even
to Meroë.[6] In Lower Egypt, on the other hand, he at
no time obtained any acknowledgment, Phthah taking
his place at Memphis, Neith at Saïs, Ra at On or Heliopolis, and other gods elsewhere.

The form under which he was worshipped was that
of a man, walking or sitting upon a throne,[7] and

---

[1] See especially the hymn to Amen-Ra published in vol. ii. of *Records of the Past*, p. 132, lines 7-9:—

Ruler of men ;
Whose name is *hudden* from his creatures,
In his name which is Amen.

Compare the *Ritual of the Dead*, ch. clxvi. 'O Ammon ! I beg to know thy name. . . . *Hidden* is thy name.'

[2] See the treatise *De Isid. et Osir.* l.s.c.

[3] Herod. ii. 42 ; Biod. Sic. i. 13; Plutarch, l.s.c., &c.

[4] In Homer Zeus is πατὴρ ἀνέρων τε θεῶν τε, as in Virgil Jupiter is 'Divom pater' or 'hominum sator, atque Deorum.' No other classical god has this title.

[5] *Records of the Past*, vol. ii. p. 129 ; vol. vi. p. 100 ; Bunsen, *Egypt*, vol. i. p. 369.

[6] Bunsen, l.s.c.

[7] See Rosellini, *Mon. del Culto*, pl. ix. fig. 1.

Y 2

crowned with a head-dress, whereof the distinguishing
feature was a pair of enormously tall stiff feathers,[1]
standing side by side, sometimes plain, sometimes
varied by four or five broad black bars.[2] The colour
of his body, when he is painted, is light blue, a tint
which has been supposed to indicate ' his peculiarly
exalted and heavenly nature.'[3]   He is clothed in the
ordinary Egyptian *shenti* or tunic, a closely fitting
garment, reaching from the paps
nearly to the knees, and confined
at the waist by a girdle, besides
which he wears only a collar,
armlets, bracelets, and anklets.
In his hands he ordinarily bears
the *ankh* and the sceptre or hooked
stick (*uas*), the symbols of life and
purity,[4] to which are added occasionally the crook and flagellum,
signs of the divine power to control and punish.

. Originally Ammon was quite
distinct from Ra, 'the Sun,' no
two ideas being more absolutely
opposed than those of ' a concealed god' and of the great manifestation of Divine power and
great illuminator of all things on
earth, the solar luminary. But from the time of the

Ammon (ordinary form).

[1] One of Ammon's titles in the
hymns addressed to him is ' Lord of
the crown high-plumed' (*Records of
the Past*, vol. ii. pp. 130, 132, &c.)
[2] In some representations of Ammon, the feathers have been covered
with thick gold leaf. (See Birch,

Guide to Museum, p. 12.)
[3] Wilkinson, *Ancient Egyptians*,
vol. iv. p. 246.
[4] Ibid. vol. iv. p. 297. Bunsen
views the *uas* as the symbol of
power (*Egypt's Place*, vol. i. p.
369).

eighteenth dynasty[1] a union of the two divinities took place, and Ammon was worshipped thenceforth almost exclusively as Ammon-Ra, and was depicted with the solar orb on his head.[2] This power of amalgamating deities arose, as already explained,[3] from the essential monotheism that underlay the Egyptian polytheism,

Ammon-Khem.   Ammon-Kneph.

whereby any two or more attributes or aspects of the Divine nature might be worshipped together. Nor was this the only combination in which Ammon had part. He appears in the sculptures not unfrequently as

---

[1] Bunsen, vol. i. p. 371; *Records of the Past,* vol. ii. pp. 20, 31, 34, &c.; vol. iv. p. 11; vol. viii. p. 3, &c.

[2] Sometimes he has also the hawk's head, which is proper to Ra, or, perhaps we should say, to solar deities.

[3] See above, page 315.

Ammon-Khem, or Ammon-Kamutf,[1] which has the
same force, and has then the form of Khem, with the
head-dress of Ammon. He is also found occasionally
as Ammon-Kneph, and has the ram's head with horns
curved downwards. Further, as Ammon-Ra, he takes
naturally, in some cases, the attributes of Tum, Harmachis, or Osiris, since they were, as will be explained
later, mere forms of the Sun-God, and so really identical with Ra.

Ammon, as Ammon, had many mystic names.
Amongst them were the following:—Iruka, Markata,
Ruta, Nasakabu, Tanasa-Tanasa, and Sharushatakata.[2]
The meaning of these terms is uncertain, and it would
seem that they were but seldom used. Ammon is
ordinarily invoked as 'Amen' or 'Amen-Ra,' 'chief'
or 'king of the gods,' and 'lord of all earthly thrones.'
The hymns addressed to him are often remarkable for
their simplicity and beauty. 'O Ammon,' says one
suppliant, 'lend thine ear to him who stands all alone
before the tribunal. He is poor; he is not rich. The
Court oppresses him : silver and gold (are needed) for
the clerks of the book, garments for the servants.
There is no other Ammon, that acteth as a judge, to
deliver a man from his misery; that, when the poor
man comes before the tribunal, maketh the poor to go
forth rich.'[3] 'Thou art He that giveth bread,' says
another, 'to him that has none; that maintaineth the
servant of thy house. Let no prince be my defender
in my troubles; let not my memorial be placed before

---

[1] *Description,* 'Antiquités,' vol.
iii. pl. 45, fig. 2.
[2] *Ritual of the Dead,* ch. clxvi.
In one of the Hymns to Amen, he
is called 'King alone, single among

the gods; of *many* names, *unknown
is their number.*' (See *Records of
the Past,* vol. ii. p. 134, § 17.)
[3] *Records of the Past,* vol. vi. p.
99.

men.. My Lord is my defender; I know his power;
He is a strong defender; there is none mighty beside
Him. Strong is Ammon, and knoweth how to make
answer. He fulfilleth the desire of all those who pray
to Him.'[1] As Ammon-Ra, the addresses made to him
are more elaborate. One, which has been translated
by Mr. Goodwin, extends to above two hundred lines,
and contains several curious and striking passages, as
for instance the following :—

'Hail to thee, Ra, Lord of truth! Whose shrine
is hidden, Lord of the gods; Creator, sailing in thy
boat; at whose command the gods were made; Tum,
the maker of men; that supportest their works, that
givest them life, that knowest how one differeth from
another; that listenest to the poor who is in distress;
that art gentle of heart when a man crieth unto thee;
Thou who deliverest the fearful man from the violent;
who judgest the poor and the oppressed; Lord of
wisdom, whose precepts are wise; at whose pleasure
the Nile overflows her banks; Lord of mercy, most
loving, at whose coming men live; Opener of every
eye; proceeding from the firmament; Causer of pleasure and light, at whose goodness the gods rejoice,
their hearts reviving when they see Thee.'[2]

KNEPH.   (Egypt. *Khnum* or *Num*.)

Kneph was the special god of Elephantiné, but he
was worshipped also in all the more southern parts of
Egypt, in Nubia, and in Ethiopia.[3] We are told that
his name was identical in meaning with the Greek
πνεῦμα, 'spirit,' or 'breath.' If we may accept this

---

[1] *Records of the Past*, vol. vi. pp. 99–100.
[2] Ibid. vol. ii. p. 131.
[3] Wilkinson, *Ancient Egyptians*, vol. iv. pp. 231, 235; Bunsen, *Egypt's Place*, vol. i. pp. 375–7.

statement on the authority of Plutarch and Diodorus,[1] and regard the root *num*, 𓊽 𓏲, as really equivalent to *nef*, 𓈖, 'breath,' we must suppose that the original notion of Kneph was that of God as a spirit, moving over matter and breathing into it form and life.[2] This special notion was, however, soon overlaid and super-

Kneph.

seded by the more general one that he was the Creator, and in a peculiar sense the creator of mankind.[3] He was also regarded as presiding in some special way over water, which was expressed by *nem*, 𓊽 𓈖, as well as by *mu*, 𓄿 𓏲 𓈖, in Egyptian.[4] In this capacity he

---

[1] Plutarch, *De Isid. et Osir.* § 26; Diod. Sic. i. 12, § 2. Neither writer mentions Kneph, but both evidently point to him.

[2] Compare Gen. i. 2: 'And the Spirit of God (רוּחַ אֱלֹהִים) moved upon the face of the waters.'

[3] Birch, *Ancient Egypt*, 'Introduction,' p. x.

[4] See the 'Hieroglyphical Dictionary' in Bunsen's *Egypt*, vol. v. pp. 425 and 452.

was 'lord of the inundation.'[1] He had further a position among the gods of the lower world,[2] which does
not belong to Ammon, who may be prayed to by the
dead,[3] but is in no sense an infernal god.

Kneph was figured as a man walking, like Ammon,
but with the head of a ram. This head has commonly
two sets of horns, both those curving downwards,
which are characteristic of the real animal, and a
second pair, spiral, growing from the top of the head,
which are properly those of the he-goat.[4] These latter
horns appear also on the head of the sitting god which
completes the hieroglyph of Kneph, ; and the
form of the entire animal is not unfrequently attached
to his name, without (as it would seem) any phonetic
force. The he-goat, with spiral horns extended, must
therefore be considered as his emblem, though the ram
was the animal especially sacred to him. Above and
between the spiral horns we see sometimes the asp or
uræus, while occasionally that place is occupied by the
vase,[5] which was the main element in his name. In his
two hands he bears, like Ammon, the sceptre, *uas*, and
the emblem of life, *ankh.* His colour is a bright
green.[6]

Kneph is also found with the peculiar crown (*atef*)
on his head which more commonly characterises Ra or
Osiris, a crown composed of the solar disk, with an

---

[1] Wilkinson, *A. E.* vol. iv. p.
238.

[2] Bunsen, vol. i. p. 377. Hence
he is 'frequently represented in the
tombs' (Wilkinson, *A. E.* vol. iv. p.
239).

[3] See the *Ritual*, § clxiii., ad fin.,
and § clxvi.

[4] So Birch, and Bunsen (*Egypt's
Place*, vol. i. p. 375). Wilkinson,

however, maintains that the long
spiral horns are also those of a kind
of sheep (*Ancient Egyptians*, vol. iv.
pp. 242–3).

[5] Wilkinson, *A. E.* vol. iv. p.
237.

[6] Ibid. p. 241 ; Bunsen, vol. i. p.
376; Rosellini, *Monumenti del Culto,* pl. lxv.

ostrich feather on either side, and between the feathers a tall striped conical cap, surmounted by a flower or a tassel.[1] Occasionally, but very rarely, he has for distinctive mark simply the uræus, which is placed on his head, or a little over it.[2]

The Greeks confused Kneph with Ammon,[3] not unnaturally ;[4] and some moderns so far agree with them as to consider Kneph ‘ a form of Ammon.’[5] This view, however, is not generally accepted, and it would seem to be no otherwise true than in so far as all Egyptian gods were, *to the initiated*, forms of the Supreme God, and so interchangeable one with another. In the minds of the vulgar, Kneph was as distinct from Ammon as from Phthah or Khem, and had his own temples, his own form, his own colour, his own proper sacrifices, ceremonies, and the like. Though the embodiment of God as a spirit, he was a less spiritual conception than Ammon. His position in the hierarchy was probably between Ammon and Khem, with both of whom he had certain points in common. Less mysterious than Ammon, less remote from matter, less purely immaterial, he was of a more ethereal nature

[1] See a representation in Wilkinson, *A. E.* ‘Supplement,’ pl. 21, part i. fig. 2 ; and compare Rosellini, *Monumenti del Culto*, pl. ii. fig. 3; pl. xx. fig. 1 ; pl. li. fig. 2 ; &c.

[2] Wilkinson, *Ancient Egyptians*, vol. iv. p. 239. When Herodotus (ii. 74) speaks of the horned snake as sacred to the Theban Jupiter (Ammon), he is probably confusing Ammon with Kneph, and the horned snake (*coluber cerastes*) with the asp (*coluber haje*).

[3] Herodotus, in the same chapter in which he identifies the Egyptian Ammon with the Greek Zeus, says that ‘ the Egyptians give their statues of Zeus the face of a ram ’ (ii.

42), which is only true of Kneph. Alexander, on his conquest of Egypt, claimed to be the son of Ammon, and thereupon adopted the curved ram’s horn which marks his coins and so many of the coins of his ‘ successors.’ Lucan has the phrase ‘ tortis cornibus Ammon ’ (*Pharsal.* ix. 514), and in Claudian (*De quarto Consulatu Honorii*, 1. 143) Ammon is ‘ corniger.’

[4] Since there was but one God in their Pantheon who could well be paralleled with either Ammon or Kneph, and since Ammon was *occasionally* represented with the head of Kneph. (See above, p. 325).

[5] Birch, *Guide to Museum*, p. 16.

than Khem, whose grosser attributes were not reproduced in him. Bunsen supposes that in order of time
Khem was anterior to Kneph;[1] but, if this were so, of
which there is no proof, still in idea Kneph must be
assigned the precedence. Kneph was the creative
spirit, Khem the generative power; Kneph presided
over men, Khem over nature. Kneph has higher
titles than any which belong to Khem. He was 'the
god who made the sun and moon to revolve under the
heaven and above the earth, and who created the world
and all things in it'—' the god who forms on his wheel
the divine limbs of Osiris '—' the god who forms the
mothers, the progenitresses of the Divine Beings '—' the
sculptor of all men.'[2]   It was not without some reason
that Wilkinson originally placed him at the head of the
Egyptian Pantheon,[3] though ultimately he assigned
that place to Ammon.

KHEM.   (Egypt. *Khem*[4] or *Khemi*.)

The full Egyptian idea of Khem can scarcely be
presented to the modern reader, on account of the
grossness of the forms under which it was exhibited.
Some modern Egyptologists[5] endeavour to excuse or
palliate this grossness ; but it seems scarcely possible
that it should not have been accompanied by indelicacy
of thought, or that it should have failed to exercise a
corrupting influence upon life and morals. Khem, no
doubt, represented to the initiated merely the generative power in nature, or that strange law by which
living organisms, animal and vegetable, are enabled to

[1] *Egypt's Place,* vol. i. p. 388.
[2] Ibid. p. 377.
[3] *Ancient Egyptians,* vol. iv. pp. 235–43.
[4] Some read the hieroglyph of

this god ⟶⟵ as Min.

[5] See Wilkinson, *Ancient Egyp-tians,* vol. iv. p. 202.

reproduce their like. But who shall say in what exact light he presented himself to the vulgar, who had continually before their eyes the indecent figures under which the painters and sculptors portrayed him? As impure ideas and revolting practices clustered around the worship of Pan in Greece and later Rome, so it is more than probable that with the worship of Khem in Egypt were connected similar excesses. Besides his Priapic or 'ithyphallic' form,[1] Khem's character was marked by the assignment to him of the goat as his symbol,[2] and by his ordinary title, *Ka-mutf*, 'the Bull of his Mother,' *i.e.* of Nature.

Apart from the gross feature here noticed, Khem's image may be readily recognised by its being enveloped in swathes, like a mummy, with the exception of the right arm, which is upraised and brandishes the flagellum. Another distinguishing mark of Khem is the long bar which descends to the ground from the back of his head, and seems intended to prevent him from falling. He wears the same head-dress as Ammon, and has very generally a cross, shaped like the letter X, upon his breast.[3]

As the god of the vegetable world, Khem is represented generally with trees or plants about him, and the Egyptian kings offer him herbs and flowers, or cut the corn or till the soil in his presence.[4] The special seat of his worship was Chemmis,[5] or, more properly, Chemmo, a place which evidently took its name from

---

[1] Bunsen, vol. v. p. 583.
[2] Herod. ii. 46. Compare Bunsen, vol. i. p. 374.
[3] Wilkinson, *A. E.* 'Supplement,' pls. 26, 76, and 77, part ii.; Bunsen, vol. i. pl. i.; *Description,* 'Antiquités,' vol. iii. pl. 14, fig. 4, &c.

[4] Wilkinson, *A. E.* vol. iv. pp. 257–8; *Description de l'Egypte,* 'Antiquités,' vol. ii. pl. 11, fig. 3; vol. iii. pl. 36, fig. 4, &c.
[5] Herod. ii. 91; with Wilkinson's note.

him, and which the Greeks appropriately called 'Pan's city' (Panopolis). But he was also worshipped in Thebes, and, to some extent, in Egypt generally. A feast was held in his honour, called 'the bringing forth of Khem,' whereat bulls, geese, incense, wine, and fruit were offered.[1]

The titles of Khem are best set forth in an inscription belonging to the time of Darius Hystaspis, which was found in the temple of Ammon at El-Khargeh.[2] He is there called 'the God Khem, who raises his lofty plumes,[3] king of the gods, lifter of the hand,[4] lord of the crown, powerful, from whom all fear emanates, the Kamutf who resides in the fields, horned in all his beauty, engendering the depths.' Like Ammon, he was occasionally identified with the Sun,[5] the source of warmth and so of all mundane life, and was worshipped as Khem-Ra, or 'Khem, the Sun-God.' He is even said in some inscriptions[6] to have been 'engendered by the Sun ;' but this can only have been

Khem.

---

[1] *Records of the Past,* vol. ii. p. 55.

[2] Ibid. vol. viii. p. 142.

[3] The allusion is to the tall plumed head-dress common to Khem with Ammon.

[4] This marked feature in the representations of Khem has been already noticed (supra, p. 332). It is mentioned by Stephen of Byzantium (ad voc. ΠΑΝΟΣ ΠΟΛΙΣ), who says the hand and whip were 'directed against the moon,' which seems very improbable.

[5] Wilkinson, *Ancient Egyptians,* vol. v. p. 264.

[6] Ibid.

a loose mode of expression, since beyond all doubt he
was regarded as a form of the Supreme God, and
so as self-originated.   Hence one of his titles was
' father of his own father.'

PHTHAH.   (Egypt. *Ptah.*)

Phthah, **∎❡**, the Egyptian god whom the Greeks
identified with their Hephaistos,[1] was the actual physical creator, the ' demiurge,' as the Greeks called him,

Ordinary forms of Phthah or Ptah.

the shaper and framer of the material universe.   The
special seat of his worship was Memphis ; but he was
also very generally adored, and figures of him are
found in all parts of Egypt.   These figures are of three
very distinct forms.   The commonest is that of a man
swathed like a mummy, but with the hands left free,
to allow of his holding in front of him the sceptre (*uas*)
and sign of life (*ankh*), with which is combined, gene-

---

[1] Herod. ii. 99; iii. 37; Dio- | *De Isid. et Osir.* § 10; Horapollo,
dorus Siculus, i. 57, § 5; Plutarch, | i. 10; &c.

rally, the so-called Nilometer, or emblem of stability. The head is covered with a close-fitting cap, and from the drapery behind the neck there comes out a string to which is appended a bell-shaped tassel.[1] Another figure is that of a man walking, dressed in the ordinary tunic (*shenti*), and holding the *ankh* and *uas*, only to be distinguished from figures of Ammon by the head-dress, which, instead of the tall plumes, is either the plain cap, or the striped head-dress of a king with lappets in front.[2] The third form is that of a pigmy, naked,[3] often with misshapen legs and feet turned inwards, and usually with a scarabæus on the top of the skull. Occasionally this figure is double, with four legs and four arms, hawk-headed at the back and human-headed in front.

The pigmy forms, and certain others—modifications, chiefly, of the second type[4]—are regarded as representing Phthah under a special character, as Phthah Sokari or Phthah-Sokari-Osiris; that is to say, Phthah viewed as having some special connection with Osiris, the lord of the lower world. In the figures which front two ways Phthah would seem to be represented by the human, and Sokari by the hawk-headed, form.[5] No wholly satisfactory explanation has as yet been given of the reasons for this union ; but perhaps they are to be found in the vivifying power of Phthah, and the supposed resurrection of Osiris from the dead,

---

[1] See Wilkinson, *Ancient Egyptians*, 'Supplement,' pl. 23, figs. 1, 4, and 6; Rosellini, *Monumenti del Culto*, pl. vi. fig. 1 ; Bunsen, *Egypt's Place*, vol. i. p. 382 ; *Description de l'Egypte*, 'Antiquités,' vol. iii. pl. 32, fig. 4.

[2] Wilkinson, pl. 23, figs. 2 and 5; pl. 24, fig. 3; Rosellini. *Mon.*

del Culto, pl. xxxvi. fig. 1, &c.

[3] See above, p. 266 ; and compare Herod. iii. 37; Bunsen, vol. i. p. 383; Wilkinson, pl. 24 A, fig. 1 ; Birch, *Guide to Museum*, p. 13 ; *Gallery*, pl. 7, fig. 18.

[4] See Wilkinson, *A. E.* vol. vi. pl. 24, figs. 1, 2, and 3.

[5] Ibid. vol. iv. p. 254.

which may have been regarded as effected through
Phthah's influence.

The principal titles of Phthah are—'the Lord of
Truth,' 'the Lord of the World,' and 'the beautiful-
faced.'[1] He is also called 'the father of the begin-
nings,' and 'the creator of all that is in the world.'[2]
Ma, 'Truth,' is sometimes represented as standing before him ; and Jamblichus was no doubt right in saying
that he was considered to have created all things, 'not
deceptively, but *with truth*.'[3] The four-barred emblem
of stability is especially characteristic of him, and,
unless when he bears the character of Phthah-Sokari,
generally appears, either in his hands, on his head, or
at his back. It is even used, together with the scarabæus and the solar disk, as emblematic of him, without
the addition of any human figure.[4]

The derivation of the word Phthah (Ptah) is, perhaps, doubtful ; but the most probable theory connects
it with an Egyptian root, *pet-h* or *pet-hu*, ' to open.'[5]
Phthah was the great ' opener ' or ' revealer '—the god
who brought everything out of the ideal into the actual
—who made the previously hidden deity (Ammon)
manifest. At Memphis he was the chief, if not the
sole, object of worship to the people ; and the kings of
Thebes, after they became masters of Lower Egypt,
were among his ardent devotees, and often called him
their ' father.'[6] His temple at Memphis seems to have
been regarded by Herodotus as more magnificent than

[1] Birch, *Guide to Museum*, p. 13; Bunsen, vol. i. p. 382.
[2] Bunsen, vol. i. p. 384.
[3] Jamblich. *De Mysteriis*, iv. 3.
[4] Wilkinson, *Ancient Egyptians*, vol. iv. p. 253.
[5] Birch, *Guide to Museum*, p. 11.

It is of course quite possible that the Egyptian root *pet-h* has a connection with the Hebrew פָּתַח, which in Kal has the same meaning.
[6] See *Records of the Past*, vol. iv. p. 35; vol. viii. pp. 6, 7, 22, &c.

any other in Egypt, though it has now almost wholly disappeared, and the traveller can with difficulty trace its site. Monarch after monarch adorned it with statues and gateways,[1] each seeking to outdo his predecessors; but the ravages of time, and the still more destructive hand of man, have swept away the entire pile, and a single colossus of the second Rameses is almost all that remains to attract attention to the place.[2]

MAUT. (Egypt. *Mut.*)

Maut, 'the mother,' which is the meaning of the word, was a 'great goddess,' worshipped especially at Thebes, in connection with Ammon (or Ammon-Ra) and Chons. She represented the passive principle in nature, and corresponded to the classical Rhea or Cybele, rather than to Latona, with whom she is identified by Herodotus.[3] Among her titles the chief were, 'Lady of Heaven,' 'Queen of the gods,' 'giver of all life for ever,' and 'mistress of darkness.'[4] In the last-mentioned phrase the darkness intended is not that of night, nor of the Lower World, but the primeval darkness of chaos, ere light was,[5] which the Egyptians regarded as, in a certain sense, 'the one principle of the universe.'[6]

Maut is expressed in Egyptian either by ⌇ or 𓅐, both forms being phonetic, and the latter emblematic

[1] Herod. ii. 101, 110, 121, § 1, 136, and 153.
[2] Brugsch, *Geschichte Aegyptens*, p. 47; Wilkinson, *A. E.* vol. iii. p. 399; Lenormant, *Manuel d'Histoire Ancienne*, vol. i. p. 552: 'Aucun monument de Memphis ne subsiste encore debout.'
[3] Herod. ii. 155. I assume the identity of Buto with Mut, about which Wilkinson was doubtful

(*A. E.* vol. iv. pp. 271–5), but which later writers regard as certain. (See Bunsen, vol. i. p. 379.)
[4] See *Records of the Past*, vol. iv. pp. 88, 94; vol. vi. p. 71; and Bunsen, l.s.c.
[5] Wilkinson, *A. E.* vol. iv. p. 274.
[6] Damascius in Cory's *Ancient Fragments*, p. 320.

as well, since the vulture was the Egyptian type of ma-
ternity.[1]   She is represented by a female figure wearing
the *pshent* or double crown, the emblem of sovereignty
both over Upper and Lower Egypt, placed upon a cap
ornamented with the head, body, and wings of a vulture.   Wilkinson notes that the *pshent* is not worn by
her as by the Egyptian kings, the one crown placed
within the other, but that the two crowns are worn
side by side,[2] that of Upper Egypt
being nearest to the spectator.   In
her two hands she bears the *ankh*
and either the hooked sceptre (*uas*)
or else one terminating in a lotus-
flower.   She is draped in the ordinary close-fitting robe, confined below the breasts by a girdle, and
wears a collar, bracelets, and anklets.

In the popular mythology, Maut
was the companion and wife of
Amen-Ra, with whom she is constantly associated in the inscriptions
and sculptures.[3]   The shrew-mouse
was dedicated to her,[4] probably as
a type of fecundity, or perhaps be-

Maut.

cause it was thought to be blind, and was thus a good
representative of ' darkness.'[5]   Besides being worshipped
at Thebes, Maut was honoured throughout Nubia, and
even in Ethiopia, where her name is often found in the

---

[1] Horapollo, i. 11.
[2] Wilkinson, *A. E.* vol. iv. p. 276. For a good *clear* representation see Rosellini, *Mon. del Culto*, pl. lvii. fig. 2.
[3] *Records of the Past*, vol. iv. pp.

88, 94; vol. vi. pp. 23, 24, 34, &c.; Rosellini, pl. xiii. fig. 1; xxx. fig. 4; xxxi. fig. 4; xxxvi. fig. 2; &c.
[4] Herod. ii. 67.
[5] Plutarch, *Sympos.* iv. Q. 5; Wilkinson, *A. E.* vol. iv. p. 273.

inscriptions.[1] If we may identify her with the Buto of
Herodotus, we must add that she was likewise among
the principal objects of worship in Lower Egypt, where
she had a famous temple and oracle at a city which bore
her name, on the western side of the Sebennytic branch
of the Nile, about twenty miles from the sea.[2]

SATI.   (Egypt. *Sat*, or *Sati*.)

Sati stood in the same relation to Kneph as Maut
to Ammon-Ra. She was his wife and perpetual companion.[3] She had not, however,
like Maut, the clear and unmistakable character of a goddess of
Nature. Rather she appears as a
sort of Queen of Heaven,[4] and was
therefore compared by the Greeks
to their Hera, and by the Romans
to their Juno.[5] The special seat of
her worship was Elephantiné; and
she was also acknowledged throughout Nubia and in Ethiopia;[6] but
in Lower Egypt she seems to have
been scarcely ever either represented or mentioned. Her name
is thought to signify 'a sunbeam,'[7]
and is expressed commonly by

Sati.

or ⪢, followed by the form of a goddess.

---

[1] *Records of the Past*, vol. iv. pp.
88, 94; vol. vi. p. 71.
[2] Herod. ii. 83, 133, 152, and
155–6.
[3] Wilkinson, *A. E.* vol. iv. p.
266; Birch, *Guide to Museum*, p.
13.
[4] According to Horapollo, Sati
(Hera) presided over the upper por-

tion of the firmament of heaven
(i. 11).
[5] The bilingual inscriptions in the
neighbourhood of Elephantiné show
this. (See Bunsen, vol. i. p. 381.)
[6] Wilkinson, *A. E.* vol. iv. p.
267.
[7] Birch, in Bunsen's *Egypt*, vol.
v. p. 583. There is no appearance,

z 2

The ordinary representation of Sati is a standing female figure, clothed in a long tight gown, with collar, belt or band, armlets, bracelets, and anklets, as usual, holding in her hands the *ankh* and lotus sceptre, and wearing on her head the crown of Upper Egypt, with cow's horns projecting from it on either side.[1]   Sometimes, however, she is found seated on a throne or chair behind her husband, clad as above described, but with bare breasts and with a snake projecting in front of her horned crown.   When coloured, her tint is of a warm red representing human flesh ; her headdress is white ; her sceptre, anklets, bracelets, and armlets are green ; and her robe is delicately patterned in narrow stripes of blue, green, and white.   The throne on which she sits, and its pedestal, are also patterned, or rather diapered, in the same colours.[2]

NEITH.   (Egypt. *Net* or *Nat.*)

Neith, according to the Greeks, corresponded to their Athêné,[3] and was thus a personification of the wisdom or intellect of God.   She was the especial goddess of Saïs, the chief city of the Delta, where she seems to have been worshipped alone, not as the member of any triad.   Her name is written with the two letters NT (⌣), after which follows an emblem, apparently non-phonetic, ⤙, in which most Egyptologists recognise a shuttle.[4]   Her most usual title was

however, of her having any solar character, and the arrow which forms an element in her name, or accompanies it, would seem rather to point to a war-goddess.

[1] Wilkinson, *A. E.* vol. iv. p. 270, and 'Supplement,' pl. xxi. part 2, fig. 1 ; Bunsen, vol. i. p. 381, and

pl. ii. fig. 2.

[2] See the *Description,* ' Antiquités,' vol. i. pl. 16.

[3] Plato, *Tim.* p. 21, E.   Compare Herod. ii. 168.

[4] Wilkinson, *Mat. Hieroglyph.* vii. ; Bunsen, *Egypt's Place,* vol. i. p. 386 ; &c.

'Lady of Saïs.' She is also called 'the mother,' 'the mistress of heaven,' 'the elder goddess,' and 'the cow that produced the sun.'[1] She is figured, ordinarily, as a female, dressed like Maut and Sati, but wearing the *teshr*, or crown of Lower Egypt, only, on her head.[2] In her right hand she bears the symbol of life, in her left either the *uas* or the lotus sceptre, to which are added in some instances a bow and two arrows.[3] Occasionally, instead of the crown, she wears the common

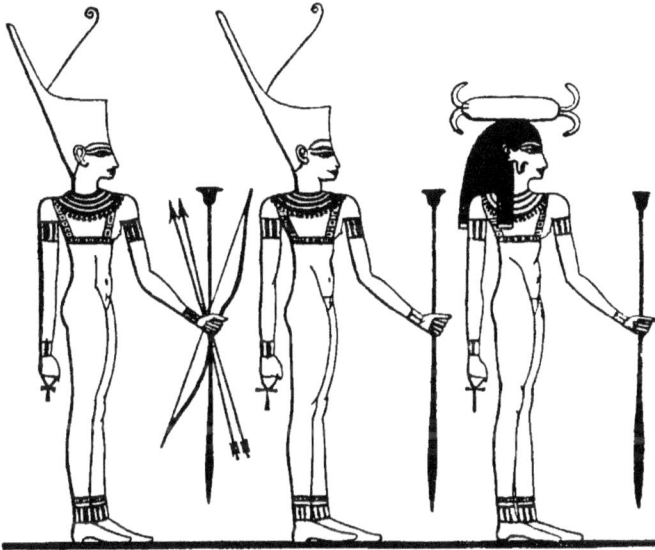

Neith.

female headdress, surmounted by the so-called shuttle.[4] It is thought that she presided specially over war and weaving.[5]

It is difficult to reconcile with this somewhat prosaic view of Neith the recondite and mystical ideas

---

[1] Bunsen, l.s.c.
[2] Rosellini, *Mon. del Culto*, pl. liv. fig. 2.
[3] Wilkinson, *A. E.* vol. iv. p.
285; 'Supplement,' pl. xxviii. figs. 1 and 2; Bunsen, vol. i. pl. 2, fig. 5.
[4] Wilkinson, pl. xxviii. fig. 3.
[5] Birch, *Guide to Museum*, p. 13.

entertained by the Greeks and Romans with respect to
the Saïtic goddess.   Plutarch says[1] that her name
meant 'I came from myself'—a meaning which would
imply self-origination, and so the highest and most supreme divinity.   Macrobius considers her 'that virtue
of the sun which administers prudence to the human
mind.'[2]   Clemens of Alexandria declares that the inscription on her shrine at Saïs ran as follows : [3]—'I am
all that was, and is, and is to be ; and no mortal hath
lifted my veil.'   It is impossible to suppose that there
was no foundation for these higher views ; and a certain
support is lent to them by her title of 'Mother' or
'Great Mother,' which would seem to imply that she
was essentially a Nature goddess, not very different
from Maut.

THE SUN-GODS, RA, KHEPRA, TUM, SHU, MENTU, OSIRIS, HORUS, HARMACHIS, ATEN.

That a large part of the Egyptian religion was connected with the worship of the sun cannot be denied,
though it seems scarcely correct to say that their worship was ' chiefly solar,'[4] or that 'most of their gods'
represented some aspect of the sun, or some portion of
his passage through the upper or the lower hemisphere.[5]
Still, the nine deities above enumerated had certainly,
all of them, more or less of a solar character, though
no two in the list can be considered as mere synonyms,
or as duplicates, the one of the other.

   Ra was the sun in the widest and most general
sense.   To the initiated he was the power of God as

---

[1] De Isid. et Osir. § 62.
[2] Saturn. i. 19.
[3] Strom. v. p. 155.

[4] Birch, Ancient Egypt, ' Introduction,' pp. ix-x.
[5] Ibid. ; Guide to Museum, p. 11.

shown forth in the material sun, which is the source of light and life to the world wherein we live, to the planets, and, as the Egyptians thought, to the universe. To the vulgar he was a created god, the son of Phthah and Neith,[1] though he was often, indeed generally, worshipped with all the highest epithets of honour, as if he were the supreme God Himself. In the 'Litany of Ra'[2] he is called 'the Supreme Power,' 'the only one,' 'the supremely great one,' 'the great eldest one,' 'the great sire that creates the gods,' 'the master of the hidden spheres who causes the principles to arise,' 'the dweller in darkness,' 'the master of light,' 'the revealer of hidden things,' 'the spirit who speaks to the gods in their spheres,' &c. His name is sometimes expressed phonetically ⊃, Ra; sometimes symbolically by a circle, with or without the addition of the asp or *uræus* (o or ᴌ⌒); sometimes by a union of the two methods ⊃₁°, or with the addition of the figure of a god ⊃₁° 𝄝. It was proposed originally to pronounce the name as Rê;[3] but modern Egyptologists seem to be agreed that the true sound was Ra,[4] which was also the name of the Supreme God in Babylon,[5] and which probably meant 'swift.'[6]

Ra is figured as a man, walking, but commonly has the head of a hawk, surmounted by the disk of the sun, with the *uræus* or asp encircling it.[7] He bears in his

---

[1] Bunsen, *Egypt's Place*, vol. i. p. 387.
[2] See the *Records of the Past*, vol. viii. pp. 105-128.
[3] Wilkinson, *A. E.* vol. iv. p. 287; *Mat. Hieroglyph.* p. 6.
[4] Bunsen, l.s.c.; Birch, *Ancient Egypt,* 'Introduction,' p. x.; Lenormant, *Manuel,* vol. i. p. 524; Brugsch, *Geschichte Aegyptens,* p. 29; &c.

[5] Rawlinson, *Ancient Monarchies,* vol. i. p. 143.
[6] *Raâ* and *rau* mean 'swift' in Ancient Egyptian. (See Birch's *Dictionary* in Bunsen's *Egypt,* vol. v. p. 466.)
[7] Bunsen, vol. i. p. 387; Wilkinson, *A. E.* vol. iv. p. 295; and compare Rosellini, *Monumenti del Culto,* pl. x. fig. 1; pl. xxx. fig. 2; pl. xxxiii. fig. 1; &c.

right hand the *ankh* or sign of life, and in his left the *uas* or sceptre. From his head depends a long cord, as from the heads of Kneph and Ammon. He wears the usual *shenti* or tunic, with armlets, bracelets, and anklets. Occasionally he is found human-headed, and in that case has the long wig with lappets.[1] In the paintings his flesh is always of a red or red-brown colour, as is also the disk of the sun superimposed upon him.

Among the emblems appropriate to Ra are, besides

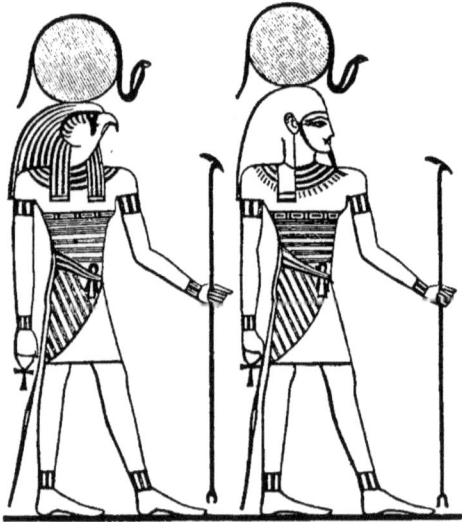

1.   2.
Ra.

the solar disk, the hawk, the *uræus* or asp, and the *scarabæus* or beetle. The hawk is said to have been 'dedicated to him as the symbol of light and spirit, because of the quickness of its motion, and its ascent to the higher regions of the air.'[2] Another ground

---

[1] Wilkinson, *A. E.* 'Supplement,' pl. xxix. fig. 3.
[2] Ibid. vol. iv. p. 295. This explanation was first given by Porphyry.

assigned is, that ' the hawk is able to look more intently towards the solar rays than any other bird, wherefore they depicted the sun under the form of a hawk, as the Lord of Vision.'[1]   The uræus probably accompanied him as ' the emblem of royalty and dominion.'[2]   Why the beetle was assigned to him is a subject on which much has been written,[3] but one which cannot be said even now to have received any satisfactory elucidation. Apion said it was because the Egyptians traced in the insect some resemblance to the operations of the sun ;[4] but the grounds for their opinion, and even the exact meaning of it, are obscure.   The beetle ordinarily re-presented in the sculptures and paintings is thought to be the *scarabœus sacer* of Linnæus, or common black beetle of Egypt ;[5] but nothing strange or peculiar has been pointed out in the habits of that creature.

Ra was worshipped more especially at On, near the old apex of the Delta, which city the Greeks therefore called Heliopolis, or ' the City of the Sun ; ' but very great respect was paid to him also in various other places.   At Thebes he was identified with Ammon, and worshipped as Amun-Ra, at the head of the local

---

[1] Horapollo, i. 6.
[2] Wilkinson, *A. E.* vol. iv. p. 297.
[3] Ibid. vol. v. pp. 256–60. Not much light is thrown on the sub-ject by the inscriptions, where, how-ever, the following passages occur : ' Hail to thee, Ra, the supreme power, the *beetle* that folds his wings, that rests in the empyrean, *that is born as his own son*' (*Records*, vol. viii. p. 105) ; and ' Homage to thee, Ra, supreme power, the god with the numerous shapes in the sacred dwelling ; *his form is that of the beetle*' (ibid. p. 108).   From the first of these passages it would seem

that the symbolism grew out of the idea that each scarab was a male, which, however, generated another (Plut. *De Isid. et Osir.* § 10), while from the second it might be con-cluded that the round or roundish form of the beetle lay at the root of the selection.
[4] See Plin. *H. N.* xxx. 11.
[5] So Wilkinson, *A. E.* vol. v. p. 253.   Dr. Birch notices that the stone and porcelain scarabæi found in Egypt do not all represent one species of beetle, since ' some have plain and others striated elytra' (*Guide to Museum*, p. 72).

triad.[1] At Memphis he was united with Phthah and
Pasht ;[2] at Silsilis with Phthah and the Nile-God, or
sometimes with Ammon and Savak.[3] His worship was
more nearly universal than that of any other Egyptian
deity, unless it were Osiris, who was also a Sun-God,
and so a form of Ra. As distinguished from Osiris,
Ra was the sun of the upper world; as distinguished
from Har or Harmachis, and from Tum or Atum
(Atmu), he was the meridian or midday sun.[4] In
litanies addressed to him, he ceases, however, to have
any partial character, and is the light at once of the
realms above and of the world below, of the heights of
the empyrean and of the 'two horizons,' both that
where he rises and that where he sets.[5] He is also, as
already observed,[6] identified in these compositions with
the Supreme God, being styled in them ' the Lord of
truth, the maker of men, the creator of beasts, the
Lord of existence, the maker of fruitful trees and
herbs, the maker everlasting, the Lord of eternity, the
Lord of wisdom, the Lord of mercy, the one maker of
existences, the one alone with many hands, the sovereign of life and health and strength.'[7]

KHEPRA.

Khepra seems to represent the creative energy of
the sun,[8] which is the source of all the life that we see

---

[1] See *Records of the Past*, vol.
viii. pp. 24, 34, 38, &c.
[2] Strictly speaking, the third god
of the Memphitic triad was Tum,
rather than Ra ; but Tum, as will
be shown later, was little more than
a form of Ra.
[3] Wilkinson, *A. E.* vol. iv. p.
231.
[4] Birch, *Ancient Egypt*, 'Introduction,' p. x.
[5] See the 'Litany of Ra' in the

Records of the Past, vol. viii. pp.
105–28, and note particularly p.
106, verse 12, p. 107, verse 27, and
p. 108, verse 31.
[6] See above, p. 343.
[7] See Mr. Goodwin's translation
of the Boulaq Papyrus, No. 17, in
the *Transactions of the Society of
Biblical Archæology*, vol. ii. pp.
253–6.
[8] *Khepr* or *Khepru* is ' to create,
make,' in Ancient Egyptian. (See

upon the earth. He is not, so far as appears, depicted
separately, but there is frequent mention of him both
in the historical and the devotional compositions.[1] The
scarabæus (*Kheprr*) forms the chief element in his
name, which is written 🪲 | ⚱, or Khepra, followed
by the figure of a sitting god.

TUM or ATUM.

Tum is the sun, as he approaches or rests upon the
western horizon, just before and when he sets.[2] His
common epithet is *nefer*, 'good,' and this is regarded
by some as a part of his name,[3] which is expressed by
⨎ Temu, ⨎ Atum, or ⨎ Nefer-Tum.
Among his other titles the commonest is 'the Lord of
the two lands,'[4] or 'countries,' by which has sometimes
been understood 'the two regions of Upper and Lower
Egypt,'[5] but which appears from the inscriptions to
have pointed rather to some division of the nome of
Heliopolis.[6] He is also styled 'the maker of men,'[7]

Birch's *Dict. of Hieroglyphics*, p.
566). The courtiers of Rameses
II. are represented in one place as
saying to their master, 'The god
Ra is like thee in his limbs; the
god Khepra *in creative force*' (*Records of the Past*, vol. viii. p. 78).

[1] See, besides the above-quoted
passage, *Records*, vol. ii. pp. 98, 131,
135; vol. viii. pp. 46, 106, 111, &c.

[2] This, which was not known to
Wilkinson (*A. E.* vol. v. pp. 23–6),
is now made clear by the inscriptions (see above, p. 144, and compare *Records of the Past*, vol. iv. p.
122), and generally admitted by
Egyptologists. (Birch, *Egypt from
the Earliest Times*, 'Introduction,'
p. x.; Lenormant, *Manuel*, vol. i.
p. 524; De Horrack in *Records of*

the Past, vol. iv. p. 122; Stuart
Poole in Smith's *Dictionary of the
Bible*, vol. ii. p. 631; &c.)

[3] Wilkinson, *A. E.* vol. v. p. 25;
Birch, 'Introduction,' p. xi.; *Records of the Past*, vol. vi. p. 27; &c.

[4] *Records of the Past*, vol. vi. pp.
23, 52, 59; vol. viii. pp. 6, 39; &c.

[5] Wilkinson, *A. E.* vol. v. p. 25.

[6] Tum is called 'Lord of the two
lands of On' repeatedly in an inscription of Rameses III. (*Records
of the Past*, vol. vi. pp. 59, 61; vol.
viii. p. 39; &c.) The two lands
seem to have been called respectively 'the land of Ra' and 'the
land of Harmachis.'

[7] *Records of the Past*, vol. ii. p.
131.

'the Universal Lord,'[1] 'the Creator God,'[2] and 'the great Lord of created beings.'[3] His worship was widespread. It was really Tum, rather than Ra, *i.e.* it was Ra under the form of Tum, who was worshipped at Heliopolis ;[4] and it was Tum who was the third god in the triad of Memphis. At Thebes he received frequent acknowledgment,[5] and throughout Egypt he was universally recognised, at any rate, as a god of the

Tum.

lower world, where he is scarcely distinguishable from Osiris. In the ' Ritual of the Dead ',the souls in Hades

[1] *Records of the Past*, vol. vi. p. 52.
[2] Ibid. vol. iv. p. 95.
[3] Ibid. vol. viii. p. 143. Other titles of Tum are, 'Creator of those who are,' 'the hidden,' 'the Maker of Heaven,' 'the producer of the gods,' 'the self-creating,' and ' the Lord of life, supplying (life to) the gods.' (See the *Ritual of the Dead*, ch. lxxix. ad init., and *Records of the Past*, vol. vi. p. 52.)
[4] Birch, *Ancient Egypt*, 'Introduction,' p. xi.; *Records of the Past*, vol. vi. pp. 52–66; and vol. iv. pp. 27 and 41, where On or Heliopolis is called ' the city of the god Tum.'
[5] See the *Records*, vol. iv. pp. 11, 13, 14, 27, &c.

call to him and style him ' father,' while he in his turn
addresses them as his ' sons.'[1]

Tum's most common form is that of a man walking, dressed in the ordinary way,[2] but bearing on his
head either the two crowns of Egypt, placed side by
side, as on Maut,[3] or else the wig with lappets, which is
worn also by Ra.[4]   Like Ra, Kneph, Ammon, and
many other gods, he carries the *ankh* and sceptre.   He

.   Nefer-Tum.

has also, like Ra, Kneph, and Ammon, the long pendent cord, ending in a tassel.   As Nefer-Tum, he
carries on his head a short shaft or stick, crowned by a
lotus-flower, or else by two feathers, and two pendent

---

[1] Bunsen, *Egypt's Place*, vol. i.
p. 398.
[2] Wilkinson, *A. E.* vol. v. p. 25;
Bunsen, vol. i. pp. 396-7.

[3] See above, p. 338.
[4] Compare the representation of
Ra, *supra*, p. 344, fig. 2.

tassels, one on either side of the shaft.   Sometimes his
sceptre terminates similarly.   In the British Museum
there is a silver figure of Nefer-Tum, wearing the lily
and also the two feathers.[1]   The ordinary colour of
Tum is, like that of Ra, red ; but he is said to be sometimes represented of a green hue.[2]

The ' house of Tum ' at Heliopolis was one of the
grandest of the Egyptian temples.   In front of it stood
a number of granite obelisks, among them that which
has been recently erected on the Thames Embankment,
and which is the second Egyptian obelisk that has been
brought to England.[3]   The temple itself was resplen-
dent with gold, and so celebrated for its magnificence,
that to say a building was ' like the house of Tum ' came
to be regarded as the highest conceivable eulogy.[4]   Large
tracts of land were assigned to it by the munificence
of the Egyptian monarchs ;[5] its sacred slaves (*hieroduli*)
were reckoned by thousands ;[6] and its furniture was
of the richest and most costly character, comprising
vessels and ornaments of gold, silver, lapis lazuli, turquoise, crystal, jasper, alabaster, green felspar, and
hæmatite.[7]

The following ' Hymn to Tum ' will show the feel-
ings wherewith he was worshipped :—

> Come to me, O thou Sun ;
> Horus of the horizon, give me help.
> Thou art he that giveth help ;
> There is no help without thee.

---

[1] See Birch, *Guide to Museum*, p. 14. A similar representation oc- curs in the *Great Harris Papyrus*, where Rameses III. addresses the great triad of Memphis, Phthah, Sekhet, and Nefer-Tum. (See the *Records of the Past*, vol. viii. p. 6.)

[2] Bunsen, *Egypt's Place*, vol. i. p. 397.

[3] The other is one dedicated to Kneph, and originally erected at Elephantiné, which was to be seen at Sion House until its demolition in 1875.

[4] *Records of the Past*, vol. vi. p. 27 ; vol. viii. p. 26 ; &c.

[5] Ibid. vol. vi. pp. 59–60.

[6] Ibid. p. 59. The total number mentioned is 12,963.

[7] Ibid. pp. 61–2.

Come to me, Tum ; hear me, thou great God ;
  My heart goeth forth towards On ;
  Let my desires be fulfilled ;
Let my heart rejoice, my inmost heart rejoice in gladness.
Hear my vows, my humble supplications every day,
  Hear my adorations every night—
My cries of terror, cries that issue from my mouth,
  That come forth from it one by one.
O Horus of the horizon, there is none other beside thee,
Protector of millions, deliverer of tens of thousands,
  Defender of him that calls upon thee,
    Lord of On !
Reproach me not for my many sins—
  I am young, and weak of body ;
  I am a man without a heart.
Anxiety preys upon me, as an ox [feeds] upon grass :
If I pass the night in [sleep], and therein find refreshment,
Anxiety nevertheless returns to me ere the day is done.[1]

SHU.

The word *shu* signifies ' light,'[2] and it is probable
that Shu was originally the light of the sun, as distinguished from the solar orb itself ; but this distinction
was known only to the initiated. The name[3] is expressed by an ostrich feather, followed by the ordinary
sign for *u*, and then by a figure of a sitting god 𓆄𓏛𓀭.
Shu is commonly spoken of as a son of Ra,[4] and frequently connected with Tafné,[5] a daughter of Ra, and
(according to some) Shu's twin sister.[6] Tum, Shu, and
Tafné are in one place called ' the great chiefs of On.'[7]

When figured, Shu is either walking or kneeling.
In the former case he has the ordinary form of a male

---

[1] This version is taken from the
Records of the Past, vol. vi. pp.
100–1. A few alterations have
been made, chiefly to improve the
rhythm.
[2] Birch, *Dictionary of Hieroglyphics*, pp. 579 and 583.
[3] Wilkinson, *A. E.* ' Supplement,'
pl. 46, part ii.
[4] *Records of the Past*, vol. vi. p.

109 ; vol. viii. p. 24 ; Wilkinson,
A. E. vol. v. p. 16.
[5] *Records of the Past*, vol. vi. pp.
105, 115, 116, 119, 124, &c. ; *Ritual of the Dead*, pp. 180, 269, 275 ;
&c.
[6] So Bunsen (*Egypt's Place*, vol.
v. p. 275), and Birch (*Guide to Museum*, p. 14).
[7] *Ritual of the Dead*, p. 180.

deity, but bears on his head either a single ostrich feather, or else a fourfold plume.[1] In the latter, he kneels upon his left knee, and elevates above his head the sun's disk, which he holds in his two hands.[2]

Shu, like Tum, was a deity of the lower world, worshipped by the spirits in Hades, and invoked by them.[3] It was his special office to stop the wicked on the steps of heaven, to prevent their entering, and effect

Shu.

their final destruction.[4] It is curious that the word *shu* meant in Egyptian both 'light' and 'shade;'[5] and thus the god of light might be represented as plunging

---

[1] Rosellini, *Monumenti del Culto,* pl. x. 2; Wilkinson, *A. E.* 'Supplement,' pl. 46, part ii.

[2] Birch, *Guide to Museum,* pp. 14–15; *Ritual of the Dead,* ch. xvi.

[3] See the *Ritual,* chs. xviii., xxxv., cxv., cxxxiv., &c.

[4] So Birch (*Guide to Museum,* l.s.c.).

[5] *Dictionary of Hieroglyphics,* pp. 579, 580.

the hopelessly wicked into the darkness of annihilation.[1]

We do not hear of any temples expressly dedicated
to Shu ; but he was probably worshipped at Heliopolis (On) in conjunction with Tum and Tefnut. Small
porcelain figures of him, kneeling and supporting the
sun's disk, are common.

MENTU.

Mentu is thought to have been originally a pro-
vincial form of the deity who presided over the sun.[2]
He is often identified with the solar orb, and bears
the name of Mentu-Ra 𓇳𓏤 𓊪 𓀭 ○ —*i.e.* 'Mentu the
Sun-God.'[3] When, however, he was accepted into the
general Pantheon, he came to have some peculiar attributes, and a peculiar form, assigned to him. He
was viewed as the special protector of Egypt and of the
monarchs, a sort of 'Mars Ultor,' but not the god of
war in a vulgar sense.[4] The kings are fond of comparing themselves to Mentu, especially when they are
fighting.[5] They celebrate his 'force' and his 'victorious arm,' and speak of him as 'very glorious.'[6] The
peculiarity of his form is, that to the hawk's head, the
disk, and uræus of Ra he joins the tall plumes of Am-

---

[1] It is remarkable that in the
Egyptian paintings the hue assigned
to Shu is black or nearly so (Wilkinson, *A. E.* vol. v. pp. 15-16).
[2] Bunsen, *Egypt's Place*, vol. i.
p. 405.
[3] Wilkinson, *A. E.* vol. v. p. 33,
and 'Supplement,' pl. 49, part ii.
Compare *Records of the Past*, vol.
viii. p. 143.
[4] Birch calls him simply 'the
Egyptian Mars' (*Guide to Museum*,

p. 14); but Wilkinson notes that
the real bloody god of war is, not
Mentu, but Reshpu, or (as he reads
the name) Ranpo (*A. E.* vol. v. p.
34).
[5] See *Records of the Past*, vol.
ii. pp. 43, 71, 74, 75, 77 ; vol. iv. p.
14; vol. viii. p. 75; &c.
[6] Bunsen, *Egypt's Place*, vol. i. p.
404; *Records of the Past*, vol. iv. p.
14; vol. viii. p. 75.

mon.[1] His hue, when he is painted, like that of Ra, is red.[2]

The chief seat of the worship of Mentu was Hermonthis, a city which appears to have derived its name from this god.[3] There he was the first deity of a local triad. In the rest of Egypt he would seem to have been but little known, unless it were in the Thebaid, of which he is sometimes said to be 'the lord.'[4] It is very rarely that the Egyptian monarchs make offerings to him. Still he occasionally attracted their regards, and is found associated in their memorials with Ammon, Ra, Phthah, Horus, and Sati, and again with Ammon-Ra and Athor.[5]

Mentu (ordinary form).

OSIRIS.

Osiris was, practically, the god chiefly worshipped in Egypt, since, while all other worships were local, his was universal.[6] Originally, perhaps, a personification of the divine goodness,[7] Osiris came to be regarded as a form of the sun, and especially as the sun of the lower

---

[1] Rosellini, *Monumenti del Culto*, pl. ii. 1.

[2] Bunsen, vol. i. p. 405.

[3] Champollion originally suggested the derivation of Hermonthis from Mentu-Ra by inversion of the two elements. Wilkinson approves his suggestion (*A. E.* vol. v. p. 33, note).

[4] *Records of the Past*, vol. ii. p. 43.

[5] Rosellini, *Monumenti del Culto*, pl. ii. 1 and pl. xxxiv. 2.

[6] Herod. ii. 42; Birch, *Ancient Egypt*, 'Introduction,' p. xi.; Wilkinson, *A. E.* vol. iv. p. 345.

[7] Wilkinson, vol. iv. pp. 317, 325, &c.

world, the great deity of Amenti or Hades.[1]   His office
as judge of the souls of men upon their entrance into
Hades has been already mentioned.[2]   This office was
peculiar to him and never assigned to any other deity;
but, except in this relation, Osiris seems to have been
little more than a name for the Supreme God. He is
called 'the eldest,' 'the chief of his brothers,' 'the
chief of the gods,' 'the master of the gods,' 'the king
of the gods,'[3] and again 'the lord of life,' 'the lord of
eternity,' 'the eternal ruler,' 'the lord of the world,'
and 'the creator of the world.'[4]   A peculiar character
of mildness, goodness, and beneficence attaches to him.
He is 'the manifester of good,' 'full of goodness and
truth,'[5] 'the beneficent spirit,' 'beneficent in will and
words,' 'mild of heart,' 'fair and beloved of all who see
him.'[6]   He 'affords plentifulness and gives it to all
the earth; all men are in ecstasy on account of him,
hearts are in sweetness, bosoms in joy; everybody is
in adoration; every one glorifies his goodness . . .
sanctifying, beneficent is his name.'[7]

The name of Osiris is expressed, most simply, by
two hieroglyphs, thus :— ; or more commonly
followed in most cases by the determinative for
'a god,' or . Sometimes, however, the human eye
is replaced by a simple circle o, and the other non-
descript sign by an animal form, . The native
pronunciation of the name would seem to have been

[1] 'Ce soleil infernal prenait plus spécialement le nom d'Osiris.' (Le-normant, *Manuel*, vol. i. p. 525.)
[2] See above, p. 318.
[3] See the 'Hymn to Osiris,' trans-lated in the *Records of the Past*, vol. iv. pp. 99-100.
[4] Compare Wilkinson, *A. E.* vol.
iv. pp. 320-1, with the above men-tioned hymn.
[5] Wilkinson, l.s.c.
[6] *Records of the Past*, l.s.c.
[7] Ibid. vol. iv. p. 103. It is not quite clear whether these expres-sions are applied to Osiris or to his son, Horus.

Hes-ar or *Has-ar*,[1] which the Greeks, adding a nomi-
natival ending, converted into Osiris.   There is some
doubt as to the true meaning of the word ; but perhaps
'the many-eyed,' which can plead for itself the authority
of Plutarch,[2] may deserve acceptance as the most probable rendering.

Osiris was represented, most commonly, in a mummied form, to mark his presidency over the dead ; but
occasionally he appears as a man, walking or standing.
Usually he bears in his two hands the crook and the flagellum, to which are sometimes added the sceptre (*uas*)
and the *ankh* or symbol of life.   On his head he carries
the crown of Upper Egypt only, sometimes unadorned,
sometimes ornamented on either side with a barred
feather, and occasionally surmounted with a disk.   When
represented as a man walking, he has the lappeted wig,
crowned with two wavy horns, above which are the
two feathers.   The wavy horns are also found with the
plumed crown above them, and serpents (*uræi*) on
either side, surmounted by disks.   In some rare instances Osiris has the head of an ibis, but with two
bills, one pointing either way.[3]   His hue, when he is
painted, is sometimes black, but more usually green.[4]

Another rare form of Osiris is that which has been
already given[5]—a form rightly termed ' barbaric,'[6] with

---

[1] So Birch, *Dictionary of Hieroglyphics*, p. 582.   Hellanicus observed that the Egyptians did not
say ' Osiris,' like the Greeks, but
' Hysiris' (ap. Plut. *De Isid. et Osir.*
§ 34).

[2] Ἔνιοι δὲ καὶ τοὔνομα διερμηνεύουσι
πολυόφθαλμον, ὡς τοῦ μὲν ΟΣ τὸ πολύ,
τοῦ δὲ ΙΡΙ τὸν ὀφθαλμὸν Αἰγυπτίᾳ
γλώττῃ φράζοντος (ibid. § 10).   Bunsen prefers the derivation, ' son of
Isis,' from HES = ' Isis' and AR =
' child, son '(*Egypt's Place* vol. i. p.

423) ; but the order of the two elements must be reversed to give this
meaning.

[3] So Bunsen, vol. i. p. 425.   But
Wilkinson thinks the head to be
that of ' a crane, peculiarised by a
tuft of two long feathers' (*A. E.* vol.
iv. p. 342).

[4] Ibid. p. 340.

[5] See above, p. 281 (central
figure).

[6] Bunsen, *Egypt's Place*, vol. i.
p. 424.

eyebrows meeting, fat cheeks, and a coarse mouth, clad in a spotted robe, and wearing ' the Nilometer ' [1] underneath the horns and plumed disk. Osiris likewise appears, but very rarely indeed,[2] seated on a throne, mummied, and wearing the disk of the moon, with which he appears then to be identified. Such figures have been called ' figures of Osiris-Aah.' [3]

Three Forms of Osiris.

The myths connected with Osiris were numerous and curious, but, like the Greek myths, frequently contradictory.[4]　He is ordinarily represented as the son of Seb and Nutpe ; [5] but sometimes his father is Ra,[6] at

[1] Or rather, the ' symbol of stability.' (See Wilkinson, vol. iv. p. 341 ; Birch, *Guide to Museum*, p. 15.)

[2] There is one specimen in the British Museum, called by Dr. Birch (l.s.c.) ' unique.' There is another in the Museum of Liverpool. (See Gatty's *Catalogue*, p. 8, No. 27.)

[3] Birch, l.s.c.

[4] On some of the contradictions, see Bunsen, *Egypt's Place*, vol. i. p. 438.

[5] Ibid. pp. 416, 439, &c.

[6] Plutarch, *De Isid. et Osir.* § 11 ; *Records of the Past*, vol. iv. p. 121.

other times Shu,[1] and his mother is Isis [2] as well as
Nutpe. Isis, at one time his mother, at another his
sister, at another his daughter, is always his wife, and
their child is Har or Horus. Osiris, according to the
common legend,[3] was once upon a time incarnate, and
reigned as king of Egypt. Having ruled for a while
beneficently, he went upon his travels, leaving Isis to
conduct the government, which she did with vigour
and prudence. Set, however, the principle of evil,
conspired against Osiris, murdered him, and, having
cut his body into fourteen pieces, disposed of them
in various parts of the country. Isis collected the remains and revivified them, while Horus, to avenge his
father, sought out Set, and, engaging him, brought him
under. Various offshoots of this stock tale were current. Isis, it was said, released Set after Horus had
made him prisoner, and Horus thereupon tore off her
crown, or (according to some) struck off her head. Set
accused Horus of illegitimacy, and the other gods were
called in to judge the cause, which they decided in
favour of Horus. The war between the two continued,
and Horus ultimately slew his enemy, who is then represented either under a human form,[4] or under that of
the great serpent Apepi or Apap.

Various explanations have been given of these legends. Osiris has been regarded by some as the sun,
and Set as night or darkness, which destroys the sun
and buries him, but is in its turn slain by the reap-
pearing, rejuvenated sun of the next day, 'Horus of

---

[1] *Records of the Past,* vol. vi. p.
119.

[2] Bunsen, *Egypt's Place,* vol. i. p.
438.

[3] See Wilkinson (*Ancient Egyp-*

tians, vol. iv. pp. 329-33), where
the entire legend is given in full.

[4] Wilkinson, *A. E.* 'Supplement,
pl. 42, fig. 2.

the horizon,' who thus avenges his father.[1] Others
have seen in Osiris the Nile inundation, in Typho
drought, in Isis the land of Egypt, and in Horus vapours
and exhalations.[2] But the truth seems to be that little
more was aimed at in the Osirid legends than to teach
and illustrate the perpetual opposition and conflict between good and evil, light and darkness, order and

Horus destroying the great Serpent Apap.

disorder, virtue and vice. Starting from this basis, the
religious imagination allowed itself pretty free play
among the minor personages of the Pantheon, the details of the stories being of little account so long as the
relative positions of Set and Osiris were maintained, so
long as the struggle was shown forth, and the final

[1] Lenormant, *Manuel d'Histoire*   §§ 13–33), who is followed by Bun-
Ancienne, vol. i. pp. 525–6.   sen (*Egypt's Place*, vol. i. p. 437) and
[2] So Plutarch (*De Isid. et Osir.*   Wilkinson (*A. E.* vol. iv. pp. 336–7).

triumph of good asserted. Interwoven into the various narratives are found religious ideas, which may be echoes from the far past of that primeval revelation which God vouchsafed to the human race, or may be merely thoughts natural to man, arising out of the constitution of his mind and its broodings upon God and nature. Such are the ideas of an incarnate god, a suffering god, a god who dies and is restored to life again ; such, too, is the connection of evil with the form of the serpent, and the ultimate bruising of the serpent's head by the Divine benefactor.

It has been observed above,[1] that Osiris was a deity worshipped throughout the whole of Egypt. And this is undoubtedly true. Indeed, it could scarcely be otherwise, since all recognised him as the god before whom they were to appear on their descent into the Lower World, and who was then and there to determine their final happiness or misery. Still, though an object of worship throughout Egypt, he had some special cities which were peculiarly devoted to him. The chief of these was Abtu, or, as the Greeks called it, Abydos, of which he is commonly called ' the lord,'[2] and where there was a great temple specially dedicated to him.[3] Another Osirid city was Philæ, situated on an island in the Nile a little below Elephantiné, where again he had a magnificent temple, adorned with sculptures illustrative of his life on earth and mysterious sufferings.[4] A third such city was Tattu, or This, which, like Abydos, claimed him as its ' lord,'[5] and worshipped him in the

---

[1] See page 354.

[2] *Records of the Past*, vol. ii. p. 119 ; vol. iv. pp. 7, 99, 126 ; vol. vi. p. 3 ; vol. viii. pp. 26, 29, &c.

[3] Wilkinson, *A. E.* vol. iv. p. 346.

[4] Ibid. pp. 189, 255, 345, &c.

[5] The most usual title of Osiris is ' lord of Abydos ; ' but we find him also termed ' lord of This ' (Birch, *Guide to Museum*, p. 15) and said to ' reside ' in This (*Records of the Past*, vol. iv. p. 99).

form which is distinguished by the *tat* or 'emblem of stability.'

HORUS, HARMACHIS.

It has been usual to distinguish two Horuses,[1] called respectively 'the elder' and 'the younger;' but the more Egyptian mythology is studied, the more doubtful does it appear to be whether any such distinction was really intended.[2] No stress can be laid upon contradictory statements of the relationship borne by Horus to other gods, for such contradictions are quite common, and include cases where no one has ever suggested that different gods are meant, as those of Isis and Osiris.[3] All the representations of Horus have a near resemblance; and the epithets attached to the name seem to mark, not different personages, but different aspects in which one and the same deity might be viewed. Primarily Horus is the youthful or rising sun, and is spoken of as Harmachis (*Har-em-akhu*), 'Horus in the horizon.' In this capacity he is one of the gods of Heliopolis,[4] and bears the title of Ra-Harmachis, to make his solar character unmistakable. ' In connection with the myth of Osiris he is Harpocrates (*Har-pa-krat*), 'Har the child,' and is dandled on the knee of Isis, or exhibited with the single lock of hair, which in Egypt was the mark of childhood, and often conjoined with Nephthys and Isis, his aunt and mother.[5] Occasionally his pe-

---

[1] Wilkinson, *A. E.* vol. iv. pp. 395–405; Bunsen, *Eggpt's Place*, vol. i. pp. 433–6; Birch, *Guide to Museum*, p. 13; Kenrick, *Ancient Egypt*, vol. i. p. 420, &c.

[2] Brugsch (*Histoire d'Egypte*, p. 22) and Lenormant (*Manuel d'Histoire Ancienne*, vol. i. pp. 525–6) seem to admit but one Horus.

[3] See Bunsen, *Egypt's Place*, vol. i. p. 438.

[4] *Records of the Past*, vol. vi. pp. 52 *et seqq.*

[5] Wilkinson, *Ancient Egyptians*, 'Supplement,' pl. 35A, part ii. fig. 2; Birch, *Guide to Museum*, p. 15; Gatty, *Catalogue of Mayer Collection*, p. 9; &c.

culiar characteristics are forgotten, and he is the sun generally, 'the sun of the two worlds,'[1] identified with Ra and Tum, or with Amen-Ra, the sun considered as informed by the Supreme Being. He then has commonly the hawk's head, which characterises Ra, surmounted by the double crown of the Two Egypts, with

1. Horus.   2. Isis nursing Horus.   3. Horus the Child (Har-pa-krat).

or without the uræus in front, while in his hands he bears, like Ra, the *ankh* and sceptre, and is represented walking, with the left foot advanced.

Horus is entitled ' Lord of Truth,' ' Lord of Heaven,' ' Lord of the Crown,' ' helper of his father,' ' Lord of the sacred bark,' ' king of the worlds,' and ' supreme ruler of gods and men.'[2] He is ' beauteous,' ' blessed,' ' self-

---

[1] *Records of the Past,* vol. ii. p. 40. | p. 131; Wilkinson, *A. E.* vol. iv.
[2] Ibid. pp. 5, 123; iv. p. 125; viii. | p. 398; *Ritual of the Dead,* ch. cxli.

sprung,' 'self-existing.'[1]   A hymn, addressed to him
as Ra-Harmachis, celebrates his countless excellences.
He was worshipped almost as universally as Osiris,
and was in special favour at Heliopolis and Abydos.[2]
The Egyptian kings held him in peculiar honour, and
delighted in identifying themselves with him and as-
suming his name and his titles.[3]   This practice, begun
(it would seem) by the monarchs of the fourth dynasty,[4]
continued down at least to the time of the twenty-
second dynasty, when we find Pianchi addressed as
'the indestructible Horus,' 'Horus, lord of the palace,'
and 'Horus, royal bull.'[5]

The name Horus is ordinarily represented by the
figure of a hawk, 𓅃, which is sometimes followed by
a vertical stroke ı the sign of the masculine gender.[6]
Harmachis is expressed by 𓅃══𓇳 ; Harpocrates
by 𓅃ı𓀔 . The hawk occurs also, as the emblem
of Horus, on mummy-cases, on wooden tablets, in the
tombs, and in bronze and porcelain figures, where the
bird commonly wears the *pschent*.[7]

ATEN.

Aten, written 𓇋𓏏𓈖 or 𓇋𓏏𓈖𓇳, was, properly speaking, the disk of the sun, and was worshipped under the
representation of a large circle, from the lower hemisphere of which projected numerous arms and hands

---

[1] *Records &c.* vol. viii. pp. 131-4.
[2] Birch, *Egypt from the Earliest Times,* 'Introduction,' p. xi.
[3] See the *Records*, vol. ii. pp. 37, 64, 76, 90, 91, 98; vol. iv. pp. 11-14, 20-3, 35, 55, &c.; vol. vi. p. 70; vol. viii. pp. 69, 74, 75, &c.
[4] See an inscription of Khufu (Cheops) given by Bunsen in his fifth volume, pp. 719-21, where that king calls himself *ankh Har—* 'the living Horus.'
[5] *Records of the Past,* vol. ii. pp. 89, 91, 92.
[6] See Birch's *Grammar,* in Bunsen's *Egypt,* vol. v. p. 621.
[7] Birch, *Guide to Museum,* p. 19.

which presented to the worshipper the *ankh* or symbol
of life.[1]   It might have been supposed that there could
be nothing very peculiar in this worship, or at any rate
nothing to make it antagonistic to the rest of the Egyptian religion.   Yet there was certainly a time when
such an antagonism developed itself, and Aten, who
had previously been only one of the many sun-gods,
was elevated above every other deity, and even worshipped almost exclusively,[2] while the adherents of the
rest of the gods were persecuted.   This time of undue
favour was followed by a reaction; the name and form
of the king who had carried the worship to its highest
pitch were mutilated and defaced; [3] disk-worship, as a
special religion, disappeared; and Aten sank back into
his old position of inferiority and subordination.

ATHOR.

With the sun-gods are closely connected two goddesses, Athor and Isis.   Athor signifies 'the abode of
Hor,'[4] and is generally expressed by a hieroglyph in
which the hawk (Horus) is enclosed within the character
representing a house. A variant mode of writing
the word is 'Eit-har' or 'Athar.' She represented most properly the lower hemisphere, from which
the sun rose in the morning, and into which he sank at
night; but in course of time came to be regarded as only
one out of the many divinities of the lower world, to

[1] See Lepsius, *Denkmäler*, vol. vi.
part iii. pls. 91–110; Wilkinson,
Ancient Egyptians, 'Supplement,'
pl. 30; and Birch, *Egypt from the
Earliest Times*, p. 109.

[2] Birch, pp. 107–10.   Compare
Wilkinson (*A. E.* vol. iv. p. 298)
and Lenormant (*Manuel d'Histoire*

Ancienne, vol. i. pp. 391–3).

[3] Lepsius, *Denkmäler*, vol. vi.
part iii. pls. 91, 106, 110, &c.

[4] Wilkinson, *A. E.* vol. iv. p.
387; Bunsen, *Egypt's Place*, vol. i.
p. 400; Birch, *Egypt from the Earliest Times*, ' Introduction,' p. xi.

be adored together with Osiris, Isis, Horus, Nephthys,
Anubis, Tum, Thoth, &c., as a goddess inhabiting the

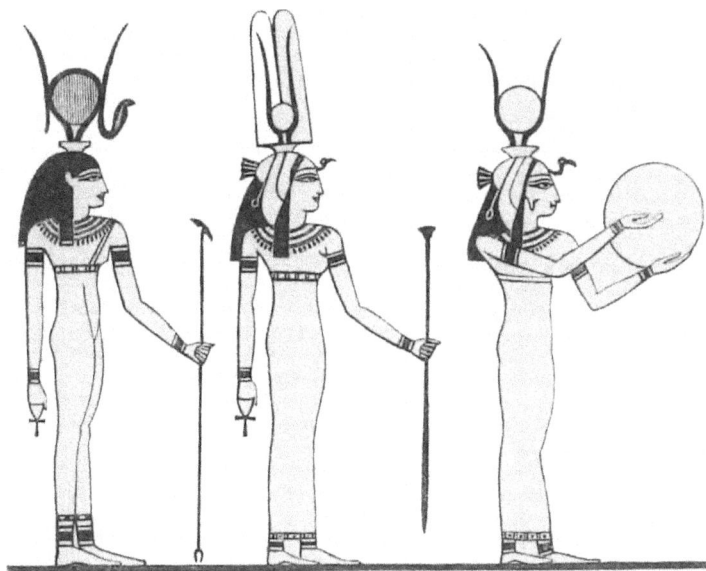

Forms of Athor.

lower region together with them.[1] She is depicted
under many forms. Sometimes she appears almost as
Isis, in the ordinary form of a female, but with horns,
a disk, and a uræus on her head, and in her two hands
the sceptre, *uas*, and the *ankh* or 'symbol of life.' Or
she has the vulture head-dress of Sati and Maut, surmounted by the disk and horns, with or without two
tall plumes, and bears in her left hand the sceptre
which only females bear, or holds in her two hands a
round object which is thought to be a tambourine.[2]
Occasionally she has a cow's head with a disk between
the horns, or is worshipped under the figure of a spotted cow, crowned with a disk and two plumes. She
appears likewise as a hawk with a female head and the
usual horns and disk.

Among the titles of Athor were those of 'mother
of Ra,' 'eye of Ra,' 'mistress of Amenti,' 'celestial
mother,' ' lady of the dance and mirth,'[3] and 'mistress
of turquoises.'[4] Like Osiris, she was worshipped in
most parts of Egypt, but especially at Tentyra, Thebes,
and Atarbechis. Cows, especially white and spotted
cows, were sacred to her, as also was a certain kind of
fish,[5] but the exact species cannot be determined. The
Greeks identified her with their Aphrodité, and the
Romans with their Venus; there does not, however,
appear to be much reason for either identification.[6]

---

[1] See the *Ritual of the Dead* in
Bunsen's *Egypt*, vol. v. pp. 211,
239, 275, &c.
[2] So Bunsen, *Egypt's Place*, vol.
i. p. 401. To me it seems that the
object, which is a simple circle, and
is sometimes held with both hands
(*Description de l'Egypte*, 'Antiquités,' vol. i. pl. xi. 1), may be merely
the sun's disk.
[3] Bunsen, l.s.c., and Birch, *Guide*

to *Museum*, p. 14.
[4] *Records of the Past*, vol. viii. p.
50.
[5] Wilkinson, *Ancient Egyptians*,
vol. iv. p. 394.
[6] The title, ' lady of the dance
and mirth,' is almost the sole monumental evidence of there being any
aspect of Athor in which she could
be reasonably compared with Venus.
But the Greeks and Romans were

ISIS.

Isis in original conception did not differ much from Athor, with whom she was sometimes identified by the Greeks,[1] and from whom even in the monuments it is often difficult to distinguish her.[2] She was called the mother, as well as the wife and sister, of Osiris. It is, however, as his wife and sister that she is chiefly presented to us. The part assigned to her in the ' myth of Osiris ' has been already spoken of ;[3] and this constitutes the main feature in all the longer notices of her which occur in the inscriptions. Thus, in the ' Tears of Isis,' we have her lamentations over her brother when slain, and her joyful address to him upon his re-appearance.[4] In the ' Book of Respirations ' we hear of the ' sighs of Isis for her brother Osiris, to give life to his soul, to give life to his body, to rejuvenate all his members, that he may reach the horizon with his father, the sun ; that his soul may rise to heaven in the disk of the moon ; that his body may shine in the stars of Orion on the bosom of Nut.'[5] A hymn to Osiris tells us how ' his sister took care of him by dispersing his enemies,' how she ' unrepiningly sought him, went the round of the world lamenting him, shadowed him with her wings, made the invocation of his burial, raised his remains, and extracted his essence.'[6] Thenceforth, as a reward for her fidelity and love, Isis ruled with Osiris in the Amenti, assisted him in judging the dead, and

---

determined to find resemblances, and often made the most absurd identifications.

[1] Plutarch, *De Isid. et Osir.* § 56.
[2] Wilkinson, *A. E.* vol. iv. pp 381-2.

[3] See above, p. 358.
[4] *Records of the Past*, vol. ii. pp. 119-23.
[5] Ibid. vol. iv. p. 121.
[6] Ibid. pp. 101-2.

received in common with him the principal worship of the departed.[1]

The name of Isis is expressed by the hieroglyph supposed to represent a throne, followed by the two feminine signs[2] of the half-circle and the egg 𓊨, to which is added sometimes the hatchet 𓌹, *neter*, or the form of a sitting goddess 𓁦. She is figured commonly as a

Forms of Isis.

female with the so-called throne upon her head, either simply, or above the horns and disk which are also characteristic of Athor. Sometimes she wears the vulture head-dress; at other times she has the head of a cow; and she is even found with the head of a cat.[3]

---

[1] See the *Ritual of the Dead*, in Bunsen's *Egypt*, vol. v. pp. 180–2, 262, 269, &c.

[2] Birch's *Hieroglyphic Grammar*

in Bunsen's Egypt, vol. v. p. 621.

[3] Wilkinson, *Ancient Egyptians*, vol. iv. p. 384.

She has commonly in her hands the *ankh* and the female sceptre. Occasionally she is sitting on the ground and nursing Horus.

Her most frequent title is 'defender' or 'avenger of her brother;'[1] but she is also called 'the goddess mother,'[2] 'the mistress of the two worlds,' and 'the mistress of Heaven.'[3] She was worshipped more or less in every part of Egypt; but her most remarkable temples were those at Philæ and Coptos. The Egyptians connected her in some peculiar way with Sothis, the Dog-Star,[4] and also with a goddess called Selk[5] or Serk, whose special emblem was the scorpion.

THE MOON-GODS, KHONS and THOTH.

The Egyptians had two moon-gods, Khons or Khonsu, and Tet or Thoth. Of these the former seems to have borne that character only, while the latter had, curiously enough, the further aspect of a god of letters. Khons was represented as the son of Ammon and Maut,[6] and formed together with those deities the third god of the Theban triad. He is frequently called 'the god of two names;'[7] and these names seem to be Khons or Khonsu and Nefer-hetp, both words being of uncertain meaning.[8] Khons's ordinary titles are, 'the great

---

[1] *Records of the Past*, vol. ii. p. 123; vol. iv. p. 101, &c.

[2] Wilkinson, l.s.c.

[3] Bunsen, *Egypt's Place*, vol. i. p. 419.

[4] Plutarch says that her soul was placed in Sirius, or the Dog-Star, after her death (*De Isid. et Osir.* §§ 21 and 61); but the *death* of Isis was scarcely an Egyptian idea. It is certain, however, that *some* very close connection was regarded as existing between the star and the

goddess. (See *Records of the Past*, vol. ii. p. 122; and compare Wilkinson, *A. E.* vol. iv. p. 371.)

[5] Wilkinson, *A. E.* vol. iv. p. 370.

[6] Birch, *Guide to Museum*, p. 13.

[7] Bunsen, *Egypt's Place*, vol. 1. p. 392. Compare *Rec'd of the Past*, vol. iv. pp. 5[5], 58, 60, &c.

[8] Khons is connected by Birch with *khens* ⊙ ⁓̶̶ ∧ 'to hunt, to chase;' and Nefer-hetp would seem to come from the two words *nefer*,

god,' ' the giver of life,' and ' the giver of oracles.' [1] He
is also called ' the expeller of spirits from the possessed,' [2]
and ' the clerk of the divine cycle.' [3]   He was generally
worshipped in combination with Ammon and Maut ; [4]
but Rameses III. built him a special temple in Thebes
' of good hewn sandstone and black basalt, having gates
whose folding doors were plated with gold, and itself
overlaid with electrum like the horizon of heaven.' [5]   It

Three Forms of Khons.

was probably from this temple that, in the time of
Rameses XII., an image of the god was sent enclosed
in a sacred ark from Thebes to Mesopotamia, for the
purpose of curing a ' possessed princess,' the daughter

'good,' and *hetp* ⚊ 'food,' ' welcome,' ' a table.' But in neither
case is the exact intention of the
name certain.

[1] *Records of the Past*, vol. iv. pp.
55, 58, 88, &c.
[2] Ibid p. 58.

[3] Ibid. p. 94.
[4] Bunsen, *Egypt's Place*, vol. i.
p. 392. Compare the *Description*,
vol. iii. pls. 32 and 33; Rosellini,
Mon. del Culto, pl. xxxiii. 2.
[5] *Records of the Past*, vol. vi. p.
32.

of a ' king of Bakhten.' [1] The cure was happily effected,
and the monarch so delighted with the result, that he
could not bring himself to part with the image, until in
the fourth year he was warned by a dream to restore
it to its proper place in Egypt.

The name Khons or Khonsu is always written phonetically ⟨glyph⟩ or ⟨glyph⟩, with or without the figure
of a bearded god. The form most commonly assigned
to the deity is that of a mummied figure, like the figure
of Phthah,[2] but with the lock of hair that characterises
Harpakrat and other *young* gods, and with the disk and
crescent that mark him as a moon deity. In his hands
he bears either ' the Nilometer' with the crook and
whip, like Phthah, or a palm-branch and pen, like
Thoth. Occasionally he is represented as hawk-headed,
and is distinguishable from Horus and Ra only by the
crescent and disk which always accompany him.

Thoth, who adds to his lunar character the features
and titles of a god of letters, is ordinarily represented
with the head of an ibis and a wig with lappets, the
head being surmounted by the crescent and disk. To
these an ostrich feather is sometimes added, while occasionally in lieu of the crescent and disk we see the
complicated head-dress which is worn more commonly
by Kneph, Ra, and Osiris.[3] In some few cases the
entire figure is that of a man,[4] attired as usual, while,
still more rarely, the form selected is that of a cynocephalous ape. Thoth commonly bears in his hands a tablet
and reed pen ; but sometimes he has the palm-branch
and pen, like Khons, sometimes the *uas* or crook-headed
sceptre.[5]

---

[1] *Records*, vol. iv. pp. 55–60.
[2] See above, p. 334.
[3] Supra, pp. 328 and 356.
[4] See Wilkinson, *A. E.* 'Supplement,' pl. 45, fig. 3.
[5] Ibid.

The titles most frequently given to him are ' lord of
Sesennu '[1] and ' lord of truth.'[2]   He is called also ' one
of the chief gods,' ' the great god ' or ' the god twice
great,' ' the great chief in the paths of the dead,' ' the
self-created, never born,' ' the lord of the divine words,'
and ' the scribe of Truth.'[3]   It is his special office to be
present in Amenti when souls are judged, to see their

. Three Forms of Thoth.

deeds weighed in the balance, and to record the result.
He is also in this world the revealer to men of God's
will.   It is he who composes the ' Ritual of the Dead,'

---

[1] *Records of the Past,* vol. ii.
p. 90; vol. iv. p. 123; vol. viii. p.
30, &c.
[2] *Ritual of the Dead,* pp. 175,
214, 236, &c. In one place (p. 275)
Thoth is ' the husband of Truth.'

[3] See, for these titles, the *Records
of the Past,* vol. iv. p. 123; the
Ritual of the Dead, pp. 161, 180;
and Bunsen, *Egypt's Place,* vol. i.
p. 393.

or at any rate its more important portions.[1] It is also he who in the realms below writes for the good souls with his own fingers 'the Book of Respirations,' which protects them, sustains them, enlightens them, gives them life, causes them to 'breathe with the souls of the gods for ever and ever.'[2] According to one legend, Thoth once wrote a wonderful book, full of wisdom and science, containing in it everything relating to the fowls of the air, the fishes of the sea, and the four-footed beasts of the mountains. The man who knew a single page of the work could charm the heaven, the earth, the great abyss, the mountains, and the seas. This marvellous composition he enclosed in a box of gold, which he placed within a box of silver; the box of silver within a box of ivory and ebony, and that again within a box of bronze; the box of bronze within a box of brass, and the box of brass within a box of iron; and the book, thus guarded, he threw into the Nile at Coptos. The fact became known, and the book was searched for and found. It gave its possessor vast knowledge and magical power, but it always brought on him misfortune. What became of it ultimately does not appear in the manuscript from which this account is taken;[3] but the moral of the story seems to be the common one, that unlawful knowledge is punished by all kinds of calamity.

The name of Thoth is written with the ibis standing upon a perch, followed by a half-circle and the two oblique lines, which are used commonly to express *i*,

---

[1] Bunsen, *Egypt's Place*, vol. v. p. 133. Compare p. 209.
[2] *Records of the Past*, vol. iv. pp. 123-5. The value of the writings of Thoth to the good souls in the Amenti is noticed also in the *Ritual*, ch. xciv.
[3] The legend is contained in the 'Tale of Setnau,' which has been translated by Dr. Brugsch, and will be found in the *Records of the Past*, vol. iv. pp. 133-48.

Birch reads the name as 'Teti,' regarding the sign ﻗ as having its usual force ;[1] but Wilkinson supposes that the two lines in this case ' double the T,' and reads the name as Tet or Tot.[2]

As a god who took part in the judgment of the dead, Thoth was an object of universal reverence throughout Egypt.[3] His main worship, however, was at Sesennu, or Hermopolis, where he had a temple,[4] and was adored together with Tum, Sa, and Nehemao.[5] Oxen, cows, and geese were sacrificed in his honour,[6] and the ibis and cynocephalous ape were sacred to him.[7] He is often represented in attendance on the kings of Egypt, either purifying them, or inscribing their names on the sacred tree, or in some other way doing them honour.[8]

Among the minor divinities of the Egyptians may be mentioned the gods Seb, Savak, Hanher, Merula or Malouli, and Aemhept, together with the goddesses Bast or Pasht, Nu or Nutpe (Netpe), Nebta or Nephthys, Anuka, Ma, Tafné, Merseker, Heka, Menh, and Nehemao ; to whom must be added the malignant deities Set or Sutech, Nubi, Bes, Taourt, and Apepi (Apap) or Apophis. A few words only can be given to each of these.

---

[1] *Dictionary of Hieroglyphics*, in Bunsen's *Egypt*, vol. v. p. 583.

[2] *Ancient Egyptians*, vol. v. p. 7, note.

[3] See *Records of the Past*, vol. vi. p. 111: 'All eyes are open on thee, and *all men worship thee as a god.*'

[4] Ibid. vol. ii. p. 90 ; Wilkinson, *A. E.* vol. v. .p. 4.

[5] *Records*, vol. ii. p. 90, note [2]. Compare the *Ritual*, chs. cxiv. and cxvi.

[6] *Records*, vol. ii. p. 90, par. 59.

[7] Ibid. vol. vi. p. 111.

[8] See the *Description de l'Egypte*, ' Antiquités,' vol. i. pl. 10, part 2 ; vol. ii. pl. 13, part 1 ; Wilkinson, *A. E.* 'Supplement,' pl. 54 A ; Birch, *Guide to Museum*, p. 15.

SEB.

Seb, the father of Osiris, is thought to have been the embodiment of 'the stellar universe,' and is spoken of as 'the father of the gods' (*atefi neteru*) or 'the leader of the gods.' His name is expressed by a goose

Seb.

or an egg, followed by the ordinary phonetic sign for *b*, and the image of a sitting god (⟨glyph⟩ or ⟨glyph⟩). He is figured in the form of a man, walking, dressed in the short tunic or *shenti*, with collar, girdle, armlets, bracelets, and anklets. In his two hands he holds the *ankh* and *uas*, and sometimes he carries on his head the figure of a goose. There is not much mention of him in the inscriptions.[1]

---

[1] Seb has an important part assigned to him in the legend called 'The Destruction of Mankind by Ra' (*Records of the Past*, vol. vi. p. 110); but otherwise his name scarcely occurs half a dozen times in the five Egyptian volumes of that series.

SAVAK.

Sabak or Savak, the crocodile-headed god, has all the appearance of having been originally a local deity, worshipped in the Arsinoite nome, and perhaps there representing the Supreme Being. Bunsen supposes that the 'tractability' of the crocodile was the quality which drew attention, and caused it to be invested with a sacred character;[1] but it is perhaps more reasonable to consider that its strength and destructiveness made it first feared and then worshipped. The crocodile is the only animal that attacks man in Egypt; and many deaths are caused by crocodiles every year.[2] If we take this view, we can understand why crocodiles, and the crocodile-headed god, were either hated, as at Tentyra, Apollinopolis, Heracleopolis, Elephantiné, and elsewhere, or else honoured and reverenced. Savak obtained at a somewhat late date[3] recognition and worship in Thebes and the adjacent parts of Egypt, just as Set obtained recognition; but he was never honoured generally.[4] The Thebans connected him with Kneph and Ra, representing him with a ram's head, or with a human head and the head-dress appropriate to sun-gods, and sometimes changing his name from Sabak into Sabak-Ra. The people of Ombos gladly adopted him, and identified him with their favourite deity,

---

[1] *Egypt's Place*, vol. i. p. 405.
[2] On the danger to life in Egypt from the crocodile, see Herod. ii. 90; Ælian, *Nat. Anim.* x. 24; Senec. *Nat. Quæst.* iv. 2; Diod. Sic. i. 35; and compare *Records of the Past*, vol. ii. pp. 143, 155, and 160.
[3] The word 'Savak' occurs as an element in a royal name as early as the twelfth dynasty (Brugsch, *Geschichte Aegyptens*, p. 164), which

would seem to imply his recognition as a god by the Thebans; but we have no clear evidence of his worship until the time of the nineteenth, when he is much honoured by Rameses II. and Rameses III. (See Rosellini, *Mon. del Culto*, pls. xxxii. 2; xxxiii. 1 and 2; xxxv. 2; xxxvi. 1 and 2; *Records of the Past*, vol. viii. pp. 29, 31.)
[4] Wilkinson, *A. E.* vol. v. p. 36.

Ombo. or Nubi, who was himself a form of Set, as will be shown later. He was also accepted at a few other places; but, generally speaking, both Sabak and the crocodile, his sacred animal, were held in horror and detestation.

Sabak's name is expressed either phonetically $\prod\rfloor$━, or by a crocodile and a sort of shrine or chapel [hieroglyph] . Where the phonetic characters are used, the others are often added. His crocodile-headed form has been already given ;[1] in his other shapes he is undistinguishable from Kneph and Phthah-Sokari-Osiris.[2]

ONURIS. (Egypt. *Han-her*).

Onuris is generally said to be the Egyptian Mars,[3] and his name would certainly seem to mean 'bringer of fear.'[4] It is written either $\bigwedge\stackrel{\bullet}{\frown}$ or $\bigwedge$━, but does not occur very frequently. Rameses III. calls him 'son of Ra,' identifies him with Shu, and speaks of him as his own father.[5] He is noted as a god who wore 'tall plumes,'[6] and distinguished in the sculptures by four upright feathers. Silsilis appears to have been the city where he was chiefly worshipped ;[7] and it would seem to have been the temple of that place which Rameses III. surrounded with a wall ninety feet high, to protect it from the attacks of the native Africans.[8]

---

[1] See above, p. 282.
[2] Compare Wilkinson, *A. E.* 'Supplement,' pl. 50, pt. 2, fig. 3, with pl. 21, pt. 1, fig. 1 ; and pl. 50, pt. 2, fig. 1, with pl. 24, fig. 2.
[3] Birch, *Egypt from the Earliest Times*, 'Introduction,' p. xii.; *Records of the Past*, vol. viii. p. 24, note, &c.
[4] See Birch's *Dict. of Hierogly-*

phics, pp. 402–3.
[5] *Records of the Past*, vol. viii. p. 24.
[6] Ibid. p. 29: 'The men which he gave to the temple of the god, Hanher *of the tall plumes.*'
[7] Rameses III. speaks of Onuris as 'resident in Tennu,' which is the same place as Silsilis.
[8] *Records*, vol. viii. pp. 24–5.

MERULA.

Merula or Malouli is a god who does not appear until the later sculptures and inscriptions, but who can scarcely be supposed an invention of the later ages. His name[1] is written ⳥ 𓊽 ⁝⁝⁝ 𓂝]. He is represented in the ordinary form of a god, but with the Osirid

Merula.

head-dress placed above a wig and fillet, or else with a still more complicated head-ornament,[2] placed above a cap resembling one sometimes worn by the kings.

---

[1] See Rosellini, *Monumenti del Culto*, pl. xv. 1; and compare Wilkinson, *A. E.* 'Supplement,' pl. 50, pt. 1.

[2] This ornament does not appear on the head of any other god. It consists of *three* spheres placed side by side over the usual wavy horns, and surmounted by three vascular forms with a disk at the top of each. On either side are the usual ostrich feathers and uræi.

Curiously enough, this ornament, which was certainly not common in Egypt, appears very slightly modified in the near vicinity of the tomb of Cyrus. (See the author's *Herodotus*, vol. i. p. 256, 3rd ed.)

At Talmis in Nubia, Merula was the third deity of a triad consisting of Horus, Isis, and himself.[1] On another Nubian site he occupied the same subordinate position, together with Seb and Nut or Netpe.[2] According to some, he is a mere form of Osiris; according to others, he is the last link in the long chain of the divine manifestations, the final member of the final triad of all, the 'last of the incarnations of Ammon.'[3] It may be suspected that he was a local (Nubian?) deity.

AEMHETP.

Aemhetp, whom the Greeks compared to their Asclepius or Æsculapius, was a god but little acknowledged and but little wor-
shipped. He seems never
to have had a temple ex-
pressly built in his honour.[4]
The form assigned to him is
the simplest that we find
given to any god, consisting,
as it does, merely of a
bearded man, wearing a
plain tunic, with a collar,
and a close-fitting skull-cap.
The *ankh* and sceptre which
he carries, alone show him

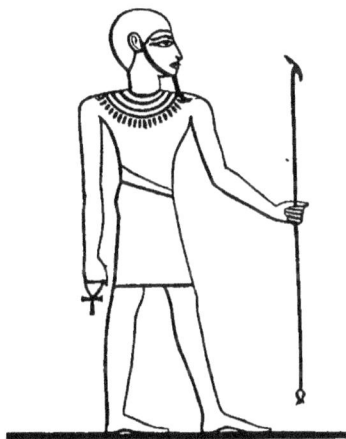

Aemhetp.

to be a god. His name is expressed by [hieroglyphs] or [hieroglyphs].

The monuments state that he was the 'son of Phthah,' but give no account of his attributes. We

---

[1] Champollion, *Lettres écrites d'Egypte*, lettre xi. pp. 155–6.
[2] Wilkinson, *A. E.* vol. v. p. 35.
[3] So Champollion, l.s.c.
[4] Wilkinson says, he 'held a post

among the contemplar gods of Upper and Lower Egypt from Philæ
to the Delta' (*A. E.* vol. v. p. 54),
but mentions no temple where he
was worshipped separately.

may conclude, however, from the notices of the classical writers,[1] that he was in some sort a 'god of medicine,' and was worshipped in the belief that his favour would avert disease from his votaries, or cure them when afflicted with any malady. Images of him, which appear to have been votive offerings, and represent him seated on a stool, unfolding a papyrus roll which lies upon his knees, are not uncommon.[2]

PASHT or BAST.

Of the goddesses not hitherto described, the most important seems to have been Pasht or Bast. Some writers have even placed her among the eight deities of the first order ;[3] but this view is scarcely tenable. She was the wife of Phthah,[4] and was worshipped together with him and their son, Tum, in the great triad of Memphis. Her common title is Merienptah ☒ 'beloved of Phthah ;' she is also called *Mut*, 'the mother,' and *ur-heku*, which is of uncertain meaning.[5]

Bast is represented in the ordinary form of a goddess, but as lion-headed in the earlier, and as cat-headed in the more recent times. In most instances she bears upon her head the sun's disk, with the uræus ; but sometimes she has the disk only, sometimes the

[1] Synes. *Encom. Calv.* p. 73, B ; Amm. Marc. xxii. 14; Macrob. *Saturnal.* i. 20, &c.

[2] See Birch, *Guide to Museum*, p. 15; Gatty, *Catalogue of Mayer Collection*, p. 8, &c.

[3] Wilkinson in the author's *Herodotus*, vol. ii. pp. 284–6.

[4] Wilkinson, *A. E.* vol. iv. p. 280. There is some doubt whether the true wife of Phthah was Bast or Sechet, or whether these two names

did not really belong to a single goddess. Individually I incline to this theory ; but Dr. Birch in a recent work distinguishes between the two, and suggests that they were sisters (*Egypt from the Earliest Times*, 'Introduction,' p. xi.)

[5] Bunsen suggests the meaning, ' the old (oldest ?) of the avengers ; ' but doubtfully (*Egypt's Place*, vol. i. p. 399).

uræus only, and occasionally neither the one nor the other.[1] Excepting by her hieroglyphic name, she is undistinguishable from Menh and Tafné. This name is expressed by three signs, thus : ╪⚬, and is read doubtfully as Pasht or Bast.

The worship of Bast was widely spread. At Thebes she held a high place among the contemplar deities there reverenced.[2] At Memphis, she was not only

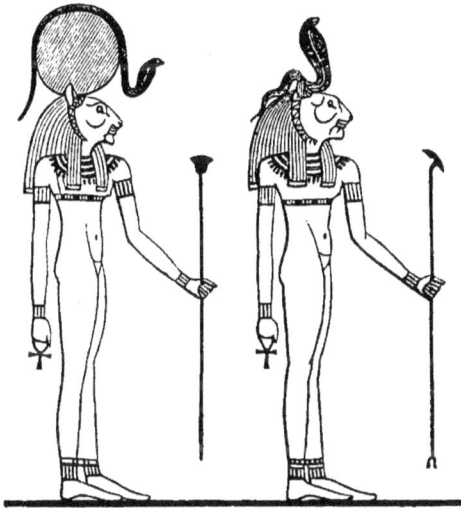

Bast or Pasht.

united with Phthah, but had a special temple of her own.[5] Her great city was, however, Bubastis (now Tel-Basta) in the Delta, which was wholly dedicated to her,[4] and contained her principal shrine, an edifice

[1] See Wilkinson, *A. E.* 'Supplement,' pls. 27, 35A, and 51. Compare *Description de l'Egypte*, 'Antiquités,' vol. i. pl. 16, No. 2 ; vol. iii. pl. 48 ; Rosellini, *Mon. del Culto*, pl. 8, No. 3 ; pl. 32, No. 1 ; and numerous statues in the British Museum, as those numbered 16, 62, 88, 517, 518, and 520.
[2] Wilkinson, *A. E.* vol. iv. p. 277.
[3] See *Records of the Past*, vol. iv. p. 143.
[4] Ibid. vol. viii. p. 31.

pronounced by Herodotus to be 'the most pleasing of
all the temples of Egypt.'[1] Once a year a great festival was held at this place, accompanied by indecent
ceremonies, which was frequented by vast numbers
of the Egyptians.[2] It does not appear that her worship was very ancient; but from the time of Rameses
III., at any rate, she was held in high repute, and
received the frequent homage of the kings, who even
sometimes called her their ' mother.'[3]

NUT or NETPE.

Nu, Nut, Nuhar, or Netpe is the rendering of a
name expressed in hieroglyphics by the three characters 𓊽, which are sometimes followed
by the feminine signs of the half-circle
and egg, 𓏏. It is doubtful whether
the third hieroglyph ▭, which is the
ideograph for 'heaven,' was sounded,
and, if it was, whether the sound was
har or *pe*. The goddess was the divinity of the firmament, and is generally
called the wife of Seb and mother of
Osiris. Her titles are, 'the elder,'
'the mother of the gods,' 'the mistress of Heaven,' and 'the nurse.' She
is at once the mother and the daughter
of Ra.[4] She was represented in the
common form of a goddess, with the *ankh* and female

Netpe.

---

[1] Herod. ii. 137.
[2] Ibid. ii. 60.
[3] Her worship by Rameses III. appears upon the monuments (Rosellini, *Mon. del Culto*, pl. viii. No. 3; pl. xxxii. No. 1), and is also noticed in the inscriptions (*Records of the Past*, vol. viii. p. 31). She

was a favourite with Sheshonk, who erected statues to her. Osorkon I. adorned her temple at Bubastis. It is Rameses III. who calls her his 'mother.' (*Records*, l.s.c.)
[4] See *Records of the Past*, vol. vi. pp. 108-9, and vol. viii. pp. 131-3.

sceptre, sometimes bearing a vase upon her head. Occasionally she appears in a fig or sycomore tree, pouring liquid from a similar vase into the hands of a deceased soul.[1] As the mother of Osiris, she is held in honour in the lower world, and thus her figure often appears in the tombs. It does not seem, however, as if she was a special object of worship in any city, or had anywhere a temple specially built in her honour.

NEPHTHYS.   (Egypt. *Neb-ta.*)

Nephthys, according to the myth, was the sister of

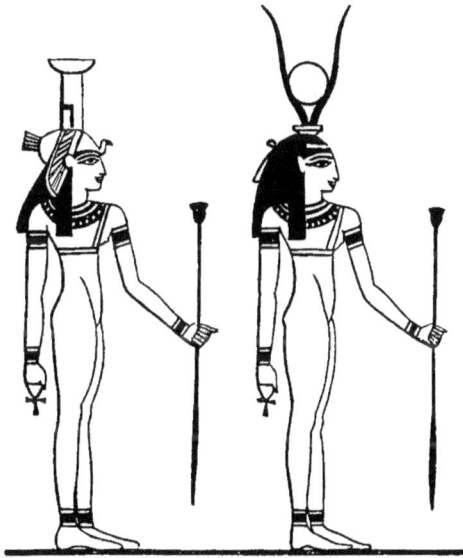

Ordinary Forms of Nephthys.

Isis, and assisted her in her painful efforts to collect her husband's scattered members and effect his resuscitation.[2] Her common titles are ' the sister,' ' the benevo-

---

[1] Wilkinson, *Ancient Egyptians,* ' Supplement.' pl. 32, fig. 3.
[2] See the ' Tears of Isis' in the

Records of the Past, vol. ii. pp. 119-24.

lent saving sister,' ' the sister goddess,' and ' the great
benevolent goddess.' [1] She held an important office in
the under world, where she is the constant associate of
Osiris and Isis,[2] and is said to ' cut away the failings ' of
deceased persons.[3] Her name is written with a sign
which seems to be a combination of a house with a
basket, ⊓⌐, followed by the half-circle and egg so
frequently attached to the name of a goddess. It has
been read Neb-tei, and translated ' lady of the abode,' [4]
but Birch reads it simply Neb-ta.[5]

Neb-ta was figured like other goddesses, but with
the house and basket upon her head, or else in a form
in which she is undistinguishable from Isis, crowned,
that is, with the sun's disk between two long cow's
horns. She often appears in the tombs, but does not
seem to have had any temple dedicated to her.

ANUKA.   (Egypt. *Ank*).

Anuka has been regarded by some as a form of
Nephthys,[6] by others as a form of Sati.[7] But she
seems to be really a distinct and substantive goddess.
There is nothing that properly connects her in any way
with Nephthys ; and though she stands connected with
Kneph, very much as Sati does, being, like Sati, his
wife and companion, yet they can scarcely be identical,
since the two are invoked together,[8] and represented
together,[9] and called, in the plural number, ' the ladies

[1] Bunsen, *Egypt's Place*, vol. i. p. 417 ; Wilkinson, *Ancient Egyptians*, vol. iv. p. 438.
[2] See the 'Ritual of the Dead' in Bunsen's *Egypt*, vol. v. pp. 180, 269, 270, 310, &c.
[3] Ibid. p. 179.
[4] Wilkinson, *A. E.* vol. iv. pp. 437–8.
[5] See Bunsen's *Egypt*, vol. v. p. 582.
[6] Ibid. vol. i. p. 421.
[7] Birch, *Guide to Egyptian Galleries*, p. 5.
[8] *Records of the Past*, vol. vi. pp. 81, 84, &c.
[9] Rosellini, *Monumenti del Culto*, pl. 6, fig. 2.

of Elephantiné.'[1] Anuka was acknowledged as a goddess only at the extreme south of Egypt and in Nubia.
There she was the third deity in a triad composed of
herself, Kneph, and Sati, or sometimes the third deity
in a 'tetrad' composed of Kneph, Sati, herself, and
Hak, who is her son by Kneph.[2] Her name is written
phonetically ⸗, or *ank*, followed by the feminine
sign ▪, and that by the form of a goddess. She is represented, like other goddesses, in the ordinary female
attire, and with the *ankh* and
lotus sceptre, but is clearly distinguished from all her rivals by
a head-dress of a very peculiar
kind. This is a high cap, ornamented at the top with a number of feathers which spread
outwardly, and form a striking
and graceful plume.[3] The Greek
conquerors of Egypt identified
her with Hestia or Vesta,[4] but
on what grounds is uncertain.
She seems to have been really
rather a war-goddess than a
protectress of the hearth.

Anuka.

MA.

Ma was the Egyptian goddess of truth. To the
initiated she was, no doubt, the truth and justice of the
Supreme God personified ; but to the vulgar she was

---

[1] *Records of the Past*, vol. vi. p.
81.
[2] Birch, l.s.c.
[3] Sometimes, instead of feathers,
the cap seems to be crowned by a
row of lotus-blossoms. (See Rosellini, *Mon. del Culto*, pl. 2, fig. 2.)
[4] This is proved by an inscription
found at Sebayl, near the first cataract, where she is called ' Anukè or
Hestia.' (See Wilkinson's *Ancient
Egyptians*, vol. v. p. 26.)

a distinct personage, a goddess who presided over all transactions in which truth and justice came into play. The kings, as supreme judges, are frequently said to be ' beloved of Ma,' *i.e.* friends of truth.[1] The chief judge in each subordinate court is said to have worn an image of Ma, and when he decided a cause to have touched with the image the litigant in whose favour his decision was made.[2] In the final judgment of Osiris Ma's image was also introduced, being set in the scale and weighed against the good actions of

Forms of Ma.

the deceased.[3] Ma was reckoned a daughter of Ra, and was worshipped together with him.[4] She is sometimes called ' chief' or ' directress of the gods.'[5] No

---

[1] *Records of the Past*, vol. x. pp. 25–7, &c.

[2] Diod. Sic. i. 76.

[3] Wilkinson, *A. E.* ' Supplement,' pl. 88. Sometimes Ma is present in person and watches the proceed-

ings (*Description de l'Egypte*, ' Antiquités,' vol. ii. pl. 35).

[4] Rosellini, *Mon. del Culto*, pl. 35, fig. 1.

[5] Wilkinson, *A. E.* vol. v. p. 31.

special temples were dedicated to her, nor was she comprised, so far as is known, in any triad. Her peculiar emblem was a single ostrich feather ⌡ ; and her name is sometimes written with such a feather, followed by the half-circle and egg, which are usual signs of femininity, thus, ⌡⌣. But the more common mode of expressing it is as follows : ⌐⌐.

Ma is most frequently figured in the ordinary form of a standing goddess, but with an ostrich feather erect above her head. Sometimes, however, she sits, and bears the *ankh* without the sceptre. She is also found occasionally with huge wings, which project in front of her body to a considerable distance. In this guise, she is often double, since the Egyptians were in the habit, for some recondite reason, of representing truth as twofold.[1]

TAENÉ.

Tafné, another daughter of Ra, has a faint and shadowy character, which does not admit of much description. She ordinarily accompanies Shu,[2] whose twin sister and wife she is, and seems to be a sort of goddess of light.[3] Both Osiris and Horus are called in places

Tafné.

---

[1] See the *Ritual of the Dead*, ch. lxxv., where the deceased person is ushered into the 'Hall of the Two Truths' (Bunsen's *Egypt*, vol. v. p. 252).

[2] See *Records of the Past*, vol. vi. pp. 105, 115, 116, 119, 124 ; *Ritual of the Dead*, pp. 180, 275, &c.

[3] See the *Records*, vol. x. p. 137 : 'Shu, the son of Ra, as Ra, navigates the heaven on high every morning ; *the goddess Tafné rests upon his head*: she *gives her fire* against his enemies to reduce them to non-existence.'

c c 2

'sons of Shu and Tafné;'[1] but this mythology is of
course exceptional.   Her name is written phonetically ⚊ ⚊, with or without the figure of a sitting goddess.   She is portrayed in the usual female form, but
with the head of a lioness, like Sekhet, and bearing on
her head the solar orb, surmounted
by the uræus.[2]   Within the limits
of Egypt, she was worshipped
chiefly at Thebes;[3] but her effigy
is found also in Nubia,[4] where she
was held in honour by the Ethiopians.

MERSEKER.

Merseker—whose name is written in two ways, ⚊ or
⚊—is a goddess not very
often mentioned.   We may gather
from her name, which means 'loving silence,'[5] that she was the
'goddess of silence,'[6] a conclusion

Merseker.

which is confirmed by our finding her called, in one of
the royal tombs at Thebes, 'the ruler of Amenti' or
'the regions below.'[7]   The form assigned to her is
very like that usually given to Isis and Nephthys,
differing only in the head-dress, which is without lappets.   She carries the *ankh*, like other goddesses, but
bears the *uas* or male sceptre.

---

[1] *Records,* vol. vi. pp. 116 and 119.
[2] Rosellini, *Monumenti del Culto,* pls. xi. and xii.; Wilkinson, *Ancient Egyptians,* 'Supplement,' pl. h. part i.
[3] Wilkinson, *A. E.* vol. v. p. 38.
[4] Rosellini, l.s.c.
[5] From *mer*, ⚊ or ⚊, 'to love,' and *skar*, ⚊ or ⚊ 'silence.'
[6] Birch, in Bunsen's *Egypt,* vol. v. p. 582.
[7] Wilkinson, *A. E.* vol. v. p. 81.

HEKA.

The goddess Hak or Heka, as commonly represented, is undistinguishable from Tafné, having the
lion's head surmounted by the solar orb and asp. She
seems, however, unlike Tafné, to have been a goddess of
the tombs, in which her effigy often
occurs. Sir Gardner Wilkinson supposed her to correspond to the Greek
Hecaté,[1] whose name he identified
with hers ; but the resemblance of
the two in character is very slight.
Hak appears on some of the older
monuments as the wife of Kneph.[2]
She is there frog-headed instead of
lion-headed, and bears neither the
disk nor the uræus. Her name is
written either ⚲ or ⚲, and has
sometimes the figure of a sitting
frog 𓆏 placed after it.

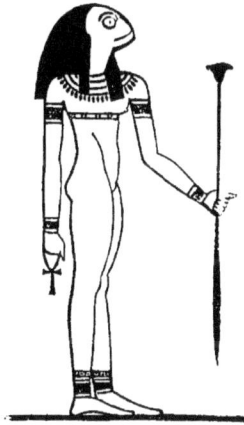

Form of Hak.

MENH or MENHI.

In form this goddess is, like Heka, an exact reproduction of Tafné, lion-headed, with the solar orb and
uræus, and bearing the *ankh* and lotus sceptre in her
two hands.[3]   Her name is written ⚲ or ⚲.
No special office can be assigned to her.

NEHEMAO.

Nehemao is another colourless and shadowy goddess, not often mentioned, and, when mentioned, given

---

[1] Wilkinson, *A. E.* vol. v. p. 39.
[2] Sharpe, *Egyptian Inscriptions,*
p. 78.

[3] Wilkinson, *A. E.* ' Supplement,'
pl. li. part iii.

no epithets that assign her any definite character. She is a 'daughter of the sun,' 'the lady of Tentyris,' and 'the mistress of the eight regions of Egypt.' [1] Her head-dress consists of a shrine, from which in some cases water plants are seen to issue on all sides. At the quarries near Memphis she was worshipped as the second member of a triad, in which she was conjoined with Thoth and Horus. Her name is expressed in Egyptian by the following group ⌇.

It has been already stated that to a certain number of the Egyptian deities an evil and malignant character very unmistakably attaches, [2] if not in the more ancient form of the religion, at any rate in that form which ultimately prevailed and established itself universally. This character belongs in some degree even to Savak, the crocodile-headed god, who was a main object of worship at the best period ; but it is intensified in such deities as Set or Sutech, Nubi or Ombo (if he is really distinct from Set), Bes, and Taouris, who are represented in grotesque or hideous forms, and whose attributes and actions are wholly or predominantly evil.

SET or SUTECH.

Set was a son of Nut or Netpe, and so a brother of Osiris. According to the myth, he rebelled against his brother, murdered him, cut his body into pieces, and reigned in his stead. Osiris was afterwards avenged by his son, Horus, who vanquished Set, and, according to some accounts, slew him. [3] Set, however, though slain,

---

[1] Wilkinson, *A.E.* vol. v. pp. 80–1.
[2] See above, p. 316.
[3] See *Records of the Past*, vol. ii. p. 121 : 'Thine enemy is vanquished ; *he no longer existeth ;*' and compare vol. vi. pp. 116–7 : 'Shu and Tefnut (Tafné) place their son, Horus son of Isis, on the throne of his father ; they upset Set ; they drag him to the secret

continued to be feared and worshipped, being recognised as the indestructible power of evil, and so requiring
to be constantly propitiated. In the time of the Old
Monarchy he seems to have held a place among the
'great gods,'[1] but was not the object either of any
special adoration or of any marked aversion. During
the rule of the Hyksos, or shepherd kings, those invaders selected him as their sole deity, refusing to
worship any of the other Egyptian gods.[2] On their
expulsion, he resumed his former place till the time of
the nineteenth dynasty, when increased prominence
was given to him by Seti I., in whose name Set was the
chief element.[3] Subsequently, but at what exact time
is unknown, Set passed wholly out of favour. His
worship ceased, and his very name was obliterated
from the monuments.[4]

The name Set is expressed commonly by ⌐ or
⌐ ; but in the latter case the Typhonian animal, ⌐,
which sometimes stands by itself for Set, is usually
added. When Sutech is the name used, it is commonly
written ⌐. The worshippers of Set call him
'the lord of the world,' 'the most glorious son of Nut,'
and 'the great ruler of heaven.'[5] His detractors view
him as 'wicked,' 'vile,' and 'the enemy of Osiris.'[6]
The form generally assigned him is curious. It is a
human figure of the ordinary type, but with a strange

place of punishment in the east.
Horus kills him in his name.'
[1] See the list of early Egyptian
gods in Manetho (ap. Euseb. *Chron.
Can.* i. 20, § 1); where Typhon
(= Set) occurs between Osiris and
Horus.
[2] *Records of the Past,* vol. viii.
p. 3.
[3] The name of Seti I. is com-

monly written ⌐, where the
sitting figure represents Set.
[4] Wilkinson, *A. E.* vol. iv. pp.
416–18.
[5] See *Records of the Past,* vol. iv.
pp. 27, 32, &c.
[6] Ibid. vol. vi. pp. 117, 122; vol.
x. p. 162, &c.

and monstrous head, halfway between that of a bird
and that of a quadruped. A pair of long, erect, and
square-topped ears, a bill like that of a stork, a small
eye, and a large wig, form an *ensemble* which is grotesque in the extreme,[1] and which naturally provokes a
laugh. Sometimes, besides this head there is a second,
which is clearly that of a hawk.[2]

Forms of Set.

NUBI or NUBTI.

It is probable that in Nubi or Nubti we have not
so much a distinct god as another name of the deity
above described,[3] Sutech or Set. The name Nubti,
written ⨍ is followed by the same grotesque animal

---

[1] Wilkinson, *Ancient Egyptians,*
'Supplement,' pl. 38, pt. ii. fig. 1;
pl. 39, fig. 1; and pl. 78, fig. 1.
[2] Ibid. pl. 38, pt. ii. fig. 2.

[3] So Canon Cook in the *Records
of the Past,* vol. ii. p. 102, and Bunsen in his *Egypt,* vol. i. p. 425.

form as the name Sutech ; and it not unfrequently
accompanies one or other of the figures which were
assigned to Set in the last paragraph. Nor is there
any other form than this which can be ascribed to Nubti.
Nubti is called ' the occupant of the south,' [1] and is said
to ' shoot his arrows against the enemies of the sun,'
and to ' shake the earth and the sky with his storm.' [2]

TAOURIS.   (Egypt. *Taour* or *Taourt.*)

Taour or Taourt, the feminine counterpart of Set,
appears commonly in the form of a hippopotamus

Forms of Taourt.

walking, with the back covered by the skin and tail of
a crocodile.[3] In one hand she generally bears an implement like a knife, while in the other she sometimes
holds a young crocodile.[4] Her mouth is commonly
furnished with huge teeth, and has the tongue pro-

---

[1] *Records of the Past*, vol. ii. p.
101.
[2] Ibid. vol. x. p. 145. This en-
listment of Nubti, or Nubi, among
the *helpers* of the sun is very re-

markable.
[3] See Rosellini, *Monumenti del
Culto*, pl. xxxi. fig. 1 ; Wilkinson,
A. E. ' Supplement,' pl. 40.
[4] See the woodcut on p. 282.

truding from it more or less.   Sometimes, instead of a
knife, the implement which she bears in her hand resembles a pair of shears.   She was worshipped at
Silsilis in combination with Thoth and Nut or Nutpe,[1]
standing there, as it seems, at the head of a local
triad.   Her name is commonly written phonetically
◂人 人 ⌣ and is sometimes followed by a uræus 𓆗,
ouro, which is redundant.

BES.

Bes, represented as a hideous dwarf, generally with
a plume of feathers on his head and a lion-skin down

Form of Bes.

his back,[2] is thought by some to be a form of Set, by
others to be the Egyptian 'god of death.'[3] He is some-

---

[1] Rosellini, l.s.c.
[2] See above, p. 266, where the

central figure is that of Bes.
[3] Wilkinson, *A. E.* vol. iv. p. 432.

times seen armed with a sword or swords, and is even
found in the act of slaying persons.[1] His name, which
is written ⫞⫟, is followed, curiously enough, by the
hieroglyph representing a skin ⫭, which occurs com-
mouly as the determinative of animals. He was worshipped at Thebes, at Tentyris, and in Ethiopia. Bronze
images of Bes are common, and appear sometimes to
connect him with the moon.[2]

APOPHIS. (Egypt. *Apep.*)

Apophis is portrayed either as a huge serpent disposed in many folds, or as a water snake with a human

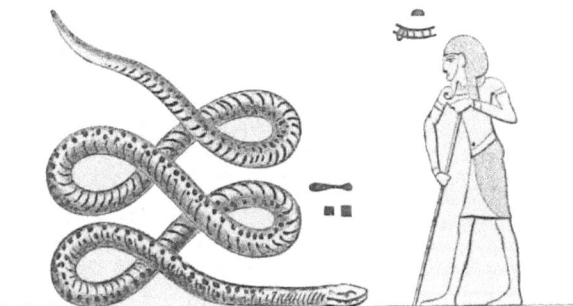

Apophis and Tum.

head.[3] He was supposed to have sided with Set
against Osiris, and to have thereby provoked the anger
of Horus, who is frequently represented as piercing his
head with a spear.[4] The place of his ordinary abode
is the lower world, where he seems to act as the
accuser of souls, and to impede their progress towards
the inner gates of Hades and the Hall of the Two Truths.[5]

[1] Wilkinson, l.s.c.
[2] Birch, *Guide to Museum*, p. 16.
[3] Wilkinson, *A. E.* vol. iv. p. 436.
[4] See above, p. 359.
[5] See the *Ritual of the Dead*, ch. xxxix. (in Bunsen's *Egypt*, vol. v. pp. 193–5).

He is thought to have been the original principle of
evil in the Egyptian system, and to have subsequently
given way to Set, when their hatred of the Asiatics,
whose great god Set was, caused the Egyptians to invest
that deity with a malignant and hateful character.[1] The
word ' Apep ' seems to be derived from *ap*, ' to mount '
or ' rise.' It is expressed in Egyptian either by ⌐⌐,
or ⌐⌐.

Besides gods, the Egyptians recognised a certain
number of dæmones or genii, who were not the objects of any worship, but figured in their religious
scenes, and had certain definite offices assigned them,
if not in this world, at any rate in the next. Such
was Anubis, the conductor of the dead, who is sometimes represented as watching the departure of the
spirit from the body of one recently deceased,[2] but
more often appears in the judgment scenes, where he
weighs the souls in the balance,[3] or superintends the
execution of the sentence which has been passed upon
them by their judge.[4] Anubis is represented with the
head of an animal which the Greeks and Romans considered to be a dog,[5] but which is now generally
regarded as a jackal. In other respects he has the
ordinary form of a god, and even, when unemployed,
carries the *ankh* and sceptre. Occasionally he bears
on his head the crown of the two Egypts.[6] He is
called ' lord of the burying-ground,' [7] and regarded as
presiding over coffins,[8] tombs, and cemeteries. In the

[1] Wilkinson in the author's *Herodotus*, vol. ii. p. 220, 2nd edition.
[2] Wilkinson, *Ancient Egyptians*,
'Supplement,' pl. 44, pt. i. fig. 3.
[3] Ibid. pl. 88.
[4] Ibid. pl. 87.
[5] Propert. iii. xi. 41; Ov. *Met.*
ix. 690; Virg. *Æn.* viii. 698; Plutarch, *De Isid. et Osir.* § 14.
[6] Wilkinson, *A. E.* 'Supplement,'
pl. 44, pt. i. fig. 2.
[7] *Records of the Past*, vol. x. p. 3.
[8] Ibid. vol. iv. p. 3; vol. x. pp.
3, 85; Wilkinson, *A. E.* vol. iv.
p. 442.

mythology he was said to be a son of Ra and Nephthys,[1] or of Osiris and Nephthys.[2]   His name is written
either ▮⌐, 'Anep,' or ▮⌐, 'Anepu.'

With Anubis may be joined the 'four genii
of Amenti,' Amset, ▮⌐, Hapi, ▮⌐, Tuamutef
▮⌐, and Kebhsnauf ▮⌐, who are repre-
sented either as mummied figures, or in the ordinary
human form,[3] and bear respectively the heads of a man,
a cynocephalous ape, a jackal, and a hawk.   These
beings presided, with Anubis, over the grave.   At the
embalmment of a corpse the intestines were taken out,

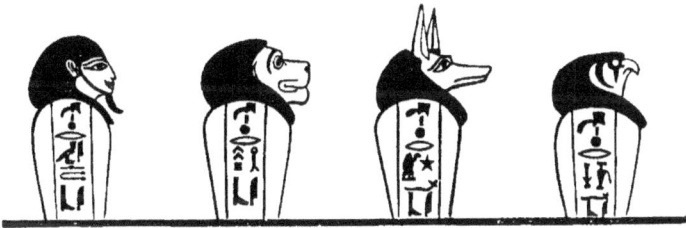

Sepulchral jars, with heads of the four Genii.

treated with medicaments, and then either deposited in
jars bearing the respective heads of the four genii, and
placed with the coffin in the tomb, or else returned
into the body accompanied by their complete figures.
Each genius had certain special intestines committed to
his care : Amset, the stomach and large intestines ;
Hapi, the smaller intestines ; Tuamutef, the lungs
and heart ; Kebhsnauf, the liver and gall-bladder.[4]

---

[1] *Records of the Past*, vol. x. p.
149.
[2] Bunsen, *Egypt's Place*, vol. i. p.
415.
[3] Wilkinson, *A. E.* vol. v. p. 71.

The mummied form is by far the
most common.
[4] Ibid. pp. 70–1. Compare Birch,
Guide to Museum, pp. 89–90.

Speeches, supposed to be made by the genii, were frequently inscribed on the exterior of coffins, and on the boxes which held sepulchral vases and sepulchral figures.[1] In the infernal regions the four genii were closely associated with Osiris, and are spoken of as ' lords of truth, chiefs behind Osiris.' [2] Their duties are not very clear, but seem rather connected with the preservation of the body than the safe passage of the soul through its ordeals.[3] Still, the genii are sometimes invoked to sustain the soul upon its way with food and light, to help it to ' pass through the secret places of the horizon,' and to cross ' the lintels of the gate.' [4]

It is usual to attach to the ' four genii of Amenti ' the ' forty-two ' who are known as ' the assessors.' In representations of Osiris upon the judgment-seat, the assessors usually appear, standing or sitting in two or more rows above him or behind him, each crowned with an ostrich feather, the emblem of truth, and carrying in his two hands an implement resembling a sword or knife.[5] All have mummied forms, and, while some have human, the majority have animal heads, chiefly those proper to certain of the gods, as hawks', lions', jackals', rams', crocodiles', and hippopotamuses'. Each assessor has his own proper name; and these names it was necessary for all persons to know, and to repeat when standing in the ' Hall of the Two Truths,' and disclaiming the forty-two sins of the Egyptian moral code. All the names appear to have been sig-

---

[1] *Records of the Past*, vol. x. pp. 86–7 ; Gatty, *Catalogue of Mayer Collection*, p. 39.

[2] *Ritual of the Dead*, ch. xvii. (in Bunsen's *Egypt*, vol. v. p. 175).

[3] See especially *Records of the Past*, vol. x. pp. 85–7.

[4] *Ritual of the Dead*, ch. cxlix. ad fin.

[5] Wilkinson, *A. E.* ' Supplement,' pl. 62 ; Rosellini, *Monumenti del Culto*, pl. lxvi. &c.

nificant, and most of them were well calculated to cause the guilty to tremble.[1] 'Eyes of flame,' 'breath of flame,' 'cracker of bones,' 'devourer of shades,' 'eater of hearts,' 'swallower,' 'lion-god,' 'white tooth,' 'smoking face,' and the like, sufficiently indicated what fate would befall those who made a false protest of innocence to the spirit whose province it was to punish some one particular crime. The assessors 'lived by catching the wicked,' 'fed off their blood,'[2] and 'devoured their hearts before Horus.'[3] They were thus not merely judges, but accusers and punishers of crime. Guilty souls were handed over to them by Osiris, but to be 'tortured' only, not destroyed.[4]

Long as is the above list of Egyptian gods and genii, let it not be supposed that the catalogue is as yet complete. A full account of the Egyptian Pantheon would have to comprise, besides the deities which have been enumerated, at least twenty or thirty others; as for instance, Nun, the god of the primeval waters;[5] Hapi, the Nile god;[6] Bahu, the lord of the inundation;[7] Repa, the wife of Hapi;[8] Uati, the goddess of Lower Egypt;[9] Khaft, perhaps the goddess of the upper country;[10] Sem, the goddess of the West;[11] Sefkh, god-

---

[1] See the *Ritual*, ch. cxxv. (Bunsen, pp. 253–6).
[2] Ibid. p. 252.
[3] Ibid. p. 256.
[4] Ibid. The final annihilation of the wicked soul, when it took place, was effected by Shu. (See above, p. 352.)
[5] Nun is often mentioned in the sacred myths, as, for instance, in the 'Destruction of Mankind by Ra,' where he is called 'the firstborn of the gods,' and said to be the father of Ra (*Records of the Past*, vol. vi. pp. 105–6).
[6] See Wilkinson, *A. E.* vol. v.

pp. 56–9; *Records of the Past*, vol. iv. pp. 107-114; vol. vi. pp. 66–9; Rosellini, *Mon. del Culto*, pl. xxx. fig. 4.
[7] *Records of the Past*, vol. x. p. 149.
[8] Ibid. vol. vi. p. 69.
[9] Ibid. vol. iv. pp. 12–13; vol. x. pp. 29, 34, &c.
[10] Ibid. vol. ii. p. 31. Khaft is called 'lady of the country' by Thothmes III. in a tablet set up at Thebes.
[11] Birch in *Records of the Past*, vol. ii. p. 29.

dess of writing ;[1] Seneb, goddess presiding over child-
birth ;[2] Rannu, goddess of the harvest ;[3] Nepra, god
of corn ;[4] Hu, touch ;[5] Sa, taste ;[6] and the foreign
importations, Anta or Anaïtis ;[7] Astaret, Ashtoreth or
Astarte ;[8] Bar, or Baal ;[9] Reshpu, or Reseph ;[10] Ken, or
Kiun ;[11] and Sapt.[12]   Rito, Sekar, and Serk would also
claim a place in any full description, though it would
probably appear on examination that they were mere
forms of the better known Athor, Phthah, and Isis.
Inquiry would also have to be made into the true character and attributes of Am, Amente, Astes, Hak, Makai,
Nausaas, Nebhept, Nishem or Nuneb, Nuhar, Urhek,[13]

---

[1] Wilkinson, *A. E.* 'Supplement,'
pls. 54 and 54A; Birch in Bunsen's
Egypt, vol. v. p. 583.

[2] Wilkinson, *A. E.* vol. v. pp.
41-5; Rosellini, *Mon. del Culto*,
pl. xlviii. fig. 2, and pl. lii. fig. 2.
Birch reads the name as ' Nub,' regarding the initial letter as ⅃ and
not ⌐. (See Bunsen's *Egypt*, vol.
v. p. 582.)

[3] Wilkinson, *A. E.* vol. v. p. 64;
and 'Supplement,' pl. 58, pt. 4;
Records of the Past, vol. x. p. 156;
Birch in Bunsen's *Egypt*, vol. v. p.
583.

[4] *Records of the Past*, vol. ii. p.14.

[5] Ibid. vol. viii. p. 78 ; Wilkinson,
A. E. 'Supplement,' pl. 64, pt. 2.

[6] *Records of the Past*, l.s.c.; Birch
in Bunsen's *Egypt*, l.s.c.

[7] Bunsen, vol. i. pp. 409-10;
Records of the Past, vol. x. p. 142;
Wilkinson, *A. E.* 'Supplement,' pl.
70, pt. 1.

[8] *Records of the Past*, vol. iv. p.
31; vol. x. p. 142, &c.

[9] Ibid. vol. ii. pp. 68, 71, 76;
Birch, *Guide to Museum*, p. 11.

[10] Wilkinson, *A. E.* vol. v. pp.
83-4; Bunsen, *Egypt's Place*, vol.
i. pp. 411-12.

[11] Bunsen, vol. i. p. 412; Birch,
l.s.c.

[12] Birch in Bunsen's *Egypt*, vol.
v. p. 583; Wilkinson, *A. E.* 'Supplement,' pl. 65, pt. 3.

[13] Am, the 'Cerberus' of Wilkinson (*A. E.* vol. v. p. 77, and 'Supplement,' pl. 63, pt. 2), seems to
have been one of the demons of
Hades. He watches the weighing of souls (Wilkinson, pl. 88).
Amente was a feminine Ammon
(Bunsen, *Egypt's Place*, vol. i. p.
378) ; Astes, one of the gods of
Hades, joined with Thoth, Osiris,
and Anubis (*Ritual of the Dead*,
ch. xviii.); Hak, a son of Kneph
and Anuka, worshipped together
with them at Elephantiné ; Makai, a
crocodile god, a son of Set (*Records
of the Past*, vol. x. pp. 139, 147,
and 154). Nausaas was a daughter
of Ra or Tum, and one of the chief
deities of Heliopolis (ib. vol. vi. pp.
56, 58). Nebhept, generally cou-
pled with Nausaas, is thought to
have been a form of Athor. Nishem
or Nuneb is joined by Horus of the
18th dynasty with Uati, Neith, Isis,
Nephthys, Horus, and Set (ib. vol.
x. p. 34). Nuhar and Urhek are
included by Birch in his list of
Egyptian deities (Bunsen's *Egypt*,

&c. But to exhaust the subject would clearly require the devotion to it of at least one whole volume. In a work of moderate dimensions, such as the present, where even the more important deities have to be sketched rather than described at length, it is impossible to do more than glance at the minor and, comparatively speaking, insignificant personages of the Pantheon.

The arrangement of the gods into classes, and the organisation, so to speak, of the Pantheon, belong to a comparatively late date, and are too artificial to be of much interest. According to Herodotus,[1] the Egyptians recognised three orders of deities, and assigned to the first order eight, to the second twelve, and to the third an indefinite number. There is some reason to question the accuracy of this statement. In the extant native monuments and papyruses, neither 'the eight' nor 'the twelve' are to be recognised. We hear sometimes of a 'holy nine,'[2] of 'nine gods of the Ta-Mera,'[3] and of 'nine gods, the masters of things,'[4] but never of eight or twelve. Still, as Manetho to some extent confirms Herodotus,[5] it has been generally thought that there must have been, at any rate under the later Pharaohs, some arrangement of the gods into groups and some recognition of a presiding 'eight;' but great difficulty has been found in determining both the principle or principles of the division, and (still more) the deities which belong to each group. Following a

---

vol. v. pp. 581-3); the former is said to be a 'god of the firmament.'
[1] Herod. ii. 145.
[2] *Records of the Past*, vol. x. pp. 41-2.
[3] Ibid. p. 35.
[4] Ibid. p. 97.

[5] Strictly speaking, Manetho's list is one of seven, not eight, deities. But Isis may perhaps be considered to be implied in Osiris. (See Euseb. *Chron. Can.* i. 20, § 1, and compare Syncell. *Chronograph*, pp. 51-2.)

hint dropped by Herodotus,[1] one writer takes, as the general principle of the grouping, genealogical succession,[2] placing in the first order original or uncreated gods, in the second gods derived or descended from them, and in the third gods derived or descended from deities of the second rank. He is unable, however, to obtain more than seven gods of the first order by this method, and, to complete the eight, has to associate with them a produced god, Ra. the son of Phthah and Neith.[3] Recently it has been thought best to lay aside this principle of division altogether, and merely to ask the question, What eight gods practically received the chief worship of the Egyptians? To this question it has been found impossible to give a simple answer, since different usages prevailed in different parts of the country. The subjoined, for instance, is given as the probable list at Memphis :—1. Phthah; 2. Shu; 3. Tafné ; 4. Seb ; 5. Nut or Netpe; 6. Osiris; 7. Isis (with Horus) ; and 8. Athor ; while at Thebes 'the eight' is supposed to have been constituted as follows :— 1. Ammon-Ra; 2. Mentu; 3. Tum; 4. Shu (with Tafné); 5. Seb ; 6. Osiris ; 7. Set (with Nephthys); and 8. Horus (with Athor).[4] It is reasonable to sup-

---

[1] Herod. ii. 43 : Ἐκ τῶν ὀκτὼ θεῶν οἱ δυώδεκα θεοὶ ἐγένοντο. Compare ch. 145.

[2] Bunsen, *Egypt's Place*, vol. i. pp. 366–8.

[3] So Bunsen, p. 387. But the Egyptian mythology is not always self-consistent. Ra is sometimes the son of Nun (*Records of the Past*, vol. vi. pp. 105–6).

[4] Birch, *Guide to Museum*, p. 12. ✦ The lists here given do not altogether agree with those contained in Dr. Birch's *Egypt from the Ear-liest Times*, which are as follows :—

Eight great Gods at Thebes.	Eight great Gods at Memphis.
1. Ammon-Ra.	1. Phthah.
2. Mentu.	2. Ra.
3. Shu.	3. Shu (with Tafné).
4. Seb.	4. Seb.
5. Nut.	5. Nut.
6. Osiris.	6. Osiris (with Isis).
7. Set.	7. Set.
8. Horus (with Athor).	8. Horus.

pose that a similar divergence would show itself, were the inquiry extended to other religious centres.[1] The recognition of a first order of gods, if we regard it as established, necessitates the recognition of a second order; but it seems very improbable that the number of the second order was limited to twelve. Whatever eight we separate off from the rest to form the first order, we shall find at least twenty with about equal claims to a place in the second.[2] It would seem most probable that in the second order were included all the proper deities below the first eight; and that the third order contained only the deities more correctly called 'dæmones' or 'genii,' such as Anubis, Amset, Hapi, Tuamutef, Kebhsnauf, Am, Astes, Maentfef, Karbukef,[3] and 'the Assessors.'

Of far more practical importance than this division into orders was the curious preference, shown by the Egyptians generally, for worshipping their gods in triads, or sets of three.[4] In almost every town of any consequence throughout Egypt, a local triad received the chief worship of the inhabitants. At Memphis the established triad consisted of Phthah, Sekhet, and Tum; at Thebes, of Ammon-Ra, Maut, and Chonsu; at Heliopolis of Ra (or Tum), Nebhept, and Horus; at Elephantiné, of Kneph, Sati, and Anuka; at Abydos, of Osiris,

---

[1] At Heliopolis, for instance, the 'Eight' would almost certainly have comprised, besides Ra and Horus, the god Tum and the goddesses Nebhept and Nausaas. (See *Records of the Past*, vol. vi. p. 52.)

[2] It is observable that Bunsen, who alone attempts to fix on a definite 'twelve,' is obliged immediately to append to his list a 'supplementary' one of thirteen others (*Egypt's Place*, vol. i. pp. 409–11).

[3] Maentfef and Karbukef appear in the *Ritual of the Dead* as companions of the 'Four Genii,' but apparently are of a lower grade (Bunsen's *Egypt*, vol. v. p. 175).

[4] Birch, *Egypt from the Earliest Times*, 'Introduction,' p. xi.; *Guide to Museum*, p. 11; Wilkinson, *A. E.* vol. iv. pp. 230–3. Bunsen objects to the word 'triad,' and thinks the grouping by threes unimportant (*Egypt's Place*, vol. i. p. 305).

Isis, and Horus; at Ombos, of Savak, Athor, and Khonsu; at Silsilis, of Ra, Phthah, and Hapi, the Nile-god. Occasionally, but not very often, a fourth divinity was associated with the principal three, as Bast or Pasht (if she be different from Sekhet) at Memphis, Neith at Thebes, Nephthys at Abydos, and Hak at Elephantiné;[1] but the fourth always occupied a wholly subordinate position. The three gods of a triad were not themselves upon a par. On the contrary, the first god of the three had a decided pre-eminence, while the last was generally on a lower footing. The middle deity of a triad was ordinarily, but not always, a goddess.

Temples were generally dedicated to a single god; but the god thus honoured was worshipped in them *together with his contemplar deities.* Worship comprised three things, prayer, praise, and sacrifices. Specimens of the first and second have been already given.[2] But we subjoin one or two more. The following is an address to Ammon-Ra, considered as the Supreme God:—

Hail to Thee for all these things,
The One alone with many hands;
Lying awake while all men sleep,
To seek the good of Thy creatures!
O Ammon, sustainer of all things,
Atum-Horus of the horizon!
Homage to Thee from all voices!
Salvation to Thee for Thy mercy towards us;
Acknowledgment to Thee, who hast created us.

Hail to Thee, say all creatures,
Salutation from every land—
To the height of heaven; to the breadth of the earth;
To the depths of the sea.
The gods adore Thy majesty;
The spirits Thou hast created exalt Thee,
Rejoicing before the feet of their Begetter.

---

[1] Birch, *Guide to Museum,* l.s.c.   [2] Supra, pp. 326-7 and 350-1.

They cry out welcome to Thee,
Father of the father of all the gods ;
Who raises up the heavens, who fixes the earth.

Maker of beings, Creator of existences,
Sovereign of life and health and strength, Chief of the Gods :
We worship Thy spirit, which alone has made us :
We, whom Thou hast made, thank Thee that Thou hast given
    us birth :
We give praises to Thee for Thy mercy towards us ![1]

The subjoined is part of a 'Hymn to the Nile ; '
but the local colouring gradually fades, and, forgetting
his special theme, the sacred bard passes to a general
expression of thankfulness to the Almighty :—

Bringer of food ! Great Lord of provisions !
Creator of all good things !
Lord of terrors, and of all choicest joys !
All are combined in Him.
He produceth grass for the oxen,
And provides victims for every god ;
The choicest incense he too supplies.
Lord of both regions,
He filleth the granaries ; he enricheth the storehouses ;
· He careth for the estate of the poor.

He causeth growth, to fulfil all desires ;
He wearies not ever of it.
He maketh His might a buckler.
He is not graven in marble ;
No image of Him bears the double crown ;
He is not beheld ;
He hath neither ministrants nor offerings :
He is not adored in sanctuaries ;
His abode is not known ;
No shrine of His is found with painted figures.

There is no building that can contain Him.
There is none that can give Him counsel.
The young men, His children, delight in Him ;
He directeth them, as their King.
His law is established in all the land ;
It is with His servants, both in the north [and in the south].
He wipeth away tears from all eyes :
He careth for the abundance of His blessings.[2]

---

[1] *Records of the Past*, vol. ii. p. 133.   [2] Ibid. vol. iv. pp. 108-10.

The great deficiency which we note in the prayers of the Egyptians is the want of any earnest appeals for pardon, of any heartfelt repentance, or deep conviction of sin. Only once or twice do we find an Egyptian making any confession of sin at all.[1] On the other hand we find abundant boasting and self-assertion. As before the assessors in the Amenti each departed soul had to protest its absolute innocence, so every Egyptian takes every opportunity of setting forth his manifold good deeds and excellences in this life. ' I was not an idler,' says one, ' I was no listener to the counsels of sloth : my name was not heard in the place of reproof. . . . All men respected me. I gave water to the thirsty ; I set the wanderer in his path ; I took away the oppressor, and put a stop to violence.'[2] ' I myself was just and true,' writes another on his tombstone, ' without malice, having put God in my heart, and being quick to discern His will. I have done good upon earth ; I have harboured no prejudice ; I have not been wicked ; I have not approved of any offence or iniquity ; I have taken pleasure in speaking the truth. . . . *Pure is my soul;* while living, I bore no malice. There are no errors attributable to me ; no sins of mine are before the judges. . . . The men of the future, while they live, will be charmed by my remarkable merits.'[3] It is, of course, possible that we

---

[1] There is one slight acknowledgment in a ' Hymn to Tum,' which has been already given at length (supra, pp. 350-1) ; and in the *Ritual of the Dead* it is admitted that the soul, after passing through the Hall of the Two Truths, and protesting five times over, 'I am pure, I am pure, &c.,' still requires cleansing in the basin of purgatorial fire. ' Extract ye all the evil out of me,' say the souls ; ' obliterate my faults ; annihilate my sins.' ' Thou mayest go,' reply the spirits ; ' we obliterate all thy faults ; we annihilate all thy sins.' (See Bunsen's *Egypt,* vol. v. p. 260.)

[2] *Records of the Past,* vol. vi. pp. 137-9.

[3] Ibid. vol. x. pp. 7-9.

have here merely the indiscriminate and overstrained
eulogium of an affectionate widow or orphan, bent on
glorifying a deceased husband or parent, and thus that
the effusion is simply parallel to those epitaphs of the
Georgian era, assigning every virtue under the sun to
the departed, which disgrace so many of our own
churches; but it was certainly the general practice in
Egypt for persons to prepare their own tombs,[1] and
the use of the first person singular is therefore, probably, not a figure of rhetoric. Beka, most likely,
saw nothing unseemly or indelicate in putting on record
his own wonderful merits, and inviting posterity to
imitate them. Similarly, Uja-hor-resenet, a government official under Amasis, Psamatik III., and Cambyses, asserts his own excellence upon a statue, which
he certainly dedicated during his lifetime, in terms such
as the following:[2]—' I was a good man before the
king; I saved the population in the dire calamity
which took place throughout all the land; I shielded
the weak against the strong; I did all good things
when the time came to do them; I was pious towards
my father, and did the will of my mother; I was kind-
hearted towards my brethren. . . . I made a good
sarcophagus for him who had no coffin. When the
dire calamity befell the land, I made the children to
live, I established the houses, I did for them all such
good things as a father doth for his sons.'[3]

Sacrifice with the Egyptians, as with the Jews and
with the classical nations, was of two kinds, bloody and
unbloody. Unbloody sacrifice was the more usual.

---

[1] Records of the Past, vol. vi. p. 150. Compare Wilkinson, A. E. vol. v. p. 400.
[2] Records, vol. x. p. 52.

[3] Contrast with these utterances those of David (Ps. xxxi. 9–10; xxxii. 1–7; xl. 12, &c.), Isaiah (vi. 5), and even Job (xl. 4; xlii. 6).

The Egyptians offered to their gods bread,[1] fiour,[2] cakes of various kinds,[3] oil, honey, fruit, incense, wine, beer,[4] perhaps spirits, and also flowers.[5]　Libations to the gods were of daily occurrence,[6] and were certainly both of beer and wine, possibly also of the spirit which is easily obtained from dates.[7]　Incense was continually offered,[8] and consisted, in part, of frankincense, in part of various aromatic gums, and sweet-scented woods.[9] The best produce of Arabia was desired for this pious practice, and expeditions were sometimes undertaken, mainly for the purpose of procuring incense of the best quality.[10]　The fruits presented were such as dates, grapes, figs, the produce of the *doum* palm, olives, mulberries, &c.[11]　Flowers were offered in bouquets, in basketfuls, and in garlands ; the lotus and papyrus being among the plants in highest favour.[12]

The sacrificial animals included certainly bulls, oxen, male calves, sheep, goats, pigs, geese, ducks, pigeons, and certain undomesticated creatures, such as antelopes and various kinds of water-fowl.　Of these,

---

[1] Bread is usually placed first in the general descriptions of sacrifices (*Records of the Past*, vol. iv. p. 3 ; vol. vi. pp. 29, 31, &c. ; vol. x. p. 44).　Ten or twelve different kinds of bread are mentioned as offered to the Theban triad by Rameses III. (ibid. vol. vi. pp. 44–5), whose total of ' good bread, different loaves,' offered in one temple during the space of thirty-one years, was 2,844,357, or above 90,000 annually.

[2] *Records of the Past*, vol. vi. pp. 45, 64, &c.

[3] Wilkinson, *A. E.* vol. v. p. 337 ; Juv. *Sat.* vi. 540; *Records of the Past*, vol. iv. p. 13 ; vol. vi. p. 45, &c.

[4] *Records of the Past*, vol. iv. p.

3 ; vol. vi. pp. 29, 31, 45, &c.

[5] Wilkinson, *A. E.* vol. v. pp. 368–9.

[6] Herod. ii. 39; *Records of the Past*, vol. vi. p. 28 ; vol. viii. p. 14 ; vol. x. p. 44, &c.

[7] ' Spirits ' are thought to occur among the offerings of the kings to the temples (*Records of the Past*, vol. vi. pp. 45, 62, &c.)

[8] Wilkinson, *A. E.* vol. v. pp. 338–40.

[9] Ibid. p. 339.　Compare *Records of the Past*, vol. viii. p. 12.

[10] See the ' Inscription of Queen Hatasu' in the *Records of the Past*, vol. x. pp. 13–19.

[11] Ibid. vol. vi. pp. 42, 46, 65, 67, &c.

[12] Ibid. pp. 48–9, 65, 68, &c.

oxen, male calves, and geese were most in request, and
served as victims universally ; [1] goats were offered at
Thebes and in most other parts of Egypt, but not at
Mendes, where sheep took their place ; [2] pigs, generally
regarded as unclean, formed the necessary sacrifice on
certain special and rare occasions ; [3] ducks and pigeons
served as convenient offerings for the poor ; [4] parts of
antelopes seem to have been occasionally offered by the
rich.[5]   It has been generally maintained that cows and
heifers, being sacred to Athor, could under no circumstances be employed as victims in Egypt,[6] and this was
certainly the belief of Herodotus ; [7] but the Egyptian
remains throw great doubt upon the truth of the Hero-
dotean statement.   Not only do cows and heifers appear
among the sacrificial animals presented to the temples
by the Egyptian monarchs, as regularly and in as large
numbers as bulls, oxen, and steers,[8] but it is distinctly
stated in numerous passages that cows were actually
offered in sacrifice.[9]   Whatever objection, therefore,
the Egyptians may have felt to eating the flesh of cows
and female calves,[10] it would seem to be certain that
they had no scruple about sacrificing them.   Probably
such victims were made in every case ' whole burnt-
offerings '—consumed, that is, entirely upon the altar,

---

[1] Herod. ii. 41, 45; *Records*, vol.
ii. pp. 90, 93, 96, &c. ; vol. vi. pp.
31, 33, &c.

[2] Herod. ii. 42.

[3] Ibid. ii. 47–8.

[4] Just as they did among the
Jews. (See Levit. v. 7 ; xii. 8 ;
and xiv. 22.)

[5] *Records of the Past*, vol. x. p.
44.

[6] Wilkinson, *A. E.* vol. v. p. 347;
Kenrick, *Ancient Egypt*, vol. ii. p.
11 ; Trevor, *Ancient Egypt*, p. 172,
&c.

[7] See Herod. ii. 41. (Herodotus
says that they were ' sacred to Isis,'
but, by mentioning *Atar*-bechis as
their burial-place, shows that it was
not Isis, but Athor, to whom they
were dedicated.)

[8] *Records of the Past*, vol. vi. pp.
47, 64, 66; vol. viii. p. 20, &c.

[9] Ibid. vol. ii. pp. 90, 96, 99 ; vol.
x. pp. 44, 62, &c.

[10] Herod.l.s.c.; Porphyr. *De Abstinent.* ii. § 11 ; Hieronym. *Adv.
Jovin.* ii. 7 ; &c.

and not partaken of, either by the priests or by the worshippers.

When a sacrifice was intended, the victim was usually decked with flowers,[1] and brought to the temple by the offerer, who submitted him first of all to the inspection of the priests, and then, if he was pronounced pure, and sealed in the appointed way,[2] conducted him to the altar, where, after a libation had been poured, he was slaughtered by the officiating minister, who cut his throat from ear to ear,[3] and let the blood flow freely over the altar, or over the ground at its base. Generally, only certain parts of the animal were burnt, the remainder being shared between the priest and the person, or persons, who brought the victim; but sometimes the whole animal was placed on the altar and consumed with fire. Cakes of the best flour, honey, raisins, figs, incense, myrrh, and other odoriferous substances were often added, together with a quantity of oil, which helped the fire to consume the whole.[4] Such sacrifices were, no doubt, in many cases, thank-offerings, mere indications of the devotion and gratitude of the worshipper; but occasionally they were of the nature of expiatory rites, and gave some indication of that sense of sin and desire of pardon which were, as already observed,[5] generally lacking in the devotional utterances of the Egyptians. Herodotus tells us[6] that it was usual, when a victim was offered, to cut off the head, and after heaping imprecations upon it, and praying that whatever evils were impending either over Egypt or over the worshippers might fall upon that head, to sell it to Greeks or cast it into the Nile—a

---

[1] Wilkinson, *A. E.* vol. v. p. 352.
[2] Herod. ii. 38.
[3] Wilkinson, l.s.c.
[4] Herod. ii. 40.
[5] See above, p. 406.
[6] Herod. ii. 39.

practice which recalls the Jewish ceremony of the
scape-goat, and likewise that commanded in Deuter-
onomy for the expiation of an uncertain murder.[1] Again,
the same writer informs us that, in sacrifices to Isis,
it was the custom for the sacrificers both to offer the
victim fasting, and to beat themselves during the burning[2]—both which practices point to the expiatory idea
as involved, to some extent at any rate, in the Egyptian
notion of sacrifice.

One of the most remarkable features of the Egyptian religion—and one in which it differed from almost
all others—was the sacred character with which it
invested various animals. A certain number of animals were held sacred universally, and might nowhere
under any circumstances be killed or injured. Others
received a veneration less than universal, but not far
short of it; while a third set enjoyed a mere local and
exceptional privilege. To the first class belonged the
cat,[3] which was sacred to Bast or Sekhet; the ibis[4] and
cynocephalous ape,[5] which were sacred to Thoth; the
hawk[6] and beetle,[7] which were sacred to Ra; the asp,
probably;[8] and either cows as a class, or at any rate
white cows, which were sacred to Athor. Generally
but not universally reverenced were sheep,[9] which
were sacred to Kneph, and dogs,[10] which do not seem

---

[1] Deut. xii. 1-9.
[2] Herod. ii. 40.
[3] Ibid. ii. 66-7. Compare Wilkinson, *A. E.* vol. v. pp. 161-8. Cat
mummies are very common (Birch,
Guide to Museum, pp. 60-1).
[4] Herod. ii. 67, 75; Wilkinson,
A. E. vol. v. pp. 217-25.
[5] Wilkinson, vol. v. pp. 128-31;
Birch, *Guide to Museum,* pp. 17, 60,
&c.
[6] Herod. ii. 65, 67; Diod. Sic. i.
87; Wilkinson, vol. v. pp. 205-

210, &c.
[7] *Records of the Past,* vol. viii.
pp. 105, 108; Birch, *Guide to Museum,* p. 72.
[8] Wilkinson expresses himself
doubtfully on this point (*A. E.* vol.
v. p. 243).
[9] Plut. *De Isid. et Osir.* § 72.
(Compare Herod. ii. 63.) Sheep
were *especially* sacred at Thebes and
at Sais.
[10] Wilkinson, *A. E.* vol. v. pp.
138-41.

to have been assigned to any special deity. Local
honours attached to lions, crocodiles, hippopotamuses,
wolves or jackals, ibexes, antelopes, goats, ichneumons, shrew-mice, vultures, frogs, certain snakes, and
certain kinds of fish. Lions, emblems of Horus and
Tum, were sacred at Heliopolis and Leontopolis ; crocodiles, emblems of Set, at Ombos, Coptos, and in the
Arsinoïte nome (or Fayoum) generally; hippopotamuses, emblems of Taouris, at Papremis in the Delta ;
wolves or jackals, emblems of Anubis, at Lycopolis ;
ibexes and frogs at Thebes ; antelopes at Coptos ; goats
at Mendes ; ichneumons at Heracleopolis ; shrew-mice
at Athribis ; vultures, emblems of Maut, at Eileithyia ;
snakes at Thebes ; and fish of different kinds at Latopolis, Lepidotopolis, Elephantiné, and elsewhere.[1] In
each locality where any kind of animal was sacred, some
individuals of the species were attached to the principal
temples, where they had their special shrines or chambers, and their train of priestly attendants, who carefully
fed them, cleaned them, and saw generally to their
health and comfort.[2] When any of them died, they
were embalmed according to the most approved method, and deposited in mummy-pits, or in tombs
specially appropriated to them, with much pomp and
ceremony.[3] All the other individuals of the species
were sacred within the locality, and had to be protected from injury. It was a capital offence to kill one
of them intentionally; and to do so even accidentally
entailed some punishment or other,[4] and necessitated

[1] Birch, *Egypt from the Earliest Times,* 'Introduction,' p. xii.; *Guide to Museum,* pp. 17-20.
[2] Herod. ii. 65; Diod. Sic. i. 83; Wilkinson, *A. E.* vol. v. pp. 91-5.
[3] Herod. ii. 67.

[4] Herodotus says that even acci-dentally killing an ibis or a hawk entailed the penalty of death (ii. 65, ad fin.). But this was not the Egyptian *law.* The fanaticism of the people may occasionally have

priestly absolution. The different towns and districts were jealous for the honour of their favourites; and quarrels occasionally broke out between city and city, or between province and province, in connection with their sacred animals, which led in some cases to violent and prolonged conflicts, in others to a smouldering but permanent hostility.[1] An appreciable portion of the religious sentiment of the nation was absorbed by these unworthy objects; but so strong and lively was that sentiment among the Egyptians, that the animal worship, widely spread as it was, does not appear to have interfered seriously with the respect and reverence which were paid to the proper deities.

In the animal worship hitherto described, it was the species and not the individual that was held in honour. But in certain cases the religious regard attached to the individual either solely or specially. The Egyptians believed that occasionally a deity became incarnate in a particular animal, and so remained until the creature's death. The occurrence was made known to the priests by certain signs;[2] and the god, greeted, as soon as recognised, with every token of respect and joy, was conducted in solemn procession to his proper temple, and installed there as the actual deity. This form of superstition prevailed at Memphis, Heliopolis, Hermonthis, and Momemphis. At Memphis, a magnificent abode, in the

---

led to such a shocking result. (See Diod. Sic. l s.c.)

[1] Plut. *De Isid. et Osir.* § 44.

[2] On the signs by which an Apis calf was known, see Herod. iii. 28, ad fin., and compare Ælian, *Nat. An.* xi. 10; Plin. *H. N.* viii. 46; Amm. Marc. xxii. 14. The chief

seem to have been a white star on the forehead, and a white mark on the back or side, in which some resemblance could be traced to the outline of an eagle. It is evident that the priests would easily find a fresh Apis, whenever they wanted one.

shape of a court surrounded by Osirid pillars,[1] was prepared for the accommodation of a sacred bull, believed to be an incarnation of the god Phthah,[2] who was thought from time to time to visit Egypt in person. When a male calf, having been examined by the priests, was pronounced to have the required marks, he received the name [3] of Apis, 𓀀𓁐𓃒, and became the occupant of this building, which thenceforth he never quitted, except on certain fixed days when he was led in procession through the streets of the city and welcomed by all the inhabitants, who came forth from their houses to greet him.[4] Otherwise he remained continuously in his grand residence, waited upon by numerous priests, fed on choice food, and from time to time shown for a short space to those who came to worship him and solicit his favour and protection. The cow which had been so favoured as to be the earthly mother of the deity was also made an inmate of the sacred edifice, being lodged in the vestibule which gave access to the building.[5] It is remarkable that the Apis bulls were not in every case allowed to reach the natural term of their lives. If a natural death did not remove them earlier, the priests drowned them when they reached the age of twenty-five,[6] after which they were buried with the usual

[1] Herod. ii. 153.
[2] So Lenormant (*Manuel d'Histoire Ancienne*, vol. i. p. 535) and Birch (*Egypt from the Earliest Times*, 'Introduction,' p. xii.) Others make the Apis bulls incarnations of Osiris (Wilkinson, *A. E.* vol. iv. p. 347; Bunsen, *Egypt's Place*, vol. i. p. 431).
[3] The hieroglyphics which represent this name are different from those expressive of the Nile-god, but identical (or nearly so) with

the group which represents the second genius of Amenti (see above, p. 397).
[4] Wilkinson, *A. E.* iv. p. 351.
[5] Strab. xvii. 1, § 31. There were also apartments provided in the temple for a certain number of other cows, Apis requiring to have the solace of female companionship. (See Ælian, *Nat. An.* xii. 10.)
[6] Plin. *H. N.* viii. 46; Amm. Marc. xxii. 14.

honours, their bodies being carefully embalmed and deposited with much ceremony in the sepulchral chambers of the Serapeum,[1] a temple at Memphis expressly devoted to the burial of these animals. Each Apis, when dead, became an Osiri-Apis,[2] or Serapis, and the object of a special cult,[3] which in Ptolemaic and Roman times received an extraordinary development. All Egypt went into mourning at the death, however produced, and remained inconsolable until it pleased the priests to declare a new *avatar*, when mourning was at once cast aside, a time of festival was proclaimed, and, amid the acclamations of the whole people, the new-found Apis was led in solemn pomp to occupy the chambers of his predecessor.[4]

At Heliopolis, another sacred bull was maintained in the great temple of the sun,[5] which was viewed as an incarnation of Ra or Tum,[6] and received the same sort of honour as the Apis bulls of Memphis. The name assigned to this animal was Mnevis. It is said by Plutarch and Porphyry to have been a black bull; but the monuments are thought to represent it as white.[7] Though highly reverenced by the Heliopolites, it did not enjoy much regard beyond the precincts of its own city.

A third sacred bull, called Bacis or Pacis, was maintained at Hermonthis,[8] not far from Thebes, on

---

[1] Recently discovered by M. Mariette. (See his *Renseignements sur les soixante-quatre Apis trouvés au Sérapéum*, Paris, 1855.)
[2] Lenormant, *Manuel d'Histoire Ancienne*, vol. i. p. 536; *Records of the Past*, vol. iv. pp. 63–4.
[3] *Records of the Past*, l.s.c.
[4] Herod. iii. 27; Ælian, l.s.c.; Plut. *De Isid. et Osir.* § 35; Diod.

Sic. i. 84; &c.
[5] Plut. *De Isid. et Osir.* § 33; Diod. Sic. l.s.c.; Strab. xvii. 1, § 27.
[6] Birch, *Egypt from the Earliest Times*, 'Introduction,' p. xii.
[7] Wilkinson, *A. E.* vol. v. p. 196.
[8] Macrob. *Saturnal.* i. 21; Strab. xvii. 1, § 47; Ælian, *Nat. An.* xii. 11.

the left bank of the river. Like the Heliopolite bull, this was regarded as an incarnation of Ra ; and was kept in the temple of Ra at Hermonthis, which was a magnificent building. Its natural colour was black ; but it is said to have changed colour frequently,[1] which would seem to have been through some priestly artifice ; and we are also told that its hairs, or some of them, grew the wrong way.[2] It was an animal of unusual size.[3]

White cows, sacred to Athor, were maintained in temples at Hermonthis, Athribis, Momemphis, and elsewhere ; but whether they were regarded as incarnations of Athor, or simply as emblematic of her, is uncertain. The fact that Athor is sometimes represented under the form of a cow [4] tells in favour of the view that they were considered to be incarnations ; but the distinction which Strabo draws [5] between Apis and Mnevis on the one hand, and most of the sacred cows on the other, points in the opposite direction. Perhaps the Momemphite cow was alone regarded as an actual incarnation.[6]

On the origin of the animal worship of the Egyptians much speculation has been expended, both in ancient and modern times. By some it is maintained that the entire system is to be referred to the prudence and foresight of the priests, who invested with a sacred character such animals as were of first-rate utility, in order to secure their continuance and increase.[7] This theory sufficiently accounts for the veneration paid to

---

[1] Macrob. l.s.c.
[2] Ibid. Compare Ælian, l.s.c.
[3] Ælian, l.s.c.
[4] Wilkinson, *A. E.* 'Supplement,' pl. 35ᴀ, pt. 2; pl. 36, figs. 2 and 3.
[5] Strab. xvii. 1, § 22.
[6] Strabo (l.s.c.) seems to place this animal on a par with the Apis

and Mnevis bulls.
[7] This is the view to which Sir G. Wilkinson inclines. (See the author's *Herodotus*, vol. ii. pp. 92–3, 2nd edition.) Among the ancients, it was held by Diodorus (i. 86) and Cicero (*De Nat. Deor.* i. 36).

the cow, the sheep, the goat, the dog, the cat, the ichneumon, the hawk, the vulture, and the ibis ; but it fails completely if applied to the great majority of the sacred animals. The lion, the crocodile, the hippopotamus, the cynocephalous ape, the cobra de capello, the wolf, the jackal, the shrew-mouse, did not benefit the Egyptians appreciably, if at all ; and indeed must have presented themselves to the general intelligence rather as harmful than as useful creatures. The sacred fish, which might not be eaten, cannot be shown to have been in any other way beneficial to man ; nor is the practical utility of beetles very apparent. These objections to the utilitarian theory [1] have prevented its general acceptance, and led to various other suggestions, both anciently and recently. Some of the ancients said, the animals worshipped were those whose forms the gods had occasionally taken when they came down from heaven to visit the earth ; [2] others that they were those which Osiris had selected and placed on the standards of his army.[3] A third theory was that the whole of the animal worship had been introduced by a politic king, with the express object of causing division and discord among the natives of the different nomes, and so making it easier to govern them.[4] In modern times the Pantheistic nature of the Egyptian religion has been alleged as the ' true reason ' of the worship by one writer,[5] while another [6] has seen in it an original African

[1] Even Wilkinson allows that they have weight, and suggests that, besides the ground of utility, the Egyptians must have had some other ' hidden motive ' on which it is idle to speculate (*A. E.* vol. v. p. 109).
[2] Diod. Sic. i. 12.
[3] Plut. *De Isid. et Osir.* § 72.
[4] Ibid. Compare Diod. Sic. i. 86.

[5] Canon Trevor (see his *Ancient Egypt*, p. 184). Porphyry, among the ancients, was an advocate of this theory (*De Abstinent.* iv. 9). It is disproved by the fact that the Egyptians worshipped some animals only, not all.
[6] Mr. R. Stuart Poole (*Dictionary of the Bible*, vol. i p. 501).

fetishism, on which was afterwards engrafted a more
elevated form of belief by an immigrant Asiatic people.
To us it seems a sufficient and probably a true account
of the worship, to say that it grew out of that exaggerated symbolism [1] which was so characteristic of the
Egyptian religion, which, beginning by tracing resemblances in certain animals to certain attributes of the
Divine Nature, proceeded to assign to particular deities
the heads of these creatures, or even their entire forms ;
after which it was but a short step to see in the animals themselves a quasi-divinity, which elevated them
above their fellows and rendered them venerable and
sacred. If this explanation does not cover the whole
of the worship, as (it must be admitted) it does not,
still the exceptions are so few and, comparatively
speaking, so unimportant,[2] that their existence is per

---

[1] See Lenormant, *Manuel d'Histoire Ancienne*, vol. i. pp. 533–4 :—
'Le symbolisme était l'essence même
du génie de la nation égyptienne et
de sa religion. *L'abus de cette ten-
dance produisit* la plus grossière et
la plus monstrueuse aberration du
culte extérieur et populaire de la
terre de Mitsraïm. Pour symbo-
liser les attributs, les qualités et la
nature des diverses divinités de leur
panthéon, les prêtres égyptiens
avaient eu recours aux êtres du
règne animal. Le taureau, la vache,
le bélier, le chat, le singe, le crocodile, l'hippopotame, l'épervier, l'ibis,
le scarabée, etc. étaient les emblèmes chacun d'un personnage divin.
On représentait le dieu sous la figure
de cet animal, ou plus souvent encore, par accouplement étrange et
particulier à l'Égypte, on lui en
donnait la tête sur un corps hu-
main. Mais les habitants des bords
du Nil, éloignés de l'idolâtrie des
autres nations païennes par un instinct de leur nature, avaient pré-

féré porter leurs hommages à des
images vivantes de leurs dieux plu-
tôt qu'à des images inertes de
pierre ou de métal; et ces images
vivantes, ils les avaient trouvées
dans les animaux qu'ils avaient
choisis pour emblèmes de l'idée ex-
primée dans la conception de chaque
dieu. De là ce *culte des animaux
sacrés*, qui paraissait si étrange et si
ridicule aux Grecs et aux Romains.'
[2] The chief apparent exceptions
are the dog, the ichneumon, the
shrew-mouse, and the fish worshipped in different localities ; to which
may perhaps be added the ibex and
the antelope, if these were really
sacred. No gods have been found
represented by the forms, or with
the heads, of these animals. I suspect, however, that originally the
Egyptians confused together the
wolf, the jackal, and the dog, and
that the ancients were not altogether wrong when they said that
Anubis had the head of a dog (see
above, p. 396). In most of the re-

haps not incompatible with the truth of the origin suggested.

The outward aspect of the Egyptian religion was, as already noticed,[1] magnificent and striking. The size and number of the temples, the massiveness and solidity of their construction, the immense height of the columns, the multiplicity of the courts and halls, the frequent obelisks and colossi, the groves and lakes,[2] the long avenues of sphinxes, the lavish abundance of painted and sculptured decoration, formed a combination which was at once astonishing and delightful, and which travellers were never weary of describing.[3] But all this was the mere exterior framework or setting within which the religion displayed itself. Life and meaning were imparted to the material apparatus of worship by the long trains of priests and the vast throng of worshippers constantly to be seen in and about the temples, by the processions which paced their courts in solemn pomp, the mournful or jubilant strains which resounded down their corridors, the clouds of incense which rose into the air, the perpetual succession of victims which smoked upon the altars. The Egyptians, as Herodotus notes,[4] 'were religious to excess.' There was certainly not a day, perhaps scarcely an hour, without its own religious ceremony, in any of the greater temples, whose ' colleges of priests'[5] could readily furnish a succession of

maining cases the worship was markedly local, and may have been connected with some local divinity of whom we have no representation.
[1] See above, p. 311.
[2] Wilkinson in the author's *Herodotus*, vol. ii. p. 202, 2nd edit.
[3] Herod. ii. 155, 169, &c.; Diod. Sic. i. 45-9; Strab. xvii. 1, §§ 28, 46, &c.

[4] Herod. ii. 37.
[5] ' Instead of a single priest,' says Herodotus (l.s.c.), ' each god has the attendance of a college, of whom one is the chief priest.' Sir G. Wilkinson observes that this statement ' is fully confirmed by the sculptures.' (See the author's *Herodotus*, vol. ii. p. 56, note [8].)

officiating ministers, always ready to offer on behalf of
those who brought victims or other oblations. Thus a
constant round of religious offices was maintained; the
voice of prayer, however imperfect or misdirected,
went up from the temples continually; and Egypt, in
whatever darkness she lay, at least testified to the need
and value of a perpetual intercession, a constant plead-
ing with God, a worship without pause or weariness.

The worship culminated in certain festivals, or great
gatherings of the people for special religious services,[1]
which were mostly either annual or monthly. A
monthly festival, on the day of the new moon, celebrated the reappearance of that luminary after its
temporary obscuration.[2] On the fourth day of each
month, a festival was held in honour of the sun.[3] Once
a year, on the day of a particular full moon, there was a
festival in which the moon and Osiris would seem to
have been honoured conjointly.[4] On this occasion,
according to Herodotus, the rites included a procession
to the sound of the pipe, wherein both men and women
participated, though the ceremony was of an indecent
character.[5] Other feasts were held in honour of Osiris
on the seventeenth day of Athyr and the nineteenth
of Pashons; in the former of which the 'loss of Osiris,'
and in the latter his recovery, were commemorated.

---

[1] Herod. ii. 58, ad init.
[2] Wilkinson in the author's *He-rodotus*, vol. ii. p. 85, note. The feast, being delayed until the moon actually reappeared, took place in reality on the day *after* the new moon.
[3] Wilkinson, *A.E.* vol. v. p. 315.
[4] Herod. ii. 47.
[5] Wilkinson doubts the state-ments of Herodotus on this point, because Osiris was not a Priapic god (*A. E.* vol. iv. p. 342). But they are confirmed by Plutarch, who declares that the Paamylia, a fes-tival in honour of Osiris, resembled the Greek Phallophoria (*De Isid. et Osir.* § 12 and § 18). Even Wil-kinson would allow that the inde-cencies in question formed a part of the Egyptian religion; but he would transfer them from the cult of Osiris to that of Khem. (See *A. E.* vol. v. p. 306.)

A cow, emblematic of Isis, was veiled in black and led about for four successive days, accompanied by a crowd of men and women who beat their breasts, in memory of the supposed disappearance of Osiris from earth and his sisters' search for him ; while, in memory of his recovery, a procession was made to the seaside, the priests carrying a sacred chest, and, an image or emblem of Osiris fashioned out of earth and water having been placed in it, the declaration was made, ' Osiris is found! Osiris is found!' amid general festivity and rejoicing.[1]

Among the most remarkable of the annual festivals were those of Bast or Pasht at Bubastis, of Neith at Saïs, and of Mentu or Onuris at Papremis. It would be uncritical to attach any great value to the details which Herodotus, in his lively manner, gives us of the ceremonies on these occasions,[2] or of the numbers by which the festivals were attended.[3] Still we may safely conclude from his account that the concourse was often very great, that the Nile was used for religious processions, and that open and flagrant indecencies disgraced some of the gatherings. We may perhaps be also justified in concluding that some of the ceremonies led actually to fighting and bloodshed, the god being regarded as honoured by the wounds of his votaries, and still more by their deaths, if the wounds received proved fatal.[4]

Processions were a conspicuous, if not a very important, part of the Egyptian ritual. On special occasions the sacred animals, and on others the images

---

[1] Wilkinson, *A. E.* vol. v. p. 301 (compare vol. iv. p. 335); Trevor, *Ancient Egypt*, p. 190.
[2] Herod. ii. 60–3.
[3] Seven hundred thousand, without counting children, at Bubastis, according to this writer (ii. 60, ad fin.).
[4] Compare the well-known bloody rites of Juggernaut.

of the gods, were taken from the *adyta* of temples, in which they were commonly kept, to be paraded openly through the towns, down their streets and along their water-courses, in the sight of admiring multitudes. The animals were led along by their respective attendants, and received the homage of their adorers as they passed.[1] The images were sometimes placed upright upon platforms,[2] and borne along the line of route upon the shoulders of a number of priests, while others, marshalled according to their various ranks and orders, preceded or followed the sacred figures, clad in a variety of vestments, and with symbolic head-dresses, chanting hymns or litanies in praise of the gods whom they accompanied. At other times, and more commonly, the images were deposited in boats of a light construction,[3] richly carved and adorned at either end with a symbol of the god, which could either be drawn along the streets upon a low sledge, or carried (like the platforms) upon men's shoulders, or launched upon the Nile and propelled by oars along its waters. These boats are favourite objects of representation upon the monuments.[4] Generally a number of priests carry them under the superintendence of a chief priest, clad in the usual leopard's skin; then follows a crowd of subordinate ministers and nobles, with sometimes even the Pharaoh of the time, who, when represented, always takes an important part in the ceremony. A portion of the priests bear flowers, another portion banners, while some have long staves surmounted by a religious

---

[1] Plin. *H. N.* viii. 46.
[2] Wilkinson, *Ancient Egyptians,*
vol. v. p. 271.
[3] Ibid. p. 275. Compare the
author's *Herodotus,* vol. ii. p. 85;
2nd edit.
[4] See Rosellini, *Monumenti del
Culto,* pls. 67 et seqq.

emblem ; occasionally there is one who offers incense, while another beats a tambourine.[1]

Besides their worship of gods, the Egyptians also practised to some extent a worship of ancestors. A sepulchral chamber, cut in the rock, or built over the mummy-pit, was an ordinary appendage of tombs ;[2] and in this apartment, which was ornamented with suitable paintings, the friends of the deceased met from time to time, to offer sacrifices to the dead and perform various acts of homage.[3] The mummies, which were kept in a closet within the sepulchral chamber, having been brought forth by a functionary, were placed upright near a small portable altar, on which the relations then laid their offerings, which consisted ordinarily of cakes, wine, fruit, and vegetables, but sometimes comprised also joints of meat, geese, ducks, loaves, vases of oil, and other similar delicacies. Sometimes a libation of oil or wine was poured by an attendant priest over the mummy-case. The relations made obeisance, sometimes embraced the mummy, sometimes tore their hair, or otherwise indicated the sorrow caused by their bereavement. Prayers were probably offered either to or for the deceased ; his mummied form was adorned with flowers, and after an interval was replaced in the closet from which it had been taken. Representations of these scenes are frequent in the tombs,[4] where, however, the deceased are generally depicted, not in their mummied forms, but dressed as they used to be in life, and seated before the

---

[1] Wilkinson, *A. E.* vol. v. pp. 271-5.
[2] Ibid. pp. 392-7.
[3] Ibid. pp. 384, 397, &c.

[4] See Birch's *Guide to the Vestibules of the Egyptian Galleries*, pp. 22-39.

table or altar, whereon are deposited the good things which their relations have brought to them.

It is impossible to say what exactly was the feeling or belief which lay at the root of these ceremonies.[1] They resembled the Roman 'parentalia,' and necessarily implied, first, the continued existence of the dead ; secondly, their exaltation to a sort of quasi-divinity ; and, thirdly, their continued need of those supports of life which had been necessary to them in this world. There is something contradictory in these last two notions ; but the Egyptians were not a logical people, and, accustomed to a mythology full of contradictions,[2] did not regard them with absolute disfavour. Moreover, their entire conception of the condition of the dead was strange, abnormal, and irrational,[3] so that the different portions of the system could not be expected to be in all cases in harmony.

It is possible that the confusion which to the ordinary observer seems to prevail, alike in the details of the Egyptian mythology and in their opinions concerning the dead, may have been superficial only, and that to those who saw below the surface into the deeper meaning of what was taught and believed, all appeared consistent, harmonious, and readily intelligible. The Egyptians, we are assured,[4] had ' mysteries ; ' and it was of the essence of mysteries, in the Greek and Roman sense of the word, to distinguish between the outer husk of a religion and its inner kernel, the shell

[1] Birch says that the scenes represented are 'acts of sepulchral homage or ancestral worship made by the children and other relatives of the dead' (*Guide to Vestibules*, p. 23). Wilkinson, on the contrary, suggests that ' it was not to the deceased that these ceremonies were performed, but to that particular portion of the Divine essence which constituted the soul of each individual and returned to the Deity after death' (*A. E.* vol. v. p. 381).
[2] See above, pp. 377, 382, &c.
[3] Compare above, p. 147.
[4] Herod. ii. 171.

of myth and legend and allegorical fable with which it was surrounded, and the real essential doctrine or teaching which that shell contained and concealed. Initiation into the mysteries conveyed to those who received it an explanation of rites, an interpretation of myths and legends, which gave them quite a different character from that which they bore to the uninitiated. If we possessed any full account of the Egyptian mysteries drawn up by themselves, or even any authentic description of them by a classical writer, we should probably be able to explain the contradictions, clear up the confusion, and elucidate the obscurity which still hangs about the subject of the Egyptian religion after all the investigation that it has undergone. But we are not so fortunately circumstanced. Though the veil of Isis has been partially lifted through the decipherment and interpretation of the hieroglyphics, though some points of the esoteric doctrine have been made sufficiently clear, and can no longer be questioned,[1] yet we are far from possessing anything like a complete account of the inner religion, or indeed any authentic account at all of the true interpretation of that great mass of legend which clustered about the Osirid deities, and formed practically the chief religious *pabulum* of the bulk of the people. The existing remains are in no case formally exegetical; and any light which they throw upon the myths is indirect and uncertain. Nor

---

[1] A good article on this subject has appeared in the *Nineteenth Century* (December 1878, pp. 1105–20) since the earlier portion of this chapter was in type. The writer takes a somewhat over-favourable view, and omits to notice the great contrast between the esoteric and exoteric systems in Egypt—the religion of the few and the religion of the many. No account of the Egyptian religion can be regarded as a fair one which is silent on the subject of the general idolatry and polytheism, of the existence of indecent rites, and of the constant occurrence of indecent emblems in the religious representations.

do the classical writers afford us much assistance. Some claim to have been initiated, but decline to tell us what they had learned thereby,[1] withheld by motives of religious reverence. Others [2] appear to have simply indulged their fancy, and to have given us conjectural explanations of myths with which they show no very full or exact acquaintance. The result is, that their comments are without any value, and leave us where they find us, uninformed and unable to do more than guess at the truth. Where examination and inquiry lead to such a result, it seems best to quit the subject with a confession of ignorance.

---

[1] Herod. l.s.c. Compare ii. 48, ad fin.; and also chs. 61, 62, 65, &c.

[2] As Diodorus and Macrobius.

(See Wilkinson, *A. E.* vol. iv. p. 326.) Plutarch's explanations (*De Isid. et Osir.* § 38 et seqq.) are scarcely more trustworthy.

CHAPTER XI.

MANNERS AND CUSTOMS.

Question of the Peculiarity of Egyptian Customs—Proposed mode of treating the subject. Division of the People into Classes—Number of the Classes. Account of the Priests—the Sacred Women. The Soldiers —Number of these last—Training—Chief divisions—The Infantry— the Cavalry—the Chariot Service—Weapons—Tactics—Mode of conducting Sieges. Treatment of Prisoners and of the Slain. Camps— Marches—Signals—Triumphs. Naval Warfare. Condition of the Agricultural Labourers—of the Tradesmen and Artisans. Principal Trades —Building—Weaving—Furniture-making—Glass-blowing—Pottery— Metallurgy, &c. Artistic Occupations—Sculpture, Painting, Music and Dancing. Musical Instruments and Bands. Professions—the Scribe's— the Physician's—the Architect's. Lower Grades of the Population— Boatmen—Fowlers—Fishermen—Swineherds. Life of the Upper Classes. Sports—Entertainments—Games. Conclusion.

THE statement of Herodotus,[1] that 'the ancient Egyptians in *most* of their manners and customs exactly reversed the common practice of mankind,' is one of those paradoxical remarks in which that lively writer indulged with the view of surprising his readers and arresting their attention. In observations of this kind, the 'Father of History' is never without some foundation for what he says, though, if we were to accept such statements literally, they would very seriously mislead us. There was certainly in Egyptian customs much that to a Greek—even to a travelled Greek—must have seemed strange and peculiar, much

---

[1] Herod. ii. 35.

428 HISTORY OF ANCIENT EGYPT. [Cn. XI.

that he was not likely to have seen elsewhere. We may even go further and say, that there was a considerable body of customs which (so far as is known) were unique, absolutely unshared by any other ancient people ; but these peculiar usages were not really so very numerous—certainly they did not outnumber those which belonged to the nation in common either with most civilised peoples, or at any rate with some. There were analogies between Egyptian customs and those of India,[1] of China and Japan,[2] of Assyria,[3] nay, of Greece itself; and if Herodotus had been as observant of resemblances as of differences, he might have found ample materials for a good many chapters in the usages which the nation possessed in common with others. Few things strike the modern inquirer so strongly, or with so much surprise, as the numerous points in which the Egyptian coincided with modern civilisation, the little difference that there seems to have been between the life of the opulent classes under the Pharaohs three thousand years ago and that of persons of the same rank and position in Europe at the present day.

In the present survey of Egyptian manners and customs, it will be impossible to treat the subject with the minuteness and thoroughness with which it has been already handled by a learned and popular English writer. Sir Gardner Wilkinson devoted to the theme more than four out of the five volumes of his *magnum opus*,[4] and illustrated it with above five hundred

---

[1] As the division into classes, which, if not actual castes, approached nearly to the caste character.

[2] As the dislike of foreigners, and the designation of one port only with which they might trade (He-

rod. ii. 179).

[3] The Egyptian chariots, arms, furniture, and personal ornaments have a considerable resemblance to the Assyrian.

[4] 'The Manners and Customs of the Ancient Egyptians, including

engravings. His elaborate treatment left little to be desired even when his work first appeared in 1837–1841 ; and the little that might have been then wanting has now been fully supplied by the 'annotations and additions' appended to the edition of 1878 by Dr. Birch. The present author cannot, within the space of fifty or a hundred pages, attempt to compete with this most excellent and exhaustive treatise. He would gladly have avoided a comparison which must necessarily be unfavourable to himself, and have omitted the matter altogether, could he have persuaded himself that to all readers of his work that of his valued friend and *collaborateur* [1] would be accessible. But, as this is not likely to be the case,[2] his duty to his readers compels him not wholly to pass over an important branch of the subject on which he has undertaken to write. He proposes, however, to limit himself to a certain number of the more essential, more salient, or more curious points, thus embracing what will be sufficient to complete in outline the picture of the people which the present volume contains, but not attempting to fill up the details, or to do more than furnish his readers with a careful *sketch*. Those who have the desire

---

their Private Life, Government, Laws, Arts, Manufactures, Religion, and Early History, derived from a comparison of the paintings, sculptures, and monuments still existing with the accounts of ancient authors, illustrated by drawings of those subjects. By Sir J. G. Wilkinson, F.R.S., M.R.S.L., &c. Five volumes, with Supplement, containing Plates and Index. London : Murray. 1837–41.'

[1] In producing his 'History of Herodotus,' the author had for many years the advantage of Sir

G. Wilkinson's kind assistance, and was in constant communication with him on Egyptian and other subjects.

[2] A work in *two* volumes, *moderately* illustrated, will penetrate to a class of British readers, to whom works in five volumes, illustrated lavishly, are a forbidden luxury. Moreover, the author's writings are largely read in America, where Sir G. Wilkinson's 'Manners and Customs' is not (he believes) to be found even in all public libraries.

and the leisure to convert the sketch into a finished
portrait, must obtain the 'Manners and Customs' of
Sir G. Wilkinson, and give that work their best
attention.

The separation of classes in Egypt was very marked
and distinct; and though these classes were not castes,
in the strict sense of that word, yet they approached to
them. In other words, although the son did not necessarily or always follow his father's calling, yet the
practice was so general, so nearly universal, there was
such a prejudice, such a *consensus* in favour of it, that
foreigners commonly left the country impressed with the
belief that it was obligatory on all, and that the classes
were really castes in the strictest sense. Such was
the conviction of Herodotus,[1] of Plato,[2] of Diodorus
Siculus,[3] of Strabo,[4] and of others; and though modern
research shows that there were exceptions to the general
practice, yet it shows also that the transmission of employments was usual, and was extraordinarily regular
and prolonged. It is enough to refer, in proof of this,
to the 'family of architects' tabulated by Dr. Brugsch
in his 'History of Egypt,'[5] where the occupation of
architect is found to have descended from father to
son for twenty-two generations, from the time of Seti I.,
the first king of the nineteenth dynasty, to that of
Darius, the son of Hystaspes, the second Persian
monarch. That the succession was equally, if not
even more, persistent in the priestly order, is indicated by the story which Herodotus tells concerning
the high priests of Thebes, who were said to have descended in a direct line from father to son for 345

---

[1] Herod. ii. 164-6.   [4] Strab. xvii. 1, § 3.
[2] Plat. *Tim.* p. 24 B.   [5] See the table, opp. p. 644; and
[3] Diod. Sic. i. 28, 73.   compare pp. 36-7.

generations,[1] from the foundation of the monarchy by Menes to the time of Artaxerxes Longimanus. On the other hand, it is proved by the monuments (1) that a man might change his occupation ; (2) that a father need not bring up all his sons, or even an only son, to his own trade or profession ; and (3) that one and the same man might pursue two or more callings.[2] Priests might serve in the army, and often did so ; and members of any class might hold civil office, if the monarch chose to give them an appointment. It is not improbable that Herodotus is right in saying that the soldiers, while they continued soldiers, liable to be called out on active service, could not engage in a trade ;[3] but when they were past the military age, it is probable that they might do as they pleased. No religious notions seem to have attached to the class distinctions ; and it is certain that, unless the swineherds formed an exception,[4] the classes were free to intermarry one with another. Thus it must be fully allowed that the essential ideas of caste were absent from the Egyptian system, which was merely one in which classes were sharply defined, and in which sons, as a rule, followed their father's calling.

The number of the classes is differently stated by ancient authors. Herodotus makes them to be seven, Plato six, Diodorus five,[5] Strabo three only. In a general way it would seem to be right to adopt the

---

[1] Herod. ii. 143. The number of generations is, of course, unworthy of credit ; but the general fact of the hereditary succession of the Theban high priests would be one within the cognisance of Herodotus's informants, and may be accepted.

[2] See Birch, *Ancient Egypt*, 'Introduction,' p. xx. ; Lenormant,

Manuel d'Histoire Ancienne, vol. i. pp. 477–8 ; Wilkinson in the author's *Herodotus*, vol. ii. p. 248, 3rd edition.

[3] Herod. ii. 166, sub fin.

[4] As Herodotus declares they did (ii. 47).

[5] The subjoined table will show the resemblances and differences be-

classification of Strabo, and to say that the entire free
population of Egypt, which did not belong to the
sacerdotal or the military order, formed a sort of 'third
estate,' which admitted of subdivisions, but is properly
regarded as politically a single body.[1] The soldiers
and the priests were privileged; the rest of the community was without privilege of any kind. The chief
subdivisions of the unprivileged class were as follows :—
1. The labourers or *fellahin* in the country, who cultivated the estates of the rich proprietors,[2] men chiefly
of the military class. 2. The tradesmen and artisans
in the towns, including merchants, shopkeepers, physicians, notaries, builders and architects, brickmakers,
weavers, upholsterers, glassblowers, potters, workers in
metal, shoemakers, tailors, armourers, painters, sculptors, and musicians. 3. The herdsmen, chiefly in the
Delta, who were either oxherds, shepherds, goatherds,
or swineherds, the last-named class forming a completely distinct and much despised body.[3] 4. The
boatmen on the Nile and its branches, who conveyed
produce up and down the stream, and ferried passen-

tween these three authorities :—

Classes of Herodotus	Classes of Plato	Classes of Diodorus
1. Priests	1. Priests	1. Priests
2. Soldiers	2. Soldiers	2. Soldiers
3. Cowherds	3. Herdsmen	3. Herdsmen
4. Swineherds	4. Husbandmen	4. Husbandmen
5. Traders	5. Artificers	5. Artificers
6. Boatmen	6. Hunters	
7. Interpreters		

[1] See Strab. l.s.c., and compare
Lenormant, vol. i. p. 481:—' Toute
la portion de la population libre qui
n'appartenait ni au corps sacerdotal
ni au corps militaire composait, en
Egypte, un troisième ordre de l'état,
qui lui-même se subdividait en plu-
sieurs classes,' &c.
[2] See above, p. 154.
[3] Herod. l.s.c.

gers across it, employments which, under the peculiar circumstances of the country, gave occupation to vast numbers. 5. The hunting class, comprising those who pursued the gazelle and other wild animals in the deserts which bordered the Nile valley ; the fishermen, who obtained a living from the produce of the Nile itself, of the canals, and of the great lake, the Birket-el-Keroun ;[1] and the fowlers, who supplied the market with edible birds of various kinds, as especially wild ducks, wild geese, and quails.[2]   6. The dragomans or interpreters, a small class and one belonging only to later times,[3] but kept very distinct from the rest by the prejudice against any intercourse with foreigners.

It does not appear to be necessary to regard the officials of the kingdom as a distinct class. 'Egypt,' no doubt, 'swarmed with a bureaucracy,'[4] a bureaucracy which was 'powerful, numerous, and cleverly arranged' in such a graduated series that the most bureaucratic countries of the modern world may with reason be said to 'have nothing superior to it ;'[5] but the official class was composed in the main of persons who belonged previously either to the priestly or to the military order.[6]   Some official posts appear to have been hereditary ;[7] but this is the exception rather than the rule, and the Egyptian, like other Oriental, monarchs seem to have been free to bestow all but a few official posts on any subject whom they chose to favour.

Of all the classes, that of the priests was the most

---

[1] Herod. ii. 149, ad fin.
[2] Wilkinson in the author's *Herodotus*, vol. ii. p. 129, and *Ancient Egyptians*, vol. iii. p. 47.
[3] Herod. ii. 154.
[4] Birch, *Egypt from the Earliest Times*, 'Introduction,' p. xix.
[5] Lenormant, *Manuel*, vol. i. p.

487.
[6] Out of twelve officials, whose inscriptions are published in the *Records of the Past*, six appear to have been soldiers, and three others priests.
[7] Birch, *Egypt from the Earliest Times*, 'Introduction,' p. xix.

powerful and the most carefully organised. At the
head of the order stood a certain number of high
priests,[1] among whom the high priest of the great
temple of Ammon at Thebes had a species of primacy.
This individual held a rank second only to that of the
king;[2] and the time came when, taking advantage of
his position, the Theban high priest actually usurped
the throne. Next in rank to the high priests were the
prophets,[3] who were generally presidents of the temples,
had the management of the sacred revenues, were
bound to commit to memory the contents of the ten
sacerdotal books,[4] and directed the details of ritual
and ceremonial according to the prescribed *formulæ*.
Below the prophets was an order of ' divine fathers,'[5]
or ordinary priests, of whom several were attached to
each temple. After these came first the *hierostolistæ*,
who had the charge of the sacred vestments and the
office of attiring in appropriate garments the statues
of the gods ;[6] next the *hierogrammateis*, or sacred
scribes,[7] who kept the accounts and registers, made
catalogues of the sacred utensils and other possessions
of the temples, and performed generally all literary
functions devolving upon the sacerdotal order ; and,
finally, a crowd of servants or attendants invested with
a semi-sacerdotal character : the *pastophori*, or bearers
of the sacred shrines;[8] the *hierophori*, or bearers of sacred

[1] Herod. ii. 37, sub fin.; *Rosetta Stone*, line 6 (in *Records of the Past*, vol. iv. p. 71).
[2] Birch, *Egypt from the Earliest Times*, ' Introduction,' p. xx.
[3] See *Rosetta Stone*, l.s.c.; and compare *Decree of Canopus*, line 2 (*Records* &c. vol. viii. p. 83) ; and Clem. Alex. *Strom.* i. p. 758.
[4] Kenrick, *Ancient Egypt*, vol. i. p. 450.
[5] Birch, l.s.c. Compare *Decree of Canopus*, line 3.
[6] *Rosetta Stone*, lines 6-7 ; *Decree of Canopus*, l.s.c.
[7] Ibid. Compare *Records*, vol. x. p. 53.
[8] Diod. Sic. i. 29 ; Porphyr. *De Abstinentia*, iv. 8. There is a famous figure of a ' pastophorus ' in the Vatican, which has been represented in various works on art.

emblems;[1] the *pterophori*, or bearers of the fans and fly-flappers;[2] the *neocori*, who were charged with the sweeping and cleansing of the sacred edifices;[3] the *hierolaotomi*, or sacred masons;[4] the *theriotrophi*, or guardians of the sacred animals,[5] and others. The exact arrangements by which this entire priestly body was bound together and enabled to act in concert without unseemly contest, or even perceptible friction, have not come down to us;[6] but there is reason to believe that the organisation was almost as perfect as that attained by the Church of Rome at the present day. When a decree went forth from the chief authority, the entire priesthood accepted it; and the religious movement, whatever it was, swept at once over the length and breadth of the land. Though there were in Egypt distinct centres of priestly learning, yet, at any rate from the time of the nineteenth dynasty, no religious difference is perceptible; one and the same spirit animates the whole of the sacerdotal order; no contest occurs; no 'heresy' shows itself; a uniform system prevails from Elephantiné to Canopus and Pelusium, and the priestly body, having no internal divisions to waste its strength, is able to exercise an almost unlimited dominion over the rest of the community.

The independence and freedom of the hierarchy was secured by a system of endowments. From a

---

(See Winckelman's *History of Art*, vol. i. pl. 7; and Visconti's *Museo Pio-Clementino*, vol. vii. pl. 6.)
[1] Wilkinson, *A. E.* vol. i. p. 238.
[2] Ibid., and compare the *Rosetta Stone*, line 7.
[3] Porphyr. l.s.c.
[4] Wilkinson, l.s.c.
[5] Herodotus, ii. 68; Diod. Sic. i.

83; &c.
[6] Birch speaks of 'chapters or synods,' by which the highest posts were filled up when vacant (*Egypt from the Earliest Times*, 'Introduction,' p. xx.); but I am not aware that there is any evidence of their existence earlier than the time of the Ptolemies.

remote antiquity [1] a considerable portion of the land of
Egypt, perhaps as much as one third,[2] was made over
to the priestly class, large estates being attached to
each temple, and held as common property by the
'colleges,' which, like the chapters of our cathedrals,
directed the worship of each sacred edifice. These
lands were probably, in part, let to tenants ; but they
seem to have been, in the main, cultivated or grazed
by *hieroduli*, or 'sacred slaves,' under the direction of
the priests themselves,[3] to whose granaries and cattle-
stalls, attached to the temples, the produce was from
time to time brought in. The priestly estates were,
we are told, exempt from taxation of any kind,[4] and
they appear to have received continual augmentation
from the piety or superstition of the kings, who constantly made over to their favourite deities fresh
'gardens, orchards, vineyards, fields,' and even 'cities.' [5]

Besides their regular revenues, the proceeds of their
own lands, the priests received, at the hands of the
faithful, a large amount of valuable offerings, whereby
they were enabled at once to live themselves and bring
up their families in luxury, and also to add year by
year to the wealth stored in the temple treasuries.
The gold, the silver, the fine linen, the precious stones,
the seals, the rings, the 'pectoral plates,' the necklaces,
the bowls and vases, the censers, the statues and statu-

---

[1] That the priests had their lands
before the time of Joseph, is apparent from Gen. xlvii. 22 and 26.
[2] This seems to be the meaning
of Diodorus Siculus (i. 73), who
may have had access to the Roman
registers.
[3] This appears especially from the
'Great Harris Papyrus,' where the
priestly lands, slave-cultivators,
barns, granaries, cattle-stalls, poul-
try-yards, &c., are repeatedly mentioned (*Records of the Past*, vol. vi.
pp. 31–34 ; vol. viii. pp. 8–39).
[4] Wilkinson, *A. E.* vol. i. p. 262.
[5] *Records of the Past*, vol. vi. pp.
31, 32, 36 ; vol. viii. pp. 14, 29, 39,
&c.

ettes in precious materials,[1] which the kings and other
donors continually offered to the various deities, and
which became really the property of the priests, were
of a value that cannot be computed, but that must have
been enormous,[2] and must have ultimately made the
priestly class by far the richest portion of the community. If it had not been for the plunder of the
temples from time to time by foreign invaders, which
dispersed the accumulated hoards, the precious metals
must have tended to become gradually locked up in
the sacred treasuries ; and Egypt, drained of these important elements of national wealth and prosperity,
would have fallen into a condition of exhaustion and
premature decay.

The advantages enjoyed by the priests were accompanied by correspondent obligations. As mediators
between men and the gods, they were bound to maintain a high standard both of internal and of external
purity. No doubt there were evasions of the former;
but from the latter it was impossible to escape. For
the preservation of perfect purity of body, each priest
had to wash himself from head to foot in cold water
twice every day and twice every night.[3] Not only
were their heads constantly shaved, but they were
bound to shave the entire body every other day, to
make it impossible that any vermin should harbour

[1] *Records of the Past*, vol. vi. pp.
37–40, 61, 69, &c. ; vol. viii. pp. 16
-17, 20-21, 32-35, &c.
[2] Rameses III. declares that he
presented to temples, in the course
of thirty - one years, gold vases
weighing 2,218,920 grains troy,
silver vases weighing 3,399,900
grains, 3,047 pieces of linen, 6,278
turquoise rings, 4,247 crystal rings,
12,256 'pectorals,' 10,463 seals, and
other ornaments in lapis lazuli, jasper, green felspar, turquoise, and
crystal, almost without number.
(See *Records of the Past*, vol. viii.
pp. 32-5.)
[3] Herod. ii. 37. Porphyry (*De
Abstinent.* iv. 7) says *thrice* a day,
and once in the night, *occasionally*.
But he is speaking of Roman times.

upon their persons.[1] Their garments, at any rate
when they were inside the temples, had to be of linen
only ;[2] and their shoes, or rather sandals, were necessarily of the papyrus plant,[3] that so no animal substance
might be in contact with them. The ' Sem,' however,
or officiating high-priest, wore, as his costume of office,
a complete leopard-skin, with head, claws, and tail ;[4]
but this sacred vestment was placed over the linen
clothes, and may have been lined with linen where it
was liable to touch the priest's arms or body. Their
food was limited to the flesh of oxen and geese, with
wine, bread, and certain kinds of vegetables.[5] Mutton,
pork, and fish, were expressly forbidden them ; and
they were bound to abstain from beans, peas, lentils,
onions, garlic, and leeks.[6] It has been conjectured
that these regulations originated in ' dietetic motives,'
and that ' the sanitary rule grew into a religious pro-
hibition ; '[7] but, as this theory fails to account for the
larger number of the prohibitions, it is perhaps better
to suppose that what were regarded as the coarser and
grosser kinds of food were considered to be unsuited
to the priestly dignity, and were therefore forbidden.
It may be objected that mutton is not coarser than
beef; but the Egyptians may have been of a different
opinion ; and certainly mutton was held generally in

---

[1] Herod. l.s.c. In the representations of priests upon the monuments, the head is either perfectly
bare, or covered with an ample wig,
which descends to the shoulders.
(See the author's *Herodotus*, vol.
ii. pp. 62–3, 3rd edition.)

[2] So Herodotus (l.s.c.); but Pliny
says that cotton dresses were particularly agreeable to the priests
(*H. N.* xix. 1). Probably we have
here an indication of the laxer discipline which prevailed ultimately.

[3] Herod. l.s.c.; Birch, *Guide to
Museum*, p. 26. Shoes were not
really worn until the Græco-Roman
period.

[4] Wilkinson, *A. E.* vol. i. p. 279.
For a representation, see above, p.
274.

[5] Herod. ii. 37 ; Plut. *De Isid.
et Os.* § 5.

[6] Plut. *De Isid. et Os.* §. 8.

[7] Kenrick, *Ancient Egypt*, vol. i.
p. 447.

disesteem among them, and was avoided even when it was not prohibited.[1]

At certain times of the year, even greater abstemiousness was necessary. The religious calendar contained a number of fasts, some of which lasted from seven to forty-two days. Throughout the whole duration of every such period, the priests were required to abstain entirely from animal food, from herbs and vegetables, and from wine.[2] Their diet on these occasions can have been little more than bread and water.

The rite of circumcision, which was practised by the Egyptians generally,[3] though not universally, must have been obligatory upon the priests, if it was a necessary preliminary to initiation into the mysteries.[4] Marriage was not forbidden them, but on the contrary was encouraged, since it was in this way especially that the priestly order was maintained and continued. Polygamy, however, was strictly prohibited;[5] and a general simplicity of living was enjoined, which it was not found possible to secure in all instances. Priests often held important political offices; they served in the army, and received rich gifts for good conduct; many of them accumulated considerable wealth through these secular employments, and their villas were on a scale which is scarcely compatible with ascetic, or even with simple, habits.[6]

The attire of the priests varied considerably. Some wore, even when officiating, no other garment than the short tunic or *shenti*, which was common to all adult males in Egypt; some added to this a mat or napkin

[1] See above, p. 175, note [2].
[2] Wilkinson, *A. E.* vol. i. p. 278.
[3] Herod. ii. 37 and 104.
[4] As Wilkinson supposes. (See the author's *Herodotus*, vol. ii. p.
62, note [9]; and compare Kenrick, *Ancient Egypt*, vol. i. p. 449.)
[5] Diod. Sic. i. 80, § 3.
[6] Wilkinson, *A. E.* vol. i. p. 282; Rosellini, *Mon. Civ.* i. p. 266.

upon the left arm.   Others wore over the tunic a long smock reaching from below the arms to the feet, and supported over the two shoulders by straps.   But the most part had a long full robe, with large sleeves, which covered the arm to the elbow, and descended to the ankles.   This outer robe was frequently of so fine a material as to be transparent, and to show through it the shape of the limbs and of the under tunic.   A dress intermediate between this and the light apparel just mentioned consisted of a loose tunic, falling in folds about the loins and legs, with a heart-shaped apron in front.   Another differed chiefly from the long full robe by commencing at the waist, and being supported by a broad strap passing over the left shoulder.[1] Most commonly the priests officiate with bare heads; but sometimes they wear wigs, carefully curled, and descending low; in the earlier times their feet are

An Egyptian Priest bare, but from about the fifth or sixth dynasty they wear sandals.   The priests are generally represented either in procession, when they usually bear an emblem, or in the act of pouring a libation, or as worshipping a god, or the king, when they have their two hands raised with the palms turned outwards.

The emblems borne in the processions are of various kinds, but seem to mark not so much the rank or dignity of the priest who carries them, as the worship to which they are attached.   In one procession [2]

[1] See the author's *Herodotus*, vol. ii. pp. 62–3; and compare Wilkinson, *A. E.* 'Supplement,' pl. 76, where a procession of priests in various costumes carries the divine emblems.

[2] Wilkinson, *A. E.* 'Supplement,' pl. 76.

we see borne the cow of Athor, the hawk of Horus, the ape of Thoth, the jackal of Anubis, the vase of Netpe, the shrine of Nehemao, and other emblems of a similar character, the priests themselves having nothing to distinguish them but such varieties of apparel as were mentioned above. It is quite possible that these varieties themselves may be connected with differences of rank ; but at present we have no means of determining which of them belonged to the higher, and which to the lower orders. We can only say that the leopard-skin marked the very highest grade of the priestly office, and was peculiarly appropriate to that rank when engaged in the very highest functions.[1]

It has been a matter of dispute among Egyptologists [2] whether or no the Egyptians allowed the sacerdotal office to be held by women. Herodotus distinctly states that they did not ;[3] and the monuments so far bear out his assertion that ' nowhere does a female appear discharging a properly sacerdotal office, nor does the hieroglyphic for priest occur with the feminine termination.'[4]   On the other hand, Herodotus himself speaks of ' sacred women ' as attached to the temple of Ammon at Thebes ;[5] and the Rosetta stone contains distinct mention of ' priestesses.'[6]   We shall best reconcile the various statements by supposing that, strictly speaking, women could not hold the priestly office, at any rate until Ptolemaic times ; but that certain functions about the temples were from the first open to them, and that among the other customs introduced by

[1] Wilkinson, A. E. vol. i. pp. 278 –279.
[2] Compare Wilkinson, A. E. vol. i. pp. 258–262, with Kenrick, Ancient Egypt, vol. i. p. 452.
[3] Herod. ii. 35.
[4] Kenrick, l.s.c.

[5] Herod. ii. 54, 56. Compare De Rougé, Monuments qu'on peut attribuer aux six premières Dynasties de l'Egypte, pp. 83, 97, &c.
[6] Records of the Past, vol. iv. p. 71.

the Macedonian kings were a relaxation of the old law, and an admission of females to certain really sacerdotal offices. Women could, however, from the first offer for themselves in the temples,[1] and they played an important part in the sacred rites accompanying funerals.[2]

In immediate succession to the priestly order, and ranking only a little below it, must be placed the class of the soldiers. This class, which, according to the numbers that have come down to us,[3] must have amounted to from two to three and a half millions of persons, and so have formed, at the least, above one-fourth of the population,[4] was settled on rich lands in various parts of Egypt,[5] but chiefly in the Delta, and, except when upon active service, employed itself mainly in the cultivation of the soil. It comprised persons of very different social rank and of manifold degrees of opulence. The statement of Herodotus that each of the 410,000 soldiers, which formed the native armed force of Egypt in his day, possessed exactly twelve *aruræ*, or nine English acres, of land,[6] is highly improbable, and can only point to a supposed original allotment, such as Diodorus says was made by Sesostris.[7] Original equality, though scarcely likely, is possible; but the extinction of some families and the expansion of others would soon lead to the same sort of inequality which we find at Sparta; the opposite results of industry and

---

[1] Wilkinson in the author's *Herodotus*, vol. ii. p. 56. (Compare *Ancient Egyptians*, vol. i. p. 260.)

[2] Wilkinson, *A. E.* 'Supplement,' pls. 83–6.

[3] Herodotus (ii. 165–6) estimates the actual soldiers at 410,000, Diodorus (i. 54) at 692,000. Taking the average of a family at five persons, the former estimate would

give for the military class a total of 2,050,000, the latter a total of 3,460,000.

[4] See above, pp. 107–8.

[5] Diod. Sic. i. 54, § 6: Πᾶσι δὲ τοῖς προειρημένοις κατεκλήρουχησε τὴν ἀρίστην τῆς χώρας.

[6] Herod. ii. 168.

[7] See above, note [5]

idleness, thrift and extravagance, would make themselves felt ; lots would be divided and subdivided,
sometimes alienated ; the thrifty would add field to
field, and in course of time become possessed of considerable estates; favourite officers would obtain grants
of land from the monarch out of the royal domains ; [1]
and thus there would ultimately come to be contained
within the military class a certain number of large
landed proprietors, a considerable body of moderately
wealthy yeomen, and a more or less numerous 'prole-
tariat.' These last, it is probable, worked as day
labourers on the estates of their wealthy brethren, or
else rented portions of them, agriculture being the
only employment open to them besides the profession
of arms, since they were positively forbidden to engage /
in any handicraft or trade.[2]

The military class was divided into two distinct
bodies, called respectively Hermotybies and Calasiries.
The Calasiries, are supposed to have been
chiefly, or universally, archers.[3] According to Herodotus,[4] they inhabited the nomes, or cantons, of Thebes,
Bubastis, Aphthis, Tanis, Mendes, Sebennytus, Athribis, Pharbæthis, Thmuïs, Onuphis, Anysis, and My-
ecphoris—districts which, with the single exception of
Thebes, lay within the Delta. They could bring into
the field, when their strength was at its greatest,
250,000 men. The Hermotybies were very much less
numerous. They inhabited six cantons only [5]—Busiris,
Saïs, Papremis, Prosopitis, and Natho, regions of the
Delta, together with Chemmis, which was in Upper

[1] See *Records of the Past,* vi. 9 ;
and compare Diod. Sic. i. 73, § 6.
[2] Herod. ii. 165–6.
[3] Wilkinson in the author's *Herodotus,* vol. ii. p. 249, note [6] ;
Birch, *Dictionary of Hieroglyphics,*
p. 410.
[4] Herod. ii. 166.
[5] Ibid. ii. 165.

Egypt.   When at their fullest strength, they furnished
to the army no more than 160,000 soldiers.

It is not to be supposed that Egypt, with its population of seven or seven and a half millions, kept this
enormous military force continually under arms.   The
great states of Europe, with populations from three to
five times as large, find the maintenance of armies
numbering 400,000 or 500,000 men burdensome in
the extreme.   In Egypt, armies were levied and dis-
banded, as occasion required ; the number of the
militia called out varied according to the supposed
strength of the enemy about to be attacked or resisted ;
campaigns were usually short; and, except the troops
kept in garrison [1] and the two thousand who formed
the body-guard of the king,[2] the men of the military
class had the greater part of the year to themselves.
No doubt, some considerable portion of this leisure
time was spent in gymnastic training and various kinds
of military exercise; but it can scarcely be questioned
that at least as much of it was given to agricultural
employments.   The wealthier members of the body
indulged also in the sports of the field.[3]

The exact mode of training and educating persons
for the military profession is not known.   It is likely
enough that, as Diodorus states of the companions of
Sesostris,[4] they underwent a special education from
boyhood, and were practised in running and other
athletic exercises, though the necessity of accom-
plishing a distance of twenty miles before breakfast [5]

[1] Herod. ii. 30, with Wilkinson's note.
[2] Ibid. ii. 168.
[3] Wilkinson, A. E. vol. i. p. 286.
[4] Diod. Sic. i. 53, § 3.   Birch, in his additions to Wilkinson, notes that military schools are alluded to, and the hardships endured at them complained of, in a letter written by a contemporary of Rameses II., and published by M. Maspero (A. E. vol. i. p. 187 ; ed. of 1878).
[5] So Diodorus, l.s.c.

can scarcely have been a regular requirement. It is also probable that hunting expeditions formed a portion of the ordinary course, and hardened the frame by exposure to sun and cold, and the constitution by the necessity of light meals and infrequent indulgence in drink.[1] When the age for active service approached, the young soldiers were formally enrolled, and taken from their homes to some military station, where they were carefully drilled by a sergeant. When pronounced fit, they were attached to existing corps or

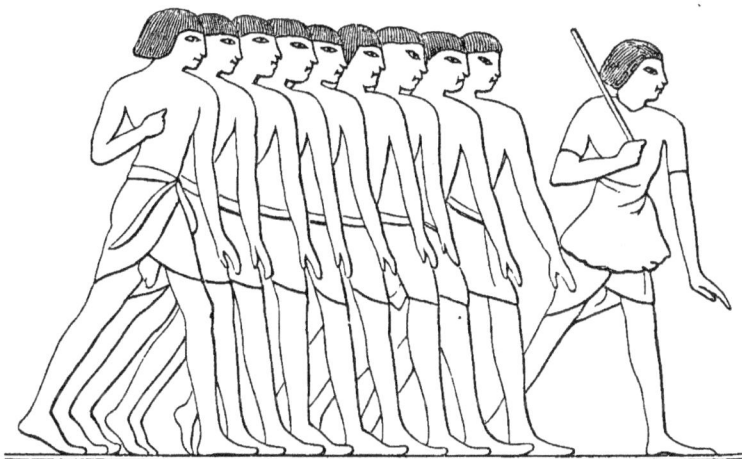

Infantry drilled by a Sergeant.

regiments, and entered upon garrison duty, or took the field and were employed against the enemy.

The bulk of an Egyptian army was always composed of infantry.[2] These were divided into heavy-armed and light-armed. The heavy-armed troops wore helmets, which were either of metal[3] or of quilted

[1] Diod. Sic. i. 53, § 5.

[2] Diodorus makes the infantry of Sesostris 600,000, the cavalry 24,000, and the chariots 27,000 (i. 54, § 4). This is not historical, but it indicates the notions which that writer obtained from the Egyptian priests of the proportion which the three main arms of the service bore one to the other.

[3] Metal helmets were but rarely worn, the weight being inconvenient

linen, descending in the latter case over the back of
the neck and the shoulders.[1]   Their bodies were protected by cuirasses or coats of mail, which were sometimes quilted like the linen helmets,[2] but often had

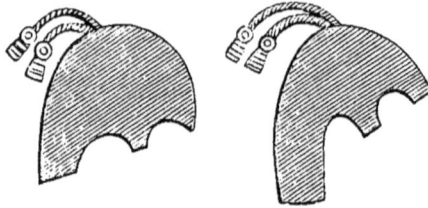

Egyptian Helmets.

overlapping plates of metal sewed on outside the linen,
and which reached from the
neck nearly to the knee.
Short sleeves, in no cases
falling below the elbow,
guarded the upper part of the
arm. The legs and feet were,
for the most part, bare ; but
sometimes a tunic or kilt, descending below the coat of
mail, gave a slight protection
to the thighs and knees.[3]
Large shields were carried,
which were generally circular
at the top and of oblong shape,
the sides being either parallel,
or contracting as they descended.[4]   Usually the shield

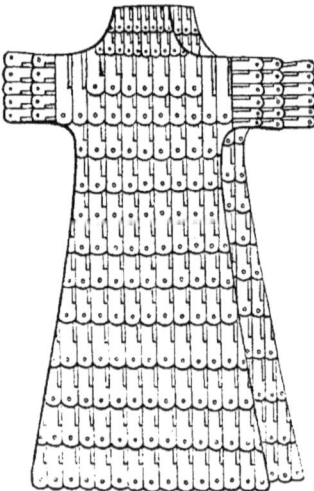

Ccat of Mail.

---

in so hot a climate. (See Wilkinson, *A. E.* vol. i. p. 330.)   Still, unless they had been in occasional use,
the story told by Herodotus of Psamatik I. (Herod. ii. 151) would
scarcely have gained acceptance.
   [1] Wilkinson, l.s.c.

[2] Herod. ii. 182, with Wilkinson's note ; and compare *Ancient
Egyptians,* vol. i. pp. 331–2.
   [3] Wilkinson, *A. E.* vol. i. p. 332,
and pl. iii. fig. 7.
   [4] Instances are found where the
shield expands instead of contract-

was of wood or wickerwork, and was covered with an untanned bull's hide, having the hair outwards;[1] it was further generally strengthened by a metal rim of considerable breadth and by a boss of metal in the centre of the circular portion. Occasionally a very much larger and more cumbrous defence was employed, the shield being nearly the height of the

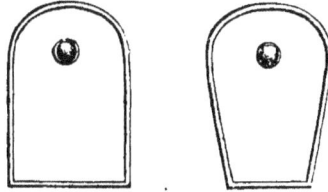

Ordinary Egyptian Shields.

warrior, who was sometimes forced to rest one corner of it upon the ground.[2] In this case, instead of a circular top, the form affected was that of the pointed arch, as will be seen by the subjoined woodcut. The offensive weapons of the heavy-armed troops were the spear, the mace, the battle-axe, the sword, straight or curved, and the hatchet. Most corps had two at least of these arms; some seem to have had three, one carried in either hand, and the third worn as a side-arm.[3]

The light-armed troops were in some cases bare-headed, but more commonly wore the quilted cap, some-

Warrior, with Shield of unusual size.

times surmounted with a crescent and ball.[4] The upper part of their person was naked; and sometimes

---

ing (Rosellini, *Monumenti Storici*, pl. xciv. line 2, &c.) But they are of rare occurrence.

[1] Wilkinson, vol. i. pp. 298–9.

[2] See Rosellini, *Monumenti Storici*, pl. cxvii. 4; and compare Wilkinson, *A. E.* vol. i. p. 202, ed. of 1878.

[3] Wilkinson in the author's *Herodotus*, vol. iv. opp. p. 402.

[4] Rosellini, *Monumenti Storici*, pls. cxxvi., cxxix. &c.

they wore nothing on their body but the ordinary
shenti or plain tunic,[1] which began at the waist and
ended a little above the knees.   Instances occur of an

Light-armed Troops marching.

even lighter equipment, the tunic being occasionally
dispensed with, and a mere cloth worn, which, after

Spearmen and Archers.

encircling the waist, was passed from front to back be-

---

[1] Rosellini, *Monumenti Storici,* | *mäler,* vol. vi. part iii. pls. 154,
pls. cxxvi. et seqq. ; Lepsius, *Denk-* | 155, &c.

tween the legs. Sometimes, however, their dress was a robe which reached from the waist to the ankles, and more frequently a full tunic with many folds, which descended somewhat below the knee.[1] A shield of moderate size and of the ordinary shape was borne by most of these troops, who carried, as their main weapons, either bows and arrows, or spears, or else javelins, and for a side-arm had a curved sword, a club, or a hatchet. A portion of them, forming probably a separate corps, were slingers, and carried nothing but their sling and a bag of stones hung round their neck.[2]

Egyptian Slinger.

It is exceedingly remarkable that on the monuments there is no representation of Egyptian cavalry. The few mounted warriors who occur are foreigners;[3] and, to judge from the monuments alone, we should say that this arm of the military service, important as most nations have considered it, was unknown to the Pharaohs. But the evidence of historical writers is directly opposed to this conclusion. Diodorus Siculus assigns to Sesostris a cavalry force of 24,000.[4] Herodotus represents Amasis as leading his army on horseback.[5] In the historical books of the Old Testament, the Egyptian horsemen obtain frequent mention;[6] and as many as 60,000 are said to have accompanied Sheshonk

---

[1] Wilkinson, *A. E.* vol. i. pp. 301, 334; Rosellini, *Mon. Stor.* pls. cxxix. cxxx., &c.
[2] Wilkinson, vol. i. p. 316; Rosellini, *Mon. Civ.* pl. cxvii. 3.
[3] Rosellini, *Mon. Civ.* pl. cxx.;

Lepsius, *Denkmäler*, vol. vi. pt. iii. pl. 145, *b*; &c.
[4] Diod. Sic. i. 54, §4.
[5] Herod. ii. 162.
[6] Ex. xv. 21; Is. xxxvi. 9; 2 Kings xviii. 23-4, &c.

(Shishak) when he invaded Palestine.[1] The hieroglyphic texts, moreover, if translated aright, make
frequent mention of Egyptian cavalry;[2] and the
‘ command of the cavalry was a very honourable and
important post, generally held by one of the king's
sons.’[3]

Still, it would seem to be certain that cavalry was
not an arm by which the Egyptians set much store.
Perhaps they were bad riders, and found it difficult to
manage a charger.[4] At any rate, it is clear that they
preferred to use the horses, of which they had abundance, in the chariot service, rather than to mount
riders upon them.

The chariot service was, beyond a doubt, considered to be the most important of all. The king
invariably went to war mounted upon a car, and
seldom descended from it excepting to give the *coup
de grâce* to a wounded enemy.[5] The chiefs of the
army, all the best and bravest, followed their monarch's
example, and as many as 27,000 chariots are assigned
to Sesostris.[6] This is, no doubt, an over-statement;
but the twelve hundred who accompanied Shishak[7]
will not appear, to any one who is acquainted with the
Egyptian monuments, to be an exaggeration. Chariots
were drawn up in line, great care being taken to
‘ dress the ranks,’[8] and were supported by columns of
infantry drawn up behind them,[9] a second line of each

[1] 2 Chron. xii. 3.
[2] See *Records of the Past*, vol. ii.
pp. 68, 70, 72, &c.
[3] Wilkinson, *A. E.* vol. i. p. 292.
[4] In the army of Xerxes they
served as sailors only (Herod. vii.
89); in the army of Artaxerxes
Mnemon at Cunaxa as infantry only
(Xen. *Anab.* i. 8, § 9).
[5] See Rosellini, *Mon. Storici*, pls.

lxii. 1; lxiv. &c.
[6] Diod. Sic. l.s.c.
[7] 2 Chron. xii. 3.
[8] Lepsius, *Denkmäler*, vol. vi.
pt. iii. pls. 155, 160; Rosellini,
Mon. Storici, pls. lxxxvii., xcvi.,
ciii., cv. &c.
[9] Lepsius, vol. vi. pl. 155; Rosellini, pl. cvii.

being sometimes kept in reserve. In fighting, this exactness of arrangement could not, of course, be maintained, though we sometimes see an Egyptian chariot force preserving its ranks unbroken, while it throws a similar force opposed to it into disorder.[1] More often, when a battle is depicted, chariots, loose horses, and footmen are mingled together in inextricable confusion. The Egyptian cars were small, and but slightly raised above the ground. Ordinarily they carried two persons only, the warrior and the charioteer. It was the business of the latter not only to manage the two steeds by which the car was drawn, but also to hold a shield in front of himself and his companion. As this double occupation was a difficult thing to achieve successfully, it would seem that he sometimes fastened the reins round his own or the warrior's waist,[2] so as to be enabled to give his whole attention to the management of the shield. Occasionally, but very rarely, a chariot has three occupants, the charioteer, and two warriors, who stand behind him, side by side.[3]

The Egyptian war-chariot had a semicircular standing-board, which was either wholly of wood, or composed of a wooden frame filled up with a network of thong or rope, which by its elasticity rendered the motion of the vehicle more easy.[4] From this rose in a graceful curve the *antyx* or rim, which first sloped a little backwards, and was then carried round in front

---

[1] Rosellini, pl. ciii.
[2] Ibid. Sometimes the warrior drives; but this, it may be presumed, was before coming into the presence of the enemy. (See Rosellini, pl. lxxxii.)
[3] Wilkinson, *A. E.* vol. i. p. 336,

fig. 1. Three warriors are frequent in the chariots of other nations. (Rosellini, pls. lxxxviii.–xci., &c.; Lepsius, vol. vi. pls. 157–60.)
[4] See Wilkinson, *A. E.* vol. i. p. 342.

of the driver at the height of about two feet and a half from the standing-board. The space between the standing-board and the rim was generally left open at the sides, connection between the two being in this part maintained merely by three leathern straps; but in front there was always a broad upright of wood, extending from the board to the rim, and interposed between the driver and the horses. Sometimes the sides themselves were filled up, either with wood or with cloth of some kind, which was ordinarily of a bright colour.[1] The whole body of the car was painted in gay patterns, and perhaps sometimes ornamented with the precious metals.[2]

The body, thus constructed, was placed upon the axle-tree and the lower part of the pole, and firmly attached to them. It was not, however, balanced evenly upon the axle-tree, but shifted towards the front, so that but little of the standing-board extended behind the wheels.[3] The ends of the axle-tree were inserted into the axles of the wheels, which worked round them, being prevented from falling off by a peg or linch-pin. The pole, after passing along the bottom of the car, rose in a gentle sweep, meeting a bar or strap, which united it to the rim in front. It terminated in a yoke, to which were attached small saddles, these latter resting on the withers of the horses. Chariot wheels had in some cases four spokes only; but the regular number was six, an amount which is not exceeded.

Each war-chariot was furnished with at least one

---

[1] Rosellini, *Monumenti Storici,* pls. lxxxii., lxxxiv., and c.
[2] Wilkinson, *A. E.* vol. i. p. 348. (For representations, see, besides the places mentioned in the preceding note, Rosellini, *M. S.* pls. lxxxi. and cii.)
[3] Wilkinson, p. 343.

quiver and one bow-case, which were placed on the side on which the warrior took up his position in the car. They hung obliquely between the body of the car and the wheel, crossing each other at right angles, and forming the most conspicuous objects in the representations which we have of chariots. Both are covered with brilliant and elaborate patterns ; and

War-chariot, with Bow-case, Quivers, and Javelins.

the bow-case is frequently further ornamented with the figure of a lion rushing at full speed, which is carefully and delicately executed. Sometimes a second quiver is provided, and placed close to the bow-case, but apparently inside the body of the car. Both the quiver and the bow-case occasionally contain a javelin or javelins.

The Egyptian chariots were drawn uniformly by two horses, harnessed one on either side of the pole. The harness comprised, besides the saddles above mentioned as attached to the yoke, only a girth, a breast-band, a head-stall, and reins. The girth and breast-baud were fastened to the saddle. The head-stall much resembled a modern one, excepting that the top of the head was covered by a close-fitting cap, through which the ears passed, and which was frequently crowned by a plume of feathers. The reins consisted of a bearing rein, drawn rather tight and secured to a hook at the top of the saddle, and a driving rein,[1] which, after passing through a ring or leathern loop on either side of the saddle, was held above the back of the horse by the charioteer. Chariot horses were usually caparisoned with elegant housings.[2]

The offensive arms of the Egyptians were somewhat peculiar. Their spears were excessively short, not much exceeding the length of five feet. Their straight swords were formidable weapons, apparently not less than from two to three feet long, and very broad at the base, tapering thence to a point.[3] But the arm more commonly used was the curved sword or falchion,[4] which was a shorter and, to all appearance, a less effective weapon. The shapes of the battle-axe and pole-axe were unusual, the former having a long blade, with a curved edge, sometimes semicircular, sometimes a mere segment of a circle, with two seg-

---

[1] The representations of chariots represent the pair of horses as driven by a single rein; but it is supposed that this is an ' economy' of the artists, and that in reality each horse had his own rein.

[2] See the woodcut, page 454.

[3] See Rosellini, *Monumenti Sto-* *rici*, pl. ci.; and compare Wilkinson, *A. E.* vol. i. p. 318.

[4] The king has in all cases the curved, and not the straight, sword. It is also more common than the straight sword in the hands of the soldiers.

ments taken out of it at the back,[1] and the latter
having its blade weighted by a massive ball at the
base, which is thought to have been about four inches

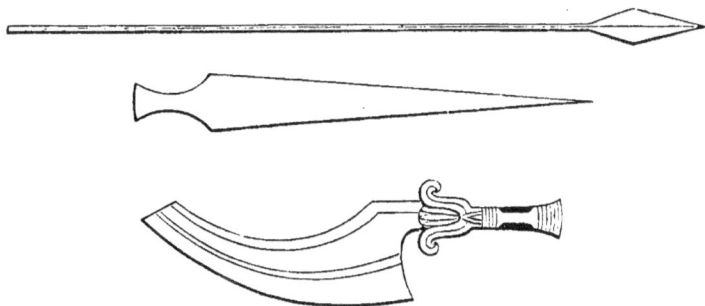

Egyptian Spear, Straight Sword, and Falchion.

in diameter.[2] Maces generally terminated in a ball,
which was no doubt of metal, but sometimes they were
mere rods, which can have been of little service, unless
they were of bronze or iron. They had a curious
curved projection at the lower end, whereto a strap

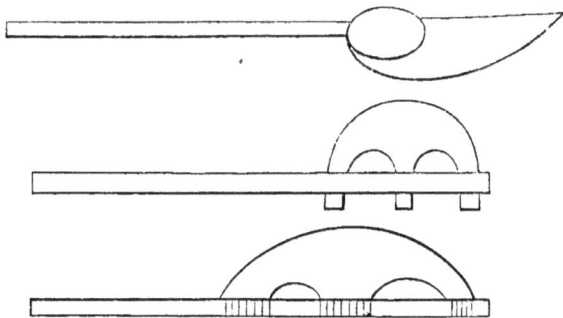

Egyptian Battle-axes and Pole-axe.

was probably attached,[3] which was then twisted round
the wrist or hand, to render the hold on the weapon

---

[1] Wilkinson, *A. E.* vol. i. pp.
324–5; Rosellini, *Mon. Civili*, pls.
cxvii. 5, and cxix. 1.

[2] Wilkinson, vol. i. p. 326.
[3] See Birch, *Guide to Museum*,
p. 39, No. 5467.

more sure. Clubs were also employed, sometimes of the ordinary character,[1] sometimes resembling the modern African *lissan*, which is a curved stick of hard

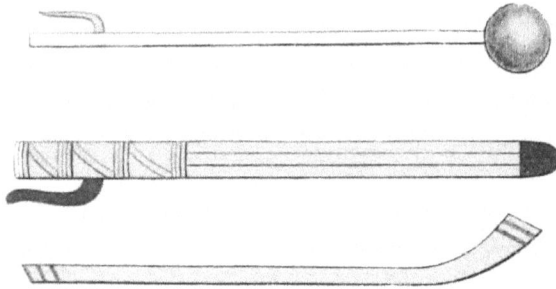

Egyptian Clubs and Maces.

wood, about two feet and a half in length, with a slight enlargement at the lower end.[2] Daggers were very commonly worn ; their place was in the belt, into the right side of which they were thrust obliquely. The blade was short, not exceeding eight or ten inches

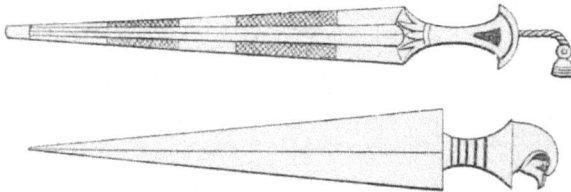

Egyptian Daggers.

in length,[3] and tapered gradually from end to end, terminating in an exceedingly sharp point. It was of bronze,[4] but so skilfully tempered, that the elasticity

---

[1] For a representation, see Rosellini, *Mon. Storici*, pl. cxxix.
[2] Wilkinson, vol. i. p. 329.
[3] Ibid. p. 319. Compare the weapons themselves in the British Museum (Nos. 5423–6).
[4] The bronze used for arms appears, upon analysis, to have been composed as follows: copper 94·0, tin 5·9, iron 0·1. (See Birch, *Guide to Museum*, p. 39.) The tin is in a smaller proportion than usual; but the slight tinge of iron was probably more than a compensation.

and spring remain after three thousand years, and almost equal that of the best steel.[1] The handles were of wood, bone, ivory, silver, or gold, and were often delicately inlaid: that of the king often ended in the head of a hawk.[2] Each dagger had its sheath, which was of leather, sometimes plain, sometimes patterned.

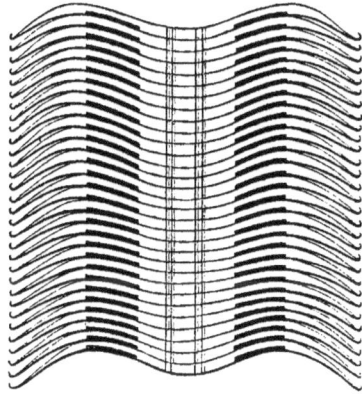

Egyptian bows, though not perhaps so powerful as Ethiopian,[3] were formidable weapons, and must have driven the arrow

Egyptian Bows.

with great force. In length they were commonly from five feet to five feet and a half,[4] and were formed of a rounded piece of tough wood, which when unstrung became nearly straight, or else curved itself into a sort of double crescent.[5] Sometimes the wood was further strengthened by pieces of leather, which were inserted at intervals into the under part of the bow. Bowstrings were made of hide, catgut, or string,[6] and appear to have been sufficiently strong.[7] The material used for arrows

Archer taking aim.

was either a light wood, or more commonly reed ; the

[1] Wilkinson, A. E. vol. i. p. 320.
[2] Ibid. p. 319.
[3] See Herod. iii. 21.
[4] Wilkinson, A. E. vol. i. p. 308.
[5] Rosellini, Mon. Civili, pl. cxxi. 25; Wilkinson, A. E. vol. i. p. 305.
[6] Wilkinson, p. 308.
[7] See the woodcut. It is notice-

heads were either of metal or stone, and were occasionally barbed;[1] the shafts were carefully notched at
the lower extremity, and winged with three feathers in
the most approved modern fashion.[2] The ordinary
length of an arrow was from twenty-two to thirty-two
inches. Archers shot either standing or kneeling ; they
drew the arrow either with the first two fingers or with
the thumb and the forefinger, and in war commonly

Archers stringing their Bows.

brought the hand to the ear. We sometimes, but not
very often, see the left forearm protected from the
blow of the string by a guard.[3] Two modes of stringing the bow are shown in the accompanying woodcut.

able that the Egyptian chariot
archers often attempt to entangle
their enemies with their strung bows,
which implies great confidence in the
strength of the string.
　[1] Wilkinson, *A. E.* vol. i. p. 310

(woodcut 33, fig. 4).
　[2] Ibid. p. 309. It may perhaps
be questioned whether two or three
feathers were used.
　[3] Ibid. p. 306 (woodcut 29).

Each bowman, unless when riding in a chariot, carried a quiver slung at his back ; and the king generally carries one even under such circumstances,[1] though he has always one or two others attached to his car. Quivers were commonly square-topped and rounded at the bottom ; but sometimes the cover was modelled into the form of a lion's head.[2] The whole of the exterior was painted in gay patterns.

Another offensive arm frequently employed by the Egyptians was the javelin, which was of a lighter kind than that used by most nations. It consisted of a long thin shaft, sometimes merely pointed, but generally armed with a head, which was either leaf-shaped, or like the head of a spear, or else four-sided,

Egyptian Quivers.

and attached to the shaft by projections at the angles.[3] At the lower extremity was either a tasseled head, or a strap,[4] which enabled the javelin-man, after throwing his weapon, to recover it.

Not very much is known concerning Egyptian tactics. The infantry was certainly divided into distinct corps, each of which had its own special arms and accoutrements; some being spearmen, some bow-

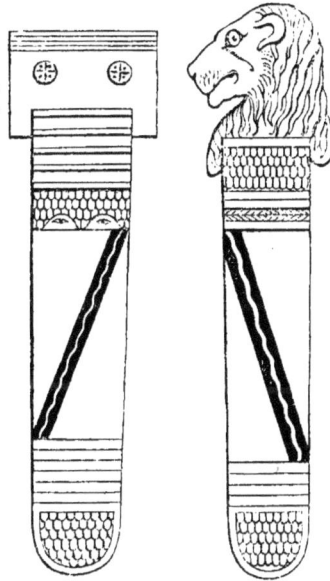

---

[1] Rosellini, *Mon. Storici*, pls. xlvi. 1; xlviii. 2, &c. Lepsius, *Denkmäler*, vol. vi. pt. iii. pls. 126 b, 160, 166, &c.

[2] Rosellini, *Mon. Civili*, pl. cxxi. 23 and 26.
[3] Wilkinson, *A. E.* vol. i. p. 315.
[4] See the woodcut overleaf.

men, some clubmen, some armed only with swords.[1]
They were drilled to march in step, and are always
represented as keeping step when in movement.
They fought commonly in dense columns, which were
sometimes drawn up ten men deep.[2] The chariots seem
ordinarily to have covered the front of the battle, and
consequently to have commenced the fight. Sometimes
they had to meet a chariot force, when the charioteers
charged at speed, shooting their arrows as they ad-

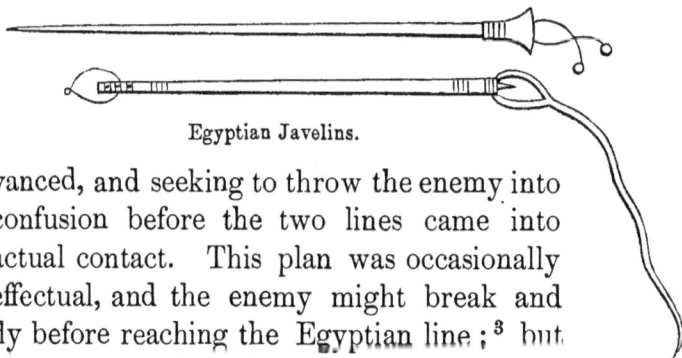

Egyptian Javelins.

vanced, and seeking to throw the enemy into
confusion before the two lines came into
actual contact. This plan was occasionally
effectual, and the enemy might break and
fly before reaching the Egyptian line ;[3] but
it was not often that such a result was
achieved. Generally the two chariot forces became
intermixed, and the battle was a mere *mêlée*, depending
on the individual prowess and strength of the com-
batants. The Egyptians are ordinarily represented as
greatly outnumbered by their adversaries, with whom,
however, they never fear to engage, and whom, in the
sculptures, they always discomfit. An important part
in the battles is often assigned to the javelin-men,[4]
whose weapons seem to inflict death at every blow.

To counteract the confusion which appears to have
been the normal condition of things in every fight, it

[1] See the representations in Rosellini, *Mon. Storici*, pls. cxxix.,
cxxx., cxxxiii., &c.
[2] Wilkinson, p. 293; Rosellini,
Mon. Storici, pl. xcvi. ; Lepsius,

Denkmäler, vol. vi. part iii. pl. 155
[3] Rosellini, *Mon. Storici*, pl. ciii.
[4] See Rosellini, *Mon. Storici*, pls
cxxvii. and cxxviii.

was important that the members of each corps should have a visible rallying-point. For this purpose standards were employed, and every battalion, indeed every company, possessed its own ensign, which was conspicuously different from all the rest. Most of them were of a religious character,[1] representing

Egyptian Standards.

either the head or ark of a god, or a sacred animal, or some emblem employed in the religion, or the cartouche of a king's name, which was viewed as sacred, since the kings were recognised as divinities. The ensigns were not embroidered on flags, but, like

[1] The plume of Ammon, the heads of Horus, Khonsu, Athor, Isis, and Tafné, the jackal of Anubis, the hawk of Horus or Ra, the crocodile of Savak, the stork of Thoth, are among the forms recognised. Sacred arks are also common. (See Wilkinson, *A. E.* vol. i. p. 294; and Rosellini, *Mon. Civili,* pl. cxxi. Nos. 1 to 15.)

the Roman eagles, consisted of solid objects ; they were
borne aloft at the top of a tall pole, standing usually
upon a cross-bar. Below the cross-bar we not infre-
quently see two streamers floating in air. It was ·
probably from their standards that the different corps
took the names by which they were distinguished.[1]

Each company of soldiers was commanded by an
officer called *menh*, whose rank was nearly that of
lieutenant in our service. Above him was the *aten*,
or captain ; then the *mer*, or major ; and finally the
haut, the colonel or general.[2] The conscripts, or
young soldiers, *neferu*, ⌋⇃⌐, were distinguished
from the rest of the army,[3] and probably filled the
posts of least danger. The archers, *masa*, were regarded as the best troops. In the field, an army was
divided into brigades, each brigade consisting of a
number of regiments. We find as many as four
brigades in one army.[4] The monarch usually led the
expeditions, and acted as commander-in-chief, while
important posts were frequently filled by his sons.[5]

In the wars between civilised nations, sieges have
always been among the most important of military
operations. Even savages construct stockades or
' kraals ; ' and it requires no very high degree of intelligence to go beyond this, and enclose spaces with
high walls protected by towers, which, according to
their size, are denominated castles, fortresses, or fortified cities. The nations with whom the Egyptians

---

[1] See *Records of the Past*, vol. ii.
p. 68, where we find the chief divisions of the army of Rameses II.
named after the gods, Ammon, Ra,
Phthah, and Set.

[2] Birch in the new edition of
Wilkinson's *Ancient Egyptians*, vol.
i. p. 193, note [8].

[3] Ibid.

[4] *Records of the Past*, l.s.c.

[5] The four chiefs who direct the
attack on the fort represented on
page 468 are the four sons of Rameses
II. (See Wilkinson, *A. E.* vol. i.
p. 361, note.)

contended, especially those of Syria and Mesopotamia, had fortified posts of all three kinds; and it was necessary, if any permanent impression was to be made upon them, that the Egyptians should possess some means of capturing these strongholds. Accordingly

A Syrian Fort.

the art of conducting sieges was early studied; and a certain amount of efficiency was attained in it by the time of the Ramesides. The simplest mode which the Egyptians employed was the bold advance of a large body of troops to the walls, a constant discharge of flights of arrows against the defenders, and the application of a number of ladders to the ramparts, which were then scaled by the besiegers.[1] If the escalade failed, a

[1] See Rosellini, *Mon. Storici*, pl. cviii.; Lepsius, *Denkmäler*, vol. vi. | pt. iii. pls. 145 c and 166.

regular siege had to be formed ; the troops surrounded
the place ; covered sheds, arched at the top, and supported by wooden sides or forked poles, were advanced

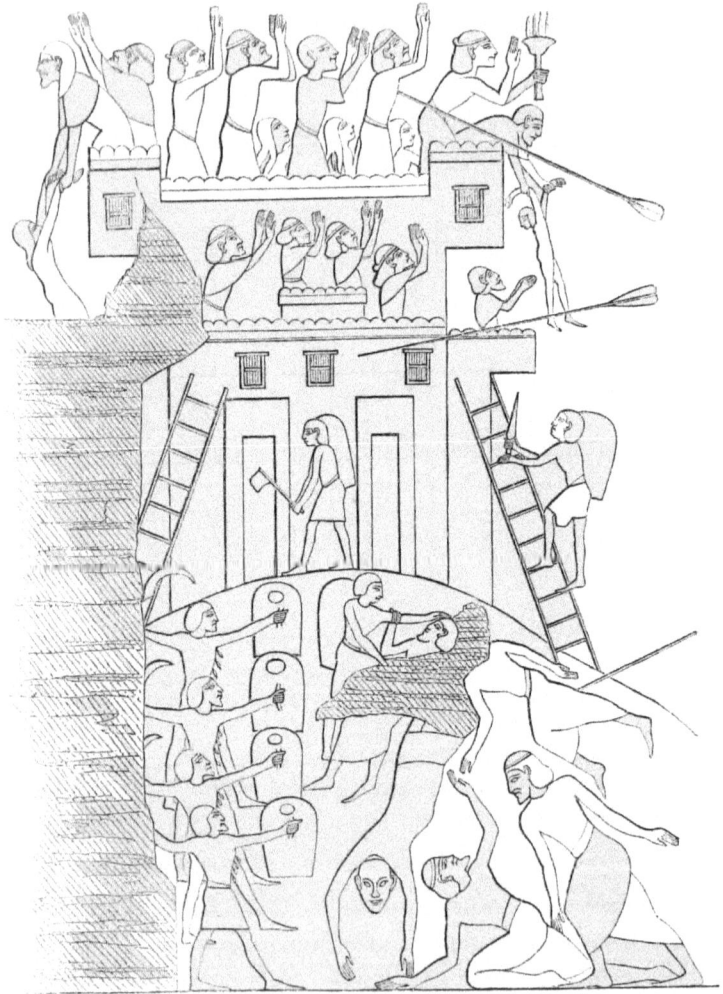

Escalading a Fort.

to the walls by a body of men posted within them,
and a long pole, pointed probably with iron or bronze,

was employed to dislodge the stones one by one, and so gradually effect a breach. Meanwhile, the attention of the defenders was distracted by archers, who shot at every one who showed himself above the battlements. After a breach had been effected, no doubt an assault was made, when the attack commonly prevailed over

Siege of a Fort.

the defence, and the place, after a longer or shorter resistance, fell.

Sometimes, instead of the means above described, an attempt was made to break open the gates of a fort or city by means of hatchets, which could be employed with good effect upon the wooden doors that blocked the entrance.[1] Fire does not appear to have been applied, as by the Assyrians;[2] but there is a paucity

[1] See the woodcut on the preceding page, and compare Lepsius, *Denkmäler*, vol. vi. pt. iii. pl. 145

c; Rosellini, *Mon. Storici*, pl. lxviii.
[2] See the author's *Ancient Monarchies*, vol. i. p. 474, 2nd edition.

in the representations of sieges, which leaves many points connected with them doubtful, and which is much to be regretted.

Attack on a Fort.

On the whole, it must be said that the Egyptians did not show much military genius, or much fertility

of resource in their conduct of sieges. The monuments give no indication of their having in any case
made use of the mine, notwithstanding their familiar
acquaintance with the art of driving underground
galleries, as evidenced in their tombs. Nor is there
any indication of their having employed moveable
towers like the Assyrians,[1] or catapults and *balistæ*,[2]
like the same people, and also the Greeks and Romans.
Even their battering ram, if it may be given the name,
was, as we have seen, a poor implement, being little
more than a spear of unusual size.[3] The natural
result seems to have followed—the Egyptians were not
very successful in their sieges. They took small places
easily enough, but could seldom capture large towns.
Ashdod resisted Psammetichus for twenty-nine years.[4]
Jerusalem was only once taken after David had fortified it, and then seems to have submitted, and not
fallen by assault.[5] It may be suspected that many
Syrian and Mesopotamian strongholds successfully resisted the Egyptian armies under the Thothmeses and
the Ramesides, and that this is the secret of that inability to retain their Asiatic conquests, which is so
marked a feature in the history of the nation.

The Egyptian troops had to contend with their

---

[1] See the author's *Ancient Mo-narchies*, vol. i. p. 471.

[2] Dr. Birch speaks of the em-ployment of catapults by the Egyp-tians (*Egypt from the Earliest Times*, 'Introduction,' p. xix.), and Canon Cook finds *balistæ* mentioned in an inscription of Pianchi (*Re-cords of the Past*, vol. ii. p. 88), who, however, is an Ethiopian and not an Egyptian. But I am not aware that any representation oc-curs in the Egyptian monuments of either a catapult or a *balista*. Still it

is not improbable that they may have been introduced from Assyria in the time of the twenty-second dynasty. The later monarchs, however, have left us no representations of their wars or sieges, so that we have no means of knowing whether or no they innovated upon the old Egyp-tian practice.

[3] See the woodcut, p. 467.

[4] Herod. ii. 157.

[5] 1 Kings xiv. 25–6, compared with 2 Chron. xii. 2–9.

enemies, not by land only, but also by sea. A certain number of the military class were, perhaps, specially trained for the sea service ; [1] but all soldiers were supposed capable of being. sailors, and the same persons were often employed alternately in the sea and in the land services.[2] The galleys used were of no great size, being impelled by not more than from sixteen to twenty rowers,[3] and apparently not exceeding a length of thirty or forty feet. The hull was rounded, and rose at either extremity, the prow terminating usually in the head of an animal, while the stern, which was

Egyptian War-galley.

higher, tapered gradually to a point. Above the hull was a bulwark, carried from end to end of the boat, for the protection of the oarsmen. The middle portion of the boat must have been occupied by a raised deck, since the soldiers fight from it at a higher level than that occupied by the rowers. They are armed chiefly with bows and arrows, but sometimes

[1] So Wilkinson, *A. E.* vol. i. p. 274 (edition of 1878).

[2] See *Records of the Past*, vol. ii. pp. 5–6; vol. vi. pp. 7–10.

[3] Rosellini, *Mon. Storici*, pl. cxxxi.; Wilkinson, *A. E.* vol. iii. pp. 203–4; *Description de l'Egypte*, 'Antiquités,' vol. ii. pl. x.

have maces or spears in their right hands, while in their left they carry shields. The boat is guided by a man who sits at the stern on a raised seat, and manages a large paddle or steering-oar, which is attached to the side of the vessel. The vessel has a single mast, a long curved yard, and a large square sail, which in time of action is reefed by means of four ropes working through pulleys fixed in the yard. At the top of the mast is a bell-shaped receptacle, sufficiently large to contain a man; and here an expert archer or slinger seems to have been generally stationed, who played a similar part to that of our sharpshooters in the maintops.

Naval tactics can scarcely be said to have existed. Attempts were, perhaps, sometimes made to run down an enemy's vessel by striking it with the bow, armed as that was with a metal figurehead; and we may presume that the special aim would be to deliver the blow upon the side rather than the stem of the adverse galley.[1] But the evidence that we possess is insufficient to enable us to come to any positive conclusions on these points. A single representation of a sea-fight is all that has come down to us, and it gives us little information. The vessels represented in it seem to be stationary; and the engagement is between the soldiers who man the galleys on either side, rather than between the navies. One enemy's boat is, however, being sunk; and this, we may presume, has been disabled by its antagonist. The engagement is fought at one of the mouths of the Nile, and takes place so near the land, that the reigning Pharaoh, who is present with four of his sons, can take a part in the fight by shooting down the enemy from the shore.

---

[1] Wilkinson, A. E. vol. iii. p. 204.

In the interior waters of the Nile, a different and much larger kind of craft was employed;[1] and there can be little doubt that on some occasions these vessels were turned to account in the wars. We find an Ethiopian invader attacking Memphis with a fleet of ' boats, yachts, and barges,' blockading its port, and seeking to enter the town by means of the river.[2] What a foreign assailant could utilise in a sudden inroad, the Egyptians themselves are tolerably sure to have been in the habit of employing, either for attack or defence.[3] The Nile boats must have been especially serviceable as transports, since they were at least 120 feet long,[4] and could carry from fifty to a hundred men.

When the enemy ceased to resist, the Egyptians readily gave quarter; and the prisoners taken in an expedition are often counted by thousands.[5] If they ran down an enemy's ship, they exerted themselves to rescue the men on board from the waves, and drew them into their own vessels at some peril to themselves.[6] On land, those who laid down their weapons and sued for mercy were ordinarily spared; their arms were bound together by a cord passed round them a little above the elbows, and they were led from the field to the camp, generally in long strings, each conducted by a single Egyptian.[7] Laggards were induced to hasten

---

[1] For representations, see Lepsius, Denkmäler, vol. iii. pt. ii. pl. 45; vol. v. pl. 17; Description de l'Egypte, 'Antiquités,' vol. iv. pl. lxv. 3; vol. v. pl. xviii. 7.

[2] Records of the Past, vol. ii. pp. 95–6. Compare Brugsch, Geschichte Aegyptens, pp. 697–8.

[3] The use of the Nile boats in warfare is indicated in the Records of the Past, vol. ii. p. 6; vol. vi. p. 7; &c.

[4] Wilkinson, A. E. vol. iii. p. 205.

[5] Records of the Past, vol. ii. p. 45; vol. iv. p. 47; vol. viii. p. 48; &c.

[6] See the Description, 'Antiquités,' vol. ii. pl. x.

[7] Rosellini, Mon. Storici, pls. lxxxv., cxxxv., &c.; Lepsius, Denkmäler, vol. vi. pt. iii. pls. cxxix., cxxx., &c.

their movements by fear of the stick, which was no
doubt freely applied by those who had the prisoners in
charge. All captives were regarded as belonging to
the king, and naturally became his slaves, and were
employed by him in forced labours during the remainder
of their lives;[1] but sometimes the monarch was pleased
to reward individual captors by making over to them
their own prisoners,[2] who in that case passed into
private servitude. The ransom of prisoners seems not
to be mentioned, much less any exchange, as is customary in modern warfare. Whether important prisoners,

Prisoners of War, escorted by their Captor.

especially when regarded as guilty of rebellion, were or
were not sometimes put to death by the monarch in
cold blood, is a moot question, upon which different
opinions will probably be always held. On the one
side there are the frequent representations of kings
holding their captive enemies by the hair with one
hand, while in the other they brandish aloft a sword or
a mace, seeming to be in the act of striking a deadly
blow;[3] on the other side there is the belief of many

---

[1] Brugsch, *Geschichte Aegyptens*,
p. 551 ; Wilkinson, *A. E.* vol. i. pp.
402-3. Compare Herod. ii. 108.
[2] *Records of the Past*, vol. vi. pp.
8-9.
[3] Rosellini, *Mon. Storici*, pls.

lxiv., lxxix., cxi.; *Description de
l'Egypte,* 'Antiquités,' vol. ii. pl.
16 ; vol. iii. pls. 6 and 22 ; vol. iv.
pl. 22, fig. 11 ; Lepsius, *Denkmäler,*
vol. vi. pt. iii. pls. 130, 139, 140,
&c.

that these representations are allegorical, and that the
Egyptians were far too civilised to be guilty of wanton
cruelties.[1] If it be urged against this that the Assyrians,
who were not much less civilised than the Egyptians,
beyond all doubt, frequently put prisoners to death in
cold blood,[2] the reply may be made that the Assyrian
monarchs distinctly acknowledge, and indeed glory in,
the practice, whereas no mention of it appears in the
Egyptian records.   Nor do the Greek writers ever tax
the Egyptian monarchs with such barbarities.[3]   It is
the *Ethiopian*, Sabaco (Shabak), who puts to death the
captive Bocchoris.[4]

The treatment of the slain was less in accordance
with modern notions.   Mere wanton ill-usage was not
indeed encouraged ; but no reverence for the dead
restrained the kings from commanding, or the soldiers
from practising, a system of mutilation, which, though
prompted by an unobjectionable motive, is shocking to
modern sentiment.   It was considered important that
the numbers of the enemy who fell in a battle should
be accurately known ; and, with this object in view,
the Egyptian soldiers regarded it as their duty to cut
off and carry to the camp some easily recognisable
portion of each fallen enemy's person.   The right hand
was the part ordinarily selected ;[5] but sometimes the
tongue was preferred, and occasionally the organ of

---

[1] Wilkinson, *A. E.* vol. i. p. 398.
[2] See the author's *Ancient Monarchies*, vol. i. pp. 447–8, 2nd
edition.
[3] The only approach to an exception, so far as I know, is in the
case of Amasis, who after a time
consented to the death of Apries
(Herod. ii. 169).
[4] Manetho ap. Euseb. *Chron.
Can.* i. 20. (See the *Fragmenta Hist.*

Gr. vol. ii. p. 593 ; Fr. 65.)
[5] Wilkinson, *A. E.* vol. i. p.393.
Compare *Description de l'Egypte,*
'Antiquités,' vol. ii. pl. 12 ; Rosellini,
Mon. Storici, pls. 94 and 132. The
practice was so usual that, instead of
saying 'I killed one of the enemy,'
a man commonly said 'I carried off
a *hand.*' (See *Records of the Past,*
vol. vi. pp. 7–8, and compare vol.
iv. p. 7.)

reproduction.[1] Heaps of each are seen in the sculptures, which the royal scribes are represented as counting in the king's presence, previously to entering them upon the register. A reward appears to have been obtained by each soldier on his presentation of these proofs of his prowess,[2] a reward no doubt proportioned to their number. Under the Persians the bodies of slain Egyptians seem to have been left to rot upon the field of battle;[3] but, while their dominion lasted, the Egyptians, we may be sure, embalmed and buried their own dead, whatever became of the corpses of their adversaries.

The camps of the Egyptians were quadrangular, sometimes square, sometimes oblong.[4] They were not, so far as appears, entrenched, but simply defended by a palisade. The royal quarters occupied a central position, and were surrounded by a double rampart or fosse, with a considerable space between the two enclosures.[5] The king's tent was within the inner circuit, the outer one being allotted to his chief officers. A special portion of the camp was assigned to the horses and the baggage animals, another to the chariots and the baggage, the chariots being arranged in rows, not far from the horses. There was a certain place in the camp which served the purposes of a hospital, the sick, whether men or animals, being there collected together and carefully tended.[6] There was also within the camp a shrine, or centre for religious worship[7]—a spot

---

[1] Wilkinson, l.s.c. Compare *Records of the Past*, vol. vi. p. 19, line 8.

[2] *Records of the Past*, vol. vi. p. 8.

[3] Cf. Herod. iii. 12.

[4] Wilkinson, *A. E.* vol. i. p. 395.

Compare Lepsius, *Denkmäler*, vol. vi. pt. iii. pl. 128.

[5] Rosellini, *Mon. Storici*, pl. cvii.

[6] Kenrick, *Ancient Egypt*, vol. i. p. 229. See Rosellini, *Mon. Storici*, pl. xcviii.

[7] Rosellini, *Mon. Storici*, pl. xcix.

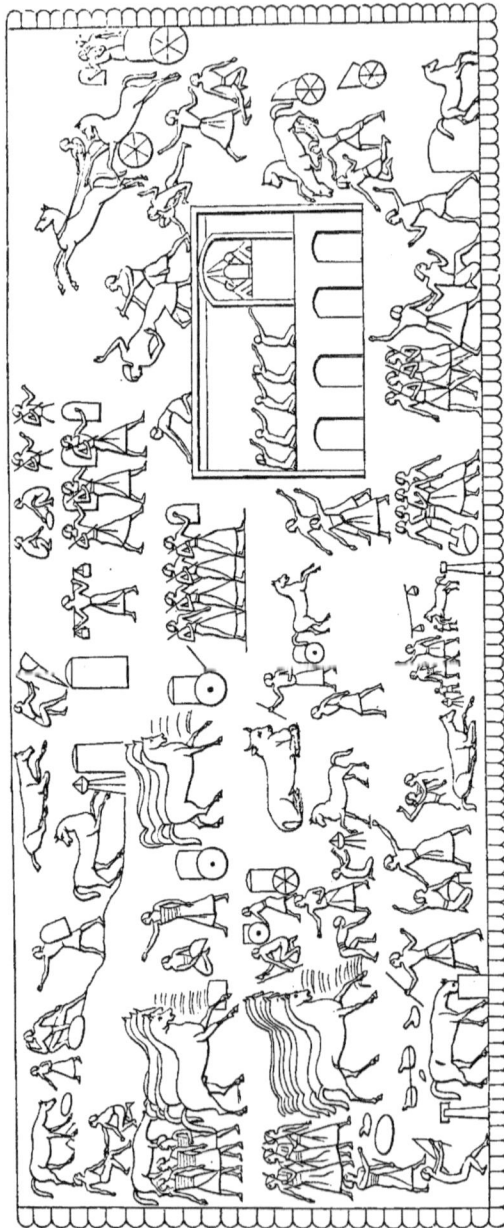

Part of the Interior of an Egyptian Camp.

where sacrifice could be offered, and the gods consulted when any doubt arose as to the proper course of action.

Within the limits of Egypt, troops were chiefly moved by water, along the Nile, its various branches, and the numerous canals ;[1] but when foreign countries —Arabia, Syria, Mesopotamia—had to be attacked, the Egyptian armies were forced, like most others, to accomplish marches. In these the chariot division commonly led the way, and was followed by a portion of the infantry ; after which came the monarch himself, mounted in his royal car, and accompanied by his chief officers and attendants, who, with their large fans or *flabella*,[2] sought at once to create a current of air, and to keep off the flies from the royal person. Behind the royal *cortége* followed the rest of the troops, arranged in the various corps of archers, spearmen, clubmen, &c. The cavalry probably covered the flanks of the army, acting upon the wings, and throwing out scouts in advance to give notice of the approach of an enemy.

Egyptian Trumpeters.

The signal for an attack was given, when the enemy's presence was reached, by the sound of the trumpet ; and the same instrument was employed, on the march of an army, both for

---

[1] *Records of the Past,* vol. ii. pp. 6, 82, 85 ; vol. vi. pp. 7, 10, &c.
[2] Wilkinson, *A. E.* vol. i. p. 391.

For an illustration, see Rosellini, *Mon. Storici,* pl. cxxxvii.

starting and halting the columns.[1] The Egyptian trumpet was a long tube, apparently of brass, expanded at the end into a large bell-shaped mouth. It was commonly held in a horizontal position with both hands, the upper end being pressed against the lips.[2] The drum and trumpet seem to have been used together upon a march for the enlivenment of the soldiers, and in order to regulate their movements. The drum employed was one of small diameter, but of considerable length, and was played by the hands without the intervention of a drumstick.[3]

Egyptian Military Drum.

On his return from an expedition, the monarch always claimed to have been successful, and made a grand display of the fruits of his victories. The troops marched in jubilant procession before him and behind him, carrying often, besides their arms, branches of trees,[4] and sometimes bearing, in their hands or on their shoulders, the most important products of the countries visited. The chariot of the monarch was accompanied by some of his great officers, and preceded or followed closely by a train of captives, with their arms bound or hands manacled, and generally united together by a long rope, the end of which was held by the Pharaoh himself, or else fastened to his car.[5] As he approached the various towns which lay upon his route, the Egyptians came out to meet him with acclamations, raising their

Egyptian Captive.

---

[1] Wilkinson, l.s.c. ; and vol. ii. p. 260.

[2] See Rosellini, *Mon. Storici*, pl. xliv. ter.

[3] Wilkinson, *A. E.* vol. ii. p. 260. Compare p. 264.

[4] Ibid. vol. i. pp. 400–1.

[5] See Rosellini, *Mon. Storici*, pls. l., lviii., and cxxxvii.

hands aloft, and bringing him bouquets of flowers, green boughs, and branches of palm.[1]   Arrived in his capital, the monarch proceeded to the principal temple for the purpose of making acknowledgments to the deity to whom he attributed his victories.   There, before the image of the god, he offered the choicest parts of the spoil, vases, incense, bags of money (?), rhytons, jars of ointment, and the like, and at the same time made presentation of a large number of his captives,[2] who were added to the sacred slaves previously possessed by the temple.   The troops seem to have attended the ceremony, though they are not often represented, and to have returned thanks for their own preservation, a priest in this case interposing between the god and the worshippers, and offering on their behalf incense, meat-offerings, and libations.[3]

The condition of the *fellahin*, or agricultural labourers, has been already indicated to some extent in what has been said, in the chapter on Egyptian Agriculture, concerning the tenure of the land and the manner in which it was cultivated.[4]   It is possible, however, that somewhat too favourable a view has been there taken.   The number of peasants rich enough to rent farms and cultivate on their own account was probably small ; and the great majority of the class had to content themselves with the position of hired labourers, and to work on the estates of others.   These persons laboured under overseers, who were generally severe taskmasters, and who, at their discretion, might punish the idle or refractory by

---

[1] Lepsius, *Denkmäler*, vol. vi. pt. iii. pl. 128.   Compare Wilkinson, *A. E.* vol. i. p. 399.
[2] Rosellini, *Mon. Storici*, pls.
xlviii., lii., and lvi.
[3] Wilkinson, *A. E.* vol. i. p. 400.
[4] See above, pp. 154-6.

blows.[1] The peasant farmer was somewhat better off; but even his position was scarcely enviable, and Egyptian authors not unfrequently hold him up to their readers as an object of pity. 'Have you ever represented to yourself,' writes Amenemun to Pentaour,[2] 'the estate of the rustic who tills the ground? Before he has put the sickle to the crop, the locusts have blasted a part of it; then come the rats and the birds. If he is slack in housing his grain, the thieves are upon him. His horse dies of weariness as it drags the wain. Anon, the tax-gatherer arrives; his

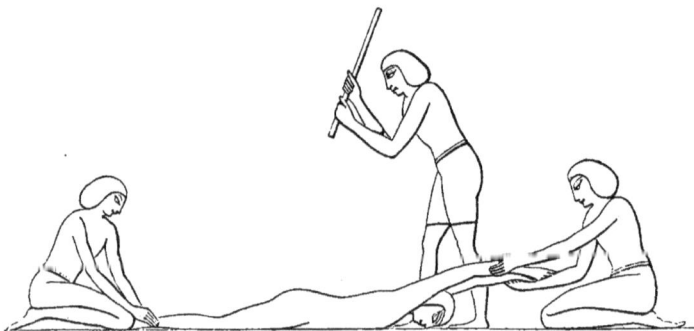

Egyptian undergoing the Bastinado.

agents are armed with clubs; he has negroes with him, who carry whips of palm branches. They all cry, "Give us your grain!" and he has no easy way of avoiding their extortionate demands. Next, the wretch is caught, bound, and sent off to work without wage at the canals; his wife is taken and chained; his children are stripped and plundered.' In the 'Praise of Learning' by Tuaufsakhrat, a very similar description is

[1] Brugsch, *Geschichte Aegyptens*, p. 26.
[2] See Mons. St. Leon's 'Egypt of the Khedive' (London, 1877), whence the subjoined passage is taken.

given.[1] 'The little labourer having a field, he passes his life among rustics; he is worn down for vines and pigs, to make his kitchen of what his fields have; his clothes are heavy with their weight; he is bound as a forced labourer; if he goes forth into the air, he suffers, having to quit his warm fireplace; he is bastinadoed with a stick on his legs, and seeks to save himself; shut against him is the hall of every house, locked are all the chambers.' It appears from these passages that not only was the weight of taxation felt by the small cultivator to be oppressive, and the conduct of the tax-gatherer to be brutal, but that forced labours were from time to time imposed on him, and the stick and cord employed if he resisted. Torn from his family and homestead, and compelled to work under the hot Egyptian sun at cleaning out or banking up the canals, no wages paid him, and insufficient food supplied, he doubtless shared too frequently the lot of modern forced excavators, and perished under the hardships which a cruel government imposed on him. If a tough constitution enabled him to escape this fate and return home, he might find his family dispersed, his wife carried off, and his mud cabin a heap of ruins!

Add to all this, that at the best of times he was looked upon with contempt,[2] not only by the privileged classes, but by their servants—perhaps even by their slaves—and it will be evident that to the cultivators of the soil Egypt under the Pharaohs was far from being

---

[1] *Records of the Past*, vol. viii. p. 149. We may suspect that the picture is somewhat over-coloured, since the writer is bent on finding fault with every occupation but that of a scribe, and abuses not only the life of the 'little labourer,' but those of the blacksmith, carpenter, mason, barber, boatman, gardener, weaver, armourer, courier, dyer, shoemaker, washerman, fowler, and fisherman, which he represents as all equally detestable.

[2] Brugsch, *Geschichte Aegyptens*, p. 23.

an Arcadia. On the whole the difference would seem not
to have been so very great between the condition of
the children of the soil in the most flourishing period
of the independent monarchy and in the Egypt of
to-day.

A more independent and enviable position was
enjoyed by the tradesmen and artisans, who dwelt
chiefly in the towns. Trade flourished under the
Pharaohs, and was encouraged not only by the lavish
expenditure of the Court, of the high ecclesiastics, and
of the great nobles, but also by the vast demand which
there was for Egyptian productions in foreign countries.
Though the Egyptians themselves rarely engaged in
foreign trade either by land or sea,[1] yet their country
was sought from very ancient times by a host of
foreign traders, Phœnicians, Greeks, Syrians, Arabs,
who brought with them the commodities of their own
lands or of other more distant ones, and exchanged
them for the finished productions of the Egyptian
manufacturers.[2] Syria took Egyptian chariots by hundreds;[3] Tyre imported ' fine linen with broidered
work;'[4] Greece, large quantities of paper;[5] India and
Arabia, linen fabrics;[6] Etruria, glass, porcelain, and
alabaster;[7] Assyria, perhaps, ivories.[8] In the earlier
times Egyptian manufactures must have been altogether unrivalled; and their glass, their pottery, their
textile fabrics, their metal-work, must have circulated

---

[1] Mr. Kenrick (*Ancient Egypt*,
vol. i. pp. 212–13) has some good
remarks on this subject.

[2] See Gen. xxxvii. 25; Herod. i.
1; ii. 178; iii. 6.

[3] 1 Kings x. 29; 2 Chr. i. 17.
On the numerous chariots of the
Syrians, see *Records of the Past*,
vol. ii. p. 69, and *Ancient Monar-*

chies, vol. ii. p. 103, note[7], 2nd edit.

[4] Ezek. xxvii. 7.

[5] Herod. v. 58.

[6] Plin. *H. N.* xix. 1, § 2.

[7] Wilkinson, *A. E.* vol. iii. p.
111.

[8] See the author's *Ancient Monarchies*, vol. i. pp. 373–5.

freely through the various countries bordering the Mediterranean and the Red Sea. All this gave a vast stimulus to trade, and encouraged the artisans to fresh efforts after improvement, which resulted in works of continually increasing excellence. Though in taste and elegance the Greeks ultimately far surpassed the dwellers on the Nile, yet in perfection of mechanical construction and finish the latter have scarcely been outdone by any nation; and their fine linen, their glass-work, their porcelain, their veneering and inlaying of wood, together with various other products and processes, excite admiration at the present day.[1]

The most important trades appear to have been those of building, stone-cutting, weaving, furniture-making, chariot-making, glass-blowing, pottery, metallurgy, boat-building, and embalming. The builders worked in three materials, wood, stone, and brick, preferring stone on the whole, and using several of the choicest and hardest kinds. The skill exhibited in many of their contrivances is great; and the mechanical excellence of their works is sufficiently evinced by the continuance of so many of them to the present day. Still, a certain timidity is observable in the employment of over-massive and over-numerous supports, and a certain rudeness and want of enterprise in the constant adherence to the simplest possible mode of roofing an edifice—viz., by laying wooden beams or long blocks of stone across the entire space to be covered in. What results they were able to achieve with brick and wood, we have no sufficient means of judging, since no works in these materials remain except some brick pyramids of the rudest kind; but they had certainly

---

[1] Wilkinson, *A. E.* vol. iii. pp. 102, 103, 120, &c.; Kenrick, *Ancient Egypt,* vol. i. pp. 214-20.

reason to be proud of their stone edifices, which are in
many respects unsurpassed by later ages. But so
much has been said on this subject in the chapter on
Egyptian architecture that it seems unnecessary to
dwell upon it any further here.[1]

Stone-cutting included the two very different occupations of quarrying and shaping blocks for the builder,
and of cutting, polishing, and engraving gems. In the
former branch the Egyptians remain still unrivalled.
The size of their blocks, the exactness and accuracy
with which the angle required was produced, the
apparent ease with which they worked the stubbornest
material, the perfect smoothness of the surface, and
excellence of the polish put on it, have often been

Egyptian Saw.

remarked upon, and are said to leave nothing to be
desired.[2] It is doubtful whether the steam-sawing of
the present day could be trusted to produce in ten
years from the quarries of Aberdeen a single obelisk,
such as those which the Pharaohs set up by dozens.
In the other branch of the business the Egyptians have
no doubt been surpassed by many nations: their
engravings have little beauty, and they do not seem to
have triumphed over the difficulty of cutting really
' hard stones.' Such gems as the diamond, the ruby,
the emerald, the sapphire, the topaz, and the chryso-
beryl, defied their skill; but they could deal with the

---

[1] See above, pp. 201, 207–8, 256, &c.

[2] Vyse, *Pyramids of Ghizeh*, vol. i. p. 289 ; Bunsen, *Egypt's Place*, vol. ii. p. 164; Fergusson, *History of Architecture*, vol. i. pp. 91–2; &c.

amethyst, the carnelian, the garnet, and the jasper,
with hæmatite, porphyry, lapis lazuli, green felspar.
obsidian, serpentine, and steatite.[1] It was not commonly their practice to engrave gems in the ordinary
way; the Egyptians preferred to shape them into
certain forms, as rings, beads, eyes, hearts, sphinxes,
and scarabæi,[2] and then (sometimes) to inscribe them
further with figures of deities or hieroglyphics.   There
is little delicacy and little grace in these engravings,
which are rough, shallow, and unfinished.

The cutting of blocks was ordinarily effected by
the saw,[3] which was single-handed, and worked by a
single sawyer.[4]   But some-
times the pick and chisel
were employed to a certain
extent, and then wedges of
dry wood were inserted,
which on being wetted ex-
panded, and split off the
required block from the
mass of stone in the quarry.[5]
It is supposed[6] that the
tools used, being mostly of
bronze, must, when em-
ployed to cut granite, ba-
salt, or stone of similar quality, have been moistened
and dipped in emery powder, and that the same

Process of smoothing Stone.

---

[1] Birch, *Guide to Museum*, pp.
70-4.   These are the materials ordinarily used.   Agate is perhaps to
be added to them.   (Wilkinson,
A. E. vol. iii. p. 376.)
[2] Birch, *Guide to Museum*, pp.
67-80.
[3] Wilkinson, *A. E.* vol. iii. p.
251, note.
[4] The sawing of stone is not re-

presented on the monuments; but
Wilkinson was of opinion that the
Egyptians possessed the single-handed saw only (*A. E.* vol. iii. p. 172).
[5] Wilkinson, *A. E.* vol. iii. p.
337; Kenrick, *Ancient Egypt*, vol.
i. pp. 218-19.
[6] Wilkinson, vol. iii. pp. 106
and 251.

substance must have lent its force to the implements
whereby the engraving and shaping of gems was effected.
Emery powder was not difficult to obtain, since it is
produced by the islands of the Archipelago. Whether
or no the Egyptians employed the lapidary's wheel
appears to be doubtful. Blocks of stone, however obtained from the quarries, were finally smoothed and
prepared for use by means of the chisel and mallet.[1]

Herodotus states that weaving in Egypt was the
occupation of men only, not of women, and declares

Women weaving.

that the woof was always worked upwards by the
Egyptians, and not downwards, as by other nations;[2]
but the native monuments show that men and women
were alike employed both in spinning and weaving,
and that the woof was worked indifferently either up

[1] Wilkinson, *A. E.* vol. iii. p.
335. (See the woodcut on the preceding page.)
[2] Herod. ii. 35.

or down.[1] The Egyptian loom was of the most primitive description,[2] the shuttle being passed across by
the hand and not thrown, and all the needful movements being effected entirely by the weaver himself,
who, if a man, ordinarily sat in front of his frame.
It is wonderful what exquisite fabrics were produced by these simple means. The Egyptians worked
in linen, in cotton, and in wool, producing good
results in every case ; but their favourite textile manufacture was that of linen, and it is in this branch that
their fabrics are most remarkable.[3] The fineness of
some equals that of the best Indian muslin,[4] while of
others it is said that ' in touch they are comparable to
silk, and in texture to our finest cambric.'[5] Originally
the linen was extremely white ;[6] but sometimes it
was dyed red,[7] and at other times the edges were
coloured with indigo, either in a single line or in
several stripes.[8] Patterns were occasionally inwrought
during the weaving,[9] while sometimes they were super-
added by a process analogous to that which in modern
times is called printing.[10] Gold threads were also in
some cases introduced to give additional richness to
the fabric,[11] which was often as transparent as lawn[12]
and of silky softness.

---

[1] Kenrick, *Ancient Egypt*, vol. i.
pp. 216–17 ; Wilkinson in the author's *Herodotus*, vol. ii. pp. 54–5,
3rd edition.

[2] Wilkinson, *A. E.* vol. iii. p.
118.

[3] The Egyptian linen corselets
were noted as most remarkable by
the ancients (Herod. ii. 182 ; iii.
47 ; Plin. *H. N.* xix. 1 ; &c.)

[4] Wilkinson, *A. E.* vol. iii. p.
121.

[5] Ibid. p. 119.

[6] Birch, *Guide to Museum*, p. 51.

[7] Wilkinson, *A. E.* vol. iii. p.
126 ; Birch, l.s.c.

[8] Wilkinson, vol. iii. p. 123.

[9] Ibid. p. 125.

[10] Ibid. pp. 126 and 128.

[11] Herod. iii. 47 ; Ex. xxxix. 3 ;
Wilkinson, *A. E.* vol. iii. p. 128.

[12] The transparency of the Egyptian fabrics is strikingly illustrated
by the painted sculptures, where
the entire form, especially of women,
is often made distinctly visible
through the outer garment.

The poet who bewails the misery of the 'little labourer' has a word of lamentation for the weaver likewise. 'The weaver,' he says,[1] 'inside the houses is more wretched than a woman ; his knees are at the place of his heart; he has not tasted the air. Should he have done but a little in a day of his weaving, he is dragged as a lily in a pool. He gives bread to the porter at the door, that he may be allowed to see the light.' Confinement, close rooms, a cramped position, are no doubt evils; but they are common to many handicrafts and scarcely separable from that of the hand-loom weaver. So far, then, the Egyptian workman had no special cause of complaint. If he was literally 'dragged in a pool' by an angry employer when he had been idle,[2] he may to some extent claim our pity, though an idle man is perhaps the better for a little punishment ; but if the poet merely meant that he *looked* like a draggled lily after a few hours' hard work in so hot a climate, we need not shed many tears over his hard lot. If the work-room was insufficiently lighted, and he had to bribe the porter to keep the door open, we may admit that he had a grievance, but one not altogether intolerable.

Upholstery must in Egypt have employed a large number of persons, since the opulent class was numerous, and took a pride in having its houses handsomely furnished.[3] The empty and bare interiors affected by

---

[1] *Records of the Past*, vol. viii. p. 151.
[2] This is one meaning assigned to the passage. (See the *Records*, vol. viii. p. 151, note [5].)
[3] The subject of the Egyptian furniture has been so copiously and so excellently discussed and illus-trated by Sir G. Wilkinson (*Ancient Egyptians*, vol. ii. pp. 190-222) that nothing new, which should also be true, can be said about it. I have therefore been content with the briefest possible summary.

modern Orientals were not at all to the Egyptian taste. Elegant chairs,[1] with or without arms, fauteuils, sofas, ottomans, and low stools of various kinds garnished the Egyptian reception rooms, where every guest expected to find a seat awaiting him, since only the attendants and the professionals stood, and sitting on the ground, though sometimes practised, does not seem to have been fashionable.[2] Tables, moreover, round, square, or oblong, sometimes delicately inlaid with ivory or with rare woods,[3] sometimes supported on a carved

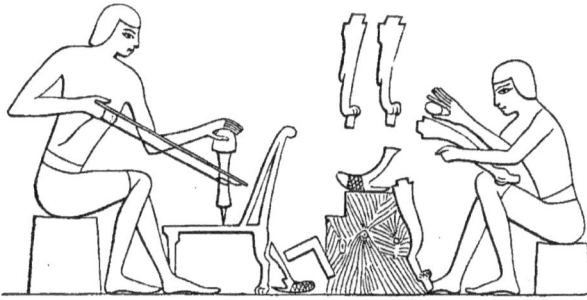

Furniture-making.

human figure,[4] were essential to the completeness of an apartment. Footstools also constituted a necessary part of the furniture of a sitting room; while stands for jars or flowers, folding-stools, and boxes or cabinets for holding various objects were also common.[5] For the sleeping apartments, rich beds or couches, with mat-

[1] See Wilkinson, pl. xi., and compare Rosellini, *Mon. Civ.* pls. lxxiv., xc., and xci. The close resemblance of the Egyptian arm-chairs and of some of their couches and ottomans to modern ones is very remarkable. (See Wilkinson, vol. ii. pp. 195, 199, 201, &c.; Rosellini, pls. xc.–xcii.)

[2] Birch says, 'the Egyptians sat on chairs or on the ground' (*Egypt from the Earliest Times,* 'Introduction,' p. xiv.); but, except on their first admission and at certain games, the *guests* in a house are almost always represented as seated either on chairs or stools. (See Wilkinson, *A. E.* vol. ii. pp. 191, 214, 390, 393, and pl. xii.)

[3] Wilkinson, *A. E.* vol. ii. p. 203.

[4] Ibid. p. 202.

[5] Birch, *Guide to Museum,* p. 22.

tresses, pillows, and cushions, were required, together
with toilet-tables, chairs, wardrobes, and wooden head-
rests of a peculiar fashion.[1] These consisted commonly

Head-rest.

of a pillar or pedestal supporting
a curved, semi-elliptical piece of
wood, acacia, sycomore, or tamarisk, adapted to receive the back
of the head, which fitted into it.
Though it is said that Egyptian
houses were, 'on the whole,
lightly furnished, and not en-
cumbered with so many articles
as are in use at the present day,'[2] yet it is clear that
to provide the objects enumerated for the very large
number of wealthy persons who dwelt in the great
cities, often possessing country villas besides their town
residences, a numerous class of skilled artificers must
have been required, who, it is reasonable to suppose,
were well paid for their labours.

Chariot-making, or coach-building, as it would be
called in modern times, was also an important trade,
and must have occupied no small number. The kings
maintained a chariot-force of at least several hundreds ;[3] and every well-to-do Egyptian gentleman had
his own private vehicle, which constituted his ordinary
means of locomotion.[4] Four-wheeled cars were required for certain sacred ceremonies.[5] The export of
chariots was also probably considerable,[6] and perhaps
extended to other countries besides Syria.[7] Coach-

---

[1] Wilkinson, A. E. vol. ii. pp.
201, 204, and 205 ; Birch, l.s.c. ;
Rosellini, Mon. Civ. pl. xcii.

[2] Birch, Guide to Museum, p. 23.

[3] See above, p. 450.

[4] Wilkinson, A. E. vol. i. p. 335.

[5] Herod. ii. 63. For a representation, see Wilkinson, A. E. vol.
ii. p. 341.

[6] 1 Kings x. 29.

[7] The native Libyans, who, according to Herodotus (iv. 189), were

makers are seen at work in the Egyptian sculptures, engaged in fashioning all the various constituent parts of the usual vehicle, the seat, the rim, the pole, the yoke, the wheels, the fittings.[1] These were chiefly made either of wood or leather, very little metal being employed in the construction. The felloes of the wheels, however, were for the most part strengthened

Chariot-making.

with bronze or brass bands, and the tire consisted always of a hoop of metal.[2] If the price which foreigners paid for a chariot was three hundred Jewish shekels,[3]

the first to yoke four horses to a chariot, probably obtained their vehicles from Egypt.
  [1] For full representations, see Wilkinson, *A. E.* vol. i. pp. 343, 349, and 350; Rosellini, *Mon. Civili,* pl. xliv. figs. 3 and 4.

  [2] Wilkinson, vol. i. p. 348.
  [3] The 'six hundred shekels' of 1 Kings x. 29 seem to be rightly regarded as paid for the chariot *and pair of horses.* (See the *Speaker's Commentary,* vol. ii. p. 545.) As the price of each horse was 150

or about forty-five pounds of our money, the trade must have been sufficiently remunerative.

The invention of glass, which the later Romans attributed to the Phœnicians of Tyre,[1] is with reason claimed for Egypt,[2] where glass-blowing appears to have been practised, at least from the time of the twelfth dynasty.[3] Really colourless transparent glass was not produced, the nearest approach to it being found in vases of a bottle-green colour, with conical or globular bodies and long necks, which are thought to belong to about the sixth century B.C.[4] The earlier

Glass-blowing.

bottles and vases are of an opaque or semi-opaque material, with backgrounds of light or dark blue, and wavy lines of yellow, light blue, and white running in horizontal bands on the surface round the body of the vessel. No objects of any large size were produced ; nor does glass appear to have been in common use at entertainments. In the main, it was reserved for the toilet and the toilet-table, being employed to contain

shekels (1 Kings, l.s.c.), the sum paid for the chariot would have been 300 shekels.

[1] Plin. *H. N.* xxxvi. 26.

[2] Wilkinson, *A. E.* vol. iii. pp. 88–92. The claim was made, before Wilkinson's time, by M. Boudet in his essay 'Sur l'Art de la Verrerie, né en Egypte,' published

in the *Description de l'Egypte*, 'Antiquités,' vol. ii. pp. 7 et seqq.

[3] Birch, *Guide to Museum,* p. 119.

[4] Ibid. Specimens will be found in the 'Second Egyptian Room' of the British Museum, Case *t*, Nos. 4750–3.

the unguents, perfumes, stibium, and other dyes for
the eyebrows and eyelids, which were in constant use
among the Egyptians of both sexes ;[1] and also for
ornaments of the person, such as necklaces, bracelets,
ear-rings, and the like.[2] Glass was also largely employed for the decoration of mummies by means of a
network of beads and bugles,[3] which was placed outside the linen wrappings, covering the entire figure,
and often terminating in a fringe below. It was likewise used for inlaying and mosaic work,[4] together with
artificial pastes, and such substances as lapis lazuli,

Specimens of Egyptian Glass Vessels.

agate, &c. Sometimes, but rarely, small figures of
gods and animals were produced in the material.[5]

Egyptian pottery embraced the varieties of a coarse
red, black, or yellow earthenware, suitable for the
wants of the common people, a finer terra-cotta, adap-

[1] Wilkinson, *A. E.* vol. iii. p.
382 ; Birch, *Egypt from the Earliest Times*, 'Introduction,' p. xv.
　[2] Birch, *Guide to Museum*, pp.
67, 70, &c.
　[3] Wilkinson, *A. E.* vol. iii. p.
101 ; Birch, *Guide to Museum*, p.
101.
　[4] Wilkinson, p. 102 ; Birch, p.
120.
　[5] Birch, *Guide to Museum*, p.
131.

ted not only for vases, diotæ, amphoræ, &c., but also
for human and animal figures, and a beautiful porcelain or faïence, which was of many different colours,
and was applied, like the terra-cotta, to a great variety
of purposes. The ordinary earthenware was used for
vases, bowls, plates, pans, bottles, amphoræ, cups, jugs,
and the like ;[1] it was not of a very good material,
and was consequently made of more than the usual
thickness. Three kinds are distinguished, the unglazed, the glazed, and the painted.[2] The glaze em-

Specimens of ordinary Egyptian Pottery.

ployed is of a vitreous character, and seems to have
been added after the vessels had been baked. In the
painted specimens, the colours have been laid on in
tempera. Almost all the various utensils found appear
to have been shaped by the wheel,[3] which must thus
have been of an extreme antiquity in Egypt, while in

---

[1] Birch, *Guide to Museum*, pp.
33-35.
[2] Ibid. p. 33.
[3] Birch, *Ancient Pottery*, p. 25.
In the representations given by Lepsius of very early pottery (*Denkmäler*, vol. iv. pt. ii. pl. 153) there
are a few which, from the irregularity of their shape, would seem to
have been wholly modelled by the
hand. (See particularly Nos. 3,
29, and 32.) But these are rare
exceptions ; and the great majority
of the vessels found with them,
which belong to the time of the
fourth and fifth dynasties, bear clear
traces of the wheel.

other countries it was a comparatively recent introduction.[1]   The shapes of the common kind of vessels,
though not so elegant and refined as those which pre-

Elegant Vases and Amphoræ.

vailed in Greece and in Etruria, are comparable with
any that were in use elsewhere at the time, and in many
instances must be pronounced decidedly graceful and

[1] At Athens it was said to have
been invented, *i.e.* introduced, by
Corœbus (Plin. vii. 56), about B.C.
776.   In Babylonia it was certainly not employed by the early
potters.   (See the author's *Ancient
Monarchies*, vol. i. p. 91.)

pleasing.[1]   The glazed vessels were of superior quality
to the unglazed, and sometimes affected human or animal shapes.[2]   They were often ornamented with bands,
and occasionally inscribed with a few hieroglyphics.[3]
The painted vases and amphoræ were either simply
decorated with ' annular bands of a black or purple
colour, running round the body or neck,' or had a
hatching of thin lines uniting the bands, or ' the representation of a collar pendent from the shoulder of the
vase, painted in blue, black, and red.'[4]   But the most
recherché and elaborate ornamentation consisted in
colouring the entire vase with a ground in distemper,
and then painting it with straight or festooned lines,
or leaves of plants, or even animals disporting themselves among shrubs and lotus-flowers.[5]

In terra-cotta the Egyptians produced chiefly vases,
especially those intended to receive the intestines of
the dead,[6] sepulchral cones,[7] mummied figures,[8] and
statuettes of deities.[9]   The material used is only of
middling quality, and was frequently concealed by
paint.[10]   It was not much affected, excepting for sepul-

[1] Birch says with reason: ' The
Egyptian potters had not, it is true,
that highly refined sense of the
beautiful which the Greeks possessed ; but they were by no means
entirely destitute of it.' (*Ancient
Pottery*, p. 33.)
[2] Examples will be found in the
First Egyptian Room at the British
Museum, Nos. 4860, 5114, and 5116.
[3] See, in the same collection, Nos.
4860, 4864, and 5117 ; and compare Leemans, *Mon. Egyptiens*, pl.
lxiii., No. 367.
[4] Birch, *Ancient Pottery*, p. 35.
[5] Ibid. p. 36. Compare Rosellini, *Mon. Civili*, pl lvi. No. 108 ;
pl. lx. No. 3 ; and see above, p. 495.
[6] See above, p. 397, and compare

Birch, *Ancient Pottery*, pp. 23–4 ;
Guide to Museum, pp. 89–94.
[7] Wilkinson, *A. E.* vol. v. p.
398 ; Birch, *Ancient Pottery*, pp.
18–21 ; Prisse, *Mon. Egyptiens*,
pls. 23, 27, and 28.
[8] Birch, *Ancient Pottery*, pp. 21–
22 ; *Guide to Museum*, p. 89.
[9] British Museum, First Egyptian
Room, No. 1296 ; Second Room,
Cases 96 and 97. These figures,
and the sepulchral or mummied
ones, are, however, regarded as of
late date. They belong probably
to Roman times.
[10] The vases for the intestines are
generally painted. (British Museum,
Second Room, Nos. 9530–5, 9547–
50, 9552–4, &c.)

chral cones, in the time of the independent monarchy, but came into more general use during the Ptolemaic and Roman periods.

The Egyptian porcelain, or faïence, as it is said to be more properly termed,[1] was composed of white sand, slightly fused,[2] and covered with a coloured glaze or enamel, the constituents of which are somewhat doubtful.[3] Porcelain was employed for vases of various kinds, for glazed tiles, sepulchral figures, pectoral plates, symbolic eyes, beads and bugles, scarabæi, rings, and statuettes. The vases are usually of a blue or apple-green colour, and have for the most part a form resembling somewhat that of a lotus flower, consisting of round basins, or bowls, or tall cups, superimposed upon a low stand or stem.[4] Some of them are ornamented with figures of men and animals, with water-plants, or with other

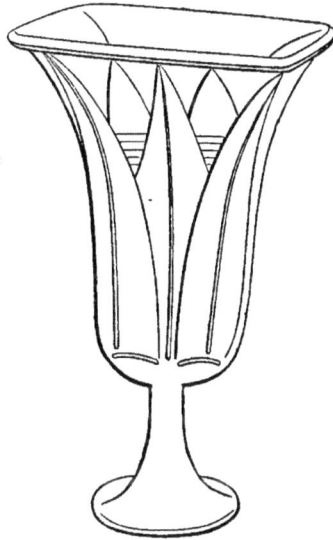

Egyptian Porcelain Vase.

objects. A few are glazed in various colours, as yellow, violet, and white. Some bear the name and titles of the reigning Pharaoh.[5]

The glazed tiles seem to have been used for mural decoration only. They have been found almost ex-

---

[1] Birch, *Ancient Pottery*, p. 47.
[2] Birch, *Guide to Museum*, p. 30.
[3] Birch (*Ancient Pottery*, p. 48) laments that 'no very recent analysis' of Egyptian glazes 'has been made;' and that consequently 'we are compelled to acquiesce in the conjectures of archæologists, rather than to adopt the tests of chemists.'
[4] Birch, *Guide to Museum*, l.s.c.
[5] British Museum, First Room, Nos. 4766 and 4796.

clusively at one place,[1] where they belonged to a palace
of Rameses III., which was composed of unbaked
bricks and ornamented with the tiles in question. Like
those which decorated the walls of some Babylonian
palaces,[2] they presented in their combination a series
of pictures, representing the king returning victorious
from his military expeditions, with prisoners and tro-
phies, and other similar subjects. In most instances
the figures were first marked out by depressions in the
tiles, which depressions were afterwards filled in with
coloured glass or pastes, with alabaster, terra-cotta, or
glazed sandstone;[3] but in some cases the figures are
in relief upon a flat ground, and the work resembles
modern Palissy ware. 'Portions of the garments and
the backgrounds are inlaid with coloured pastes of
various colours; the features and flesh of the limbs are
appropriately glazed, and the hair, or head-dress, especially of the negroes, of coloured pastes. They are well
made, and fine specimens of toreutic work in relief.'[4]

Pectoral plates were borne by almost all mummies,
being suspended on the neck or throat. They are
usually shaped like an Egyptian doorway, with its re-
curved cornice,[5] and represent, in outline or in relief,
some sacred scene connected with the lower world, as
the adoration of Anubis, the boat of the sun bearing
the scarabæus and saluted by Isis and Nephthys, the
worship of Osiris by the deceased, the human-headed
hawk (Horus), or a train of goddesses. Occasionally,
portions of the design are coloured by inlaying with
pastes.[6]

[1] The *Tel-el-Yahoudeh*, or supposed 'Place of Oneias.' (See Birch,
Ancient Pottery, p. 49.)
[2] *Ancient Monarchies*, vol. ii. p.
552.
[3] Birch, *Guide to Museum*, p.
118.
[4] Birch, *Ancient Pottery*, p. 50.
[5] Ibid. p. 60.
[6] British Museum, Second Room,
No. 7866.

The porcelain statuettes are representations of gods or genii. They are usually not more than from one to two inches in height; but some have been found which a little exceed a foot. Ordinarily they are of no great merit, the forms being conventional and stiff, the spaces between the limbs 'reserved,'[1] and the workmanship indifferent; but a few exceptions occur. 'Some of these figures are of exquisite style, and rather resemble gems than porcelain in the fineness of their details.' Others 'have the limbs detached,' and show some 'freedom of position.'[2] But the forms of the Egyptian gods are for the most part so disagreeable, and the head-

Potters at Work.

dresses so disfiguring, that even in the best specimens of porcelain or other statuettes there is little beauty.

It will be evident to the reader that the various branches of the potter's art which have been here described must have given employment to a very large number of persons, some of whom must have possessed considerable artistic talents and advanced technical knowledge. The Egyptian glazing is often of the very finest character; the colours used are sometimes exqui-

---

[1] That is, not cut away. On this peculiarity of Egyptian figure-work, see above, p. 263.
[2] Birch, *Ancient Pottery*, p. 64.

K K 2

site ; and the skill displayed in suiting the glaze to the material great. A high class of artists was no doubt employed for much of the work, and these persons, we may presume, were well remunerated and lived comfortable lives. But in the lower walks of the trade no great skill was needed ; and the class which produced the ordinary coarse ware, and which is seen at work in the sepulchral chambers of Beni Hassan,[1] was probably composed of persons who were not held in much account, and may have consisted in part of slaves.[2]

Metallurgy in Egypt comprised the working in gold, in silver and lead to a small extent, in copper, in iron, and in bronze. Tin appears to have been scarcely used except as an alloy,[3] while zinc was wholly unknown. The Egyptians found gold in considerable quantities within the limits of their own land, chiefly in veins of quartz towards the south-eastern parts of the country.[4] After digging out the quartz they broke it up by hand into small pieces,[5] which were then passed on to the mill, and ground to powder between two flat granite mill-stones of no great size, this work again being performed by manual labour. The quartz thus reduced to powder was washed on inclined tables, furnished with one or two cisterns, until all the earthy matter was separated and washed away, flowing down

[1] See the woodcut on p. 499; and compare Rosellini, *Mon. Civ.* pl. l.; Wilkinson, *A. E.* vol. iii. p. 164.
[2] So Birch, *Ancient Pottery*, p. 37 : 'Potters held a low position in Egypt; and the occupation was pursued by servants or slaves.'
[3] A few plates of pure tin seem to occur among the objects found with mummies. They are placed as amulets to guard the incisions on the flanks, through which the intestines were extracted, and commonly have

on one side the right symbolic eye, the emblem of the god Shu. (See Birch in his edition of Wilkinson's *Ancient Egyptians*, vol. ii. p. 232; and compare *Guide to Museum*, p. 81.)
[4] See above, p. 93.
[5] The whole of this description is taken from Diodorus (iii. 12–14), who describes, no doubt, the process employed in his own day. It is probable, however, that the very simple method then in use had come down from a remote antiquity.

the incline with the water. The gold particles which remained were carefully collected and formed into ingots by exposure to the heat of a furnace for five days and nights in earthen crucibles, which were allowed to cool and then broken. The ingots having been extracted were weighed, and laid by for use.

The manufacture of objects out of gold was effected by goldsmiths, who, after melting down an ingot, or a portion of one, in a crucible, with the help of a blow-pipe,[1] proceeded to work the material into shape

Goldsmith at Work.

with the forceps and tongs,[2] and finally to fashion it with graving tools.[3] Among the objects produced the commonest were solid rings of a certain size and weight, which seem to have passed current as money,[4] vases, bowls, baskets, armlets, bracelets, anklets, necklaces, ear-rings, and other ornaments of the person, cups,

[1] Blowpipes are represented more than once in the tombs. (See Rosellini, *Mon. Civ.* pl. li. 4, and pl. lii. fig. 4.)

[2] The forceps is sometimes represented on the monuments. (See the above woodcut.) Both tongs and forceps have been found in the tombs (Birch in Wilkinson's *A. E.* vol. ii. p. 235, note).

[3] The existing gold objects show this. Compare Ex. xxxii. 4.

[4] *Records of the Past,* vol. ii. p. 26; Wilkinson, *A. E.* vol. ii. p. 11.

goblets, rhytons, and other drinking-vessels. Statuettes also were sometimes made of gold,[1] and figures of the

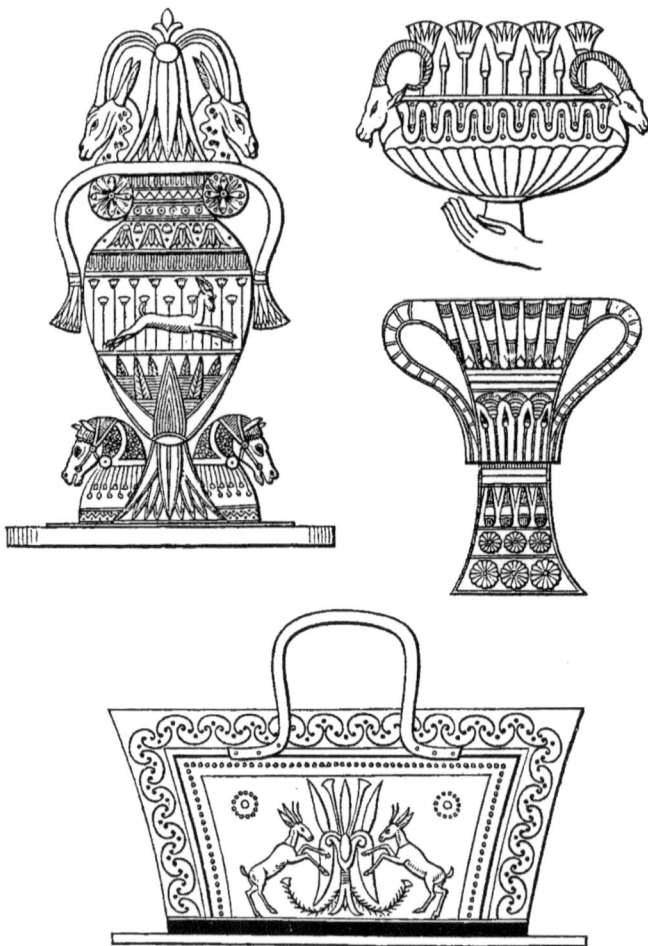

Egyptian Gold Vases.

sacred animals were inlaid with it.[2] The gold vases appear to have been most elaborately chased, and con-

---

[1] British Museum, First Egyptian Room, Nos. 86 and 285.   [2] Ibid. No. 1422.

structed in most elegant forms. Very few of them have escaped the ravages of time and the cupidity of man ; but, if we accept the representations in tombs as probably not exceeding the reality, we must ascribe to the Egyptian goldsmiths a very refined and excellent taste. Rosellini has six pages of vases,[1] above a hundred specimens in all, taken from the sculptures and paintings, almost all graceful, some quite exquisite, which show the Egyptians to have possessed a feeling for the beautiful in toreutic art that, without this proof of it, we should scarcely have expected. The few specimens which can be here reproduced will give a most inadequate idea of their power in this respect ; and those who wish to appreciate it as it deserves should consult the ' Monumenti Civili.'

A good deal of taste was also shown by the Egyptian goldsmiths in their armlets, bracelets, ear-rings, and finger-rings. Armlets were of elastic metal, the two ends, which did not quite meet, being sometimes fashioned into the heads of snakes or other animals.[2] Bracelets were generally solid bands of metal, plain, or else ornamented with *cloisonné* work, and sometimes enamelled and inlaid with lapis lazuli and glass pastes.[3] Occasionally the form of a snake was preferred, and a bracelet composed of three or four coils, carefully chased so as to imitate the skin of the reptile.[4] Ear-rings were mostly ' penannular,' one end being pointed, and the other shaped into the form of some animal's head. They had sometimes pendants,[5] and occasionally were set with pearls or other jewels.[6] Finger-rings were

[1] *Monumenti Civili*, pls. lvii. to lxii.
[2] See a specimen in Wilkinson, *A. E.* vol. iii. p. 347, No. 1.
[3] Birch, *Guide to Museum*, p. 69.
[4] Wilkinson, l.s.c. (No. 14.)
[5] Birch, *Guide to Museum*, pp. 66–7.
[6] Wilkinson l.s.c. (No. 17.)

most commonly intended to be used as signets, and consisted of a plain gold circle with a fixed, or else a revolving, bezel, bearing usually the name of the owner, and, if it revolved, some other engraved figures.

In silver the objects produced were, principally, rings used for money,[1] vases, bracelets, plates to be employed as ornaments of mummies,[2] figures of gods and sacred animals,[3] and finger-rings. The forms affected resembled for the most part those of the same objects in gold, but were on the whole less elaborate. It is worthy of observation that the silver is sometimes gilt.[4]

Leaden objects seem scarcely to be found; and the only proof which exists of the metal being known and worked by the Egyptians is its employment as a solder in combination with tin,[5] without which it will not serve the purpose. Egypt did not produce it, so far as appears; but it was sometimes taken as tribute from foreign nations in considerable quantities.[6]

It has been much questioned whether iron was employed at all by the Egyptians until the time of the Greek conquest. The weapons, implements, and ornaments of iron which have been found on the ancient sites are so few,[7] while those of bronze are so numerous, and the date of the few iron objects discovered is so uncertain, that there is a strong temptation to embrace the simple theory that iron was first introduced into Egypt by the

---

[1] *Records of the Past*, vol. ii. pp. 24, 26, and 49; Wilkinson, *A. E.* vol. ii. p. 11; vol. iii. p. 237.
[2] Birch, *Guide to Museum*, p. 81.
[3] British Museum, First Egyptian Room, Nos. 6, 310, and 1887.
[4] Ibid. No. 8412. Compare Wilkinson, *A. E.* vol. iii. p. 234.
[5] Wilkinson, p. 259.

[6] *Records*, vol. ii. pp. 27, 52, &c.
[7] The British Museum seems to possess no more than about seven or eight specimens of Egyptian iron. (First Room, Nos. 2435, 2464, 2916, 2918, 2954, 5410, 5423, and 6113.) Of these three (Nos. 2464, 2954, and 6113) are decidedly of a late period.

Ptolemies. Difficulties, however, stand in the way of the complete adoption of this view. A fragment of a thin plate of iron was found by Colonel Vyse imbedded in the masonry of the Great Pyramid.[1] Some iron implements and ornaments have been found in the tombs, with nothing about them indicative of their belonging to a late period. The paucity of such instances is partially, if not wholly, accounted for, by the rapid decay of iron in the nitrous earth of Egypt,[2] or when oxidised by exposure to the air. It seems moreover very improbable that the Hebrews and Canaanites should for centuries have been well acquainted with the use of iron,[3] and their neighbours of Egypt, whose civilisation was far more advanced, have been ignorant of it. On these grounds the most judicious of modern Egyptologists seem to hold, that while the use of iron by the Egyptians in Pharaonic times was, at the best, rare and occasional, it was still not wholly unknown,[4] though less appreciated than we should have expected. Iron spear-heads, iron sickles, iron gimlets, iron bracelets, iron keys, iron wire, were occasionally made use of; but the Egyptians, on the whole, were contented with their bronze implements and weapons, which were more easily produced, and which they found to answer every purpose.

The manufacture of bronze was by far the most extensive branch of Egyptian metallurgy. Arms, implements; household vessels such as cauldrons, bowls, ewers, jugs, buckets, basins, vases, ladles, &c.; articles

---

[1] This is now in the British Museum, and forms No. 2435 in the Egyptian collection.
[2] Wilkinson, A. E. vol. iii. p. 246.
[3] Deut. iii. 11; iv. 20; Judg. i. 19; iv. 3.
[4] Birch in Wilkinson's *Ancient Egyptians* (edition of 1878), vol. ii. pp. 250–1; Deveria, *Mélanges d'Archéologie Egyptienne*, vol. i. p. 2.

of the toilet, mirrors, tweezers, razors, pins, ear-rings, armlets, bracelets, finger-rings ; artistic objects, figures of gods, of sacred animals, and of men ; tools, such as saws, chisels, hatchets, adzes, drills, and bradawls ; are usually, or at any rate frequently, of this material,[1] which must have been employed by the Egyptian metallurgists to as large an extent as all the other metals put together. The bronze was very variously composed ; sometimes it contained as much as fourteen parts of tin, and one of iron, to eighty-five parts of copper,[2] a very unusual proportion ; more often the copper stood to the tin as eighty-eight to twelve ;[3] while sometimes the proportion was as high as ninety-four to six. In bronze of this last-mentioned quality, a tinge

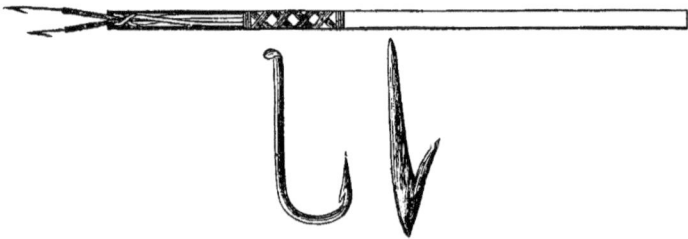

Harpoon and Fish-hooks.

of iron, amounting to about one part in a thousand, is usual.[4] The bronze arms included swords, daggers, battle-axes, maces, spear-heads, arrow-heads, and coats of mail; the implements, ploughshares, sickles, knives, forceps, nails, needles, harpoons, and fish-hooks.[5] Bronze was also used, as already observed,[6] in the con-

---

[1] Birch, *Guide to Museum*, pp. 13-21, 28-9, 35-41, &c.
[2] Birch, *Guide to Museum*, p. 28.
[3] Wilkinson, *A. E.* vol. iii. p. 253, note.
[4] Birch, *Guide to Museum*, p. 39.

[5] Specimens of most of these may be seen in the British Museum, First Egyptian Room, Nos. 5408a to 5497.
[6] See above, p. 491.

struction of chariots, and perhaps to some extent in furniture and house-building.

The process of melting bronze is not shown upon the monuments. It must have required furnaces, melting pots, and moulds of considerable dimensions, and must have given occupation to a very large class of artisans. Among these, perhaps the most important was the armourer, who provided the offensive and defensive arms on which the safety of the country depended. It would seem that there was nothing particularly unpleasant in his occupation, since the poet, who seeks to disparage all other callings except that of the scribe, is unable to point out anything whereof the ' maker of weapons ' has to complain, except the fatigue and expense of his journeys,[1] which can only have been accidental and occasional.

Boat-building must also have been a flourishing trade, and have employed the energies of a large number of persons. Besides their war vessels or galleys, which were rather large boats than ships, the Egyptians made use of a great variety of craft, adapted for peaceful purposes, and differing according to the exact service for which they were wanted. A sort of light canoe, formed (we are told) of the papyrus plant, and propelled either by a single paddle or by a punting-pole, furnished the ordinary means of transport from one side of the Nile to the other, and was also used by fishermen in their occupation, and by herdsmen, when it was necessary to save cattle from an excessive inun-

---

[1] See *Records of the Past*, vol. viii. p. 151: ' The maker of weapons suffers extremely, going forth to foreign countries; he gives a great deal for his asses, more than the labour of his hands. He gives a great deal for their being in a field; he gives on the road. He arrives at his garden; he reaches his house at night. He must be off [again].'

dation.[1]   The stem and stern of these vessels rose considerably above the water ; they must have been flat-bottomed and broad, like punts, or they could have

Building a Boat.

possessed no stability.   They are probably the ' vessels of bulrushes,' spoken of by Isaiah,[2] which were common to the Egyptians with the Ethiopians.

But the ordinary Nile boat of Pharaonic times was built of wood.   Planks of the acantha or *Mimosa nilotica* were cut with the hatchet, a yard or two in length, and arranged in rows one above another, very

Nile Boat.

much as builders arrange their bricks.[3]   These planks were probably united together by glue and by wooden bolts and nails, in the same way as articles of furniture ;

---

[1] See above, p. 172.
[2] Is. xviii. 2.
[3] See Herodotus, ii. 96, where this comparison is made, and compare Rosellini, *Mon. Civ.* pl. xliv. 1.

but they were sometimes further secured by means of

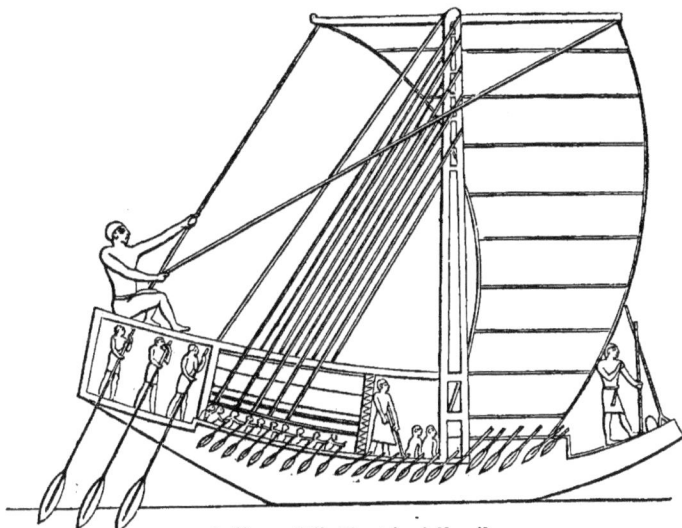

Ordinary Nile Boat in full sail.

a number of short poles or stakes, placed internally at

An Egyptian Gentleman's Pleasure-boat.

right angles to the planks, and lashed to them by means

of cord or string.[1]   On a boat of this kind a sort of
house of lattice-work was sometimes raised, and cattle
were embarked upon it and conveyed from place to
place.[2]   Occasionally the house was of a more solid
character, being formed of boards which were continuous and only pierced by a few windows.[3]   Some
boats of this construction had a mast and sail ; others
were without these conveniences, and depended entirely upon the rowers.   These varied in number from
twelve to forty-four ; their oars were of rude construction, and they appear sometimes to have rowed
standing.   Steering was managed either by a rudder,
worked through a notch in the centre of the stern, or
by two or more steering-oars on either side, each entrusted to a separate steersman.   The only sail used
was a square sail, and the rigging was of the most
simple character.   Sails were often coloured, and sometimes patterned, or embroidered with quaint devices.[4]

The embalmers of dead bodies must also, like the
boat-builders, have been a numerous class, and must
have driven a profitable trade, if the prices mentioned
by Diodorus[5] were really those commonly exacted.
According to the Sicilian historian, the expense of
preparing a corpse for interment in the most approved method was a talent of silver, or something
more than 240l. of our money ; and even for a secondary and far inferior method, a payment had to be
made exceeding 80l.   For the lowest and poorest class
of persons a third method had necessarily to be employed, the cost of which was, comparatively speaking,

---

[1] Herod. l.s.c. ; and compare
Wilkinson's illustration in the author's *Herodotus*, vol. ii. p. 132.
[2] See Wilkinson, *A. E.* vol. iii.
p. 195.

[3] Ibid. and p. 196.
[4] See Rosellini, *Mon. Civ.* pls.
cvii., cviii. and cix. ; and Wilkinson,
A. E. vol. iii. pl. xvi. opp. p. 211.
[5] Diod. Sic. i. 91.

moderate ; but even here, taking the numbers into account, the profit made must have been considerable. It has been calculated that between B.C. 2000 and A.D. 700, when embalming ceased, there may have been interred in Egypt 420,000,000 mummied corpses.[1] This would give an average of 155,000 yearly. If we calculate that, of these, five-sixths, or 130,000, would belong to the lower orders, while two-fifteenths, or 20,000, may have been furnished by the class which was fairly well off, and one-thirtieth, or 5,000, by the really opulent ; and if we suppose the poor man to have paid, on an average, no more than one-twentieth of the price paid by those of the upper middle class, the annual sum received by the embalmers would have exceeded three millions sterling.[2]

The embalmers' trade was certainly ancient in Egypt,[3] and by the time of the eighteenth dynasty the art had attained an extraordinary pitch of perfection.[4] In the most expensive system, the brain was skilfully extracted by a curved bronze implement through the nostrils, and the skull was then washed out with certain medicaments ; the nostrils were plugged up ; the eyes removed and replaced by artificial ones in ivory or obsidian, and the hair sometimes also removed and placed in a separate packet, covered with linen and bitumen.[5] The right side was opened by a cut with a flint knife,[6] and the whole of the intestines were re-

---

[1] See Birch, *Guide to Museum*, p. 54.

[2] At the rates suggested, the exact sum would be 3,320,000*l*. It may be doubted, however, whether Diodorus does not considerably exaggerate the mere cost of embalming.

[3] A considerable number of the mummies are regarded as belonging to the time of the first six dynasties. These ' have been only slightly preserved, and drop to pieces on exposure to the air.' (Birch, *Guide to Museum*, l s.c.)

[4] Ibid.

[5] See the specimens in the British Museum (First Egyptian Room) numbered from 6725 to 6728.

[6] Herod. ii. 86.

moved by the hand[1] and placed in sepulchral urns;[2] the cavity was then cleansed by an injection of palm-wine, and sometimes by a subsequent infusion of pounded aromatics;[3] after which it was filled with bruised myrrh, cassia, cinnamon, and other spices. Next, the entire body was plunged in natron and kept covered with it for seventy days. Silver gloves or stalls were put on the fingers, to keep the nails in place, or else they were secured with thread;[4] a plate of tin, inscribed with the symbolic eye, was laid over the incision in the right side; the arms were arranged symmetrically, either along the sides, or on the breast or groins; and the process of bandaging commenced. The bandages used were always of linen;[5] they were usually three or four inches wide and several yards in length; coarser kinds of linen were employed near the body, and finer towards the exterior. In some cases the entire length of the bandages wherein a single corpse was swathed exceeded 700, or, according to one writer, 1,000 yards.[6] To unite the bandages together, and keep them in place, gum was employed. When the swathing was completed, either an outer linen shroud, dyed red with the *carthamus tinctorius*, and ornamented with a network of porcelain beads, was placed over the whole; or the swathed body was covered by a 'car-tonnage,' consisting of twenty or forty layers of linen tightly pressed and glued together, so as to form a sort of paste-board envelope, which then received a thin coating of stucco, and was painted in bright colours with hieroglyphics and figures of deities.[7] This was

---

[1] Biod. Sic. i. 91.
[2] See above, p. 397.
[3] Herod. ii. 86.
[4] Birch, *Guide to Museum*, p. 53.
[5] Herod. l.s.c.; Wilkinson, *A. E.*

vol. iii. p. 115; vol. v. p. 463; Birch, l.s.c.
[6] Pettigrew, quoted by Wilkinson (*A. E.* vol. v. p. 471).
[7] 'Cartonnages' may be seen in

placed within a wooden coffin shaped similarly, and in
most cases similarly ornamented, which was often enclosed within another, or within several, each just
capable of holding the preceding one. Finally, in the
funerals of the rich, the coffined body was deposited
within a stone sarcophagus, which might be of granite,
alabaster, basalt, breccia, or other good material, and
was either rectangular, like that of Mycerinus,[1] or in
the shape of the mummied body. Some sarcophagi
were plain ; but many were covered with sculptures in
relief or intaglio, consisting chiefly of scenes and passages from the most sacred of the Egyptian books, the
' Ritual of the Dead.'

When the relatives were not able, or not disposed,
to incur the large outlay which this entire process required, there were various ways in which it might be
cheapened.[2]　The viscera, instead of being placed
together with spices in separate urns, might be simply
returned into the body, accompanied by wax images of
the four genii ; the abdominal cavity might be merely
cleansed with cedar oil,[3] and not filled with spices ; the
silver finger-stalls and artificial eyes might be omitted ;
the bandages might be reduced in number and made of
less fine linen ; the ornamentation might be simpler :
a single wooden coffin might suffice ; and the sarcophagus
might be dispensed with. In this way the cost could be
reduced within moderate limits, so as perhaps not greatly
to exceed that of funerals in our own upper middle class.

---

the British Museum Collection, Nos.
6662, 6665, 6679, 6680, &c.
　[1] See above, p. 192.
　[2] Herodotus speaks of a single
' moderately cheap ' method; and so
Diodorus. But modern research
proves that no sharp and decided
line can be drawn, either between
the ' expensive ' and the ' moderate,'
or between the ' moderate ' and the
' cheap' system. (See Wilkinson,
A. E. vol. v. pp. 468–473.)
　[3] Herod. ii. 87.

But some still cheaper process was necessary, unless
the poor were to be debarred from the privilege of
embalming their dead altogether.   One cheap mode
employed seems to have been the submersion of the
bodies for a short time in mineral pitch;[1] another,
the merely drying and salting them.   Bodies thus prepared are sometimes found swathed in bandages, but
often merely wrapped in coarse cloths or rags ; they
are without coffins, and have been simply buried in the
ground, either singly, or in layers, one over the other.[2]
The cost of preparing the body for burial under either
of these two systems must have been trifling.

We are assured that the class of embalmers was
held in high consideration among the Egyptians, parti-
cipating to some extent in the respect which was entertained for the priestly order.[3]   Yet, if any credence is
to be given to a tale told by Herodotus,[4] it must have
comprised individuals capable of almost any atrocity.
Probably the heads of embalming establishments were
alone persons of high respectability; the actual evis-
cerators (*paraschistæ*) and embalmers (*taricheutæ*) being
generally of a low grade, and more or less untrustworthy.   It is to be hoped, however, that the degree of
brutality indicated by Herodotus was of rare occurrence.

Besides the trades and handicrafts in which so
many of the Egyptians found occupation for their time
and talents, a considerable portion of the population

---

[1] Rouger, *Notice sur les Embaume-
ments des anciens Egyptiens,* quoted
by Wilkinson, *A. E.* vol. v. p. 472.
[2] Belzoni, *Researches,* p. 156.
[3] Wilkinson, *A. E.* vol. iii. p. 184.
[4] The story can only be given in
the author's own words :—Τὰς γυ-
ναῖκας τῶν ἐπιφανέων ἀνδρῶν, ἐπεὰν
τελευτήσωσι, οὐ παραυτίκα διδοῦσι

ταριχεύειν, ἀλλ' ἐπεὰν τριταῖαι ἢ τε-
ταρταῖαι γένωνται, οὕτω παραδι-
δοῦσι τοῖσι ταριχεύουσι· τοῦτο δε
ποιέουσι οὕτω τοῦδε εἵνεκεν, ἵνα μή
σφι οἱ ταριχευταὶ μίσγωνται τῇσι
γυναιξί. Λαμφθῆναι γάρ τινά φασι
μισγόμενον νεκρῷ προσφάτῳ γυναι-
κός· κατεῖπαι δὲ τὸν ὁμότεχνον. (Herod. ii. 89.)

pursued employments of a more elevated and intellectual character. Sculpture,[1] painting, and music had their respective votaries, and engaged the services of a large number of persons who may be regarded as artists. If dancing is to be viewed as a ' fine art,' we may add to these the paid dancers, who were numerous, but were not held in very high estimation. There were also employments analogous to our ' professions,' as those of the architect, the physician, and the scribe.

The merits of Egyptian painting and sculpture have been considered in an earlier chapter, and no more need be now said on that subject; but a few words on the mechanical processes employed, and the social status of artists and sculptors, are requisite in such a review of Egyptian manners and customs as we are at present engaged in. The sculptors may be divided into those who produced complete figures ' in the round,' and those who carved reliefs or intaglios on plain surfaces. The complete figures were either ideal, of gods

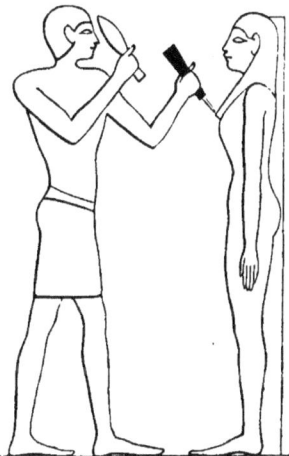

Chiselling a Statue.

and demi-gods, or portrait-statues representing individuals. Those of the former kind, being systematic and conventional, required but little artistic ability, and could be produced mechanically by a number of workmen, who at one and the same time employed themselves on different parts of the figure.[2] Portrait-statues

---

[1] Ch. viii. pp. 261–285.
[2] Representations of persons so employed may be seen in Rosellini,

Mon. Civ. pl. xlvii. Nos. 3 and 4; and Wilkinson, *A. E.* vol. iii p. 336.

required a different treatment, and must have been the creation of individual artists, who often showed themselves possessed of considerable talent. The implements employed by the Egyptian, as by all other, sculptors were two only, the chisel and the mallet, the sole peculiarity being that in Egypt the chisel was probably of bronze and not of iron.[1] After the form had been in this way completely rendered,[2] according to the notions of the artists, a final polish was produced by rubbing the statue with a round ball of some hard material.

Statues, even colossal ones, were completed some way from the place where they were to be set up, and had to be transported considerable distances by muscular force. Human agency seems to have been alone employed to effect the transport, gangs of labourers being engaged to drag the mass, after it had been attached by ropes to a sledge.[3] To prevent injury to the statue by friction, pads of leather, or some other similar substance, were introduced between the ropes and the stone at all the points of contact; and to facilitate the movement of the mass, the ground in front of the sledge was lubricated with a copious stream of oil or melted grease.

As reliefs and intaglios were far more common than statues, the sculptors engaged in executing them must have constituted a much more numerous class. In general, owing to the existence and enforcement of conventional rules, they had little opportunity of showing originality or genius. Sacred subjects were repeated a thousand times with scarcely any variety; domestic

---

[1] Wilkinson, *A. E.* vol. iii. pp. 251-2.

[2] See the woodcut on the preceding page.

[3] See Rosellini, *Mon. Civ.* pl. xlviii. 1. Compare the author's *Herodotus*, vol. ii. pl. opp. p. 150.

subjects were treated with almost equal monotony; even in historical subjects there was much that was fixed and invariable, as the representations of marches and processions, of the reception of prisoners and of tribute, the counting of hands and tongues, the *emblematic* execution of conquered enemies;[1] and the like: but the various incidents of a campaign, or a royal progress, afforded occasional scope to the sculptors for novel compositions, and enabled them to vindicate their claims to a really artistic character. Compositions occur in which the monarch singly puts to flight the host of the enemy,[2] or in which the Egyptians are engaged in a hand-to-hand conflict with their foes by land [3] or sea,[4] or where the flying foe is driven from the field in utter rout;[5] or, lastly, where the monarch is employed in the chase of the king of beasts,[6] in all of which the conventional is discarded, the artist is thrown entirely upon himself, and qualities are called forth by the opportunity for their employment, with which, but for these specimens, we should scarcely have credited the Egyptian artists. The drawing is no doubt far from faultless; in some of the scenes mere confusion prevails; in others there is an unartistic exaggeration of the size of the royal person; in most there is a want of unity, of grouping, and of picturesque effect; but still ability is shown; talent, skill, even genius, make themselves apparent; and we see that, as in other countries, so

---

[1] The usual representation consists of a gigantic figure of the king, holding a conquered king, or a number of conquered kings, by the hair with one hand, while with the other he brandishes aloft a sword or mace. (See Rosellini, *Mon. Storici*, pls. lx., lxiv., lxvi., &c.; *Description de l'Egypte*, ' Antiquités,' vol. ii. pl. xvi. &c.)

[2] See the woodcut opp. p. 276.
[3] See the woodcut on p. 452.
[4] Rosellini, *Mon. Storici*, pl. cxxxi.; *Description*, ' Antiquités,' vol. ii. pl. x.
[5] Lepsius, *Denkmäler*, vol. vi. pt. iii. pls. 158, 165, &c.; Rosellini, *Mon. Storici*, pls. cx., cxxxvi., &c.
[6] See the woodcut opp. p. 278.

even in Egypt there was a reserve of artistic power
which favourable circumstances might at any time call
forth, and which was capable of producing very remarkable and in some respects very admirable results.

Egyptian painting was far inferior to Egyptian
sculpture ; and it may be questioned whether the
Egyptian painter ought to be regarded as an artist in
the true sense of the word.   It was his principal business to add brilliancy to walls and ceilings, either by
colouring them in patterns, or by painting in a conventional way the reliefs and hieroglyphics with which they
had been adorned by the sculptor.   Still, occasionally,
he seems to have been called upon to produce pictures
in the modern sense, as, for instance, portraits,[1] and
figures of men or animals.   Of the portraits we have no
specimens;[2] but it is not likely that they had much merit.
Outlines of men and animals occur in unfinished tombs,
boldly and clearly drawn, as a guide to the chisel of
the sculptor.[3]   We have also some representations of
painters at work upon animal forms,[4] from which it
would appear that they must have possessed great
steadiness of hand and power over the pencil.   The
painter seems to have held his pot of colour in his left
hand, while with his right, which he did not support in
any way, he painted the animal.   A similar absence of
support is observable when painters are employed in
colouring statues.[5]   When the artist was engaged in
any complicated work, instead of a single paint-pot, he

[1] Amasis, B.C. 540, sent a portrait of himself as a present to the
people of Cyrene (Herod. ii. 182).
We may presume that it was painted
by a native artist.

[2] The coarse representations on
cartonnages and mummy-cases can
scarcely be considered as portraits.

[3] Wilkinson, A. E. vol. iii. p.
313.

[4] Ibid. p. 311 ; Rosellini, Mon.
Civ. pl. xlvi. 3.

[5] Rosellini, pl. xlvi. 5, 6, 8, and
10.

made use of a palette. This was ordinarily a rectangular piece of wood, porcelain, or alabaster, containing a number of round depressions, or 'wells,' for holding the various colours. Palettes are found with as many as eleven or twelve of these cavities,[1] which indicate the employment of at least eleven or twelve different tints.[2] The cakes of paint, which filled the cavities, were moistened, at the time of use, with a mixture of water and gum arabic.[3] The painter used slabs and mullers for grinding his colours.[4]

The materials that exist for determining the social status of artists are but scanty ; and different opinions may no doubt be formed with respect to it. But there is some reason for believing that the status was higher than that of the same class of persons in most ancient countries. Iritisen, a statuary in the time of the eleventh dynasty, had a funeral monument prepared for himself, which is pronounced to be 'one of the masterpieces of Egyptian sculpture.'[5] He is represented upon it 'holding in the left hand the long baton used by elders and *noblemen*, and in his right the *pat* or sceptre.'[6] In the inscription he calls himself the 'true servant' of the king Mentu-hotep, 'he who is in the inmost recess of his (i.e. the king's) heart, and makes his pleasure all the day long.'[7] He also declares that he is 'an artist, wise in his art—a man *standing above all men* by his learning.'[8] Altogether, the monument is one from which we may reasonably conclude that Iritisen occu-

---

[1] British Museum, First Egyptian Room, Nos. 5515 and 5525 *b*.

[2] It has been already shown (supra, pp. 286-7) that the Egyptian painters employed about fourteen tints.

[3] Wilkinson, *A. E.* vol. iii. p. 301.

[4] Birch, *Guide to Museum*, p. 41.

[5] De Rougé, *Catalogue des Monuments égyptiens de la Salle du Rez-de-chaussée*, 1849, p. 47.

[6] *Records of the Past*, vol. x. p. 2.

[7] Ibid. p. 3.

[8] Ibid. l.s.c.

pied a position not much below that of a noble, and
enjoyed the personal acquaintance of the monarch in
whose reign he flourished.

Musicians seem scarcely to have attained to the same
level. Music was used, in the main, as a light entertainment, enhancing the pleasures of the banquet, and
was in the hands of a professional class which did not
bear the best of characters. The religious ceremonies
into which music entered were mostly of an equivocal
character.[1] There may perhaps have been some higher
and more serious employment of it, as in funeral lamentations,[2] in religious processions,[3] and in state ceremonies ; but on the whole it seems to have borne the
character which it bears in most parts of the East at
the present day—the character of an art ministering to
the lower elements of human nature, and tending to
corrupt men rather than to elevate them.[4] Still, as an
amusement or entertainment, music was much cultivated in Egypt, even from the earliest times, a great
variety of instruments was invented ; several forms of
most instruments were tried ; and both playing and
singing in concert were studied and practised. Of
instruments, we find employed, besides cymbals and
castanets, the flute, the single and double pipe, the
lyre, the harp, the tambourine, the sistrum, the drum,
the guitar, and the cylindrical maces. Flutes were long,
and had a small number of holes,[5] placed very near the
lower extremity. Pipes, on the other hand, were short,

---

[1] See Herod. ii. 48 and 60.
[2] Ibid. ii. 79.
[3] Wilkinson, A. E. vol. ii. pp.
237, 240, 316, &c. Rosellini, Mon.
Civ. pl. xcix. 2.
[4] See Diod. Sic. i. 16. The contrary statement of Plato in his

'Laws' cannot be depended on (De
Leg. ii. p. 656, E).
[5] One flute in the British Museum (No. 6388) has six holes ; but
four or five were more usual (Wilkinson, A. E. vol. ii. p. 304).

not exceeding a length of fifteen inches;[1] they had ordinarily either three or four holes, and were furnished
with a narrow mouthpiece of reed or straw. Lyres
and harps varied greatly, both in the number of their
strings and in their shapes. Lyres had from five to
eighteen strings, and were played either by the hand or
with the plectrum;[2] the two arms of the frame were
sometimes of equal, but more usually of unequal
lengths, to allow of a variety in the length of the
strings. The sounding-board at the base was ordinarily square, but sometimes its sides were curved, and
occasionally there was a second smaller sounding-board
projecting from the main one, whereto the strings were
attached. Harps had any number of strings from four
to twenty-two,[3] which were made of catgut,[4] and were
always of different lengths. Some harps were above
six feet high,[5] and when played stood upon the ground,
having an even broad base: others had to be held
against the body, or rested upon a stool or other support,[6] and had a height of from two to four feet. The
frame of most was curved like a bow, but with an enlargement towards the lower extremity, which served
as a sounding-board. Some harps, however, were triangular, and consisted of a single straight piece of wood
and a cross-bar, placed at a right or an acute angle.[7]
The subject has been so abundantly illustrated by Sir
G. Wilkinson, that it seems unnecessary to give representations here.

Tambourines were of two kinds, round and oblong

---

[1] Wilkinson, A. E. vol. ii. p. 308.
[2] For the use of the plectrum see
Wilkinson, A. E. vol. ii. p. 291
(woodcut No. 217, fig. 1).
[3] Birch, Guide to Museum, p. 48.
[4] Wilkinson, A. E. vol. ii. p. 283.

[5] Rosellini, Mon. Civ. pl. xcvii.;
Wilkinson, A. E., frontispiece to
vol. ii.
[6] Wilkinson, A. E. vol. ii. pp.
234, 274, 275, &c.
[7] Ibid. pp. 280, 282, and 287.

square. They seem to have been composed merely of a membrane stretched upon a framework of wood, and not to have been accompanied by metal rings or balls in the frame.[1] Drums were also of two kinds : one, like the drum of the soldiers,[2] was a long barrel-shaped instrument of small diameter, not unlike the ' tomtom ' of the Indians. The other resembled the *darabooka* drum of modern Egypt, which consists of a sheet of parchment strained over a piece of pottery shaped like the rose of a watering-pot.[3] Both kinds of drums were played by the hand, and not beaten with drumsticks.

Egyptian guitars had several peculiarities. The body of the instrument was unusually small,[4] though not perhaps so small as that which characterised the guitar of the Assyrians.[5] The neck or handle was at once long and narrow ; the strings were three only,[6] and were disengaged from the instrument by means of a bridge at the upper end and by attachment at the lower end to a projection from the body. They seem not to have been tightened by pegs, but to have been passed through holes in the neck and then tied as tightly as was necessary.[7] The mode of playing was nearly the same as in modern times, the left hand being employed in shortening or lengthening the strings, and the right in striking the notes. These, however, were produced, not by the actual fingers, but by the plectrum

[1] Sir G Wilkinson (*A. E.* vol. ii. p. 315) comes to an opposite conclusion ; but, as it seems to me, on insufficient grounds.
[2] See above, p. 477.
[3] Wilkinson, *A. E.* vol. ii. p. 254. A third sort of drum, not unlike our own, has been found among the Egyptian remains (ibid. p. 268), but is not represented upon the monuments, and apparently was

not employed by musicians. This was played with drumsticks.
[4] Rosellini, *Mon. Civ.* pl. xcvi. 2, 3 ; pl. xcviii. 2, 3, &c.
[5] See the author's *Ancient Monarchies*, vol. ii. p. 156.
[6] Wilkinson, *A. E.* vol. ii. p. 297. Birch says ' from two to four' (*Guide to Museum*, p. 48).
[7] Birch, l.s.c.; Wilkinson, p. 234, woodcut No. 185, fig. 2.

or short pointed rod. The performer on the guitar usually played it standing, and sometimes danced to his own melody.[1]

The sistrum, or rattle, seems to have been a sacred instrument, used only in religious ceremonies. It was generally of bronze, and consisted of an open loop of that metal, crossed by three or four moveable bars,[2] which sometimes carried two or three rings apiece ;[3] the whole when shaken producing a loud jingling sound, which, according to Plutarch, was supposed to frighten away Set or Typhon. The religious purpose of the instrument is often indicated by its being surmounted with the figure of a cat or lion—the sacred animals of Pasht or Sekhet—or else supported on the head of Athor. It was played only by females, and was often highly ornamented.

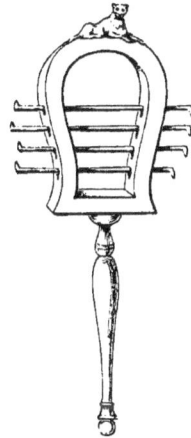

Cylindrical maces were also no doubt of bronze. They consisted of a straight or slightly curved handle,[4] surmounted by a ball, which was often shaped into the resemblance of a human or animal head. The performer held one in each hand, and played them by bringing the two heads into collision with greater or less force, producing thus a loud clash or clang. Such music was sufficient to mark time, and was sometimes employed without other accompaniment to guide the dance.

Egyptian Sistrum.

The 'triple symphony,' as musicians call it, was

[1] See Wilkinson, A. E. vol. ii. p. 235, woodcut No. 167, fig. 2 ; p. 301, woodcut No. 222.

[2] For examples, see the British Museum Collection, First Egyptian Room, Nos. 6355 and 6365.

[3] Wilkinson, A. E. vol. ii. p. 323.

[4] Ibid. pp. 257 and 260.

well known in Egypt; and mixed bands of vocal and
instrumental performers appear in the sculptures almost
as frequently as bands of either kind separately.[1] In
one ancient tomb near the Pyramids, belonging probably to the times of the first six dynasties, we see a
band composed of two harpers, four singers, a piper,
and a flute-player.[2] In another sculpture, two singers
are accompanied by a flute-player and two harpers.[3] In
a third, three sing, while one plays the harp, one the
lyre, and one the double pipe.[4] Instrumental bands

Band of Six Musicians.

consist of any number of performers from two to six;
but the number of different instruments played together
does not exceed five.[5] Where the performers are more
numerous, the same instrument is played by two or
more of them.[6] Most commonly all the members of a
single band are of one sex; but occasionally the two
sexes are intermixed.[7]

---

[1] Wilkinson, *A. E.* vol. ii. pp.
237 and 239, woodcuts 190 and 193.
Compare Rosellini, *Mon. Civ.* pl.
xciv. and xcvi. 1.
[2] Wilkinson, p. 233.
[3] Ibid. p. 236, woodcut 189.
[4] Ibid. p. 237, woodcut 190.
[5] Rosellini, *Mon. Civ.* pl. xcviii.
Nos. 2 and 3; Wilkinson, *A. E.*

vol. ii. p. 235.
[6] The harp and the guitar are the
instruments most frequently multiplied.
[7] Rosellini, *Mon. Civ.* pl. lxxix.
line 6; pl. xcvi. 1; Wilkinson,
A. E. vol. ii. p. 234, woodcut 185;
p. 237, woodcut 190; p. 238, woodcut 192.

Dancing and music are constantly united together in the sculptures ; and the musicians and dancers must, it would seem, have been very closely connected indeed, and socially have ranked almost, if not quite, upon a par. Musicians sometimes, as already observed,[1] danced as they played; and where this was not the case, dancers generally formed a part of the *troupe*, and intermixed themselves with the instrumental performers. Dancing was professed both by men and women ; but women were preferred ; and in the entertainments of the rich the guests were generally amused by the graceful movements of trained females,[2] who went through the steps and figures, which they had been taught, for a certain sum of money. If we may trust the paintings, many of these professionals were absolutely without clothes,[3] or wore only a narrow girdle, embroidered with beads, about their hips. At the best, their dresses were of so light and thin a texture as to be perfectly transparent, and to reveal rather than veil the form about which they floated. It is scarcely probable that the class which was content thus to outrage decency could have borne a better character, or enjoyed a higher social status, than the *almehs* of modern Egypt or the *nautch* girls of India.

Of learned professions in Egypt, the most important was that of the scribe. Though writing was an ordinary accomplishment of the educated classes,[4] and scribes were not therefore so absolutely necessary as they are in most Eastern countries, yet still there were a large number of occupations for which professional

---

[1] See above, note [1], p. 523.
[2] Rosellini, *Mon. Civ.* pls. lxxix. and xcix. ; Wilkinson, *A. E.* vol. ii. p. 390.
[3] Wilkinson, p. 333.
[4] Birch, *Egypt from the Earliest Times,* ' Introduction,' p. xvi.

penmanship was a pre-requisite, and others which demanded the learning that a scribe naturally acquired in the exercise of his trade. The Egyptian religion neces-sitated the multiplication of copies of the ' Ritual of the Dead,' and the employment of numerous clerks in the registration of the sacred treasures, and the management of the sacred estates. The civil administration depended largely upon a system of registration and of official reports, which were perpetually being made to the court by the superintendents in all departments of the public service.[1] Most private persons of large means kept bailiffs or secretaries, who made up their accounts, paid their labourers, and otherwise acted as managers of their property. There was thus a large number of lucrative posts which could only be properly filled by persons such as the scribes were, ready with the pen, familiar with the different kinds of writing, good at figures, and at the same time not of so high a class as to be discontented with a life of dull routine, if not of drudgery. The occupation of scribe was regarded as one befitting men from the middle ranks of society, who might otherwise have been blacksmiths, carpenters, small farmers, or the like.[2] It would seem that there were schools[3] in the larger towns open to all who desired education. In these reading, writing, and arithmetic were taught, together with ' letters ' in a more extended sense ; and industry at such places of instruction was certain to be rewarded by opening to the more advanced students a

[1] Birch, *Egypt from the Earliest Times*, ' Introduction,' p. xix.
[2] This may be concluded from the Egyptian poem, which has been called ' The Praise of Learning ' (*Records of the Past*, vol. viii. pp. 147–156), where the occupation of scribe is compared with these and similar ones.
[3] Ibid. p. 147, line 6; p. 153, line 189. Compare Brugsch, *Geschichte Aegyptens*, p. 24.

variety of situations and employments. Some of these
may have been of a humble charac*t*er, and not over
well paid;[1] but among them were many which to an
Egyptian of the middle class seemed very desirable.
The posts under government occupied by scribes included some of great importance, as those of ambas-
sador,[2] superintendent of store-houses,[3] registrar of the
docks,[4] clerk of the closet,[5] keeper of the royal li-
brary,[6] ' scribe of the double house of life.'[7] It is indicative of the high rank and position of government
scribes, that in the court conspiracy which threatened
the life of the third Rameses as many as six of them
were implicated, while two served upon the tribunal
before which the criminals were arraigned.[8] If persons failed to obtain government appointments, they
might still hope to have their services engaged by the
rich corporations which had the management of the
temples, or by private individuals of good means.
Hence the scribe readily persuaded himself that his occupation was above all others—the only one which had
nothing superior to it, but was the first and best of all
human employments.[9]

The great number of persons who practised medicine in Egypt is mentioned by Herodotus,[10] who further
notices the remarkable fact that, besides general practitioners, there were many who devoted themselves to
special branches of medical science, some being ocu-

---

[1] The unremunerative nature of
the scribe's office is thought to be
alluded to in lines 228-237 of the
poem. (See *Records of the Past*,
vol. viii. p. 155, note [4].)
[2] Ibid. p. 148, line 31.
[3] Ibid. vol. ii. p. 3.
[4] Ibid.
[5] Ibid. p. 4.

[6] Ibid. vol. viii. p. 57.
[7] Ibid. pp. 62 and 63.
[8] Ibid. pp. 57-65.
[9] Ibid. p. 153: 'Consider, there
is not an employment destitute of
superior ones except the scribe's,
which is the first.'
[10] Herod. ii. 84.

lists, some dentists, some skilled in treating diseases of
the brain, some those of the intestines, and so on.   Ac-
coucheurs also we know to have formed a separate
class, and to have been chiefly, if not exclusively,
women.[1]   The consideration in which physicians were
held is indicated by the tradition which ascribed the
composition of the earliest medical works to one of the
kings,[2] as well as by the reputation for advanced knowledge which the Egyptian practitioners early obtained
in foreign countries.[3]   According to a modern authority,[4] they constituted a special subdivision of the sacerdotal order; but this statement is open to question,
though no doubt some of the priests were required
to study medicine.[5]

A third learned profession was that of the architect,
which in some respects took precedence over any other.
The chief court architect was a functionary of the highest importance, ranking among the very most exalted
officials.   Considering the character of the duties entrusted to him, this was only natural, since the kings
generally set more store upon their buildings than upon
any other matter.   ' At the time when the construction
of the Pyramids and other tombs,' says Brugsch,[6] ' demanded artists of the first order, we find the place of
architect entrusted to the highest dignitaries of the
court of the Pharaohs.   The royal architects, the *Murket*, as they were called, recruited their ranks not unfrequently from the class of princes ; and the inscriptions engraved upon the walls of their tombs inform us

---

[1] Ex. i. 15–19.
[2] Manetho ap. Euseb. *Chron.*
Can. i. 20, § 4.
[3] Hom. *Od.* iv. 231-2 ; Herod.
iii. 1,129 ; Jerem. xlvi. 11.
[4] Wilkinson in the author's *He-*

rodotus, vol. ii. p. 117.
[5] Clem. Alex. *Strom.* vi. 4, p.
758.
[6] *Geschichte Aegyptens*, ch. v. p.
50.

that, almost without exception, they married either the
daughters or the granddaughters of the reigning sove-
reigns, who did not refuse the *Murket* this honour.'
Semnofer, for instance, an architect under the third or
fourth dynasty, was married to a lady named Amon-
Zephes, the granddaughter of a Pharaoh ; Khufuhotep,
belonging to about the same period, had for wife a person of the same exalted position ; Mer-ab, architect
under Khufu, or Cheops, was an actual son of that
monarch ; Pirson, who lived a little later, married
Khenshut, of the blood royal ; and Ti, though of low
birth himself, married Nofer-hotep, a princess. This
last-named architect united in his own person a host of
offices and dignities : he was the king's secretary in all
his palaces, the secretary who published the king's de-
crees, the president of the royal Board of Works, and
a priest of several divinities. His magnificent tomb is
still to be seen at Saccarah in the neighbourhood of the
pyramids, a little to the north of the Serapeum, and at-
tracts the general attention of travellers.[1]

Though a position of such eminence as this could
belong only to one man at a time, it is evident that the
lustre attaching to the head of their profession would
be more or less reflected upon its members. Schools of
architects had to be formed in order to secure a succession of competent persons, and the chief architect of
the king was only the most successful out of many aspi-
rants, who were educationally and socially upon a par.
Actual builders, of course, constituted a lower class,
and are compassionated in the poem above quoted, as
exposed by their trade both to disease and accident.[2]

---

[1] Brugsch, *Geschichte Aegyptens,*
ch. vii. p. 89.

[2] *Records of the Past,* vol. viii.
p. 149 : 'I tell you also of the

But architects ran no such risks ; and the profession
must be regarded as having enjoyed in Egypt a rank
and a consideration rarely accorded to it elsewhere.
According to Diodorus, the Egyptians themselves said
that their architects were more worthy of admiration
than their kings.[1]   Such a speech could hardly have
been made while the independent monarchy lasted and
kings were viewed as actual gods ; but it was a natural
reflection on the part of those who, living under foreign
domination, looked back to the time when Egypt had
made herself a name among the nations by her conquests, and still more by her great works.

At the opposite extremity of the social scale were a
number of contemned and ill-paid employments, which
required the services of considerable numbers, whose
lives must have been sufficiently hard ones.   Dyers,
washermen, barbers, gardeners, sandal-makers, blacksmiths, carpenters, couriers, boatmen, fowlers, fishermen, are commiserated by the scribe, Tuaufaakhrat,[2] as
well as farmers, labourers, stone-cutters, builders, armourers, and weavers ; and though he does not often
point out any sufferings peculiar to those of his own
countrymen who were engaged in these occupations,
we may accept his evidence as showing that, in Egypt,
while they involved hard work, they obtained but small
remuneration.   The very existence however of so many
employments is an indication that labour was in request ; and we cannot doubt that industrious persons
could support themselves and their families without
much difficulty, even by these inferior trades.   The

---

builder of precincts. Disease tastes
him ; for he is in draughts of air ;
he builds in slings, tied as a lotus
to the houses.'

[1] See the passage placed as a
heading to ch. vii. (supra, p. 181).
[2] *Records of the Past*, vol. viii.
pp. 148–153.

Egyptians, even of the lowest class, were certainly not crushed down by penury or want ; they maintained a light heart under the hardships, whatever they may have been, of their lot, and contrived to amuse themselves and to find a good deal of pleasure in existence.[1]

If the boatman, for instance, led a laborious life, 'doing beyond the power of his hands to do,'[2] he had yet spirit enough to enter into rivalry with his brother boatmen, and to engage in rude contests, which must have often caused him a broken head or a ducking.[3]

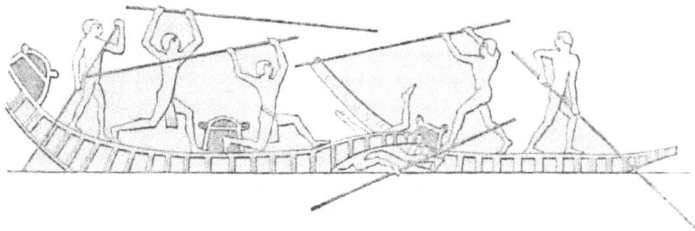

Boatmen quarrelling.

If the fowler and the fisherman had sometimes hard work to make a living, yet they had the excitement which attaches to every kind of sport, and from time to time were rewarded for their patient toil by 'takes' of extraordinary magnitude. The drag-nets and clap-nets which they used to entrap their prey are frequently represented as crowded with fish [4] or birds, as many as twenty-five of the latter being enclosed on some occasions.[5] The fish were often of large size, so that a man could only just carry one ; [6] and though these monsters

<hr>

[1] Brugsch, *Geschichte Aegyptens,* p. 22.
[2] *Records of the Past,* vol. viii. p. 149, l. 56.
[3] See Rosellini, *Mon. Civ.* pl. civ. 9.
[4] See Rosellini, *Mon. Civ.* pl.
xxiv. 1 ; Wilkinson, *A. E.* vol. ii. p. 20 ; vol. iii. p. 37, &c.
[5] Wilkinson, vol. iii. p. 37. Compare vol. ii. p. 19, and Rosellini, *Mon. Civ.* pls. iv. and v.
[6] Wilkinson, vol. iii. p. 57, fig. 3. Compare p. 56, figs. 3 and 4.

were perhaps not in very great request, they would have sufficed to furnish three or four meals to a large

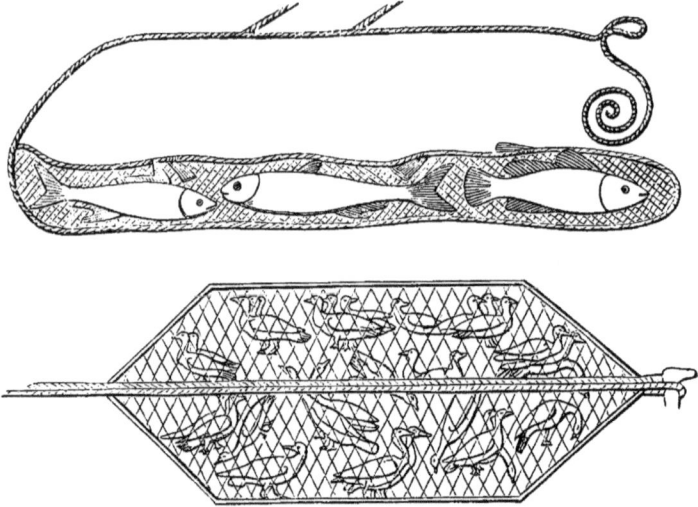

Egyptian drag-net and clap-net.

family. Fish were constantly dried and salted,[1] so that the superabundance of one season supplied the deficiency of another ; and even birds appear to have been subjected to a similar process, and preserved in jars,[2] when there was no immediate sale for them.

An occupation held in especial disrepute was that of the swineherd. According to Herodotus,[3] persons of this class were absolutely prohibited from entering an Egyptian temple, and under no circumstances would a man of any other class either give his daughter in marriage to a swineherd, or take a wife from among them. This prejudice was connected with the notion

---

[1] Herod. ii. 92, ad fin.; Diod. Sic. i. 36; Rosellini, *Mon. Civ.* pl. xxv. 3; Wilkinson, vol. iii. pp. 37 and 56.

[2] Rosellini, *Mon. Civ.* pl. iv.; Wilkinson, vol. ii. p. 19 ; Herod. ii. 77.

[3] Herod. ii. 47.

of the pig being an unclean animal,[1] which was common to the Egyptians with the Jews, the Mohammedans, and the Indians. If it existed to the extent asserted, the swineherds, the Pariahs of Egypt, must have
approached nearly to the character of a caste, as inter-
marrying wholly among themselves, and despised by
every other section of the population.

But if Egyptian civilisation had thus its victims, it
had also its favourites. There stood in Egypt, outside
the entire number of those who either belonged to a
profession or exercised a trade or calling, that upper
class of which we have more than once spoken,[2] owners
of a large portion of the soil, and so possessed of hereditary wealth, not very anxious for official employment,
though filling commonly most of the highest posts in the
administration,[3] connected in many instances more or
less closely with the royal family,[4] and bearing the rank
of *suten-rech* or ' princes '—a class small, compared
with most others, but still tolerably numerous—one
which seemed born to enjoy existence and ' consume
the fruits ' of other men's toil and industry.[5] Such
persons, as has been said,[6] ' led a charmed life.' Possessed of a villa in the country, and also commonly of
a town house in the capital, the Egyptian lord divided
his time between the two, now attracted by the splen-
dours of the court, now by the simple charms of rural
freedom and retirement. In either case he dwelt in a
large house, amply and elegantly furnished—the floors

---

[1] The unclean habits of the pig
are no doubt the chief cause of this
notion; but it is also said that the
flesh is unwholesome in Eastern
countries (Wilkinson in the author's
Herodotus, vol. ii. p. 72; Houghton in Smith's *Dictionary of the
Bible,* vol. iii. p. 1393).

[2] Supra, pp. 154, 442, &c.
[3] Brugsch, *Geschichte Aegyptens,*
p. 24.
[4] Ibid.
[5] ' Fruges consumere nati ' (Hor.
Epist. i. 2, 1. 27).
[6] Birch, *Egypt from the Earliest
Times,* p. 44.

strewn with bright-coloured carpets [1]—the rooms generally provided with abundant sofas and chairs, couches,
tables, faldstools, ottomans, stands for flowers, footstools, vases, &c.[2]—the household numerous and well
trained, presided over by a major-domo or steward, who
relieved the great man of the trouble of domestic management.[3]　Attached to his household in some way,
if not actual members of it, were ' adepts in the various
trades conducive to his ease and comfort ' [4]—the glass-
blower, the worker in gold, the potter, the tailor, the
baker, the sandal-maker.　With a prudent self-re-
straint not often seen among orientals, he limited himself to a single wife, whom he made the partner of his
cares and joys, and treated with respect and affection.
No eunuchs troubled the repose of his establishment
with their plots and quarrels.　His household was composed in about equal proportions of male and female
servants; his wife had her waiting-maid or tirewoman,
his children their nurse or nurses ; he himself had his
valet, who was also his barber.　The kitchen depart-
ment was entrusted to three or four cooks and scullions,[5]
who were invariably men, no woman (it would seem)
being thought competent for such important duties.
One, two, or more grooms had the charge of his stable,
which in the early times sheltered no nobler animal
than the ass,[6] but under the New Empire was provided
with a number of horses. A chariot, in which he might
take an airing, pay visits, or drive a friend, was also
indispensable [7] in and after the time of the eighteenth

---

[1] Wilkinson, *A. E.* vol. ii. p.
200; vol. iii. pp. 141–2; *Records
of the Past,* vol. ii. p. 12.

[2] See above, p. 489.

[3] Birch, *Egypt from the Earliest
Times,* p. 44.

[4] Ibid.

[5] Wilkinson, *A. E.* vol. ii. p.
388, woodcut No. 278.　Compare
Rosellini, *Mon. Civ.* pls. lxxxiii. to
lxxxv.

[6] Birch, l.s.c.

[7] Wilkinson, *A. E.* vol. i. p. 335;
vol. ii. p. 211.

dynasty ; and the greater lords had no doubt several of such vehicles, with coach-houses for their accommodation. Litters were perhaps used only for the aged and infirm, who were conveyed in them on the shoulders of attendants.[1]

Egyptian Noble carried in a Litter.

Egyptian men of all ranks shaved their heads and their entire faces, except sometimes a portion of the chin, from which a short square beard was allowed to depend.[2] The barber was in attendance on the great lord every morning, to remove any hair that had grown, and trim his beard, if he wore one. The lord's wig was also under his superintendence. This consisted of numerous small curls, together sometimes with locks and plaits, fastened carefully to a reticulated ground-

---

[1] Rosellini, *Mon. Cir.* pl. xciii. 2 ; Wilkinson, *A. E.* vol. ii. p. 208.
[2] Birch, *Egypt from the Earliest Times,* 'Introduction,' p. xv. Wil-

kinson thought the beard, when worn, was artificial (*A. E.* vol. iii. p. 362). Some beards certainly seem to be tied on.

work, which allowed the heat of the head free escape.[1]
The dress, even of the highest class, was simple.   It
consisted, primarily, of the *shenti*, or kilt, a short garment, folded or fluted, which was worn round the
loins, and fastened in front with a girdle.   The material might be linen or woollen, according to the state of
the weather, or the wearer's inclination.   Over this the
great lord invariably wore an ample robe of fine linen,
reaching from the shoulders to the ankles, and provided
with full sleeves, which descended nearly, if not quite,
to the elbows.   A second girdle, which may have been
of leather, confined the outer dress about the waist.
The arms and lower parts of the legs were left bare ;

Egyptian Sandals.

and in the earliest times the feet were also bare, sandals being unknown ; but they came into fashion at the
beginning of the fifth dynasty,[2] and thenceforward were
ordinarily worn by the rich, whether men or women.
They were either of leather lined with cloth, or of a
sort of basket-work composed of palm leaves or the
stalks of the papyrus.[3]   The shape varied at different
periods.   Having dressed himself with the assistance of
his valet, the Egyptian lord put on his ornaments,
which consisted commonly of a collar of beads or a
chain of gold round the neck, armlets and bracelets of
gold, inlaid with lapis lazuli and turquoise, round the
arms, anklets of the same character round the ankles,

---

[1] Wilkinson, vol. iii. pl. 355-6.   26-7; Rosellini, *Mon. Civ.* pl. lxv.
[2] Birch, 'Introduction,' p. xv.   figs. 1-8.
[3] Birch, *Guide to Museum*, pp.

and rings upon the fingers of both hands.[1] Thus attired, the lord took his *bâton* or stick,[2] and, quitting his dressing-room, made his appearance in the *salon* or eating-apartment.

Meanwhile, his spouse had performed her own toilet, which was naturally somewhat more elaborate than her husband's. Egyptian ladies wore their own hair, which grew in great abundance,[3] and must have occupied the tirewoman for a considerable period. A double-toothed comb was used for combing it,[4] and it may also have been brushed, though hair-brushes have not been discovered. Ultimately, it was separated into numerous distinct tresses, and plaited by threes into thirty or forty fine plaits, which were then gathered into three masses, one behind the head and the others at either side of the face, or else were allowed to fall in a single continuous ring round the head and shoulders. After it had been thus arranged, the hair was confined by a fillet, or by a head-dress made to imitate the wings, back, and tail, and even sometimes the head, of a vulture.[5] On their bodies some females wore only a single garment,[6] which was a petticoat, either tied at the neck or supported by straps over the shoulders, and reaching from the neck or breast to the ankles; but those of the upper class had, first, over this, a coloured sash passed twice round the waist and tied in

---

[1] Birch, *Egypt from the Earliest Times,* 'Introduction,' p. xv.
[2] Ibid.
[3] Wilkinson, *A. E.* vol. iii. pp. 369–70.
[4] Egyptian combs may be seen in the British Museum (First Egyptian Room, Nos. 2678 and 2683). They are either of wood or bone, and generally have two rows of teeth, one row of larger teeth at widish intervals, the other with small teeth, very close together. (See Wilkinson, *A.E.* vol. iii. p. 381.)
[5] See above, p. 282, and compare the vulture head-dress of certain goddesses, as Maut (p. 338), Athor (p. 365), Isis (p. 368), and Nephthys (p. 383).
[6] Birch, *Egypt from the Earliest Times,* 'Introduction,' p. xv. Compare Herod. ii. 36.

front, and, secondly, a large loose robe, made of the
finest linen, with full open sleeves, reaching to the
elbow.[1] They wore sandals from the same date as the
men, and had similar ornaments, with the addition of
earrings. These often manifested an elegant taste,
being in the form of serpents or terminating in the
heads of animals or of goddesses.[2] The application of
kohl or stibium to the eyes seems to have formed an
ordinary part of the toilet.[3]

It is unfortunately impossible to follow throughout
the day the husband and wife, with whose portraits we
are attempting to present our readers. We do not
know the hours kept by the upper classes in Egypt,
nor the arrangements which prevailed respecting their
meals,[4] nor the mode in which a lady of rank employed
herself from the time when her morning toilet was
completed until the hour of dinner. We may conjecture that she looked after her servants, superintended
the teaching of her children, amused herself in her
garden,[5] or visited and received visits from her acquaintance; but the evidence on these various points
is scanty, and scarcely sufficient to justify general conclusions. It is somewhat different with respect to the
men. The sculptures show us that much of the Egyptian gentleman's day was spent in sports of various

---

[1] Wilkinson, *A. E.* vol. iii. p. 368.

[2] Ibid. p. 374.

[3] Birch, l.s.c.; Wilkinson, *A. E.* vol. iii. p. 380. Birch adds that the nails were often dyed with henna, and the breath sweetened with pastilles.

[4] It may be suspected that, like the *early* Greeks and Romans, the Egyptians took but two regular meals in the day: one about ten or eleven o'clock, and the other in the evening. (See for the former of these, Herod. ii. 193, and for the latter, Herod. ii. 78.) Bread, meat, and wine or beer, were probably taken at both.

[5] One amusement in which ladies indulged was certainly archery (Wilkinson, *A. E.* vol. ii. p. 189). Another was boating (Rosellini, *Mon. Civ.* pls. cv. 1, and cix.) They also accompanied their husbands or brothers in some of their sporting expeditions.

kinds; that he indulged in fishing and fowling, as well as in the chase of various wild beasts, some of which were sought as delicacies for the table, while others seem to have been attacked merely to gratify that destructive instinct which urges men to take delight in field sports.

Ponds commonly existed within the pleasure-grounds attached to an Egyptian country house,[1] and were often of considerable dimensions. Formal in shape, to suit the general character of the grounds, they were well stocked with a variety of fish, and often furnished the Egyptian noble with a morning's amusement. The sport was of a kind which in these days would not be considered exciting. Reclined upon a mat, or seated on a chair,[2] under the shade of a tree, and with a short rod in his hand, apparently of one joint only, the lord threw his double or single line into the preserved pool, and let his bait sink to the bottom. When he felt the bite of a fish, he jerked his line out of the water,[3] and by this movement, if the fish was securely hooked, he probably landed it; if not, he only lost his labour. Hooks were large and strong, lines coarse, fish evidently not shy; there was no fear of the tackle breaking; and if a few fish were scared by the clumsy method, there were plenty of others to take their place in a few minutes.

A less unskilful mode of pursuing the sport was by means of the fish-spear. Embarking upon his pond, or the stream that fed it, in a boat of bulrushes, armed with the proper weapon, and accompanied by a young son, and by his wife or a sister,[4] the lord would direct

---

[1] Rosellini, *Mon. Civ.* pl. lxix.;
Wilkinson, *A. E.* vol. ii. pp. 129,
143, &c.

[2] Wilkinson, vol. iii. p. 52.
[3] Ibid. p. 53.
[4] Ibid. p. 41, woodcut, figs. 18,

his gaze into the water, and when he saw a fish passing, strike at him with the barbed implement.   If the
fish were near at hand, he would not let go of the
weapon, but if otherwise, he would throw it, retaining
in his grasp a string attached to its upper extremity.[1]
This enabled him to recover the spear, even if it sank,
or was carried down by the fish ; and, when his aim
had been true, it enabled him to get possession of his
prize.   Some spears had double heads, both of them

Spearing Fish.

barbed ; and good fortune, or superior skill, occasionally secured two fish at once.

The fowling practised by the Egyptian gentleman
was very peculiar.   He despised nets, made no use of
hawks or falcons, and did not even, except on rare occasions, have recourse to the bow.   He placed his
whole dependence on a missile, which has been called
a 'throw-stick'[2]— a thin curved piece of heavy wood,
from a foot and a quarter to two feet in length, and
about an inch and a half broad.   Gliding silently in a
light boat along some piece of water, with a decoy bird
stationed at the head of his vessel, trained perhaps to

19, and 20. Compare Rosellini, *Mon.*   [1] Wilkinson, *A. E.* vol. iii. pp.
Civ. pl. xxv. 1, and Lepsius, *Denk-*   60–1.
mäler, vol. iv. pl. 130.   [2] Ibid. p. 38.

utter its note, he approached the favourite haunt of
the wild fowl, which was generally a thicket of tall
reeds and lotuses.[1] Having come as close to the game
as possible, with his throw-stick in one hand and a
second decoy bird, or even several, in the other, he
watched for the moment when the wild fowl rose in a
cloud above the tops of the water-plants, and then flung
his weapon in among them. Supplied by a relative or
an attendant with another, and again another, he
made throw after throw, not ceasing till the last bird
was out of reach, or his stock of throw-sticks exhausted. We sometimes see as many as four sticks in
the air, and another upon the point of being delivered.[2]
Skilled sportsmen seem to have aimed especially at
the birds' necks, since, if the neck was struck, the bird
was pretty sure to fall. This sport appears to have been
an especial favourite with Egyptians of the upper class.

The chase of wild beasts involved more exertion
than either fishing or fowling, and required the sportsman to go further afield. The only tolerable hunting-
grounds lay in the desert regions on either side of the
Nile valley; and the wealthy Egyptians who made up
their minds to indulge in this pastime, had to penetrate
into these dreary tracts, and probably to quit their
homes for a time, and camp out in the desert. The
chief objects of pursuit upon these occasions were the
gazelle, the ibex, the oryx, and perhaps some other
kinds of antelopes. The sportsman set out in his chariot, well provided with arrows and javelins, accom-

[1] For representations, see Wilkinson, *A. E.* vol. iii. pp. 39, 41,
and 42.
[2] Wilkinson, woodcut No. 335
(vol. iii. p. 39). Sportsmen are
sometimes accompanied by a cat,
which is represented as taking an
interest in the sport, and sometimes
as even springing into the air and
catching one of the wild fowl (Wilkinson, woodcut No. 337). But
this can scarcely have been a usual
incident.

panied by a number of dogs, and attended by a crowd of menials, huntsmen, beaters, men to set the nets, provision and water carriers, and the like. A large space was commonly enclosed by the beaters, and all the game within it driven in a certain direction by them and the hounds, while the sportsman and his friends, stationed at suitable points, shot their arrows at such beasts as came within the range of the weapon, or sought to capture them by means of a long thong or cord ending in a running noose. Nets were also set at certain narrow points in the wadys or dry water-courses, down which the herd, when pressed, was almost sure to pass, and men were placed to watch them, and slaughter each animal as soon as he was entangled, before he could break his way through the obstacle and make his escape. When the district in which the hunt took place was well supplied with beasts, and the space enclosed by the beaters was large, a curiously mixed scene presented itself towards the close of the day.[1] All the wild animals of the region, roused from their several lairs, were brought together within a narrow space—hyænas, jackals, foxes, porcupines, even ostriches, held on their way, side by side with gazelles, hares, ibexes, and antelopes of various descriptions—the hounds also being intermixed among them, and the hunter in his car driving at speed through the thickest of the mêlée, discharging his arrows right and left, and bringing down the choicest game. Attendants continually supplied fresh arrows; and the work of slaughter probably went on till night put an end to it, or till the whole of the game was killed or had made its escape.

---

[1] See this scene represented in Rosellini, *Mon. Civ.* pl. xv., and compare Wilkinson, *A. E.* vol. iii.

p. 22. For a portion of the scene, see above, p. 276.

Occasionally, instead of antelopes, wild cattle were the object of pursuit. In this case, too, dogs were used, though scarcely with much effect.[1] The cattle were, most likely, either stalked or laid in wait for, and, when sufficiently near, were either lassoed,[2] or else shot with arrows, the place aimed at being the junction between the neck and the head. When the lasso was employed, it was commonly thrown over one of the horns.

According to one representation,[3] the lion was made use of in the chase of some animals, being trained to the work, as the *cheeta* or hunting leopard is in Persia and India. That the Egyptians tamed lions appears from several of the sculptures,[4] and is also attested by at least one ancient writer;[5] but the employment of them in the chase rests upon a single painting in one of the tombs at Beni Hissar.

Lions themselves, when in the wild state, were sometimes hunted by the monarchs;[6] but it is doubtful whether any Egyptian subject, however exalted his rank, ever engaged in the exciting occupation. The lion was scarcely to be found within the limits of Egypt during any period of the monarchy; and though occasionally to be seen in the deserts upon the Egyptian borders,[7] yet could scarcely be reckoned on as likely to

[1] Wilkinson, *A. E.* vol. iii. p. 18.
[2] Ibid. p. 15, woodcut No. 325.
[3] Ibid. p. 16.
[4] Rosellini, *Mon. Storici*, pls. lxvi., lxxxiv., and cvii. Compare above, p. 454.
[5] Diod. Sic. i. 48.
[6] Amenembat I. in his instructions to his son Osertasen says, 'I hunted the lion' (*Records of the Past*, vol. ii. p. 14), referring apparently to an occasion when he had gone into Nubia. Rameses III. represents himself as engaged in the chase of the lion on the walls of his palace at Medinet-Abou. (See above, pl. opp. p. 278.) The scene of this chase is thought to have been Southern Palestine (Birch, *Egypt from the Earliest Times*, p. 140).
[7] Wilkinson, *A. E.* vol. iii. p. 20.

cross his path by a private sportsman.   The kings who
were ambitious of the honour of having contended
with the king of beasts, could make hunting expeditions beyond their borders, and have a whole province
ransacked for the game of which they were in search.
Even they, however, seem very rarely to have aspired
so high ; and there is but one representation of a lion-
hunt in the Egyptian sculptures.

A similarly exceptional character attached to the
chase of the elephant by the Egyptians.   One monarch on one occasion only, when engaged in an
expedition which took him deep into Asia, ' hunted a
hundred and twenty elephants on account of their
tusks.'[1]   Here a subject had the good fortune to save
his royal master from an attack made upon him by the
leading or ' rogue ' elephant of the herd, and to capture the brute after inflicting a wound upon its trunk.

The pursuit of the hippopotamus and the crocodile
was, on the contrary, a favourite and established practice with Egyptian sportsmen.   The hippopotamus was
hunted as injurious to the crops,[2] on which it both fed
and trampled by night, while at the same time it was
valued for its hide, which was regarded as the best
possible material for shields, helmets, and javelins.[3]   It
appears to have been thought better to attack it in the
water than upon the land, perhaps because its struggles
to escape would then be, comparatively speaking, harmless.   Spears, with strings attached to them, were
thrown at it ; and when these had taken effect, it was
drawn to the surface and its head entangled in a strong
noose by which it could be dragged ashore ;[4] or, if

[1] Records of the Past, vol. ii. p. 62.
[2] Plin. H. N. viii. 25.
[3] Diod. Sic. i. 35; Herod. ii. 71;
Pliny, l.s.c.
[4] See Wilkinson, A. E. vol. iii. p. 70, and pl. xv.

this attempt failed, it was allowed to exhaust itself by repeated rushes and plunges in the stream, the hunters 'playing' it the while by reels attached to the strings that held their spears, and waiting till it was spent by fatigue and loss of blood, when they wound up their reels, and brought their booty to land.[1]

There were two modes of chasing the crocodile. Sometimes it was speared,[2] like the hippopotamus, and was then probably killed in much the same way; but another method was also adopted, which is thus described by Herodotus:[3]—'They bait a hook with a

Spearing the Crocodile.

chine of pork, and let the meat be carried out into the middle of the stream, while the hunter on the bank holds a live pig, which he belabours. The crocodile, hearing its cries, makes for the sound, and encounters the pork, which he instantly swallows down. The men on the shore haul, and when they have got him to land, the first thing the hunter does is to plaster his eyes with mud. This once accomplished, the animal

---

[1] Wilkinson, vol. iii. pp. 71-3.
[2] Rosellini, *Mon. Civ.* pl. xxiv. 4;
Lepsius, *Denkmäler*, vol. iv. pl. 105.
[3] Herod. ii. 70.

is despatched with ease ; otherwise, he gives much trouble.' Very similar modes to both of these are still in use on the Nile.[1]

It is of course not to be supposed that the Egyptian of high rank was so enamoured of the chase as to devote to it all the time that he spent in the country. There would be days on which he inspected his farm,[2] his cattle-stalls, his live stock, his granaries, his wine-presses, his olive-presses, moving from place to place, probably, on his favourite ass, and putting questions to his labourers. There would be others on which he received his steward, went through his accounts, and gave such directions as he thought necessary ; others again on which his religious duties occupied him, or on which he received the general homage of his subordinates.[3] His life would be in many ways varied. As a local magnate, he might be called upon from time to time to take part in the public business of his nome. He might have civil employment thrust upon him, since no one could refuse an office or a commission assigned him by the king. He might even find him-

[1] Wilkinson says: 'One mode, which is now adopted, is to fasten a little puppy on a log of wood, to the middle of which a strong rope is tied, protected to a certain distance by iron wire ; and this, when swallowed by the crocodile, turns, on being pulled, across the throat. It is then dragged ashore, and soon killed by blows on the head from poles and hatchets. They have also another mode of catching it. A man swims, having his head covered by a gourd with two holes for his eyes, to a sandbank, where the crocodile is sleeping ; and when he has reached it, he rises from the water with a shout, and throws a spear into its side or armpit if pos-sible, when feeling itself wounded it rushes into the water. The head of the barbed spear having a rope attached to it, the crocodile is thereby pulled in, and wounded again by the man, and his companions who join him, until it is exhausted and killed.' (See the author's *Herodotus,* vol. ii. p. 99, note [4].)

[2] Birch, *Egypt from the Earliest Times,* p. 44: 'The chief occupation of the period, or at all events that most often represented in the tombs, was the inspection of the farm.' Compare Lepsius, *Denk-mäler,* vols. ii. and iii. *passim.*

[3] Rosellini, *Mon. Civ.* pl. lxxxii. ; Lepsius, *Denkmäler,* vol. iii. pt. ii. pls. 19, 21, &c.

self called upon to conduct a military expedition. But, apart from these extraordinary distractions, he would have occupations enough and to spare. Amid alternations of business and pleasure, of domestic repose and violent exercise, of town and country life, of state and simplicity, he would scarcely find his time hang heavy on his hands, or become a victim to *ennui*. An extensive literature was open to him, if he cared to read ;[1] a solemn and mysterious religion, full of awe-inspiring thoughts and stretching on to things beyond the grave, claimed his attention ; he had abundant duties, abundant enjoyments. Though not so happy as to be politically free, there was small danger of his suffering oppression. He might look forward to a tranquil and respected old age ; and even in the grave he would enjoy the attentions and religious veneration of those whom he left behind him.[2]

Among the duties continually devolving on him, the most important were those of charity and of hospitality. It was absolutely incumbent upon him, if he would pass the dread ordeal in the nether world, that during this life he should be careful 'to give bread to the hungry, drink to the thirsty, clothes to the naked, oil to the wounded, and burial to the dead.'[3] It was also incumbent on him, in the general opinion of those with whom he lived, that he should show towards men of his own class a free and open-handed hospitality. For this purpose it was necessary that, both in the town and in the country, he should provide his friends with frequent grand entertainments. With a description of one of these we may terminate our account of the manners and customs of the higher classes of society in

---

[1] See above, pp. 134–151.
[2] See above, p. 422.

[3] Birch, *Egypt from the Earliest Times*, p. 46.

ancient Egypt, and with that account we may be content to bring to an end the present too extended chapter.

The preparations for an entertainment had to commence some days previously. Game had to be procured, professionals engaged, extra attendants hired, a stock of fresh flowers and perhaps of unguents laid in. Great activity prevailed in the kitchen ;[1] confectionery was prepared, spices pounded, macaroni made,[2] cooking utensils scoured, the larder stored with provisions. The reception-rooms were then arranged for guests, chairs being placed in rows or groups, extra carpets and mats strewn about, flowers put into the vases, and the house generally decorated. When the guests began to arrive, they were first of all received in the vestibule by attendants, who presented them with bouquets,[3] placed garlands of lotus upon their heads, and sometimes collars of lotus round their necks, anointed their hair with unguents, and offered them wine or other beverages. At this time the visitors commonly sat on the floor, probably for the convenience of those who had to anoint and adorn them. Having received these attentions, the guests, ladies and gentlemen intermixed, passed on to the main apartment, where they were greeted by their host and hostess, and begged to take their seats on the chairs and fauteuils which had been arranged for them. Here more refreshments were handed round, more flowers offered, while the guests, generally in pairs, but sometimes in groups, conversed one with another.[4] Music was now com-

---

[1] This is often represented. (Rosellini, *Mon. Civ.* pls. lxxxiii. to lxxxvi.; Wilkinson, *A. E.* vol. ii. pp. 383, 385, 388, &c.)

[2] Wilkinson, *A. E.* vol. ii. p.

385; woodcut, No. 277, *l, n.*

[3] Rosellini, *Mon. Civ.* pl. lxxix.; Wilkinson, *A. E.* vol. ii. p. 215, &c.

[4] Wilkinson, *A. E.* vol. ii. pl. xii., and pp. 367, 390, and 393.

mouly introduced, sometimes accompanied by dancing, the performers in both arts being professionals, and the dancing-girls being nearly, if not quite, naked.[1] Sometimes, at the same party, there would be two bands,[2] who, we may suppose, played alternately. Pet animals, dogs, gazelles, or monkeys,[3] might be present, and the young children of the house in some instances gave animation to the scene, and enlivened the entertainment with their prattle. As it was not customary for children under ten or twelve years of age to wear any clothes,[4] the nudity of the dancing-girls might seem less strange and less indelicate.

It is possible that on some occasions the music, dancing, and light refreshments constituted the whole of the entertainment, and that the guests after a while took their departure without any formal meal being served ; but more often the proceedings above described were the mere prelude to the real piece, and the more important part followed. Round tables, loaded with a great variety of delicacies, as joints of meat, geese, ducks, and waterfowl of different kinds, cakes, pastry, fruit, and the like, are seen interspersed among the guests,[5] to whom no doubt the dishes were handed in succession, and who must have helped themselves, as Orientals commonly do, with their hands. Knives and forks, spoons for eating with,[6] even plates, were an unknown luxury ; the guest took what his hands could manage, and after eating either dipped

[1] See above, p. 525.
[2] Wilkinson, *A. E.* vol. ii. pl. xii.
[3] Ibid. and p. 389. Compare Herod. ii. 36. The fondness of the Egyptians for such pets, especially monkeys, is very observable.
[4] Birch, *Egypt from the Earliest Times,* ' Introduction,' pp. xiv.-xv.
[5] Wilkinson, *A. E.* vol. ii. p. 393.
[6] Egyptian spoons exist. (See, in the British Museum Collection, Nos. 5951 to 5976; and compare Wilkinson, *A. E.* vol. ii. pp. 403-4.) But there is no evidence of their being used to eat with.

them in water, or wiped them with a napkin brought him by an attendant.[1]   The dishes offered him would include probably two or three kinds of fish ; meat, generally beef, boiled, roasted, and dressed in various ways ; venison and other game ; geese, ducks, or water-fowl ; vegetables in profusion, as especially lentils, endives, and cucumbers ; pastry, cakes, and fruits of twenty kinds, particularly grapes and figs.[2]   To quench his thirst, he would be supplied with frequent draughts of wine or beer,[3] the wine probably diluted with water.

Herodotus tells us[4] that it was customary, when the feast was over, for an attendant to bring in a wooden mummied form, from a foot and a half to three feet long, painted to resemble a corpse, and to show it to each guest in turn, with the words :—' Gaze here, and drink and be merry ; for when you die, such will you be.'   If the expressions used are rightly reported, we must suppose the figure brought in when the eating was ended and the drinking began, with the object of stimulating the guests to greater conviviality ; but if this were so, the custom had probably lost its original significance when Herodotus visited Egypt, since it *must* (one would think) have been intended at the first to encourage seriousness, and check undue indulgence, by sobering thoughts concerning death and judgment to come.[5]   The Egyptians were too much inclined to the pleasures of the table, and certainly required no stimulus to drinking.   Both gentlemen and ladies not

---

[1] The attendants often carry napkins in their left hands.

[2] See Wilkinson, *A. E.* vol. ii. p. 400 ; and compare Birch, *Egypt from the Earliest Times*, p. 45.

[3] Wilkinson, *A. E.* vol. ii. pp. 170–3.

[4] Herod. ii. 78.

[5] So Wilkinson (*A. E.* vol. ii. pp. 410–11), whose remarks appear to be reasonable.

unfrequently indulged to excess.[1] The custom mentioned by Herodotus and alluded to also by Plutarch,[2] can only have proceeded from the priests, who doubtless wished, as guardians of the public morality, to check the intemperance which they were unable to prevent altogether.

After the banquet was entirely ended, music and singing were generally resumed,[3] and sometimes tumblers or jugglers, both male and female, were introduced, and feats of agility were gone through with much dexterity and grace.[4] The women played with three balls at a time, keeping two constantly in the air ; or made somersaults backwards ; or sprang off the ground to the height of several feet. The men wrestled, or pirouetted,[5] or stood on their heads,[6] or walked up each other's backs, or performed other tricks, and feats of strength. Occasionally, games seem to have been played. As the kings themselves in their leisure hours did not disdain to play draughts with their favourites,[7] so it may be presumed that the Egyptian lord and his guests would sometimes relieve the tedium of a long evening by the same or some similar amusement. Chess does not appear to have been known ; but a game resembling draughts, one like the modern *morra*, and several which cannot be identified, certainly were ;[8] and, though there is more evidence of their being in

---

[1] Wilkinson, *A. E.* vol. ii. pp. 167-8.   Ladies are represented as sick from excessive drinking, and gentlemen as carried home dead drunk by their attendants.

[2] Plut. *De Isid. et Osir.* § 15.

[3] Wilkinson, *A. E.* vol. ii. p. 414.

[4] Rosellini, *Mon. Civ.* pls. xcix. to civ. ; Wilkinson in the author's

Herodotus, vol. ii. pp. 272-7.

[5] Wilkinson, *A. E.* vol. ii. p. 335.

[6] See the author's *Herodotus*, vol. ii. p. 277.

[7] Wilkinson, *A. E.* vol. ii. pp. 420-1.

[8] Ibid. pp. 417-435 ; Rosellini, *Mon. Civ.* pls. ciii. and civ.

favour with the lower than with the higher orders, yet
it can scarcely be supposed that the royal example was
not imitated by many among the nobles.

In conclusion it may be observed that Egyptian
society under the Pharaohs, if in many respects it was
not so advanced in cultivation and refinement as that of
Athens in the time of Pericles, was in some points both
more moral and more civilised. Neither the sculptures nor the literary remains give any indication of
the existence in Egypt of that degrading vice which in
Greece tainted all male society from the highest grade
to the lowest, and constituted ' a great national disease,'
or ' moral pestilence.' [1] Nor did courtesans, though
occasionally they attained to a certain degree of cele-
brity among the Egyptians,[2] ever exercise that influence
which they did in Greece over art, literature, and even
politics. The relations of the sexes were decidedly on
a better footing in Egypt than at Athens, or most other
Greek towns Not only was polygamy unknown to
the inhabitants of the Nile valley, and even licensed
concubinage confined to the kings,[3] but woman took
her proper rank as the friend and companion of man,
was never secluded in a harem, but constantly made
her appearance alike in private company and in the
ceremonies of religion, possessed equal rights with man
in the eye of the law, was attached to temples in a
quasi-sacerdotal character, and might even ascend the
throne and administer the government of the country.[4]
Women were free to attend the markets and shops ; [5]
to visit and receive company, both male and female ;

[1] Döllinger, *Jew and Gentile*, vol.
ii. p. 239, E. T.
[2] Herod. ii. 135.
[3] On the concubinage of some of
the kings, see Wilkinson, *A. E.*
vol. ii. pp. 420–1; Birch, *Egypt
from the Earliest Times*, p. 160, &c.
[4] Birch, ' Introduction,' p. xiv.
[5] Herod. ii. 35.

to join in the most sacred religious services ;[1] to follow the dead to the grave ; and to perform their part in the sepulchral sacrifices.[2]

Again, the consideration shown to age in Egypt was remarkable, and, though perhaps a remnant of antique manners, must be regarded as a point in which their customs were more advanced than those of most ancient peoples. 'Their young men, when they met their elders in the streets,' we are told,[3] 'made way for them and stepped aside ; and if an old man came in where young men were present, the latter rose from their seats out of respect to him.'

In arrangements with respect to education they seem also to have attained a point not often reached by the nations of antiquity. If the schools wherein scribes obtained their instruction were really open to all,[4] and the career of scribe might be pursued by any one, whatever his birth, then it must be said that Egypt, notwithstanding the general rigidity of her institutions, provided an open career for talent, such as scarcely existed elsewhere in the old world, and such as few modern communities can be said even yet to furnish. It was always possible under despotic governments that the capricious favour of the sovereign should raise to a high, or even to the highest position, the lowest person in the kingdom. But, in Egypt alone of all ancient States, does a system seem to have been established, whereby persons of all ranks, even the lowest, were invited to compete for the royal favour, and, by distinguishing themselves in the public schools,

---

[1] Rosellini, *Mon. del Culto*, pls. v. 2, xxxi. 1 ; Lepsius, *Denkmäler*, vol. vi. pls. 91, 97 c, 106 b, &c.
[2] Wilkinson, *A. E.* vol. v. p. 383, woodcut, No. 492 ; 'Supplement,'
pls. 83–5.
[3] Herod. ii. 80.
[4] See Brugsch, *Geschichte Aegyptens*, p. 24.

to establish a claim for employment in the public service. That employment once obtained, their future depended on themselves. Merit secured promotion; and it would seem that the efficient scribe had only to show himself superior to his fellows, in order to rise to the highest position but one in the empire.

END OF VOL. I.